INSIDE VIEW OF THE ABBEY CHURCH, PAISLEY.

FROM THE NORTH EAST.

Published by Hugh Crichton Paisley 1818.

A

GENERAL DESCRIPTION

OF THE

SHIRE OF RENFREW,

INCLUDING AN ACCOUNT OF THE

NOBLE AND ANCIENT FAMILIES,

WHO, FROM THE EARLIEST TIMES, HAVE HAD PROPERTY IN THAT COUNTY, AND THE MOST REMARKABLE FACTS IN THE LIVES OF DISTINGUISHED INDIVIDUALS.

TO WHICH IS ADDED,

A GENEALOGICAL HISTORY

OF

THE ROYAL HOUSE OF STEWART,

AND OF THE SEVERAL

NOBLE AND ILLUSTRIOUS FAMILIES OF THAT NAME,

FROM THE YEAR 1034, TO THE YEAR 1710;

COLLECTED FROM PUBLIC RECORDS, CHARTULARIES OF MONASTERIES, AND THE BEST HISTORIANS AND PRIVATE MSS.

PUBLISHED IN 1710,

By GEORGE CRAWFURD,

AUTHOR OF THE PEERAGE OF SCOTLAND, &c. &c.

AND CONTINUED TO THE PRESENT PERIOD,

By GEORGE ROBERTSON,

AUTHOR OF THE AGRICULTURAL SURVEY OF MID LOTHIAN, &c.

PAISLEY:

PRINTED BY J. NEILSON.

SOLD BY H. CRICHTON, BOOKSELLER, PAISLEY, THE PUBLISHER; JOHN SMITH & SON, GLASGOW; ARCHIBALD CONSTABLE & CO. EDINBURGH; AND REST FENNER, LONDON.

1818.

Entered in Stationers' Hall.

TO

HIS ROYAL HIGHNESS

GEORGE AUGUSTUS FREDERICK,

PRINCE OF GREAT BRITAIN, HEREDITARY PRINCE OF HANOVER,

PRINCE OF WALES,

DUKE OF CORNWALL AND ROTHESAY,

MARQUIS OF THE ISLE OF ELY,

EARL OF CHESTER, CARRICK, AND ELTHAM,

VISCOUNT LAUNCESTON,

BARON OF RENFREW AND SNAWDON,

LORD OF THE ISLES, AND STEWARD OF SCOTLAND,

PRINCE REGENT,

THE FOLLOWING WORK IS RESPECTFULLY INSCRIBED

BY THE EDITOR.

PREFACE.

The county of Renfrew, though, in point of extent, one of the least in Scotland, has many claims to general notice. It was for ages the peculiar patrimony and chief place of residence of the illustrious family, which for several centuries gave sovereigns to these realms, and whose descendants, in a line direct or lateral, are still found on the thrones of the first kingdoms in Europe. The Noble families of Abercorn, Blantyre, Cathcart, Dundonald, Eglinton, Glencairn, Lenox, Lyle, Ross, and Sempill, had their origin, or early residence, in this county, and have their history necessarily blended with that of the county itself. Among its principal proprietors, it had the Brisbanes, Crawfurds, Cunninghames, Dennistouns, Flemings, Hamiltons, Houstouns, Maxwells, Mures, Napiers, Polloks, Porterfields, Ralstouns, Shaws, Walkinshaws, and Wallaces, of whom, nearly the whole, have great possessions in it until this day.

In other circumstances, which confer distinction, Renfrewshire ranks very high. Its commerce and manufactures have risen to a pitch almost unrivalled; its agriculture is most respectable; while its population, in proportion to extent, is believed to be the first in Scotland.

This important county found in Crawfurd a historian equally distinguished for profound research and minute accuracy. His history is still considered a first authority, particularly as to the origin and progress of families. But this book is now rarely to be met with, and can only be obtained at a high price. In the present work a copy of it is reprinted verbatim. There was a new edition of it published in 1782, by William Semple, but even it has now become scarce. That edition has been carefully consulted, and the useful additions in it are all retained in this.

In presenting this new edition to the public, the editor will, in few words, state the authorities from which the additional matter has been compiled.

So far as regards the localities of Renfrewshire, he has made great use of Ainsley's map, on a scale of two inches to a mile, published in 1796. With this he has combined his own knowledge, obtained by frequently traversing the county in all directions, not only, as lately, in the view of this publication, but for several years before it was thought of. To all that personal observation has furnished, is to be added much distinct information received from the different proprietors, from the ministers of most of the parishes, and from the active friendship of intelligent individuals in different parts of the county.

PREFACE.

The valued rent of the different lands was taken from the Cess books in 1817, (see note, page 266). Their extent has been estimated, partly from authentic information, partly from probable conjecture. In cases in which no satisfactory information could be obtained, it was in vain to endeavour to ascertain it. Individuals, however, from their own knowledge, may be able to place the extent of property in the blanks which have been left for that purpose in the proper column in the table.

On the subject of manufactures, the Editor owes much to information communicated by William Carlyle, Esq; Provost of Paisley; and, on that of commerce, to different gentlemen in Greenock and Port Glasgow.

With respect to the main subject of the work, the descent of Families; so far as regards those of the nobilty, the circumstances have been collected chiefly from the Peerage of Scotland, published in 1813, by Wood, the best work on the subject that has appeared; the account here given is greatly abridged from the original of that correct writer, who is not answerable for the manner in which it is drawn up. The continuation till the present time has, in most cases, been obligingly communicated by the noble families themselves. The genealogy of the many respectable families of the other proprietors of the county, has been continued from Crawfurd by materials, in nearly every case, furnished by themselves, or which have been submitted to their inspection, and have met with their approbation.

From the great influx of new matter, during the time of printing, it became necessary to abridge greatly the accounts previously written, in order that the work might not much exceed the extent originally proposed. After all, it has been lengthened out considerably beyond those limits. This abridgement extends less or more to every branch discussed, and will account for the brevity in them all.

The additional size of the volume has rendered it impracticable to give a list of subscribers; but those highly respectable names will appear in a supplemental, though separate work, to be entituled, " Views of the Noblemen and Gentlemens' Seats in the County of Renfrew," to which will be prefixed a concise History of Renfrewshire, a curious work, written in 1696, by that eminent antiquary, Hamilton of Wishaw; copied, by permission, from a M.S. in the advocate's library, a prospectus of which will soon be issued.

INDEX.

Parishes.

	Craw-furd. P.	Conti-nuation. P.		Craw-furd. P.	Conti-nuation. P.
Cathcart,	28	262	Kilmalcolm,		395
Eagleshame,	28	245	Lochwinnoch,	75	348
Eastwood,	35	275	Mearns,	35	286
Erskine,	113	387	Neilston,	39	298
Greenock,	124	411	Paisley,		309
Houstoun,	98	378	Paisley Town,	44	331
Inchinnan,	105	382	Port Glasgow,	119	407
Innerkip,	129	422	Renfrew,	65	341
Kilbarchan,	82	361			

Towns, Villages, Estates, &c.

	Craw.	Cont.		Craw.	Cont.
Abbey of Paisley,	134		Elderslie,	86	311
Abbot's Inch,		342	Eliestoun,	80	350
Achinames,	80	362	Erskine House and Lands,	107	388
Ardgowan,	128	422	Ferguslie,	90	311
Arthurlie,	39	299	Finlayston,	114	396
Bargarran,	112	238	Freeland,	107	383
Barrhead,		302	Fulbar,	88	311
Barochan,	102	379	Fulwood,	103	379
Beltrees,	79	350	Gavin,	79	350
Bishopton,	113	388	Glanderston,	40	299
Blackhall,	58	312	Gourock,	126	424
Blacksolm,	94	397	Greenock Town,	124	411
Blawarthill,	67	341	Hawkhead,	54	310
Boghall,	104	379	Househill,	45	310
Bogtoun,	30	263	Houstoun House,	98	379
Bredieland,	89	311	Johnstone House,	82	362
Bridge of Weir,		364	Johnstone Village,		316
Bruntchels,	96	362	Jordanhill,	68	342
Cairncurran,	94	396	Kelly,	129	422
Caldwell,	44	299	Kilbarchan Village,	82	364
Cardonald,	51	310	Killallan,	103	378
Cartsburn,	123	411	Kirkland,	64	342
Castlesemple,	75	349	Knoc,	61	342
Cochran,	82	311	Langside Village,	30	263
Craigbett,		397	———— Battle,	186	271
Craigton,	107	388	Linwood,		364
Crawfurdsdyke,	123	418	Merksworth,	92	312
Crockston,	39	310	Millbank,	78	349
———— ancient Castle,	45		Newton,	88	311
Cross-my-loof,		266	Newtown of Mearns,	36	289
Dargeval,	104	388	Newton Ralston,		302
Denniestoun,	94	396	Newark,	118	369
Duchal,	92	396	Northbar,	106	382

INDEX.

Estates, &c.	Crawfurd. P.	Continuation. P.	Estates, &c.	Crawfurd. P.	Continuation. P.
Park of Erskine,	113	388	Ramphorlie, or Ranforlie,	95	363
Park of Inchinnan,	106	382	Scotstoun,	68	341
Partick,	67	275	Shutterflat, meeting at,		300
Pollok, Nether,	31	276	Southbar,	104	382
Pollokshaws,	31	277	Stanley,	89	311
Pollok, Upper,	37	286	Thirdpart,	80	362
Porterfield,	62	342	Thornliebank,		278
Pulnoon,	23	248	Walkinshaw,	90	343
Raiss,	56	310	Waterstoun,	96	362
Ralstoun,	57	310	Whiteford,	56	310
Ranfield, or Renfield,	64	342	Williamwood,	31	264

Families.

	Crawfurd. P.	Continuation. P.		Crawfurd. P.	Continuation. P.
Abercorn, Marquis of,		317	Hamilton of Fingalton, &c.	39	293
Adam of Garpel,		360	Harvey of Castlesemple,		360
Alexander of Newton & Southbarr,	88	386	Hay of Renfield,	64	
Bannatyne of Kelly,	129	422	Houstoun of Houstoun,	98	413
Belhaven, Lord,		402	———— of Johnstone,	82	328
Brisbane of Bishopton, &c.	113	390	How of Damton,		378
Brown of Capelrig,		298	Hutcheson of Scotstoun,	68	
———— of Langside,		271	Hyndman of Lunderstoun,		425
Buchanan of Hillington,		331	King of Drums,		394
Caldwell of that-ilk,	44	301	Knox the Reformer,	95	
Campbell of Blytheswood,	64	347	Lennox, Duchess of,	52	
Cathcart, Lord,	28	267	Lindsay of Dunrod,	128	
Cochran of Ladyland,		361	Lyle Lord Lyle,	92	401
Crawfurd of Cartsburn,	123	416	MacGilchrist of Northbarr,	106	382
———— the historian,		417	M'Dowall of Castlesemple,		357
———— of Achinames,	80	364	Marr, Earl of,	107	
Cuningham of Cairncurran,	94	405	Maxwell of Caerlaverock,	36	
———— of Corsehill,	115	399	———— of Blawert-hill,	68	284
———— of Craigends,	97	371	———— of Brediland,	89	329
Darroch of Gourock,		425	———— of Dargeval,	104	392
Dennistoun of that-ilk,	94	406	———— of Freeland,	107	
Douglas, Lord,		344	———— of Merksworth,	92	329
Dundonald, Earl of,	83	322	———— of Nether Pollok,	31	278
Dunlop of Househill,	45	328	———— of Newark,	118	
Eglinton, Earl of,	23	248	———— of Stainly,	89	
Fleming of Barrochan,	102	381	———— of Southbarr,	104	
Fulton of Park,		331	———— of Williamwood,	31	270
———— of Hartfield,		ibid.	———— of Irvine,		385
Glasgow, Earl of,		325	Montgomery of Skelmurly,	42	258
Glencairn, Earl of,	114	398	———— —— of Scotstoun,	68	
Glen of Barr,	74		Montrose, Duke of,	46	
Hall of Fulbar,	88	329	Mure of Caldwell,	43	304
Hamilton, Aikenhead & Holmhead,	30	264	Napier Milliken, Bart. of Napier,		372
			Napier of Blackstoun,	99	377

INDEX.

Families.

	Craw-furd. P.	Continuation. P.		Craw-furd. P.	Continuation. P.
Orr of Ralstoun,		330	Stewart of Arthurlie,	39	
Oswald of Scotstoun,		347	——— of Cardonald,	51	
Paterson of Craigton,	107	394	——— of Blackhall,	58	412
Pollok of that-ilk,	37	289	Speirs of Elderslie,		346
Porterfield of that-ilk,	62	402	Sibbald, Sir Robert,	80	
Ralstoun of that-ilk,	57	330	Walkinshaw of that-ilk,	9b	
Ross, Lord,	66	323	Walkinshaw of Scotstoun,	68	
Ross of Balnagown,		324	Wallace of Elderslie,	86	
Sempill, Lord,	75	356	——— of Neilstonside,	41	
——— of Beltrees,	79		——— of Kelly,		426
——— of Cathcart,	80	262	Waterstoun of that-ilk,	96	
Shaw of Bargarran,	112		Whitefoord of that-ilk,	56	
——— of Greenock,	124	416			

Index to the Stewarts.

	Craw.	Cont.		Craw.	Cont.
Origin of,	130	433	Stewart Earl of Buchan,	234	
Walter the first Steward,	133	434	Stuart Earl of Traquair,	234	466
Robert II. the first King,	150	437	Stewart Earl of Galloway,	235	463
Successors till James VII.—155	206	437	Stuart Earl, and since Marquis of Bute,	238	455
Prince James Francis,		443	Stuart Lord Blantyre,	240	467
——— Charles Edward		444	Stuart of Dunearn,		460
——— Cardinal York,		ib.	Steuart of Allanton,		468
——— Duchess of Albany,		445	——— of Coltness,		477
Royal family from the revolution till the present time		446	——— of Goodtrees,		481
Stuart Duke of Lennox,	219	452	——— Barclay of Collerney,		486
Lennox Duke of Lennox,	225	453	——— of Allanbank,		488
Stewart Duke of Albany,	226		——— of Mitcham,		490
Stewart Lord Ochiltree,	228		——— of Castlemilk,		491
Stuart Earl of Moray,	229	458	——— of Fettercairn,		493
Stewart Lord Methven,	231		——— of Blairhall,		494
Stewart Lord Lorn,	232		——— S. M. Fullarton of Fullarton,		ib.
Stewart Earl of Athol,	233				

b

APPENDIX.

	Page.
No. 1. Copy of the Original Charter of the Principality of Scotland,	497
No. 2. Copy of a Charter from King Robert the III. as Tutor to his Son, the Prince of part of the Principality,	ibid.
No. 3. Titles of the Prince of Wales, according to the Charters of the present day, granted by his Royal Highness, as Prince and Steward of Scotland,	498
No. 4. Letter from Queen Mary to Sir John Maxwell before the battle of Langside, 5th May 1568.	ibid.
Letter from King James VI. to Sir John Maxwell to attend at Holyroodhouse, December 1593,	ibid.
No. 5. Letter from King James the VI. to the Laird of Caldwell,	499
No. 6. Transcript of the Charter by Robert the II. (see page 392),	500
No. 7. Description of the Lordship of Paisley according to the Charter by King James the VI. dated 3d May 1621, in favour of James, first Earl of Abercorn,	ibid.
No. 8. Notes Respecting the Constitution and Records of the Burgh of Paisley,	501
No. 9. Supplementary Notices respecting Renfrewshire,	505
Miscellaneous Notices,	509
No. 10. Commission of the Peace for the County of Renfrew, dated 26th March 1818,	510
Ross Pedigree,	513
Dunlop of Househill,	522
Annual Revenues of the Hostages given in Security of the Ransom of King James I. in 1424,	ibid.

A GENEALOGICAL HISTORY

OF THE

ROYAL AND ILLUSTRIOUS

FAMILY OF THE STEWARTS,

FROM THE YEAR 1034 TO THE YEAR 1710;

GIVING

AN ACCOUNT OF THE LIVES, MARRIAGES, AND ISSUE OF THE MOST REMARKABLE PERSONS
AND FAMILIES OF THAT NAME.

TO WHICH ARE PREFIXED, FIRST,

A GENERAL DESCRIPTION

OF

THE SHIRE OF RENFREW,

THE PECULIAR RESIDENCE AND ANCIENT PATRIMONY OF THE STEWARTS:

AND, SECONDLY,

A Deduction of the Noble and Ancient Families,

PROPRIETORS THERE FOR UPWARDS OF 400 YEARS, DOWN TO THE PRESENT TIMES: CONTAINING THE DESCENT, ORIGINAL CREATIONS,
AND MOST REMARKABLE ACTIONS OF THEIR RESPECTIVE ANCESTORS; ALSO THE CHIEF TITLES OF HONOUR THEY
NOW ENJOY; WITH THEIR MARRIAGE AND ISSUE, CONTINUED DOWN TO THIS PRESENT YEAR,
AND THE COAT OF ARMS OF EACH FAMILY IN BLAZON.

COLLECTED FROM OUR PUBLICK RECORDS, ANCIENT CHARTULARIES OF THE MONASTERIES OF PASLY, ARBROTH, KELSO, DUMFERMLING,
MELROSS, BALMERINOCH, SCOON, DRYBURGH, CAMBUSKENNETH, ABERDEEN, AND MURRAY; AND FROM
THE BEST HISTORIANS AND PRIVATE MANUSCRIPTS.

EDINBURGH:
PRINTED BY JAMES WATSON, ON THE NORTH SIDE OF THE CROSS.

1710.

TO THE QUEEN.

MADAM,

The hereditary virtues and glorious actions of your royal ancestors have employed our ablest historians; as the peculiar glories of your Majesty's victorious and most happy reign shall for ever afford matter of history and panegyrick to latest posterity.

I have, with a great deal of industry and pains, collected, from original papers and authentic records, the genealogical account of the lives, marriages, and issue of your Majesty's royal ancestors for these seven hundred years past: and how far soever I go back in the tracing your line and pedigree, find it always royal: for all historians agree, that Bancho, grandfather to Walter the first Stewart upon record, was descended of the Kings of Scotland; and from him I trace your royal line down to your Majesty's person.

Hence it is I presume to offer, in all humility, this performance to your Majesty's protection, which I hope will not be unacceptable: And that the almighty and gracious God may long preserve your royal person, to be the support of the protestant religion at home and abroad, is and shall be the constant prayer of,

May it please your Majesty,
Your Majesty's most dutiful,
Most humble and devoted
Subject and Servant,
GEORGE CRAWFURD.

THE PREFACE.

INSTEAD of a long and tedious preface, I shall briefly acquaint my reader whence I have collected my materials for this history; and withal, mention my hearty acknowledgements to those honourable and worthy persons by whose means and assistance I have carried it on.

And, in the first place, my best acknowledgements are ever due to the Right Honourable John Earl of Dundonald, who was pleased to allow me the perusal of the Register of the Monastery of Pasly, by which I had some special advantages of discovering the antiquities of the most of the noble and ancient families in the shire of Renfrew, and of the illustrious family of Stewart. Having so often mentioned the Register or the Chartulary of Pasly, I shall presume so far upon the reader's patience as to give a brief account of the same.

In the old monasteries of Scotland there were three sort of Register-Books; as, I. A general one, which, by way of Annals or Chronicle, gave the yearly occurrences relating to the public. II. Their Obituaries, wherein were recorded the times of the death and the places of interment of their Abbots, Priors, and other great men of their respective houses, and their chief benefactors. III. Their Chartulary or Register, wherein were recorded the charters of the kings and other great men, bulls of the popes, and the more private grants of inferior benefactors which had pass'd in their favours; such as this book I am now to give account of, which is a large folio, all writ on Lombard paper, in a fair legible hand.

The first leaf begins with an alphabetical index of all the charters therein contain'd. Then follows the charter of foundation, which is confirmed by the Pope's bull, with another from King William; as also several privileges and exemptions from the bishops of Glasgow, Argile, and the Isles. Then we have through the whole book promiscuously, Popes' bulls, grants from the Sovereigns, and donations by the High Stewards of Scotland, who were its patrons and greatest benefactors. In the 161 leaf, we have " Carta Erectionis " Villæ de Pasleto in liberum Burgum," by King James the IVth, anno 1488; the grounds of the erection are, his devotion to St. Mirin, the holy confessor;. and his love and respect to the venerable father, George Shaw, Abbot of the monastery of Pasly. Then we have several grants by the Abbots to their vassals, brought down to the year 1545.

I had also considerable assistance from the Honourable Sir James Dalrymple of Killoch, a learned antiquary, who was pleased to show me several very valuable pieces of antiquity: as also, from the fam'd antiquary Mr. William Hamilton of Wishaw: and the learned Sir Robert Sibbald allowed me to peruse his descriptions of the shire of Renfrew, which he has among his curious geographical collections. But I cannot forbear to mention how much I am obliged to Thomas Crawfurd of Cartsburn, my brother german, who furnished me with a much exacter description of the shire than ever hitherto had been given, with many curious genealogical notes for illustrating the families, and and several other good helps. The Right Honourable and learned Sir Alexander Seton of Pitmedden, Baronet, sometime one of the Senators of the College of Justice, was pleased to allow me the favour of some of his curious manuscripts relating to Scots antiquities, of which his lordship has a very handsome collection. The learned and curious antiquary, Mr. Alexander Baillie of Castlecarie, who hath made considerable genealogical collections relative to Scots Antiquities, gave me what notes made for my purpose. As also the ingenious Mr. David Symson, my worthy friend lately deceased, freely interchanged his observations on the royal family for those I had observed.

I was at the pains to go through and take notes from the public records, which I had access to by the favour of Mr. Alexander Baillie, from some rolls of King Robert Bruce, down to the beginning of King James the IV's reign. And since that time I had, by the favour of Robert Miln, Writer in Edinburgh, a person well known to be indefatigable in the study of Scots antiquities, his vast collections from the public records, frankly communicate to me. I likewise had access, by the favour of the curators and keepers of the lawyers library, to peruse the Chartularies of most of the Monasteries mentioned in the title-page.

I must acknowledge how unfit I am, both in years and experience, for an undertaking of this kind; but several of our most learned and judicious antiquaries having perused my collections, both relating to the shire of Renfrew and the royal family, prevailed with me to publish them, which gives me encouragement to hope they have escaped with very few material faults: yet as in a work of this nature it would be next to an imposibility; so it would be vain in me to suppose, that either through inadvertency or omission of the pen, some errors should not have escaped me, as some slight faults may be owing to the press; but where any such have come to my knowledge, they are corrected in the errata.

I have avoided all reflections wherever I found them in the histories I have followed; for next to being free of errors, I shall reckon myself happy to have given no offence.

I shall not say any thing as to the usefulness of the work; I think it may be of some use to our nobility and gentry, to whom it is chiefly, with submission, recommended. This is all I shall say by way of preface.

ADIEU.

A

HISTORY

OF THE

SHIRE OF RENFREW.

THE Shire of Renfrew lies to the west of the sheriffdom of Lanerk, (commonly called Clydsdale) of which once it was a part, and is bounded, on the east, with the western parts of Clydsdale; and, on the south and west, by the Bailiary of Cuninghame in the shire of Air; and, on the north, by the river of Clyde, the boundary of this shire from the sheriffdom of Dunbartoun, excepting a little part of it, about a mile and a half in length, and a mile broad, that's upon the north side of the river of Clyde, comprehending the lands of Jordanhill, Scotstoun, Blawerthill, and Wester Partick, and makes a part of the paroch of Renfrew. The length of this shire, from the south-east, in the paroch of Eaglesham, adjoining to Evandale and Kilbride, in Clydsdale, and Loudonhill, in Cuninghame, to the north-west, in the paroch of Innerkip, adjoining to the Largs, in the shire of Air, is about twenty-four miles; and its bredth, from north to south, where broadest, is about twelve miles, viz. From Greenock lying on Clyde, to the southern places in the paroch of Lochwhinyeoch, bordering with Beeth in Cuninghame.

The ancient denomination of this country was Strath-Grief, so called from one of its principal rivers, as appears from a donation by Balduin de Bigres, Vicecomes de Lanerk, of the kirk of Innerkip to the monastery of Pasly; by which he gives that kirk to be possessed as freely by the monks of that Abby as the rest of the kirks of Strath-Grief were, " ex dono Walteri, filii Allani, Dapiferi

Regis Scotiæ." This donation is in the reign of Malcolm the IV[1]. As also, in the same reign, the lands of Kilpeter, in Strath-grief, are given by Balduin de Bigres, Vicecomes Regis, to Hugh de Padvinan; from which Hugh, these lands were called Hugh's Town, of whom is lineally descended Sir John Houstoun of that Ilk, Baronet[2].

This country came afterward to be designed, THE BARONY OF RENFREW; so called from the principal town of the same name, and was the chief part of the patrimony of the GREAT STEWART OF SCOTLAND: and, after the accession of that illustrious family to the crown, the Barony of Renfrew was dissolved from the shire of Lanerk, and erected into a distinct sheriffdom by King Robert the III. when he erected the ancient patrimony of his ancestors, which was, the baronies of Renfrew, King's-Kyle and Kyle-Stewart in the sheriffdom of Air, the isles of Bute, Aran, and Cumbraes; the Baronies of Ratha and Innerweek in the sheriffdom of Edinburgh, into a principality, in favours of James, Prince and Stewart of Scotland, his son; as is evident from the original charter of erection yet extant, dated at Perth the 10th of December, in the year 1404. The most part of this shire is holden of the Prince and Stewart of Scotland.

This country, lying next to Clydsdale, partakes of the fertility of that soil, particularly those parts that ly upon the rivers of Clyde, Cart white and black, and upon the river of Grief, being champaign and level, but having many pretty risings of the ground, from whence there are very agreeable prospects of the most part of this shire, as also of the Nether-ward of Clydsdale, and of many places both of the shires of Dunbartoun and Stirling, the south and western places being mountanous. All of it is very fertile and of a good soil, especially the lower country, which abounds with corns; as the higher abounds with grass and choise pasturage, where there is made excellent butter and cheese; and, beside what is made use of in the country, there are considerable quantities carried to the neighbouring shires.

But to be more particular in the description of this shire, its rivers, lakes, and what is rare of its natural product of several kinds. The principal rivers are three, viz. White and Black Cart, and the river of Grief.

' White Cart hath its source betwixt Eagelsham in this shire, and Evandale and Kilbride, in Clydsdale; its course for some miles is northward, till, at the castle of Cathcart, (within two miles of the city of Glasgow) it turneth north-west to Pasly, and from thence northward to the kirk of Inchenan, where, meeting with Black Cart, they have their influx into Clyde, betwixt the Ranfield and some part of

---

[1] Chartulary of Pasly.   [2] Carta penes D. Johan. Houstoun de Eodem. Bar.

the lordship of Inchenan, a little below that church. In this river of White Cart, above the town of Pasly, there are found pearls so fine and big, that they may compare with many oriental, and have been taken notice of by some of the most famous jewelers in Europe : They are found in the ground of the river among the sand, in a shell larger than that of a musle. The proper season of fishing them is in the summer.

The river of Black Cart hath its rise from Castle-Semple Loch, and taketh its course eastward, till near the house of Blackstoun : It runneth northward thro' the mosses, which maketh the water somewhat blackish, from whence it taketh the denomination of Black Cart. It hath its influx into Grief at the Walkinshaw, and both meet and mix themselves with White Cart, opposite to the point on which stands the kirk of Inchenan : How they have their influx into Clyde is above described.

The third principal river of this shire, is that of Grief, which hath its source in the western parts of this country, in the lands of Garvock, a part of the Barony of Houstoun (but lying in the paroch of Greenock) and runs eastward, till near the influx of Cart into it, and thence northward, till, as said is, it fall into Clyde in manner above described. The tide flows up the river of Cart to the bridge of Pasly, and is reckoned to flow about three foot, by which fishing boats from Clyde are carried up to that place. All these rivers are well replenished with fish and fowl; but, none of them being rare, I insist not on them.

There are several lakes in this shire, but the most considerable is that of Castle-Semple, (or Lochwinyeoch Loch) which hath communication with the Loch of Kilbirny, in Cuninghame, by a small rivulet : Its extent is about two miles in length, and near a mile in bredth. In the middle of the loch, opposite to the church of Lochwhinyeoch, there is a little rock, on which Robert, the great Lord Semple, did raise a small tower, called, The Peel of Castle-Semple, which, as it was of use for security, against the insults of rambling parties, in time of our ancient feuds, so was it for pleasure, when the family of Semple did recreate themselves by diversion in their boats of pleasure on that lake. There are also several lesser lochs in this shire, such as Queenside Loch, out of which the river Calder hath its source, which empties itself into Lochwhinyeoch Loch below the house of Barr. As also, Lochlibo in Nielstoun, and Bennen in Eagelsham, about a mile in circumference; in all of which there is plenty of fish and fowl; but, being only such as are common, I insist not on them. The country is well stored with springs of water; and, particularly, there is a spring in the lands of Woodside, the possession of Hugh Crawfurd, my brother-german, that flows and ebbs at spring tides, though at three miles from any part of the river of Clyde, and half a mile from the bridge of Pasly, where the river of Cart ebbs and flows; the ground, where that spring is, being much higher than that river.

And though the river of Clyde hath not its rise in this shire, yet, being its northern boundary, from the royal burgh of Renfrew to the Cloch, in the paroch of Innerkip, which is about 17 miles; its fresh water mixeth with the salt, a mile below Erskine, where the river is a mile broad. Some of its chief ports and havens upon the coast are, the Bay of Newark, Port-Glasgow, Crawfurds-dike, Greenock, Gourock, and Innerkip, all particularly described in the following History, and raised of late by trade and the herring fishing, which, though it may more properly belong to the river of Clyde in general, than to any particular shire lying on its banks; yet, of all the shires that border on it, this may most justly claim a right to it, the inhabitants thereof, at Greenock, Crawfurds-dike, Gourock, Newark, and Innerkip, making the greatest number of the fishers. I shall here take occasion to give some account of the Herring Fishing, which sometimes is in the Firth of Clyde. The herrings which are caught there being larger, firmer, and of a better taste, and taking better with the salt, than any other the kingdom affords, are more valued, both fresh and salted, at home and abroad. When the fishing was considerable in the river of Clyde, there have been of boats imployed in catching herrings about nine hundred, built after the form of little galleys, each boat having on board four men and twenty-four nets, every net being six fathom long, and a fathom and an half in bredth, all join'd together, making a considerable length. Anciently none were allowed to fish till the 25th of July, about which time the shoals used to come from the sea which is called Lochin; and such as went a-fishing before that day were liable to a certain pecunial mulct. I understand that, anciently, the boats went a-fishing three times a-year, which times were called the Drave; and there was payable to the crown, out of each boat, of such a bigness as was then determined, a thousand herring each Drave, and were afterward paid by a measure of a fixed size and bigness, from whence that duty came to be called the Assyze Herring; which, by act of parliament, in the reign of King James III. was annexed to the crown, of which the Most Honourable His Grace John Duke of Argile, as also his ancestors, have for a long time had tacks, with a jurisdiction annexed, for regulating the fishing, and punishing crimes committed by any employed about it, betwixt the Firth of Pictland and the Mule of Galloway (the isles of Orkney and Zetland excepted). The herrings are sold by the fishers to the coopers, (viz. such as retail them for the service of the country) and packers, (i. e. such as are employed by merchants to buy herrings, to be barrell'd for export and foreign sale) by the maze, which contains 500. The curing and right packing of herring for export is under good regulations, by several acts of parliament, in the reign of King Charles II. and his successors; and particularly, that the herring barrel is to contain 8 gallons and a quart of Scots measure: And, for encouraging merchants, there are, by some late acts, considerable drawbacks appointed to be allowed, in consideration of the duty upon salt made use of in curing herring. And, that this so profitable product of this country may be in good esteem in foreign mercats, no merchant can have the benefit of any drawback, except he or the curer depone on oath, that the herring have been cured with foreign salt, without any mixture of home-made salt; and which herring, before export, are to be inspected by an overseer, appointed for that purpose, and sealed, if found sufficient, with a certain seal, to testify their sufficiency. There was, about the year 1670, a company erected, which employed a considerable stock of money for curing herring; and because His Majesty King Charles II. put in a share of the stock, they were called the Royal Company: They built a large house at Greenock, and made that place the seat of their trade, where they had large cellars for keeping their salt and herring till exporting. By this erection, none, except that company, were allowed to cure herring before the 20th day of September yearly; which being represented to the government as a very hard restraint upon the merchants, the said company was dissolved in the year 1684. Their houses at Greenock being exposed to roup, were purchased by the magistrates and town council of the city of Glasgow. The fishing continues from the 25th of July to the 25th of December; after which there is no allowance to fish that season. The number of herring taken in the Firth of Clyde, some years, is almost incredible, considering what hath been made use of by those employed in fishing, cooping, packing, and barrelling, and the home consumption, beside what has been exposed to foreign mercats; and, particularly, I'm told that in the year 1674 there were exported to the port of Rochel in France, 1700 last; beside what were exported to other ports in France, Sweden, Dantzick and other places within the Baltick. When there is a good tack of herrings in Clyde, they are mostly the food of all commons in the shires adjacent, especially in the harvest time, where they are a chief part of the diet made use of by the reapers. There is, near to, and within the liberties of, the city of Glasgow, a considerable mercat for herring during the whole fishing season. There has also been excellent Red Herring dried at Crawfurd's-dike, by Mr. John Spreul, merchant in Glasgow, author of the "Accompt Current betwixt Scotland and England," who has large conveniences at that place for making red herring.

This country fell likeways under the Roman arms, and did, on this hand, set a bound to their conquest; the Romans having never passed the Firth of Clyde to Argileshire: For, at Pasly, there are the vestiges of a large Roman camp, with a Prætorium on the westend, on a rising ground, called Oak-shaw-head, upon the descent whereof stands the town of Pasly: The Prætorium is not large, but has been well fortified with three fosses and dikes of earth; it seems to have included all that ground which the town stands upon, and may have been a mile in compass. When one treads upon the ground of the Prætorium, it gives a sound as if it were hollow, occasioned, probably, by some vault underneath, such as are at Cameleon and Ardoch, two other Roman camps; and about a quarter of a mile distant from this Prætorium, upon two little hills, the one to the west, upon the lands of Woodside, the other to the south, on the lands of Castle-head, almost in a triangular form: by the vestiges yet remaining they appear to have been larger than the other Prætorium, and probably were stations for the out-guards; which I find, was the opinion of the Reverend and curious Antiquary, Mr. William Dunlop, late principal of the University of Glasgow, in a description, by him, of the shire of Renfrew, in MS. in the hands of Sir Robert Sibbald, and is taken notice of by Doctor Nicolson, Bishop of Carlile, in his Scotish Historical Library. At Langside, also, within a mile and an half of the city of Glasgow, there is an appearance of an old camp, on the top of the hill: Here the battle was fought betwixt Queen Mary's troops, against those of her son, King James VI. under the command of James, Earl of Murray, his Regent, which fell out the 10th of May 1568, and is called Langside field.

The inhabitants of this shire are generally frugal, both nobility, gentry, and commons: The gentry, most of them, have a tolerable measure of learning, and are given to all the ordinary exercises performed by gentlemen, such as haulking, hunting, gunning, &c. and live in good friendship among themselves, being all of them related to one another by frequent intermarriages.

This country abounds much with coal and excellent quarries of free stone. The several curiosities found in this shire, which the accurate Mr. Robert Woodrou, minister of the Gospel at Eastwood, has observed, shall be taken notice of in the description of the several places where they are found.

As to the government of this shire: beside the several jurisdictions of Regalities and Barony, to be taken notice of in the subsequent History. As it is a shire, the heritable sheriff is the Right Honourable Alexander Earl of Eglintoun, who officiats by his deputes. The present sheriff depute is John Maxwel of Williamwood. His lordship is also heritable baillie of the Regality of Pasly. Both these jurisdictions were acquired by Alexander Earl of Eglintoun, from Hugh Lord

Semple, Anno 1686, whose ancestors had enjoyed the heritable sheriffship, from the erection of the Barony of Renfrew into a distinct shire, by King Robert III. as, before that time, the Barons of Elieston, ancestors to the Lord Semple, were Stewarts of this Barony. I have seen Robert Semple design'd, " Senescallus Baroniæ de Renfrew," in a Charter granted by James, High Steward of Scotland, grandfather of Robert II. of that name, king of Scotland, and first of the Stuarts, to Stephen the son of Nicol, one of the ancestors of Robert Hall, now of Fulbar [1], of several lands, (" juxta oppidum de Renfrew, ubi aqua de Grief cadit in aquam de Clyde") which is before the year 1309, that the granter of that Charter died; as the Bailliary of the Regality of Pasly was bestowed upon Robert, Master of Semple, by John Hamilton, Abbot of Pasly, Anno 1545, which was enjoyed by that family until the reign of King Charles I. that with the sheriffship both these jurisdictions came to the family of Eglintoun.

In relation to the church, this shire, in time of Episcopacy, is a part of the diocess of the Archbishop of Glasgow; and, in the time of Presbytery, all its paroches, except two, viz. Eaglesham and Cathcart, being in the Presbytery of Glasgow, are united unto one Presbytery, whose seat is at Pasly, and makes a part of the Synod of Glasgow. The rest, viz. Eastwood, Mearns, Pasly, Neilston, Lochwhinyeoch, Innerkip, Greenock, Port-Glasgow, Kilmalcolm, Kilbarchan, Killelan, Houstoun, Erskein, Inchenan, and Renfrew, are all in the Presbytery of Pasly.

There was one monastery in the shire, at Pasly, pleasantly situate on the river Cart, within two miles of Clyde, founded in the reign of king Malcolm IV. Anno 1160, by Walter, the son of Allan, Dapifer regis Scotiæ, as the original Charter of foundation, in the chartulary of that Abby [2] testifies, and bears as follows. " Sciant præsentes & futuri, quod, ego, Walterus, filius Allani, dapifer regis " Scotiæ, pro anima quondam regis David, & anima Henrici regis Angliæ, & " anima Comitis Henrici, & pro salute corporis & animæ regis Malcolmi, & " pro animabus omnium Parentum meorum & Benefactorum, nec non, & mei " ipsius salute, constituam quandam Domum religionis, infra terram meam de " Pasletto, secundum ordinem Cluniacensem." (Which order was institute in the year 910, by Bruno, in France, where they have their principal Abby; and then this Abby was planted with Monks of the Cistertian order, distinguished by a white habit, from the Benedictines, who went in black: But afterwards Pasly was replenished by Monks of Cluny again, as an accurate author [3] ob-

---
[1] Carta penes Rob. Hall de Fulbar.   [2] Chartulary of Pasly, Fol. 3.   [3] Mr. William Forbes on Tithes.

serves.) " Cum consensu & assensu Prioris & Conventus de Wenlock," (in the diocess of Hereford in [1] England) " & ad domum illam construendam, habeo, de " Domo de Wenlock XIII. Fratres. Et Prior qui de illis XIII. præcedere, domum " illam regendo præficitur, per me & meum consilium eligetur; & si contingat " ipsum Priorem, vel per mortem vel per criminalem prævaricationem, a prioratu " suo deponi, per me & consilium meum deponetur; & qui ei in prioratum succe- " dat per me & consilium meum eligetur." This foundation is confirmed by King William of Scotland, as also by Pope Innocent, and Stephen Abbot of Cluny. This monastery was endowed with large revenues by the Great Stewards of Scotland, who were both patrons and constant benefactors to it. King Robert III. erected all their lands, which were either in the baronies of Renfrew, or in Kyle-stewart; as also their lands of Molla, Huntlaw, and Hassenden, in Roxburgh-shire; and the lands of Orde in the shire of Peebles, in a regality, " in " honorem Dei, Beatæ Virginis Mariæ & beati Jacobi Apostoli & sancti Miri- " ni confessoris, pro salute animæ suæ & animarum antecessorum Regum & Se- " nescallorum Scotiæ: reddendo inde, nobis & successoribus nostris, dicti " Monachi & eorum successores, orationem tantum, pro omni alio servitio secu- " lari," as the original Charter bears [2]. This Abby had under its patronage these Churches, viz.

Inerweek in Lothian
Legerwood in the Merss
Rutherglen
Carmonock, and
Dalziel, in Clydsdale
Riccartoun
Craigie
Dundonald
Monktoun
St. Ebox
Prestwick
Auchinleck and
The Chappel of Corsby, all in Kyle
Cumbra in Bute
The kirk of St. Oswald, of Turnberry in Carrick

Rosneth, and
Kilpatrick in the Lennox
Killcolmenel
Kilkeran, and
Kilfinian in Argile-shire
Cathcart
Eastwood
Mearns
Neilston
Pasly
Kilbarchan
Lochwhinyeoch
Innerkip
Erskin
Houstoun, and
Killelan in the shire of Renfrew.

[1] Chartu'ary of Pasly.   [2] Chartulary of Pasly.

The fabrick of this monastery yet remaining, is both large and spacious. There was at this place a stately Cross-church, which was built after the model of a Cathedral, with a very lofty steeple, which went to decay about the reformation; the chancel is only now standing, which is a fair building. The Abby and Church, with its large orchards and gardens, are enclosed with one of the most magnificent walls in Britain, all built with square stone upon both sides, about a mile in circuit: This wall, with most of the fabrick of the Abby, that now stands, was built in the reign of King James III. by George Shaw, Abbot of Pasly (of the family of Sauchie) Anno 1484, which appears from this inscription, on the corner of that wall, viz.

> Thy calit the abbot George of Shaw
> About my Abby gart make this waw,
> An thousand four hundreth Zear
> Eighty-four the date but weir;
> Pray for his salvation
> That laid this noble foundation.

The Monks of this Abby wrote a Chronicle of Scotland, called the Black Book of Pasly, an authentic copy of which was burnt in the Abby of Holy-roodhouse, during the English usurpation [1]; as also another copy of it was in Sir Robert Spotiswood's Library, and after his death carried to Englaud by general Lambert [2]. There is yet extant the Chartulary of the Monastery, wrote all in a very fair legible hand, containing the Charter of foundation of that Abby, with Charters and Bulls of confirmations, from Kings and Popes, with privileges and exemptions from the Bishops of Glasgow, Argile, and the Isles: There are a great many donations given by the High Stewarts of Scotland, both before and after their accession to the Crown; as also many grants from other great men, who have been branches of that illustrious house, with less considerable mortifications from private persons, and is brought down to the year 1548. John Hamilton, the last Abbot of Pasly, natural brother of James Duke of Chatlerault, upon his promotion to the episcopal See of St. Andrews, Anno 1546, resign'd the Abbacy of Pasly in favours of Lord Claud Hamilton, third son of James Duke of Chatlerault, his nephew; which resignation is confirmed afterwards by Pope Julius III. Anno 1553 [3]. This Lord Claud Hamilton, titular

---

[1] Description of the shire of Renfrew, by Mr. William Dunlop. [2] Theatrum Scotiæ.
[3] Carta penes J. Comitem de Dundonald.

Abbot of Pasly, upon the distribution which King James made of these lands which fell to the Crown upon the dissolution of the monasteries, obtained from that Prince a Charter, erecting the possessions belonging to the Abby of Pasly into a temporal Lordship, dated, at Edinburgh, July 29, Anno 1587; and afterwards was, by the same Prince, created a Lord of Parliament, by the title of Lord Pasly, Anno 1591. He deceased Anno 1621, leaving issue by Margaret his wife, daughter of George Lord Seaton, James, his son and heir; which James, in the year 1604, was nominate one of the commissioners for Scotland, to treat of an Union with England; and, at the same time he was created Lord Abercorn, and that honour improven by James, first Monarch of Great Britain, to the dignity of Earl of Abercorn, by Letters Patent, bearing date, at Whitehall, July 10, Anno 1606; which dignity is now enjoyed by the Right Honourable Thomas Earl of Abercorn, Baron Hamilton of Straband in Ireland, descended of Mr. George Hamilton, younger son of James, first Earl of Abercorn, by Marion his lady, daughter of Thomas Lord Boyd: The Lordship of Pasly was disponed by James Earl of Abercorn, to Archbald Earl of Angus, in the year 1652, and acquired by William Lord Cochran, afterwards Earl of Dundonald, Anno 1653 [1], and is now the principal residence of the Right Honourable John Earl of Dundonald, his Great Grand-child, by whom it hath been of late repaired, and much beautified, having most pleasant orchards and gardens, and one prettily adorn'd with statutes, with a deer park adjoining to them.

This Abby was honoured with being the burial-place of the Great Stewarts of Scotland, (for King Robert III. says, in a Charter to the Monks of Pasly, " ubi plurima corpora progenitorum nostrorum sepeliuntur & requiescunt in " pace [2]," as also of King Robert II. and of Marjory Bruce his mother, daughter of the renowned K. Robert I. where there is a monument erected to her memory, cut in the form of a woman, raised about two foot above the surface of the ground, and is called Queen Blearey's tomb. A small portion of the ancient Church yet stands, which shows much of the magnificence of that structure.

[1] Carta penes J. Comitem de Dundonald.   [2] Chartulary of Paisly.

A Succession of the Abbots of Pasly.

THOUGH many of them be buried in oblivion, these few I have collected from the Register-books of the Monastery, and other ancient documents, as follows. The first I have found is,

Roger; who, with consent of the Convent, gives allowance to Robert de Croc to build a chappel of ease, in the reign of King William. To whom succeeded

William; who, in 1225, makes an agreement with Sir Hugh, the son of Reginald (ancestor of Sir John Houstoun) about the lands of Auchincloss.

Then these succeeded in order:

Andrew, de Kelcow, is Abbot of Pasly, in the reign of King Robert Bruce, and in 1318 makes an agreement with Sir Reginald Mure of Abercorn. To whom succeeded

John, Abbot of Pasly; who in 1327, obtained a confirmation of the kirk of Kilkeran, from the Bishop of Argile: who was succeeded by another

John, Anno 1369; who was succeeded by

Another of the same name, 1409. His successor was

William Chisholm, abbot of Pasly; whose successor was

John Lithgow, in 1432. To whom succeeded

Thomas, Abbot of Pasly; who obtained from Robert Lord Lyle the fishing of Crockat-Shot upon Clyde, Anno 1452 [1], whose successor was

Henry, Abbot of Pasly; of whom I have found little more mention, than that he obtained from John Laumund of that-ilk, a confirmation of the Patronage of the kirk of Kilfinan, Anno 1466. His successor was

George Shaw, (of the family of Sauchie) who built much of the fabrick of the Monastery; and being a Privy Counsellor to King James IV. it was in his favours the town of Pasly was erected into a Burgh and Barony, Anno 1488, as the Charter of Erection, yet extant, testifies[2]. To George Shaw succeeded

Robert Shaw his kinsman; who in 1509 was promoted to the episcopal See of Murray; his successor being

Robert Stewart, of the house of Lennox; whom I find granting Charters to his vassals, from the year 1511 to the year 1529; whose successor was

[1] Chartulary of Pasly.   [2] Chartulary of Pasly.

John Hamilton, natural son of James Earl of Arran; who, being promoted to the episcopal see of St. Andrews, as I formerly observed, Anno 1546, his successor was

Lord Claud Hamilton, third son of James Duke of Chatlerault; who was titular Abbot and Commendator of Pasly; and being forfaulted after the field of Langside, an. 1568, that dignity was conferred upon

Mr. William Erskine, Parson of Campsy, afterwards titular Bishop of Glasgow, which he enjoyed until the Road of Stirling, an. 1685, that Lord Claud Hamilton was, with others of his kindred, restored.

The next and last I have found designed Commendator of Pasly, was

Claud Hamilton of Shawfield, second son of Claud Lord Pasly; who in 1601, resign'd his right of that commendatory in favours of James, Master of Pasly, his brother[1]. And this much as to the succession of the Abbots of Pasly.

There was also, in this country, the Collegiate Church of Lochwhinyeoch, commonly called the College of Castle-Semple, (near to the house of Castle-Semple) founded by John, first Lord Semple, an. 1505. " In honorem Dei & Bea-
" tæ Virginis Mariæ; & pro prosperitate Jacobi quarti Regis & Margaretæ Regi-
" næ suæ; & pro anima Margaretæ Colvil, quondam sponsæ suæ; nec non pro
" salute animæ suæ & Margaretæ Crichtoun, sponsæ suæ modernæ, omnium an-
" tecessorum & successorum suorum & omnium fidelium defunctorum;" which the orignal Charter of Foundation, yet extant, bears. This foundation was confirmed by King James IV. at Edinburgh, the 5th of June 1506[2]. It was richly endowed with a large revenue, for the maintainance of a Prebend and three Chaplains, for celebrating divine service, by mortifying to it the lands of Upper and Nether Pennelds, and the mill thereof, and the lands of Achlodmont; as also the teinds of Glasford were annexed to it: And since our happy reformation, 'tis now of no other use than a place of sepulture to that noble family, where John, Lord Semple, and Janet Colvil his lady, ly under a monument, carrying that inscription; as also his successors ly in a vault below ground, some of them in leaden coffins.

There were also several Chappels of Ease in this country; but one of the most ancient was near Neilstoun, founded by Robert de Croc, in the reign of King William; and to which Roger, Prior of Pasly, with consent of the convent, gave " infirmis fratribus hospitalis quod Robertus Croc construxit in terra sua, ut ha-
" beant capellam & capellanum qui iis divina celebret officia, ita quod Robertus

[1] Carta penes, J. Comitem de Dundonald. [2] Carta penes Francisc Dom. Semple.

"Croc, eidem capellano stipendia & omnia alia necessaria providebit, quæ divini "officii usibus conveniet." As there were likeways Chappels at Pollock, Upper and Nether: at Ranfurly there was a Chappel founded by the family of Ranfurly, and dedicated to St. Mary, to which the lands of Kirkland were annexed. At the Side, in Kilmalcolm, there was also a Chappel founded by the Lord Lyle: I have seen Magister David Stonyer designed, " Hermita Capellæ de Syde," Anno 1555. And at Greenock there were two Chappels of Ease upon both the lands of Easter and Wester Greenock; and at several other places through the country.

There are now no forrests in this country, tho' anciently there was one upon the south-west of Pasly, out of which Walter, the founder of the monastery of Pasly, grants several privileges, as the Chartulary of that Abby testifies. Also I have seen " John Le Hunter de la Forreste de Pasly," in Ragman's Roll, Anno 1296[1]. There was another at the Fernieneese, an ancient possession of the family of Semple. There are many woods in this shire, almost one upon the possession of every proprietor; the most considerable are at Eastwood, Pollock, Halkhead, Ralstoun, Erskine, Houstoun, Craigends, Barochan, Duchal, and Greenock.

[1] Prin's History of King Edward I.

A HISTORY

OF THE

SHIRE OF RENFREW.

PART SECOND.

HAVING thus briefly finish'd the Geographical Description of the Sheriffdom of Renfrew, which I only designed as an introduction to the following parts of this History, I proceed to the second part, wherein I propos'd to give a description of the several seats of the nobility and gentry, with the Genealogical Account of their families, in this method; following the several courses of the rivers, as they are above described.

As I observed in the Geographical Description of this shire, that the river of White Cart had its source betwixt Kilbryde in Clydsdale, and Eagelsham in this shire; upon the bank of which (some few miles from its source) stands, first, the Castle of Punnoon, the principal messwage of the Barony of Eagelsham, an ancient possession of the Montgommeries, a family originally of Norman extraction [1], who have been of great antiquity in Renfrewshire, and for well nigh 600 years possessed of a fair inheritance in those parts, is clear enough from

[1] Cambden in his Description of Scotland, and the learn'd Sir James Dalrymple, in his Preface to his Observations on the Scots History.

the following account. For Robert de Mundegumbri is a witness in the Charter of the foundation of the monastery of Pasly, Anno 1160. (Reg. Malcolmo IV [1].) As Allan de Mundegumbri, in the same register of Pasly, is mention'd a witness in the confirmation of that donation of the kirk of Inerweek, to the Monks of Pasly, which Allan, the son of Walter the Founder, made " pro sa-" lute animæ Willielmi regis [2]:" " Robert de Mundegumbri & Johannes frater " suus," are both witnesses to that Donation which Walter, the son of Allan High Stewart of Scotland, made to the Monks of Pasly, in the reign of King Alexander II. about the year 1234. The principal family of this name was of Eagelsham; Sir John Montgomery is so design'd in the Register of Pasly, in the reign of Robert II. Anno 1388. And the same valiant and heroic person being at the battle of Otterburn, took Henry Piercy, sirnam'd Hotspur, prisoner with his own hand, and with his ransom-money built the castle of Punnoon [3]. This Sir John Montgomery of Eagelsham obtained the Baronies of Eglintoun and Ardrossan, in Cunninghame, by marriage of the Heiress of Sir Hugh Eglintoun of that-ilk [4], and of Giles, his lady, daughter of Walter, High Stewart of Scotland, and sister to King Robert II. by reason of which marriage, the Earl of Eglintoun bears the Coat of Eglintoun of that-ilk, which is; Gules, three Annulets, Or; Stoned, Azure; quarter'd with the Coat of Montgomery, viz. Azure, three Flower-de-Luce's, Or. This family afterwards took designation of Ardrossan: I have seen Sir Alexander Montgomery so design'd, in a Commission which he had from King James I. Anno 1430 [5], to be Governour of Kintyre and Knapdale: which Sir Alexander was advanced to the degree and dignity of a Baron of this Realm, with the title of Lord Montgomery of Ardrossan, Anno 1445. He deceased Anno 1453, leaving issue, three sons; Alexander, his son and heir; Robert, author of that branch of the Montgomeries of Giffen, a son of which family was James Montgomery, commonly called Count De Montgomery, who was captain of the Scots Guard du Corps, that was institute by Charles V. King of France, for a guard to him, as a signal mark of their fidelity and favour, who in a Tournament slew Henry II. of France with a splinter of his spear, which penetrated through his eye into his brain, of which he died.

Of George Montgomery, a third son of Alexander, first Lord Montgomery, descended the Honourable family of Skelmurly: (" quod vide infra") beside these sons he had likeways several daughters, viz. Christian, who married John

---

[1] Chartulary of Pasly. [2] Chartulary of Pasly. [3] Holinshed and Lesly.
[4] Dalrymple. [5] Haddingtoun's Collections in Bib. Juridica.

first Earl of Lennox, of whom that noble family descended; and Janet, wife of Sir Robert Cunninghame of Kilmaures, ancestor to the Earl of Glencairn.

To Alexander, Lord Montgomery, succeeded Alexander, his son and heir; who in Anno 1454, acquired the Heritable Bailliary of Cunninghame from Sir Alexander Cunninghame of Kilmaures, his nephew; whose successor was Alexander, Lord Montgomery; and of Robert, his second son, descended the family of Braidstane: for this I have [1] seen a Charter granted by Alexander, Lord Montgomery, an. 1452, of these lands " dilecto suo Nepoti Roberto Montgomery," from which Robert lineally descended Sir Hugh Montgomery, son and heir of Adam Montgomery of Braidstane, who was raised to the dignity of Lord Viscount of Airds in the Kingdom of Ireland, by King James VI. of Scotland, and first Monarch of Great-Britian; and in the person of Hugh, Viscount of Airds, his son, improven to the dignity of Earl of Mount-Alexander in that Kingdom, by King Charles II. to whom the Right Honourable the Earl of Mount-Alexander is lineal heir.

But to return to the principal branch of this family: the first, who laid the foundation of that honour, which his posterity have ever since enjoyed, was Hugh, son and heir of Alexander, Lord Montgomery, who was by the bounty and favour of King James IV. (the 14th year of his reign) Anno 1503, created Earl of Eglintoun [2]. This noble Peer was married with the Lady Helen Campbel, daughter of Archbald Earl of Argile, by whom he had several sons; of which, John Master of Eglintoun was the eldest, killed in that conflict upon the street of Edinburgh, betwixt the Earls of Angus and Arran, the 30th of April 1520. Earl Hugh's second son was Sir Niel, author of that branch of the Montgomeries of Langshaw; who obtained the lands of Skeldone and Holy-Chapel, by the marriage of Margaret, daughter and sole heir of Quintine Muir of Skeldone, of whom James Montgomerie, now of Langshaw, is lineally descended. His third son was William, who obtained the lands of Stane in Cunninghame, by marriage of Janet Frances, daughter and heir of   Frances of Stane; which family produced the Montgomeries of Achinhood, of whom issued the Montgomeries of Broomlands, Wrae and Sloss [3]. Robert, a 4th son of Earl Hugh, was Bishop of Argile: and beside these sons, he had likeways six daughters; first Margaret, who married William, 2d Lord Semple, and had issue; the 2d, Marjory, married William Master of Somerveil, and had issue; the 3d Maud, was married to Colin Campbel of Arkinglass, and of her that family is descended. The 4th daughter was married to John Blair of that-ilk, and had issue.

c

[1] Carta D. Johannis Shaw de Greenock, Bar.   [2] Productions at the Decreet of Ranking.
[3] Genealogy of Eglintoun.

The 5th   was first married to Robert Montgomery of Giffen, and afterwards she became the wife of John Mure of Caldwall, of whom the Mures of Caldwall and Glanderstoun are descended. The 6th daughter, Agnes, was married to John Ker of Kersland, and had issue. As to the precise time of Earl Hugh's death, I know not, but he was immediately succeeded by Hugh, his grandson and heir, viz, son of John, Master of Eglintoun, who died in his lifetime, by Janet his wife, daughter of Sir Archbald Edmonstoun of Duntreath, by whom he had also a daughter, Christian, married to Sir William Douglass of Drumlenrig, of whom James Duke of Queensberry is the lineal heir; which Hugh Earl of Eglintoun, was appointed one of the Governours of Scotland, upon King James V.'s. going for France, in the year 1536 [1]. He was married to Marion Seatoun, daughter of George Lord Seatoun, by whom he had Hugh his successor, who after his father's death, in an. 1558, is a Minor, and under the tutory of Sir Richard Maitland of Lethintoun, and Mr. Andrew Crawfurd, Rector of Eagelsham. He married Agnes, daughter of Sir John Drummond of Innerpeffer, by whom he had two sons, and as many daughters; Hugh his successor, and Robert Montgomery of Giffen, commonly called Master of Eglintoun, who took to wife Margaret, daughter of Sir Matthew Campbel of Loudoun, by whom he had a daughter, Elizabeth, married to Hugh Earl of Eglintoun (her cousin): his lady surviving him, was afterwards married to Ludovick Duke of Lenox. This Earl's daughters were, first, Margaret, married George Lord Seatoun, and had issue, Robert, of whom the family of Wintoun is descended; and Alexander, of whom the Earl of Eglintoun is come. Earl Hugh had a 2d daughter, Agnes, married to Robert, 4th Lord Semple, and had issue. Upon his death, which happened about 1582, his estate and honours devolved upon Hugh, his son and heir, who survived him but a short time, being killed at Stuartoun, in 1586, by the Cunninghames, leaving issue by Giles his wife, daughter of Robert Lord Boyd, Hugh, his only son and heir, a Minor at his death, and under the tutory of Robert, Master of Eglintoun, his uncle. This Earl Hugh was twice married: first, to Lady Jean Hamiltoun, daughter of James, Duke of Chatlerault; she deceased in December 1596, without issue, and was buried in the Abby Church of Holy-rood-house. 2dly, He took to wife Elizabeth Montgomery, his first cousin, only daughter of Robert Master of Eglintoun, his uncle. He departed this life, without any succession, in the year 1612. His estate and honours, according to his destination, descended on Mr. Alexander Seatoun, his cousin german, son of George, Lord Seatoun, by Lady Margaret Montgomery, daughter of Hugh, third Earl of

[1] Holinshed.   [2] Spotiswood's History.

Eglintoun and aunt to this last Earl, with this Proviso, that he and his successors carry the Name and Arms of Montgomery¹ : which Alexander married Ann, eldest daughter of Alexander, first Earl of Linlithgow, by Helen his wife, daughter of Andrew, Earl of Errol, by whom he had Hugh his successor. The 2d, Sir Hary of Giffen, died without succession. The 3d, Colonel James of Coilsfield, father of Hugh Montgomery now of Coilsfield. The 4th, Major General Robert; who by Margaret his wife, daughter of James Viscount of Kilsyth, had issue, Mr. James Montgomery his son and heir. This Earl had likeways one daughter, Margaret, married first to John Earl of Tweeddale, for his 2d wife, and had issue, Mr. William Hay, now of Drumellior ; she, surviving her first husband, married secondly William Earl of Glencairn, Lord Chancellor of Scotland, but to him had no issue. This Earl Alexander, surviving his first lady, he secondly took to wife Margaret Scot, daughter of Walter, Lord Buccleugh, and Dowager of James Lord Ross ; but by her he had no issue : he was Captain of his Majesty's Guards, when in Scotland, an. 1650. He survived the Restauration of King Charles II, and departed this life an. 1661 :

To whom succeeded Hugh his son and heir ; which Hugh was twice married, first, with the Lady Ann, daughter of James Marquis of Hamilton, by whom he had only one daughter, Ann, married to James Earl of Finlator, and had issue. Secondly he married Mary, daughter of John Earl of Rothes ; by whom he had two sons ; Alexander his successor, and Mr. Francis of Giffen ; who married, first, Margaret, Countess and sole heiress of Alexander Earl of Leven ; but she dying soon after, he remarried Elizabeth, daughter of Sir Robert Sinclair of Lochermachouse, by whom he had two sons and a daughter ; John Montgomery younger of Giffen, who is married with Mary, daughter of John Earl of Hyndford, and hath issue, the 2d, Colonel Alexander : his daughter Elizabeth is married to Colonel Patrick Ogilvie of Longmay. This Mr. Francis hath been since the Revolution one of the Commissioners of the Thesaury, as also sometime Captain and Governour of Her Majesty's Castle of Dunbartoun, and one of those nominate by Her Majesty to treat on the Union with England an. 1706 : he is also at present a Member of Parliament for the Shire of Air, an. 1709. Earl Hugh had likeways several daughters, viz. Mary, married George Earl of Wintoun, but had no issue : the 2d, Margaret, James Earl of Loudoun : the third Christian, was married to John Lord Balmerinoch, and had issue : the 4th Elenor, to Sir David Dunbar of Baldoon, and had issue: the 5th, Ann, to Sir Andrew Ramsay of Abbotshall, and had issue. Earl Hugh dying an. 1669,

To him succeeded Alexander, his son and heir, who departed this life at London, an. 1701, and his corps were transported to Scotland, and buried at Kilwinning among his ancestors ; leaving issue, by Elizabeth his Countess, daugh-

¹ Spotiswood's History.

ter of William, 2d Earl of Dumfries; Alexander now Earl of Eglintoun, his son and heir; likeways a daughter, Mary, married to Sir James Agneu of Lochnaw, and hath issue. Which Alexander now Earl of Eglintoun hath been thrice married: first, to Margaret Cochran, daughter of William Lord Cochran son and heir of William Earl of Dundonald; by whom he had Hugh, then Master of Eglintoun, who died at the University of Glasgow, an. 1696: and four daughters; Catharine married James Earl of Galloway; hath issue. The second, Euphem, to George Lockhart of Carnwath; hath issue. The third, Lady Grace: the fourth Lady Jean; both yet unmarried. His second Lady was Ann, daughter of George Earl of Aberdeen, by whom he has one daughter, Lady Mary. He is thirdly married to Susanna, daughter of Sir Archbald Kennedy of Colzean, Baronet.

The Armorial bearing of the family of Eglintoun is, Two Coats quarterly; first; Azure, Three Flower-de-luces, Or: secondly; Gules, Three Annulets, Or, stoned, Azure: all within a Border, Or; Flower'd and Counter-flower'd Gules; supported by two Dragons, Vert: and for Crest, a Maid holding in one hand a Man's Head, and in the other an Anchor: with this Motto, " Garde bien."

West from the Castle of Punnoon stands the Paroch Church of Eagelsham, a Parsonage, and an ancient Dependency upon the Cathedral of Glasgow. In the reign of King James VI. Mr. Andrew Boyd, natural son of Thomas Lord Boyd, Parson of Eagelsham, was an. 1613, advanced to the Episcopal See of Argile, where he continued till his death, an. 1638. The Reverend Mr. John Stewart is present minister of Eagelsham. South from this Church stands the house and lands of Auchinhood, an ancient possession of the Montgomeries, a branch of the family of Eglintoun, and is now the property of Mr. John Montgomery of Wrae, Depute Secretary for North Britain, descended of the family of Auchinhood.

North-west of Eagelsham, and upon the bank of Cart, lies the Barony of Cathcart, where, upon an eminence, stands the Castle of Cathcart, the principal messwage of a fair Lordship of the same denomination; whose ancestors (without doubt) have taken Sirname and Designation from their hereditary lands, when fixed Sirnames came to be used: for in the reign of King William, and about the year 1179, Rainaldus de Cathcart is a witness to the Donation of the Church of Cathcart, by Allan the son of Walter, Dapifer regis Scotiæ, to the Monks of Pasly[1]. But the first of this family I have found design'd of Cath-

[1] Register of Pasly.

cart, was " Dominus Allanus de Cathcart, Dominus ejusdem, Miles," an. 1387, (regnante Roberto II.) [1], who obtained the Baronies of Sundrum and Auchincrew in Kyle, in right of Sir Duncan Wallace of Sundrum his uncle.

But, the first of this family stood ranked with the Peers of this Realm, was Sir Allan Cathcart of that-ilk, who was dignified with the Honour of Lord Cathcart of Cathcart, by King James II. an. 1447. I have seen him then designed, " Nobi-" lis & Magnificus Dominus Allanus de Cathcart Dominus ejusdem." The same Prince gave a Charter of Confirmation of the Barony of Cathcart, " dilecto " Consanguineo suo, Allano Domino Cathcart." To Allan Lord Cathcart, formerly mentioned, succeeded John his grandson and heir; (his own immediate son dying in his lifetime) which John was married, first with Margaret Kennedy, a daughter of Kennedy of Balquhan, by whom he had Allan his successor: secondly he took to wife, Janet daughter of Sir William Douglass of Drumlenrig (ancestor to the Duke of Queensberry), and of Elizabeth Crichtoun, daughter to the Lord Sanquhar. By the contract, yet extant, the said Elizabeth Crichtoun Lady Drumlenrig, obliges herself to pay to the said John Lord Cathcart, 700 Merks of Tocher with the said Janet Douglass her daughter. The issue of this marriage were two sons, John and James. The first brother obtained the Barony of Carltoun, by marriage of Margaret, daughter and sole heiress of Allan Cathcart of Carltoun, an ancient family of that name; to whom Sir Hugh Cathcart of Carltoun, Baronet, is now the lineal heir. Mr. Andrew Cathcart of Glasgow, merchant, is his brother german: as James Cathcart, the 2d son of John Lord Cathcart, obtained the lands of Carbiestoun, by marriage of Margaret, daughter and co-heir of William Cathcart of Carbiestoun, of whom is lineally descended Mr. James Cathcart of Carbiestoun.

To John Lord Cathcart, who lived till the year 1530, succeeded Allan his son; who in 1507, obtained a Charter of the Barony of Cathcart, upon the resignation of his father: he was married to Agnes, daughter of Robert Lord Lyle [2], by whom he had Allan his successor; which Allan and Helen his wife daughter of William Lord Semple, obtained a Charter of the Barony of Cathcart, from King James V. an. 1537. He alienate the Lordship of Cathcart about the year 1546, to Gabriel Semple, of Ladymure; and was killed at the

---

[1] Genealogy of the Lord Cathcart, in the hands of the Honourable and learned Antiquary, Sir James Dalrymple, Baronet; excerpted from the Writs of that Family, and courteously communicate to me. [2] Carta penes Allanum Domin. Cathcart.

battle of Pinkie, an. 1547 ¹. The Right Honourable Allan Lord Cathcart, is his lineal heir,

The Barony of Cathcart being sold by Allan Lord Cathcart to Gabriel Semple of Ladymure, who was one of the younger sons of John Lord Semple, by Janet Colvil his lady, took thence designation of Cathcart. I have found him so designed, an. 1547. He married Janet Spreul, daughter of John Spreul of Coudon, and relict of John Pollock of that-ilk. William Semple of Cathcart was his son: he had likeways a daughter, Margaret, married John Pollock of that-ilk, and had issue ². To William succeeded another Gabriel, who was father of Bryce Semple of Cathcart; whose son and heir is Sir William Semple now of Cathcart: whose Armorial bearing is, Argent, a Cheveron Checquie, Argent and Gules; betwixt two Bugles, Sable, in chief, stringed Gules; and a Flower-de-luce in base, of the third: and for Crest, a Stag's Head': with this Motto, " Keep Tryst."

At the Castle of Cathcart, there is a stone bridge over the river, near to which stands the Paroch Church of Cathcart, an ancient Dependency on the Monastery of Pasly, given to that Abby by Walter, the son of Allan, " Dapifer regis Scotiæ." The patronage of this Church was in the family of Dundonald. The Church at present is vacant.

West from the Church of Cathcart lies the village of Langside, a place only memorable for the defeat given to Queen Mary's troops, by these of her son King James VI. under the command of James Earl of Murray, Regent, an. 1568. A part of which is the property of James Hamilton of Aikenhead, by purchase of James Hamilton of Aikenhead, his Grandfather, who was a merchant in Glasgow, and Provost of that city; and a younger son of Robert Hamilton of Torence, who was descended of a younger brother of that noble family of Hamilton; whose Armorial bearing is, Gules, a Hunting Horn, betwixt three Cinquefoils, Argent.

South from Langside lies the house and lands of Bogtoun, built by John Blair of that-ilk, and Grissel his lady, daughter of Robert Lord Semple, in an. 1580, after these lands were acquired from the Lord Cathcart, by the laird of Blair, an ancient family in Cunninghame, where their principal residence is, and who, as appears from unquestionable documents, have been possessed of the lands of Blair before the twelfth Century, that William de Blair is mentioned, an. 1205, in a contract of agreement betwixt Ralph de Eglintoun and the village

---

¹ Precept for Infefting Allan Lord Cathcart, as heir to Allan his father, kill'd at Pinkie, 1547. ² Carta penes Dom. Rob. Pollock, de eadem, Bar.

of Irvine[1]. From the family of Blair, the lands of Bogtoun came to Sir Adam Blair of Bogtoun, nephew of Bryce Blair of that-ilk, by Robert his Brother German; which Sir Adam sold the lands of Bogtoun to James Hamiltoun of Aikenhead, about the year 1679.

Near Bogtoun is the house of Williamwood, the Seat of, and from whence, John Maxwell, Sheriff Depute of Renfrew, takes his Designation, and is descended from the Maxwells of Aldhouse, who were of a son of the ancient family of Pollock; and gives for his Armorial bearing the Coat of that family, viz. Argent, on a Saltyre, Sable; an Annulet, Or ; Stoned, Azure; with a suitable distinction.

South from Bogtoun lies the house and lands of Newlands, which were acquired from Hugh Earl of Eglintoun, by John Anderson, merchant in Glasgow, and soon afterward disponed by him to John Leckie, a wealthy merchant in that city, (who was descended from the Leckies of Wester Catter, in the Sheriffdom of Dunbartoun) whose son John Leckie of Newlands dying an. 1707, his estate came, by marriage of Susanna his daughter and sole heir, to Francis Dunlop of that-ilk, chief of that name, and head of an ancient family in Cunninghame.

West from the Paroch of Cathcart is Eastwood; where, first, we have the village of Pollockshaws, the property of Sir John Maxwel of Pollock, Baronet, one of the Senators of the College of Justice; at which place there is a stone bridge of two arches over the river of Cart: and not far from this, towards the west, stands the Castle of Nether Pollock, the principal Manour of an ancient family of the Sirname of Maxwel, a branch of those of Carlaverock (ancestor to the Earl of Nithsdale) adorn'd with curious orchards and gardens; with large parks and meadows, excellently well planted with a great deal of regular and beautiful planting, which adds much to the pleasure of this Seat. Upon an eminence near to this, stood the old Castle of Pollock, the ancient Seat of that family, where are still the remains of a draw-bridge and a fossy.

This ancient family derive their descent from John Maxwel of Pollock, who was brother to Sir Herbert Maxwel of Carlaverock, in the reign of King Alexander III.[2], and is a witness to that Donation, which Sir Herbert Maxwel gave to the Monks of Pasly, out of his lands of Mearns, about the year 1273 [3],

---

[1] In the Charter Chest of the Burgh of Irvine, an Excerpt of which I have seen by the favour of Richard Cunninghame of Bedland. [2] Sir James Dalrymple in his Appendix to the Observations of the Scotish History. [3] Chartulary of Pasly.

and design'd, " Johanni Maxwel Domino de Nether Pollock:" of which John, did Sir John Maxwel of Pollock lineally descend; who lived in the reign of King David Bruce, and in that of his successor, Robert II. and is frequently found in Charters granted by the Prince; particularly I find he was a witness to that Confirmation, which Robert Earl of Strathern, and John Lord Kyle, his eldest son and apparent heir, gave of that Mortification, by Sir William Mure of Abercorn, to the Monks of Pasly, an. 1367. The same Sir John Maxwel and Elizabeth Lindsay his spouse, niece to King Robert II. obtained from Robert Earl of Strathern, a part of the lands of Badruel, in the Earldom of Strathern; of which lands he also obtained a Charter of Confirmation from David Earl of Strathern, eldest son of King Robert II. by Euphem Ross his Queen, which is dated at Edinburgh the 10th of May, 1372 [1]; which lands of Badruel the same Sir John Maxwel exchang'd with Sir Bernard Hauden, ancestor to the laird of Gleneagles, for the lands of Jacktoun, in the Barony of Kilbride and Sheriffdom of Lanerk, an. 1398, as is evident from the original Charter of Excambion, yet extant [2]: he had issue by Elizabeth Lindsay his lady, daughter of Sir James Lindsay of Crawfurd, and of Giles his wife, daughter of Walter High Stewart of Scotland, and sister of King Robert II. two sons; Sir John his successor, and Robert, author of that branch of the Maxwels of Calderwood (which produced the family of Newark, of whom issued the Maxwels of Stainly, Dargavel, &c.) for this I have seen a Charter granted by Sir John Maxwel of Pollock, " dilecto filio suo Roberto Maxwel," of the lands of Calderwood, dated at Pollock, the 4th May 1401 [3]: he obtained the lands of Mauldsley, Nether Finlaystoun and Stainly, by marriage of Elizabeth, daughter and one of the co-heirs of Sir Robert Dennistoun of that-ilk. I have seen, by the favour of my Lord Pollock, a contract in the year 1405, betwixt Duncan Earl of Lenox, upon the one part; and Sir William of Cuninghame, Lord of Kilmaures, and Sir Robert of Maxwel, Lord of Calderwood, with consent of Margaret and Elizabeth Dennistouns, their spouses, daughters and co-heirs of Sir Robert Dennistoun, Knight, upon the other part, relative to the division of their lands; on account of which marriage, the family of Calderwood carry the Coat of Dennistoun of that-ilk, viz. Argent, a Bend Dexter, Azure; quarter'd with the paternal coat of Maxwel: of whom William Maxwel of Calderwood is lineally descended.

---

[1] Sir James Dalrymple's edition of Cambden.   [2] Carta Dom. Johan. Maxwel de Nether Pollock, Baronet.   [3] Carta penes Dom. Joh. Maxwel de Pollock, Baron.

To Sir John Maxwel of Pollock, formerly mentioned, succeeded Sir John, his son and heir, who lived in the reign of King James I. To whom succeeded another Sir John Maxwel of Pollock; who, an. 1477, obtained the lands of Glanderstoun from John Lord Darnly, "pro homagio & servitio suo," as the original Charter, yet extant, bears. When he died I find not; but he left two sons, Sir John his successor, and Mr. Robert, first Rector of Torboltoun; I find him so designed, an. 1521 [1]. He was afterwards Provost of the Collegiate Church of Dunbartoun; and from thence, in the reign of King James V. advanced to the Bishoprick of Orkney.

Which Sir John, last mentioned, was co-temporary with King Jams IV. and from that Prince obtained the honour of Knighthood: He was married to a daughter of the family of Houstoun of that-ilk; by whom he had only one daughter, Elizabeth Maxwel, his sole heir: which Elizabeth took to husband John Maxwel, her first cousin, who was son of George Maxwel of Cowglen, a brother of the family of Pollock, and in an. 1558, she is retoured heir of Sir John Maxwel of Pollock, her great grandfather [2]. This Sir John was knighted by Queen Mary, and adhered zealously to that misfortunate Princess; and after her escape from Lochlevin, an. 1568, he being a person in whom she had assurance, both of his fidelity and affection to her interest, orders him to meet her at Hamiltoun with his friends and servants, "boden in feer of Weir," as the Original Letters, yet extant, bear, and continued with Her Majesty until the defeat of her troops at Langside: He deceased an. 1578. To whom succeeded John his son and heir; who also obtained the honour of Knighthood from King James VI. and being at the conflict at Lockerby, an. 1593, assisting the Lord Maxwel against the Laird of Johnstoun, he was there slain; leaving issue, by Margaret his lady, daughter of William Cunninghame of Caprintoun, Sir John his son and heir; likeways a daughter, Agnes, who was married to John Boyle of Kelburn, whose ancestors have been possessed of these lands upwards of Five Hundred years, as the Writs of that ancient family do sufficiently demonstrate. The Right Honourable David Earl of Glasgow is the great grandchild of the above mentioned John Boyle of Kelburn, by the said Agnes Maxwel his lady.

Sir John, son and heir of Sir John his father, formerly mentioned, was twice married; first with   Campbel, daughter of Sir Matthew Campbel of Loudoun; and, surviving her, he secondly took to wife Grisel, daughter of John Blair of that-ilk; but, he dying without succession, as appears by the Probate of his Testament, the 1st of November 1647, his estate devolved upon Mr. George

[1] Chartulary of Pasly.   [2] Carta penes D. Joa. Maxwel de Pollock. Baronet.

Maxwel of Aldhouse, his cousin and nearest heir male; which Mr. George was lineally descended of Hugh Maxwel, brother of Sir John Maxwel of Pollock, in the reign of King James IV. For this I have seen a Remission granted by that Prince, an. 1500, dated at Renfrew, to John Maxwel, son and apparent heir of Sir John Maxwel of Pollock, and to Hugh Maxwel, brother german to the said Sir John, for a slaughter committed by them on Hector Mure, son to the Laird of Caldwel: from which Hugh did lineally descend John Maxwel of Aldhouse, Father of Mr. George Maxwel of the same place, who was thrice married; first, with Janet, daughter of John Miller of Newtoun, and of Giles his wife, daughter of John Pollock of that-ilk; by whom he had Mr. John his son and heir: He secondly took to wife, Jean, daughter of William Mure of Glanderstoun, by whom he had William Maxwel, who was author of that branch of the Maxwels of Sprinkel, whose son is Sir Patrick Maxwel now of Sprinkel, Baronet. He was thirdly married to Janet Douglass, daughter to the Laird of Waterside, by whom he had a son, Hugh, who obtained the lands of Dalswintoun, by marriage of Elizabeth, daughter and heir of John Maxwel of Dalswintoun, whose son is George Maxwel now of Dalswintoun.

To Mr George Maxwel of Aldhouse, above mentioned, succeeded Mr. John his son and heir; who married Elizabeth Stewart, Daughter of James Stewart, Tutor of Blackhall, by whom he had two sons, Mr. George, who succeeded to Sir John Maxwel of Pollock: And the second was Zacharias of Blawarthill (" quod vide") father of Mr. John Maxwel now of Blawarthill; which Mr. George Maxwel of Pollock obtained the honour of Knighthood from King Charles II. He was a gentleman of singular accomplishments, and justly esteemed a person eminent for piety, learning, and other good qualifications: He was married to Anabel, daughter of Sir Archbald Stewart of Blackhall, by Margaret his wife, daughter of Bryce Blair of that-ilk; by whom he had John, his successor, and three daughters; first, Marion married William Stewart of Rosyth; had no issue: secondly, she married Sir Charles Murray. The second daughter Anabel, married, first, John Cathcart of Carltoun, but had no issue; she afterwards married Sir Robert Pollock of that-ilk, and had issue. The third daughter was Margaret, married to Alexander Maxwel younger of Calderwood. This Sir George deceased an. 1677: to whom succeeded John, his son and heir; which John was raised to the dignity of Baronet, by King Charles II's Letters Patent, bearing date, at Whitehall, the 12th of April 1682. And that dignity is since confirmed to his heirs of Tailzie: and being unanimously chosen by the Freeholders of the Shire of Renfrew, as one of their Commissioners to the Convention of Estates, which met at Edinburgh, March 14, an. 1689, he was by his late Majesty, King William, nominate one of his Privy Council for Scotland, upon the first Constitution thereof; and afterwards, in the year 1696, was appointed one of the Lords Commissioners of the Thesaury and Exchequer; and in 1699, constitute one of the Senators of the College of Justice, and Lord Justice Clerk. He married Marion, daughter of Sir James Stewart of Kirkfield.

The Armorial bearing of this ancient family is ; Argent; on a Saltyre, Sable; an Annulet, Or; Stoned, Azure; supported by two Monkies; and for Crest, a Stag's Head; with this Motto, " I am ready."

South of Nether Pollock stands the house and lands of Aldhouse, situate upon a rivulet of the same denomination, where there are found a great many fossile shells, collected by the Reverend Mr. Robert Woodrow, minister of the Gospel at Eastwood, (my very worthy friend,) a gentleman well seen in the curious natural products of this country. The lands of Aldhouse are now the property of Robert Sanders, Printer in Glasgow, a Vassal to my Lord Pollock. And south from this stands the Paroch Church of Eastwood, an ancient Dependency on the Monastery of Pasly, well provided with a large manse. The present minister is the Reverend Mr. Robert Woodrow; his predecessor was that Reverend and learn'd Divine, Mr. Matthew Crawfurd, who was descended of the house of Carse, and deceased in the month of December, an. 1700. and left a compleat History of the Church of Scotland, of his own composure, collected from several rare manuscripts, from the planting of the Christian Faith, down to the late Revolution; wherein that Reverend author hath given sufficient proof of his indefatigable pains, as well as of his profound judgement and industry. He hath given an account of a great many transactions, from the year 1638 to the year 1662, from original papers. The manuscript is in two large volumes in folio, all writ in a fair legible character, and is in the hands of Mr. Matthew Crawfurd, his son, preacher of the Gospel, and keeper of the Library of the University of Glasgow, who designs with all expedition to publish the same.

South from this Church lies the Castle of Eastwood, the principal Manour of that Barony; an ancient possession of the family of Eglintoun, of which noble family I have already treated, page 23, &c.

Some two miles south from Eastwood lies the Paroch of Mearns; the southern places of which bound the Shire of Renfrew from the Bailliary of Cunninghame; where, upon an eminence, stands the Castle of the same name, the chief messwage of that Barony, a Seat of the Lord Maxwel; but the first using that designation is Rolandus de Mearns, who is mentioned a witness in the donation, which Eschina de Molla, wife of Walter, High Stewart of Scotland,

Founder of the Monastery of Pasly, gave to the Monks of that Abby, " pro sa-
" lute Domini sui Willielmi regis Scotiæ [1]." But this Barony of lare extent,
came to the Maxwels of Carlaverock, by marriage of an heiress of the Sirname of MacGeachin, as the Genealogy of the family of Maxwel bears [2], in
the days of King Alexander II. For, in that reign, I have seen Eumerus de
Maxwel a witness to the Confirmation of the Church of Dundonald, to the
Monks of Pasly, by " Walter Senescallus regis Scotiæ ;" as also Herbertus
Maxwel, Miles, in a donation to the Monastery of Pasly, in the reign of King
Alexander III. gives " pro salute animæ suæ & animarum omnium Anteces-
" sorum & successorum suorum, octo acras & dimidium, & viginti octo parti-
" catas terræ, in nova villa sua de Mearns ; & sex mercas argenti de proventi-
" bus molendinorum suorum de Mearns [3]." I have also seen Johannes Maxwel Dominus de Mearns, granting a Charter to John Pollock his grandchild,
by Agnes Maxwel his daughter, an. 1372 [4]. Sir Herbert Maxwel of Carlaverock
and Mearns, was created a Lord of Parliament, with the title of Lord Maxwel, by King James II. about the year 1445 ; whose successor, John Lord
Maxwel, in the reign of King James VI. in right of Elizabeth Douglass his
lady, daughter and one of the co-heirs of James Earl of Morton, upon the forfaulture of James Earl of Morton, Regent, (his brother-in-law) who had married another of the daughters and co-heirs of that Earldom, did, in the year 1581,
obtain the Earldom of Morton, with that dignity : But Archbald Earl of Angus,
nephew to the Regent (Morton), being restored to the Earldom of Morton, an.
1585, the Lord Maxwel was obliged to relinquish that title, and returned to his
former dignity of Lord Maxwel ; and Robert Lord Maxwel, his son, was declared Earl of Nithsdale, by King James VI. in the Parliament, an. 1617, with precedency from the time of his predecessor's being created Earl of Morton, which
was in an. 1581. Robert, Earl of Nithsdale, alienate the Barony of Mearns,
about the year 1648, to Sir George Maxwel of Pollock ; from whom those lands
were soon after acquired by Sir Archbald Stewart of Blackhall, and is now the
property of Sir Archbald Stewart of Blackhall, Baronet, his grandchild.

West from the castle of Mearns stands the Paroch Church of the same denomination, which was a Dependency upon the Monastery of Pasly. The Reverend Mr. James MacDoual is the present minister.

West from the castle of Mearns lies the Newtoun, the Seat of the Burgh and
Barony of Mearns, erected in favours of the Lord Maxwel. The lands of

[1] Register of Pasly. [2] Genealogy of the Lords Maxwel. [3] Chartulary of Pasly.
[4] Carta penes, D. Rob. Pollock de eodem, Bar.

Newtoun were anciently possessed by the Rankins; and, by marriage of Margaret, daughter and sole heir of John Rankin of Newtoun, these lands came to Matthew Stewart, who was descended of the house of Blackhall; and are now the propertie of Lieutenant Matthew Stewart, his son.

And a little west from this stands the castle of Upper Pollock, the principal messwage of that Barony, situate upon a rising ground: It had a handsome old tower, according to the ordinary model, with a large battlement: But the present Sir Robert Pollock thought fit to demolish that fabrick, and in place of it raised a stately large house, of a new model: 'Tis also well planted, and hath good orchards, and large and commodious parks.

This ancient family have been possessed of these lands for many ages, and derive their known descent from one Peter, the son of Fulbert, who assumed both Sirname and Designation from his hereditary lands, when Sirnames were commonly used. I have seen him design'd, " Petrus de Pollock, filius Fulberti:" He is an early donator to the Monastery of Pasly; for, in the reign of King Malcolm IV. Petrus de Pollock mortifies to the Abby of Pasly, " Ecclesiam de
" Pollock cum pertinentiis suis; pro anima Domini David regis & regis Malcol-
" mi; nec non pro salute Willielmi regis, & David fratris sui; & pro anima Do-
" mini Walteri filii Allani; pro animabus patris & matris suæ, & pro salute sua
" & uxoris suæ Helenæ." Which donation is confirmed by Joceline, Bishop of Glasgow; who died[1], an. 1199. The same Petrus de Pollock is witness in a Charter by King William, of the lands of Burgin, to the Abby of Kinloss, in Murray, an. 1190[2]. He is also witness, with Robertus, filius Fulberti, his brother, to the Confirmation of the Kirks of Bute, to the Abby of Pasly, by Allan the son of Walter, " Dapifer regis Scotiæ[3],

Whose successor, Robert of Pollock, son of another Robert, mortifies to the Monks of Pasly, " Duodecem denarios de firma terræ suæ de Pollock, pro ani-
" mabus Walteri filii Allani, & Allani filii sui; & pro animabus Petri de Pollock
" & Roberti filii Fulberti fratris; & pro animabus omnium Antecessorum suo-
" rum; nec non pro salute sui ipsius & uxoris suæ & hæredum suorum." Which donation is in the reign of King Alexander II.[4]. And in the same reign Thomas de Pollock is a witness to the resignation, by " Dungallus filius Christini Ju-
" dicis de Lenox," of the lands of Caltbeth, to the Monks of Pasly[5], an. 1234.

I have also seen Petrus de Pollock, in the year 1296, mentioned, as one of the Scots Barons that gave Allegiance to Edward I. of England, by Prin

---

[1] Chartulary of Pasly. [2] Sir James Dalrymple's Appendix to the Observations on the Scots History. [3] Chartulary of Pasly. [4] Chartularly of Pasly. [5] Chartulary of Pasly.

in his History of that Prince; as also, in the reign of King Robert II. John Pollock, son and heir of Robert Pollock of that-ilk, by Agnes his wife, daughter of Sir John Maxwel of Mearns, obtained a Charter of his lands of Pollock, from the said Sir John Maxwel, his grandfather; therein designed, " Johanne de " Pollock filio & hærede Roberti de Pollock, & Agnetæ Maxwel filiæ dicti Do- " mini Johannis Maxwel;" and is dated, at Carlaverock, in the year 1372, as the original extant shows [1]. As also Charles Pollock of that-ilk, his successor, obtained a Charter of his lands of Pollock, from Robert Lord Maxwel, an. 1486. He married Margaret Stewart, daughter to the Laird of Minto, by whom he had two sons, John and David, successively Lairds of Pollock. Which Charles dying, an. 1508, to him succeeded John, his son and heir, whose posterity failzieing, his estate devolved upon David Pollock, his brother, who obtained a Charter of the lands of Pollock, an. 1523, and departed this life, an. 1543; leaving issue, by Marion his lady, daughter of William Stewart of Castlemilk, John his successor; and of a younger son, descended the Pollocks of Balgray. Which John Pollock of that-ilk was married with Margaret, daughter of Gabriel Semple of Cathcart; and departed this life in 1567. To him succeeded John, his son and heir; which John took to wife, Janet, daughter of William Mure of Glanderstoun, by whom he had John, his son and heir: who was married, first, with Maud, daughter of Sir Neil Montgomery of Langstoun; and then to Dorothea Stewart, daughter of James Stewart of Cardonald; and being at the conflict at Lockerby, an. 1593, assisting the Lord Maxwell (his cousin) against the Laird of Johnstoun, was there slain; leaving Robert, his son and heir, (by his second wife.) Which Robert was married to Jean, daughter of James Mowat of Busbie, by whom he had Robert, his son and heir, who died in the year 1675; leaving issue, Robert, by Jean his lady, daughter of Cornelius Crawfurd of Jordan-hill and of Mary his wife, daughter of Sir James Lockhart of Lee. Which Robert was one of the Commissioners to the Scots Parliament for the Shire of Renfrew, and was one of the Scots members to the Parliament at Westminster, on commencing the Union: he was also, by Her present Majesty, in consideration of his early and seasonable appearances for the Government, with his being chief of an ancient and honourable family, advanced to the degree and dignity of a Baronet, in the year 1703. He hath been twice married; first with Anabel, daughter of Sir George Maxwel of Pollock; and, secondly, he married Anabel, daughter of Walter Stewart of Pardovan; by whom he has issue, Robert, his son and apparent heir.

[1] Carta Dom. Rob. Pollock, de eodem, Bar.

The armorial bearing of Pollock of that-ilk, is, Vert; a Saltyre, Gules; betwixt three bugles, Or; stringed of the Second; supported by two Ratches: and for Crest, a Boar, pierced with a Dart: and this motto, " Audacter et Strenuè."

West from the place of Upper Pollock lie the house and lands of Balgray, an ancient inheritance of a Family of the sirname of Park. Alexander Park of Balgray alienate those lands, an. 1603, to David Pollock in Lee; whose successor, David Pollock of Balgray, dispon'd his lands to Thomas Pollock, a wealthy merchant of the city of Glasgow; which Thomas was son of Mr. David Pollock, minister at Glenluce, by Margaret his wife, daughter of Mr. James Boyd at Trochrig, Archbishop of Glasgow. This Mr. David was descended of a brother of the family of Pollock, in the reign of Queen Mary; whose grandchild is Thomas Pollock, now of Balgray; whose armorial bearing is the coat of the family of Pollock, and adds a Molet in Chief, for a brotherly difference.

South from the house of Balgray lie the house and lands of Fingletoun, an ancient inheritance of the Hamiltons of Prestoun; whose original ancestor, Sir John Hamilton of Rosaven, obtained a charter of the lands of Fingletoun, from Sir David Hamilton of Cadzow, his newhew, an. 1359. (regnante Davide Secundo,) which lands came from the family of Preston, to Sir James Oswald of Fingletoun.

South West of the Paroch of Mearns lies Neilstoun, an ancient possession of the Crocs of that-ilk, a family of great antiquity in this Shire: for Robert de Croc is a witness in the foundation of the Monastery of Pasly, an. 1160. Which Robert gives the patronage of the kirk of Neilstoun to the Monastery of Pasly, " pro salute animæ suæ¹," in the reign of King William.

To Robert de Croc succeeded Allan his son; for this I have seen in the Register of the Monastery of Pasly, a donation of the mill of Pasly to the Monks of that convent, by Allan, the son of Walter founder of that Monastery; to which Roberto de Croc & Allano filio suo, are witnesses: and, by Marion de Croc, daughter and heiress of another Robert de Croc, the lands of Crocstoun, Darnly and Neilstoun, came, by marriage, to a younger brother of the illustrious Family of Stewart; of whom issued the Stewarts, promiscuously designed, of Crocstoun and Darnly, afterwards Earls, and then Dukes, of Lenox (quod vide). In Neilstoun are the seats of several ancient and respective families: as, Arthurly, anciently the inheritance and designation of a family of the sirname of Stewart, a branch of the noble Family of Darnly. Walter Stewart of Arthurly obtain'd from King James the III. Anno 1452, a Charter

¹ Chartulary of Pasly.

of the lands of Wester Partick. By Margaret Stewart, his daughter and heir, these lands came by marriage to William Cunninghame, a son of Alexander, first Earl of Glencairn, ancestor of the Cunninghames of Craigends: upon which account that Family carries the coat of Stewart, quartered in their achievement. The lands of Arthurly are now the property of Allan Pollock of Arthurly.

In this paroch of Neilstoun is also Glanderstoun, the residence of William Mure, upon a small rivulet, adorn'd with regular orchards and large meadows, beautified with a great deal of regular and beautiful planting. The house was of an old model, which the present Glanderstoun thought fit to demolish; and, in place of the old one, hath raised a pretty house, of a new model, with several well finished apartments. The lands of Glanderstoun being a part of the Lordship of Neilstoun, were given by Matthew, first Earl of Lenox, to John Stewart his brother, in the year 1507, who leaving only one daughter, Margaret Stewart, who became the wife of John Frizel of Knock[1]; the lands of Glanderstoun came to the Family of Caldwel, and were disponed by John Mure of Caldwel, to William Mure his brother-german, an. 1554. He was married with Elizabeth Hamilton, a daughter of the Family of Raploch, and aunt to Gavin, Commendator of Kilwinning; by whom he had William, his successor, and several daughters; viz. Janet, married John Pollock of that-ilk, and had issue: Jean, married to Mr. George Maxwell of Aldhouse: the third, Margaret, to William Hamilton of Duncarnock. To William Mure of Glanderstoun, formerly mentioned, succeeded William, his son and heir; who took to wife Jean Hamilton, daughter of Mr. Hans Hamilton, Minister of the Gospel at Dunlop, and sister of James Hamilton, Earl of Clanbrysal in the kingdom of Ireland: by whom he had two sons and six daughters: William his eldest son and heir; the second, James of Bellybregach, in the County of Doun, in the kingdom of Ireland. His Daughters were, first, Ursula, who was married to William Ralstoun of that-ilk, and had issue. The second, Jean, to John Hamilton of Halcraig, and had issue. The third, Margaret, to Mr. Zacharias Boyd, Minister of the Barony of Glasgow; and afterward she became wife of that eminently learn'd and pious divine; Mr. James Durham of Pourie, Minister of the Gospel at Glasgow; but had no issue. The fourth daughter, Janet, to Mr. John Carstairs, Minister of the Gospel at Glasgow; they were father and mother to the Reverend Mr. William Carstairs, principal of the University of Edinburgh. The fifth daughter, Elizabeth, was married to Mr. Alexander Dunlop, minister of the Gospel at

---

[1] Carta penes W. Mure de Glanderstoun.

Pasly, whose son was the Reverend Mr. William Dunlop, Principal of the University of Glasgow, and Historiographer for Scotland. The sixth, Agnes, married William Porterfield of Quarreltoun. This William Mure of Glanderstoun deceased an. 1640. To whom succeeded William, his son and heir: Which William deceased in the year 1658, leaving issue two sons and three daughters, by Barbara his wife, daughter of Robert Mure of Caldwel: viz. William his successor; the second, James of Rhoddens, in the County of Doun and kingdom of Ireland; whose eldest son and apparent heir, is Mr. William Mure of Duncarnock, Advocate. His daughters were Jean, married to James Lindsay of Dovehill; but had no issue. The second, Elizabeth, to James Stewart of Hartwood, and had issue. The third, Barbara, to Captain James Mure of Bellybregach, and had issue.

To William, formerly mentioned, succeeded William his son and heir: which William Mure, now of Glanderstoun, hath married Margaret, daughter of Sir George Mowat of Inglistoun, descended from the ancient family of Balquhollie in Aberdeen Shire; but as yet hath not any issue.

The armorial bearing of this family is, Argent; on a Fess, Azure; three Molets, of the First; within a Border, Gules; with a Crescent in base, of the Third: and for Crest, a Hand holding a sword; with this motto, Help at Hand, Brother.

West from Glanderstoun stands the Paroch Church of Neilstoun, the Patronage of which was given by Robert de Croc, " pro salute animæ suæ," to the Monks of Pasly, in the reign of William. And near to that Church lie the lands of Kirktoun, the property of the Reverend Mr. John Miller, present minister of the Gospel at Neilstoun; which he obtained by marriage of Janet, daughter and sole heiress of James Adam of Kirktoun, merchant in Glasgow; which Mr. John was son and heir of Mr. Robert Miller, minister at Ochiltree, by Grissel his wife, daughter of Colonel Hugh Cochran, brother-german to William Earl of Dundonald.

South from the Church of Neilstoun lie the house and lands of Neilstounside, a part of the Lordship of Neilstoun; of which lands I have seen a charter granted by John Earl of Lenox, to John Maxwell of Stainly, and Agnes Lyle his spouse, an. 1522 [1]; but these lands came afterwards to the Stewarts: and by marriage of Margaret, daughter and sole heir of Hugh Stewart, came to William Wallace, of the family of Eldersly, whose son is John Wallace now of Neil-

---

[1] Carta penes J. Com. de Dundonald.

stounside, heir and representative of the ancient family of Eldersly: (quod vide.)

West from this Church lies the barony of Syde, an ancient possession of the Montgomeries of Skelmurly, who derive their descent from George Montgomery, a younger son of Montgomery of Ardrossan. But of this family I have not found any thing memorable, until the reign of Queen Mary, that Robert Montgomery of Skelmurly married Mary, daughter of Robert Lord Semple, by whom he had two sons, William and Robert; as likeways a daughter, Margaret, married to William Cochran of that-ilk, of whom the Right Honourable John Earl of Dundonald is lineally descended: which Robert Montgomery of Skelmurly, above-mentioned, and William, his eldest son and apparent heir, were both killed, by Patrick Maxwel of Newark[1], an. 1584: to whom succeeded Robert, his second son and heir: Which Robert, being a person of an ample fortune, was the seventeenth in number, as to precedence, of those Barons, whom King Charles I. raised to the degree and dignity of Baronet, the third year of his reign; his patent bearing date the first day of January 1628[2]. He was married with Margaret, daughter of Sir William Douglas of Drumlanrig, by Elizabeth his Lady, daughter of Sir John Gordon, of Lochenvar; by whom he had Sir Robert, his son and heir, who wedded the Lady Mary Campbel, daughter of Archibald Earl of Argile, and of Ann Douglas, daughter to the Earl of Morton, by whom he had, Sir Robert, his successor, who departed this life an.

leaving issue two sons, by Ann his Lady, daughter and one of the co-heirs of Colonel Sir James Scot of Rossie, viz. Sir James Montgomery of Skelmurly, and Hugh Montgomery now of Busbie, Esquire, and late Provost of the City of Glasgow: Which Sir James Montgomery, being chosen one of the Commissioners for the Shire of Air, to the Convention of Estates which met at Edinburgh the 14th of March 1689, was one of the Scots Commissioners nominate in that great meeting, with Archibald Earl of Argile, and Sir John Dalrymple, afterward Earl of Stair, to wait on their late Majesties, King William and Queen Mary, with an offer of the Crown: but afterwards retiring to France, he died there an.   leaving issue, by Margaret his Lady, daughter of James Earl of Anandale, two sons, Sir Robert Montgomery now of Skelmurly, Baronet, and Lieutenant-Colonel William Montgomery, his brother-german.

The Armorial bearing of this Family, is, Two coats quarterly: First; Azure; Three Flower de Luce's, Or; within a double Tressure, Flower'd and Counter-

---

[1] Carta penes Alex. Porterfield, de codem.   [2] An exact list of Baronets, in the hands of the Honourable and learn'd Antiquary Sir James Dalrymple, Baronet.

flower'd of the 2d: Secondly: Gules; Three Annulets, Or; stoned Azure: Third, as Second: Fourth, as First: And for Crest, an Anchor: with this motto, Garde, Garde.

West from the barony of Syde lie the lands and castle of Caldwel, the possession of an ancient family of the Mures, descended of the family of Abercorn in West Lothian, who obtained the Lands of Caldwel by marriage of an heiress of the same sirname: But, that the descent of Caldwel from the family of Abercorn, may not be received without a sufficient document, you'll find from the Chartulary of Pasly[1], presently in my hands, by the favour of the Right Honourable John, Earl of Dundonald, a submission, an. 1328, betwixt And. de Kelchor, Prior of Pasly, and Procurator for the said Abby, on the one part; and Reginald Mure, Procurator for the Master, Chanons and Monks of Simpringhame, on the other; concerning fourty merks of annuity, payable by the Monastery of Pasly to Simpringhame, and assigned by them to the said Sir Reginald: on which submission, the Abbot is decerned to pay the fourty merks to the said Sir Reginald and his successors; he getting a sufficient writ from those of Simpringhame, to secure Pasly for what they pay: and, for further security to the said Sir Reginald and his son Sir William Mure, designed of Abercorn, consign a writ, disponing his lands of Sanackar, Camsestrang, Donlarigs, Cowdams, Staflour and Hormsdale, lying in the Baronies of Renfrew and Cowal, in warrandice to the said Abby, for securing them; until he produced the said Writing from Simpringhame; and the Monks of Pasly afterwards addressing to Robert Earl of Strathern, High Stewart of Scotland, and to John Lord Kyle, his eldest son and apparent heir, who were superiors of the lands disponed to them for their security, desiring a charter, whereby they might be seased in the said lands: which Robert Earl of Strathern, and John Lord Kyle, his son, did grant an. 1367. These lands above-mentioned continued, many ages, a possession of the Mures of Caldwel; and the lands of Cowdams are held of that family to this day. But, not having seen the writs of this honourable family, I can say but little about them, save that they were honoured with diverse matches from sundry noble houses, as the families of Eglintoun, Semple, Valyfield, Rouallan, Knox of Ranfurly, and many others. William Mure, late of Caldwel, in the reign of King Charles II. married Barbara, daughter of Sir William Cunninghame of Cunninghame-head; but having no mail issue, that estate came to Barbara Mure, his daughter and sole heiress; who hath taken to husband John Fairly, second son of William Fairly of that-ilk, who assumes the

---

[1] Chartulary of Pasly.

name and arms of that ancient Family, viz. Argent; on a Bend, Azure; Three Molets, of the First; within a Border, Ingraled, Gules.

Near the Castle of East-Caldwel stand the House and Lands of Wester Caldwel, the possession of an ancient family of the same Sirname, and representative of the old Caldwels of that-ilk; most of whose estate went to a son of Abercorn, who was ancestor of the Mures of Caldwel above-mentioned: which family continued in reputation for several hundreds of years, and made intermarriages with these honourable Families, as, the Wallaces of Craigie, Semples of Milbank, Montgomeries of Langshaw, Mures of Rouallan, and Stewarts of Allantoun; and failizied in the person of John Caldwel of that-ilk, who was one of the Commissioners for the Shire of Renfrew to the Parliament, since the Revolution. These lands belong now to the Right Honourable John Earl of Dundonald.

In the Paroch of Neilstoun lie the lands of Coudoun, which gave first title of Lord to Sir William Cochran, afterwards Earl of Dundonald. An ancient family of the Spreuls, did possess the forementioned lands for many ages: but the first of that name I have found mentioned in charters, was Walter Spreul, "Senescallus de Dunbartoun," who obtain'd from Malcolm Earl of Lenox, a charter of the lands of Dalquhern, "pro homagio & servitio suo," as the charter testifies[1], and by the witnesses appears to be in the beginning of the reign of Robert Bruce: as also I have seen a resignation of the lands of Coudoun, by Walter Spreul, so design'd, in favours of Thomas Spreul, his son and apparent Heir, an. 1441[2]: Which Thomas was father of John Spreul of Coudoun, who had a charter of these lands, an. 1481, as Robert Spreul, his son, had a charter of the same lands, an. 1515. Which Robert, last mention'd, was father of John Spreul of Coudoun; who was succeeded by a son of the same name; who was father of James Spreul of Coudoun, in whose person this family failed: he sold his estate to Alexander Cochran of that-ilk, an. 1622: which lands became the patrimony of Mr. William Cochran his son, afterwards Lord Coudoun and Earl of Dundonald, and is now the property of the Earl of Dundonald.

The armorial bearing of Spreul of Coudoun, was, Or; a Cheveron Checquie, Azure and Argent; betwixt three Purses, Gules. Of this family of the Spreuls of Coudoun, are several of good note descended; as John Spreul now of Miltoun, and my very good friend Mr. John Spreul of Glasgow, merchant, author of the Accompt Current betwixt Scotland and England.

To the north from the Paroch of Neilstoun lies the Paroch of Pasly, in the

---

[1] A collection of Charters belonging to the Earls of Lenox, in the Burgh of Dunbarton's Charter-chest. [2] Writs of Coudoun, in the hands of the Earl of Dundonald.

south part whereof stands the place of Househill (situate on the rivulet Levran, which hath its influx unto Cart near to this place) a neat and handsome dwelling, the seat of James Dunlop of Househill, son and heir of James Dunlop his father; who was son and heir of Thomas Dunlop of the same place, by Grissel his wife, daughter of Alexander Cochran of that-ilk; which Thomas was one of the younger sons of James Dunlop of that-ilk, and acquired those lands from the Laird of Minto.

In the same Paroch of Pasly, and near to the River of Cart, stand some considerable remains of that noble and stately edifice, the Castle of Crockstoun, the principal messwage of the regality of Crockstoun; which regality comprehends the lordship of Darnly and Inchenan in this Shire, and the lordship of Torboltoun in the Shire of Air, where was one of the principal seats of the noble family of Darnly. This ancient building did consist of a large quarter, with two very lofty and high towers, with battlements on the wings thereof, in which there has been many spacious and large rooms: it had a very agreeable prospect through a great part of the Country; and had, adjoining to it, some square and level pieces of ground, where (no doubt) there were orchards, and surrounded with pleasant woods. Hard by the Castle is to be seen that noble monument, the Ew-tree, called, the tree of Crockstoun; of so large a trunk, and well spread in its branches, that 'tis seen at several miles distance from the ground where it stands; the impress of which is on the Reverse of the large pieces, of an ounce weight, coined by Queen Mary, after her return from France, that she had taken Henry Lord Darnly for her husband; as that coin is described at large by the Reverend Dr. Nicolson, Bishop of Carlyle, in his Scottish Historical Library, page 322. But, because what that learn'd author has writ is in few hands, and all the Scots coin, except what is now in the cabinets of the curious, is called in by the proclamations of Council, since the late Union, I presume it will not be unacceptable to the reader, to insert the said Author's words, more particularly, concerning that coin, viz. " After the " Queen's return from France, she coined the large pieces of an ounce weight; " on the first of these is the Shield of Scotland, crowned, and supported by Two " Thistles, " Maria & Henricus Dei Gratia R. & R. Scotorum :" On the re- " verse, a Palm-tree, (the Author should have nam'd it an Ew) crowned; with " this motto on a schedule hung in it, " Dat gloria vires," and subscribed 1565, " and circumscribed, " Exurgat Deus, dissipentur inimici ejus." Some call the " Tree on the reverse, an Ew-tree, and report, that there grew a famous one of " that kind in the park or garden of the Earl of Lenox; which gave occasion " to the Impress." This Reverend and curious Author, being a stranger, having writ at second hand, speaks thus dubiously; but, if he had thought fit, might have seen the Tree himself, when in Scotland: and it stands at this day as I have described it. The same Author says further, " Wherein the Tree " being bound, denotes the advancement of the Lenox's Family, by Henry, " Lord Darnly, his marriage with the Queen; and the Lemma of Dat gloria " vires, is observed very well to comport with the device." Thus far that Reverend Author.

The ancient proprietors of this Barony and fair Lordship, were of the Sirname of Croc; having (no doubt) taken their Sirname from their hereditary lands, when fixed Sirnames came to be used: and this is a good document of their antiquity, their Sirname being local, from the place of their habitation. I find Robert de Croc a witness to the Charter of Foundation of the Abby of Pasly, in King Malcolm IV's time. This Barony of Crocstoun, with many other lands, came, by marriage of the heiress of Robert de Croc, to a son of the illustrious family of Stewart, ancestor of the Dukes of Lenox (quod vide): and, Charles, now Duke of Lenox, having lately sold his fortune in Scotland, to his Grace James Duke of Montrose, the head of the ancient and eminent family of the Grahames, who in all ages have been persons of the greatest valour and renown; and his Grace (the Duke of Montrose) being now a considerable proprietor in this shire; I shall take occasion to descend upon the history of this most noble family, who are said to derive their descent from that heroick and valiant Grahame, whose valour was especially seen, when he made that breach upon the trench, or wall, which the Emperour Severus had made, and set up for the outmost limit of the Roman empire, betwixt the Scottish Firth and the River of Clyde, whence that trench retains the name of Grahame's Dyke. But, not to insist upon so remote an origine, and also to give unquestionable documents for the antiquity of this family, from the evidents thereof, in the hands of his Grace the Duke of Montrose; I find, King William gave a Charter of the lands of Kinabyre, Charltoun, and Borrowfield, " cum earum " pertinent ac piscariis aquæ de Northesk, ubicunque aqua currit infra Vice- " comitatum de Forfar, Davidi de Grahame, Militi, pro homagio & servitio " suo [1]." The same Sir David de Grahame obtained from Maulduin, Earl of Lenox, " Carrucatam Terræ quæ vocatur Muckram [2]." He had also a Charter from the same Earl of Lenox, with consent of Malcolm, his son and apparent heir, of the lands of Strathblane, an. 1248: (regnante Alexandro Secundo.) To Sir David de Grahame succeeded Sir David, his son and heir, who lived in the

---

[1] Carta penes Jacobum Ducem de Montrose. [2] Carta penes Jac. Ducem Montrose.

reign of King Alexander III. and from that Prince obtain'd a Charter of Confirmation, the twentieth-second year of his reign, of the lands and barony of Kincardine, granted by Maliss Earl of Strathern, to this Sir David de Grahame[1]. The next of this noble family, of whom I have found any memorable mention, is "Dominus Patricius Grahame, Miles, Vicecomes de Striveling," who was employed in several foreign embassies, by King Alexander III.[2]. As another Sir David de Grahame, successor to the former Sir Patrick, was one of these Scottish Barons, that's insert in the Letter to the Pope, asserting the Independency of the Kingdom of Scotland, an. 1320[3]. The same Sir David, design'd of Dundaff, obtained from the heroick King Robert Bruce, " pro homagio, & servitio suo, & in excambium pro terra de Cardross, quam ha-" buit ab ipso Dom. Davide, totam terram de vetere Montrose infra Viceco-" mitatum de Forfar. Apud Sconam, quinto Martii, an. regni nostri vicesimo[4]." As also in the reign of King David Bruce, "Dom. Dav. Grahame, Dom. de Dundaff," is nominate one of the Scottish Commissioners to treat for the ransom of that Prince, taken prisoner at the battle of Durhame, 1348[5].

To this Sir David, succeeded Sir Patrick his son; for this I have seen a Charter granted by " Dominus Angusius Halkincross, Dominus ejusdem, Domino " Patricio Grahame, Militi, filio & hæredi Domini David de Grahame, Domi-" ni de Dindaff, & Dominæ Matildæ, sponsæ dicti Domini Patricii;" whereby he gives " tertiam partem terræ suæ de Halkincross, quæ tertia pars vocatur " Polcair, in Comitatu de Lenox, & Vicecomitatu de Stirling, pro quinquaginta " Marcarum Sterlingorum, an. 1372, regnante Roberto Secundo." The same Sir Patrick Grahame, then design'd Fitz and heir, "Seigneur David de Grahame de Dindaff," is one of the Hostages sent to England, for the ransom of King David II. an. 1357[6]. Which Sir Patrick was the first of this noble family who assumed the designation of Kincardine, and is frequently found so designed in Charters of King Robert II. He left two sons; Sir William his successor; and Sir Patrick, who married Eupham, daughter and sole heiress of David Stewart, Earl of Strathern, eldest son of King Robert II. by Eupham Ross his Queen, and was ancestor of the Grahames, Earls of Monteith; of whom descended the Grahames of Kilbryde; which produced those of Esk; of whom the Viscount of Prestoun in England descended; and the Grahames of Gartmore; Robert Grahame is now of Gartmore; as also the

[1] Appendix to Sir James Dalrymple's Observations on the Scottish History. [2] Spotiswood's History. [3] Carta penes Jac. D. Montrose. [4] Rymer's Fœdera Angliæ. [5] Rymer's Fœdera Angliæ. [6] Carta penes Jac. D. de Montrose.

family of Gartur, &c. Which Sir William above mention'd, promiscuously design'd of Kincardine and Mugdock, obtained from Patrick, Count Palatine of Strathern, his brother, a Charter of the lands of Dalruach, in the Earldom of Strathern, which is dated at Perth the 19th of June 1406 [1]. He obtain'd also, from Duncan Earl of Lenox, with consent of Murdo Duke of Albany, and of Isobel Dutchess of Albany, daughter to the said Earl Duncan, a Charter of Confirmation of the Barony of Mugdock. I have also seen, by the favours of that industrious antiquary, Mr. David Sympson, late Historiographer for North Britain, (my worthy friend) a Tailzie of the Lordship of Grahame, in the year 1424, by Sir William Grahame of Mugdock, in favours of Patrick Grahame, his grandchild, son to the deceased Alexander Grahame his eldest son. This Sir William married for his second wife, Lady Mary Stewart, daughter of King Robert III. and widow both of William Earl of Angus, and of James Kennedy of Dunnure; by whom he had three sons; Robert, author of that branch of the Grahames of Fintrie in Angus, of whom descended the Grahames of Claverhouse, afterwards Viscount of Dundee; which produced the families of Potento and Duntroon [2]: Patrick Archbishop of St. Andrews, was his second son; and Walter his third son, who obtained, from Patrick Lord Grahame, his nephew, the lands of Wallacetoun in Dunbartoun Shire, an. 1444, " pro ho-" magio & servitio suo," as the original Charter, yet extant, testifies [3]. Which Walter was author of that family of the Grahames of Knockdolian in Carrick, now extinct; and of them descended the Grahames now of Dougalstoun.

But the first of this noble family, who arrived to the dignity of Peerage, was Sir Patrick Grahame of Kincardine, grandson and heir of Sir William above mentioned, (by Alexander his eldest son; who died in his lifetime) who was by King James II. created Lord Grahame, about the year 1445. And his successor, another William Lord Grahame, was by King James IV. the 15th year of his reign, an. 1504, created Earl of Montrose; and, in consideration of the said Earl's services to the Crown, had the lands of Ald-Montrose erected into a free Barony and Earldom, by a Charter, dated, at Edinburgh, the 3d of March 1504 [4]. He was one of the generals of the Scottish army at the battle of Floudoun, which fell out the 9th day of September 1513, where he was slain. He was married with Margaret, daughter of Archbald Edmonstoun of Duntreath, leaving issue, William, his son and heir: And of Patrick (another of his sons) descended the Grahames of Inchbrackie; a younger son of

---

[1] Mr. David Simpson's Collections. [2] Nisbet's Herauldry. [3] Carta penes Geo. Napier de Kilmahew. [4] Haddingtoun's Collections in Bibliotheca Juridica.

which family, in the reign of King James VI. was Mr. George Grahame, first minister at Scone, and then, an. 1606, advanced to the Bishoprick of Dunblain; and in 1615 translated to the Episcopal See of Orkney, where he continued until the year 1638; that, being threatened with the censures of the Assembly of Glasgow, he renounced his Episcopal Office, and betook himself to a particular charge. He was ancestor of the Grahames of Gorthie, Grameshall and Brackness.

To William, first Earl of Montrose, who was killed at Floudoun, succeeded William, his son and heir; which Earl was one of those loyal Lords, to whom John Duke of Albany, Governour of Scotland, in the minority of King James V. committed the tuition of that Prince, upon his going for France, an. 1515 [1]. He married Janet Keith, daughter of William Earl Marischal of Scotland; by whom he had four sons; Robert, Master of Grahame, who, being at the battle of Pinkie, which fell out the 10th day of September 1547, had the hard fate to be killed by the English, after he and several other Scottish Peers had both asked and obtained quarter; as the Masters of Buchan and Erskine, &c. [2]. His second son was Alexander of Wallacetoun; which lands he obtained from Robert Grahame of Knockdolian, in the reign of Queen Mary [3]; but he died without succession. Of William and Mungo, his third and fourth sons, descended the family of Kilearn and Orchil; for this I have seen a Charter, granted by William Earl of Montrose, of the lands of Orchil, "Kentigerno Grahame filio suo," in an. 1560. As also in the same year, William Earl of Montrose gave a Charter of the lands of Trimbeg, to William Grahame, Parson of Kilearn, his son; of whom John Grahame of Kilearn is now the lineal heir; as James Grahame, now of Orchil, is lineal successor to the above mentioned Mungo Grahame, his ancestor.

Beside these sons, Earl William had also several daughters; viz. Jean, married John Earl of Caithness, and had issue. The second, Ann, to Sir William Murray of Tullibardin, ancestor of John Duke of Athol; and of whom his Grace is descended. The third, Margaret, married Sir Andrew Murray of Balvaird, and had issue. As to the precise time of Earl William's death, I have not found, but he was immediately succeeded by John, his grandson and heir, viz. son of Robert, Master of Grahame, who died in his lifetime, by Margaret his Lady, daughter of John Lord Fleeming: Which John was one of the Peers that sat upon the trial of James Earl of Morton, Regent, an. 1581: and being Lord High Chancellor of Scotland at that time, when King James came to pos-

---

[1] Holinshed's History. [2] Balfour's Annals in MS.
[3] Carta Dom. Humphr. Colquhoun de Luss, Bar.

sess the Crown of England, upon Queen Elizabeth's death, an. 1603, he was nominate his Majesty's High Commissioner for holding the Parliament, 1604. In which eminent station he continued till his death. He was married with the Lady Margaret Drummond, daughter of John Lord Drummond, by whom he had John Earl of Montrose, his son and heir. The second, Sir William of Braco, whose grandchild, Sir William Grahame, died without succession, an. 1689. He had likeways a daughter, Lilias, married John, first Earl of Wigtoun, and had issue.

To John Earl of Montrose, succeeded John, his son and heir; who, being a person of singular endowments and large abilities, having performed several honourable embassies, for his Majesty King James VI. was called to be President of the Council, by King Charles I. He died an.   leaving issue, by the Lady Margaret Ruthven, his wife, daughter of William Earl of Gourie, by Dorothea his wife, daughter of Henry Lord Methven, and of Janet his Lady, daughter of John Earl of Athol, James, his only son and heir; and four daughters, viz. the first, Lilias, married to Sir John Colquhoun of Luss, Baronet, and had issue. The second, Margaret, to Archbald Lord Napier, and had issue. The third, Dorothea, to Sir James Rollo of Duncrub, but had no succession. The fourth, Beatrix, to David Lord Maddertie, and had issue.

Which James Earl of Montrose, was a person of a very martial spirit, in the time of our late civil wars, under King Charles I. and whom that Prince entrusted most with the management of the war in Scotland; and, for that end, did constitute this noble and heroick Peer, His Majesty's General, and Lieutenant Governour of the Kingdom of Scotland; and, as a special mark of this royal favour, did raise him, in an. 1643, to the dignity of Marquis of Montrose. He fought, in that great character, in the royal cause, successively, in the several battles of Tippermure, Alfuird, Aldern, Aberdeen, Innerlochie, and Kilsyth: But in September 1645, was defeat at Philiphaugh, by a strong party of horse, under the command of General David Lesly, afterward Lord Newark, detached from the Scottish army, then in England; but escaping, retired abroad, where he continued several years, in the character of his Majesty's ambassadour, to the Court of Denmark, and several of the Protestant Princes of Germany. He returned to Scotland, an. 1650, after the murder of King Charles I. for the service of his Majesty King Charles II. who, as a signal mark of that Prince's favour, and of the merit of this noble Lord, made choice of him as one of the Knights companions of the most noble order of the Garter. But, an exact memorial of the life and actions of James, the Great Marquis of Montrose, being no part of the subject I now treat of, I refer to our publick Historians of the transactions of that time, and particularly to a History of his Life and Actions, by the learn'd Doctor George Wishart, late Bishop of Edinburgh, and sometimes his Lordship's Chaplain; that there is no need to say any thing further about him here. He was married to the Lady Magdalen Carnegie, daughter of David, first Earl of Southesk, and of Elizabeth his Countess, daughter of Sir David Lindsay of Edzel, sometime Earl of Crawfurd; bv whom he had only James, second Marquis of Montrose, his son and heir, who died an. 1669, leaving issue, by the Lady Isobel Douglass, his wife, daughter to William Earl of Morton, Lord High Thesaurer of Scotland, and Dowager of Robert, first Earl of Roxburgh, James, his son and heir; and three daughters, Ann married Alexander Earl of Calender, mother to the Right Honourable George Earl of Linlithgow and Calender: Lady   to Sir Jonathan Urquhart of Cromarty, and had issue: The third, Lady Grissel, married to Mr. William Cochran of Kilmaronock, son of William Lord Cochran, and has issue.

Which James, third Marquis of Montrose, was first constitute Captain of his Majesty's troup of Guards, and afterwards President of the Privy Council; he died young, about the 27th year of his age, universally lamented; leaving issue, by the Lady Christian his wife, daughter of John Duke of Rothes, by Ann Lindsay, his Lady, daughter of John Earl of Crawfurd and Lindsay, Lord High Thesaurer of Scotland, only James, his son and heir: Which James, Marquis of Montrose, was, by her present Majesty Queen Ann, constitute Lord President of the Privy Council, and, by her royal favour, raised to the dignity of Duke (and Marquis) of Montrose, an. 1707; and since the commencing of the Union, he was made Lord Privy Seal for Scotland. His Grace hath married Lady Christina Carnegie, daughter of David, second Earl of Northesk, by the Lady Elizabeth Lindsay his wife, daughter of John Earl of Crawfurd and Lindsay, Lord High Thesaurer of Scotland, by whom he hath issue, David, Marquis Grahame.

The Armorial bearing of this noble family is, quarterly; first and fourth Or; on a Chief, Sable, three Escalops, of the first; for the name of Grahame: second and third; Argent; three Roses, Gules; for the title of Montrose: supported by two Storks; and for Crest   with this Motto, " Ne oubliez."

Near to the castle of Crocstoun, upon the opposite side of the river, stand the place and lands of Cardonald, well planted and beautified with pleasant gardens; one of the Seats of the Right Honourable Walter, Lord Blantyre. An ancient family of the Stewarts did possess the lands of Cardonald, and were originally descended of Al: Stewart, natural son of John, first Earl of Lenox;

which Al: and Marion Semple his spouse, obtained these lands, an. 1487 [1], and failed in the person of James Stewart, the last of that race; leaving three daughters; first, Elizabeth married Robert Stewart, of the family of Garlies, whom I have found designed of Cardonald: Another of his daughters, Margaret, married Sir Sohn Stewart of Minto; as the third, Dorothea, did John Pollock of that-ilk, of whom Sir Robert Pollock of that-ilk is descended.

The lands of Cardonald, in the reign of King James the VI. came to Walter Stewart, Prior of Blantyre, son of Sir John Stewart of Minto, by Margaret his wife, daughter of James Stewart of Cardonald, above mentioned: But whether he obtained these lands by right of succession or conquest, I have not found. The family of Minto was a Caddet of the ancient family of Dalswintoun and Garlies, ancestor to the Earl of Galloway; for I have seen a Charter granted by Sir William Stewart of Dalswintoun and Garlies, with consent of Alexander Stewart of Garlies, his son and apparent heir, of the lands of Minto and Morbatle in Teviotdale, in favours of Thomas Stewart his son; which family failed in the person of Sir John Stewart of Minto, who died in the expedition to Darien, an. 1699. The Lord Blantyre became the next heir and representative of that family. Which Walter, above-mentioned, was one of the Privy Council to King James VI. one of the Senators of the College of Justice, and Lord Privy Seal, in an. 1595. He was appointed one of these eight persons, called the Octavians, which that Prince made choice of to rule the affairs of his Exchequer; and the same year he was constitute Lord High Thesaurer of Scotland, upon the demission of Sir Thomas Lyon of Albar, Master of Glames [2]: And, upon the dissolution of the Monasteries and their dependencies, the Priory of Blantyre, a cell depending on the Abby of Kelso [3], and the Barony of the same denomination, were by James, first Monarch of Great Britain, erected into a temporal lordship, in favours of this Walter, prior of Blantyre: And in consideration of his many faithful services to that Prince, he created him unto the dignity of Lord Blantyre, by Letters Patent, bearing date, at Whitehall, the 10th of July, an. 1606. He was married with Nicolas Somervell, daughter of Sir James Somervell of Camnethan, by whom he had three sons and a daughter, viz. Sir James Stewart, Master of Blantyre, killed by Sir James Whartoun, in a duel near the city of London, an. 1609 [4]. The second, William his successor. The third, was Walter Stewart, Esquire, Doctor of Phisick, father of the Lady Frances Stewart, late Dutchess Dowager of Lenox and Richmond,

[1] Genealogy of the family of Lenox.   [2] Spotiswood's History.
[3] Mr. William Forbes on Tithes.   [4] Scotstarvet's Memoirs.

relick of Charles Duke of Lenox, who being ambassadour extraordinary from King Charles II. of England, to the Crown of Denmark, died at Elsinore the 2d of December 1672. The Dutchess continued his widow, and departed this life the 15th of October 1702, and thought fit to leave her estate, which was very considerable, and in money, to Walter then Master of Blantyre, with which he is enjoined to purchase land in Scotland, which is to be called Lenox-Love. The Trustees were the Earl of Rochester, Alexander late Lord Blantyre, Sir William Whitelock, and one Mr. Gray[1] *.

Walter, first Lord Blantyre, had likeways a daughter, Margaret, who married Alexander Abernethy, Lord Saltoun.

To Walter, Lord Blantyre, succeeded William his son and heir, who (by Mary his Lady, daughter of Sir William Scot of Ardross, and of Margaret his Lady, daughter of Sir John Skeen of Currie-hill, Lord Clerk Register) had two sons, Walter and Alexander, successively Lords Blantyre. For, the first brother dying without any succession, his estate and honours descended to Alexander, his brother: Which Lord Alexander took to wife Margaret, daughter of John Shaw of Greenock, by Helen his wife, daughter of John Houstoun of that-ilk, by whom he had Alexander, his only son and heir, who died, an. 1704; leaving issue, by Ann his Lady, daughter of Sir Robert Hamilton of Presminnan, and sister to John, late Lord Belhaven, Walter, now Lord Blantyre, his son and heir. The second, Capt. Robert. The third, Mr. John. The fourth, Hugh: besides these sons, he had likeways three daughters; Marion, married to James Stirling of Keir, and has issue. The second, Frances, to Sir James Hamilton of Rosehall, Baronet. The third, Ann, as yet unmarried.

The Coat Armorial of the Right Honourable the Lord Blantyre, is, Or; a Fess Checquie, Azure and Argent; surmounted of a Bend Ingraled, Gules; with a Rose in Chief, of the Third; supported upon the Dexter, with a Savage, proper, wreathed about the middle with Laurel; and on the Sinister with a Lion Ram-

---

[1] State of Europe, for the year 1702.

* This Gentleman had another daughter, Sophia, who married the Hon. Henry Bulkeley, and was mother of Anne, second wife of the renowned James Duke of Berwick, from whom, by this Lady, is descended the Ducal House of Fitz-James in France; in this manner derived from the house of Blantyre.

Editor.

pant; for Crest, a Pigeon, with an Olive Leaf in its Mouth; with this motto, " Sola juvat virtus."

South-West from the Castle of Crocstoun lie the Castle and Barony of Halkhead, situate upon the River of Cart, the principal residence of the Right Honourable William Lord Ross. This Fabrick is built in the form of a Court, and consists of a large old tower, to which there were lower buildings added, in the reign of King Charles I. an. 1634, by James Lord Ross, and Dame Margaret Scot his Lady, and adorn'd with large orchards, fine gardens and pretty terrasses, with regular and stately avenues, fronting the said Castle, and almost surrounded with woods and inclosures, which adds much to the pleasure of this seat.

This ancient family of the Rosses derive their descent from Robert Ross of Wark[1], an English gentleman, who came to Scotland in the reign of King William, upwards of five hundred years ago: but that the family of Ross, in this country, is of great antiquity, the Chartulary of the Monastery of Pasly doth plainly demonstrate: for " Godofridus de Ross, Miles, filius & hæres quondam Godofridi Ross," confirms " illam terram in villa de Stewartoun, ex collatione Domini Jacobi Ross, bonæ memoriæ, Monasterio de Pasletto, an. 1201[2]."

The Barons of Halkhead were eminent in the reign of King Robert II. for then it was, that Sir John Ross of Halkhead obtained the Barony of Melvil, in the Sheriffdom of Edinburgh, by marriage of Agnes, daughter and sole heiress of Sir John Melvil of that-ilk[3]; by whom he had issue, Sir John his son and heir, who had a charter of these lands, as heir of D. Agnes Melvil, his mother, as is clear enough from the originals yet extant; by reason of which marriage the family of Ross carry the Coat of Melvil, viz. Gules; Three Crescents within a Border, Argent, charged with Eight Roses, of the First, quartered in their Achievement. And in the reign of King Robert III. an. 1401, there is a perambulation betwixt John Stewart of Darnly and Sir John Ross of Halkhead; whose successor, another Sir John Ross of Halkhead, obtained from King James II. an. 1450, a charter of confimation of the lands of Tarbart and Achinbach, upon the resignation of Robert Ross of Tarbart: but what relation in blood this Sir John Ross of Halkhead had to the family of Tarbart, I have not seen, nor can yet discover.

But the first of this family, who laid the foundation of that hereditary honour, which his successors have ever since enjoyed, was Sir John Ross of

---

[1] Sir James Dalrymple's Edition of Cambden, printed 1695. [2] Chartulary of Pasly.
[3] Carta penes Guliclmum Dominum Ross.

Halkhead; who being a favourite of King James IV. was, by that Prince, created a Baron of this Realm, with the title of Lord Ross of Halkhead and Melvil, about the year 1492. He was slain at that fatal battle of Floudoun, which was fought the 9th of September 1513, leaving issue, by Margaret his lady, daughter of William, second Lord Ruthven[1], Ninian Lord Ross, his son and heir; whose eldest son and apparent heir, Robert, Master of Ross, being kill'd at the battle of Pinkie, the 10th of September 1547, his estate and honours devolved upon James, his second son and heir: Which James, Lord Ross, is one of the Peers that sat upon the trial of James Earl of Bothwel, for the murther of King Henry, an. 1567[2], and constantly adhered to the interest of Queen Mary, and was one of those Lords that met Her Majesty at Hamiltoun, after her escape from Lochlevin, Anno 1568. He was married with Jean Semple, daughter of Robert Lord Semple, by Elizabeth Carlile his wife, daughter to the Lord Torthorald, by whom he had two sons, Robert his successor, and Sir William Ross of Murestoun: Which Robert Lord Ross took to wife, Jean, daughter of Gavin Hamilton of Raploch. He departed this life, an. 1596; to whom succeeded James, his son and heir: Which James, Lord Ross, married Margaret Scot, daughter to Walter Lord Buccleugh, by whom he had William his successor, and several daughters; viz. Margaret, married to Sir George Stirling of Keir; and Elizabeth to Sir Robert Innes of that-ilk, and had issue.

To James Lord Ross, formerly mentioned, succeeded William his Son, who dying without succession, his estate and honours devolved upon Sir William Ross of Murestoun, his grand-uncle; which Lord William was twice married; first, to Elizabeth, daughter of Sir Patrick Houstoun of that-ilk, and widow of John Whitefoord of that-ilk, but had no issue. He afterward took to wife Helen, eldest daughter of George Lord Forrester of Corstorphine, and of Margaret his lady, daughter of Sir William Livingston of Kilsyth, by whom he had George, his only son and heir: Which George Lord Ross, was one of the Privy Council to His Majesty King Charles II: and upon the death of the Earl of Kelly, the Lord Ross succeeded, as Lieutenant-Colonel of the Royal Regiment of Guards, commanded by the Earl of Linlithgow, and deceased Anno 1682, and was buried, among his ancestors, at Renfrew. He was twice married; first, to Grissel Cochran, daughter of William, first Earl of Dundonald, by whom he had William, his successor; and a daughter,   married to Sir Alexander Gilmore of Craigmiller, and had issue, surviving his first lady. He was secondly married to Jean, daughter of George Lord Ramsay, and Earl of Dalhousie,

[1] Miscellany Collections of Alex. Baillie of Castlecary   [2] Spotiswood's History.

by whom he had a Son, Mr. Charles, now a Lieutenant-General in the service of Her Majesty Queen Ann.

To George Lord Ross succeeded William, his son and heir; which William, now Lord Ross, was one of the Privy-Council, both to the late King William, and to her present Majesty Queen Ann, and was her High Commissioner to the General Assembly of this National Church; which his Lordship discharged with universal applause. He was one of the Scottish Peers nominate by Her Majesty Queen Ann, to treat on the union with England, an. 1706; and one of the Commissioners of the Thesaury, when that commission was dissolved on commencing of the union, 1707. His Lordship married, first, Agnes, daughter and sole heiress of Sir John Wilkie of Fouldoun, by Mary his lady, daughter of James Lord Carmichael; by whom he had George, Master of Ross; and three daughters, viz. Eupham, married William now Earl of Kilmarnock, and hath issue. The second, Mary; the third, Grissel, as yet both unmarried. He married secondly,   daughter of Philip Lord Whartoun, but by her he had no issue.

The Armorial bearing of the family of Ross, is, Two Coats quarterly; first; Or; a Cheveron Checquie, Argent and Sable; betwixt three Water-Budgets, of the third: secondly; Gules; three Cresents, within a Border Argent, charged with eight roses, of the field: third, as second; fourth, as first; and for Crest, a Haulk's Head, erased; supported by two Gosehaulks; The Motto, "Think on."

South from this place lie the lands of Raiss, now the property of the Right Honourable William Lord Ross: An ancient family, of the Sirname of Logan, did possess these lands. I have found John Logan of Raiss an arbiter betwixt the Abbot of Pasly and the Burgh of Renfrew, an. 1488 [1].

South from this is the house and lands of Stewart's Raiss, an ancient possession of the family of Halrig, a branch of the noble family of Darnly. I have seen a Charter granted by John Lord Darnly and Earl of Lenox, of the lands of Halrig and Raiss, to Alexander Stewart, " Consanguineo suo," upon the resignation of Hector Stewart of Raiss, his father, an. 1484 [2]: They are now the property of Charles Stewart, writer in Glasgow.

Lower upon the bank of Cart, lie the house and lands of Whitefoord, the seat, and whence an ancient family, of the same Sirname, took appellation, who, for many ages, were both of great antiquity, and possessed of a plentiful fortune in those parts; as is clear enough from the following account. For Walter de Whitefoord obtained these lands, which he so called, in the Barony of Renfrew,

---

[1] Chartulary of Pasly. [2] Carta penes D. Jacob. Dalrymple de Killoch, Baron.

from the Stewart of Scotland, for his good service at the battle of the Largs, against the Norvegians, an. 1263, in the reign of King Alexander III.[1]; of whom descended John Whitefoord of that-ilk, who lived in the reign of King James I. whose son, Patrick Whitefoord of that-ilk, obtained from the King a confirmation of these lands, upon the resignation of John Whitefoord of that-ilk, his father, an. 1431 [2]. Which Patrick was father of another John; and he, of Quintine Whitefoord of that-ilk, who had Seasin of the lands of Whitefoord, an. 1507. (regnante Jacobo Quarto). Which Quintine above mentioned, was father of Adam Whitefoord of that-ilk, retoured an. 1519: Whose son, John Whitefoord of that-ilk, lived in the reign of Queen Mary; as John his eldest son and successor, did in that of King James VI. and died without succession, an. 1606. His estate devolved upon Adam Whitefoord of Miltoun, his brother: Which Adam was son of John Whitefoord of that-ilk, by Margaret his wife, daughter of Robert Lord Semple: This Adam had, by   Somervell his wife, daughter of Sir James Somervell of Camnethan, two sons; James his successor; and Dr. Walter Whitefoord, first, Sub-Dean of Glasgow, after that, Parson of Moffat; and, in an. 1635 advanced to the Episcopal See of Brichen, where he continued till the revolution of that government, an. 1638. By progress, from the family of Whitefoord, these lands came to the Earl of Dundonald.

But the principal branch of this ancient family is Whitefoord of Blaquhan in Carrick, who descended from that family, several ages ago. Sir Adam Whitefoord is now of Blaquhan, Baronet, who bears the Coat of that ancient family, viz. Argent; a Bend cotised, Sable; with a Garb in chief, of the second; and for Crest, a Pigeon upon the top of a Garb; with this Motto, "Tout est "d'en hault." Bryce Whitefoord of Dindaff is brother german to Sir Adam Whitefoord of Blaquhan.

A little north from Whitefoord lie the lands of Ralstoun, the possession of an ancient family of the same Sirname, who are said to derive their pedigree from Ralph, a younger son of one of the Earls of Fife, who having obtained these lands from the High Stewart of Scotland, they were afterwards called Ralphstoun, from the proper name of their predecessor. The Sirname is of great antiquity in this country: For, Nicolaus de Ralphstoun is witness to the donation, which Sir Anthony Lombard made to the Monks of Pasly [3], an. 1272,

---

[1] Genealogy of Whitefoord of that-ilk, by the accurate and judicious Antiquary, Mr. William Hamilton of Wishaw. [2] Carta penes J. Com. de Dundonald. [3] Chartulary of Pasly.

as " Jacobus Ralstoun, Dominus ejusdem," is witness in an Instrument, electing an Abbot of the Monastery of Pasly, an. 1346. And John Ralstoun of that-ilk, successor to the former, is one of the arbiters betwixt the Abbot of Pasly and the Burgh of Renfrew, an. 1488. As Thomas Ralstoun of that-ilk obtained a Charter of his lands of Ralstoun, from John Lord Ross, an. 1505[1]. From whom the seventh, in a direct line, is Gavin Ralstoun of that-ilk: whose Armorial bearing, is, Argent; on a Bend, Azure, three Acorns in the Seed, Or.

From the castle of Haulkhead, a little toward the west (upon the river of Cart) lie the house and Barony of Blackhall, which is well adorned with beautiful planting; it is one of the seats of Sir Archbald Stewart, Baronet, who derives his descent from Sir John Stewart of Ardgowan, one of the natural sons of King Robert III.; which is instructed from three several Charters, in the hands of Sir Archbald Stewart of Blackhall, granted by that Prince, " Johanni Senescallo, filio suo naturali:" The first, of the lands of Achingoun, in the Shire of Renfrew, which is dated the 20th of May, the first year of his reign (an. 1390): Another, of the lands of Blackhall, an. 1396, (Anno reg: sexto): As also he obtain'd the lands of Ardgowan, in the 14th year of his reign; (an. 1404) which original lands are yet enjoyed by his successors: From which Sir John Stewart of Ardgowan above-mentioned, did John Stewart of Blackhall and Ardgowan lineally descend; who obtain'd from King James IV. an. 1508[2], a confirmation of King Robert's Charter, made to his ancestor, of the lands above-mentioned; as also James Stewart of Ardgowan, his lineal successor, obtained from King James VI. a Charter, erecting his lands of Ardgowan, Blackhall, and Achingoun, into a Barony, an. 1576. Which James, last mentioned, by Margaret his wife, daughter of William Wallace of Johnstoun, had John his son and heir; father of another Archbald Stewart of Blackhall, by Margaret his wife, daughter of Archbald Stewart of Castlemilk: Which Archbald was a person of singular wisdom, prudence and consummate experience in business: For, being chosen one of the Commissioners to the Parliament, for the Shire of Renfrew, in the reign of King Charles I. in that great Convention he made his parts so conspicuous, that that Prince chose him to be one of his Privy Council, and advanced him to the dignity of Knighthood: He was also of the Privy Council to King Charles II. when in Scotland, an. 1650. He was married to Margaret, daughter of Bryce Blair of that-ilk, by whom he had John his eldest son, who died in his lifetime. The second, Archbald, who obtained the lands

---
[1] Carta penes Gavinum Ralstoun, de eodem.
[2] Carta penes D. Arch. Stewart de Blackhall, Baronet.

of Scotstoun, by marriage of Margaret, daughter and heiress of Mr. John Hutcheson of Scotstoun. His third son was Walter; who, by marriage of Elizabeth, daughter and sole heiress of Robert Stewart of Pardovan, obtained these lands; whose son and heir is Walter Stewart now of Pardovan. He had likeways a daughter, Anabell, married to Sir George Maxwel of Pollock, and had issue: he deceased an. 1665. To whom succeeded Archbald his grandson and heir, viz. Son of John, (his eldest son, who died in his lifetime,) by Mary his Lady, daughter of Sir James Stirling of Keir, by whom he had also several younger sons, viz. Walter of Kincarachi, David of Kirkwood, and James of Lumloch; as also two daughters; Mary, married to Sir Alexander Cunninghame of Corsehill, and had issue: the 2d, Anabell, to William Porterfield of that-ilk, and had issue.

Which Archbald Stewart of Blackhall was, by King Charles II. raised to the degree and dignity of Baronet, by Letters Patent, bearing date, at Whitehall, the 27th of March 1667. He married Ann, daughter of Sir John Crawfurd of Kilbirny, by whom he had Mr. John Stewart younger of Blackhall, his eldest son and apparent heir, who was one of the Commissioners to the Parliament, for the Shire of Renfrew, upon commencing the Union. Sir Archbald had also several other children; viz. Patrick, and Mr. Walter Stewart, Advocate; as likeways a daughter, Margaret, who married John Brisbane of Bishoptoun, and had issue.

The Armorial bearing of this family is, Or; over a Fess Checquie Azure and Argent, a Lion rampant, Gules, arm'd and langu'd Azure; for Crest, a Lion's head erased, Gules; with this Motto, "Spero Meliora."

To the westward of Blackhall, on the north side of the river (Cart), pleasantly situate in a fair soil, stands the Abby and Church of Pasly, which I have already described, (Part I. page 15.) And, south from that, on the opposite side of the river, (adjoined by a bridge of two very large arches) stands the Burgh and Barony of Pasly, the principal town of that Regality, erected into a Burgh and Barony by King James IV; and, because I'm concern'd to give some account of the Burghs and Baronies in this shire, I shall give the original Charter of Erection, yet extant, in the Register of the Monastery of Pasly, Fol. 161. The tenor whereof is,

" JACOBUS, D. G. Rex Scotorum: Sciatis, quod, ob singularem devo-
" tionem, quam habemus glorioso Confessori Sancto Mirino & Monasterio nos-
" tro de Pasletto, per nostros nobilissimos Progenitores fundato, ubi plurima
" Progenitorum nostrorum corpora sepeliuntur & requiescunt, & ob singularem

" favorem & amorem quem gerimus venerabili in Christo Patri, Georgio Shaw,
" moderno dicti Monasterii Abbati, nostro Consiliario apprime dilecto ; ac pro
" fideli obsequio, per dictum venerabilem Patrem, nobis, temporibus retroac-
" tis, multipliciter præstito ; & præcipue, ob virtuosam educationem & nutritio-
" nem charissimi fratris nostri, Jacobi Ducis Rossensis, in sua tenera ætate ; Fe-
" cimus, Infeodavimus, Ereximus ; ac, tenore præsentis Chartæ nostræ, Faci-
" mus, Infeodamus, Erigimus & Creamus villam de Pasletto, jacen: infra Vice-
" comitatum de Renfrew, liberum Burgum in Baronia : concessimus etiam
" dictum Burgum inhabitantibus & in posterum inhabitaturis, plenam & liber-
" am potestatem emendi & vendendi, in ipso Burgo, vinum, ceram, pannum
" laneum & lineum, amplum seu arctum, & quæcunque alia bona & mercimonia
" illuc advenientia ; cum potestate & libertate habendi & tenendi ibidem pis-
" tores, brasiatores, carnifices, & tam carnium quam piscium macellarios, & ar-
" tium quarumquunque operarios, ad libertatem Burgi in Baronia spectant :
" seu spectare valent : Concessimus etiam burgensibus & inhabitantibus dictum
" Burgum de Pasletto, ut in ipso Burgo habeant & possideant crucem &
" forum, pro perpetuo, singulis hebdomadis, die Lunæ ; & duas nundinas publi-
" cas quolibet anno in perpetuum ; unam videlicet in die Sancti Mirini, & ali-
" am in die Sancti Marnoci ; cum Tholoniis & aliis libertatibus, ad hujusmodi
" nundinas spectant : seu spectare valent : in futurum tenendi & habendi præ-
" fatam villam de Pasletto perpetuis futuris temporibus in merum & liberum
" Burgum in Baronia, ; cum prædictis privilegiis, libertatibus, concessionibus
" ac universis aliis libertatibus, adeo libere, quiete, plenarie, integre, honorifice,
" bene & in pace, in omnibus & per omnia, sicut Burgi de Dunfermling, New-
" burgh & Aberbrothock, aut aliquis alius Burgus in Baronia, in regno nostro,
" quibuscunque temporibus retroactis liberius infeodatur seù tenetur : ac insu-
" per concessimus, dicto venerabili Patri & successoribus suis Abbatibus de
" Pasletto, facultatem & protestatem, eligendi annuatim, Præpositum, Balivos
" & alios Officiarios dicti Burgi, & eosdem toties quoties opus fuerit removendi
" & alios in eorum locis de novo eligendi, &c. In cujus rei testimonium,
" huic præsenti Cartæ nostræ, Magnum Sigillum nostrum apponi præcepimus.
" Testibus Reverendis in Christo Patribus, Roberto, Episcopo Glasguensi; Geor-
" gio, Episcopo Dunkelden ; dilectis Consanguineis nostris, Colino, Comite de
" Argyle, Domino Campbel, Cancellario nostro ; Arch: Comite Angusiæ,
" Domino de Douglass ; Patricio Domino Halys, Magistro Hospitii nostri ;
" Roberto Domino de Lyle, Justiciario nostro ; Andrea Domino le Gray ;
" Laurentio Domino Oliphant ; Johanne Domino Drummond : apud Stirling,
" decimo nono die mensis Augusti, 1488, & regni nostri primo.

The town consists of one principal street, well built with handsome houses, about half a mile in length, with several other lanes and a large Town-House, where the Sheriff Court is kept, also the Courts of the Regality of Pasly: Both the Sheriffship and Regality are now in the family of Eglintoun, by purchase from the Lord Semple, in the reign of King Charles I. as I have already observed. At Pasly is likeways kept the Justice of Peace Courts, called the Quarter Sessions. This Burgh has a Weekly Mercat, on Thursday, where there is store of provisions: But that which renders this place considerable, is its trade of Linnen and Muslin, where there is a great weekly sale in its Mercats of those sorts of cloath; many of their inhabitants being chiefly imployed in that sort of manufactory. It has several fairs, the greatest of which is on the 25th of July, called St. James's-day; to which there is a great concourse of people from many places, about business; as there is of others, for diversion, to see their Horse and Foot-Races, which are run on ground excellently fitted for that purpose: 'tis governed by two Baillifs, one of which used to be annually nominate by the Abbot of Pasly, before the Reformation, and afterwards, by the Lord of the Erection. But that privilege was disponed by William, Earl of Dundonald, to the Community of that Burgh, an. 1654. The most part of their revenue is held immediately off the Crown; whereby one, commissioned from the Town Council, hath right to vote at the Election of the Commissioner to the Parliament for the Shire of Renfrew.

There is a prospect both of the Abby and Town of Pasly in Mr. Sletzer's Theatrum Scotiæ.

From the Town of Pasly the river of Cart hath its course northward; upon the east side whereof lie the lands of Knoc, or Knox, an ancient possession of a family of the same name, promiscuously designed of that-ilk, and of Ranfurly. I have seen a Charter granted by Uchter Knox of Ranfurly, of the half of the lands of Knoc, to George Knox his son, and Janet Fleeming his Spouse, an. 1503 [1]; from whose successor, Sir Matthew Knoc, a churchman, these lands are acquired by William Cunninghame of Craigends, an. 1526: and, from Alexander Cunninghame of Craigends, Anno 1654, by Colin Campbel of Blythswood. At this place there is a high Cross standing, called Queen Bleareie's Cross; but no Inscription is legible: Tradition hath handed down, that it was erected on this occasion. Majory Bruce, daughter of the renowned Robert I. and wife of Walter, Great Stewart of Scotland, at that time Lord of this country, being hunting at this place, was thrown from her horse, and by

[1] Carta Colini Campbel de Blythswood.

the fall, suffered a dislocation of the vertebræ of her neck, and died on the spot; she being pregnant, fell in labour of King Robert II.; the child or Fœtus was a Cesar: The operation being by an unskilful hand, his eye being touched by the instrument, could not be cured; from which he was called King Bleareie. This, according to our historians, fell out in the year 1317 [1]. She lies buried at Pasly, where there is a Monument erected to her memory.

Somewhat lower, upon the bank of the river of Cart, lie the lands of Porterfield, an ancient possession of a family of the same sirname, and from whence they, without doubt, have taken both Sirname and designation. But, that what is to be said of the antiquity of the Porterfields, may not be received without a document, you'll find, in the register of the Abby of Pasly, that in the reign of King Alexander III. an. 1262, John de Porter was a witness to that donation of the Kirk of Dundonald, by Alexander, High Stewart of Scotland, to the Monks of that Abby. Likeas I find, Walter le Porter is mentioned in Ragman-Roll, an. 1296 [1]. But to descend a little more particularly upon the genealogy of the Porterfields: in the reign of King David II. Stephen de Porter obtained a charter of his lands of Porterfield, from Robert Earl of Strathern, about the year 1362 [2]. But of this Stephen de Porter I have not seen any more than that he mortified to the Monastery of Pasly, " pro salute animæ suæ, annuum " reditum duodecem denariorum ex Burgagio Michaelis Sperlin in Renfrew [3]." To Stephen succeeded Robert, his son and heir: Which Robert, out of his charity to the church and poor, (according to the opinion of those times, that they did a very agreeable service to God Almighty, to be liberal to the churclr and clergy) mortified to the Monastery of Pasly, " pro salute animæ suæ, patris " & matris ejus, & pro salute omnium antecessorum & successorum, annuum; " reditum sex decem denariorum de Burgagio Johannis Walker in Renfrew, in " liberam, puram & perpetuam eleemosinam, ad duos anni terminos, per æquales " portiones, viz. ad Festum Pentecostes & Festum Sancti Martini; & insuper, " Ego præfatus Robertus Porter Dominus de Porterfield, ratifico, approbo, & hac " præsenti Charta mea, confirmo, illam donationem & concessionem, quam Ste- " phanus Porter, quondam pater meus, fecit Deo & Beatæ Virgini Mariæ, & " Beato Jacobo & Beato Mirino Confessori de Pasletto, & Monachis ibidem. " Deo servientibus."

From Robert Porterfield, formerly mentioned, did John Porterfield of that-ilk lineally descend, who obtained from King James III, a charter of confirma-

---

[1] Description of Renfrewshire, by Mr. William Dunlop. [2] Prin's History, page 663.
[3] Carta Alex. Porterfield, de eodem. [4] Chartulary of Pasly.

tion of his lands of Porterfield, an. 1460. Which John was father of another John Porterfield of that-ilk, who married Catherine, daughter of Patrick Mackgrigor of Ardinconel, by whom he left issue. Robert his successor obtained a charter of the lands of Porterfield, from King James IV. an. 1500 ; and, by Isobel Maxwel his wife, a daughter of the house of Newark, had two sons, Alexander and Mr. John. Which Alexander died without succession, having resign'd the lands of Porterfield in favours of his brother Mr. John Porterfield of that-ilk, an. 1540. Which Mr. John being a person of great learning, (at that time) raised his family by several considerable purchases, viz. the Barony of Duchal from John Lord Lyll, with consent of James, Master of Lyll, his eldest son and apparent heir, an. 1544; as the original Writs, yet extant, sufficiently testifie [1]. He acquired the lands of Spangow in Innerkip, from Sir Matthew Campbel of Loudoun, an. 1565. He was twice married; first, with Beatrix, daughter of William Cunninghame of Craigends, by whom he had William his son and heir : secondly, he took to wife Jean Knox, daughter to the laird of Ranfurly, by whom he had two sons; Gabriel, who had a charter of the lands of Blairlin, from his father, an. 1568 ; and John, who obtained from his father the lands of Greenend, an. 1573. He had likeways a daughter, called Elizabeth, married to Sir James Maxwel of Calderwood. He deceased an. 1575. To whom succeeded William his son and heir; who married (an. 1565) Isobel, one of the daughters of John Cunninghame of Glengarnock, by Margaret his lady, daughter to the Lord Fleeming, by whom he had Alexander his eldest son, who died in his lifetime ; and three daughters; Jean, married first to Alexander Cunninghame of Waterstoun, and after his death became the wife of Sir William Mure of Rouallan. The second, Mary, to Alexander Cunninghame of Corshill. The third, Marion, to Patrick Maxwell of Dargevell. Which William Porterfield of that-ilk deceased an. 1612, and was immediately succeeded by Alexander his grandson, viz. (Son of Alexander his eldest Son, who died in his lifetime, by Agnes his wife, daughter of Sir Patrick Houstoun of that-ilk): Which last Alexander Porterfield of that-ilk departed this life in the year 1675, leaving issue, by Agnes his lady, daughter of John Blair of that-ilk, and of Isobel his wife, daughter of Thomas Lord Boyd, three sons and a daughter, viz. John his successor; the second, William of Quarreltoun ; the third, Alexander, father of Mr. Alexander Porterfield, Chirurgion in Glasgow ; and Grissel, married to John Semple of Fulwood. Which John Porterfield of that-ilk took to wife Jean, daughter of Sir James Hamilton of Broomhill, by whom he had, William his eldest son, who died in his lifetime ; Alexander, now of Fulwood ; and several

[1] Carta penes Alex. Porterfield de eodem.

daughters; Ann, married James Hamiltoun of Aikenhead, and Margaret, to Archibald Crawfurd of Achinames.

William Porterfield younger of that-ilk, in his father's time, married Anabel, daughter of John Stewart younger of Blackhall, by whom he had Alexander, who immediately succeeded his grandfather, and died an. 1690. Which Alexander was one of the Commissioners to the Parliament for the Shire of Renfrew, upon the dissolving thereof on Her Majesty's accession to the Crown. He hath married the lady Catharine Boyd, daughter of William Earl of Kilmarnock; by whom he hath issue William, his eldest son and apparent heir.

The armorial bearing of this family is, Or; a Bend; betwixt a Stag's head, erased, in chief, and a bugle, in base, Gules; supported by two   : for Crest, a Laurel; with this motto, "Sub pondere sursum."

Near Porterfield lie the lands of Kirkland, a part of which has, for some considerable time, been the possession of Robert Ross, Portioner of Kirkland's ancestors, who were descended from the Rosses of Tartriven, an old Cadet of the family of Halkhead. They have made intermarriages with these following respective families in this Country, viz. Semples of Fulwood, Whitefoords of that-ilk, and Cunninghames of Quarreltoun. Which Robert Ross, above-mentioned, was married with   Hamiltoun, daughter of Major Alexander Hamiltoun of Forehouse, (descended of the family of Torrence), by whom he had Mr. Andrew Ross, his eldest son, now Professor of Humanity in the University of Glasgow.

And below Kirkland, upon the confluence of Clyde and Grief, in a plain field, stand the house and lands of Ranfield, adorn'd with pleasant orchards and gardens, beautified with very much planting and regular avenues, from both the rivers of Clyde and Grief, to the Ranfield House; which adds much to the beauty of this seat. Who were its ancient proprietors, I have not found, before the year 1568, that Mr. Andrew Hay, design'd Chanon of Glasgow, (and afterwards Parson of Renfrew, a younger brother of the family of Linplum, who were a branch of the ancient and noble family of Locherwart, afterward Lord Yester, and now Marquis of Tweeddale) obtained from James Earl of Murray, Regent, a Charter of these lands; as did also Mr. John Hay, Parson of Renfrew, his son; and whose son, Mr. John Hay of Ranfield, also Parson of Renfrew, sold these lands, an. 1654, to Colin Campbell of Blytheswood, a wealthy merchant, and Provost of the City of Glasgow; whose original ancestor was a younger brother of the ancient family of Ardkinlass; whose ancestor was John Campbel, a brother of the illustrious family of Argile, in the reign of King Robert II; whose grandchild is Colin Campbel now of Blythswood. Whose

Armorial bearing is¹; Two Coats quarterly; first, Gironnè of eight pieces, Sable and Or; each Giron charged with a Trefoil, slipt and counter-changed: secondly; Argent; a Gally with her Oars in action; for Crest, a Ship with her Sails trussed up; third, as second; fourth, as first; with this Motto, " Vincit labor."

Mr. John Hay of Inchnoch is the representative of the Hays of Ranfield.

Two miles north of Pasly, upon the river of Clyde, stands the Royal Burgh of Renfrew, the principal town of this country, both before and after its erection into a distinct Shire, and seems to be Randuara mentioned by Ptolomy, as a learned author observes² : but that the Burgh is of great antiquity, the Chartularies of Dunfermling and Pasly do plainly demonstrate : For, in the first of these, " Walterus, filius Allani, Dapifer Regis Scotiæ, pro amore Dei & salute " corporis & animæ suæ," gives " Ecclesiæ Sanctæ Trinitatis de Dunfermling, in " perpetuam eleemosinam, unum toftum plenarium in Burgo suo de Renfrew³." And the same " Walterus filius Allani," gave to the Monks of Pasly, " Insul- " am juxta oppidum suum de Renfrew, cum piscatura inter ipsam insulam & " Portheck, & dimidiam Marcam Argenti de firma ipsius Burgi ad Luminare " Ecclesiæ de Pasletto⁴.

At Renfrew, the Lord High Stewart of Scotland had a castle, the chief manour of this fair Barony : for this I have seen a Charter granted by James, High Stewart of Scotland, (grandfather to King Robert II.) " Stephano filio " Nicolai"⁵, (one of the ancestors of Robert Hall now of Fulbar) " pro homa- " gio & servitio suo, totam terram illam quæ data fuit Patricio de Selvinland, " quæ terræ jacent apud Burgum de Renfrew, ubi aqua de Grief descendit in " aquam de Clyde: Reddendo inde dictus Stephanus & hæredes sui, nobis & " successoribus nostris, quolibet anno, duodecim denarios argenti, nomine feo- " di-firmæ. Apud Manerium nostrum de Renfrew ; Testibus Tho. Randolph, " Roberto Boyd, Willielmo Fleeming de Barughan, Finlaio de Houstoun, Mili- " tibus : Roberto de Coningsburgh, Gilesio de Eastwood ; Roberto Semple, " tunc Senescall : Baroniæ de Renfrew." This castle was situate upon a pretty rising ground, called Castle-hill, upon the brink of the river of Clyde ; from whence there has been a very agreeable prospect of the country, many miles distant every way, and surrounded with a large and deep fossie. I have also seen, by the favour of the judicious and learned Antiquary, Mr. Alexander Baillie of Castlecary, a tack of the castle of Renfrew, with the orchards and

H

¹ Nisbet's Heraldry. ² Cambden's Britannia. ³ Chartulary of Dunfermling.
⁴ Chartulary of Pasly. ⁵ Carta penes Rob. Hall de Fulbar.

meadows, to Robert Lord Lyll, and to his heirs male, for the payment of iiii lib. vi sh. viii d.; Anno 1468. The Barons Ross of Halkhead have been heritable Constables of this castle, of a long time; by virtue whereof the Lord Ross hath power to uplift customs at the principal fairs of this Burgh. It was erected into a Royalty, by King Robert III. when the Barony of Renfrew was disjoin'd from the Sheriffdom of Lanerk, and erected into a distinct Shire by that King, the 14th year of his reign. They obtained from that Prince a Charter, confirming their privileges, granted by himself or his predecessors, the 6th year of his reign [1]. As also King James VI. in the year 1577, confirms the privileges of this Burgh; and, in an. 1703, the Royal Burgh of Renfrew hath obtained an ample Charter from her present Majesty Queen Ann.

This Burgh was, in the Scots Parliament, the 30th in number, as to precedency, among the Burrows, and ranked immediately after Dunbartoun, and before Dunbar; and since the late Union, 'tis joined in that district with the city of Glasgow, the Burghs of Dunbartoun and Rutherglen.

The town consists of one principal street, about half a mile in length, with some small lanes; it has a spacious Market-place, and a handsome Townhouse, with a Steeple covered with lead. It hath one Paroch Church, very large, also of an old model: It was anciently a parsonage, and a dependency on the Cathedral of Glasgow, from the time of King David I, that " Ecclesia " de Renfrew, cum decimis & consuetudinibus suis," are given to the Cathedral See of Glasgow, " quas tenuit a tempore regis David [2]," as the learned Antiquary Sir James Dalrymple has observed. And, since the Reformation, (in an. 1617,) it was annexed to the University of Glasgow, with the burden of twelve chalders of victual to the minister of Renfrew. Adjoining to the Church there is a spacious Isle, the burial place of the family of Ross; as also on the south side of this Church lies the Statue of Sir Josias Ross of Halkhead, and Marjory Mure, a daughter of Caldwel, his wife, as big as the life, with their Coats of Arms over them, each carved in one stone: About the verge of the tomb I find this inscription:

" Hic jacet Josias Ross, Miles, quondam Dominus de Halkhead,
& Marjoria uxor ejus. Orate pro illis."

The present minister of Renfrew is the Reverend Mr. Patrick Simpson, now the eldest minister of the Church of Scotland who is in Office.

[1] Carta penes Burgum de Renfrew. [2] Excerpta ex Regist. de Glasgow.

This Burgh had once some little foreign trade; but the business in which its inhabitants are mostly imployed now, is in trade to Ireland. It has a very convenient harbour, called Puddoch, made by the tract of the ancient channel of the river of Clyde, into which the tide flows, and whereby vessels of considerable burthen, at spring tides, are carried up to the bridge of Renfrew.

'Tis governed by a Provost and two Bailliffs: The present Provost is Colin Campbel of Blythswood; their revenue consists of land rents, ground annuals, customs, &c. and it has also belonging to it a publick ferry boat over the river of Clyde, betwixt the isle, called the King's Inch, and Blawart-Hill, upon the north side of the river, whereby there is considerable intercourse betwixt the Shires of Renfrew and Dunbartoun.

At the Burgh of Renfrew, in the reign of King Malcolm IV. an. 1164, was that signal defeat given to the Arch-Rebel Sumerled, Thane of Argile, who, upon that Prince's accession to the Crown, being a man of unbounded ambition, rose in rebellion against him: But Gilchrist, Earl of Angus, the King's Lieutenant, being sent against him with an army, put him to flight, and obliged him, with a few more, to fly to Ireland; but, some years afterwards, landing with a considerable company, he plundered the country as far as Renfrew; there his forces were put to flight, and himself being apprehended, as Buchanan[1] says, and brought to the King, was hanged on a gibbet. But the Chronicle of Melross bears, " Sumerledus Regulus Argatheliæ, per duodecem annos, " contra Regem Scotiæ Malcolmum, Dominum suum natalem, impiè rebel- " lans, cum, copiosum de Hibernia & diversis locis exercitum trahens, apud " Renfrew applicuit, tandem, ultione divina, cum filio suo, ibidem occisus. " M.C.LXIIII.[2].

Near this Burgh, upon the river of Clyde, stands the Inch Castle, one of the ancient Seats of the Barons Ross of Halkhead, and is now the property of the Right Honourable William Lord Ross.

Opposite to that, upon the north side of the river of Clyde, ly the lands of Wester Partick and Blawert-hill, anciently a possession of the Stewarts of Arthurly: For, of these lands I have seen a Charter granted by King James II. an. 1452, to Walter Stewart of Arthurly; and, by marriage of one of the co-heirs of that branch of the Stewarts of Darnly, these lands came to the family of Minto, and are now the property of Sir John Maxwel of Pollock, Baronet, one of the Senators of the College of Justice: as the lands of Blawert-hill are

---

[1] Buchanan's History of Scotland.
[2] Chron. de Melross, in Bibliotheca Universitatis Glasguensis.

of Mr. John Maxwel; whence he takes designation, being only son and heir of Zacharias Maxwel of Blawert-hill, (brother german to Sir George Maxwel of Pollock) by Jean his wife, only daughter of John Maxwel of South-Bar, by Elizabeth his wife, daughter of William Cunninghame of Craigends. He hath married the Lady Ann Carmichael, daughter of John Earl of Hyndfoord.

Not far from this, toward the east, are the house and lands of Scotstoun, an ancient inheritance of the Montgomeries, a branch of the family of Eglintoun: Robert Montgomery of Scotstoun is recorded in the Chartulary of the Abby of Pasly, to have been an arbiter betwixt the Abbot of that Convent, and the town of Renfrew, an. 1488 [1]. John Montgomery of Scotstoun, the last of this race, alienated these lands, in the reign of King Charles I. to Mr. John Hutcheson; and they came, by marriage of Margaret, his daughter and heiress, to Archbald Stewart, second son of Sir Archbald Stewart of Blackhall; and from George Hutcheson of Scotstoun, their son, these lands were acquired (an. 1691) by William Walkinshaw, (son of John Walkinshaw of Borrowfield, descended from a younger brother of the family of Walkinshaw of that-ilk, in the reign of King James VI.) by whom this place is much improven, by a very handsome house, well finished and adorned with curious orchards and gardens, stately avenues, and large inclosures, sheltered with a great deal of beautiful planting: so that it has become one of the sweetest seats, upon the river of Clyde, in this Shire.

The present William Walkinshaw of Scotstoun was married with Marion, daughter of Thomas Crawfurd of Cartsburn, by whom he had John, his son and apparent heir. Their Armorial bearing is; Argent; upon a Mount, a grove of Firrs, proper; surmounted with a Mullet, for a brotherly difference; and, for Crest, he bears a Martlet; with this Motto, " In season."

Towards the north from Scotstoun, pleasantly situate upon an eminence, stands the house of Jordan-hill, the principal Manour of these lands, of late repaired by Laurence Crawfurd now of Jordan-hill, beautified with pleasant orchards and gardens, and likeways well planted. These lands have, for near 150 years, been the possession of a family of the Sirname of Crawfurd, the latest Cadet of the ancient and honourable Family of Kilbirny, in the Shire of Air, now dignified with the title of Viscount of Garnock. Their ancestor was that brave gentleman, Captain Thomas Crawfurd, who was a younger son of Laurence Crawfurd of Kilbirny, by Helen his Lady, daughter of Sir Hugh Campbel of Loudoun, Sheriff of Air (ancestor to the Right Honourable Hugh, now Earl of

[1] Chartulary of Pasly.

Loudoun.) This gentleman gave very early proof of his courage and bravery: for, being at the battle of Pinkie, where was a bloody conflict, the 10th of September 1547, betwixt the Scotish army, under the leading of James Earl of Arran, Governour to Queen Mary of Scotland, and Edward Duke of Somerset, uncle and protector to King Edward VI. of England, on occasion of the Scots refusing to bestow their young Queen Mary in marriage to the said King Edward; where eight thousand brave Scots were slain, and many taken prisoners, of which number Captain Thomas Crawfurd was one. After his release he went for France, where he became so much valued by King Francis I. that he made him one of the guard of Scotsmen, that waited on his royal person, as a special mark of their fidelity and favour. He continued in that kingdom till the death of Francis II. husband of our Queen Mary, an. 1561: And, returning home with his Princess, he lived privately and loyally, until the execrable murder of King Henry, that he thought himself bound in duty to associate, with other loyal subjects, to revenge that murder, and obtained from the Earl of Murray, then Regent, the command of a body of men; after which, he was known by the designation of Captain Crawfurd. He accus'd Sir William Maitland of Lethingtoun, secretary of state, at a Convention at Stirling, an. 1569, as being accessory to King Henry's murder: Upon which accusation the Secretary was sent prisoner to the castle of Edinburgh. As also, during the Regency of Matthew Earl of Lenox, he surprised the castle of Dunbartoun, the 2d of April 1571, a strength at that time thought impregnable'[1]: which memorable adventure is mentioned by all our historians of the time. In consideration of his many faithful services to his King and country, he obtained the lands of Bishop's Meadow, Blackstoun Barns, and Mills of Partick, with a pension of 200 l. yearly, payable out of the Priory of St. Andrews; of all which lands he obtained, from King James, a Charter, confirming a former, granted by James Boyd, Archbishop of Glasgow, dated the 10th of March 1573, as is evident from the original yet extant, viz,

" JACOBUS, D. G. Rex Scotorum; Sciatis: Nos dedisse, Thomæ Crawfurd
" de Jordan-hill, Capitaneo, Militi prudenti, ac in rebus bellicis audaci & ex-
" perto, pro remuneratione ejusdem Thomæ Crawfurd, ob Castrum Dunbarto-
" nense, non solum viris rebellibus, Regi regnoque & legibus resistentibus,
" sed etiam victulalibus, machinis bellicis & armorum copia repletum, sed ob

---

[1] Crawfurd's Memoirs of the four Regents.

" portentuosum illius situm in summitate rupis asperrimæ, munitissimum, omni-
" um judicio inexpugnabile, labore & industria ipsius Thomæ, captum & ex-
" pugnatum, ' " &c.

He was also one of the commanders under the Earl of Morton, at that conflict which happen'd the 10th of June 1571, at the Gallow-Lee, betwixt the Earl of Huntly, Lieutenant for the Queen, and the said Earl of Morton, for the young King; where Huntly was defeat, and some fifty or sixty of his men slain: In memory of which action, Morton gave Captain Crawfurd for Motto these words, " God shaw the Right," and is ever since borne by his family; which words were expressed by Sir William Drury, the English Resident, when he had rode betwixt the two parties, endeavouring to mediate a peace betwixt them. The story is particularly related by Mr. Hume of Godscroft, in his History of the family of Douglass: And, upon the dissolution of the religious houses, he acquired the lands of Jordan-hill, from Sir Bartholomew Montgomery, Chaplain of the Chappel of Drumray, an. 1562: To which the lands of Jordan-hill had been originally mortified; and afterwards that Chappel was richly endowed with a plentiful revenue, by Laurence Crawfurd of Kilbirny, (father of Captain Crawfurd) about the year 1546, " pro salute animæ suæ &
" Helenæ Campbel, sponsæ suæ², &c. & omnium Antecessorum & Successo-
" rum suorum."

King James VI. had so grateful a sense of the Captain's services, that he writes him a letter, I thought fit, as a proof, thereof to subjoin.

CAPTEN CRAWFORD,

" I have heard sic report of your guid service done to me from the beginning of the wars against my onfriends, as I shal sum day remember the same, GOD willing, to your greit contentment: In the mein quhyle be of guid comfort, and reserve you to that time with patience, being assured of my favour. Fareweil.

15, Sept. 1575.   Your guid friend,

JAMES REX.

[1] Carta penes Laurentium Crawfurd de Jordan-hill.
[2] Carta penes Patricium Vice-comitem de Garnock.

He was also Provost of the city of Glasgow, an. 1577, then in the hands of the most considerable gentlemen in the country ; which is evident from original documents, yet extant, in the hands of his descendants [1] : About which time he built a great part of the bridge of Partick, over the river of Kelvin, consisting of four arches, on which is his name and arms, viz. The quarter'd Coat of the family of Kilbirny ; first ; a Fess, ermine : secondly ; a Cheveron, betwixt three Cross-molins, for the name of Barclay ; and, in base of the Coat of Crawfurd, for distinction, two Swords saltyre ways ; which is carried by all his descendants ; and underneath his arms is this inscription. :

" He that by labour does any honestie,
" The labour goes, the honour bides with thee ;
" He that by treason does any vice also,
" The shame remains, the pleasure soon agoes."

He was twice married ; first, with Marion Colquhoun, daughter of Sir John Colquhoun of Luss, and Dowager of Robert, Master of Boyd, by whom he had only one Daughter, called Marion, married to Sir Robert Fairly of that-ilk, an ancient Baron in the Shire of Air ; and surviving his first lady, he remarried Janet Ker, eldest daughter and heiress of Robert Ker of Kersland, the head and representative of an ancient family of that name, in the Shire of Air, where they have been seated for upwards of 500 years. For, William de Ker is recorded witness in a contract betwixt Bryce of Eglintoun and the Burgh of Irvine, an. 1205 [2] The issue of this marriage were two sons and a daughter, viz. Daniel, of whom the Kers of Kersland descended : The second, Hugh, of whom issued the Crawfurds of Jordan-hill : His daughter Susanna was married to Colin Campbel of Elengreg, of whom Sir Neil Campbel of Elengreg is lineally descended. By his testament, bearing date, in November 1602, he bequeathed his body to be buried at Kilbirny, having erected a stately tomb at that church, with the statues of himself and his wife, as big as the life, in stone, with this inscription :

" Here lies Captain Thomas Crawfurd of Jordanhill, sixth son to Lawrence Crawfurd of Kilbirny ; and Janet Ker, eldest daughter of Robert Ker of Kersland, his spouse."

[1] Carta penes Thomam Crawfurd de Cartsburn.
[2] Carta penes Burg. de Irvine.

He departed this life the 3d of January 1603, as appears from the probate thereof, yet extant.

To Captain Thomas Crawfurd of Jordanhill, formerly mentioned, succeeded Hugh his son, who obtained the lands of Jordanhill from his father, an. 1586 [1], and took to wife Elizabeth, daughter of William Stirling of Law; by whom he had Cornelius, his son and heir; the second, Lawrence, who went to Sweden, Anno. 1629, where he served Gustavus Adolphus, in his wars in Germany, in the quality of a Lieutenant-Colonel, and behaved himself honourably, until the battle of Lutzen, where that brave Prince fell; at which time he returned home, and was made Colonel of a Regiment of Foot (in the service of King Charles I.) which was sent to Ireland, for suppressing the horrid Rebellion that fell out in that kingdom, an. 1641; where he gave many signal proofs of being a brave and valiant General: but afterwards quitting that side, he engaged in the Parliament's service, and was made Major General to the Earl of Manchester's Brigade; and in the year 1643, leaving the English service, he went to the Scottish Army, where he was made Major General, Commissary General, Colonel and Captain of a troup of horse, and one of the Council of war: He was immediately sent to command at the siege of Hereford, where he was killed with a musket bullet, from the walls of the town, as he was riding about, viewing its fortifications, in September 1645. He was interred in the Cathedral of Glocester, and had a marble Monument erected to his memory, with his statue as big as the life. He was married with Elenora, daughter of Sir Robert Merideth, by whom he had a son, Lawrence, who died in his infancy. His estate, which was very considerable in money, came to Cornelius Crawfurd of Jordanhill, his brother german. The Major General's armorial bearing was, Gules; a Fess Ermine; betwixt three Mulets Argent; on a Canton of the second, two Swords saltyre ways, proper, hilted and pomeled, Or; for Crest, a Lawrel, with this motto, " Calcar honeste."

There was a third brother, Mr. John, who was Rector of Halden, in the County of Kent.

The fourth, Thomas, who went to Sweden in the year 1629, and afterwards to Muscovy, where, for his good service, he was made a Colonel: he was at the taking of Smolensko, an 1652, where he was blown up with powder, by which he lost an eye, and was disabled for any service; so that the Emperor gave him a handsome allowance till his death, an. 1685. He was married to Agnes,

---

[1] Carta penes Laurent. Crawfurd de Jordanhill.

daughter of Colonel Alexander Crawfurd, a son of the Baron of Fedret, in the North of Scotland.

The fifth, Daniel, who was Lieutenant Colonel to his brother the Major General's Regiment, in Ireland: He had a considerable share in all the fights and skirmishes wherein his brother was concerned; and during his abode there, he behaved himself both bravely and loyally: For when his brother, Major General Lawrence, went into the Parliament's service, he refused to serve the King's enemies, but came over to Scotland, and lived privately, till the time of Duke Hamilton's Engagement, an. 1648, when he entered into that service, and was with the Duke at Prestoun, in no other quality than that of a Volunteer; and after the defeat of the Scots Army, he retired to Scotland, where he continued to appear for his His Majesty's service in the hills, several years, in conjunction with, and on the head of, some of those loyal Scots who opposed the troops of the usurper, Oliver Cromwel; but was afterwards, in one of those rencounters, betwixt Jordan-hill and Glasgow, taken, and sent prisoner to London, where he continued for sometime: but being released, upon condition of leaving the Kingdoms of England, Scotland, and Ireland, within two months, and never to meddle with any thing prejudicial to the state of England; he went first for France, and soon after to Muscovy; and, on his arrival, was by His Imperial Majesty declared Colonel of a Regiment of 1600 men. He was afterwards made Governour of Smolensko by the Emperor, and declared a Major General, and governour of Muscovy, a place which no stranger had ever enjoy'd, and which he kept till his death, about 1674. He left issue, by Mary his wife, daughter of Colonel John Crawfurd, a Scots Gentleman in the Muscovite service, two sons, both captains of horse in the Prussian service, in the year 1690; and a daughter, Mary, married to Colonel Robert Duncanson. But the particular lives of martial Scotsmen being no part of the subject I treat of, I refer my reader to the learned and accurate Historian Doctor Patrick Abercromby, who designs, with all expedition, to publish the lives of our martial Scots Gentlemen.

But to return to the principal branch of this family, Hugh Crawfurd of Jordanhill, who paid his last debt to nature, an. 1626. To him succeeded Cornelius, his son and heir; who took to wife, Mary, daughter of Sir James Lockhart of Lee, by Jean his lady, daughter of Sir George Auchinleck of Balmanoe, an ancient family in Perthshire, by whom he had two sons and as many daughters: Hugh, his eldest son, died in his own time; and Thomas, author of the Crawfurds now of Cartsburn: his daughters were; Margaret, married to James Grahame of Kilearn, and had issue; and Jean, married to Robert Pollock

I

of that-ilk, and mother of Sir Robert Pollock now of that-ilk, Baronet: Which Cornelius deceased an. 1687. To whom succeeded Laurence his grandson and heir, by Hugh his eldest son. But before I proceed, 'tis proper to take notice, that, having married Bethia Hamilton, daughter to the Laird of Woodhall, he departed this life in the year 1684, (his father then living) leaving issue by the said Bethia his wife, two sons and as many daughters, viz. Lawrence, and James, late Sheriff Depute of Renfrew (father of Mr. Hugh Crawfurd, writer in Edinburgh.) His daughters were Jean, married to Andrew Colquhoun of Garscadan, and Mary to Ninian Hill of Lambhill, and both had issue.

Which Lawrence Crawfurd, now of Jordanhill, hath been twice married; first, to Elizabeth, daughter and co-heiress of John Dove of Arnhall, by whom he had one daughter called Anna, married to James MackGilchrist of Northbar: He hath, secondly, married Margaret, daughter and sole heiress of John Hamilton of Woodhall, by whom he had John, his son and heir, &c.

The Armorial bearing of Jordanhill is, Two Coats quarterly; first; Gules, a Fess Ermine, with two Swords Saltyre ways in base. Secondly; Gules, a Holly leaf Vert, betwixt three Cinque Foils Argent. Third, as second; and Fourth, as first: and for Crest a Castle, (relative to his ancestor Captain Crawfurd's surprising the castle of Dunbartoun) with this Motto, " Expugnavi ;" and, on a compartment, " GOD shaw the Right."

HAVING thus finished the Description of the several places upon the river of White Cart, I come next to give a Description of the several Seats of the nobility and gentry upon the river of Black Cart; which, as I observed in the Geography of this Shire, hath its source from the Loch of Castle-Semple: Upon the north side whereof stands the house of Barr, the Seat of an ancient family of the Sirname of Glen: But the first of this family, touching whom I have found any thing on record, is Allanus Glen, Armiger, who was a witness to the donation of the fishing of Crockat-Shot, by Robert Lord Lyll, to the Monks of Pasly, an. 1452. His successor James Glen obtained a grant from Robert Abbot of Pasly, of his lands of Barr, Bridge-End, and Lyntchels, in the Lordship of Glen and Regality of Pasly, in the year 1506. Another James Glen of Barr, obtained a Charter from John, Abbot of Pasly, with consent of the Convent, of the lands above-mentiond, an. 1544. Which James Glen of Barr, being with Queen Mary's troops at the field of Langside, an. 1568, was forfaulted by the Regent, and restored by the treaty of Perth, in 1573. William Glen of Barr was his son; whose son, of the same name, dying without male issue, his only daughter, Isobel, was married to Thomas Boyd of Pitcon. The estate of Barr devolved upon Alexander Glen, his brother and heir, in whose person that family failed. I have seen their Armorial bearing; Blasond; Argent; a Fess, Gules; betwixt three Martlets, Sable.

The lands of Barr are now the property of John Hamilton of Barr, representative of the Hamiltons of Fergusly.

North-east from Barr stands the Village and Church of Lochwhynoch, a Chaplainry in old times depending of the Abby of Pasly. The Reverend Mr. John Pasly is the present Minister.

And a little towards the east of this village, upon the brink of the Loch, stands the Castle of Semple, the principal messwage of a fair lordship of the same denomination; which consists of a large court, part of which seems to be a very ancient building; adorned with pleasant orchards and gardens.

As to the origine of this noble family, I can make no conjecture; neither shall I insist upon what is tradition relative to it, that being for the most part trifling and confus'd: 'Tis sufficient to know, that for more than 400 years they have been Barons of great account in this Shire, which, I think, the following account will sufficiently document. But to omit the obscurer Barons of Eliestoun, in the reign of King Alexander III. Robert Semple is Stewart of the Barony of Renfrew. I have seen little more of this Robert, but that he was a witness to a Charter granted by James, High Stewart of Scotland: " Stephano " filio Nicolai de terra illa, quæ data fuit Patricio de Selvinland, ubi aqua de " Grief, descendit in aquam de Clyde [1]," which is before the year 1309, that the granter of that Charter died. And, in the Chartulary of the Monastery of Pasly, in the reign of King Robert Bruce, Robert Semple is witness to the donation of the church of Largs; which Walter, High Stewart of Scotland, father of King Robert II. gave to the Monks of Pasly, for the health of his soul, and for the soul of Marjory Bruce his deceased wife, an. 1318 [2]. The Barons of Eliestoun were eminent in the reign of King David II. For, Thomas Semple, Lord of Eliestoun, is recorded in the Register of Pasly, a witness to that confirmation which Robert, Earl of Strathern, and John Lord Kyle, his son and apparent heir, gave to the Monks of that Abby, of the lands of Sanaquhar, Coudams, and Staflour, about the year 1367 [3]; as John Semple of Eliestoun is a witness to that mortification which Sir Adam Fullertoun of that-ilk

[1] Carta penes Rob. Hall de Fulbar. [2] Register of the Monastery of Pasly.
[3] Chartulary of Pasly.

made out of his lordship of Corsby to the Abbot and Convent of Pasly, an. 1392, for the health of his soul and for the souls of his ancestors. The same John Semple of Eliestoun, knight, appends his seal to a resignation of the lands of Fultoun to the Monks of Pasly, an. 1409. His successor, another John Semple of Eliestoun, is witness to a Charter of confirmation, by Robert Duke of Albany, Governour of Scotland, of the lands of Edingtoun, in favours of Sir Robert Lauder, knight [1]. His successor Sir William Semple, Lord of Eliestoun, knight, Sheriff of Renfrew, obtained from King James III. a Charter of the Baronies of Eliestoun and Castletoun, upon his own resignation, dated the 4th of October 1474 [2]. To whom succeeded Sir Thomas Semple of Eliestoun, Sheriff of Renfrew, his son, who departed this life in the year 1486, and was succeeded by his son, Sir John Semple of Eliestoun; which Sir John, being a person of an ample fortune, was, by the bounty and favour of King James IV. the first year of his reign, an. 1488, created into the dignity of Lord Semple: He obtained from that monarch, in the year 1505, a Charter of the lands of Eliestoun, Castletoun, Shuterflat, Hairs-Pennell, Nether-Pennell, Barr in Kilbarchan, Whitelands, Bordland, Craiginfeoch, and Fairnieniese, in the Shire of Renfrew; the lands of Southenen, with their pertinents, in the Shire of Air; and the Barony of Glassford in Lanerk. Lord John, in the year 1505, founded the Collegiate Church of Castle-Semple, to the honour of God and of the blessed Virgin Mary, for the prosperity of his Sovereign Lord King James IV. and Queen Margaret, his royal consort; and for the soul of Margaret Colvil, his former wife; and for the health of his own soul, and of Margaret Creighton his wife, then living; as also for the souls of all his ancestors and successors. Lord John was twice married; first to Margaret Colvil, a daughter of the house of Ochiltree: Secondly, he took to wife Margaret Creighton, Lady Keir, and sister of Sir Adam Creighton. By the first he had two sons; William his successor, and Gabriel, ancestor of the Semples of Cathcart: and being at the battle of Floudoun, which was fought the 9th of September 1513, had the hard fate to be there slain.

To him succeeded William, his son and heir, who obtained a Charter of the lordship of Semple, from King James V. with consent of John Duke of Albany, Governour of Scotland, during the minority of that Prince, Anno. 1515. He was, by the same monarch, appointed one of the Lords of Justiciary of the Regality of Pasly, with consent of his Privy Council [3]. He augmented his pater-

[1] Carta penes Dom. Alex. Seaton de Pitmedden, Baron.
[2] Carta penes Franciscum Dom. Semple. [3] Chartulary of Pasly.

nal inheritance, and acquired the lands of Leven, Kirkpennyland, and Thirdpart, in the Shire of Renfrew. He married, first, Margaret Montgomery, daughter of Hugh, first Earl of Eglintoun; by whom he had Robert his successor: David, one of his younger sons, obtained the lands of Craiginfeoch from Robert Master of Semple, his brother, an. 1546 [1], He had likeways several daughters; viz. Helen, married to Allan, Lord Cathcart, and had issue; Marion was married to the Laird of Keir. He 2dly, took to wife, Dame Elizabeth Arnot: and 3dly, he married Marion Montgomery, daughter to the Laird of Haslehead. He deceased in the year 1547: his estate and honours devolving upon Robert, his son and heir: Which Robert was called the great Lord Semple; who being a person of a very martial spirit, was at the field of Pinkie, an. 1547, where he had the misfortune to be taken prisoner by the English; and after that, continued most affectionately devoted to the interest of Queen Mary, until the murther of King Henry, that this noble Lord did, with other Scots Peers, enter into a bond of association, to defend the young Prince, King James, and was with the Regent at the field of Langside; and in consideration of his many good services to king and government, he obtained from the Regent Murray, a Charter of the Abby of Pasly, during life, an. 1569, upon the forfaulture of Lord Claud Hamilton [2]; and continued indefatigable in the service of his Prince till his death, which was an. 1572. He was twice married: first, to Isobel Hamilton, a daughter of the house of Hamilton, by whom he had two sons; Robert Master of Semple, who died in his father's time; and Andrew, commonly called Master of Semple, ancestor of the Semples of Bruntshells and Milbank [3]. He married 2dly, Elizabeth Carlile, daughter to the Lord Carlile; by whom he had John, author of that branch of the Semples of Beltrees. His daughters were married in the families of Ross, Blair, Broomhill, Whitefoord, Stanhouse, Haslehead, Skelmurly, Barochan, &c. of whom these several families descended.

To Robert, the great Lord Semple, succeeded immediately Robert his grandson, viz. son of Robert Master of Semple, (who deceased in the year 1569) by Barbara Preston his Lady, daughter to the Laird of Valyfield. He was left under the tutory of James Earl of Morton, Regent: He was of the Privy Council to King James VI. and in the year 1596, was constitute his Majesty's Ambassador to Spain [4]. He was married, first, to Agnes Montgomery, daughter of Hugh Earl of Eglintoun, by whom he had Hugh his successor, and

[1] Carta penes Alexand. Porterfield de Eodem. [2] Carta penes Francisc. Dominum Semple.
[3] Carta penes J. Comitem de Dundonald. [4] Genealogy of the family of Semple.

four daughters; Ann, married to Sir Archbald Stewart of Castlemilk, (by whom he had two sons, Sir Archbald Stewart of Castlemilk, and James, ancestor of the Stewarts of Torence) the 2d, Barbara, married Sir Coll Laumont of that-ilk, and had issue. The 3d, Grissel, to John Logan of Raiss. The 4th, to Robert Brisbane of Bishoptoun. Lord Robert married 2dly, Dame Joanna Evieland, a Dutch Lady, by whom he had Sir William Semple of Letterkeny, in the Kingdom of Ireland.

To Robert Lord Semple succeeded Hugh, his son and heir: Which Lord Hugh was one of the Peers that sat upon the trial of Patrick Earl of Orkney, an. 1614 [1]. He married, first, Ann Hamilton, daughter of James Earl of Abercorn, by whom he had one daughter, called Marion, who married Sir George Preston of Valyfield, and had issue. Secondly, he took to wife Elizabeth Hay, daughter of Francis Earl of Errol; by whom he had Francis and Robert, successively Lord Semple: the third, Arch: of Dykehead: and daughters, Elizabeth, married William Lord Mordingtoun; and Jean to William Menzies of Pitfodel, and had issue. He departed this life in the year 1687, his estate and honours devolving upon Francis, his son and heir: Who dying without succession, his estate and honours descended to Robert his brother; who died in the year 1675, leaving issue, by Ann Douglass his wife, daughter of James Lord Mordingtoun, Francis, his son and heir; and two daughters, Ann, married to Francis Abercromby of Fiterneer; and Jean to Alexander Saintclair of Rosline, and had issue: Which Francis, Lord Semple, took to wife Grissel, daughter of Sir Archbald Primrose of Dalmeny; but having no succession, he departed this life, an. 1684. His estate and honours devolved upon Ann, Lady Semple, his sister and sole heiress; who, by Francis Abercromby of Fiterneer, afterwards dignified with the title of Lord Glassfoord, (son and heir of Alexander Abercromby of Fiterneer, who was son and heir of Hector Abercromby of Fiterneer, second son of Sir Alexander Abercromby of Berkenboig, an ancient family in Bamff-Shire) had Francis, now Lord Semple, her son and heir, who succeeded his mother, (who deceased an. 1691.) His Lordship's Armorial bearing is, Argent; a Cheveron Checquie, Gules, and of the first; betwixt three Bugles, Sable, garnished of the second; supported by two Ratches; for Crest, a Stagg's head couped, proper; with this Motto, " Keep Tryst."

Near to the Castle of Semple are the lands of Milbank, from which James Semple, son of Andrew, Master of Semple, took designation. I have seen him so designed in a Charter granted by Robert Lord Semple, in the year 1603, of several

---

[1] Spotiswood's History.

lands in the Shire of Renfrew, to James Semple of Milbank, and Sibilla Glen his spouse (a daughter of the house of Barr) son of Andrew Master of Semple, his uncle[1] : Which James above-mentioned was father of Robert Semple of Milbank, who sold these lands, and died an. 1663 ; leaving issue, by Elizabeth his wife, daughter of John Boyle of Kelburn, and of Marion his Lady, daughter of Hugh Crawfurd of Kilbirny, Andrew, his son and heir : who, by Jean his wife, daughter of William Algoe of Easter-Walkinshaw, had two daughters, his co-heirs ; Jean, married to Thomas Crawfurd of Cartsburn, and had issue ; Margaret, wife of Robert Hall of Fulbar, and had issue.

Near to this, towards the north, ly the lands of Balgreen, which came to a natural son of the family of Semple, by marriage of Margaret Atkine, the heiress of these lands.

Opposite to Castle-Semple, upon the south side of the Loch, ly the lands of Beltrees : A family of the Sirname of Stewart did anciently possess these lands. I have seen a Charter granted by King James III. anno 1477, of the lands of Beltrees, to William Stewart and Alison Kennedy his spouse, which failed in the person of another William Stewart of Beltrees, an. 1559. These lands came to Robert Lord Semple, and became the patrimony of John Semple, son of Robert Lord Semple, by Elizabeth Carlile (his second wife) a daughter of the Lord Torthorald, who was ancestor of the Semples of Beltrees : He was married to Mary, sister to William Lord Livingstoun, and one of the maids of honour to Queen Mary ; by whom he had Sir James Semple of Beltrees, his son and heir ; from whom Robert Semple, now of Beltrees, is the fourth in a direct descent. The intermarriages of the Semples of Beltrees, beside these above-mentioned, are with these following ancient and considerable families ; Elphinstouns of Blythswood, Lyons of Albar, Campbels of Arkinglass, Mackfarlans of that-ilk, Maxwels of Newark, Pollocks of that-ilk. Their Armorial bearing is the Coat of the Lord Semple, and in base of the 3d Bugle, a Rose Gules.

And a little towards the east ly the lands of Gavan and Rysk, an old possession of the Boyds, an ancient family in Airshire. The first I have found of this family, is " Dominus Robertus Boyd, Miles," a witness in a contract of agreement betwixt Bryce de Eglintoun and the village of Irvine, in the year 1205, as the original, extant in the Charter-chest of Irvine, testifies ; and excerpt of which I have seen, (subscribed by the Provost of that Burgh), by the favour of George Ross of Gaustoun, a gentleman well seen in the antiquities

[1] Carta penes Hugh Crawfurd de Woodside.

of his country. The lands above-mentioned came afterwards to the Boyds of Benheath, an early Caddet of the noble family of Kilmarnock: (for this I have seen a Charter granted by King Robert III. to William Boyd, son and apparent heir of William Boyd of Badenheath, upon his father's resignation, in the year 1405 [1],) and continued for several hundreds of years, a possession of that family: And in the 1518, these lands came to Mr. Robert Boyd of Kipps, descended of the family of Badenheath; and by marriage of Margaret, his daughter and heiress, the lands of Kipps came to Mr. David Sibbald, of the house of Rankeilor: They were father and mother of that learned gentleman and curious Antiquary, Sir Robert Sibbald of Kipps, Doctor of Medicine. The superiority of the lands of Gavan and Rysk, was lately acquired from William, first Earl of Kilmarnock, by Francis Lord Glasfoord.

Near to this stands the Castle of Eliestoun, the principal messwage of a Barony of large extent, of the same name; and ancient designation of the Barons Semple. I have seen a Charter granted by King Robert Bruce, " Dilecto & " fideli suo Roberto dicto Sympel, de tota terra in tenemento de Largs cum " pertinent: quæ fuere quondam Johannis de Baliolo, Militis [2].

Lower upon the river of Cart, lie the lands of Thirdpart, an ancient inheritance of the Crawfurds, a branch of those of Achinames. I have seen a Charter of alienation of these lands from John Crawfurd, son and heir of Archbald Crawfurd of Privick and Drumvier, for the sum of three hundred merks, to be paid upon St. James's altar in St. Giles's kirk of Edinburgh, in the year 1523 [3], to William Lord Semple; and is now the residence and property of Robert Semple of Beltrees.

And near to this, a little towards the north, stand the Castle and Barony of Achinames: an ancient family of the Crawfurds have possessed these lands well nigh 400 years, and are certainly a branch of the Crawfurds of Loudoun, heriditary Sheriff of Air in the days of King Alexander II. For in the Register of Pasly, in a Charter by " Walterus Senescallus Scotiæ," in the same reign, to the Abby of Pasly, " de terra de Dalmulin," among the witnesses, is " Reginaldus de Crawfurd, Vicecomes de Air, & Hugo filius Reginal- " di:" But afterwards, in the reign of King Robert Bruce, the Barony of Loudoun, came, by marriage of Susanna, daughter and heiress of another Sir Reginald Crawfurd of Loudoun, to Sir Duncan Campbel of the family of Lochow in Argileshire: For there is a Charter granted by King Robert I.

[1] Carta penns Will. Comitem de Kilmarnock. [2] Carta in Publicis Archivis.
[3] Carta penes Franciscum Dominum Semple.

" Anno regni duodecimo, Duncano Campbel, Militi, & Susannæ, Sponsæ suæ,
" omnes terras suas de Loudoun & Stevenstoun, cum pertinentiis per dictos
" Duncanum & Susannam, Sponsam suam hæreditarie contingentes, ratione
" dictæ Sponsæ;" and so by Susanna the heiress of Crawfurd, the lands of
Loudoun and Stevenstoun came to the Campbels, hereditary Sheriffs of Air, afterwards Lords, and then Earls, of Loudoun, who carry the figure of the arms of Crawfurd in their atchievement. The Right Honourable Hugh, Earl of Loudoun, is the lineal heir of the ancient family of Loudoun[1].

Of this family (of Loudoun) there are descended many ancient families, of the Sirname of Crawfurd, in the Shires of Air and Renfrew; and among the first of these, the Crawfurds of Achinames may be justly reckoned for; as a document of this, I have seen a a mortification by Thomas Crawfurd of Achinames, of the lands of Lyndnocht and Glenlean, with their pertinents, and an annuity of three merks out of his lands of Achinames, for the maintainance of a Chaplain to celebrate divine service at the altar of the Virgin Mary, in the kirk of Kilbarchan, for the health of his soul and of his wife, and for the soul of Sir Reginald Crawfurd, his grandfather; as also for the souls of his father and of his mother: Which mortification is confirmed by King Robert III. in the year 1401[2]. But of this Thomas Crawfurd I have found nothing more on record, than that he was a witness to the resignation of the lands of Fultoun, to the Monks of Pasly, an. 1409[3]. From this Thomas did Robert Crawfurd of Achinames descend, who is recorded one of the arbiters betwixt the Abbot and Convent of Pasly, and the Burgh of Renfrew, in the year 1488[4]. Which Robert, being at the battle of Floudoun with King James IV, had the hard fate to be there slain, the 9th of September 1513.

Thomas Crawfurd of Auchinames, his successor, lived in the reign of King James V. and died an. 1544, leaving issue, by Marion Montgomery, his Lady, a daughter of the family of Haslehead, three sons, John, William, and Patrick, all successively Lairds of Achinames: John Crawfurd of Achinames, the eldest of the three brothers being killed at the battle of Pinkie, the 10th of September 1547, his estate devolved upon William, his brother and heir; who took to wife Anabel Chalmers, daughter to the Laird of Gadgirth, by whom he had only James, his son and heir; who married Elizabeth, daughter of William Earl of Glencairn, by whom he left only one daughter, named Jean, who was heiress of the lands of Corsby in Cunninghame. The estate of Achinames descended

K

[1] Preface to the Observations upon the Scottish History. [2] Carta penes Pat. Fleeming de Barochan. [3] Chartulary of Pasly. [4] Register of the Monastery of Pasly.

to Patrick Crawfurd, uncle to James Crawfurd of Achinames, last mentioned; whose grandchild, Patrick Crawfurd of Achinames, married Jean Crawfurd, heiress of Corsby, by which the ancient estate of Corsby and Achinames was re-unite: Their grandchild, Archbald Crawfurd of Achinames, died without male succession, and his estate devolved immediately on Helen Crawfurd, only daughter and heir of William Crawfurd, younger of Achinames, his grandchild.

The intermarriages of this family, beside these already mentioned, were with these following considerable families, viz. Frazers of Knock, Houstouns of that-ilk, Hunters of Hunterstoun, Laumonts of Ineryne, Boyds of Trochrig, Kennedies of Kilhainzie, Porterfields of that-ilk, Bruces of Poufouls, and Crawfurds of Drumsoy.

The armorial bearing of the family of Achinames is, Argent; Two Spears Saltyre ways; betwixt Four Spots of Ermine.

A little towards the north from the Castle of Achinames, stand the church and village of Kilbarchan, lately erected into a Burgh and Barony, in favours of William Cunninghame now of Craigends. The present Minister is Mr. Robert Johnston.

And near to this ly the house and lands of Johnstoun: An ancient family, of the Sirname of Wallace, did possess these lands for several ages; they descended from the house of Eldersly, by Thomas, a younger son of John Wallace of Eldersly, in the reign of King Robert III. I have seen a resignation of the lands of Achinbothy, into the hands of Robert, Duke of Albany, Governour of Scotland, an. 1398, by John Wallace of Eldersly, in favours of Thomas Wallace his son. This family obtained the lands of Johnstoun by marriage of the heiress, who was of the Sirname of Nisbet. The family failed in the person of William Wallace of Johnstoun, in the reign of King Charles I. The lands were acquired by Sir Ludovick Houstoun of that-ilk, and became the patrimony of George Houstoun, his second son: Which George Houstoun now of Johnstoun, hath married Elizabeth, daughter of Alexander Cunninghame of Craigends; by whom he has Ludovick, his son and apparent heir.

Opposite to Johnstoun, upon the east side of the river, ly the house and barony of Cochran, the principal manour of the Cochrans, a family of great antiquity in this Shire, whose ancestors have possessed these lands well nigh 500 years, and, without doubt, have taken appellation from their hereditary lands, when fixed Sirnames came to be used: For, as a learned author observes, that Sirnames at first were only used by the first families, and for the most part were local from the places of their habitation, nativity or country, and assumed by those who before were known by patronymicks; and that it was a sufficient proof of ancient descent, where the inhabitant had his Sirname of the place he inhabiteth: Of this sort with us is the Sirname and family of Cochran, whereof I'm now to speak: And though none of this family stood ranked with the Peers of this realm, until the reign of King Charles I. yet were they Barons of eminent note, many ages before, and possessed of a fair inheritance in this Shire. But that what is to be said of the antiquity of the Cochrans, may not be received without sufficient authority, you'll find in the reign of King Alexander the III. Waldenus de Cochran was a witness to that charter, which " Dungallus, filius Suvyn," gave to Walter Stewart, Earl of Monteith, of the lands of Skipnish in Argile-shire, in the year 1262, as the original, yet extant, testifies [1]. I further find William de Cochran is mentioned by Prin in his history, as one of the Scottish Barons that gave allegiance to King Edward I. of England, in the year 1296 [2]. And, as further proof, take the authority of the Chartulary of the Monastery of Pasly, presently in my hands, by the favour of the Right Honourable John Earl of Dundonald; where I find Johnnes de Cochran, a witness in an instrument, electing an Abbot of Pasly, Anno 1346 [3], (reg. Dav. 2do.) And in the following reign, Gosolinus de Cochran seems to have had a considerable share of favour with King Robert II. for I have found him frequently a witness in charters, granted by that Prince; particularly he is a witness to a charter of confirmation, which King Robert II. gave to the Monks of Pasly, of the lands of Sanakar, Camsestrang and Dullarigs, in the year 1367 [4]. His successor, William de Cochran, obtained from that Monarch, a charter of the Barony of Cochran, upon his own resignation, dated, at the Monastery of Kilwinning, the 22d of September 1389, as is evident from the original yet extant, in the hands of the Earl of Dundonald. Of which William Cochran of that-ilk, last mentioned, did Allan Cochran of that-ilk lineally descend, who lived in the reign of King James II. but of him I have found little more memorable, than that he was a witness to the donation, which Robert Lord Lyll made to the Monks of Pasly, of the fishing of Crockatshot, in an. 1452, by the designation of Allanus Cochran, Armiger. To Allan, formerly mentioned, succeeded Robert, his son and heir; who was father of John Cochran of that-ilk, who had sasine of his lands of Cochran and Corsefoord, in an. 1498. I have seen a licence under the Great Seal, granted by King James IV. dated at Edinburgh Octob. 31, an. 1509 [5], to John Cochran of that-ilk, to sell either his lands of Easter-Cochran

---

[1] Carta penes Jo. Ducem de Argyle. [2] Ragman's Roll in Prin's History. [3] Chartulary of Pasly. [4] Chartulary of Pasly. [5] Carta penes Alex. Porterfield de Eodem.

in Renfrewshire, or his lands of Pitfour in Perthshire; which deed is sealed with the Coat of Cochran, viz. Three Boars heads Erazed. He wedded Elizabeth, daughter of John Semple of Fulwood, and departed this life an. 1537, leaving issue by the said Elizabeth, his wife, John his son and heir; who deceased an. 1556, leaving issue, William his successor, by   Lindsay his wife, a daughter of the ancient family of Dunrod: Which William Cochran of that-ilk obtained a charter of confirmation from Queen Mary, of the lands of Cochran, in an. 1576: He took to wife Margaret Montgomery, daughter of Robert Montgomery of Skelmurly, by Mary his lady, daughter of Robert Lord Semple; by whom he had issue, one daughter, called Elizabeth, his sole heir: He tailzied his estate to his daughter, and to the heirs of her body; and for want of such issue, to several others therein specified, upon condition that every such heir should bear the name of Cochran, with the Arms of his family: Which Elizabeth Cochran of that-ilk, took to husband Alexander Blair, one of the younger sons of John Blair of that-ilk, and of Grissel his lady, daughter of Robert Lord Semple; obliging him to assume the Sirname and Arms of Cochran of that-ilk; and by him she left issue, seven sons; first, Sir John Cochran, their son and heir; the 2d, Sir William Cochran of Coudoun; the 3d, Colonel Alexander, whose grandson is Laird of Mainshill; the 4th, Colonel Hugh, whose son and heir is William Cochran of Fergusly; the 5th, Sir Bryce, a Colonel; the 6th, Captain Ochter; the 7th, Captain Gavin of Craigmuir, whose son and heir is Alexander Cochran now of Craigmuir; and two daughters, viz. Margaret, married to John Lenox of Woodhead, an ancient family in the Shire of Stirling; the second, Grissel, married to Thomas Dunlop of Househill.

To Alexander Cochran, succeeded Sir John, his son, who married Buttler, a lady of the family of Ormond, and died without male issue. He was a gentleman of great parts, and beloved by King Charles I. who imployed him for his resident at the Court of Denmark. To him succeeded Sir William Cochran of Coudoun, his brother; who being a person of singular wisdom and prudence, was esteemed by King Charles I. as one very fit to promote the Royal interest in Scotland, at that critical juncture. He was, by the bounty and favour of that Prince, by letters patent, bearing date, Skarsborow the 26. December 1647, advanced to the degree and dignity of a Lord of Parliament, by the title of Lord Cochran of Coudoun and Dundonald: And in the Parliament 1648, he gave sufficient evidence, that his Prince's favour was bestowed for the interest of the Royal cause, by contributing much for the furthering that design, of sending the Scots army into England, under the command of His Grace, James Duke of Hamilton, for the relief of the King's Majesty, from his unjust restraint in the isle of Wight. And upon the restauration of King Charles II. His Majesty being fully sensible of his great sagacity, consummate experience and conduct in business, did make choice of him to be of his Privy Council for Scotland, and was constitute one of the Commissioners of His Majesty's Thesaury: In which honourable and eminent stations he continued a great many years, much to his honour, as well as to the improvement of the Royal Revenue: And, as an additional mark of His Majesty's just esteem of his good services, he was advanced to the dignity of an Earl, by letters patent, bearing date, at Whitehall, the 12th of May 1669, by the title of Earl of Dundonald. He married Eupham, daughter of Sir William Scot of Ardross, by Margaret his lady, daughter of Sir John Skein of Curriehill, by whom he had two sons and a daughter, viz. William Lord Cochran, and Sir John Cochran of Ochiltree; and a daughter, Grissel, who married George Lord Ross, and had issue, William now Lord Ross: Earl William deceased an. 1686, his estate and honours immediately devolving upon John his grandson and heir, viz. son of William Lord Cochran, his eldest son.

But before I proceed, 'tis proper to take notice, that William Lord Cochran, having married the lady Catharine Kennedy, daughter of John Earl of Cassils, by the lady Jean Hamilton, daughter of Thomas, first Earl of Haddingtoun, he departed this life an. 1679, (his father then living) leaving issue, by the said lady Catharine his wife, John, his son and heir; the 2d, William of Kilmaronock, married the lady Grissel Grahame, daughter of James Marquis of Montrose; the 3d, Thomas of Pollockely, married Diana, daughter and sole heiress of Sir David Cunninghame of Robertland, and died without succession; the 4th, Alexander of Bonshaw. Beside these sons, he had likeways several daughters; Margaret, married to Alexander, Earl of Eglintoun, and had issue; the 2d, Helen, to John Earl of Sutherland, and had issue; the 3d, Jean, to John Grahame, Viscount of Dundee; and surviving him, she afterward married William, Viscount of Kilsyth.

To William Earl of Dundonald, succeeded John his grandson; he departed this life an. 1690, in the flower of his age; leaving issue, by the lady Susanna, daughter of William and Ann, late Duke and Dutchess of Hamilton, two sons, William and John, successively Earls of Dundonald: Which William, late Earl of Dundonald, died at his house of Pasly, the 19th of November 1705; his estate and honours devolving upon John, now Earl of Dundonald, his brother, who hath wedded the lady Anna Murray, daughter of Charles Earl of Dunmore, son of John Marquis of Athol, by the lady Æmilia Stanly, daughter of James Earl of Darby, by whom he has issue, William Lord Cochran.

The armorial bearing of the family of Dundonald is, Argent; a Chevron Gules; betwixt three Boars heads Erazed, Azure; supported by Two Gray hounds; and for Crest, a Horse; with this motto, "Virtute & Labore."

Towards the east from the place of Cochran lie the lands of Easter Cochran, (which comprehends the lands of Quarreltoun, Lonbank, Hag, Greenend and Nether Cartside,) they were anciently possessed by the family of Cochran, until the reign of King James V. that John Cochran of that-ilk and of Pitfour (for so he is designed) alienated these lands to James Bethune, then Archbishop of Glasgow, in the year 1519, as appears from the original yet extant[1]; and the same Prelate, when Archbishop of St. Andrews, an 1535, sold the lands of Easter Cochran, to William Cunninghame of Glengarnock, and Elizabeth Saintclair, his spouse, who being killed at the battle of Pinkie, an. 1547, his estate came to John Cunninghame of Glengarnock, his son and heir: One of his younger sons, William Cunninghame, obtained the lands of Quarreltoun, an. 1583; and in the year 1654, they were purchased from William Cunninghame of Quarreltoun, his successor, by Alexander Porterfield of that-ilk, and are now the property of George Houstoun of Johnstoun.

A little towards the east of Cochran stand the Castle and Barony of Eldersly, a place most memorable for giving designation to the valiant and renowned Sir William Wallace of Eldersly, Governour of Scotland, who is still remembered as one of the greatest patriots and champions that ever Scotland had, and as such had his exploits recorded by several hands: He was son and heir of Sir Malcolm Wallace of Eldersly, by . . . . Crawfurd his wife, daughter of Sir Reginald Crawfurd of Loudoun, Sheriff of Air; which Sir Malcolm was a younger son of the ancient family of Riccartoun, in the Shire of Air; one of whose ancestors, Richardus Wallensis, is a witness in the Charter of foundation of the Monastery of Pasly, in King Malcolm IV. his time; and from Richard, the proper name of their predecessor, the lands of Riccartoun, in Kyle, were probably called; which was the seat and designation of Wallace, before the marriage of . . . Lindsay, heiress of Craigie, about the beginning of the reign of King Robert II, whose lineal heir is Sir Thomas Wallace of Craigie, Baronet.

Our brave champion, Sir William Wallace of Eldersly, as he proceeded in the course of his victories, was betrayed by Sir John Monteith, near Glasgow, to Aymer de Valence, Earl of Pembroke, or, as others write, to Robert Umphrevil, then Regent of the north part of Scotland, the 7th of September 1305, and sent to London; where, by King Edward of England's order, he was barbarously executed, being drawn at horse tails, affixed to gibbets, and his dis-

[1] Carta penes Alex. Porterfield de Eodem.

sected members hung up in the publick places of Scotland, to the terror of others. He left issue only one daughter, who was married to Sir William Baillie of Hoprig, of whom William Baillie, now of Lamingtoun is the lineal heir: the lands of Eldersly returned to the family of Craigie; a younger son of that ancient family obtaining them in patrimony, about the beginning of the reign of King Robert III. The first of whom I have found mention, is John Wallace of Eldersly, who resigns the lands of Achinbothy in favours of Thomas Wallace his son, in the year 1398[1], who was author of the Wallaces of Johnstoun. Further, I have found John Wallace of Eldersly appending his seal to a resignation of the lands of Fultoun to the Monks of Pasly, an. 1409[2]; like as " Johannes Wallace de Eldersly, Scutifer," is to be found in the Chartulary of the Monastery of Pasly, an. 1432[3]; as George Wallace of Eldersly is recorded a witness to the donation of the patronage of the kirk of Kilfinan, by John Laumont of that-ilk, to the Monks of that Abby, an. 1468. Which George last mentioned was father of Patrick Wallace of Eldersly; (who made a considerable figure in the reign of King James IV.) and he of William Wallace of Eldersly, who was father of another John Wallace of Eldersly, who added to his paternal inheritance the lands of Elientoun, of which he and Catharine Cunninghame, his spouse, obtained a Charter in the year 1530[4]. William Wallace of Eldersly, his son and successor, obtained a Charter of his lands, an. 1554: He married .... Crawfurd, daughter of Hugh Crawfurd of Kilbirny, (ancestor to the Viscount of Garnock,) by whom he had two sons; William his successor, and John a younger son, who obtained the lands of Fergusly by marriage of Margaret, daughter and sole heiress of John Hamilton of Fergusly, a branch of the Hamiltons of Orbiestoun, of whom descended the Wallaces of Neilstoun-side. The principal branch of the Wallaces of Eldersly, failing in the person of Hugh Wallace of Eldersly, who died without succession, (John Wallace, now of Neilstoun-side, his cousin, was his heir) the lands of Eldersly, in the year 1678, came to Sir Thomas Wallace of Craigie, and became the patrimony and designation of Sir Thomas Wallace now of Craigie, Baronet, during the life of Sir William, his elder brother; and are now the property of John Wallace of Eldersly, nephew and apparent heir male of John Wallace of Neilstoun-side, his uncle, by Mr. William Wallace, his brother-german, the representative of the family of Eldersly; which John Wallace of Eldersly hath married Jean, only daughter and sole heiress of Dr. Thomas Kennedy, physician in Glasgow,

[1] Carta penes D. Arch. Stewart de Blackhall, Bar. [2] Chartulary of Pasly.
[3] Chartulary of Pasly. [4] Carta penes J. Com. de Dundonald.

The Armorial bearing of Wallace of Eldersly, as it is Blazon'd by Sir George Mackenzie in his Herauldry, is, Gules; a Lion rampant, Argent; within a Border, compound Azure and Argent.

Not far from this lie the lands of Craigmuir, the property and designation of Alexander Cochran, son and heir of Captain Gavin Cochran of Craigmuir, brother-german of William, first Earl of Dundonald.

And a little towards the east from the Castle of Eldersly, lie the lands of Newtoun, the possession and designation of Robert Alexander, son and heir of Claud Alexander of Newtoun, who was a younger son of Robert Alexander of Blackhouse.

South of this stand the house and lands of Fulbar, the seat of, and whence an ancient family of the Halls take designation. The first I have found of this Sirname and family is Thomas de Aula, design'd Surgico, who obtained from King Robert II. " illas quatuor mercatas terræ, in Tenemento de Stanle, in " Baronia de Renfrew, quas dudum, eidem Thomæ pro tempore vitæ, conces- " simus, Anno regni primo:" which is the year of our Lord 1370 [1]. These lands above-mentioned are the lands of Fulbar by the bounding, which lands continue yet with their descendents. The direct line of the Halls of Fulbar, in the reign of Queen Mary, extinguished in the person of William Hall of Fulbar, who deceased about the year 1550 without issue. His estate descended on Adam Hall of Tarquinhill, his cousin, who was son of Adam Hall, and he of another Adam Hall, who with the flower of the Scottish nobility and gentry was killed, in the defence of his king and country, at the battle of Floudoun, Anno 1513, where King James IV. died. My authority for this is a discharge, granted to Adam Hall of Fulbar, of the non-entries of the lands of Fulbar and others, which devolved to him as heir of Adam Hall his grandfather, killed at the field of Floudoun: Which Adam last mentioned was married with Jean, daughter of John Wallace of Cairnhill, by whom he had Mr. William, his suscessor; whose son, Robert Hall of Fulbar was father of another Robert, who deceased in 1692, whose son is Robert Hall now of Fulbar. This family have made several alliances with respectful families, viz. The Semples of Fulwood, Cunninghames of Waterstoun, Hamiltons of Torrence, Semples of Milbank, and Maxwels of Dargevil. Their Coat Armorial is, Argent; a Fess Checquie, Sable and of the first; betwixt three Falcons heads, couped, of the second.

[1] Carta in publicis Archivis.

And a little towards the east from this lie the castle and Barony of Stainly, an ancient possession of the Denelstouns of that-ilk; for I have seen in the publick rolls of King Robert III. a Charter granted to Sir Robert Denelstoun knight, of these lands, the second year of his reign (1372.) His estate, by marriage of Elizabeth, one of his daughters and co-heirs, came to Sir Robert Maxwel of Calderwood, in the same reign, and so to George Maxwel, son of Sir John Maxwel of Calderwood, ancestor of the Maxwels of Newark, about the year 1477; and became the patrimony of Archbald Maxwel, younger son of this George Maxwel, first of the house of Newark. They continued a family in good reputation, until at last they failed in the person of John Maxwel of Stainly, who, with consent of Janet Crawfurd, (a daughter of the house of Ferme) his wife, and John his eldest son and apparent heir, alienated the lands of Stainly, in the year 1629, to Dame Jean Hamilton, Lady Ross.

Near to this lie the lands of Achinbach, a possession in times past of the Robertons of Earnock, an ancient family in Lanerkshire; they were anciently Barons of Robertoun in that county, and are to be early met with in the Chartulary of Kelso; as a mortification made by " Robertus, filius Waldevi de " Bigris," for the welfare of his soul, to the cell of Lesmahagoe, " tota decima " bladi terræ Ricardi Baird," to which " Roberto de Robertoun" is a witness, in the reign of King Alexander the II. shows. John Robertoun of Earnock resigned the lands of Achinbach in favours of Sir John Ross, (ancestor to the Lord Ross,) which is confirm'd by King Robert II. the 20th year of his reign; as a Charter, in the public Rolls of King Robert II. testifies. Of two brothers of that ancient family, are the Robertouns of Earnock, and those of Bedlay lineally descended.

A little towards the north from the Castle of Stainly lie the house and lands of Bredieland, which has been possessed by the Maxwels of this race for upwards of two hundred years; but of what family they derive their pedigree I know not. Their original Charter, which I have seen, is granted by Robert, Abbot of Pasly, to Thomas Maxwel, designed son of Arthur Maxwel, Clerk of of Neilstoun, Anno 1488, in the reign of King James IV: Of whom John Maxwel, now of Bredieland, is the lineal heir. The Maxwels of Bredieland have furnished some considerable Cadets; as John Maxwel, predecessor, by the mother, to George Maxwel now of Dalswintoun; and several considerable families of this name in Ireland.

And north from Bredieland lie the house and lands of Woodside, the seat and designation of Hugh Crawfurd, second son of Thomas Crawfurd of Cartsburn.

And hard by Woodside stand the house and lands of Fergusly, beautified with pleasant planting. The first proprietor of these lands I have found, is John Hamilton, descended of the Hamiltons of Orbiestoun, who obtained a grant of the lands of Fergusly, from John Hamilton, Abbot of Pasly, with consent of the Convent, in the year 1544[1]; and, by the heiress of the family, they came to John Wallace, a younger son of William Wallace of Eldersly; whose successor and representative is John Hamilton now of Barr. The lands of Fergusly are the property of William Cochran of Fergusly, son of colonel Hugh Cochran, brother-german of William Earl of Dundonald; who carries the Armorial Coat of Cochran, with a suitable brotherly difference.

Lower upon the river of Black Cart stands the house of Blackstoun, adorned with large orchards, and beautified with planting. This place was the summer dwelling (or the country-house) of the Abbot of Pasly, and was built by George Shaw, Abbot of that Monastery, in the reign of King James IV. And, after the erection of the lands belonging to the Monks of Pasly, in favours of the family of Abercorn, the house of Blackstoun was much improven, by James the first Earl of Abercorn. From that family the lands came to Sir Patrick Maxwel of Newark, and so to John Maxwel of Blackstoun, one of his younger sons; and (by marriage of Catharine, his only daughter and sole heiress,) to Alexander Napier now of Blackstoun, nephew of Archbald, first Lord Napier, by Adam his brother-german.

A little towards the north from [Blackstoun, upon the confluence of Black Cart and Grief, stand the house and lands of Walkingshaw, the seat of an ancient family in this Shire; who derive their pedigree from one " Dungallus, " filius Cristini, Judicis de Levenax," (who was the person that exercised a jurisdiction over the vassals and tenants of the Earldom of Lenox, and was a very ancient officer,) for he is so designed in an Excambion he makes, with consent of Maud his spouse, of his lands of Knoc, with the Abbot and Convent of Pasly, for the lands of Walkingshaw, in an. 1235. the 21st year of the reign of King Alexander II. of Scotland, as is evident from the original, yet extant in the Chartulary of the Monastery of Pasly, folio 105. And from his hereditary lands of Walkingshaw, which he so obtained, probably he assumed his Sirname and designation. His descendants continued in a direct line until that, the Laird of Walkingshaw having only two daughters, his co-heirs, the lands of Easter Walkingshaw came to the Mortons by marriage, and the same way to the Algoes; and by the other co-heiress, the lands of Wester Walkingshaw came to Walkingshaw of Little Fulwood.

[1] Register of Pasly.

The principal branch of this family failing in the person of Walkingshaw of that-ilk, (as said is,) the Walkingshaws of Little Fulwood became the next heirs of that ancient family ; James Walkingshaw of Little Fulwood having married one of the co-heiresses of Walkingshaw, and by that marriage obtained the lands of Wester Walkingshaw, from whence his successors took designation of that-ilk. For, Patrick Walkingshaw of that-ilk obtained a Charter of confirmation of the lands of Wester Walkingshaw from the Abbot of Pasly, upon the resignation of his father, an. 1464. Which Patrick, last mentioned, was father of John Walkingshaw of that-ilk, who, with Margaret Fleeming his wife, a daughter of the family of Barochan, obtained a Charter of these lands from the Abbot of Pasly, an. 1511 [1], in the reign of King James IV. John Walkingshaw of that-ilk, his successor, in the subsequent reign, added to his paternal inheritance the lands of Achincreich, in the year 1532 [2], and died Anno 1562; leaving issue, by Margaret Maxwel his wife, of the house of Newark, John his son and heir; who, by Janet his wife, a daughter of the family of Houstoun of that-ilk, had two sons; John his successor, and Mr. Patrick, Sub-Dean of Glasgow, who was author of that branch of the Walkingshaws of Garturk; of whom John Walkingshaw now of that-ilk is the lineal heir. The principal branch of the family of Walkingshaw failing a second time in the person of John Walkingshaw of that-ilk, who died without male succession, an. 1636, his estate descended to Mr. John Walkingshaw of Garturk, his cousin-german; who took to wife Margaret Hamilton, daughter of   Hamilton of Orbiestoun; by whom he had Gavin his son and heir; who, by Beatrix his wife, daughter of Mr. Henry Maul of Melgum, and a grandchild of the family of Panmure, had John Walkingshaw now of that-ilk, his son and heir : Whose Armorial bearing is, Argent; upon a mount a grove of Firrs proper ; and supported by two Forresters in long robes, (relative to his predecessor's being Forrester to the High Stewart of Scotland, in the Barony of Renfrew,) and for his Crest he bears a Pigeon with an Olive leaf in its mouth ; with this Motto, " In Season."

The above-mentioned Gavin Walkingshaw of that-ilk thought fit, in the year 1683, to alienate his estate of Walkingshaw to James Walkingshaw, merchant in Glasgow, second son of John Walkingshaw of Borrowfield, a Cadet of his family, who died in the year 1708; his estate devolved upon John Walkingshaw now of Walkingshaw, his son and heir.

Near to this lie the lands of Easter Walkingshaw, which went early, by marriage of one of the co-heiresses of that ancient family, to the Mortons. The

---

[1] Chartulary of Pasly.   [2] Carta penes Jo. Com. de Dundonald.

first of this family I have found mentioned is Robert Morton of Walkingshaw, who is recorded an arbiter betwixt the Abbot of Pasly and the Burgh of Renfrew, an. 1488 [1]. Adam Morton obtained from Robert, Abbot of Pasly, a Charter of his lands of Easter Walkingshaw, an. 1511 [2]: As another Adam Morton, whom I have found designed of Leven and Walkingshaw, alienated the 10 lib. land of Leven in Innerkip, to William Lord Semple, an. 1547 [3]: And his lands of Easter Walkingshaw came, by marriage of Marion Morton his heiress, to Peter Algoe, a gentleman originally from Italy; his ancestor came from that country with one of the Abbots of Pasly; and for some considerable time his posterity possessed a plentiful fortune in this Shire, and failed in the person of John Algoe of Easter Walkingshaw, in the reign of King Charles I.

Near to this lie the lands of Marksworth; (the Algoes of Easter-Walkingshaw did anciently possess these lands,) and are now the property of James Maxwel of Marksworth, son of Hugh Maxwel of Bredieland.

The river of Black Cart hath its influx into Grief at the Walkingshaw house.

I Observed in the Geography of this country, that the river of Grief had its source in the western places of this Shire, its course being eastward till it meeteth with Cart, and thence northward till its influx into Clyde. From this river the country of Renfrew was anciently called Strathgrief.

Near to this river upon the confluence of two rivulets, stand the Castle and Barony of Duchal, the seat and designation of the Barons of Lyll: The first mention I find of this family is in that grant which "Baldwin de Bigres" made to the Monks of Pasly, of the church of Innerkip, where "Radulphus de In-"sula" is mentioned among the witnesses thereto [4]. Likeas "Radulphus de "Insula Dominus de Duchal" is mentioned in the Register of that Monastery, as a witness to several donations to that Abby, an. 1243, in King Alexander II's time: Of which Ralph last mentioned, descended John de Lisle, who, with Margaret de Vauss his wife, obtained from King David II. the lands of Buehquhan in the Sheriffdom of Stirling. But omitting the Barons Lyll of more ancient and obscure times, I come to Sir Robert Lyll of Duchal, who, being a Baron of an ample fortune, was by King James II. created into the dignity of Lord Lyll of Duchal, an. 1445; which Robert Lord Lyll was a benefactor to the Monks of Pasly, by the gift of the fishing of Crockat-Shot, in an. 1452 [5]. Ro-

[1] Chartulary of Pasly.   [2] Chartulary of Pasly.   [3] Carta Joh. Stewart Junioris de Blackhall.
[4] Chartulary of Pasly.   [5] Chartulary of Pasly.

bert Lord Lyll, his son, was Justiciar of Scotland, in the reign of King James IV. He married Elizabeth Douglass, daughter of the Earl of Angus, by whom he had John Lord Lyll, his son and heir, and a daughter called Agnes, married Allan Lord Cathcart, and had issue ¹.

Which John Lord Lyll was seased of the Barony and Manour of Duchal in Renfrewshire; the lands of Achintorly and Glenavert in Dunbartounshire; the lands of Buchquhan, Kerse and Dryfield, in the Shire of Stirling; the Barony of Lundy in Forfar; the lands of Milhill and Blairflat in Perth, as an ample Charter from King James V. dated in the year 1540, yet extant, doth plainly show ². He alienated most part of the lordship of Duchal, in the year 1544, to John Porterfield of that-ilk, with the special consent of James Master of Lyll, his eldest son and apparent heir: Which James, the last of this family, died without succession, about the year 1556. The reversion of that lordship descended to Sir Neil Montgomery of Langshaw, in right of Jean Lyll his mother, sole heir of John Lord Lyll. My authority for this is a contract of agreement betwixt Sir Neil Montgomery of Langshaw, and Neil Montgomery younger of Langshaw, his son and apparent heir, upon the one part, and William Porterfield of that-ilk, upon the other; wherein Sir Neil Montgomery laying claim to the Manour of Duchal and diverse other lands, as heir and nearest of line to John Lord Lyll and James Master of Lyll, his son, and of Jean Lyll his mother, nearest of kin (I keep by the original) by succession to the foresaid persons; and, both parties submitting to the decision of John Blair of that-ilk, William Mure of Rouallan, and Alexander Fleeming of Barochan, by these arbiters William Porterfield of that-ilk was appointed to pay the said Sir Neil Montgomery a certain sum of money in satisfaction of his claim; which contract is dated an. 1599 ³. James Montgomery now of Langshaw, great grandchild to Sir Neil Montgomery, formerly mentioned, as heir of line to the Lord Lyll, carries the Coat armorial of that noble family, viz. Two Coats quarterly; first; Azure; a Bend Argent; betwixt six cross Croslets, of the second: being the Coat of Marr (one of the Lord Lyll's ancestors having married one of the co-heiresses of that Earldom: My authority for this is Fordoun ⁴, who writes, that, Alexander Stewart " Comes de Marr obiit " an. 1436, &, quia Bastardus erat, Rex sibi successit de facto; licet de jure, " secundum quosdam, Domini Erskine & de Lyll Jure hæreditario successisse " debuissent") secondly: Or; a Frette Gules; supported by two Cats; for

---

¹ Carta penes Allanum D. Cathcart.   ² Carta penes Alexander Porterfield de Eodem.
³ Carta penes Alex. Porterfield de Eodem.   ⁴ Fordoun in Vita Jacobi primi.

Crest, a Cock crowing ; with this Motto, " An I may :" all which quarter'd Coat and Crest, Langshaw bears quarterly, quarter'd with the Coats of Montgomery and Eglintoun.

Near to the Castle of Duchal stand the house and lands of Carncuren, the seat and designation of   Cunninghame, lineally descended of William Cunninghame, younger son of William Cunninghame of Craigends ; which lands were acquired from John Lord Lyll, an. 1544, by Giles Campbel lady Craigends, and disponed to the said William her son.

Lower upon the bank of Grief, lie the lands of Blacksolm, the seat and designation of a family of the Sirname of Lindsay, a branch of the ancient family of Dunrod, before that George Lindsay of Blacksolm obtained the lands of Balquharage, by marriage of Margaret, daughter and sole heiress of Alexander Fleeming of Balquharage ; which George was son and heir of John Lindsay of Blacksolm, by Janet his wife, daughter of John Crawfurd of Kilbirny, lineally descended of John Lindsay, who acquired the lands of Blacksolm from John Lord Lyll, an. 1544, as the original Charter, yet extant, testifies.

Upon the Grief lies the Barony of Denniestoun, of which the Castle of Finlaystoun was the principal messwage. When the Denzelstouns obtained these lands is not certain ; but that from the proper name of their predecessor they assumed both Sirname and designation, is without all doubt ; for I have seen the original Charter of the Barony of Houstoun, which is in the reign of King Malcolm the IV. which is bounded with the lands of Danziel[1] ; which by the situation clearly appears to be the lands of Denniestoun. But the first mention of this family I have found in our Public Records is a Charter given by King David Bruce to Robert de Denzelstoun, son and heir of Sir John Denzelstoun, Knight, his father, of the Barony of Glencairn, upon his own resignation, the 40th year of his reign, which is 1370[2] ; which Sir John, designed " Dominus ejusdem," is mentioned one of the witnesses to that Charter, by Robert Earl of Strathern, wherein he ratifies all grants by himself or his predecessors to the Monks of Pasly, an. 1361. I have moreover seen a Charter[3] granted by King Robert II. the 14th year of his reign, an. 1374, of the lands of Mauldsly and Kilcadyow, to Sir Robert Denzlestoun, upon his own resignation : As also he obtained a Charter of the lands of Denzelstoun and Finlaystoun, in the Barony of Renfrew, from King Robert the II. upon his own resignation, the third year of his reign, an. 1373. By Margaret and Elizabeth, daughters of Sir Robert de

---

[1] Carta penes D. Joh. Houstoun de Eodem, Baronet.   [2] Carta in Publicis Archivis.
[3] Carta in Publicis Archivis.

Denzelstoun, that great inheritance was shared betwixt Sir Robert Cunninghame of Kilmaures, and Sir Robert Maxwel of Calderwood: the first, by marriage of the said Margaret, had the Baronies of Denzelstoun, Finlaystoun, Kilmaronock in Dunbartonshire, and the Barony of Glencairn in the Shire of Dumfries: and, to the last, in right of Elizabeth de Denzelstoun, his wife, came the lands of Mauldsly, Kilcadyow, Stainly, &c. and so ended the family of Denzelstoun. Denzelstonn of Cougrain, in the Shire of Dunbartoun, is repute heir male of this ancient family

And, south-west from Denzelstoun lie the Castle and Barony of Ranfurly, the seat and designation of an ancient family of the name of Knox. But that what is said of the antiquity of the family of Ranfurly, may not be received without a document, you find in the Registers of the Abby of Pasly, frequent mention made of the Knoxs, in the reigns of Alexander II. and III. as witnesses to the Charters of that Abbacy: They were promiscuously designed of Ranfurly and Craigends: for this I have seen a grant of the half of the lands of Knock, by Uchter Knock of Ranfurly, to George Knox, his son, in the year 1503 [1]. of Uchter Knox of Craigends is one of the Arbiters betwixt the Abbot of Pasly and the Burgh of Renfrew, in the year 1488 [2]. And, in our public records, I have seen a Charter of confirmation by King James III. of a resignation of the Barony of Ranfurly and Grief Castle, by John Knox of Craigends, in favours of Uchter Knox, his son, about the year 1474. This family failed in the person of Uchter Knox of Ranfurly, who left one daughter, (by Elizabeth his wife, daughter of Sir William Mure of Rouallan,) called Elizabeth, married to John Cunninghame of Caddel. The Barony of Ranfurly was alienate by Uchter Knox of Ranfurly last mentioned, an. 1665, to William first Earl of Dundonald.

Of this family, several eminent persons in this church descended; as the famous Mr. John Knox; who, (as my author, the Prefacer of the Church History of Scotland that goes under his name, tho' by the by there are many strong presumptions that that worthy and eminent person wrote it not, as we have it; as also Mr. Matthew Crawfurd, late Minister of the Gospel at Eastwood, in a collection of the Lives of the Scottish Reformers, writes) was a grandnephew of this family; whom GOD was pleased signally to honour as one of the most eminent instruments in our happy reformation from Popery. But our histories are so copious in giving account of his Life, who well deserves that epithet given him by the great Beza, of being the Scottish Apostle, that there is no

[1] Carta Col. Campbel de Blythswood.   [2] Chartulary of Pasly.

need of saying ought further about him in a treatise of this kind: And, since I'm upon the family of Ranfurly, I think it not improper to take notice of Mr. Andrew Knox, being a younger son of John Knox of Ranfurly, (and grand uncle to Uchter Knox, the last of this family,) who, applying himself to the work of the Ministery, was first settled in that character at Lochwhinyeoch, and translated from that to Pasly, about the year 1585, where he continued until the year 1606, that King James VI. with consent of his Parliament, having restored the estate of Bishops in Scotland, Mr. Knox was promoted to the Bishoprick of the Isles; and, in the year 1622, he was translated to the Episcopal see of Rapho, in the kingdom of Ireland: (His Majesty King James being pleased to advance Mr. Thomas Knox, the Bishop's son, to the Episcopal see of the Isles, who died soon after his promotion to it.) He was a person of considerable learning, moderate temper, and averse from all manner of persecution for matters of church Government, and very much disposed to oblige his countrymen, who had left Scotland, from their aversion to the then established government of this church: He concurred in ordaining some Presbyterian Ministers, in conjunction with several Ministers of that communion, saying, "he thought his old age prolonged of little other purpose, but to do such " good offices for the propagation of the Gospel [1]." This Reverend Person died Anno 1632.

A little towards the south from the Castle of Ranfurly lie the lands of Bruntchels, the seat, of old times, of Bruntchells of that-ilk. John Bruntchels, the last of that race, resigned his lands in favours of William Lord Semple, an. 1547. Robert Lord Semple gave these lands to Andrew Semple his son, by Isobel Hamilton his lady, daughter of Sir William Hamiltoun of Sanquhar, an. 1560 [2]; which Andrew was commonly called Master of Semple: He was married to Margaret Stirling, daughter to the Laird of Craigbarnet, by whom he had two sons; William, of whom descended the Semples of Bruntshells, now failed; and James, ancestor of the Semples of Milbank. (quod vide p. 78.)

And near to this lie the lands of Waterstoun, the possession anciently of a family of the same Sirname. In the reign of King Robert II. William Waterstoun of that-ilk, alienate these lands to Sir William Cunninghame of Kilmaures, an. 1384 [3]: And, in the reign of King James V. William, Master of Glencairn, gave the lands of Waterstoun to Hugh Cunninghame his son, an. 1538 [4]; whose lineal heir is Alexander Cunninghame of Carlung.

[1] Vita R. M. Jo, Livingston. [2] Carta penes J. Com. de Dundonald, [3] Carta penes Alex. Porterfield de Eodem, [4] Carta penes Alex. Porterfield de Eodem.

Lower, upon the bank of the river of Grief, stands the house of Craigends, adorned with pleasant orchards and gardens, the seat of an ancient family of the Sirname of Cunninghame, a Cadet of the noble family of Glencairn, lineally descended from William Cunninghame, one of the younger sons of Alexander, first Earl of Glencairn (who was created into that dignity by King James III, an. 1488) and obtained from his father the lands of Craigends, an. 1477 [1]. He is one of the arbiters betwixt the Abbot of Pasly and the Burgh of Renfrew, an. 1488 [2]: He married Elizabeth Stewart, daughter and co-heiress of Sir William Stewart of Arthurly, who was of the Stewarts of Darnly; by whom he obtained the lands of Arthurly. By reason of this marriage the family of Craigends carry the Coat of Stewart, viz. Or; a Fess Checquie, Azure and Argent; quarter'd with their paternal bearing, which is, Argent; a Shake-Fork Sable. By the said Elizabeth his wife, he had issue William, his son and heir: He secondly took to wife Dame Marion Achinleck, daughter and one of the co-heirs of Sir John Achinleck of that-ilk, an ancient family in Kyle, and Dowager of Campbel of Loudoun; by which marriage he obtained the Barony of Achinleck, an. 1499, and to their heirs male, bearing the name and arms of Achinleck: But the conveyance being without the consent of the king, who was superior, the Barony of Achinleck fell in the king's hands, by recognition. King James IV. in the year 1505, gave these lands " dilecto & familiari suo " Thomæ Boswel, pro suo bono & gratuito servitio nobis impenso," as the original bears [3]. Which Thomas was a younger son of the ancient family of Balmutoe in Fife, and married . . . . Achinleck, another of the daughters and co-heiress of Sir John Achinleck of that-ilk; whose lineal heir is Mr. James Boswel of Achinleck, advocate.

William Cunninghame of Craigends left issue, by the said Dame Marion Achinleck his wife, David Cunninghame of Bartenholm, ancestor of the Cunninghames of Robertland; of whom Sir John Cunninghame, Baronet, is now the lineal heir male.

To William Cunninghame of Craigends last mentioned succeeded William, his son and heir; who, by Giles his wife, daughter of Sir John Campbel of Loudoun, had three sons; Gabriel his successor; William, ancestor of Carncuren; and Robert, of whom the Cunninghames of Bedland, Achinharvie, and Suthhook descended. Beside these sons he had several daughters who were married

[1] Carta penes Will. Cunninghame de Craigends. [2] Chartulary of Pasly. [3] Carta in Publicis Archivis.

in the families of Castlemilk, Porterfield, Eldersly, Achinames, Newark, &c. of whom these familes descended.

Gabriel Cunninghame, son and heir of William his father, being at the battle of Pinkie in the year 1547, was there slain; leaving issue, by . . . Livingstoun his wife, a daughter of the family of Kilsyth, two sons; William his successor, and James, ancestor of Cunninghame of Achinyards; and daughters, Janet married to Sir Patrick Houstoun of that-ilk, and had issue; the second married Andrew Stirling of Portnallan and Law, and had issue.

To Gabriel Cunninghame of Craigends, formerly mentioned, succeeded William his son, who departed this life, Anno 1568, leaving issue, by Margaret his wife, daughter of William Cunninghame of Cunninghamehead, Alexander his son and heir, who wedded Elizabeth Cunninghame, daughter of William Earl of Glencairn; by whom he had William his successor, who took to wife Elizabeth, daughter of Archbald Stewart of Castlemilk, by whom he had William his eldest son, and a daughter Janet, married in 1630, to John Crawfurd of Crawfurdland. But before I proceed, it is proper to take notice, that having married Elizabeth Napier, daughter of Sir John Napier of Marchistoun, he died in the year 1636, (his father then living) leaving issue by the said Elizabeth his wife, Alexander his son, who immediately succeeded his grandfather, and three daughters, married in the families of Bargarran, Southbar, and Dargevel.

Alexander Cunninghame, grandson and heir of Alexander Cunninghame of Craigends, married Janet Cunninghame his cousin, daughter of William Cunninghame of the family of Achinyards, by whom he had William his successor; and daughters, Elizabeth, married to George Houstoun of Johnstoun, and had issue; Rebecka, to John Hamilton of Grange; the third, Janet, to John Alexander of Blackhouse; the fourth, Marion, to Alexander Porterfield of Fulwood, and had issue.

Which William Cunninghame, now of Craigends, was elected, by the Freeholders of the Shire of Renfrew, one of their Commissioners to the Convention of Estates, which met at Edinburgh the 14th of March 1689, and to the several Sessions of Parliament subsequent to it: In which trust, he gave sufficient proof of honour, integrity, and fidelity, to the satisfaction of the Shire; he hath married Christian, daughter of Sir John Colquhoun of Luss, Baronet, by whom he has Alexander his son and apparent heir.

Upon the opposite side of the river stand the Castle and Barony of Houstoun, situate upon an eminence, which affords a very agreeable prospect of most of this Shire; the fabrick is a large court, which has been of late much improven by Sir John Houstoun now of that-ilk; it has a most beautiful avenue fronting the said castle, regularly planted; and has orchards, gardens, and parks, equal to many in this place of the kingdom, with delectable woods surrounding almost the house.

That the family of Houstoun, originally assuming their Sirname from a place long since called Kilpeter, has been of great antiquity in these parts, doth appear from unquestionable documents, and derive their descent from "Hugo de "Padvinan," who obtained a grant of the Barony of Kilpeter from "Balduin "de Bigres, Vicecomes de Lanerk," in the reign of King Malcolm the IV. whereupon his descendants assumed appellation from their hereditary lands; which Barony continueth with them in the male line to this day; for it is a received observation by antiquaries, that when Sirnames became fixt and hereditary, these are the most ancient, which were derived from Baronies and lands; and when these lands have only been injoyed by the same family, it is a manifest proof, that that name and family is of great antiquity. But of this "Hugh de Padvinan" I have found nothing more on record, but that he was one of these witnessess to Walter High Stewart of Scotland's foundation Charter of the Abby of Pasly, about the year 1160 [1].

To Hugh, formerly mentioned, succeeded Sir Reginald his son, who obtained a Charter from Robert, the son of Walden, son of Balduin of Biger, of the lands of Kilpeter in Strathgrief, ratifying a former grant by the said Balduin his grandfather, "Reginaldo filio Hugonis de Padvinan [2] Terrarum de Kil- "peter cum terrâ illâ quam Bodricus & Arkenbaldus, fratres ejus tenueret. "His Testibus; Allano Dapifero Regis Scotiæ, Waltero Filio suo, Roberto "Croc, Reginaldo de Cathcart, & multis aliis."

To Reginald succeeded Hugh his son, who obtained from Walter High Steward of Scotland, then Lord of the country of Strathgrief, a Charter of confirmation of the lands "quod Hugo Avus ejus tenuit de Balduino de Bigres "Vicecomes Regis, & postea de Waldeno Filio ejus, & postea de Roberto filio "Waldeni, sciz. Terras de Kilpeter." He was also a benefactor to the Monks of Pasly, bestowing upon them an annuity of half a merk out of his lands of Achenhoss in the year 1225 [3]. His successor, Sir Finlay de Houstoun, knight, lived in the reign of King Alexander III. I have found him frequently mentioned witness to Charters granted by James High Steward of Scotland; and is one of those Scots Barons, mentioned by Prin, subscribing that bond of submis-

[1] Chartulary of Pasly.   [2] Carta penes D. Joan. Houst. de Eodem, Bar..
[3] Chartulary of Pasly, & penes D. Joan. Houst.

sion to King Edward the first of England, commonly called "Ragman Roll," in Anno 1296 [1], designed Finlay de Houstoun Chevalier.

But, from these ancient Barons of Houstoun, descending to the reign of King James II. that Sir Patrick Houstoun of that-ilk, departing this life Anno 1450, was buried in the Chapel of Houstoun, where there is a fair monument erected to the memory of him and his wife, with this inscription,

" Hic jacet Patricius Houstonn, de Eodem, Miles, qui obiit
Anno MCCCCL.
" Et D. Maria Colquhoun, Sponsa dicti Domini Johannis, quæ obiit
MCCCCLVI."

leaving issue, Sir John his son and heir, who died Anno Dom. 1456, and was interred in the Paroch Church of Houstoun, under a canopy of free stone, with the effigies of himself and his lady, as big as the life; about the verge of which tomb, I find this inscription in Saxon Capitals.

Here lyes John of Houstoun Lord of that-ilk, and Annes Campbel
his Spouse, who died Anno 1456.

To whom succeeded Sir Peter his son and heir; who, being at the battle of Floudoun, which was fought upon the 9th day of September, in the year 1513, was with his sovereign King James the IV, and the flower of the nobility and gentry of Scotland, killed in that fatal engagement; leaving issue, by Helen his wife, a daughter of the ancient family of Schaw of Sauchy (now represented by Sir John Schaw of Greenock, Baronet) Patrick his son and heir; who obtained the honour of knighthood from King James V. and associating with John Earl of Lennox, to rescue the Prince out of the custody of the Earls of Arran and Angus, was slain in a conflict at Aven, near the town of Linlithgow, in the year 1526 [2]: leaving issue by Janet Cunninghame, his Lady, John his son and heir; who obtained a Charter of the Baronies of Houstoun, &c. from King James V. Anno 1528. He was married with Agnes Hopepringle, a daughter of Hopepringle of Torsonce; and departing this life Anno 1542, was succeeded by Patrick his son; who obtained the honour of knighthood from King James VI. He died in the year 1605, leaving issue, by Janet his wife, daughter of Gabriel Cunninghame of Craigends, four sons; John his successor, Patrick of Colt, Mr.

---

[1] Prin's History. [2] Hathornden's History of the 5 King Jameses.

Peter of Wester Southbar, and James of Commonside; as also several daughters, viz. Janet married John Fulerton of Dreghorn, and afterward to George Crawfurd of Liffnoris; the 2d, Elizabeth, to John Whitefoord of that-ilk; and surviving him, she married William Lord Ross, but had no succession; the 3d, Agnes, to Alexander Porterfield of that-ilk and had issue; the 4th, daughter Marion married James Hamilton of Barduie, and had issue; the 5th, Margaret, to William Crawfurd of Achinames, and had issue.

To Sir Patrick, formerly mentioned, succeeded John his son and heir, who deceased Anno 1609, leaving issue, by Margaret his Lady, daughter of Sir James Stirling of Keir, Sir Ludovick his son and heir, and several daughters; 1st, Jean married William Semple of Fulwood, and had issue; 2d, Helen to John Schaw of Greenock, and had issue; 3d, Margaret, to William Livingstoun of Kilsyth, and had issue; 4th, Mary to Alexander Cunninghame of Corshill, and had issue; 5th . . . . to Adam Cunninghame of Buchquhan.

Which Sir Ludovick, was married to Margaret daughter of Patrick Maxwel of Newark, by whom he had Patrick his successor; and George, first of the Houstouns of Johnstoun; and daughters married in the families of Orbiestoun, Langshaw, Pearstoun, and Kilcroich. He departed this life Anno 1662, his estate devolving upon Patrick his son and heir: Who, being a Baron of an ample fortune, and representing an ancient family, was by the favours of King Charles II. the 19th year of his reign, advanced to the degree and dignity of Baronet; his patent bearing date, at Whitehall, the last day of February 1668. He departed this life in the year 1696, leaving issue, by Ann his Lady, daughter of John Lord Bargany, and of Margaret his wife, daughter of William first Marquiss of Douglas, Sir John his son and heir; the 2d Patrick; the 3d Mr. William; the 4th James; the 5th Archbald; and daughters, 1st, Margaret married Sir Humphry Colquhoun of Luss, Baronet, and had issue; the second, Ann to Sir John Inglis of Cramond, Baronet, and had issue; and surviving him, she married 2dly Sir William Hamilton of Whitelaw, one of the Senators of the College of Justice; and thirdly, she became the wife of Adam Cockburn of Ormistoun, one of the Senators of the College of Justice, and Lord Justice Clerk, and had issue. The 3d, Jean, to Walter Dundas of that-ilk; 2dly to Richard Lockhart of Lee; and now wife of Ludovick Grant of that-ilk. The 4th, Henrietta, to Andrew Brown of Braid, and had issue; and after his death she married Mr. Colin Mackenzie, Advocate, son of Sir Alexander Mackenzie of Coul.

Which Sir John Houstoun, now of that-ilk, Baronet, served Commissioner to our Parliament for this Shire, upwards of twenty years, which trust he discharged to his own honour and the great satisfaction of the Freeholders there: He hath married the Lady Ann Drummond, daughter of John Earl of Melfort, by Sophia his Lady, daughter and sole heiress of Robert Lundin of that-ilk, an ancient family in the Shire of Fife, (lineally descended of Robert de Lundin, son of King William of Scotland, as is evident from many unquestionable documents:) By which Lady Ann Drummond he has issue John, his son and apparent heir, one of the members of the current Parliament for the Sheriffdom of Linlithgow.

The Coat Armorial of this ancient family is, Or; a Cheveron Checquie, Azure and Argent; betwixt three Martlets Sable; supported by two Hinds; and for Crest, a Sand-glass; with this Motto, " In time."

From the Castle of Houstoun, about a mile towards the north, lie the house and Barony of Barochan, the seat of, and whence, an ancient family of the Sirname of Fleeming take designation. The original ancestor of that name came from Flanders to Scotland very early, and assumed their Sirname and designation from their country. But the first mention I have found of the Fleemings of Barochan is in a Charter granted by Malcolm Earl of Lenox, in the reign of King Alexander III. to Walter Spruel, " Senescallo de Lenox," of the lands of Dalquhurn, " Willielmo Flandrense de Barochan" being a witness thereto [1]. As also I have seen a Charter granted by James High Stewart of Scotland, grandfather to King Robert II. (who died in the year 1309,) " Stephano filio " Nicolai, de Terra quæ data fuit Patricio de Selvinland, juxta Burgum de " Renfrew:" To which " Willielmus Fleeming de Barochan, Miles," is a witness. From this time I have seen nothing of the Fleemings of Barochan, until the reign of King James IV. that in 1488 William Fleeming of Barochan is Sheriff of Lanerk, who was killed at the battle of Floudoun, with King James IV. an. 1513, leaving issue, by Marion his Lady, a daughter of the family of Houstoun, James his son and heir; who was father of William Fleeming of Barochan, from whom Patrick Fleeming now of Barochan is the fifth in a direct line: Whose Armorial bearing is, a Fess Checquie, surmounted of a Bend, with a Martlet in Base. This family hath intermarried with the families of Semple, Houstoun, Bishoptoun, Rouallan, Robertland, Ladyland, &c.

Near the house of Barochan, and within that Barony, was born the learned Mr. William Jameson, Preacher of the Gospel and Professor of History in the University of Glasgow; a miracle for learning, considering he is deprived of the sense of seeing; (being born blind) yet his learned works give sufficient proof of his being a very able scholar.

[1] Carta penes Burgum de Dunbartoun.

West from the house of Barochan stands the Paroch Church of Kilellan, an ancient dependency of the Monastery of Pasly, from the year 1225. The present minister is Mr. John Fork.

Lower, upon the banks of Grief, stand the house and lands of Fulwood, the seat of, and whence, an ancient family of the Semples, took designation, from the time of King Robert the II. that their ancestor, a younger brother of the family of Eliestoun, became possessed of these lands, which before that pertained to the Fleemings, Earls of Wigtoun; for I have seen Thomas Fleeming designed " Dominus de Fulwood, dudum Comes de Wigtoun," in a Charter which he gave " Willielmo Boyd, filio Thomæ Boyd de Kilmarnock Militis, " de omnibus terris ejusdem Thomæ in Baronia de Lainzie," which is confirmed by King Robert II. an. 1374 [1].

But the first of the Semples of Fulwood I have found mentioned is John Semple of Fulwood, who is a witness to the resignation of the lands of Fultoun to the Monks of Pasly, an. 1409 [2]. Likeas William Semple of Fulwood is witness to the donation of Crockat-Shot, by Robert Lord Lyle, to the Abbot and Convent of Pasly, an. 1452. Moreover I have seen a Charter of the Barony of Kirkmichael in Dunbartounshire, in favours of John Semple, son and heir of William Semple of Fulwood, an. 1476 [3]. And, in 1515, John Semple of Fulwood gave to Robert Semple his brother, and Margaret Crawfurd his wife, a daughter of the house of Achinames, the lands of Noblestoun; (whose lineal heir is Robert Grahame of Gartmore.) Robert Semple of Fulwood, successor to the former John, obtained a Charter of his lands of Fulwood, an. 1502 [4]. This ancient family failed in the person of John Semple of Fulwood, who about the year 1679 alienated the lands of Fulwood to John Porterfield of that-ilk. His son is Robert Semple, late Sheriff Depute of Renfrew. The Laird of Porterfield in an. 1680, gave the lands of Fulwood in patrimony to Alexander Porterfield his 2d son, who is now of Fulwood, and married Marion, daughter of Alexander Cunninghame of Craigends, by whom he has John his son and apparent heir.

Near Fulwood lie the lands of Blackburn; an ancient family of the Semples. A branch of those of Fulwood did for some time possess these lands, and failed in the person of Robert Semple of Blackburn, who died without male succession; so that John Semple of Closs, his brother-german, became his heir: Which John I have seen designed lawful son to John Semple of Blackburn,

---

[1] Carta in publicis Archivis. [2] Chartulary of Pasly.
[3] Carta penes Joa. Comitem de Dundonald. [4] Carta penes Joa. Comitem de Dundonald.

an. 1583 [1]; whose grandchild, John Semple of Balgoun, dying without male issue, his estate went with Marion, his daughter and sole heir, to Sir George Suty now of Balgoun. So the lineal heir male of that family is William Semple, writer in Edinburgh.

Northwest of Fulwood stand the house and lands of Boghall, (now gone to decay) the seat of an ancient family of the Fleemings, descended of a younger son of the family of Biggar, now Earl of Wigtoun. By the death of John Fleeming of Boghall these lands came to John Lord Fleeming, an. 1581, and became the patrimony of James Fleeming, his 2d lawful son, to whom he disponed them an. 1593, and are now the property of the Right honourable John Earl of Dundonald.

And a little towards the east from this stands the house of Dargevel, the seat and designation of a family of the Sirname of Maxwel, an early Cadet of the house of Newark. Their ancestor was John Maxwel, eldest son of Patrick Maxwel of Newark, by Marion Crawfurd his 2d wife, a daughter of the house of Carse: For this I have seen, in the hands of John Maxwel of Dargavel, a Charter granted by John Earl of Lenox to Patrick Maxwel of Newark and Marion Crawfurd his spouse, of the lands of Dargevel, and to John Maxwel, their eldest son, in Fee, which is dated Anno 1522. To him succeeded James Maxwel of Dargevel his son; and to him Patrick his son, who was slain at the conflict which happen'd betwixt the Maxwels and Johnstouns at Lockerby, an. 1593; leaving issue John his son and heir; who wedded Margaret, daughter of James Wallace of Johnstoun, by whom he had John his successor; who, by Jean his wife, daughter of William Cunninghame of Craigends, had John Maxwel now of Dargevel; who hath married Margaret, daughter of John Campbel of Succoch.

The Armorial bearing of Maxwel of Dargevel is, Argent, a Saltyre Sable, with a Stagg's head in Base.

And east from Dargevel stand the house and lands of Southbar, adorned with pleasant planting; the possession, for well nigh three hundred years, of a family of the Sirname of Maxwel, descended of a younger son of the Lord Maxwel, in the reign of King James III. But not having seen the writs of this family, I can say but little about them, save that they were honoured by diverse matches with several ancient and honourable families, as Stewart of Barscube, Hamilton of Haggs, Houstoun, Cunninghame of Craigends, &c.

[1] Carta penes M. Joan: Semple.

Lower upon the river of Grief lie the lands of Barnhill, Alands, Newlands, and diverse others; which Walter High Stewart of Scotland, in the reign of King Robert I. gave to Sir Walter Hamilton,¹ ancestor to his Grace the Duke of Hamilton; and from Sir David de Hamilton his successor, they were acquired by Sir Robert Erskine of that-ilk; and from the Earl of Marr by Sir John Hamilton of Orbiestoun; and are now the property of John Grahame of Dougalstoun, descended of the Grahames of Knockdolian in Carick, who was a younger son of the illustrious family of Grahame in the reign of King James I.

From this the river of Grief hath its course some short way eastward, till meeting at the church of Inchenan with White Cart, they mix, and empty themselves into the river of Clyde, a little below that church.

The church of Inchenan, before the reformation, belonged to the Knights Templars, who had all their lands within the Shire of Renfrew, erected into a Regality, called the Regality of Greenend. And, because some may have the curiosity to know somewhat concerning the Templars, I shall furnish my reader with the history of them, hoping he'll pardon the digression.

The order of Templars was set up first at Jerusalem; frequent incursions being made into Godfrey's kingdom, by Saracens, Turks, and Egyptians; and the roads leading to Jerusalem being infested by robbers, so as travellers to the holy Sepulchre were much exposed to danger. Nine generous Knights undertook the defence of the sacred Sepulchre, and to clear the high-ways, that passengers and pilgrims might safely go and come thither, without hazard or interruption. This order was first established, an. 1118. They were called Templars, because they had apartments allowed them by Baldwin II. King of Jerusalem, near to the temple. This order was confirmed by Honorius II. an. 1182. They had a white habit assigned them in token of their innocence, to which Pope Eugene III. ordered them to wear, above their habit, for a distinguishing badge, a red cross, to signify their readiness to spend their blood in defence of the Holy Land: They lived according to the rule of the Chanon Regulars. They came first to Scotland in the reign of King David, where they flourished to that degree, that there were few Paroches wherein they had not some lands. The Prior of the order in Scotland resided at Torphichen, (as another of their principal houses was at St. Germans in Lothian;) their priests and chaplains had benefices, and were ministers of the churches of Tulloch, Aboyn, Inchenan, Mary-Culter, &c. Sir James Sandielands of Calder was preceptor of Torphichen and Lord St. John, at the Reformation, in Scotland; he

¹ Mr William Forbes on Tithes.

resigned all the Temple lands in Scotland in Queen Mary's hands, and obtained an erection thereof into a temporal lordship, with the dignity of Lord Torphichen, an. 1563. And, from the Lord Torphichen, the Temple lands in Renfrewshire, afterward erected into a Regality, came to Semple of Cathcart.

Upon the west side of the river of Grief, in a plain field, upon the bank of the river of Clyde, stand some considerable remains of the old palace of Inchenan, one of the seats of the illustrious family of Lenox, which hath been builded by Matthew, Earl of Lenox, and Elizabeth Hamilton his Countess, daughter of James Earl of Arran, in the year 1506.

And west from this stands the house of Barr, the seat of the Stewarts of Barscube, a branch of the Stewarts of Darnly. As to the precise time of Barscube's descent, I cannot determine; but this much I certainly know, that they were a younger son of that noble family: For I have seen a Charter granted by Matthew Earl of Lenox, " dilecto consanguineo suo Thomæ Stewart, de " Terris de North Bar, Craigtoun, Barscube, & Rashielee: Apud Crocstoun 5° " Julii, Anno 1497 [1]." This family continued in good reputation, was esteemed among the first of quality in this Shire, and well allied in the country, and failed in the person of Thomas Stewart of Barscube, who died without issue, in the last Irish wars. He alienated most of his estate, about 1670, to Donald MacGilchrist, a wealthy merchant of the city of Glasgow. The first of this Sirname I have found is " Donaldus MacGilchrist, Dominus de Tarbart", who was a benefactor to the Monastery of Pasly, by giving the Monks and their successors the privilege of cutting wood, for supporting of the fabrick of the Monastery, in any part of his woods that lay most convenient for them; which deed he expresses to be made " for the health of the souls of his ancestors, and for the welfare of his own soul:" which I take to be about the beginning of the reign of King Robert Bruce [2]. And from this last Donald MacGilchrist of Tarbart probably descended Donald MacGilchrist of North Bar, who built the house of North Bar in an. 1676, which is in form of a court, adorned with pleasant orchards and gardens. He departed this life an. 1684, leaving issue James, his son and heir; who hath married Ann, daughter of Laurence Crawfurd of Jordan-hill, by whom he hath issue.

His Armorial bearing is, Gules; a Lion Rampant, Argent; within a Border ingraled, of the 2d; and for Crest, a Lion's Paw; with this Motto, " Cogit in hostem."

Near North Bar lie the lands of Park of Inchenan; of which I have seen a grant by John Earl of Lenox, " dilecto consanguineo suo Willielmo Stirling de

---

[1] Carta penes Jac. MacGilchrist de North-Bar. [2] Register of the Monastery of Pasly.

"Glorat, & Margaretæ Houstoun Sponsæ suæ, Anno 1522." Andrew Stirling of Portnallan and Law, their son, obtained the said lands in patrimony; whose lineal heir is John Stirling of Law.

And south from this lie the lands of Freeland, the inheritance of the Stewarts of Kilecroy in old times, and now the property of William Maxwel of Freeland, brother to the Laird of Dargevel.

Near to the place of North Bar lie the lands of Craigtoun, the possession of Walter Paterson of Craigtoun; which lands were acquired from Stewart of Barscube.

Lower, upon the bank of the river of Clyde, stand the castle and Barony of Erskine, the seat and designation of an ancient family of the same denomination, who, without all question, have taken their Sirname from their hereditary lands, when fixed Sirnames came to be used: For 'tis universally received among Antiquaries, that, when Sirnames became fix'd and hereditary, these are the most ancient which were derived from Baronies and lands; and that it is a sufficient proof of ancient descent, where the inhabitant had the Sirname from the place he inhabiteth. But the first mention I have found of the name of Erskine, is a confirmation of the Church of Erskine or Iriskyn, by Florentius Bishop of Glasgow, to the Abbot and Convent of Pasly: which must be in an. 1207, that the Chronicle of Melross bears Anno MCCVII. Florence, elect Bishop of Glasgow, with the Pope's licence, resigned his Episcopal office, and that Walter, Chaplain to the king, was elected Bishop in his place, upon the 5th of the Ides of December, and consecrate, an. 1208 [1]. But the first of this noble family I have found is " Henricus de Iriskyn," mentioned a witness to that grant, which Ameleck, brother of Malduin Earl of Lenox, made to the Monks of Pasly, of the patronage of the church of Rosneth, " pro salute Domini sui " Alexandri Regis, Anno 1226 [2]." Moreover I have found " Dominus Johannes Iriskyn, Miles," witness to that confirmation, which Walter Stewart, Earl of Monteith, gave of the patronage of the kirk of St. Colmonel in Kintyre, to the Abbot and Convent of Pasly; which is dated " Apud Parcum de Irschyn, Anno 1262." Whose successor, Sir William Erskine, was co-temporary with the renowned King Robert Bruce: Whose son, Sir Robert Erskine of that-ilk, was one of those noble Scots patriots who firmly adhered to the interest of King David Bruce; and, in reward of his faithful services performed to that Prince, obtained an heritable grant of the keeping of Stirling castle, as also the Sheriffship of that Shire during life; the 40th year of his reign [3]. As further, in consideration

[1] Chron. de Melross.   [2] Chartulary of Pasly.   [3] Carta in Publicis Archivis.

of his good and faithful services, obtained, " tertiam partem totius annui " reditus, nobis debiti de Burgo nostro de Dundee; nec non tertiam par- " tem totius terræ de Pothcaroch, juxta dictum Burgum [1]." Our famous Historian Buchanan writes, that Sir Robert Erskine, at the death of King David Bruce, was Governour of the castles of Edinburgh, Stirling, and Dunbartoun, in the year 1370; and that he contribute very much to King Robert II's peaceable accession to the Crown; he was no less favourite with that Prince than he had been with King David; for I find he obtained a confirmation of a former grant, by King Robert before his accession to the Crown, of the lands of Nisbet and Edinham, in the Sheriffdom of Roxburgh. In exchange of the lands of Edinham, he obtained " centum libras Sterlingorum, de firmis Burgi " de Aberdeen, nobis debit. annuatim, in excambium pro Baronia de Edin- " ham, quam dictus Robertus Erskine, Miles, in manibus nostris sursum red- " didit, Anno Regni tertio;" which is the year 1373 [2]. His piety was also very conspicuous, according to the sentiments of those times, which was, that they did a very agreeable service to God Almighty, if they were liberal to the church; for he gave to the Monks of the Abby of Cambuskenneth, Anno 1361, in pure alms, the lands of Fintalach in Strathern, with the patronage of the church of Kinoule, therein designed " Robertus Erskine, Dominus ejusdem & " Baroniæ de Kinoule:" Which grant he expresses to be made " for the healthful estate of himself and Christian Keith his spouse, during their lives here, and for the safety of their souls after their departure out of this frail life; as also for the souls of their ancestors, parents, and successors, and all the faithful deceased."

Sir Robert had two sons; Sir Thomas Erskine of that-ilk, his son and heir; and Sir Nicol Erskine, first of the Erskines of Kinoule. For authority of this, I have seen a confirmation of the patronage of the church of Kinoule to the Monastery of Cumbuskenneth, by Sir Nicol Erskine of Kinoule: ratifying the donation thereof, formerly made by Sir Robert Erskine of that-ilk, his father, to the Monks of that Abby, an. 1400 [3]; which family failed in an heiress, in the reign of King James III. married to Sir Robert Crichton of Sanquhar, ancestor to the Earl of Dumfries.

Which Sir Thomas Erskine of that-ilk is witness in a Charter granted by King Robert III. an. 1396, wherein he ratifies and confirms to the Monks of Pasly all grants by himself or ancestors to that Monastery [4]: He is also one of

[1] Carta in Rotulis Regis David. [2] Chartulary of Aberdeen. [3] Chartulary of Cambuskenneth.
[4] Chartulary of Pasly.

the hostages sent to England for the ransom of King David Bruce, taken prisoner at the battle of Durham an. 1348 [1]. He married, first, Janet Keith, (daughter and sole heir of Sir Edward Keith of Sintoun, and of Christian Monteith his wife, daughter of Sir John Monteith of Rusky, by Helen his wife, daughter of Gratny Earl of Marr,) by whom he had Sir Robert his son and heir. Afterwards he married Jean Barclay, a daughter of the family of Brichen, by whom he had John, author of that branch of the Erskines of Dun in Angus: For this I have seen a Charter by King Robert III. in the year 1398, to Sir John Erskine, of the Barony of Dun, upon the resignation of Sir Thomas Erskine his father; reserving the liferent to the said Sir Thomas Erskine, and Dame Jean Barclay his Spouse, mother to the said Sir John; whose lineal successor, Sir John Erskine of Dun, was Provost of Montrose, and one of the Scots Commissioners nominate by the estates of Scotland to attend the celebration of the Nuptials betwixt Queen Mary of Scotland and Francis II. then Dauphin of France, an. 1558. And, upon the establishing of the Reformation, by Parliamentary authority, in the year of GOD 1560, he was chosen Superintendant for Angus and Mearns, which he worthily discharged, and ought always to be honourably remembered as one of the greatest instruments in that blessed work. He died in 1591.

But to return to the family of Erskine: To Sir Thomas, formerly mentioned, succeeded Sir Robert his son and heir, who claimed the Earldom of Mar, upon the death of Lady Isobel Douglass, Countess of Mar, only daughter of William Earl of Douglas, by Margaret his wife, daughter of Thomas, and sister of Donald, last Earl of Mar, who died without succession: So that in 1438, Sir Robert Erskine is served heir to the Lady Isobel Douglass, " tanquam legi-" timus & propinquior hæres dictæ Dominæ Isobellæ." For illustration of this, I have seen an indenture, dated at Stirling, the 10th of August, an. 1440, betwixt King James II, with consent of his Privy Council, on the one part, and Sir Robert, Lord of Erskine, with deliverance of his Council, on the other.

Wherein " The King, for the good and quiet of the land, obliges him-
" self to cause deliver to the said Lord Erskine, the castle of Kildrumy (the
" messwage of the Earldom of Mar) in all goodly haste, to be kept by the said
" Lord Erskine, for the King's behoof and age; and then to be delivered to the
" King but obstackle: The whilk done, the said Lord of Erskine, or his heirs,

[1] Rymer's Fœdera Angliæ.

" shall come before the King, and the three estates, and there purport and
" shew his claim and right; which seen and considered, shall be admitted as
" far as they are of force and of value. Furthermore it is accorded, that all the
" fruits and revenue belonging half to the Earldom of Mar, the which the Lord
" Erskine claims as his property, shall remain with the said Lord until the ish
" of the said time, and then to be comptable, gif the castle bees judged to the
" king; allowing till then, a sufficient fee for the keeping of the said castle.
" And attour it is accorded, that whatsoever time the said Lord be freely en-
" tered into the castle of Kildrumy foresaid, be the deliverance of the said
" Council, the said Lord shall truly, but any obstackle, deliver the castle of
" Dunbarton freely, at the advice of the king and the three estates, he having
" to his warrand the king's letter, under his great seal, of discharge, together
" with letters of quitt claim and remission for him and his son, and all his men,
" from all tyd down from the day of his entry in the said castle of Dunbarton, to
" the day of the making of thir letters, and till all sundry the foresaid conditions
" and appointments be leally and truly kept: the King has gart affix his Privy
" Seal, and the said Lord Erskine has gart affix his seal thereto, at day, place,
" and year, fore-written: And these are the names of them being in the foresaid
" Council present; that is to say, John and Michael, Bishops of Glasgow and
" Dunblain; Thomas and David, Abbots of Pasly and Cumbuskenneth; Dun-
" can Lord Campbel; Alexander Lord Montgomery; David Hay of Locher-
" wart; Alexander Livieston of Calender; John of Ruthven of that-ilk; John
" Sibbald of Balgony; Robert of Livieston of Drumray; John of Dun-
" bar of Cumnock; John of Ogilvie of Linthrachren; Alexander Ramsay of
" Dalhousie; Andrew Stewart of Albany; Robert of Crichton of Sanquhar;
" John of Cockburn; Walter of Ogilvie; William of Cranstoun; Gilbert of
" Seton, and James of Hamilton, Knights; John of Semple of Eliestoun;
" William of Cockburn of Ormistoun; Robert of Cunninghame; and Robert
" Stewart of Bute, Esquires; James of Parkly; Lancelot of Abernethy; John
" of Dumfries; William Bully; David of Galbraith, and Mr. John of Cadyow;
" Commissars of Burrows."

Which Sir Robert, Lord of Erskine, I have seen designed " Comes de Mar,
" Dominus de Erskine & de Garioch," in a Charter to . . . Galbraith his
Armour bearer, of the lands of Garscaden; dated the 8th day of June, in the
year 1444.

But King James II. reducing the Lord Erskine's right of the Earldom of
Mar, an. 1457, it was annexed to the Crown, and became the patrimony of

John, a younger son of the Royal family, stiled Earl of Mar; and the Lord Erskine re-assumed his ancient dignity: This Lord Erskine, above-mentioned, was father of Thomas Lord Erskine, who was cotemporary with King James III; as Alexander his son was with King James IV; who was father of another Robert Lord Erskine, who being with King James IV. at the battle of Floudon, had the hard fate to be there slain; leaving issue, by Elizabeth his wife, daughter of . . . Campbel of Loudoun, two sons; John his successor, and James, ancestor of the Erskines of Balgouny.

John Lord Erskine wedded Margaret, daughter of Archbald Earl of Argile, by whom he had Robert, Master of Erskine, killed at Pinkie; Thomas Master of Erskine died without succession; John his successor; and Sir Alexander of Gogar, commonly called Master of Mar, ancestor to the Earl of Kelly, which hath furnished some considerable Cadets; as Sir George Erskine of Inertill, one of the Senators of the College of Justice; and Sir Alexander Erskine of Cambo, Baronet, Lord Lion King at arms.

To John Lord Erskine, formerly mentioned, succeeded John his son and heir, who obtained the estate and dignity of Mar from Queen Mary, an. 1562, with the precedency of the ancient Earls, and confirm'd in the Parliament 1567. He was chosen Regent of Scotland, in King James's minority, after Lenox's death, an. 1571. When he had governed the kingdom 13 months, he died the 28th of October 1572, with the reputation of a very honest and brave gentleman. He married Arabella, daughter of Sir William Murray of Tullibardine, by whom he had John Earl of Mar, his son and heir, who was Lord High Thesaurer of Scotland, and Comptroller of His Majesty's household: He was commissioned Ambassador from King James VI. an. 1601, to Queen Elizabeth, congratulating Her Majesty's suppressing the audacious attempt of the Earl of Essex; which he managed so wisely, that it was not a little instrumental to King James's peaceable accession to the Crown of England. He was one of those Peers that Monarch made choice of to accompany him in his journey to England, when he went to take possession of that Crown, in the year 1603; and, on His Majesty's first celebration of the feast of St. George, on the 2d of July that year, he was invested into the noble order of the Garter. His Lordship was twice married; first, with Margaret, daughter of David Lord Drummond, by whom he had John his son and heir; 2dly, with Lady Mary Stewart, daughter of Esme Duke of Lenox, by whom he had James, who obtained the estate and dignity of Buchan, by right of marriage with Christian Douglass, daughter and sole heir of Robert Earl of Buchan: the second, Henry, Lord Cardross, whose lineal heir is David Earl of Buchan: the third Sir Alexander of Cumbuskenneth, one of the Senators of the College of Justice: the 4th, Sir Charles of Alva: the 5th, Sir John of Otterstoun: the 6th, Sir Arthur of Scotscraig: the 7th, Sir William, died without issue. Besides these sons he had likeways several daughters; first, Mary, married to William Earl of Marishal; 2dly, to Patrick first Earl of Panmure, and had issue: the 2d, Margaret, to John Earl of Rothes, and had issue: the 3d, Martha, to John Earl of Kinghorn: the 4th, Catharine, to Thomas Earl of Haddingtoun, and had issue. He deceased in the year 1634, his estate and honours devolving upon John his son and heir, who was made a Knight of the Bath, at the creation of Henry Prince of Wales, an. 1608. He was also one of the Senators of the College of Justice, and departed this life in the year 1654, leaving issue, by Jean Hay his Lady, daughter of Francis Earl of Errol, John his son and heir; and a daughter, Elizabeth married Archbald Lord Napier, and had issue: Which John, Earl of Marr, married . . . Scot, daughter of Walter Earl of Buccleugh; and surviving her, he espoused Jean Mackenzie, daughter of George Earl of Seaforth, by whom he had Charles Earl of Marr, his son and heir, and three daughters; Barbara, married James Marquis of Douglass; Mary, to John Earl of Glencairn, and had issue; and Sophia, to Alexander Lord Pitsligoe, and had issue.

To John Earl of Marr succeeded Charles his son and heir, who died in the year 1689, leaving isssue, by Mary Maule his wife, daughter of George Earl of Panmure, John, now Earl of Marr, his son and heir; the 2d, Mr. James of Grange, one of the Senators of the College of Justice; the 3d, Lieutenant Colonel Hary, killed at the battle of Almanza.

Arms of the family, Two Coats quarterly; 1st, Azure; a Bend, betwixt Six cross Croslets, Or; for the name of Marr: 2d; Argent; a Pale, Sable; the Paternal Coat of Erskine; supported by Two Griffons. The Crest is a Hand holding a crooked Sword; the Motto, "Je pense plus."

In the year 1638, John Earl of Marr alienated the Barony of Erskine to Sir John Hamilton of Orbiestoun, one of the Senators of the College of Justice, lineally descended of Gavin, a younger son of James First Lord Hamilton. William Hamilton of Orbiestoun, his grandchild, sold these lands, an. 1703, to Walter Lord Blantyre.

A little towards the south from the Castle of Erskine stands the house of Bargaran, the seat of John Shaw of Bargaran, whose ancestors for nigh three hundred years have possessed these lands, and derive their descent from a younger brother of the family of Sauchie (now represented by Sir John Shaw of Greenock) and carry the Coat of Arms of that house, viz. Azure; Three covered Cups, Or; and, for difference, add a Cheveron Checquie; as most of the gentry of this Shire wear, of affection to their superior Lord the Great Stewart of Scotland; just so as many of the families in Annandale carry the Arms of Bruce, Lord of Annandale, as the Johnstons, Kirkpatricks, Jardens, Tweidies, as a learned author observes [1]. But the first of the Shaws of Bargaran I have found mentioned is John Shaw, who was co-temporary with King James the II. and in Anno 1454, resigned the lands of Bargaran in favours of John Shaw his son [2], whose lineal heir is John Shaw of Bargaran, making from him the ninth descent in a direct male line. The intermarriages of this house have been with some of the most considerable gentry of this country; as, the families of Kelsoeland, Mains, Raiss, Woodhead, Glorat, Livingstoun of Haining, Craigends and Northbar.

A little south west of the Castle of Erskine stands the Paroch Church of that name; a Parsonage in latter times depending on the Church of Glasgow. Mr. Menzies is the present Minister.

Half a mile west from Erskine, upon the bank of the river of Clyde, on an eminence, stands the house of Bishoptoun, well planted, the ancient inheritance of the Brisbanes, chief of that name. The first of whom I found any memorable mention, is " Allanus de Brysbane, filius Willielmi de Brysbane," who obtained a grant from Donald Earl of Lenox, of the lands of Macherach in Stirlingshire, to which Malcolm Fleeming, Earl of Wigtoun, is a witness, who was created into that dignity by King David Bruce, in the year 1334 [3]; I am informed the Brisbanes of this race did anciently possess these lands; but I have not perused the writs of John Brisbane of Bishoptoun, to know the connection he has with this Allan, who seems to be his predecessor. Of this family several worthy persons descended; as the Reverend Mr. William Brisbane, Parson of Erskine, son of John Brisbane of Bishoptoun, (by Margaret his second wife, daughter of John Hamilton of Broomhill,) father of the Reverend Divine, Mr. Matthew Brisbane, also Parson of Erskine; whose son was the learned Doctor Matthew Brisbane, Physician in Glasgow.

John Brisbane of Bishoptoun alienated lately the lands of Bishoptoun and Wester Roslin, retaining the superiority, to John Walkingshaw of that-ilk; as also the lands of Drum, Kirkland, and Glenshinies; which Walkingshaw holds immediately of the Crown, and hath obtained a Charter of Novo Damus of these lands, to be called in all time coming Walkingshaw.

o

[1] Mackenzie's Herauldry.   [2] Carta penes Jo. Shaw de Bargaran.
[3] Carta penes Burgum de Dunbartoun.

South from Bishoptoun lie the lands of Park of Erskine, anciently possessed by the Parks of that-ilk. William Park of that-ilk, the last of this race, in the reign of King James IV. left his estate to his three daughters, among whom it was shared; Christian, the eldest, got the lands of Park, and married Robert Cunninghame of Achinharvie, by whom she had a daughter, Janet Cunninghame, heiress of Park, who married George Houstoun. They were original of Houstoun of Park, whose posterity ended not long ago in the person of George Houstoun of Park.

Another daughter of William Park of that-ilk married Alexander Cunninghame of Drumquhasle; by her he got half of the lands of Spangow in Innerkip: and the 3d daughter of Park was married to George Stirling of Craigbarnet, with whom he obtained the other half of the lands of Spangow and Flattertoun.

Three miles towards the west from Erskine, upon the coast, on a rising ground, is situate the castle of Finlaystoun, the seat of the Earl of Glencairn, well planted. The house is a noble and great building round a court.

That the family of Cunninghame, whose principal seat was at Kilmaures, in the country of Cunninghame, and from thence took designation, hath been of great antiquity in those parts, is evident from the Register of Kelso Abbacy, whereunto, in King William's time, some of them were benefactors; for in that reign, Robert, the son of Vernebald of Cunninghame, gave the patronage of the church of Kilmaures, with half a carucate of land thereunto beloging, for the welfare of himself, and for the souls of his ancestors and descendants [1]; which donation is confirmed by Richard Morvil, Constable of Scotland and Lord of Cunninghame; who, according to the Chronicle of Melross, died, Anno Dom. 1189 [2]. I have moreover seen a mortification by Robert the son of Vernebald and Richenda Barclay his wife, daughter and heiress of Umphry de Barclay, of the lands of Glenfarquharlin, in the Sheriffdom of Mearns, to the Monastery of Arbroth, about the same time of the first grant [3]: which donation is ratified by " Rob. filius Roberti filii Vernebaldi de Cunninghame, pro salute animæ sui " patris & matris suæ, & pro animabus omnium antecessorum, & successorum " suorum." But the first of this noble family who possessed the Barony of Denniestoun, was Sir William Cunninghame of Kilmaures, by marriage of Margaret, eldest daughter and co-heiress of Sir Robert Denniestoun of that-ilk, in the reign of King Robert III. This being the substance of what I have found

---

[1] Register of the Abby of Kelso. [2] Chron: de Melross.
[3] Chartulary of Arbroth.

memorable of him, I shall only take notice, that, for the health of his soul, and for the souls of his ancestors, he gave in pure alms to the Monks of the Abby of Kilwinning, the lands of Grange. As to the precise time of his death I know not; but, by the said Margaret his wife, he left issue Robert his son and heir, who was knighted by King James I. at the solemnity of his Coronation, in the year 1424 [1]. He was one of those Barons that sat upon the trial of Murdach Duke of Albany, who was attainted of Treason, upon King James I.'s return from his captivity in England. And, in 1434, he obtained from that Prince a commission to command the countries of Kintyre and Knapdale [2]. He married Janet daughter of Alexander Lord Montgomery, by whom he had Alexander his son and heir; whom King James II. an. 1445, as a reward of his faithful services, did advance to the dignity of a Baron of this Realm, with the title of Lord Kilmaures; and standing loyal to King James the III. in those turbulent times, was by that Monarch created Earl of Glencairn, an. 1488. And, when that Prince became much distressed through the potency of the turbulent Barons of that age, he stood firm to the royal cause; and, fighting gallantly in behalf of his Sovereign, in the battle of Bannockburn, which action happened upon the 11th day of June 1488, was there slain. He left issue, by his wife Margaret Hepburn, daughter to the Lord Hales, two sons: Robert his successor; and Alexander, of whom descended the family of Craigends: Which Robert so succeeding his father, used only the title of Lord Kilmaures, and died in the year 1490; leaving issue, by Marion his wife, daughter of . . . Lord Lindsay, Cuthbert his son and heir, who reassumed the title of Earl of Glencairn, in 1491. He wedded Marjory Douglas, daughter of Archbald Earl of Angus, by whom he had William his son and heir, who was cotemporary with King James V. He is one of those Scots Peers taken prisoner at the field of Soloway, in the year 1542, and was afterwards one of the Commissioners sent by the Estates of Scotland to treat with King Henry VIII. of England, about a marriage betwixt Prince Edward his son, and our Queen Mary. This Earl deceased in an. 1547, leaving issue, by Margaret his wife, daughter and sole heir of John Campbel of Stevenstoun, three sons: Alexander his successor: the 2d, Andrew, of whom issued the Cunninghames of Corsehill: for this I have seen a grant of the lands of Corsehill, by William Master of Glencairn, dated at Edinburgh the 28th day of September 1532, to Andrew Cunninghame his son; of whom Sir Alexander Cunninghame of Corsehill, Baronet, is lineally descended: the 3d, Hugh, progenitor of the Cunninghames of Waterstoun.

[1] Sir James Balfour's Annals, in MS. [2] Haddingtoun's Collections.

To William Earl of Glencairn succeeded Alexander his son; which noble person was among the first of quality that made profession of the Protestant religion; his house, before the Reformation, being a special place of refuge to those then called hereticks: he did show a more than ordinary zeal in advancing our happy Reformation. Our Historians write, that, in 1559, Queen Mary, Dowager and Regent of Scotland, using her utmost endeavours for suppressing the beginnings of the Reformation, did use great severity upon the inhabitants of the town of Perth, whereby the heat of the people was raised to that pitch, that they broke in upon the houses of the Monks and Friars, which they pulled down to the ground: this provoked the Queen so much, that she resolved to punish the town in a most exemplary manner; so she gathered the French souldiers together, with such others as would join with her: but this noble patriot, Alexander Earl of Glencairn, having gathered 2500 men together, with incredible haste, marched to that place, where there were in all about 7000 armed men. This made the Queen Regent afraid to engage with them; so an agreement was made up, and oblivion promised for all that was past, and matters of religion were referred to a Parliament. And upon Queen Mary's return from France, after the death of her husband Francis II. Her Majesty nominate Alexander Earl of Glencairn to be of her Privy Council. This worthy Peer, who deserves to have his name celebrated amongst the most eminent patriots of the age in which he lived, departed this life in the year 1576; leaving issue, by Jean his wife, daughter of James Earl of Arran, three sons: William his successor; Andrew of Halsyde; and James, Prior of Lesmahagoe; and by Jean his second wife, daughter of William Cunninghame of Capringtoun, he had Alexander, Commendator of Kilwinning, author of that branch of the Cunninghames of Mongreenend; and a daughter, Jean, married to Archbald Earl of Argile, and surviving him, she married Humphry Colquhoun of Luss.

To Alexander Earl of Glencairn succeeded William his son and heir; who wedded Janet, daughter of Sir Alexander Gordon of Lochinvar, by whom he had James his son and heir: moreover he had several daughters married in the families of Glencagles, Maclean, Achinames, Craigends, and Kilmahew. Which James Earl of Gleneairn is one of the Peers that sat upon the trial of William Earl of Gourie, an. 1582. And in an. 1604, when King James set the design of an Union betwixt the two kingdoms on foot, he was chosen one of the Commissioners to negotiate that important affair. He deceased an. 1627; leaving issue, by Margaret his wife, daughter of Sir Duncan Campbel of Glenurchie, William his son and heir; and John of Kilmaronock, (whose daughter and heir married Sir Alexander Cunninghame of Robertland): He had moreover five daughters: viz. Catharine, married Sir James Cunninghame of Glengarnock: Ann, to James Marquis of Hamilton, and had issue: Margaret, to Sir James Hamilton of Evandale; and, surviving him, she remarried Sir James Maxwel of Calderwood, and had issue: Susanna, to Lauder of Hatoun: Mary, to John Crawfurd of Kilbirny, of whom Patrick, Viscount of Garnock is lineally descended.

To James Earl of Glencairn succeeded William, his son and heir; who espoused Janet Ker, daughter of Mark Earl of Lothian, by whom he had William his son and heir; and four daughters: Elizabeth married to Sir Ludovick Stewart of Minto: Margaret to David Betoun of Cricht: Jean to John Blair of that-ilk, and had issue: Marion to James Earl of Finlator; and, surviving him, she married Alexander Lord Saltoun, sans issue.

Which William Earl of Glencairn did, in a very signal manner, distinguish himself in his loyalty to King Charles I. and II. and headed that small party of those loyal Scots, that, for some time, successfully oppos'd the troops of the usurper Oliver Cromwel; but at last were routed by a strong party of horse detach'd from the English army, under the command of Colonel Morgan, an. 1654: And, upon the Restauration of King Charles II. an. 1660, His Majesty was pleased, in consideration of the great and eminent services of this noble Peer, who had an equal talent both for camp and court, to confer on him the office of Lord High Chancellor of Scotland, which he enjoyed till his death, 1664. He was twice married; first with Ann, daughter of James Earl of Finlator; and then to Margaret, Countess Dowager of Tweeddale, daughter of Alexander Earl of Eglintoun: By the first he had issue, James Lord Kilmaures, who wedded Elizabeth, daughter of William Duke of Hamilton, but died sans issue, his father then living; the 2d, Alexander; the 3d, John, successively Earls of Glencairn. He had moreover three daughters, viz. Jean married William Earl of Kilmarnock and had issue; the 2d, Mary, to William Lord Bargeny; the 3d, Elizabeth, to William Hamilton of Orbiestoun, and had issue.

To William Earl of Glencairn succeeded Alexander his son and heir, who married . . . Stewart, daughter of Sir Lovis Stewart of Kirkhill, by whom he had only one daughter; Margaret, married John Earl of Lauderdale, and had issue; and, departing this life, an. 1670, his estate and honours descended to John his brother, who died Constable of the Castle of Dunbartoun in the year 1708; leaving issue, by Mary his wife, daughter of John Earl of Mar, William now Earl of Glencairn, his son and heir; who hath wedded Henrieta Stewart, daughter of Alexander Earl of Galloway, by whom he hath William Lord Kilmaures.

Arms; Argent; a Shake-Fork, Sable; supported by two Rabbits, proper: and for Crest, an Unicorn's Head, Coupe. Motto " Over fork over."

Of this noble family descended many ancient and opulent Barons of the Sirname of Cunninghame, in the Shire of Air; and among the first of those was the family of Capringtoun, whose original ancestor was Thomas, a younger son of Sir William Cunninghame of Kilmaures, in the reign of King Robert III. and became possest of the Barony of Capringtoun, in right of . . . . . Wallace his wife, daughter and one of the co-heirs of Wallace of Sundrum: In memory of that match this family carried, quarterly, the Coat of Wallace, viz. Gules, a Lion Rampant, Argent, in their atchievement. To Thomas succeeded Adam Cunninghame of Capringtoun; and to him another Adam his son; who in 1489 married Isobel, daughter of Malcolm Crawfurd of Kilbirny. This family failed in the person of Sir William Cunninghame of Capringtoun, Baronet.

Of the house of Capringtoun descended the Cunninghames of Legland, which hath furnished some considerable Cadets; as Cunninghame now of Capringtoun, Baronet; and Cunninghame of Enterkine.

Two miles west of Finlaystoun, upon the coast, stands the Castle of Newark, the principal messwage of the Barony of Finlaystoun Maxwel, which, with diverse other lands, came to Sir Robert Maxwel of Calderwood, a younger son of the family of Nether Pollock, in right of Elizabeth his wife, second daughter, and one of the co-heirs, of Sir Robert Denniestoun of that-ilk, whose successor, Sir John Maxwel of Calderwood, disponed the Barony of Newark to George Maxwel his son: Which grant is confirmed by a Charter from King James III. dated, at Edinburgh, the 3d day of January 1477 [1]. Whose son, Patrick Maxwel of Newark, obtained a Charter of these lands, in the year 1483, and died, an. 1522. To whom succeeded John his son and heir; and of John, a younger son, descended the Maxwels of Dargevel: Which George was cotemporary with Queen Mary. He married Marion, daughter of William Cunninghame of Craigends, by whom he had Patrick his son and heir; who being at the conflict betwixt the Lord Maxwel and the Laird of Johnston, at Lockerby, an. 1593, he escaped with his life very narrowly. He was twice married; first, with Margaret, daughter of William Mure of Rouallan; and afterwards, Margaret, daughter of David Crawfurd of Carse; by the last he had George, his son; who added to his paternal inheritance the lands of Teiling in Angus, by marriage of Helen, daughter and sole heir of Hugh Maxwel of Teiling; by

---

[1] Haddingtoun's Collections from the Publick Records.

whom he had Patrick, who immediately succeeded his grandfather, and was knighted by King Charles: He espoused Marion, daughter of Sir Dougal Campbel of Achinbreck; by whom he had Sir George his son and heir; and of his younger sons, Patrick, John, and Dougal, descended the Maxwels of Teiling, Blackstoun, and Cowhill. Sir Patrick deceased an. 1678; as Sir George his son did in the year 1684; leaving issue, by Elizabeth his wife, daughter of Robert Semple of Beltrees, and of Mary his wife, daughter of Sir Thomas Lyon of Albar, Patrick his son and heir: who married Margaret, daughter and heiress of John Napier of Kilmahew; by whom he had George Maxwel, alias Napier of Kilmahew, his son and heir, who lately sold the Barony of Newark to Mr William Cochran of Kilmaronock.

West from the Barony of Newark, on a Bay of the sea, stands the Burgh and Barony of Newark; and contiguous to that the Burgh of Barony of Port-Glasgow, (formerly called Devols Glen) erected by King Charles II. in favours of the City of Glasgow, who in an. 1668, acquired these lands from Sir Patrick Maxwel of Newark, where they have built a large harbour, which they called Port-Glasgow, and a good number of houses has been lately built there. But this place is chiefly considerable for being the seat of the Custom Office for the precinct of Clyde; as also the merchants of the City of Glasgow being obliged to discharge their goods here. In the year 1694, the Burgh of Barony of Port-Glasgow, and the Bay of Newark was dissolved from the Paroch of Kilmalcolm and erected into a distinct Paroch, which at present is vacant by the translation of the Reverend Mr. Robert Millar, in the month of November 1709, to the Town of Pasly. Above this Coast the country riseth high upon the shore.

A mile west off Port-Glasgow, upon the shore, stands the ruinous Castle of Easter-Greenock, a possession till of late, and for 300 years past, of the Crawfurds of Kilbirny; which came to that family by right of marriage of . . . . Galbraith, daughter, and one of the coheirs, of Malcolm Galbraith of Greenock, in the reign of King Robert III. The common ancestor of the Crawfurds, as our renown'd Historian and Antiquary Mr. Thomas Crawfurd, Professor of Philosophy and Mathematicks in the University of Edinburgh, and author of the Notes on Buchanan's History, (who also wrote an Historical account of of some of the ancient families of his name) says, was one Mackornock; who, as the story goes, signalized himself at an engagement by the water of Cree in Galloway, by discovering of a Foord, which gave a signal advantage to his party. The story may carry some show of truth; for it is observed, that most of our Sirnames at first were taken from places, accidents, and the most remarkable actions of a man's life: but this I wave, as not being so well attested.

But the first using this Sirname, I have found, is Galfridus de Crawfurd, who is witness in a Charter by Roger Bishop of St. Andrews, to the Abbacy of Kelso, declaring that Monastery independent of the Episcopal See[1] Which Charter has probably been about the year 1189, when Roger was elected Bishop of St. Andrews[2], in the reign of King William: so it is clear that the family of Crawfurd, seated at a place of that name, in the County of Lanerk, and from their hereditary lands took designation, when fixed Sirnames came commonly to be used. But the principal family of this name failed in the reign of King Alexander II, in the person of Sir John Crawfurd of that-ilk, who departed this life an. 1248. His Estate went to his daughters and co-heirs; Margaret the elder being married to Hugh de Douglas, ancestor of the duke of Douglas; and the 2d daughter married David de Lindsay, ancestor to the Earl of Crawfurd[3].

The principal family of the Crawfurds thus failing, a part of the old estate remained with the male issue of the ancient proprietors, as the learned Sir James Dalrymple observes[4]. For, in a Donation by David de Lindsay to the Monastery of Newbottle, out of the lands of Crawfurd, he bounds his gift " inter terram meam & terram Johannis, filii Reginaldi de Crawfurd, usque ad " terram Ecclesiæ de Crawfurd." That the lands of John, the son of Reginald de Crawfurd, are excepted out of the foresaid Donation, the same celebrated author thinks, gave rise to the distinction of the lands of Crawfurd Lindsay, from Crawfurd John.

And that a family of the Sirname of Crawfurd had possessions in Clydesdale, near Crawfurd, and a distinct family from the Crawfurds of Loudoun, who was the first and most considerable branch of the principal stemm, and seated in the Shire of Air, while the family of Crawfurd of that-ilk existed, the following authority will sufficiently document. For Mr. Thomas Crawfurd, our learned Antiquary and Historian, makes Loudoun's ancestor Grand Uncle to Sir John the last Baron of Crawfurd; and in the reign of King Alexander II. " Reginaldus de Crawfurd, Vicecomes de Air," who is of Loudoun, is frequently mention'd in the Registers of the Abbies of Kelso and Pasly, about the year 1226, and in the same reign obtained the Barony of Loudoun, by marriage of

---

[1] Regist: of Kelso. [2] Chron; de Melross. [3] Mr. Thom. Crawfurd's History of the Crawfurds, MS. and a late History of the family of Douglas. [4] Preface to the Observations upon the Scots History. [5] Ibid.

the Heiress of James Loudoun of that-ilk [1], of whom the Right Honourable Hugh Earl of Loudoun is the lineal heir. So that I think probably John, the Son of Reginald de Crawfurd, who had lands contiguous to the Barony of Crawfurd, mentioned from the Chartulary of Newbottle, was a son of the first Sir Reginald Crawfurd of Loudoun. Moreover I have seen, in the Register of the Abby of Kelso, in the Advocates Library at Edinburgh, a Writ an. 1271, wherein Andrew, Abbot of Kelso, acknowledges " Dominum Hugonem Craw- " furd, Militem, & Aliciam sponsam ejus, in possessione terræ de Draffan, in " Vicecomitatu de Lanerk:" which lands they held of that Convent. And, that this Sir Hugh Crawfurd was not of Loudoun, our national histories do sufficiently evidence. They mention Sir Reginald Crawfurd of Loudoun the father, and Sir Reginald the son, among other Scots Patriots, who stood firm to the interest of their country, after King Alexander III.'s death, in opposition to the oppression of King Edward I. of England, and were cotemporary with Sir Hugh above-mentioned.

There is also extant, in the Viscount of Garnock's Charter-chest, a contract of Excambion betwixt Laurence Crawford of Kilbirny, his ancestor, upon the one part, and Sir James Hamilton of Finnart, with consent of Margaret Livingston his spouse, upon the other, dated Jan. 29, 1528; whereby Kilbirny excambed his part of the lands of Crawfurd-John, with Sir James Hamilton's lands of Drumray in the Shire of Dunbartoun; which continues with his descendents, and gives the title of Lord to the Right Honourable Patrick Viscount of Garnock. Which Laurence Crawfurd of Kilbirny, was son and heir of Robert Crawfurd of Kilbirny, by Marion his wife, a daughter of the family of Semple; and he, of John Crawfurd of Kilbirny; and he, of Malcolm Crawfurd of Kilbirny, who obtained the Barony of Kilbirny and diverse other lands, by marriage of Marjory, daughter and sole heir of John Barclay of Kilbirny, who was a branch of the Barclays of Ardrossan, a family of great antiquity in the shire of Air. Richard de Barclay their ancestor, is mentioned a witness in the foundation Charter of the Abby of Kilwinning, founded by Hugh Morvel, Constable of Scotland, in King Malcom IV.'s time.

But to return to the family of Kilbirny: Of Laurence above-mentioned, I have found nothing more on record, but that in the year 1547, he settled upon his Chapel of Drumray, a liberal fund, for the better support of certain Priests, to celebrate Divine Service " for the soul of his late Sovereign Lord, King James V. and for the good estate of himself, and of Helen Campbel his wife, daughter of Sir Hugh Campbel of Loudoun; and for all the faithful deceased." He

[1] Preface to the Observations upon the Scots History.

departed this life in the month of June 1547, leaving issue, by the said Helen his wife, Hugh his son and heir; John of Easter-Greenock; and Captain Thomas, ancestor of the Crawfurds of Jordanhill and Cartsburn. He had moreover a daughter, Catharine, married to David Fairly of that-ilk, and had issue.

To Laurence Crawford of Kilbirny succeeded Hugh his son and heir; who, adhering to the interest of Queen Mary, at the field of Langside, join'd Her Majesty's troops with a considerable number of his vassals; for which he took a Remission from the Regent Lenox, in the year 1571. He was twice married; first, with Margaret, daughter of Sir John Colquhoun of Luss; and afterwards he espoused Elizabeth, daughter of David Barclay of Ladyland: By the first he had Malcolm his son and heir; and, of the last, he had William, author of that branch of the Crawfurds of Knightswood. He had moreover four daughters; viz. Marion, married to John Boyle of Kelburn, of whom the Right Honourable David Earl of Glasgow is lineally descended; Margaret, to James Galbraith of Kilcroich, an ancient family in Stirlingshire; Catherine, to William Wallace of Eldersly; Elizabeth, to David Brady of Castletoun in Clackmannanshire: He deceased in the year 1576, and had for his successor, Malcolm his son and heir; who wedded Margaret, daughter of John Cunninghame of Glengarnock, by whom he had John his son and heir, and a daughter, Anne, married to William Cunninghame of Leglan; which Malcolm deceased Anno 1595: to whom succeeded John his son, who departed this life Anno 1622, leaving issue, by Margaret his wife, daughter of John Blair of that-ilk, John his successor; Malcolm of Newtoun, and James of Knightswood; and a daughter Margaret, married to Hugh Kennedy of Ardmillan.

To John, last mentioned, succeeded John his son; who married Mary daughter of James Earl of Glencairn, by whom he had John his son and heir; and daughters, Anne, married to Alexander Cunninghame of Corsehill, and had issue; Margaret, to Colonel William Crawfurd, elder brother to Thomas Crawfurd of Carse, sans issue; and departed this life in November 1629, his estate descending on John his son.

Which John did, in a very singular manner, distinguish himself in his loyalty to King Charles the First; in consideration whereof, His Majesty was pleased to confer on him the dignity of Baronet, in the year 1642; he deceast at Edinburgh in the year 1661, and his corpse were] transported to Kilbirny and buried among his ancestors. He was twice married; first, with Margaret daughter of Robert Lord Burleigh; and, secondly, to Magdalen daughter of David Lord Carnegy, son and heir to David first Earl of Southesk, by whom he had two daughters; Anne, married to Sir Archbald Stewart of Blackhall, and had issue; the second, Margaret, on whom he settled his estate, and to the heirs of her body, obliging them to carry the Sirname of Crawfurd, with the Arms of his family; which Margaret took to husband Mr. Patrick Lindsay, second son of John Earl of Crawfurd, by whom she had issue, three sons and as many daughters; viz. John Crawfurd of Kilbirny her son and heir; the second, Patrick; third, Captain Archbald: and daughters, Margaret, married to David Earl of Glasgow, and had issue; the second, Anne, to Mr. Hary Maule, only brother of James Earl of Panmure, and hath issue; third, Magdalen, to George Dundas of Duddiestoun, and hath issue. Dame Margaret Crawfurd, Lady Kilbirny, died in the month of October 1680.

To whom succeeded John her son and heir, who was created into the dignity of Viscount of Garnock, Lord Kilbirny, Kingsburn and Drumray, by Her Majesty Queen Anne, by Letters Patent, bearing date, at Whitehall, the 10th of April 1703: he deceased upon the 24th of December 1708; leaving issue, by Margaret his wife, daughter to James Earl of Bute, Patrick now Viscount of Garnock, his son and heir; whose Armorial bearing is; Two Coats quarterly; 1st, Gules; a Fess, Ermine; 2dly, Azure; a Cheveron, betwixt three Cross patees, Or; supported by two Greyhounds: and Crest; an Ermine, Motto " Si- " ne labe nota."

Dame Margaret Crawfurd, Lady Kilbirny, with consent of her husband, in the year 1669, alienate the Barony of Easter Greenock, to Sir John Shaw of Greenock.

A quarter of a mile west from the Castle of Easter Greenock, at the east end of a large bay, stands the town of Crawfurdsdike, built of one street, with a convenient harbour, capable to contain ships of a considerable burden. It was erected into a Burgh of Barony, with the privilege of a weekly market and several fairs, in favours of Thomas Crawfurd of Cartsburn, by a Charter from King Ch: the II. dated the 16th of July, an. 1669. The town is chiefly inhabited by seamen and mechanicks.

A little towards the south of Crawfurdsdyke, stands the house of Cartsburn, well planted, the principal messwage of that Barony, and the seat of Thomas Crawfurd of Cartsburn: which lands were anciently a part of the Barony of Kilbirny, and became the patrimony of a younger brother of that ancient family, (in the reign of Queen Mary,) whose posterity ended in the person of David Crawfurd of Cartsburn, in the reign of King Charles the I. So the lands of Cartsburn came to Malcolm Crawfurd of Newtown, a son of the family of Kilbirny; and acquired from his heirs, an. 1657, by Sir John Crawfurd of Kilbirny. And in the year 1669, disponed by Dame Margaret Crawfurd, Lady Kilbirny, with consent of her husband, to Thomas Crawfurd her cousin, 2d son of Cornelius Crawfurd of Jordanhill, (by Mary his wife, daughter of Sir James Lockhart of Lee,) lineally descended of Captain Thomas Crawfurd, younger son of Laurence Crawfurd of Kilbirny. Which Thomas deceased the 15th of October 1695, leaving issue, by Jean his wife, daughter of Andrew Semple, son and heir of Robert Semple of Milnbank, Thomas Crawfurd now of Cartsburn, his son and heir; who hath married Bethia, daughter of Mr. Archbald Robertoun of Bedlay, by whom he has issue, Thomas his son and apparent heir.

His Armorial bearing is, Gules; a Fess, Ermine; betwixt a Crescent in chief, and two Swords saltyre-ways, hilted and pomel'd Or, in Base: for Crest, a Sword with a Balance; with this Motto, " Quod tibi hoc alteri."

Near Crawfurdsdyke, at the west end of a large bay, stands the town of Greenock, the chief town upon the coast, well built, consisting chiefly of one principal street, about a quarter of a mile in length; erected into a Burgh of Barony, by King Charles I. about the year 1642, in favours of John Shaw of Greenock, with the privilege of a weekly market upon the Friday, to which there is a considerable resort. It has belonging to it a great many vessels, which are employed in trade to foreign parts: there is also lately built one of the largest harbours in the kingdom, by Sir John Shaw of Greenock, without any publick fund: and at the west end stands the church, a handsome structure, after the modern fashion. The Reverend Mr. Andrew Turner is present minister. And above the town, on an eminence, stands the castle of Greenock, which overlooks it, surrounded with pleasant parks and inclosures, having on all sides a great deal of regular and beautiful planting, with spacious avenues and terrasses. The Barony of Greenock, as I noticed before, pertained to the Galbraiths of old, and by . . . . daughter and coheiress of Malcolm Galbraith of Greenock, by marriage, came to the family of Shaw of Sauchie, whose ancestor, according to the famous Antiquary Sir George Mackenzie, was descended of Shiach, a son of MacDuff Earl of Fife; and that his descendents took Sirname from the proper name of their predecessor, when fixed Sirnames came to be used.

In the Register of the Abby of Pasly, frequent mention is made of the Sirname of Shaw. In the reign of King Alexander III. John de Shaw was a witness to that donation, which John, the son of Reginald, made of the lands of Auldhouse to the Monks of Pasly, in the year 1284 [!].

Thus the family of Sauchie became possess'd of the Barony of Wester Greenock, by marriage of one of the coheirs of Galbraith of Greenock, in the

[!] Chartulary of Pasly, Fol. 138.

reign of King Robert III. After which they were promiscuously design'd of Sauchie and Greenock. For authority of this, I have seen a grant, by Andrew Abbot of Dunfermling, of the lands of Gartinker, to James Shaw of Greenock, in the year 1439. The lands of Greenock continued in the family of Sauchie until the reign of King James V. that Alexander Shaw of Sauchie gave the lands of Greenock in patrimony to John Shaw his eldest son, by Elizabeth his 2d wife, daughter of William Cunninghame of Glengarnock. And since the death of George Shaw of Sauchie, without succession, his estate descended to the family of Greenock, who is now the chief of the name, and representative of that ancient family. John Shaw, Greenock's ancestor, built the church of Greenock after the Baronies of Easter and Wester Greenock were dissolved from the Paroch of Innerkip, and erected into a distinct Paroch; which is ratified by an Act of Parliament, in the year 1592. He married, in an. 1565, Jean, daughter of John Cunninghame of Glengarnock, his uncle ; by whom he had five sons and as many daughters : viz. first, Alexander, who died without succession; the 2d, James his successor ; the 3d, Mr. William of Spangow ; the 4th, Patrick of Kelsoeland ; the 5th, Robert, author of that branch of the Shaws of Ganoway in Ireland. His daughters were, Elizabeth married Hugh Montgomery of Braidstane, and Lord Viscount of Airds in the kingdom of Ireland, ancestor to the Earl of Mount-Alexander in that kingdom ; Isobel married John Lindsay of the family of Dunrod ; Marion married . . . . Campbel of Dovecoathall ; Christian married Patrick Montgomery of Craigbouie Esquire ; Giles married James Crawfurd of Flattertoun. He departed this life an. 1593.

To whom succeeded James his son and heir ; who wedded Margaret, daughter of Hugh Montgomery of Haslehead ; and departing this life, in the year 1620, as appears from the probate of his testament yet extant, left issue, by the said Margaret his wife, John his only son and heir, who rais'd his fortune considerably, and died in the year 1679 ; leaving issue, by Helen his wife, daughter of John Houston of that-ilk, John his son and heir ; and a daughter, Margaret, married Alexander Lord Blantyre, and had issue. Which John, during the late usurpation, did engage in the royal cause : and when His Majesty King Charles the II. marched with his army into England, an. 1651, he was constitute Lieutenant Colonel to the regiment of horse commanded by the Earl of Dumfermling ; and, at the battle of Worcester, which fell out the 3d day of September that year, betwixt his Majesty's army and the army of the Rump, under the command of Cromwel and Lambert, the said John did, in a most signal manner, manifest his valour and loyalty to his Sovereign ; of which His Majesty was so fully sensible, that, as a token of his royal favour, he was pleased to confer on him the honour of Knighthood: and when he obtained the hereditary honour of Baronet, from King James VII. by his Patent dated, at Windsor June 28th 1687, his services to King Charles the II. and his zeal for the interest of the Crown, are particularly mentioned, as the causes of bestowing that dignity. He married Jean, daughter of Sir William Mure of Rouallan; by whom he had Sir John his son and heir, and several daughters; . . . married Patrick Mackdowal of Logan, and had issue; Margaret married to John Hamilton of Ladyland, and had issue; Sarah to Sir Robert Dickson of Inveresk, sans issue; Ann to Tobias Smollet of Bonhil, and had issue.

Which Sir John died, an. 1694, at Edinburgh, and was buried at the Abby Church of Holy-rood-house; his estate and honours devolving on Sir John his son and heir, who departed this life at Edinburgh, an. 1702, and was buried, at Greenock, among his ancestors: leaving issue, by Eleonor his wife, daughter, and one of the coheirs, of Sir Thomas Nicolson of Carnock, Sir John his son and heir, member of the present Parliament for the Shire of Renfrew, and hath married Margaret, daughter of Sir Hugh Dalrymple of North Berwick, Lord President of the College of Justice; by whom he has one daughter, Marion.

The Armorial bearing of this family is, Azure, three covered Cups, Or; supported by two Savages, wreathed about the middle; and, for Crest; a Demi-Savage: with this Motto, ".I mean well."

West from the Barony of Greenock lie the lands of Finnart, a part of the patrimony of the great and noble family of Douglas; which, upon their forfaulture, in an. 1445, came, by a gift of King James II, to James first Earl of Arran, an. 1457, and were given, in the year 1510, in patrimony to James Hamilton his natural son by Mary Boyd, a daughter of Boyd, of Bonshaw: He was legitimate in the year 1512; and, in the reign of King James V. was Lord High Treasurer of Scotland; and in the latter end of that King's reign forfaulted in an. 1540, and his estate annexed to the Crown; and the lands of Finnart were bestowed by King James the V. upon Alexander Shaw of Sauchie; who, in 1542, disponed Finnart, with the Barony of Wester Greenock, to John Shaw his son.

Two miles west of Greenock, upon the shore, stands the Burgh of Barony of Gourock, erected in favours of Sir Archbald Stewart of Castlemilk, with the privilege of a weekly market upon the Tuesday: and above the town stands the castle of the same denomination, the principal messwage of the Barony of Finnart-Stewart; which in the reign of King James II. by the forfaulture of the Earl of Douglas, came to Stewart of Castlemilk, whose ancestor was

William Stewart, a younger son of Sir John Stewart of Darnly, in the reign of King Robert II.[1]. John Stewart of Castlemilk, his son, who lived in the reign of King Robert III. is a witness in that resignation which William Urrie made of the lands of Fultoun to the Monks of Pasly, an. 1409. He was killed at the battle of Vernoil in France, an. 1424. Archbald Stewart of Castlemilk, his successor, obtained the lands of Finnart-Stewart, in the reign of King James the II. To him succeeded Alexander Stewart of Castlemilk, who is retoured in his lands, an. 1500. To him succeeded Archbald his son, who resigns the lands of Finnart in favours of Archbald his son, in an. 1528. Which last Archbald was father of David Stewart of Castlemilk, who was cotemporary with Queen Mary. His successor was Archbald his son, who, by Janet his wife, daughter of Stewart of Minto, had Sir Archbald his son and heir; who was married to Ann, daughter of Robert Lord Semple, by whom he had two sons; Sir Archbald, and James, of whom descended the Stewarts of Torrence: which Sir Archbald had issue, by . . . . Fleming his wife, daughter of John Earl of Wigtoun, Archbald, who succeeded his grandfather. He was created a Baronet, by King Charles II. the last of February 1668, and died an.   leaving issue, by Mary his wife, daughter of William Master of Carmichael, Sir William Stewart of Castlemilk, his son and heir; who hath married Margaret, daughter and sole heiress of John Crawfurd of Miltoun, whose grandfather, James Crawfurd, was a younger son of Patrick Crawfurd of Cartsburn.

The Armorial bearing of Stewart of Castlemilk is, Or; a Bend, Gules; surmounted of a Fess, Checquie, Azure and Argent.

Of the family of Castlemilk several other families of good note are descended: As the Stewarts of Allantoun, which hath furnished some considerable Cadets; as Stewart of Cultness, whereof the heir is Sir David Stewart, Baronet. Sir James Stewart of Goodtrees, late Lord Advocate, and Sir Robert Stewart of Allanbank, Baronet, are two younger brothers of Cultness.

At Gourock the river of Clyde taketh its course southward: upon the shore stands the ruinous Castle of Leven, an ancient possession of a family of the Sirname of Morton, which failed in the person of Adam Morton, of Leven, who alienated these lands, an. 1547, to William Lord Semple[2]. Robert Lord Semple disponed the lands of Leven to Andrew Master of Semple, his uncle, in the year 1584[3].

[1] Hist: of the Stewarts of Darnly, by the learn'd Sir Rob. Gordon of Gordonstoun. [2] Carta penes Dom. Archib. Stewart de Blackhall. [3] Carta penes Francisc. D. Semple.

A mile south from this lie the lands of Flattertoun, the possession, for several ages, of the Crawfurds, who are said to be descended of Kilbirny. Their ancestor, James Crawfurd of Sydehill, obtained the lands of Flattertoun and Spangow, an. 1489, in exchange of the lands of Kilwinet in Stirlingshire, by excambion with George Stirling of Craigbarnet; of which lands he became possest in right of Elizabeth his wife, daughter, and one of the co-heirs, of William Park of that-ilk[1]. From whom, James Crawfurd of Flattertoun was the sixth descendent in a direct line, who sold his estate to Sir Archibald Stewart of Blackhall, in the reign of King Charles I.

A little towards the south of this stands the Castle of Dunrod, whence an ancient family of the Sirname of Lindsay took designation, and descended of Sir James Lindsay, the constant companion of King Robert Bruce. John Lindsay of Dunrod, his successor, obtained from King Robert II. the Mains of the Barony of Kilbride in Clydesdale, for his good and faithful services; which he confirmed an. 1382[2]. This family continued to make a considerable figure for many ages, and were honoured with diverse matches from several noble families, as Eglintoun, Semple, Elphinstoun; and came to an end in the person of Alexander Lindsay of Dunrod, who alienated that Barony in the year 1619, to Sir Archibald Stewart of Blackhall. The family of Dunrod is now represented by Lindsay of Blacksolm.

North from this, upon the shore, stands the house of Ardgowan, consisting of an old tower, to which there have been lately lower buildings added, adorned with pleasant planting, the principal seat of Sir Archbald Stewart of Blackhall, lineally descended of John Stewart, natural son of King Robert III. who had a grant of the lands of Ardgowan, in the year 1404. But having touched this family already, page 58, I shall not repeat what I have said there. But since the printing of that sheet, I have seen a Donation by John Stewart of Achingoun (Blackhall's ancestor) to the Church of Dunoon, of a fourth part of the lands of Finvachun in Cowall. Which grant he expresses to be made " for the safety of his soul, and for the souls of his ancestors and successors;" dated an. 1402[3]. Moreover, I have seen a Charter granted by King James the III. an. 1472, " Johanni Stewart de Achingoun, de terris de Kilmichil & Glen-
" conby, in Dominio de Arran, cum officio Coronatoris dicti Dominii de
" Arran [4].

[1] Carta penes Dom. de Blackhall. [2] Charter in the Publick Register of Charters.
[3] Haddingtoun's Collections from the Publick Records, in the Lawyers Library at Edinburgh. [4] Carta in Rotulis Jacobi Tertii.

A little towards the south from Ardgowan stands the Paroch Church of Innerkip, so denominate from the rivulet Kipp, that here empties itself into the sea. In the register of the Monastery of Pasly, there is a Donation by Balduin de Bigres, Sheriff of Lanerk, to the Monks of Pasly, " de Ecclesia de Innerkip, " cum tota illa terra inter tumulos ubi Ecclesia est fundata[1], in liberam elee- " mosynam, ita libere & quiete quam possident reliquas Ecclesias de Strathgreif, " ex Don. Walteri filii Allani, Dapiferi Regis Scotiæ." The Reverend Mr. William Fleming is present Minister of Innerkip.

Near this Church stands the Burgh and Barony of Innerkip, erected in favours of Sir Archbald Stewart of Blackhall.

And a little towards the south of this stands the house of Christwall, the seat of James Stewart of Christwall, descended of the Stewarts of Blackhall.

South from the Church of Innerkip lie the lands of Finnock, anciently a possession of the Stewarts of Bute, descended of John Stewart, natural son of King Robert II. I have seen a resignation of these lands, by John Stewart, Sheriff of Bute and Arran, in favours of William Stewart his son, which is ratified by King James II. in the year 1444[2], and from his posterity was purchased by the Stewarts of Ardgowan.

And a mile south of this stands the house of Kelly, situate on a rivulet of the same name, the boundary of this Shire from the Shire of Air, the seat of an ancient family of the Sirname of Bannantine, a branch of the House of Keames in the Shire of Bute. The first of whom I found was James Bannatine, who had a grant of the lands of Kelly from King James III. above 220 years ago, as appears from the original yet extant[3]. Of whom Archbald Bannatine of Kelly is lineally descended; whose Armorial bearing is the Coat of Bannatine of Keames, viz. Gules; a Cheveron, Argent; between three Molets, Or, with a Brotherly difference. The intermarriages of Bannatine of Kelly have been with Stewart of Blackhall, Crawfurd of Cartsburn, Crawfurd of Flattertoun, Boyd of Portencross, Stewart of Pardovan, MackGilchrist of Northbar.

THUS I have prosecuted the Historical and Genealogical account of the Sheriffdom of RENFREW, and of the Proprietors Ancient and Modern;

---

[1] Register of Charters of the Monastery of Pasly. [2] Carta in Publicis Archivis.
[3] Carta penes Archibald. Bannatine de Kelly.

I proceed to give a Genealogical and Chronological History of the royal and illustrious Family of STEWART. This Shire was their ancient patrimony, and where, for a long time, they had their special residence; from whence they had the designation of Baron, a title afterwards peculiar to the Prince and Stewart of SCOTLAND. And so I conclude the History of this Shire.

THE

HISTORY

OF THE

ROYAL AND ILLUSTRIOUS

FAMILY OF STEWART.

THE family of STEWART is one of the most ancient in Europe: Our best Historians derive the descent of this illustrious house from Bancho Thane of Lochaber, (a title unto which that of Earl afterwards succeeded,) a great man, and of the blood royal [1], who was son of Ferquhard Thane of Lochaber; and he a younger son of Kenneth III. King of Scots, as a fam'd Antiquary writes [2]. Which Bancho was a person of great consideration in the reign of Duncan I. King of Scots, (who succeeded to the Throne in the year 1034,) and was one of the principal men whom that Monarch employ'd in all matters of importance. During whose reign, Sueno, King of Norway, invaded Scotland, and landing a considerable army at Kinghorn in Fife, ravaged the adjacent country: but by the extraordinary courage and resolution of Bancho Thane of Lochaber, the Norvegian army was worsted [3]. He was also the chief instrument in delivering his country from a second ruin it was threatened with, by an in-

[1] Buchan. in Vita Reg. Duncan. Joh. Lesly Episc. Rossen. de Rebus Gest: Scotorum.
[2] Sir Geo. Mackenzie's MS. History of the Stewarts.   [3] Buchan. Histor.

vasion from Canute, King of Denmark, whose army was overthrown near Perth, by a stratagem devised and execute by Bancho; the circumstances of which are related at large by our Historians. They also report, that the future greatness of the posterity of Bancho was foretold after this manner.

Duncan, King of Scots, had two principal favourites, MacBeath and Bancho. These two travelling on their way to Forres, where the court was then, on a sudden were met by three women, in an uncommon dress; whereof the first making obeisance unto MacBeath, saluted him Thane of Glames; the second, by the appellation of Thane of Calder; and the third, King of Scotland. "This " is unfair dealing," said Bancho, " to give my friend all the honour, and none " to me." To which one of the women replied, " That indeed he should not " be a King, but of him should descend a race of Kings, that should for " ever sway the Scots Scepter." And having thus said, they all suddenly evanished. What truth may be in this story, I cannot tell; but MacBeath, upon his arrival to court, was created into the dignity of Thane of Glames, and not long after honoured with the title of Thane of Calder. Seeing then how the prediction of the women fell out in the former, he resolv'd not to be wanting to himself in fulfilling the third; and therefore killed King Duncan: and, by reason of his command in the army, he succeeded to his throne, in an. 1040. Then calling to mind the prediction given to his companion Bancho, whom hereupon he suspected as his supplanter, to prevent which, he most barbarously caused him to be murthered an. 1050. And intending to have execute the same villany on Fleance, his son, who was no less aimed at than the father, he, with no small difficulty, made his escape into Wales, where he spent the rest of his days, under the protection of Grifith Aplevelen, Prince of the country, who bestowed upon him Nesta his daughter in marriage, by whom he had a son Walter; which Walter, after the death of the tyrant MacBeath, went for Scotland, in the reign of King Malcolm the III. and being a valiant man, was employed, as his Majesty's General, against a formidable rebellion, where he did great service, killing their General, and putting the rebels to flight. Which eminent service recommended him so much to his Prince, with the consideration of his royal descent, and great merits, that he created him " Senescallus Domus Regis," (Stewart of his houshold,) which was the same office with that of the Dapifer; which came afterwards to be extended over the whole kingdom, without any alteration or addition to the same. From this office, his family afterwards took their Sirname; and, besides their royal family, spread itself into diverse noble branches; he obtained from that Prince a grant of the lands of Kyle and Strathgreif, the ancient denomination of the Barony of Renfrew[1]. As to the precise time of his death, I have not found; but he left Allan his son for his successor; who, according to the account of our best Historians, was a man of great action in his days, especially in martial affairs. They relate, that he accompanied diverse other Christian Princes in that famous expedition to the Holy Land, in the year of our Lord 1099 [2]. He left issue,

Walter his son, who was greatly in favour with King David I. (commonly called Saint David) who, in reward of all his signal services, advanced him to be " Senescallus Scotiæ," (Lord High Stewart of all Scotland;) and continuing in the same favour and high offices with King Malcolm IV. he confirmed and ratified to him and his heirs, that hereditary office of High Stewart of Scotland. For this there is extant a Charter, an extract of which, presuming it will not be unacceptable to the curious, I have insert [3].

" Malcolmus, Rex Scotorum, Episcopis, Abbatibus, Comitibus, Baronibus,
" Justitiis, Vicecomitibus, Præpositis, Ministris, cunctisque aliis probis homini-
" bus, Clericis & Laicis, Francis & Anglis, Scotis & Galovidiensibus, totius terræ
" suæ, tam præsentibus quam futuris, Salutem : Notum sit omnibus, quod pri-
" usquam arma suscepi, concessi, & hac meâ Cartâ confirmavi hæreditarie,
" Waltero, filio Allani, Dapifero meo, & hæredibus suis, in feodo & hæredi-
" tate, Seneschalliam meam, tenendam sibi & hæredibus suis, de me & hæredi-
" bus meis; ita bene & plenare, sicut Rex David Senescalliam suam ei dedit
" & concessit : præterea confirmo donationem illam, quam Rex David, Avus
" meus, ei dedit, scilicet de terris de Reinfrew, Paisleth, Pullock, Tulloch, Ker-
" kert, Le Drip, Egilsham, Lochynoc, & Inerwick, Inchenan, Hastenden, Le-
" gerwood & Birchensyde, cum omnibus istarum terrarum pertinentiis ; &,
" in unoquoque Burgo & Dominio meo, unum plenarium toftum, & cum uno-
" quoque tofto, Viginti acras terræ, ad Hospitia sibi in eo facienda ; quare
" volo ut idem Walterus et hæredes sui teneant in capite, omnia præno-
" minata, tam illa, quæ ipse habuit ex donatione Regis David, quam illa, quæ
" habuit ex meâ donatione : REDDENDO mihi & Hæredibus meis, de illo feodo,
" servitium quinque militum. Apud Castrum de Roxburgh in Festo Sancti

---

[1] Lesly's History of Scotland. [2] Ibidem. [3] Charter in Sir James Balfour of Kinaird, Lord Lion, King at Arms, his Collections, in the hands of the learned Antiquary Sir Rob. Sibbald, M. D.

" Johannis Baptistæ, Anno Regis nostri quinto (which is the year of GOD
" 1158.) His testibus,

" Ernesto Episcop, St. Andræ.	Roberto de Bruss
Herberto Episc. de Glasgow	Radolpho de Souls
Johanne Abbate de Kelcow	Philippo de Colvill
Will: Abbate de Melross	Willielmo de Sumervilla
Waltero, Cancellario	Hugone Riddel
Willielmo & David Fratribus Regis	Davide Olifard
Comite Cospatrick	Waldeno, Filio Comitis Cospatrick
Comite Duncano	Willielmo de Morvil
Ricardo de Morvil	Balduino de la Mar
Gilberto de Umphravil	Liolpho, Filio Macus."

Thus much as to his secular actions: I come to take notice of his works of piety, which, according to the superstition of these times, were great and many; for Princes and great men, not satisfied to enrich religious houses already founded, were acted by a strange zeal to erect new Monasteries and Priories, and to endow them with lands and tithes, as the most compendious way to save their souls. So Walter High Stewart of Scotland founded the Monastery of Pasly, in the year of our Lord 1160, the 7th year of the reign of King Malcolm IV. which he dedicated to the honour of GOD, and of the blessed Virgin, and amply endowed the same with lands and tithes, as by the authorities I have here cited, will appear. The Charter of foundation, which I transcribed from the Register of that Monastery, courteously afforded me by the favour of John Earl of Dundonald, I thought fit to insert, bears:

" SCIANT præsentes & futuri, quod Ego, Walterus, Filius Allani, Dapifer
" Regis Scotiæ, pro anima Regis David, Regis Henrici, & Comitis Henrici;
" nec non pro salute corporis & animæ Regis Malcolmi, & mei ipsius, & uxo-
" ris meæ, & hæredum meorum, etiam pro animabus omnium parentum & be-
" nefactorum meorum, ad honorem Dei, & Beatæ Virginis Mariæ, constituam
" quandam Domum Religionis infra terram meam de Paselet, ordinis Fratrum
" de Wenlock, viz. secundum Ordinem Cluniacensem, communi consensu Con-
" ventus de Wenlock; & ad domum illam construendam habeo de Domo de

" Wenlock, tredecem Fratres; & Prior qui de illis tredecem præcedere Domum
" regendæ preficiatur per me & per meum Concilium eligatur; et si contin-
" gat ipsum Priorem, vel per mortem, vel per criminalem prævaricationem, a
" Prioratu suo deponi, per me & per meum Concilium, deponetur; qui ei in
" Prioratum præfatum succedat, per me et meum Concilium eligetur; pro his
" autem libertatibus habendis Domum Prædicti de Wenlock, dabo in perpetu-
" am eleemosynam unam plenariam mensuram in Burgo meo de Reinfru, &
" unum rete piscatorum ad Salmones capiendos, per proprias aquas meas, & un-
" um rete ad Halecia capienda, & unum batellum. Monachis autem de Pasleto
" dabo etiam in perpetuam eleemosynam, & ab omni alio temporali servitio li-
" beram & quietam, Ecclesiam de Inerweek, cum molendino ejusdem, cum per-
" tin : suis; præter unam marcam argenti, quam dedi in eo Radulpho de Kent;
" & Ecclesiam de Legerdswode, cum omnibus pertin : suis; & unam Carucatam
" terræ, quam Grimketel tenuit; & Ecclesiam de Kethkert, cum pertin : suis;
" & omnes Ecclesias in Strathgrief, excepta Ecclesia de Inchenan; & Ecclesiam
" de Paselet cum pertin : & duas carucatas terræ, mensuratas & perambulatas
" circa aquam de Kert juxta Ecclesiam; & illam terram ultra Kert, quam ego
" & Allanus Filius meus eis perambulavimus; & illam portionem terræ, quæ est
" sub dormitorio Monachorum; & totam insulam juxta oppidum meum de
" Reinfru, cum Piscatura inter ipsam insulam & Pertheck; & unum toftum
" plenarium in dicto Burgo, & dimidiam marcam argenti de firma ipsius Burgi
" ad luminare Ecclesiæ; & Molendinum de Reinfru, cum terra ubi Monachi
" prius habitaverunt; & illam carucatam terræ, quæ est inter Kert & Grief;
" dedi iis similiter & confirmavi Ecclesiam de Prestwick, & totam terram
" illam quam Donenaldus Filius Yveni eis perambulavit, inter terram Simonis
" Loccardi & Prestwick, usque Pulprestwick, & secundum Pulprestwick, usque
" in mare, & a mare secundum torrentem, inter terram Arnoldi & Prestwick,
" usque ad divisas Simonis Loccardi; & Ecclesiam de Burgo meo de Prest-
" wick; & totam Salinam in Kalenter, quæ fuit Herberti Camerarii. Præ-
" terea eis dedi quatuor solidas de Molendino de Paselet, ad luminare Ecclesiæ,
" & ut molant ibi absque multura; & decimam de ipso Molendino, & de omni-
" bus Molendinis quæ habeo vel habiturus sum. Insurper eis concessi decimas
" de cunctis vastis meis, & de omnibus terris, infra forestum meum de Pasleto,
" quæ ædificata sunt vel ædificabuntur, et pasturam in eo animalibus suis, Huic

"autem prædictæ eleemosynæ meæ, cum dignitatibus et libertatibus suis con-
"cedo, scilicet Sac et Soke, Thol et Them. His testibus:"

"Engelramo Episcopo Glasguensi Cancel. Gaufrido de Costentin
Ricardo Episcopo Sancti Andreæ   Alexandro de Hesting
Johanne Abbate de Kelcou   Roberto Filio Fulberti
Osberto Abbate de Jedwart   Hugone de Padinan
Magistro Marco Salomone Decano   Ricardo Walas
Elia Clerico   Roberto Croc
Roberto de Mundegumbri   Rogero de Ness
Balduino de Bigres   Ricardo Clerico meo, & multis aliis."
Roberto de Costentin

He was also a benefactor to the Monastery of Dumfermling, founded by King Macolm III. inhabited by Monks of the order of S. Benedict, by bestowing upon them "Viginti acras & unam toftam terræ in Dumfermling, cum tofta in "Burgo suo de Reinfru[1]." The Monks of Kelso, of the Cistercian order, founded by King David I. shared also of his liberality; for, in the Register of that Monastery, there is a mortification, by "Walterus Filius Allani, Dapifer "Regis Scotiæ, de terra quam habuit in Burgo de Rocasburc, & unam acram "terræ in villa de Molla, illam, scilicet, quæ fuit in calumnia inter ipsum et "Ecclesiam ejusdem; et in villa sua de Reinfru, illam terram quæ est juxta "toftum, quam Rex David dedit prædictis Monachis usque ad rivulum qui "descendit de Molendino de Clyde." Which donation he expresses to be made "for the safety of the souls of David and Malcolm, Kings of Scotland, and for the good estate of his Sovereign Lord, King William, and for the safety of his own soul, and of the souls of his ancestors and successors." He married "Eschina de Londonia, Domina de Molla." Of the Sirname of Londonia, there were several families, eminent in King David and King William's time; "Thomas de Londonia" is "Hostiarius Domini Regis Willielmi: He was a benefactor to the Monasteries of Aberbroth and Couper, his gift being confirm'd by his son Allanus, "Hostiarius Regis, Comes Atholiæ[2]." There was also, at the same time, an ancient family of that Sirname in Fife; "Robertus "de Londonia Filius Richardi, Filii Maurici, Filii Thomæ de Londonia,"

[1] Regist: Monasterii de Dunfermling, in Bibl. Juridica Edinburg.
[2] History of the Shire of Fife.

confirms " Ecclesiam de Lassedwyn, Canonicis de Dryburgh[1]." The heiress of this family married Robert, a son of King William of Scotland. I have seen a grant by that Prince, " Roberto de Londoun, Filio suo, de uno plenario tofto " in Burgo suo de Melross ;" as also there is a grant by " Robertus de Lon-" donia, Frater Reg. Scotiæ Monasterio Sanctæ Mariæ de Dryburgh de annuo " redditu tribus solidis argenti, et unam liberam piperi de Lassedwyn [2]. By marriage of the said " Eschina de Londonia," Walter, High Stewart of Scotland, obtained the Baronies of Molla and Huntlaw, in the county of Roxburgh. She was also a benefactor to the Abbies of Kelso and Pasly : On the first she bestowed the patronage of the church of Molla, " for the salvation of her soul, and of Walter, the son of Allan, her husband [3] : And to Pasly she gave, in pure alms, one carucat of land, with pasturage for fifty oxen, " for the soul of " King William, and of David, Earl of Huntingtoun, his brother", &c. [4]. Walter, High Stewart of Scotland, departed this life in the year of our Lord 1177, according to the Chronicle of Melross [5], and was buried at Pasly ; but Fordoun says in the year 1178. The disagreement may be easily reconciled, by the different ways of beginning the year. By the said Eschina his wife he left issue,

Allan, his son and heir, who was a person of great consideration in the reign of King William, and seems to have been a special favourite of that Prince, and a great benefactor to religious houses ; out of a principle of pious zeal, (according to these times) great persons being mightily forward to signalize, and even outdo one another, by extraordinary acts of charity, in making liberal provision for the Monks, who had gain'd so far upon the minds of people, by an outward show and profession of more than ordinary holiness of life, every body being possessed with a fancy, that the prayers of so many devote men, assembled in one place, would be more effectual than the devotion of a single priest, to draw down mercies and blessings upon the benefactor. The vain opinion of the merit of good works, and intercession of saints, and the doctrine of Purgatory, so prevailed with people, that they thought the bestowing a part of GOD's liberality to them, upon his servants and the church, was a ready way to attone for a sinful life, and save their souls, and ransom them out of the place of torment. Many of our Kings and other great men fre-

[1] Regist: Monast. de Dryburgh, in Bib: Jurid. [2] Ibidem. [3] Chartulary de Kelso, in Bib. Jurid. [4] Regist: of the Abby of Pasly, in the hands of the Earl of Dundonald.

[5] Chronic: de Melross, An. Dom. 1177. obiit Walterus Filius Allani, Dapifer Regis Scotiæ, qui fundavit Paaleto cujus Beata Anima vivit in Gloria.

quently mortified churches, whereof they were patrons, with large endowments of lands and tithes, to religious houses. Thus Allan, the son of Walter, " Dapifer Regis Scotiæ," gave the patronage of the church of Kingaff in the Isle of Bute to the Monks of Pasly, with the tithes of all the churches and chappels within that isle [1]: And, moreover, gave the lands of Monabroc in Strathgrief, with an annuity of five Merks, payable to him out of Mauchlyn, by the Monks of Melross [2]; and made a most ample confirmation of all grants, by himself or his father, to that Abby: Which (grant) he makes " for the soul of Walter, the son of Allan, his father, and of Eschina de Molla his mother ;" for which they covenanted to celebrate his Obit, as solemnly as for any Monk of their own convent [3]. His liberality was not confined to his own Monastery of Pasly; but the Abby of Melross, founded by King David I. for Monks of the Cistercian order, shared also of his munificence, by his gift of the lands of Mauchlyn, in pure alms, " per devisas suas inter terram de Mauchlyn, et ter-" ram Gilberti filii Richeri, cum tota pastura forestæ suæ usque ad divisas de " Duneglass et Lismahague et de Glengavil :" which donation is ratified by King William. He is an ordinary witness in that King's Charters, under the designation of " Dapifer Regis Scotiæ," as appears from many ancient documents. I conclude all that I have further to say of this Allan, with an account of his marriage with Eve, daughter of " Suanus filius Thori," a person of great account of that time. My authority for this is a confirmation by " Walterus Senescallus," to the Abby of Scone, " de terris in Tippermure quas " Suanus filius Thoraldi, avus ejusdem Walteri, dedit dictis Monachis [4]." The same " Suanus filius Thoraldi" ratifies to the the Abbacy of Holy-rood-house, the claim he had in the church of Travernent [5]: Which Allan, " Dapifer Regis," departing this life, Anno 1204 [6], was buried in the Monastery of Pasly, before the High Altar. And to him succeeded his son,

Walter the First, commonly called Senescallus, who fix'd the office of Stewart, as the Sirname of his family, as a learned author observes [7]. He was a particular favourite of King Alexander II. who bestowed on him the office of Justiciar of Scotland, in the year 1231, as Fordoun relates : And in an. 1238, he was commissioned Ambassador to France, to negociate a marriage betwixt

---

[1] Chartulary of Pasly. [2] Chron: de Melross, in Bib. Jurid. [3] Chartulary of Pasly.
[4] Chartulary of Scoon, from which I had this extract, courteously afforded me by the favour of the honourable and learned Antiquary Mr. Hary Maule of Kelly, brother to the Earl of Panmure. [5] Appendix to the Collections concerning the Scots History. [6] Fordoun's MS. Preface to the Collections concerning the Scots History.

King Alexander, and Mary, daughter of Ingeram Count de Coucy, whom he also attended in her voyage to Scotland.

Thus much as to his civil actions: In his acts of charity and liberality towards the Church, the ordinary test of piety in those superstitious times, he in a manner strove to outdo his ancestors; for, besides his ample confirmation to the Monastery of Pasly, he moreover gave to that Convent, the patronage of the Churches of Seneschar, Dundonald and Auchinleck, with the tithes thereof, and an annuity of six chalders of meal, for the support of a Priest, to celebrate Divine Service, for the soul of Robert Bruce, (Lord of Annandale:) and to the Abby of Balmerinoch, founded by King Alexander II. replenished with Cistercian Monks, he gave " Terras suas in Burgo de Perth¹."

But now the erecting of Monasteries, being discouraged by the Pope's usurping the right of patronage, reserved by the founders, in their Charters of foundation; this diverted the thoughts of persons inclin'd to liberality towards the Church, from building Abbacies, to the setting up of Collegiate Churches and Chaplaries: To promote which, the Ecclesiastical Chanons allowed, to the founders and their heirs, the right of patronage. So Walter, High Stewart of Scotland, founded a religious house of this kind at Dalmulin in Kyle, (a Cell depending on the Monastery of Pasly,) which he endowed with diverse lands and tithes, as will appear from the foundation Charter, and runs thus in the original ² ;

" WALTERUS, Senescallus Scotiæ, Salutem in Domino. Sciatis me,
" divinæ charitatis intuitu, in Honorem Dei & Beatæ Mariæ, fundasse domum
" Canonicorum & Monachorum, Ordinis de Simpringham, in loco qui dicitur
" Dalmulin super Air: Et dictis Monachis concedo, & confirmo in perpetuum,
" totam Terram de Merns, cum omnibus infra istas divisas contentis, sicut
" rivulus descendit in Air, inter novam Villam & fundum Capellæ Sanctæ
" Mariæ; & sic ascendendo per eundem rivulum usque ad divisas de Hauch-
" increw, usque ad terram Ricardi Wallensis de Hauchincrew, & sic per divisas
" ipsius Ricardi usque in Air; & præterea liberam & plenam communem in
" turbariis de Prestvick; & medietatem omnium piscariorum meorum, quæ sunt

---

¹ Register of Balmerinoch, in Bib. Jurid. Edinb.   ² Chartulary of Pasly.

" inter castrum de Air & villam de Irvin. In cujus rei Testimonium, sigillum
" meum apposui. His testibus,

" Waltero Episcopo Glasguensi   Hugone, Filio Reginaldi
" Reginaldo de Crawfurd, Vicecomite de Air Ricardo Wallensi
" Waltero Oliphard, Justitiario Loudoniæ   Johanne de Mungumri
" Malcolmo Locard, &   Hectore de Currie."
" Malcolmo Loccard, Filio ejus

 This renowned person died in the year 1246, and was buried in the Monastery of Pasly; not in 1241, as the Chronicle of Melross bears: For the illustration whereof, I have seen, in the year 1246, a discharge by him to the Convent of Pasly, of an Annuity of two chalders of meal[1]. He left issue (but by whom, I have not found any good authority for), three sons; Alexander his successor; Walter, who became Earl of Monteith, by marrying the Heiress of Walter Cuming Earl of Monteith: Which Walter, Earl of Monteith, is a benefactor to the Monastery of Pasly, by his confirmation of the Church of St. Colmonel in Kintyre, " pro salute animarum Antecessorum suorum, sepultorum " in Monasterio de Pasleto, Anno 1262[2]." But of this Walter, I have seen nothing more on record, but that he, with Alexander and John his sons, and diverse other Scots Peers, enter into an association with Gilbert de Clare Earl of Glocester, wherein they bind themselves to adhere to one another upon all occasions, against all persons whatsoever, their allegiance to their respective sovereigns only excepted; which indenture bears date at Turnberry in Carrick, in the year 1286[3]. But the title of Earl of Monteith went no further in his race, his successor relinquishing the Sirname of Stewart, assumed that of Monteith from their hereditary lands, which in the reign of King Robert the II. determined in a daughter, married to Robert Earl of Fife, son to that King.

 Of Robert, 3d son of Walter, High Stewart of Scotland, issued that illustrious branch of the Stewarts of Darnly, ancestor of the Earls and Dukes of Lenox. (quod vide) To Walter, High Stewart of Scotland, succeeded

 Alexander his son, frequently so designed in Charters recorded in the Register of Pasly. He flourished in the reign of King Alexander III. During which reign, Acho King of Norway, with a great fleet, had transported a numerous army from his country to dispute the right of the western Isles with King

[1] Chartulary of Pasly. [2] Ibid. [3] Dugdale's Baronage of England.

Alexander, landing near the Town of Air. Alexander Stewart of Dundonald, High Stewart of Scotland, being one of the Generals of the Scots Army, they joined battle in a large plain field, near the Burgh of Largs in Cunninghame, where happen'd a terrible and bloody conflict, in which the Scots were victorious, and gave the Norvegians a total defeat, which put a period to their pretensions to the Isles, and forced Acho their King, with the remains of his broken army, to retire in great disorder; which was very much owing to the conduct and valour of this Alexander Stewart, who, according to Fordoun, had the hard fate to lose his life in the battle, which happen'd upon the 8th day of August in the year of our Lord 1263 [1].

I find that he, intending an expedition to Jerusalem, to visit the Holy Grave, which superstitious custom, did very early begin (some authors say) from the time that Helen, the mother of Constantine the Great, did travel to Jerusalem; and her steps were traced by many, both men and women, notwithstanding the great dangers that attended such a journey: Among others, Alexander High Stewart of Scotland, who, to obtain the approbation of the Convent of Pasly to countenance his intended expedition, ratified and confirm'd to the Monastery, all the donations formerly made by his ancestors: and provides, that, in case he should lose his life in that expedition, his successor shall confirm to the Abbacy all grants and privileges bestowed by him or his ancestors on them, " sub periculo Animarum suarum," as the original bears [2].

And having married Jane, daughter of Roderick Lord of Bute, he had issue, two sons, James his successor, (not John, as our Historians have mistaken; for clearing of which, there is a Charter granted by King Robert the II. ratifying a former, " quas Jacobus Senescallus Scotiæ, avus noster fecit Adæ de Fullertoun, Militi, filio quondam Allani de Fullertoun, de terras de Fullertoun in Kyle [3].)" His 2d son was Sir John of Bute, commonly design'd " Frater ger-" manus Domini Jacobi, Senescalli Scotiæ:" He was one of those worthy patriots, who signalized their valour in defence of the liberty of his country, from the oppression of King Edward I. of England; and, at the battle of Falkirk, he contended with Sir William Wallace for the leading the Van of the Scots army: in which engagement he evidenced an equal share of courage and zeal for his country; and fighting gallantly, was there killed upon the . . day of . . . 1298. He mortified to the Abby of Melross, an Annuity of two Pounds of Wax, to light at the Tomb of St. Waldave, for the health of his soul, and of Margaret his wife and their children, dated on Candlemass-day, Anno 1296; leaving issue, by the said Margaret his wife, daughter and heir of Alex-

---

[1] Scoti Chronicon. [2] Chartulary of Pasly. [3] Carta in Publicis Archivia.

ander de Bonkill of Bonkill, Sir Alexander Stewart of Bonkill, his son, who was one of those worthy patriots, who signaliz'd themselves in assisting King Robert Bruce to recover their country. He was father of John, first Earl of Angus, who became possest of the Barony of Abernethy, by marriage of Margaret, the eldest of the three daughters and co-heirs of Alexander Abernethy, Lord of that-ilk. I have seen a Donation, by Margaret, Lady Abernethy, and Countess of Angus, of the lands of Bilicken, Kenbraid, and Bracke, to the Monastery of Arbroath, for the maintenance of a Priest, to celebrate Divine Service every day, at the Altar of St. Catharine the Virgin, within that Monastery, for the safety of the soul of John Stewart, late Earl of Angus, her deceased husband, and for the safety of her own soul and of her ancestors; which is confirmed by King David Bruce, an 1345 [1]. Thomas Stewart, Earl of Angus, his son, dying sans issue, his estate and dignity descended to Margaret, his sister, who married William First Earl of Douglas; of which marriage was born George Douglas Earl of Angus, of whom Achbald Duke of Douglas is now the lineal heir; who carries the Coats of Stewart Earl of Angus, quartered in his Achievement.

James, son and heir of Alexander High Stewart of Scotland, last mentioned, succeeded his father; which James was chosen one of the six Governours of Scotland, appointed by the Estates after the death of King Alexander III. who lost his life by a fall from his horse, upon the sands of Kinghorn, the 18th of April 1285. The Crown thereby devolving upon Margaret his grandchild, (commonly called the maid of Norway) daughter of Erick King of Norway, by Margaret daughter of King Alexander. This young lady, the Scots Queen, King Edward I. of England, by his Ambassadors, demanded in marriage for his son Prince Edward, that thereby the two kingdoms might be united: The Estates of Scotland entertained the proposal, and commissioned James, High Stewart of Scotland, with diverse other Scots Peers, to treat with English Commissioners, authorized by King Edward for that effect, who met at Salisbury, the 26th March 1289 [2], where the match was agreed to, on these terms, that the Kingdom of Scotland should continue free and independent of England; and in case there were no succession of the marriage, the Crown should return to the next heir, and the Kingdom retain both name and dignity of a Kingdom, as before, in holding of Parliaments, making of laws, deciding of all cases within the kingdom; and in a word, to enjoy all the laws, liberties, and customs, they had formerly enjoyed. These articles were agreed to by the commissioners,

---

[1] Register of the Monastery of Arbroth, in the Lawyers Library at Edinburgh.
[2] Mr. Tyrel's History.

as they were also by the estates of Scotland. But this design'd Union came to nothing; for before the arrival of the Scots commissioners in Norway, the Queen was deceased; by whose death there arose a competition of no less than twelve for the Crown: But Robert Bruce and John Baliol were the principal, submitting their claim to the decision of Edward King of England, who assigned them a meeting at Berwick, the 2d of June 1292, for the further prosecuting of their respective claims; appointing also a select number of the nobility of each nation to attend, where King Edward and the commissioners of both kingdoms met on the day appointed, with the auditors of claims that had been elected by them.

For Robert Bruce were elected, Robert Bishop of Glasgow, Matthew Bishop of Dunkeld, the Abbots of Melross and Jedburgh, Patrick Earl of March, Donald Earl of Mar, Walter Earl of Monteith, John Earl of Athol, Malcolm Earl of Lenox, James Lord High Stewart of Scotland, William of Soulis, Nicol of Grahame, John of Lindsay, John Stewart, Alexander of Bonkill, William of Hay, David of Torthorald, John of Calentyr, William of Fenton, Reginald of Crawfurd, Nicol of Campbel, William of Strivelyn, John of Strivelyn, John of Inchmartin, Knights; William of Coningburgh, William of Preston, Gilbert of Coningburgh, and Galfrid of Caldcote.

And by Baliol were chosen, William Bishop of St. Andrews, Henry Bishop of Aberdeen, William Bishop of Dunblain, Henry Bishop of Galloway, Maurice Bishop of the Isles, R. Bishop of Ross; the Abbots of Dunfermling, Holyrood-house, Cumbuskenneth, Kelso, Tungland, and Scone; John Earl of Buchan, Gilbert Earl of Angus, Malise Earl of Strathern, William Earl of Ross; Alexander of Argile, Andrew of Murray, Galfrid of Moubray, Herbert of Mackeswell, Symon Fraser, Patrick of Grahame, William of Santeler, Reginald of Scheen, Nicol of Hay, Richard Frazer, John of Strivelyn of Carse, Michael of Weens, Robert Combron, Michael Scot, Richard of Straton, William of Murray of Tullibardin, William of Meldrum, Ralph of Lasceles, and David of Grahame, Knights.

Now that my reader may more clearly understand their claim, it will be necessary to give the descent of those two noble persons.

Henry Prince of Scotland, son to King David I. who died before his father, left three sons; Malcolm, sirnamed the Maiden, died without issue; William, sirnamed the Lyon, both Kings of Scotland; and David Earl of Huntingtoun. King William had but one son, called Alexander the II. who was father of King Alexander III. who had one daughter, (as was said before) married to Erick King of Norway, by whom she had one daughter, Margaret, Queen of Scotland, who dying without issue, the whole line of King William the Lyon failing, the right of the Crown devolved upon the posterity of David Earl of Huntingtoun; but to which of them it belonged, it seemed hard to determine; for this Earl David had three daughters; Margaret, married to Allan, Lord of Galloway, by whom he had one daughter, Dornagilla, married to John Baliol, by whom she had John Baliol, one of the competitors for the Crown.

The second daughter of David Earl of Huntingtoun, Isobel, married Robert Bruce, Lord of Annandale; (descended, as Sir William Dugdale saith, of Robert Bruce, a noble Norman, who came into England with William the conqueror;) by whom she had Robert Bruce, the competitor with Baliol.

The question was, whether Robert Bruce, the son of the 2d daughter, and the first male, or Dornagilla, the grandchild by the 1st daughter, is to be preferred to the succession of the Crown? Bruce claimed preference to John Baliol, albeit his mother was a younger daughter of David Earl of Huntingtoun, in regard he was a degree nearer than John Baliol; and standing in the same degree with Dornagilla, John Baliol's mother, he a male, was preferable to her a female. The controversy continued for several years; at length, King Edward resolved to decide in favours of him who would subject the Crown to the authority of the King of England; and therefore, applies first to Robert Bruce, but he rejected the proposal with contempt, and replied, That he scorned to enjoy a Crown as thereby to infringe the liberty of his country. King Edward makes the like offer to Baliol, who accepts the base conditions, and so obtains the Crown. Robert Bruce the competitor deceased in an. 1295, leaving issue, by his wife, (who was one of the daughters of Gilbert de Clare, Earl of Glocester) Robert his son and heir, who became Earl of Carrick, in Right of Martha his wife, daughter and sole heir of Alexander Earl of Carrick. For this I shall give the authority of the Chronicle of Melross, which bears an. 1270. " Obiit " Adam de Kilconcath Comes de Carrick, cujus uxorem Comitissam de Carrick, " postea Robertus de Bruce junior accepit in sponsam." They were father and mother of the most renown'd Robert Bruce King of Scotland.

Baliol having thus obtained the Crown, was the first of all the Kings of Scotland, who acknowledged the King of England as superior Lord of that Realm; but on an affront offered by King Edward, in consequence of his subjection, he threw off the English yoke, proclaim'd war against England, and renew'd the league with France, which so incensed that monarch, that he not only deprived him of the Earldom of Huntingtoun in England, but also invaded Scotland both by sea and land; took the town of Berwick by storm, where, our historians say, there were slain 50000 persons. At the same time diverse of the Scots nobility, under the command of Baliol, laid siege to the town of Carlile, and ravaged the adjacent country as far as Hexham, without any opposition. But King Edward encountring the Scots army, gave th͒ m battle, and overthrew them. The English Historians write, the Scots lost an incredible number of men. Baliol having thus lost the most of his country, and entirely the affections of his people, applies to King Edward for peace, and pays him homage a second time: after which he sent him prisoner to the tower of London.

Scotland being brought to this sad and miserable condition, then the famous Sir William Wallace gets up; who, being prompted with a generous ambition of being instrumental in delivering his country from the bondage they were groaning under, carries on the war against the English with good success, having overthrown them in several encounters, with very unequal numbers: In consideration of these signal services, he was chosen Governour of Scotland, in the year 1294. In which character, he behaved with so much resolution and valour, that having obtained several victories over the English, in a short time he reduced all the south parts of Scotland to his obedience, whereby he gain'd immortal honour, and will always be remembered among the most celebrated persons of the age in which he lived. But the Scots, being afterwards defeated by the English at Falkirk, under the conduct of the brave Sir John Stewart of Bute, brother of James High Stewart of Scotland; where, fighting with a great deal of gallantry, he lost his life in that action, which fell out in the year of our Lord 1298: and after this, Scotland did almost entirely submit England. But the tyrannical government of King Edward made the Scots conspire together to recover the liberty of their country, the chief of whom were Robert Bruce Earl of Carrick, (son of that Robert Bruce Lord of Annandale, who had been one of the competitors for the Crown of Scotland,) and John Cuming Earl of Buchan; and for that end, having met together, and conferring about the distressed state of their native country, they agreed between themselves, by indentures mutually sealed and subscribed, That, if by their endeavours, they could be instruments of recovering their country out of the hands of the English, Bruce should be King, and Cuming should be rewarded with the Bruce's estate. But this league lasted not long, for Bruce knowing himself to be suspected by King Edward, in respect of his title to the Crown, thought not fit to stay long in Scotland, and therefore, immediately upon the delivery of the writs foresaid, he went with all expedition to London; but Cuming began to doubt of the success of this conspiracy, and revealed the same to King Edward; and to certify him thereof, sent his part of their indenture. Whereupon King Edward, calling for Bruce, and shewing the indenture, asked him, if he knew his hand writ? Bruce denying that he knew any thing of the matter, desired to have it for one night to puruse at leisure, offering to prove, that it was maliciously forged by Cuming, to take away his life; which if he did not, he should forfeit his estate both in England and Scotland. Upon this seeming confidence of Bruce, King Edward thought it might be a meer trick in Cuming, and therefore granted him his desire. He was not long out of the King's presence, when the Earl of Glocester, Bruce's cousin, sent him a pair of spurrs and some Crowns of Gold: Bruce understanding the meaning of this message, caused immediately horses, for himself and his servants, to be shod the contrary way, to prevent their being followed; and departing out of London about midnight, he came with all expedition to his own house of Lochmaben in Scotland; where, our historians say, he found Edward Bruce his brother, Robert Fleming, James Lindsay, Roger Kilpatrick, and Thomas Charters, to whom he gave an account of the danger he escaped: upon which he had resolved to go in search of Cuming. The motion being entertained by the above-named gentlemen, who still stood firm to his interest; and understanding by a servant of Cuming's, whom they apprehended on his way for London, with letters to King Edward, desiring Bruce might be dispatch'd in haste; for being a nobleman much favoured by the people, he might prove a troublesome enemy: and by this means they not only made a further discovery of Cuming's treachery, but came also to understand he was at Dumfries, where they hasted, and found him in the church at his devotion. Having shewed him his letters, Bruce stabbed him, the blow being followed by the rest of his retinue. This slaughter fell out on the 9th of February 1306. And by this treachery of Cuming, his family, which was then one of the greatest and most potent of any in Scotland, was brought so low, that there are but few gentlemen of the name of Cuming in Scotland remaining.

Bruce having thus rid himself of his principal enemy, was immediately joined by some of those brave Scots, who had opposed the English usurpation; such as, Malcolm Earl of Lenox, John Earl of Athol, Sir Neil Campbel of Lochhow, Sir Gilbert Hay of Errol, Sir Christopher Seaton of that-ilk, Sir Thomas Randel, Sir John Summervel of Carnwath, Sir David Barclay, Sir Alexander Frazer, Sir Robert Boyd (afterwards) of Kilmarnock, and Sir William Haliburton. With this company he went to Scoon, where, upon the . . . day of April, in the year of our Lord 1306, he was crowned King of Scotland, with as much solemnity as the state of affairs would allow of. But the actions of this most celebrated Monarch, who, by invincible courage and valour, retrieved his country from the English subjection, and overthrew their numerous army with a terrible slaughter at Bannockburn, consisting of one hundred thousand men, with an army of resolute and well disciplined men, not above thirty thousand in all; and after a reign of twenty-five years full of war, died in peace, the 7th day of June, an. 1329, I leave to the relation of our historians, in regard these things would be too long to descend on here.

But to return to James High Stewart of Scotland, who, as I observ'd, was very much concerned in all the transactions of the kingdom, from the time of King Alexander III.'s death, when he was chosen one of the Governours of Scotland, until King Robert was settled on the Throne, which he survived only three years; his death happened July 16th, in the year 1309: he was buried in the Monastery of Pasly among his ancestors, to which he was also a benefactor, by his ample confirmation of all donations, by his predecessors, to that Abby, in the year 1294. He was married to . . . . Dunbar, daughter to the Earl of March, then one of the most potent families of Scotland; by whom he had Walter, his son and heir, and James, who obtained the Barony of Duiresdeer from King Robert I. He was ancestor of the Stewarts of Rosyth in Fife, whose posterity failed but lately in the person of William Stewart of Rosyth.

Walter, son of James High Stewart of Scotland, was a person of a very martial spirit, being one of those noble Scots who assisted King Robert in his wars, for recovering the liberty of Scotland, and one of the generals of the Scots army, at the famous battle of Bannockburn, which was fought the 25th of June 1314, where the English received the greatest overthrow they ever met with from this nation; which so much discouraged the English, that a hundred of them, says Walsinghame, would flee from three Scots. In this engagement Walter High Stewart of Scotland, did so eminently signalize his valour and conduct, that King Robert, as a mark of his royal favour, did confer on him the honour of knighthood.

And in Anno 1316, when King Robert passed over to Ireland, to assist his brother Edward, Earl of Carrick, then King of Ireland, he appointed Sir Walter Stewart, and Sir James Douglas, Governours, in his absence; and upon the taking of Berwick by the Scots, Sir Walter Stewart of Scotland was made Governour thereof, which he most valiantly defended against the English; the circumstances of which are related at large by some of our historians: yea, the King had such an esteem of his worth, that, as a reward of his eminent services, he bestowed upon him in marriage, with consent of his Parliament, the Lady Marjory, his only daughter, (by Isobel his first Queen, daughter of Gratney Earl of Marr,) and at that time the apparent heir of his crown. By this royal match the Stewart of Scotland, obtained by a Charter, dated at Berwick, in portion with her, many lands, which will best appear from an extract of that grant yet extant [1].

" ROBERTUS Dei Gratia Rex Scotorum; Sciatis, me dedisse dilecto & fi-
" deli nostro Waltero Senescallo Scotiæ, in liberum maritagium cum Marjoria Filia
" nostra Baroniam de Bathgeto, Baroniam de Rathoe, cum terra de Riccartoun,
" & terras de Barns juxta Linlithgow, & terram quæ vocatur le Brome, prope
" lacum ejusdem, & terras de Bonningtoun, Kingalach & Gallowhill juxta Lin-
" lithgow, & annuum reditum de Carse, Stirlyn, quas Abbas & Canonici Monas-
" terii Sanctæ Crucis de Edinburgh tenent de nobis, & annuum reditum centum
" solidorum percipiendi de terra de Kinpunt, & terram de Ednam in Vicecomi-
" tatu de Roxburgh; tenend: eodem Walt: & hæredibus suis inter ipsum & dic-
" tam Marjoriam Filiam nostram procreandis," &c.

But this Lady died upon the . day of October, Anno 1317, as some relate, in this manner: Riding betwixt Pasly and the Castle of Renfrew, then the principal residence of the Great Stewart of Scotland her husband, she was thrown from her horse, and by the fall suffered a dislocation of the vertebræ of her neck; she being pregnant fell in labour (of King Robert II.) the child or fœtus, as they report, was a Cæsar: The operation being by an unskilful hand, his eye was touch'd by the instrument, which afterwards proved incurable, from which he was called King Bleareie. She died upon the spot; and on the fatal place where this accident happened, there was erected a cross, yet standing, called Queen Bleareie's Cross.

By the said Lady Marjory Bruce, Walter High Stewart of Scotland had a son, Robert, of whom afterwards. I have seen a donation, by Walter High Stewart of Scotland, in an. 1318, of the patronage of the Church of Largs, with the tithes thereto belonging, to the Monks of Pasly, " for the welfare of the soul of Marjory Bruce, his deceased wife." He married a second wife, by whom he had a son, Sir John Stewart, who is designed brother to Robert Earl of Strathern, in a donation by that Earl to the Church of Glasgow, an. 1364. I'm informed he was ancestor of Stewart of Ralstoun. He had likeways a daughter, called Giles, married to Sir James Lindsay, son and heir of Sir James Lindsay of Crawfurd. Take for authority of this a Charter granted by King Ro-

[1] Haddingtoun's Collections.

bert II. to Sir James Lindsay his nephew, of the Castle and Barony of Crawfurd. The said Giles married for a second husband, Sir Hugh Eglintoun of that-ilk. For this I have seen a Charter granted by King Robert II. " Dilecto " fratri suo Hugoni de Eglintoun, Militi, de tota terra de Bonnietoun, & di- " midietatem terrarum de Nortoun, in Vicecomitatu de Edinburgh." As also I have seen, in the Publick Register, a Charter granted by that King to Sir Hugh Eglintoun of that-ilk and Giles his wife, the King's sister, of the lands of Lochliboeside in Renfrewshire, in the year 1374.

This much as to the civil actions of this illustrious person; what respected his works of piety, I find only this memorable note; that he gave in pure alms to the Abby of Dryburgh, (founded by Hugh Morvel, Constable of Scotland, inhabited by the Monks of the order of Premontre,) the patronage of the church of Maxtoun, with the church lands thereto belonging. Which gift he expresses to be made for the safety of his soul, &c. and thereto appends his seal. And, departing this life in the 1326, at Bathget, he was solemnly interred at Pasly; which Mr. Barbour, in the Life of King Robert Bruce, expresses thus:

> When long time they their dule had made
> The corps to Pasly have they had,
> And there with great solemnity,
> And with great dule eirded was he.

To Walter, High Stewart of Scotland, succeeded,

Robert his son; which Robert obtained from King Robert Bruce, his grandfather, the lands of Langnewtoun, Maxtoun and Cavertoun, fallen to the Crown by the forfaulture of William de Soules. During the war against the English, he did, in a most signal manner, manifest his conduct and valour in defence of the independency of his country, and of his uncle, King David Bruce's title, against Edward Baliol, to his immortal honour: He was unanimously chosen Governour of Scotland, in his uncle's (King David) absence, in the year 1338, which he retrieved from the English and Baliol's claim, and established King David in possession of his Crown: But in the year 1348, the Scots being defeat at the battle of Durham, and the King taken prisoner, he was a second time elected Governour of the kingdom; which eminent station he discharged faithfully, until the King returned, in an. 1359, who bestowed on his nephew, Robert, High Stewart of Scotland, the Earldom and dignity of Strathern, in reward of his faithful services; which title he enjoyed until the death of King David, in an.

1370, that the Crown devolved upon him, and he was crowned at Scoon the 27th of March that year. In the beginning of his reign, he had some encounters with the English, wherein he was successful; which the French King hearing of, sent his ambassadour to Scotland, to congratulate his happy success, and requesting him never to lay down arms till he was reveng'd of the English; and also to renew the league betwixt the two Crowns, which was solemnly done at Edinburgh: and to confirm the same league, King Robert sent Cardinal Wardlaw, Bishop of Glasgow, to France; which accordingly was done at Paris, to the satisfaction of both parties. But the history of the wars King Robert had with the English, I leave to the relation of our historians, and so I proceed to take notice of his marriage and issue.

Our historians relate, That before his marriage with Eupham Ross, he had three sons by Elizabeth More, a concubine, while he was Earl of Strathern and Stewart of Scotland; which Elizabeth, say they, was not his wife until the 3d year of his reign, that his Queen died. This scandalous aspersion, that's not only injurious to the succeeding kings of Scotland, but to many other foreign Princes, who have intermarried with our Royal Family, is absolutely false in itself, as will appear from many original Charters, and other authentick records yet extant, such as;

I. That the said Elizabeth More was the first and lawful wife of King Robert II. when Stewart of Scotland, doth evidently appear from an authentick Charter, in the Archives of the Scots College at Paris, which bears date Jan. 12. Anno Dom. 1364, wherein he founds a Chaplanry in the Cathedral Church of Glasgow, and that in performance of an obligation he lay under to the Bishop of that see. The Pope's Legate dispensing with a marriage betwixt him " et " quondam Elizabeth More dum ageret in humanis, non obstante impedimento " consanguinitatis & affinitatis." Which Grant is six years before his accession to the Crown; which proves it false that she died the third year of his reign.

II. John Lord Kyle and Earl of Carrick, King Robert's eldest son by Elizabeth More, was not only owned by his father, by several public instruments, both before and after his accession to the Crown, as his eldest lawful son and apparent heir; but also by King David Bruce and Queen Eupham Ross his mother-in-law. For authority of this, though very many proofs might be given, yet I shall only adduce these. There is a Charter of confirmation by Robert Earl of Strathern, and John Lord Kyle, his son and apparent heir, of a mortification of the lands of Coudams and Camesestrang, by Reginald More, father of

Sir William More of Abercorn, to the Monks of Pasly[1]. And under that title and relation he was owned by King David Bruce his grand uncle, in a confirmation of the Pope's Bull, allowing the Bishops to dispose in testament upon their own moveables: In which Charter " Robertus Senescallus, Comes de " Strathern, Nepos noster, & Johannes Senescallus, Comes de Carrick, filius " suus primogenitus & hæres," are mentioned witnesses. As also there is a Charter granted, an. 1371, of the lands and castle of Kinross, by King Robert, in favours of Eupham Ross his Queen; " Joannes Comes de Carrick, filius " noster natu maximus & hæres," is a witness thereto: Which is an unanswerable proof of the legitimacy of his birth.

III. For a further vindication of the Royal line, it appears evidently, on record, that the three Estates conveen'd in Parliament, upon King Robert's coming to the Crown, yea on the very day of his Coronation, His Majesty declared, " that, whenever it should happen him to depart this life, that, John, Earl of Carrick and Stewart of Scotland, should and ought to be his lawful heir, and succeed him in the Kingdom." Which Act of Parliament is yet extant in the Publick Records, to which the great seal is appended, with 52 seals of the Prelates, Noblemen and Barons assembled in Parliament. By which it plainly appears there was no bastardy in the case of King Robert III. and that he needed not the assistance of an Act of the Estates, to capacitate him to succeed; but that his title is clear beyond all controversy and dispute.

And it is also evident, that Elizabeth More, daughter of Sir Adam More of Rouallan, was so far from being an obscure person, or a concubine, that she was a lady of good quality, and so nearly related to Robert Earl of Strathern, her husband, that he was obliged to procure the Pope's dispensation to marry her. And I'm informed, one of the Barons of Rouallan was married with a daughter of one of the High Stewarts of Scotland; and they standing in the degree of consanguinity, forbidden by the Cannon Law, gave occasion to the dispensation for their marriage. The family of Rouallan is one of the ancientest in the Shire of Air, and possest of an opulent fortune, for many ages. Their ancestor " David de More," in the reign of King Alexander II. is mentioned witness in a Charter to Hugh Crawfurd, of the lands of Stevenstoun, an 1246[2]. Which family is now represented by Jean, daughter and sole heir of William More of Rouallan, wife to David Earl of Glasgow.

[1] Chartulary of Pasly.

[2] Preface to the Observation concerning the Scots History.

The Children of King Robert II. by Elizabeth More.

I. John Earl of Carrick, afterwards King of Scotland, by the name of Robert III.

II. Walter, who married Isobel MacDuff, daughter and sole heir of Duncan Earl of Fife; but he died without succession.

III. Robert, who obtained the Earldom of Monteith, by marriage of Margaret, daughter and heir of Murdoch Earl of Monteith. He was afterwards created Duke of Albany, by King Robert III. an. 1399, and chosen Governour of Scotland: but of him and his posterity I shall treat afterwards.

IV. Alexander of Badenoch, created Earl of Buchan by his father, the fifth year of his reign. He married Eupham, daughter and coheir of William Earl of Ross, in right of whom he assumed that title: Alexander Stewart, Earl of Mar, was his son, who obtained that Earldom by marriage of Isobel Douglas, Countess of Mar, only daughter of William first Earl of Douglas, and of Margaret his wife, sister and heir of Thomas Earl of Mar. For this I have seen a resignation, in the year 1404, by Isobel Countess of Mar, in favours of Alexander Stewart, eldest son of Alexander Earl of Buchan, " causa matrimonii " contracti inter eundem Alex. & nos." He was commander in chief of the army at the battle of Harlaw, an. 1411, where he gave sufficient proof of his being a brave General. He deceased without succession in the year 1436.

V. Marjory, married John Dunbar, son of George Earl of March, with whom he obtained the Earldom of Murray. For this I have seen a Charter granted by King Robert II. " Dilecto Filio suo Johanni de Dunbar, & Mar- " joriæ sponsæ suæ, filiæ nostræ charissimæ, de toto comitatu Moraviæ," in the year 1372 [1]. Whose successor, James Earl of Murray, dying without succession, his estate and dignity went, by Ann his daughter and heiress, to Archbald Douglas, brother of James Earl of Douglas, who was forfeited with others of their kindred, by King James II. Anno 1455.

VI. Jean, to Sir John Lyon, (called the White Lyon, from his complexion,) with whom he obtained the Baronies of Glames and Kinghorn, an. 1379 [2]. And in honour of this royal match he got the double Tressure added to his arms, and the Crest belonging thereto, viz. A lady above the middle, enh circled with laurels. He was preferred by that King to the office of Lord Hig-

---

[1] Carta in Publicis Archivis. [2] Carta penes Jo. Comitem de Strathmore.

Chancellor of Scotland. John now Earl of Strathmore is his lineal heir. After the death of Sir John Lyon, the Lady Jean Stewart married Sir James Sandelands of Calder. For this I have seen a Charter by King Robert II. of the lands of Slamanan, &c. " Jacob. Sandelins, Militi, & hæredibus inter ipsum " & Jeanam, filiam nostram procreandis, quam Deo duce, ducet in uxorem[1]."

VII. Elizabeth was married to Sir Thomas Hay of Errol, by whom he obtained the lands of Inchtuthill. There is a grant by King Robert, an. 1372, of an annuity out of the said lands, " Tho. Hay Constabulario Scotiæ, & Eliza- " beth sponsæ suæ filiæ nostræ charissimæ;" of whom is Charles Earl of Errol lineally descended.

VII. Margaret, to John MacDonald, Lord of Yla. There is a Charter in the publick rolls, by King Robert II. an. 1376, to Joh. of Yla and Margaret his spouse, the King's daughter, of the lands of Lochaber and Knoydart[2].

IX. Catherine, married David Lindsay, Earl of Crawfurd. I have seen a Charter by King Robert II. to David Lindsay of Glenesk, his son-in-law, of the lands of Glenesk and Strathnairn, upon his own resignation; whose successor is John Earl of Crawfurd.

X. Giles, married William Douglas, son to the Lord of Galloway, with whom he obtained the Lordship of Nithsdale; for which there is extant a Charter in the publick records, by King Robert II. " Willielmo Douglas & Egidiæ " sponsæ suæ, filiæ nostræ charissimæ." His great endowments both of body and mind, and his approven merit, procured him the honours of Duke of Spruce and Prince of Danskin. He was treacherously kill'd by the Lord Clifford, in an. 1390, leaving issue, by the said Giles his wife, one daughter, called Giles, married to Henry Santclair Earl of Orkney, of whom is descended Henry Lord Santclair.

King Robert II. after the death of Elizabeth More, married Eupham Ross, daughter of Hugh Earl of Ross, and Dowager of John Randolph Earl of Murray.

The Issue of King Robert II. by Eupham Ross.

I. David, on whom he conferred the Earldom of Strathern, and created him into that dignity, in the year 1370; but dying without male succession, his estate and honours devolved on Eupham, his daughter and sole heir, who married Patrick Grahame, younger son of Sir Patrick Grahame of Kincardine,

T

[1] Carta in Publicis Archivis.   [2] Carta in Rotulis Rob: II.

ancestor to the Duke of Montrose, of whom descended the Earls of Monteith; which came to a period but lately in the person of William Earl of Airth.

II. Walter, who obtained the lands of Badenoch from his father, in the year 1370, and was afterwards created Earl of Athol. He married Margaret, daughter and heiress of Sir David Barclay of Brichen, by whom he had David his eldest son, who died in England, one of the hostages for the ransom of King James I. Allan, his second son, was created Earl of Caithness by that Prince; He was killed at the battle of Innerlochy, by Donald Balloch, an. 1428; so his estate returned to the Crown. This Walter, Earl of Athol, was the principal actor in the murther of King James I. his nephew, which proceeded (if we believe our historians) from a response he had from some of his Highlanders, in whom he had great confidence, who assured him, that before his death he should be crown'd in a solemn assembly. For which horrid and unnatural crime, the sentence of death was execute upon him in a most exemplary manner, famous over all Europe.

III. Isobel, married to the brave James Earl of Douglas, to whose personal valour was in a great measure owing that signal victory obtained over the English at Otterburn; which action fell out in the year 1388, but with the loss of himself. By this lady he had no issue. She married, secondly, Sir John Edmonstoun: For this there is a Charter by King Robert II. " Jo. Edmonstoun " de Baronia de Edenham, & Isobellæ Comitissæ de Douglas, filiæ nostræ."

Natural Issue of King Robert II.

I. Sir John Stewart, Sheriff of Bute, commonly called the Black Stewart: For this I have seen a Charter under the great seal, by King Robert III. of an annuity of 10 Merks Sterling, to Sir Adam Forrester, out of the customs of Edinburgh. In which grant " Johanne Senescallo Vicecomite de Bute, fratre " nostro naturali," is a witness; and is dated, 15th of February, in the year 1404 [1]. Moreover, there is a Charter in the publick records, by Robert Duke of Albany, when Governour of Scotland, dated, at Rothsay, the 24th of August 1408, to John Campbel of Loudoun, of the lands of Chaluckbreks in Carrick; to which " Johanne Senescallo fratre suo naturali, Vicecomite de Bute," is a witness.

II. Sir John Stewart of Dundonald, commonly called the Red Stewart, from his complexion; on whom King James I. his nephew, conferr'd the honour of

---

[1] Charter in the hands of Mr. James Robertoun, Advocate.

Knighthood, at the solemnity of his Coronation, an. 1424. But the same year James Stewart, son of Murdoch, Duke of Albany, upon his father's imprisonment, accompanied with a number of outlaws, came to the town of Dunbartoun, set it on fire, and surprized Sir John Stewart of Dundonald, whom he killed, with several others.

III. Thomas, Arch-Deacon of St. Andrews; who, upon the death of Walter Trail Bishop of that See, an. 1401, was elected Bishop of St. Andrews: but he, affecting a retired life, would never accept the Episcopal Dignity; so that the See continued vacant till his death, which happened an. 1404.

Natural Children of King Robert II. by Marion de Cardney, daughter of John Cardney of That-ilk.

I. John, who obtained the lands of Kincleven in Perthshire, from his father, as appears from a Charter yet extant in the public rolls, " dilecto filio " nostro Johanni Senescallo, genito inter nos & Mariotam de Cardney, Anno " regni nostri 12."

II. James, who obtained the lands of Kinfauns in Perthshire.

III. Alexander, who had a grant from his father of the lands of Lunan in Forfarshire, of whom the Stewarts of Doually descended.

King Robert II. departing this life at his castle of Dundonald, the 13th day of May 1390, the 20th year of his reign, and 74th of his age, his Crown and imperial dignity devolved upon John Earl of Carrick, Prince and Stewart of Scotland, his eldest son; but the name of John being ill liked by the nation, on account of John Baliol, he chang'd it, and was crowned King by the name of Robert III. (John Fairnyear.) The universal mistake of our historians, concerning the illegitimacy of his birth, which I have touched already, is now effectually removed by the learned Earl of Cromarty, in his Vindication of that Prince from the imputation of bastardy; who has shown, from undeniable and authentick records, that his father (King Robert) was first married to Rouallan's daughter: to which I refer my reader. This king being but a weak Prince, and disabled to travel, by a stroke he had accidentally received from a horse of Sir James Douglas of Dalkeith's, he appointed Robert Earl of Fife, his brother, Governour of the kingdom, whom he created Duke of Albany, an. 1399: during whose administration the English invaded Scotland, and wasted the southern countries, but were repulsed by the valour of the Earl of Douglas; which Buchanan, our renown'd historian, relates at large; to which I refer my reader. King Robert was married to Annabella, daughter of Sir John Drummond of Stobhall, ancestor to the Earl of Perth.

Children of King Robert III. by Annabella Drummond.

I. David Prince and Stewart of Scotland; who being a youth of a riotous temper, was committed, by his father, to the care and inspection of his uncle Robert, Duke of Albany, Governour of the Realm; but he being an ambitious man, and aspiring at the Crown, caused imprison his nephew in the Castle of Faulkland, and ordered him to be starved; yet his life was preserved, as our historians relate, for some time, by the charity of two poor women, one of which afforded him some oat bread through a chink of the wall, and the other gave him milk from her breasts: but the Governour having discovered them, they were both put to death; the poor Prince being reduced to feed on the members of his own body, and to die amidst the agonies of famine and torture, in an. 1401, and was buried at Lindors Abby. But the punishment due such an unnatural and inhuman crime, which himself, by the long suffering patience of GOD, felt not, his son Murdoch Duke of Albany, and two of his sons, suffered, being condemn'd for treason, upon King James I.'s return from England, in an. 1424, for which they lost their heads.

II. James Prince of Scotland, of whose preservation the King became very solicitous; and, to secure him from the attempts of the Duke of Albany, sends him to Charles VI. of France, appointing Henry Santclair, Earl of Orkney, his Governour; who taking shipping with him at the Bass, with several others of the Scots nobility and gentry, either by stress of weather or sea sickness, they were necessitated to land upon the English coast: and, notwithstanding there was then a truce betwixt the two nations, yet he and his whole company were detained prisoners. This fell out upon the 30th of March in the year 1404.

III. Margaret, married to Archbald Duke of Tourainne, Earl of Douglas, Lord Longueville, and Mareschal of France; by whom she had issue Archbald and James, successively Earls of Douglas.

IV. Mary, married first to George Earl of Angus, in an. 1396, as is evident from the contract yet extant. This Earl was taken prisoner at the battle of Homilden, an. 1402, and died that year in his return from England, leaving issue, by the said Lady Mary his wife, William Earl of Angus, who was General of the Scots at Piperdein, an. 1436. His Lady surviving him, remarried James Kennedy of Dunnure, in an. 1404, and by him she had issue Gilbert, first Lord

Kennedy; (created into that dignity by King James II.) He was one of the Governours to King James III. David Lord Kennedy, his son, was created Earl of Cassils, by King James IV. and was killed at the battle of Floudoun: Of whom John now Earl of Cassils is the lineal heir. She married 3dly, Sir William Grahame of Mugdock and Kincardine, ancestor to the Duke of Montrose; by whom she had Robert, author of that branch of the Grahames of Fintrie in Angus; and Patrick, who was Archbishop of St. Andrews.

A Natural Son of King Robert III.

John Stewart of Ardgowan, who by three several Charters obtained the lands of Blackhall, Ardgowan and Achingoun: of whom Sir Archbald Stewart of Blackhall, Baronet, is lineally descended.

After King Robert III.'s death, an. 1406, Robert Duke of Albany was Governour of Scotland; in which eminent station he continued till his death, which fell out an. 1419. The Government of the Realm was committed to Murdoch, Duke of Albany, his son; who being but a weak Prince, and of an easy nature, all things went into disorder, and his own sons became not only a grievance to their father, but to the bulk of the nation. To remeid all which disorders, the Duke called a Parliament, wherein it was agreed, that some of their number should be sent to England, to treat about the redemption of their King; and accordingly the states nominated, for that effect, Archbald Earl of Douglas, William Hay Earl of Errol, Constable of Scotland, Alexander Irvine of Drum, Henry Lighton, Bishop of Aberdeen, and Alexander Cornwal, Arch-Dean of Lothian. These, coming to London, were very favourably received by the English, and had several conferences with their Sovereign King James: At length, having desired audience in Council, they were admitted, where Bishop Lightoun delivered the following speech:

" MY LORDS,

" THE respect and reverence, which the Scots nation carrieth towards all
" Kings, is every where known, but most that love and loyalty which they have
" to the sacred persons of their own native Princes; for as Monarchy is the most
" ancient form of government, so have they ever esteem'd it the best, it being
" more easy to find one instructed and train'd up in heroical virtues, than to find
" many: and how well soever Governours and Vicegerents rule the common-

"wealth, yet is that Government but as the light of the moon or stars in ab-
"sence of the sun, and but representations of shadows for real bodies. This
"hath moved the three Estates of that Kingdom to direct us here unto you.

"Our King these many years hath been kept from us, upon just or unjust
"grounds, we will not argue. That Providence, which hath appointed every
"thing to its own end, hath done this for the best, both to you and us; and we
"are now to treat with you for his delivery, beseeching you to remember, that
"his father, of sacred memory, recommended him, out of that general duty
"that one Prince oweth to another, to your King's protection, in hope of
"sanctuary, and in request of aid and comfort against his secret, and conse-
"quently his most dangerous enemies: and we must confess, that, hitherto, he
"hath been better and more secure amongst you, than if he had been in his
"own native country; for your favours have been many ways extended to-
"wards him, having brought him up in all liberal sciences and arts; so that
"his abode with you seemeth rather to have been a remaining in an academy
"than in any captivity, and that he had been lost if he had not been lost. Be-
"sides, though we have the happiness to claim his birth and stem, ye have the
"claim of his succession and education, he being now match'd with the royal
"blood of England (for he had married the Earl of Sommerset's daughter) so that
"his liberty, which we ask, is a benefit to yourselves and those Princes which
"shall claim the descent of his offspring. For if it should fall forth (as what
"may not, by the variable changes of kingdoms, come to pass) that this Prince
"should be dethron'd, 'tis your swords that should restore him to the posses-
"sion of his royal diadem; and we expect, that as you have many times ren-
"dered him yours, you will not refuse to engage him yet more by his liberty,
"which he must acknowledge wholly and freely to receive from you; and, by
"benefits and love, to overcome a king, is more than by force of arms. And
"since he was not your prisoner by chance of war, (since he never rais'd arms
"against you) but by way of protection detained here and entertained; so we
"expect, that you will act according to your ancient honour and generosity,
"and send him freely back to his own. Yet if it be so, that you will have an
"acknowledgement for what ye have bestowed on his education, the distress
"of the present state of his Subjects and Crown considered, we will not stand
"upon trifles of money; for the redemption of a Prince is above all price."

The Governour and Estates of Scotland, being acquainted with the sum
required for the ransom of the Prince, a part of it was quickly raised, and hostages sent for the rest; who were, David Stewart, eldest son of Walter Earl of

Athol; Alexander Earl of Crawfurd; Alexander Master of Huntly; Malis Grahame Earl of Strathern; Patrick Lyon, son and heir of Sir John Lyon of Glames; Sir William Ruthven; Sir David Ogilvy; and David Moubray. These were honourably received at the English Court; but several of them died before they were redeemed.

The King was accompanied to the borders of Scotland by several of the English nobility and gentry, who there taking their leave, returned back. And the King, with a splendid retinue, arrived at Edinburgh in the month of April; and passing from thence to Perth, in the month of May following, with his Queen, they were solemnly crowned at Scoon. At which solemnity, His Majesty was pleased to confer the honour of Knighthood on the following persons, viz. Alexander Stewart, son to Murdoch Duke of Albany; Archbald Earl of Douglas; William Earl of Angus; George Earl of March; Adam Hepburn of Hales; Thomas Hay of Locheret; Walter Ogilvy; Walter Haliburton of Dirltoun; David Stewart of Rosyth; Alexander Seton of Gordon; Patrick Ogilvy of Auchterhouse; John Stewart of Dundonald; David Mackay of Gask; John Stewart of Cairdin; William Hay of Errol; John Scrimzeor Constable of Dundee; Alexander Irvine of Drum; Herbert Maxwel of Carlaverock; Herbert Herris of Teregles; Andrew Gray of Foules; Robert Cunninghame of Kilmaures; Alexander Ramsay of Dalhousie; and William Crichton of that-ilk.

Upon the King's return to Edinburgh, he called a Parliament, in which was enacted a subsidy for relieving the hostages then remaining in England for his ransom: and dissolving the Parliament, he went for Perth, where, having assembled all the present officers, and such as had born authority in the state during the Government of the Dukes of Albany, he understood that most part of the Royal revenue was bestowed by the Governours on their friends and dependents. Upon this, Sir Walter Stewart, the Duke of Albany's son, was sent prisoner to the Bass, as also Malcolm Fleming of Cumbernauld, and several others, were committed to prison, but afterwards released. The King called a second Parliament, wherein Murdoch Duke of Albany, the late Governour, Walter and Sir Alexander Stewarts, his sons, and Duncan Earl of Lenox, his father-in-law, were attainted of treason, and found guilty by a jury, consisting of the following persons, viz.

Walter Earl of Athol	Sir Thomas Sumerveil of Carnwath
Archbald Earl of Douglas	Sir Herbert Herris of Teregles
Alexander Earl of Ross, Lord of the Isles	Sir James Douglas of Dalkeith
Alexander Stewart Earl of Mar	Sir Robert Cunninghame of Kilmaures

William Earl of Angus	Sir Alexander Livingston of Callender
William Earl of Orkney	Sir Thomas Hay of Yester,
George Earl of March	Sir William Borthwick of that-ilk
James Douglas of Balveny,	Sir Alexander Ogilvy, Sheriff of Angus
Gilbert Hay of Errol, Constable of Scotl:	Sir John Forrester of Corstorphine,
Robert Stewart of Lorn	Sir Walter Ogilvy of Lintrethan
Sir John Montgomery of Ardrossan	

And the same day upon which the sentence was pronounced, the Duke's two sons, Walter and Alexander, were beheaded ; and the next day, the Duke himself and the Earl of Lenox lost their heads.

The war continuing betwixt the English and the French, Charles VII. of France sent Sir John Stewart of Darnly, Archbald Earl of Douglas, both Mareschals of that kingdom, with the Archbishop of Rheims, Ambassadors to Scotland, to renew the ancient League betwixt the two Crowns, and to propose a match betwixt Lewis the Dauphin, King Charles's son, and the lady Margaret, King James's daughter; which was agreed to. Whereupon four thousand soldiers were levied and sent to France, in the year 1426.

The English foreseeing the inconveniences that would arise from this match, sent the Lord Scroop Ambassador into Scotland, with the proposal of a breach with France, and a marriage betwixt the lady Margaret, King James's daughter, and Henry VI. their King; but it was resolved that the French should be satisfied in their demands. Whereupon the English Ambassador from fair words went to threatning ; but the King was so far from being moved by this, that he immediately caused prepare a fleet of 46 good ships, under the command of Henry Earl of Orkney, Admiral of Scotland ; and putting to sea with the lady Margaret, she landed safely at Rochel, and from thence, passed to Tours, where, with extraordinary pomp and magnificence, she was married to the Dauphin, on the 24th of June 1436. The English, after this disappointment, invaded Scotland with an army of 4000 men, under the command of Henry Earl of Northumberland, against whom the King sent an army, under the conduct of William Earl of Angus, his nephew, who defeat the English in battle at a place called Piperdein. The action happened in the year 1436.

The King, encouraged by this victory, resolved to invade England with an army, and accordingly marched the length of Roxburgh, and laid siege to the Castle. But when the English garrison was just about to surrender, the Queen came to the camp, representing to her husband a conspiracy against his life;

FAMILY OF STEWART. 161

upon which he immediately disbanded his army, and returned home, and, for his greater safety, retired to the Monastery of the Carthusians at Perth.

The conspirators were, Robert Grahame Tutor of Strathern, Robert Stewart, grandchild of Walter Earl of Athol; but the prime contriver and actor was the Earl of Athol himself, the King's uncle. These having concerted the measures they were to follow, came in the night to Perth, and, entering the Monastery, they made their way with little difficulty, where the King was, whom they most cruelly murthered, upon the 21st day of February an. 1436, in the 44th year of his age, and the 13th of his reign.

This Prince was, both for the endowments of body and mind, one of the bravest Kings of the age he lived in. He was a great master in all the liberal arts and sciences, but especially in poetry, mathematicks, and politicks: and though he used to complain of the prodigality of his ancestors in exhausting so much of the Revenue, to found and enrich religious houses, and used to call King David I. (commonly called St. David) " a sore Saint to the Crown;" yet did he not refrain from building a beautiful Monastery at Perth for Carthusian Monks, where he was interred.

He was married to Jean, daughter of John Beaufort Earl of Somerset, son to John Duke of Lancaster, by whom he had these children:

I. James, born an. 1430, who succeeded him in the kingdom: Of whom afterwards.

II. Margaret, married Lewis XII. of that name, King of France; she died in the year 1449 without succession [1].

III. Isobel, married Francis I. Duke of Bretaigne, who deceased Anno 1450; by whom she had three daughters; (1) Margaret, married to Francis of Bretaigne, Count de Estampes, and Lord of Clisson; (2) Catharine, to John Lord of Rohan, and Viscount Lyons; (3) Frances, to John Lord d'Albret.

IV. Jean, married James Earl of Angus, who seasonably assisted Sir Alexander Livingston and Sir William Crichton, Governours of Scotland in the minority of King James II. against his chief the Earl of Douglas. He died, an. 144 , without issue. She married afterwards George, 2d Earl of Huntly, by whom she had (1) Alexander, 3d Earl of Huntly, his successor, of whom George Duke of Gordon is lineally descended; (2) Adam Gordon, who married Elizabeth, sister and sole heir to John Earl of Sutherland; of whom John now Earl of Sutherland is the lineal heir. (3) Sir William Gordon, slain at the battle of Floudoun; (4) Catharine Gordon, given in marriage, by King James

U

[1] History of France.

III. to Perkin Warbeck, the impostor, Duke of York; but to him she had no issue. After his death she married Sir Matthew Craddock in Glamorganshire in Wales[1]. The Lady Jean surviving her 2d husband, was married a third time unto James Lord Dalkeith, created into the dignity of Earl of Morton, by King James II. an. 1457, by whom she had John Earl of Morton his son and heir.

IV. Helenor, married Sigismund, Arch-Duke of Austria and Earl of Tyrol, son and heir of Arch-Duke Frederick, sirnamed The Old; but he died an. 1497[2], without any issue.

V. Mary, married to John Lord Camphere and Zealand.

King James, cut off in this manner in the very prime of his days, the Estates of the Kingdom assembled at Edinburgh, on the 26th of August 1437, and solemnly crowned James his son, in the 6th year of his age, and appointed Sir Alexander Livingstoun of Callender, Governour of the Kingdom; and committed the custody of the young King, with the command of the Castle of Edinburgh, to Sir William Crichton then Chancellor.

Archbald Earl of Douglas, declining to give obedience to the Governour and Chancellor, pretended royal grants and exemptions to him and his ancestors, from such a jurisdiction in the minority of a King; but his death, which happened in an. 1438, made way for William Earl of Douglas, his son, a youth about 14 years of age: the vanity of whose followers, and want of experience, made him guilty of a great many misdemeanors. And being on his journey to a Parliament, on his way to Edinburgh, he was met by Chancellor Crichton, and nobly entertain'd at his house of Crichton; who taking occasion to mind him of the greatness and merit of his family, and of his own duty to his Sovereign, he, in return, acknowledged his bypast escapes, promised amendment for the future, and, after all this, was invited by the Chancellor to the Castle of Edinburgh. Being set at the King's table, amidst the entertainment he was suddenly removed, together with David his younger brother, and Sir Malcolm Fleming of Cumbernauld, his constant friend, and most treacherously murthered by the Governour's order, an. 1441, the 16th year of his age, neither regarding the tears and entreaties of the young king, the laws of hospitality, nor the honour contained in the invitation he had received. The Earl of Douglas, thus taken away, his Estate and honours descended on James Lord Abercorn; but he leaving this world, an. 1443, left for his successor William his son, who, in King James II.'s minority, getting into that Prince's favour, in a short time had

---

[1] History of the Family of Huntly.
[2] Opus Catholicum Genealogicum, ab Elia Reusneri.

the government of the whole affairs of the nation: and having turned the Governour and Chancellor out of their posts, got them denounced rebels in a Parliament, and orders given to Sir John Forrester of Corstorphine to prosecute them with fire and sword: the Castle of Crichton was taken, plundered, and a garrison put into it. But all this time the Chancellor kept out the Castle of Edinburgh, which the Earl of Douglas laid siege to: and, after nine months stay before it, he was forced to capitulate with the Chancellor, upon condition he should be restored to his office, and whatsoever had been withheld from him by his enemies; that all former discontents should be done away; and that he should pass out of the Castle with bag and baggage.

Shortly after this, in an. 1447, the King calls a Parliament, wherein Sir Alexander Livingston, the late Governour, Alexander Livingston his son, Sir Robert Livingston of Drumray, late Thesaurer, Sir David Livingston, Sir James Dundas of that-ilk, and Sir Robert Bruce of Clackmannan, were forfaulted for converting the King's treasure to their own private use. The old Governour, with the Lairds of Dundas and Clackmannan, were remitted; but Alexander Livingston, the Governour's son, Sir Robert and Sir David Livingstons, were executed at Edinburgh.

The Earl of Douglas, for the further securing himself against the Chancellor and his faction, enter'd, in an. 1445, into a league with the Earls of Crawfurd, Ross, Murray, Ormond, the Lord Balveny, Sir James Hamilton of Cadzow, and many other Barons; wherein they engaged solemnly, never to desert one another, and that the injury done to one of them should be as done to all, and reveng'd as their common quarrel. After this, the Earl became so insolent, that he had no regard to the King's authority; and the King, endeavouring to reduce him to his obedience by fair means, in order thereto wrote him a very obliging letter, wherein he desired him to meet him at Stirling, that affairs might be peaceably accommodated. But the Earl, conscious of the crimes he had committed, refused to come, unless he got a publick assurance, under the great seal, for safe coming and returning; which being granted him, he came to Stirling Castle, where the Court then was, with a powerful retinue. The King having received him very graciously, towards the evening, the gates of the Castle being shut, His Majesty took the Earl aside, and urged him to break the league, which he absolutely refusing, the King stabb'd him, on the 13th of February 1452.

The Earl's friends, who had accompanied him thither, hearing what was done, got immediately to arms; and James Earl of Douglas, Earl William's brother, proclaimed the King and the whole Court Faith-breakers.

Amidst these confusions, the King called a Parliament to meet at Edinburgh; to which the Earl of Douglas and his adherents were summon'd to compear: but they not thinking fit to obey, the Parliament having met, they declared James Earl of Douglas, Archbald Earl of Murray, Hugh Earl of Ormond, John Lord Balveny, his three brothers, and Alexander Earl of Crawfurd, publick enemies to the Government. And after this, in an. 1455, being driven to the necessity of a battle against the King, his brother the Earl of Murray was killed, and the Earl of Ormond taken prisoner and beheaded; but himself, with his brother the Lord Balveny, escaped, fled afterwards to England, and in an. 1456, with the assistance of Henry Earl of Northumberland, invaded the borders; but in an. 1457, were overthrown by the valour of George Earl of Angus, and James Lord Hamilton.

The same year came ambassadors from Henry VI. of England, imploring K. James's aid and assistance against the rebellion of Richard Duke of York; offering, provided he would assist them with an army, he should have restored whatsoever lands his ancestors had possessed in England: and about the same time came the like message from the Duke of York. King James answered the English ambassadors indirectly; and having dismis'd them, he raises an army, and marches towards England, layeth siege to the Castle of Roxburgh, where, by the accidental bursting of a piece of ordnance, he was killed on the 3d of August 1460, the 30th year of his age, and 24th of his reign. This Prince was married with Mary, daughter of Arnold Duke of Gelders, and niece to Philip Duke of Burgundy.

Children of King James II. by Mary his Queen.

I. James his successor, the third of that name, King of Scotland: Of whom afterwards.

II. Alexander Duke of Albany; a Prince, who, by the restlessness of his own disposition, occasioned much disquiet, both to the King his brother and to himself. He was imprisoned in the Castle of Edinburgh, from whence he escaped, and fled to France, where he was kindly received by Lewis XI. and was afterwards killed at a tournment, by Lewis Duke of Orleans, by the splinter of a spear, which penetrated into his brain, an. 1484. He was married, first, to Catharine Santclair, daughter of William Earl of Orkney, from whom he divorced, because of their consanguinity, forbidden by the Canon Law, in the year 1477, (which was ratified in Parliament, an. 1516) leaving issue by the said lady, Alexander, Abbot of Inchaffrey and Scoon, and afterwards promoted to the Episcopal See of Murray, an. 1534. Before he was a Church-man, he married Margaret Crichton, daughter to the Lord Crichton: by whom he had a daughter, Margaret, married to David Lord Drummond'. Alexander Duke of Albany, being divorced from Catharine Santclair, was remarried to Agnes, daughter of the Earl of Boulogne: by whom he had John Duke of Albany, Governour of Scotland, in King James V.'s minority; who married Anna, daughter and heir of John Count de Lauraguez, but had no succession.

III. John, created Earl of Mar by his father, in the year 1460, but died in 1479, without issue.

IV. Mary, married Thomas Master of Boyd, son and heir of Robert Lord Boyd, Chancellor and Governour of Scotland, in King James III.'s minority; a youth of extraordinary endowments, both of body and mind; with her he obtained the Isle of Arran and many other lands, and was created into the dignity of Earl of Arran, an. 1467. But in 1468, being commissioned ambassador to Denmark, to attend Margaret, daughter of Christian King of Denmark, King James III's Queen, home to Scotland, his greatness procured him envy; and, in his absence, his enemies plotted his ruin. Robert Lord Boyd his father, and Sir Alexander Boyd his uncle, were summoned to answer such points as should be exhibited against them in Parliament; and were declared enemies to the State. Robert Lord Boyd retired to England, an. 1469, where he, in a very short time, ended his days. Sir Alexander, his brother, was challenged and convicted of treasonably carrying his Majesty in person, against his inclination, on his way to the Castle of Callender, to Edinburgh; which Sir Alexander offering to produce an Act of Parliament for, approving it good service, (and is yet extant,) it was kept up, and he condemned to lose his head; which sentence was execute on him. Thomas Earl of Arran, arriving with the Queen in the Firth, in July 1469, and preparing himself to come ashore, resolving to throw himself upon the King's clemency; his Lady coming to him disguised, gave him particular information of the circumstances of his family, the weakness of his interest at Court, and the many snares laid by his enemies to cut him off: and, resolving to partake with him in his misfortunes, returned back to Denmark, from thence to France, and thereafter to Antwerp. King James writes to his sister very kindly to return home: the Lady believing her presence might influence the King her brother to restore her husband to his favour, comes for Scotland, leaving him at Antwerp, where, in a very short time, he died; leaving issue by the said Lady Mary his wife, James, who by the

' History of the Family of Drummond, in MS.

bounty of his uncle was restored to the dignity of Lord Boyd, and to the lands of Kilmarnock, Dalry, Kilbride, Nodsdale, &c. in 1482; but he was killed, in a feud, by the Montgomeries, an. 1487, and died without succession. He had likeways a daughter, Margaret, married first unto Alexander Lord Forbes; and surviving him, she remarried with David first Earl of Cassils, but had not any succession.

In the year 1474, some two years after the death of Thomas Earl of Arran, the Lady Mary was, by the King her brother, given in marriage to James Lord Hamilton; by whom she had issue James Lord Hamilton, and a daughter, Elizabeth, married to Matthew first Earl of Lenox, of whom that illustrious family descended. Which James Lord Hamilton, nephew to King James III. obtained from King James IV. the Isle of Arran, as a gratification to him for his great charge in negociating the King's marriage with Margaret, daughter of King Henry VII. and was created by him into the dignity of Earl of Arran, the 9th day of January 1503. James Earl of Arran, his son, was declared Governour of Scotland, upon the death of King James V. during the minority of Queen Mary; and, by an Act of Parliament, declared successor to the Throne, if the Queen died without issue. He was honoured with the title of Duke of Chatlerault, by King Henry II. of France, in 1548. He stood firm to the interest of Queen Mary, until his death, which happened the 22d of January 1576.

V. Cecilia, married William Lord Crichton, by whom she had only one daughter, Margaret, who married George Earl of Rothes, from whom he divorced upon the score of consanguinity, (others say they were not married) but by her he had issue, (1) Norman Lesly master of Rothes, a gentleman of great endowments and singular valour. But his misfortune in killing Cardinal David Beatoun, Bishop of St. Andrews, very much lessen'd his esteem in Scotland, so that he thought fit to retire to France, where he was preferred by King Henry II. to the command of the Scots troop. He was kill'd at Renton in Picardy, and died without succeession. (2) Robert Lesly, of whom descended the family of Findaressie. (3) Janet Lesly, married to Grant of that-ilk. (4) Helen Lesly, to John Seton of Parbroath: and surviving him, she was remarried unto Mark, commendator of Newbottle, ancestor to the Marquis of Lothian, and had issue.

JAMES III. of that name, succeeded his father, when a child of seven years of age, and was crowned at the Abby of Kelso: his education was committed to the Queen his mother. Andrew Stewart, Lord Evandale, William Earl of Orkney, John Lord Kennedy, Robert Lord Boyd, Chancellor, Patrick Lord

Grahame, James Bishop of St. Andrews, William Bishop of Glasgow, and Thomas Bishop of Dunkeld, were declar'd Governours of the Realm.

About this time, Edward Earl of March, having defeat King Henry the IV. of England, at Tantoun in Yorkshire, came to the Crown of England, by the name of Edward IV. King Henry, with his Queen, and Edward Prince of Wales, his son, fled to Scotland for assistance to recover his Crown, delivering up to the Scots the Town of Berwick, and at the same time, the better to engage them to his interest, treated of a match betwixt Edward Prince of Wales, and the lady Mary, the King's sister, which took no effect.

In the year 1468, Andrew Stewart, Lord Evandale, then Chancellor of the kingdom, ... Bishop of Glasgow, and William Earl of Orkney, were sent Ambassadors to Denmark, to demand Margaret, daughter of Christian I. King of Denmark, in marriage for King James, which was agreed to, the Danes resigning their claim to the isles of Orkney, Shetland, &c. in lieu of her dowry. They were solemnly married in the Abby Church of Holy-rood-house, the 10th of July 1469.

In an. 1473, the publick peace of the kingdom was disturbed, by the insurrection of John Lord of the Isles, who proclaimed himself King of them, and imposed taxes on the country: But, by the courage and conduct of John of Earl of Athol, the King's Lieutenant, he was reduced, and brought to submit to the King's clemency; and the Earldom of Ross, which he then stood possess'd of, was annexed to the Crown. His Majesty, in 1476, was pleased to restore him to the dignity and Lordship of the Isles.

About this time, Alexander Duke of Albany, the King's brother, was imprisoned in the Castle of Edinburgh, for treasonable practices, who, having made his escape to France, and from thence coming over to England, prevailed with King Edward to send the Duke of Glocester with an army to invade Scotland; and having gained the factious nobility to his party, the English entered the country with an army of 22000 men: And the King levies an army, and marches to Lauder, in order to invade England, much against the mind of the nobility, who were highly dissatisfied with the present administration of the Government, and particularly with his favourites, men of a mean birth; for Robert Cochran, from a mason, he raised to be Earl of Mar; and one William Roger, a musician, he promoted to the Honour of Knighthood. Whereupon, several of the nobility (the principal of whom were Archbald Earl of Angus, Alexander Earl of Huntly, John Lord Darnly, and Robert Lord Lyle) met at the Church of Lauder, where they resolved to rid the King of his wicked counsellors: And, as the nobility, were making towards the King's tent, to seize them, His Majesty, upon notice of the meeting of the nobility, sent Robert Cochran, Earl of Mar, to know what was the matter; but he was taken by the Earl of Angus in his way, and put under custody: The Earl going forward to the King's tent, he took thence the rest of his courtiers, viz. Sir William Roger, and one James Homil, who were immediately tried before the army. The principal crimes they were charged with were, advising the King to coin base money, and to cut off his relations. Cochran was immediately hanged over Lauder Bridge, in his own scarf, and the other two on a gibbet, erected for that purpose, as the authors of the mismanagement of the publick affairs. The execution being done, the army was disbanded, and the King convoyed to the Castle of Edinburgh, under the custody of John Earl of Athol, Alexander Duke of Albany, Colin Earl of Argile, John Earl of Athol, Andrew Lord Evandale, and William, Bishop of St. Andrews, were constituted Governours of the kingdom, which they held nine months. But the Duke of Albany, being daily importuned by the Queen, and imagining he was not so much respected by the rest of the Governours as his birth and merit deserved, by the assistance of the citizens of Edinburgh, set the King at liberty; in recompence of which that City got a Charter, containing many ample privileges, which they yet enjoy. But the Duke of Albany, falling again into the King's displeasure, fled to England, where he was assisted by Richard III. to invade Scotland, with James Earl of Douglas; But by the valour and conduct of the Laird of Johnston, then Warden of the Marches, and the Laird of Cockpool, they were entirely defeated; the Duke escaped to France, where he died next year, and the old turbulent Earl of Douglas was taken prisoner, and confined to the Abby of Lindores, where he died an. 1488, which put a period to the principal family of Douglas.

In the year 1488, matters coming to an open rupture betwixt the King and many of his nobility, he takes arms; the Lords do the like, choosing the Prince their General. Both armies encountering at Bannockburn, the King's troops were defeat and himself slain[1]. The action was upon the 11th of June 1488. His body was solemnly buried in the Abby of Cambuskenneth, near Stirling.

[1] Buchanan, Lesly, and Drummond.

Children of King James III. by Margaret, daughter of Christian King of Denmark, his Queen.

I. James, who succeeded him in his Throne, by the name of James the IV.

II. Alexander Duke of Ross, who was provided to the Archbishoprick of St. Andrews, upon the death of Bishop Schevez, in an. 1496. He died an. 1503, without issue.

III. John Earl of Mar, created into that dignity by his father 1480; but he also died an. 1481, without any succession.

JAMES, son and heir of King James III. upon his father's death, was crowned, at Edinburgh, June . . 1488, in the 16th year of his age; he nominated Colin, Earl of Argile, Lord High Chancellor; Patrick Earl of Bothwel, James Earl of Buchan, Robert Lord Lyle, Laurence Lord Oliphant, William Lord Ruthven, Matthew Stewart, son and apparent heir of John Earl of Lenox (of the nobility) to be of his Privy Council, and calls a Parliament to meet at Edinburgh, in February 1490, wherein it was enacted, That they who had assisted the late King at Bannockburn, and enjoyed hereditary offices, should be suspended for three years; and such as enjoyed places during life, should lose them entirely; and all promotion to honour, by the late King after he took the field, reduced. Thus the Earl of Crawfurd was divested of the title of Duke of Montrose, the Lord Kilmaures of his dignity of Earl of Glencairn, and John Ramsay of Balmain of being Earl of Bothwel. At the same time Patrick Lord Hales, created Earl of Bothwel, is sent ambassador to Spain, James Arch-Bishop of Glasgow, to France, and Sir James Ogilvie of Airly to Denmark, to renew the ancient leagues with these Crowns.

The same year 1490, Perkin Werbeck, pretending himself Richard Duke of York, son of King Edward the IV. arrives in Scotland, and cajol'd the King and Council unto a belief, that he was the person he pretended; whereupon he was honourably entertained as a Prince: And King James, to perswade the world that he thought him so indeed, gave him in marriage his cousin Catharine Gordon, daughter of George Earl of Huntly, and assissted him with an army to invade England; but King James perceiving the English did not join him, he wasted Northumberland; at which Perkin seemed to be concerned, saying, " It grieved him to the heart to see such havock made of his people:" To which the King answered, " You take care for them, who, by any thing yet " appears, are none of yours." King Henry, to revenge this injury, acquaints his Parliament, that he was under necessity of making war upon the Scots; and in all haste an army is provided, and sent into Scotland, under the conduct of the Lord Daubeny : But before he arrived, he was called back to appease a commotion in Cornwal; and while the English army were on their march to London, King James invades England, and in person besieges the Castle of Norham : but understanding the Earl of Surrey was advancing towards him, he thought fit to return home. Surrey, the English General, entered Scotland, and took the Castle of Aitoun : but, the weather proving unseasonable, the Earl returned into England. Shortly after this, by the mediation of one Peter Hilias, the Spanish ambassador, a truce was concluded betwixt Scotland and England, for several years.

In the year 1503, King James was married to Margaret, eldest daughter of King Henry VII. of England the portion being 10000 lib. Objections being made, at the Council-Board, against this marriage, viz. That thereby the Crown of England might come to the Scots. King Henry made answer, " That if any such thing should happen, I see (says he) it will come to pass " that England shall lose nothing thereby, because there will not be an acces- " sion of England to Scotland, but of Scotland to England ; seeing the less " accrueth always to the greater." From this match proceeded the Union of the two kingdoms afterwards, in the person of King James VI. of Scotland, the great grandson of this noble marriage, sole Monarch of the Island of Great Britain. King Henry accompanying Margaret his daughter, on her way to Scotland, as far as Coleivestoun, beside Northamptoun ; having given her his blessing, with fatherly counsel and exhortation, committed the guard and conduct of her person to the Earls of Surrey and Northumberland, who, with a splendid retinue, attended her as far as Berwick. And at St. Lambert's kirk, in Lamermore, in the Merse, King James, attended by the principal of his nobility, espoused her.

This conjugal alliance produced perfect peace and amity between the two Realms of England and Scotland for a long time after, but did not take away the standing animosity between the two nations, nor interrupt the alliance between France and Scotland : For King Henry having invaded France, King James sent an ambasssdor to him, while he lay at the siege of Tournay, desiring he might desist from troubling the French his allies ; which not being yielded unto by King Henry, he denounced war against England, and raises an army, invades that Kingdom, and in person takes the Castles of Norham, Wark, &c. By this time the Earl of Surrey, the English General, having gathered an army, was come within three miles, where the Scots were so advantageously encamped, that it was impossible to attack them without great disadvantage. The

Earl of Surrey sends a Herauld, to desire King James to leave that place, and come to some indifferent ground, where he would be ready to bid him battle; and both armies encountering upon the 9th September 1513, at Floudoun-field, the Scots were defeat, and the King, who showed a great deal of valour in the battle, had the ill fate to lose his life, with the flower of his nobility and gentry, the chief of whom were, Archbald Earl of Argile, Matthew Earl of Lenox, William Earl of Errol, Patrick Earl of Bothwel, John Earl of Athol, David Earl of Cassils, William Earl of Montrose, Alexander Earl of Crawfurd, William Earl of Rothes, Alexander, Bishop of St. Andrews, the King's natural son, David Bishop of the Isles, George Master of Angus, Alexander Lord Elphinstoun, Robert Lord Erskine, John Lord Maxwel, Andrew Lord Herris, George Lord Seton, John Lord Forbes, William Lord Borthwick, John Lord Semple, John Lord Ross, William Lord Ruthven, Sir Thomas Maule of Panmure, Sir John Summerveil of Camnethan, John Murray younger of Tillibardin, Sir John Hadden of Gleneagles, Sir William Maitland of Lethingtoun, Kenneth Mackenzie of Kintail, Robert Douglas of Lochlevin, David Home of Wedderburn, Thomas Maclellan of Bomby, Sir Robert Livingstoun of Easter Weems, &c.

Children of King James IV. by Margaret his Queen, eldest daughter of King Henry VII. of England.

I. James, born at Holy-rood-house, the 21st of February 1507, died in his infancy, July 14, 1510.

II. Arthur, born the 20th October 1509. He deceased an infant.

III. James, born the 5th of April 1511, was, after his father's death King of Scotland.

IV. Alexander, born the 30th of April 1514, after his father's death created Duke of Rothsay, deceased the 15th of January 1516.

Natural Issue of King James IV. by Mary Boyd, daughter of Archbald Boyd of Bonshaw.

I. Alexander, Commendator of Dunfermling and Coldingham, was sent abroad for his education, and followed his studies under the direction of the most famous Erasmus, from whom he got a very noble character. He was elected Bishop of St. Andrews, an. 1506, and afterwards Lord High Chancellor of Scotland; he was killed in the battle of Floudoun.

II. Catharine, married James Earl of Morton, by whom she had issue three daughters; (1) Margaret married to James Duke of Chatlerault, and Earl of Arran, and had issue; (2) Elizabeth to James Douglas, son to Sir George Douglas of Pittendreich, in right of whom he became Earl of Morton; (3) Beatrix to Robert Lord Maxwel, and had issue.

A natural son of King James IV. by Jean Kennedy, daughter to the Earl of Cassils, afterwards Countess of Angus.

James, created Earl of Murray by John Duke of Albany, in the year 1515. He deceased in 1544, leaving issue, by Isobel his wife, daughter of Archbald Earl of Argile, one daughter, married to John Master of Buchan, killed at Pinkie.

A natural daughter of King James IV. by Margaret, daughter of John Lord Drummond.

Margaret, married first John Master of Huntly, son and heir of George Earl of Huntly; by whom she had two sons, (1) George Earl of Huntly; (2) Alexander, Abbot of Inchaffrey, provided to the Arch-Bishoprick of Glasgow, by Mary the Queen Regent. But, while he travelled to Rome for consecration, James Beatoun, by the interest of the Duke of Chatlerault, is promoted to that See. Upon this disappointment, he got the Bishoprick of the Isles, and by Pope Paul the III. was made Titular Arch-Bishop of Athens, and, in an. 1558, was translated to the Episcopal See of Galloway. He was one of our Popish Bishops that embraced the Reformation, and enjoyed his office till his death, in 1576 [1]. She was secondly married with Sir John Drummond of Inerpeffer, by whom she had four daughters; (1) Agnes, married to Hugh Earl of Eglintoun, and had issue; (2) Isobel, to Sir Matthew Campbel of Loudoun, and had issue; (3) Margaret, to Robert Lord Elphinstoun, and had issue; (4) Jean, to Sir James Chisholm of Cromlix, and had issue.

A natural daughter of King James IV. by Isobel Stewart, daughter of James Earl of Buchan.

Jean, married Malcolm Lord Fleming, Great Chamberlain of Scotland, by whom she had, (1) James Lord Fleming, who died without male succession;

---

[1] History of the Family of Sutherland, in MS.

(2) John Lord Fleming, a constant friend to Queen Mary; (3) Margaret, married to Robert, Master of Grahame, and afterwards to John Earl of Athol, and had issue.

James IV. thus cut off, his son JAMES, a child of two years of age, is crowned at Scoon, the ordinary place of inauguration of our Kings, the 21st of December 1513; and the Queen his mother is declared Regent so long as she continued a widow, with this limitation, to conclude nothing in the administration of the Government, but by the advice of James Bishop of Glasgow, Lord Chancellor, Alexander Earl of Huntly, Archbald Earl of Angus, and James Earl of Arran. In the meantime she writeth to King Henry VII. her brother, imploring his royal and brotherly favour, particularly, that he would be pleased, out of regard to her and the infant King her son, not only to abstain from prosecuting a war against Scotland, but take them into his special protection, and defend them, as well, from foreign injuries, if offered, as from the factions of the nobility at home. To which he returned answer, " That " if the Scots would live in peace, they should have it from him; and that he " was willing to prohibit all acts of hostility against Scotland, during the mi- " nority of her son; and, for a remedy against present evils, to make a truce " for a Year." But the Queen marrying Archbald Earl of Angus, soon after thereby lost her Regency; and in 1514, John Duke of Albany, the nearest of the royal line, was chosen Regent, and ambassadors dispatched to France, to acquaint him with their proceedings; who, being furnished with a noble equipage by the French King, arrives in Scotland, an. 1515. And some time after him came an ambassador from France, to renew the ancient league betwixt the two nations: the Parliament made choice of the Duke of Albany, the Governour, to accomplish that solemn action upon their part.

The Duke going to France, an. 1517, deputed six others to manage the affairs of the Kingdom during his absence, viz. the Earls of Arran, Angus, Argile, Huntly, and the two Arch-Bishops of St. Andrews and Glasgow. And, to prevent disorders among themselves, he assigned to each of them his particular province: notwithstanding this care, several disorders were committed. After some years absence the Governour returned, October 28th 1521, and indicts a Parliament, wherein it was agreed, that an army should be rais'd to invade England, to divert the English then warring in France; but a truce was concluded betwixt the two nations for some years. The Governour goeth again to France to demand assistance against England, and arrives again in Scotland, in October 1533, with 4000 well armed men. In the mean time

King Henry raises an army of 40000 horse and foot, and marches towards Scotland; but this expedition ended also in a truce with England for some time.

In an. 1524 the Duke passeth again into France; during his absence the King, then arrived to the 12th year of his age, taketh the management of the Government in his own hands, and made choice of James Bishop of St. Andrews, Archbald Earl of Angus, Archbald Earl of Argile, John Earl of Lenox, Gavin Bishop of Glasgow, Gavin Bishop of Aberdeen, and George Bishop of Dunkeld, to remain with, and advise him in all affairs relating to the welfare of the country. But Archbald Earl of Angus, in a short time seizes the young King, takes the entire management of the Government upon himself, and retains him in effect a prisoner. The rest of the nobility being discontented that the King should be kept in this manner a prisoner by Angus, the Laird of Buccleugh, by the King's secret command, endeavoured to relieve him, but was defeat in the attempt, which happened at Melross, July 20th 1526. Afterwards, John Earl of Lenox, at the King's earnest desire, reneweth the design, but his party was worsted (by Angus) and himself slain in the field. This action fell out at Aven, in the month of September 1526. But at length in an. 1527, the King escaped privately out of Angus's custody, by night, from the Castle of Faulkland, to Stirling, where the Earls of Huntly, Argile, Glencairn, Athol, Montrose, Monteith, Eglintoun, Rothes, the Lords Drummond, Livingstoun, Santclair, Lindsay, Evandale, Ruthven, Semple, Maxwel, repaired to him; by whose advice his Majesty issued out a proclamation, discharging Angus to meddle any further in publick affairs, or him or any of his name to come near the Court by 12 miles, under pain of treason. He was forfaulted in the ensuing Parliament, and declared an enemy to the King and country.

In the year 1532, King James V. instituted the College of Justice, or the Lords of the Session, confirmed by the Pope an. 1534, and ratified afterwards in Parliament an. 1537.

At the same time, King Henry VIII. invades Scotland, and spoils the country towards Dunse: the main cause pretended for the war was, to have the Earl of Angus restored. But a peace was soon afterwards concluded betwixt the two nations.

King James, weary of a single life, commissions David Beatoun, Abbot of Arbroth, to France, to treat concerning a marriage with Magdalen, eldest daughter of Francis I. which was agreed to. The King himself in person goes to France, and commits the government of the Realm to the Earls of Huntly and Eglintoun, and was solemnly married on January 1st 1537, and arrived in

Scotland the 29th of May thereafter. It is reported, that as soon as she set her foot on the shore, she kiss'd the ground, and pray'd for all happiness to the country; but contracting a fever, she deceased July 22, the same year, to the great grief of the King and the people, and was solemnly buried in the Abby Church of Holy-rood-house, with the greatest funeral solemnity ever before that time known in Scotland.

But the King, desirous of succession, commissions Robert Lord Maxwell, and David Abbot of Arbroth, Ambassadors, to propose for a marriage betwixt him and Mary of Lorrain, daughter of Claud Duke of Guise, and widow of Lewis of Orleans, Duke of Longueville; which was agreed, and she espoused by proxy June 19, 1538: and, arriving in Scotland in a few months, they were solemnly married at St. Andrews. King Henry VIII. of England had several times desired an interview with his nephew King James, and sometime before had sent Dr. Barlow, Bishop of St. Davids, with the complement of some books, written in defence of his proceedings, and desired him to examine them impartially: he also proposed the interview at York. The Clergy of Scotland were very apprehensive of his seeing his uncle, lest King Henry might have perswaded him to follow his example, in abolishing the Pope's authority, and making some advances in a reformation. The church-men used such perswasions, that these, seconded by a message from France, diverted the King from his purpose.

Which King Henry resented to that degree, that he declared war against Scotland, pretending, that the Crown of Scotland owed him homage. The Scots, on the other hand, asserted they were a free and independent kingdom.; that the homages anciently made by their kings, were only for lands which they had in England. King Henry sends an army, consisting of 3000 men, under the command of Sir Robert Boues; but, after he had wasted the country of Teviotdale, he was repulsed with considerable loss, by the valour and conduct of the Earl of Huntly, at Haldenridge, the 24th of August 1541. In the mean time, King Henry next summer raises an army of 20000 men, under the command of the Duke of Norfolk; but after he had burnt some small towns, and wasted Teviotdale, he returned back to England. King James was resolved to follow him, which the nobility absolutely refused: so the King returned to Edinburgh, and immediately disbanded his army. But he was encourag'd by the clergy to engage in a war against King Henry, who both assured him of victory, since he fought against an heretical Prince, and advanced an annuity of 50000 Crowns for prosecuting the war. Whereupon, in the end of November 1542, he brought together an army of 15000 men, with a good train of artillery, intending to march into England by the western road. The King himself in person, came to Lochmaben, attending the event, and sent a commission to Oliver Santclair, a private gentleman, a brother of the family of Roslin, to command in chief; which so much disgusted the nobility, that they refused to march, and were beginning to separate. While they were in this disorder, the English, under the command of Sir Thomas Wharton, took advantage of their disorder, fell upon them, and dispers'd them: they took all their ordnance and baggage, and a thousand prisoners, of whom two hundred were gentlemen of quality. The news of this voluntary defeat coming to the King at Lochmaben, he retired to his Palace of Faulkland, where he fell into such extremity of grief, that in a few days it caus'd his death, December 13, 1542; and in January thereafter, his body was carried to Edinburgh, and buried in the Abby Church of Holy-rood-house.

Children of King James V. by Mary of Lorrain his Queen.

I. James Duke of Rothsay, born 1538, deceased in his infancy.

II. Arthur, born 1540, and on the day of his baptism created Earl of Fife, and Duke of Albany. He died an infant.

III. Mary, born the 5th of December 1542. The heir of his crown and misfortunes.

Natural issue of King James V. by Margaret, daughter of John Lord Erskine, afterwards wife of Robert Douglas of Lochlevin.

James, provided first to the priory of St. Andrews, an. 1540; and, because of his non-age, Alexander Miln, Abbot of Cambuskenneth, was appointed administrator in " Spiritualibus & Temporalibus:" He was, by Queen Mary his sister, created Earl of Murray, by letters patent, bearing date the 10th of February 1563. And, upon her resignation of the Crown and imperial dignity, an. 1567, (whether extorted or not I shall not determine), she appointed him tutor and regent to her son King James. He was murthered in the 4th year of his regency, by James Hamilton of Bothwel-haugh, in the Town of Linlithgow, upon the 23d of January 1570. His body was, few days after, removed from Linlithgow, and interred in St. Giles' Church of Edinburgh, where there was a monument erected to his memory, with this inscription:

" Pietas sine vindice luget : Jus exarmatum est.
23, Januarii 1570.

" Jacobo Stewarto, Moraviæ Comiti, Scotiæ Proregi, Viro, ætatis suæ,
" longè optimo, ab inimicis omnis memoriæ deterrimis, ex insidiis extincto, ceu
" Patri communi, Patria mœrens posuit.

In English thus:

" Godlines mourns without a defender: Law is disarmed.

" To James Stewart, Earl of Murray, Regent of Scotland, the far best man
" of the age he lived in, treacherously murthered by his enemies, the worst
" persons in all memory, as to a common father, the mournful country erected
" this monument."

This Earl of Murray was one of the principal persons, whom God honoured
to promote our happy reformation; a nobleman of rare abilities and eminent
zeal for religion; who, notwithstanding of all the aspersions cast on his memory
by some of late, will always be known by the character of the Good Regent,
and celebrated among the most illustrious persons this nation ever produced.
He left issue, by Agnes his lady, daughter of William Earl Marishal, a daughter, Isobel, on whom his estate and honours did descend: Of whom, and of
James Stewart, Lord Doun, her husband, is lineally descended Charles now
Earl of Murray.

*Natural Children of King James V. by Eupham, daughter of Alexander Lord
Elphinstown.*

Robert, Prior of Holy-rood-house: He made an exchange of that Abby
with Adam Bothwel, Bishop of Orkney, for his right of that Bishoprick, an.
1570; and was created into the dignity of Earl of Orkney, by King James VI.
his nephew, by letters patent, bearing date, at Edinburgh, 21st of October 1581.
He was married unto Jean, daughter of Gilbert Earl of Cassils, by whom he had,
(1) Patrick his son and heir, forfaulted for treason, for which he lost his head
in the year 1614. (2) John, created Lord Kincleven, by King James VI. the
the 5th of August, in the year 1607, and improven by King Charles I. in the
year 1633, to the dignity of Earl of Carrick; but, so much as I know, the

dignity at present is not claimed by any. (3) Sir James Stewart, one of the Gentlemen of the bed-chamber to King Charles I. (4) Mary, married to Patrick Lord Gray, and had issue. (5) Jean, to Patrick Lord Lindores, had issue. (6) Elizabeth, to Sir James Santclair of Murthill, and had issue.

Natural Children of King James V. by Elizabeth, daughter of Sir John Carmichael, Captain of Crawfurd; afterwards wife of Sir John Summerveil of Camnethan.

I. John, Prior of Coldingham, who, by marriage of Jean, daughter of Patrick, and sister and sole heir of James Hepburn, Earl of Bothwel, sometime Duke of Orkney, obtained the reversion of that fair Lordship. Francis Stewart, his son, had also the dignity of Earl of Bothwel: he was forfaulted for his rebellious practices against the Government, in an. 1593, and retired to France, thence to Italy, where he lived until the year 1624.

II. Janet, married Archbald Earl of Argile, but had not any succession.

A natural son of King James V. by Elizabeth Stewart, daughter of John Earl of Lenox.

Adam, Prior of the Charter house of Perth, had not any succession.

A natural son of King James V. by Elizabeth Shaw, of the family of Sauchie.

James, Abbot of Kelso: died in the year 1458, sans issue.

Mary, Queen of Scotland, the only lawful child of King James V. was born, at Linlithgow, on the 8th day of December 1542, and succeeded him in his crown and imperial dignity the 8th day of her age. The administration of the Government was committed to James Earl of Arran, during the Queen's minority; and, by an Act of Parliament, he was declared successor to the Throne, if the Queen died without issue. King Henry VIII. of England, conceiving this young Queen would be a fit match for Prince Edward his son, and thereby make an Union betwixt the two kingdoms, to this purpose conferred with the Scots Lords taken prisoners at Solway-field; who liked the proposal very well, and promised to promote it all they could: and so, upon their giving hostages for the performing their promises faithfully, they were sent home; and, at the same time, King Henry sent Sir Ralph Sadler ambassador to the Governour, and, to induce him to set forward the match, offered him the Lady Elizabeth, his daughter, in marriage to his son. He (the Governour) calls a meeting of the Estates, wherein the match was agreed to, and confirmed in Parliament, in August 1544. By this Union both nations were to enjoy all the reciprocal advantages of an incorporating Union; that is, an equality of all things, especially in matters of trade; yet so, as to remain two distinct nations, as before, though under one name of Britain, and to be governed by laws made, and to be made, in their respective Parliaments. But the Queen's mother and Cardinal Beatoun, an utter enemy to King Henry, so crossed and perplexed the matter, that it came to nothing, but ended in a war between the two kingdoms. So King Henry invaded the country both by sea and land, in an. 1544, under the command of the Earl of Hartford and Viscount Lisle. They demanded the young Queen to be delivered up to them; and, upon the Governour's refusal, they set the city of Edinburgh on fire, laid siege also to the Castle, but were repulsed by the conduct and valour of James Hamilton of Stanhouse, the Governour. They revenged themselves upon the neighbouring country, which they ravaged and laid waste some seven or eight miles every way. All the ships in the harbour of Leith were seized and carried off, and the town burnt to the ground; and so they marched homeward. But the Governour following them close with an army, killed and took a great many of them prisoners.

King Henry VIII. leaving this world in the year 1547, his son Edward VI. succeeded him, in the 10th year of his age: Edward Earl of Hartford was chosen Tutor to the young king, and Protector of England; who, according to the charge King Henry had left with his Council, to proceed in the marriage betwixt his son and the Scots Queen, sent a message to the Governour, inviting the Scots to consent to the marriage; but before he would commit any act of hostility, caused proclamation to be made, that his coming was only to demand performance of the marriage articles, which if they consented to, he would peaceably return. And, that he might more effectually perswade them to accept the proposition, he desisted from that demand of King Henry, about the giving up the Queen to be educate at the English Court; for he was willing she should continue in Scotland till years of maturity. This demand appeared reasonable to most of the moderate party of Scotland; but those of the French and Popish faction opposed it. Upon which ensued the battle of Pinkie, wherein the English had the victory; 8000 Scots being killed in the field of battle. The action fell out the 10th day of September 1547. The English, in their return home, placed garrisons in the towns of Haddingtoun and Lauder. The

Governour and so many of the nobility as had escaped in the fight, assembled at Stirling, where they determined to send the young Queen unto France, (lest she should fall into the hands of the English,) accompanied by Arran the Governour, James Prior of St. Andrews, John Lord Erskine, and William Lord Livingstoun; and at the same time ambassadors were dispatched to France to crave assistance, according to the league with that kingdom. Six thousand men were granted, and arrived in Scotland, in 1548; by whose assistance the Governor laid siege to Haddingtoun, which the English had fortified. But in Anno 1550, a peace was concluded with that kingdom.

In an. 1553, James Duke of Chatlerault and Earl of Arran, Governour of Scotland, demits the Regency in favours of Mary the Queen-mother, who was a daughter of the Duke of Guise, the family of all Europe most zealously addicted to the Church of Rome. In the year 1558, Queen Mary of Scotland, being now arrived to the 14th year of her age, was married to Francis the Dauphin, upon the 24th of April that year. The French king having desired that certain commissioners should be sent from Scotland to the solemnity, a Parliament was called for that effect, wherein they made choice of James Arch-Bishop of Glasgow, James Stewart Prior of St. Andrews, the Queen's natural brother, Gilbert Earl of Cassils, George Earl of Rothes, James Lord Fleming, George Lord Seton, Robert Bishop of Orkney, and Sir John Erskine of Dun. These commissioners were desired by the French king to offer the Dauphin the crown in right of his wife; but they said, that exceeded the bounds of their commission; so they only promised to represent the matter to the Estates of Scotland, which displeased the French king exceedingly. Four of the seven that were sent over died, and the fifth escaped narrowly; it being generally suspected they were poison'd. When the rest return'd to Scotland, an Assembly of the Estates was called, in which it was agreed to allow the Dauphin the title of King of Scotland, and to bear the royal arms of the kingdom impal'd with those of France, under the same crown; and commissioned the Earl of Argile and the Prior of St. Andrews to France to give an account of their proceedings.

During the Government of the Queen Regent, the Popish Clergy of Scotland were not idle, but persecuted all the professors of the reform'd religion their inquisitors could find out: and though she had given them all imaginable assurances of protection, yet resolved to suffer the Clergy to strike a terror into the people by some severe execution. They began with one Walter Miln, an old infirm Priest: He was accused, particularly, for asserting the lawfulness of the marriage of the Clergy, and for having condemned the sacrifice of the Mass and Transubstantiation, all which he confess'd; and upon his refusal to abjure them, he was condemned to be burnt. Yet so averse were the people from those cruelties, that it was not easy to find any that would execute the sentence: nor, in the town of St. Andrews, would any do so much as sell a cord to tie him to the stake; so that the Arch-Bishop was forced to send for the cords of his own Pavilion. The old man expressed great firmness of mind, and such chearfulness in his sufferings, that the people were much affected at it. And this being every where looked on as a prologue to greater severities that were to follow, many of the nobility and gentry began to consider what was fit to be done. These went under the name of the " Lords of the Congre-" gation :" They had made open profession of the truth, and supported and countenanced some worthy persons, as Mr. Knox and others, who, to the danger of their lives, made open profession of the Protestant Religion, and zealously preach'd down the error, superstition and idolatry, of the Church of Rome. They challenged the Popish Clergy to dispute upon the controverted points of religion, to be decided by the scripture; but they refused to be determined by any other rule than the authority of Councils and the Canon Law. But the Queen Regent, being unwilling to irritate so great a party, promised that they should have granted them whatever they pleased in matters of religion; but soon after she ordered a citation to be served on all reformed Ministers. The Earl of Glencairn was, upon that, sent to put her in mind of her former promises; she answered him roughly, " That maugre all that would take these " mens parts, they should be banished Scotland;" and added, " That Princes " were only bound to observe their promises so far as they found it convenient " for them to do it." To this he replied, " That if she renounced her pro-" mises, they would renounce their obedience to her." The Ministers coming from all parts to answer the citation, great numbers of nobility, gentry, and commons, came with them. The Queen Regent, apprehending the ill effects of so great a confluence of people, sent them word not to come; and upon this, many went home again; yet, because of their not appearance, they were declared rebels. This unfair dealing made many leave her, and go over to the reformed party, who then were assembled at Perth, where they broke in upon the houses of the Monks and Friars. After they had distributed all they had found in them to the poor, they pull'd them down to the ground; and, do the Queen what she could, they invaded all Cloisters and Monasteries in the kingdom, many of which they spoiled and demolished. This provoked the Queen so much, that she resolved to punish the town of Perth in a most exemplary manner; so she gathered the French souldiers together, with such others as would join with her. But the Earl of Glencairn, having gathered together 2500 men with incredible haste, marched to that place where there were in all about 7000 armed men. This made the Queen afraid to engage with them; so an agreement was made up, and oblivion promised for all that was past, matters of religion referred to a Parliament, and the Queen was to be received unto St. Johnston, without carrying the French with her; but she carried them notwithstanding of this into the town, and put a garrison in it, and punished many for what was past, contrary to the articles of pacification; and, when her promises were objected to her, she answered, " Princes were not to be strictly charged with their " promises, especially when they were made to hereticks." This turned the hearts of the most part of the nation from her. So she represents the state of the kingdom to the King of France her son-in-law, desiring a greater force might be sent over to reduce the country to her obedience. On the other hand, some were commissioned from the Lords of the Congregation to give a true representation of the matter, and to let him know, that an oblivion for what was past, and the free exercise of their religion for the time to come, would give them full satisfaction. But the death of the Queen Regent, which happened soon after, delivered them at that time from all fear of a war from France.

In the year 1560, it pleased GOD, that, by authority of Parliament, the Pope's authority and jurisdiction was abolished, and our Church reformed from the errors of Popery, according to the rule of GOD's word in the holy Scriptures, and a Confession of Faith, penn'd by Mr. Knox, ratified the 24th of August, that memorable year. These acts were only opposed by three Temporal Lords, viz. The Earl of Athol, the Lords of Borthwick and Summerveil, who said they would believe as their fathers had done. When these Acts, thus agreed on in the Parliament of Scotland, were sent over to France, for the Queen's ratification, and the King of France her husband's, they were rejected; so that the Scots began to apprehend a new war. But Francis II. Queen Mary's husband, being violently seized with a catarrh in his ear, it caused his death, the 5th of December 1560, which delivered them from all their fears. The Queen returned home in August 1561; and, in the September following, she made choice of James Duke of Chatlerault, George Earl of Huntly, Archbald Earl of Argile, John Earl of Athol, James Earl of Morton, William Earl of Marishall, Alexander Earl of Glencairn, William Earl of Montrose, Andrew Earl of Errol, James Prior of St. Andrews, John Lord Erskine, John Bishop of Ross, William Maitland of Lethingtoun, Sir James Balfour Clerk Register, and Sir John Ballantyne of Achinoul Justice Clerk, to be of her Privy Council.

In the year 1563, Matthew Stewart Earl of Lenox, who had been forfaulted during the Duke of Chatlerault's Government, was restored to his estate and honours; Henry Lord Darnly, his son, came to Scotland a few months after him. This noble Peer was one of the handsomest men of that age, and accounted the best skill'd in warlike exercises of any in his time. The Queen, it is said, no sooner saw him but she fell in love with him; he was certainly the most proper marriage she could have made; for, next to herself, he was heir of the crown of England; and if he had married with any of the great families of that kingdom, it might have inclined the English nation to settle the succession of their crown upon a native of their own kingdom; which she thought was a wise part in her to prevent. And to make this noble person the fitter match for her, she created him into the dignity of Duke of Albany and Earl of Ross, by Patent, dated the 7th of July 1564, and solemnly married him the 28th day of the same month, with consent of many of the Peers, and the next day caus'd proclaim him king. Of this marriage was born James the VI. first Monarch of Great Britain, in the Castle of Edinburgh, the 19th of June 1566. But her affection to King Henry began soon to cool, the unkindness being chiefly fomented by one David Rizio, an Italian, her Secretary for the French tongue; by means whereof he had frequent conferences with the Queen, when (they say) the king was not admitted: which indignity he reveng'd, by causing apprehend Rizio, being at the by-table in the Queen's Chamber; and, dragging him into the next room, killed him. This action, in which the king was concerned, proved the cause of all those evils which befel that royal couple and this nation for many years after.

King Henry, to the detestation of all good men, was murthered as he lay asleep on a bed, upon the 9th day of February 1567. The manner was variously reported, some thought the Earls of Murray and Morton to be the authors, as Bothwel gave out[1]; but the opinion of most was, that the Earl of Bothwel himself both contrived and executed the villany. But being accused of the murther, by Matthew Earl of Lenox, the king's father, he willingly surrendered himself a prisoner, desired he might be brought to a public trial, and was acquit, by a very honourable jury, of all suspicion, as well as action in the murther, though the suspicion of his guilt by the people was nothing diminished: but that he really was the regicide, was, and is, generally believed by most men, though the fact was never fully proven against him, though at his death he solemnly protested, that the Queen was wholly innocent; as is confidently reported by several persons of reputation and honour.

Bothwel, as he thought, having now defeat the contrivances of his enemies,

[1] Spotiswood.

began to think of marrying the Queen; and indeed his design was so far favoured by a considerable number of the nobility, that they subscribed an address, wherein they extol his merits, and lay before Her Majesty the advantages which infallibly would redound to herself and the nation, by the choice of a husband so very reasonable and necessary. The misfortunate Princess, abused by the treacherous counsels of some about her, knew not whom to trust: the Earl, having obtained a divorce from Lady Jean Gordon his wife, a daughter of the family of Huntly, upon the score of consanguinity, was created Duke of Orkney, and married the Queen, the 15th of May 1567; the most unfortunate action of her life, by this strengthening her enemies, who had cast the scandal of the king's murther on her, the credit of the aspersion being thereby supported. But some of the nobility, who had signed the address for the marriage, began now openly to condemn it; the chief of these were, the Earls of, Murray, Morton, Mar, Athol, and Glencairn, the Lords Lindsay and Boyd, who assembled at Stirling, and entered into an association for defence of the young Prince, who they thought was in danger of being murthered by Bothwel, his father-in-law. The Queen at the same time proposed a counter-association for the safety of her person and dignity.

In the mean time, the Borderers growing unruly, and committing daily depredations upon the neighbourhood, the Queen proposed to make a progress towards the borders, charging her subjects to attend her thither armed, and with fifteen days provision. This rendezvous of the Queen, the associating Lords thought she designed to employ against them. Her Majesty retired to the Castle of Borthwick; the associators take arms, lay siege to the same, wherein the Queen and Orkney lay; but next day Orkney escaped, and the Queen after him, in man's apparel, and came to the Castle of Dunbar. Upon this the Lords retired to Edinburgh, and the next day issued out a proclamation, wherein they declared, that they had betaken themselves to arms, to bring the regicide Bothwel (now Duke of Orkney) to a fair trial, who had laid violent hands upon his Sovereign's person, forced her, when in his power, to an unlawful marriage, and now designed to destroy the young Prince, as he had done his father. For these ends, and to procure to themselves, and the nation, such laws as should appear necessary for their safety and the security of the protestant religion, they charged all and sundry the lieges to be in readiness upon three hours warning, to assist them for delivering the Queen from captivity; and such as would not join with them, in so good an undertaking, were ordered to depart from the City of Edinburgh in four hours after the publication of the said proclamation, under the pain of being reputed enemies. The Queen having escaped from

Borthwick, there resorted to her in all about 4000 men, with whom she thought it to take the field; and, abandoning Dunbar, came forward to Seton, and next morning to Carberry hill. The associating Lords, being advertised of her march from Dunbar, and that she was advanced as far as Carberry, mustered their troops, and abandoned Edinburgh, marching directly to Musselburgh. As soon as they came within view of the Queen's army, and were ready to join battle, the Queen, out of tender regard of the shedding of the blood of her own subjects, Orkney retiring to Dunbar, surrendered herself to the Lords, who that night brought her to Edinburgh; and, in a few days, she was sent prisoner to the Castle of Lochleven, a place surrounded half a mile every way with water from the nearest point of land. The associators directed Patrick Lord Lindsay and William Lord Ruthven thither, to deal with Her Majesty, to make a resignation of the Government, with a power to invest her son in the same; which Her Majesty, much importuned by the Lords, was pleased to yield to, appointing the Earl of Murray Regent, during his minority, if he thought fit to accept the same; and in case he should not, the Duke of Chatlerault was nominated, with the Earls of Lenox, Argile, Athol, Morton, Glencairn and Mar, who were jointly to govern. The next day, being the 26th of July 1567, both the resignation and commission were proclaimed at the Cross of Edinburgh; and, on the 29th of the same month, in the Church of Stirling, the Prince was anointed King, by Adam Bishop of Orkney, assisted by two of the Superintendents¹, and crowned by John Earl of Athol; the sermon on that occasion being preached by Mr. John Knox. But the Queen, after ten months imprisonment, made her escape on the 2d of May 1568, in the habit of one of her servants, by means of George Douglas, the Laird of of Lochlevin's brother. As soon as she came to land, to prevent a surprise, Her Majesty, attended by George Lord Seton and James Hamilton of Ruchbank, came that night to Nidrie, a house of the Lord Seton, and the next day to Hamilton, where she was received by the Earls of Argile, Cassils, Eglintoun and Rothes, the Lords Summerveil, Yester, Borthwick, Livingstoun, Herris, Maxwel, Sanquhar and Ross, with their friends and followers, to the number of a thousand men. The Queen, calling a general council, solemnly declared, That the resignation of the Government was extorted from her: thereupon they decerned the resignation void and null, and determined, That, in the mean time, she should take possession of the Castle of Dunbartoun, and there remain, until her loving subjects came to her assistance. In pursuance of this resolution, she began her march on the 13th of May; but

¹ Spotiswood History of the Church of Scotland.

the Earl of Murray, Regent, being at Glasgow, posted himself in her way to oppose her passage, with an army of 3000 men, the Queen's consisting of near 6000. Thus prepared, both armies met at a little village, called Langside, about a mile south of the City of Glasgow; and, joining battle, the Queen's troops were defeat. This action fell out on the 13th day of May 1568. Whereupon the unfortunate Queen fled towards England, sending Sir Robert Melvil express to Queen Elizabeth, with a ring she had formerly received from that Princess, certifying her, That, if at any time she wanted her protection, she might be assured of it; and a letter, in which, after a short account of her misfortunes, she begg'd her protection and assistance, or, at least, a safe passage through England to France. But the unfortunate Queen, without waiting for an answer, relying entirely upon the honour of the Queen of England, accompanied with John Lord Fleming, who ever stood firm to her interest, and the Lord Herries, taking boat at Kircudbright, she landed at Wickeringtoun in Cumberland, the 17th day of May 1568, and, the same night, wrote the following letter to Queen Elizabeth, with her own hand.

" YOU are not ignorant (My very good sister) how some of my subjects, whom I have raised to the highest pitch of honour, conspired to imprison me. I nevertheless received them again into favour, after they had, by the force of arms, been driven out of my kingdom. Yet these very men broke violently into my chamber, cruelly murthered my servant before my face, though I was then big with child, and forcibly detained me in their custody. I nevertheless pardoned them a second time; but behold, they pretended a new crime against me, which they plotted themselves, and signed with their own hands, and were now ready with an army in the field to charge me. Trusting however to my innocence, and desirous to prevent the shedding of blood, I willingly put myself into their hands; upon which they immediately thrust me into prison, removed all my servants from me, excepting one or two waiting maids, my physician and my cook; constrained me, by threats and terror of death, to resign my kingdom; and, in an assembly of the Estates, convocated by their own authority, refused to hear me or my advocates; despoiled me of my goods, and barred me from all conference with any man. Afterwards, by GOD's guidance, I escaped out of prison; and, being guarded by the flower of the nobility, which gladly flocked into me from all parts, I put my enemies in mind of their duty and allegiance; I offered them pardon, and proposed that both parties might be heard in an assembly of the

" Estates, that the commonwealth might no longer be distracted with civil
" combustions. Two messengers I sent about this matter, both of them they
" cast into prison; those who aided me they proclaimed traitors, and commanded
" them by publick Proclamation presently to leave me. I prayed them, that
" the Lord Boyd might, upon publick faith and assurance, treat with them
" about composing matters; but this also they flatly denied: yet I hoped, by
" your mediation, they might have been recalled to their duty. But when I saw
" that I must have undergone either death or a new imprisonment, I resolved
" to go to Dunbartoun. They in the way opposed themselves against me, kill'd
" and put my men to flight in battle. I betook myself to the Lord Herries,
" with whom I am come into your kingdom, trusting assuredly in your singular
" kindness, that you will assist me, and excite others by your example. I do
" therefore earnestly entreat you, that I may be forthwith conducted unto you,
" who am now in very great straits, as I shall more fully inform you, when it
" shall please you to take pity upon me. God grant unto you a long and safe
" life; and to me patience and consolation, which I hope and pray that I may
" obtain of Him, by your means."

This moving letter was so far from prevailing with Queen Elizabeth, that, instead of the friendly reception Queen Mary expected, she was confin'd to Carlile, under the custody of the Lord Scroop. This unexpected treatment very much surprized her; and then she began, too late, to perceive her error, in coming into England, against the advice of her best friends: but, dissembling her inward grief, she sent the Lord Herries to intreat Queen Elizabeth for a hearing, in her own presence, where she might both clear herself, and shew how injuriously she had been dealt with by those, whom, at her intercession, she had recalled from banishment; or, if that could not be obtained, to crave, she might be allowed to depart out of England, and not be detained as a prisoner, since she had come voluntarily thither, in confidence of her friendship, often promised and confirmed, as well by letters as by repeated messages. This request was also rejected by Queen Elizabeth, as the former; only she was so far moved, that she promised to write to the Regent to delay all proceedings against those subjects that stood in her defence. And, instead of England's being a sanctuary to the distressed Queen of Scots, it became only a change of air, but not from confinement to liberty. And being tossed from one prison to another, for the space of eighteen years, she was at last charged with being privy to a treasonable design of invading the Realm of England, to depose Queen Elizabeth, and to take away her life. All which she denied, and with great presence of mind and modesty of behaviour, vindicated her own innocency, and refused to answer as a subject, she being an absolute Queen. They nevertheless went on, and pronounced the sentence of death upon her; which being intimated to her, she was so far from being dismayed at the news, that she gave thanks to GOD for delivering her from a miserable life, into a state of glory.

In the mean time, King James her son omitted nothing that became a dutiful son, and a wise and prudent king: for he most earnestly solicited Queen Elizabeth, by his ambassador, for sparing her life; representing to her, that he thought it strange the nobility and counsellors of England should take upon them to give sentence upon a Queen of Scotland; and would think it more strange if she should stain her hands with the blood of his mother; which, (as he could not believe would ever enter into her heart to do,) if it should be, he desired her to consider, how much it concerned him, in honour, to be revenged of so great an indignity. This being all that the king was in condition to do at that time, the French King, by his ambassador, interceded for her life; but it had the same effect with the former: for she lost her life with the stroke of an ax, at Fotheringham Castle, the 8th of February 1586.

This deplorable end had Queen Mary in the 46th year of her age: a Princess of many virtues, but still crossed with the frowns of fortune, which she bore with great courage and magnanimity to the last. Her death was lamented by many; and some particular friend had the courage to show it, in affixing, near her Sepulchre, the following inscription; the author unknown.

" MARY, Queen of Scotland, daughter of a king, widow of the King of
" France, kinswoman and next heir to the Queen of England, adorned with
" royal virtues and a princely spirit; having often, but in vain, implored to
" have the right done her that was due to a Prince, the ornament of our age
" and mirror of Princes, by a barbarous and tyrannical cruelty was cut off;
" and by one and the same infamous judgement, both Mary Queen of Scot-
" land is punished with death, and all kings living made liable to the same
" stroke. A strange kind of grave is this, wherein the living are included with
" the dead; for, with the ashes of this blessed Mary, thou shalt know, that the
" Majesty of all Kings and Princes lies here depressed and violated. But, be-
" cause the regal secret admonishes all kings of their duty, Traveller, I will
" say no more."

Her corps was solemnly interred in the Cathedral Church of Peterborough, where her body rested, until King James, coming to the Crown of England, prepared a vault in the Chappel of Westminster, to which her corps was privately conveyed; and over the same was erected a magnificent monument, with this inscription, in Roman capitals.

" D. O. M.

Bonæ Memoriæ & Spei æternæ

" MARIÆ STEWART, Scotorum Reginæ; Franciæ Dotariæ; Jac: v.
" Scotorum Regis Filiæ & Hæredis unicæ; Henrici vii. Angl: Regis, ex Mar-
" gareta majori natu Filia (Jacobi iiii. Regi Scotorum matrimonio copulata)
" Proneptis; Edwardi iiii. Angl: Regis, ex Elizabetha filiarum suarum natu
" maxima, Abneptis; Francisci ii. Gallorum R: Conjugis; Coronæ Angl: dum
" vixit, certæ & indubitatæ Hæredis; & Jacobi, Magnæ Britanniæ Monarchi
" potentissimi, Matris."

Issue of Mary Queen of Scotland, by Henry Lord Darnly and Duke of Albany, her husband.

JAMES VI. King of Scots, and first Monarch of Great Britain. This peaceable and wise Prince was born on the 19th of June 1566, and, at thirteen months old was crowned king, and James Earl of Murray appointed Regent; who, in the 4th year of his Regency, met with a violent death, at Linlithgow. Matthew Earl of Lenox, grandfather to the young king, was chosen Regent, the 12th of July 1570; who, after he had governed the kingdom about fourteen months, was killed at Stirling, the 4th of September; and, on the 5th, the Earls of Argile, Morton, and Mar, stood candidates for his post: the last of these was preferred; who, when he had governed thirteen months, died at Stirling, the 28th of October 1572; and, in the beginning of November thereafter, James Earl of Morton was elected Regent: after he had for seven years enjoyed the post, the administration of affairs was translated to the king himself, in 1579, then thirteen years of age. The Regent Morton, being accused afterwards by Captain James Stewart son to the Lord Ochiltree, as accessory to the murther of the king's father, was thereupon beheaded, the 2d of June 1581.

Some few months after the king had taken the Government into his own hands, arrived Esme Stewart, Lord Aubigny, from France. He was son of

John Lord Aubigny, younger brother of Matthew Earl of Lenox, and so cousin-german to King Henry, King James's father. He was so very graciously received by the king, that, in a few days time, he was created Earl of Lenox; the king's granduncle, Robert Earl of March, who then possessed that title, being, in place thereof, created Earl of March; and, to support his dignity, the Abbacy of Arbroth (which fell by the forfaulture of Lord John Hamilton, Commendator thereof) was bestowed on him at the same time. In Anno 1580, he was made Lord High Chamberlain of Scotland; and, as a further testimony of the royal favour, he was, by Letters Patent, dated the 5th day of October 1581, created Duke of Lenox. He was in so great favour at court, that, to prevent the Duke of Guise, the King's kinsman, from employing his interest with the king, in favour, as they pretended, of that faction, John Earl of Mar, William Earl of Gourie, Patrick Lord Lindsay, Robert Lord Boyd, and others, endeavoured to remove the Duke of Lenox and Captain James Stewart, then called Earl of Arran, from the king. Accordingly they invited His Majesty to the Castle of Ruthven, where they detained him, changed his servants, imprisoned Captain Stewart, and dismissed the Duke of Lenox into France: but the king rescued himself, and escaped to St. Andrews, where several of the nobility resorted to him, with some forces, to protect him. But Gourie and others, plotting a second surprize of the king, were discovered; Gourie imprisoned, condemned and beheaded, and his complices forced to fly.

King James, in the year 1589, was married to Ann, daughter of Frederick II. king of Denmark and Norway, by proxy, the 20th of August. Upon which she sailing for Scotland, was, by a stress and storm of weather, carried to Norway; where being forced to stay, by reason of contrary winds, the king sailed over thither; and the marriage was solemnized at Upsal, by Mr. David Lindsay, Minister at Leith, afterwards Bishop of Ross. The King and Queen arrived at Leith the 20th of May 1590, where they were received with all imaginable demonstrations of joy; and Her Majesty was crowned by Mr. Robert Bruce of Kinnaird, Minister in Edinburgh, in the Abby Church of Holyrood-house.

King James being arrived to the 36th year of his age, had always wisely continued a good correspondence with Queen Elizabeth, as the only way to secure the succession to the crown of England; she having a little before her death (which happened upon the 24th of March, 1603) declared him her successor, he deriving title from Margaret, his great grandmother, eldest daughter of King Henry VII. and of Elizabeth his Queen, daughter of King Edward IV. of England, (married to James IV. of Scotland.) So that to him descended the rights, together with the blood, of all the ancient kings of England, both Saxon and Norman. For the Lady Margaret, sister and sole heir of Edgar Atheling, the last Prince of the English Saxons, being married to Malcolm Canmore King of Scots, conveyed to him the Saxon, as Margaret, King Henry VII.'s daughter, did bring to him the Norman, titles and blood. Whereupon he was the same day proclaimed King of England, Scotland, France, and Ireland, at Whitehall. And, having settled the affairs of Scotland, set forward for England, on the 5th of April, attended by the Duke of Lenox, the Earls of Mar, Argile, and Murray, and the Lord Home, with a noble retinue; whence, by easy journies, he came to London on the 7th of May, and was solemnly crowned at Westminster, the 25th of July; where the antique Regal Chair of Inthronization, carried to England by King Edward I. did receive, with the person of His Majesty, the full accomplishment of that prediction of this his coming to the crown of England.

This learned and peacible Prince, in the 60th year of his age, fell sick of a quartan ague, the common messenger of death to aged people: after a month's languishing, he departed this mortal life on the 27th of March 1625. He was a Prince excellently skill'd in all the liberal arts, but excelled in divinity, as appeared at a conference at Hampton Court, betwixt the Episcopal and Presbyterian party, and by the writings he left to posterity; and in that part of politicks relating to monarchy, which he used to call king-craft, he was a great master. In a word, he was the Solomon of his age, as our learned historian Spotiswood says. Many epitaphs were composed to express the sorrow conceived by his death. The following I thought fit to subjoin:

> All who have eyes awake and weep,
> For he, whose waking wrought our sleep,
> Is fall'n asleep himself, and never
> Shall wake again till wak'd for ever:
> Death's iron hand hath clos'd those eyes
> Which were, at once, three kingdoms spies,
> Both to foresee, and to prevent
> Dangers, as soon as they were meant.
> That head, whose working brain alone
> Wrought all mens quiet but his own,
> Now lies at rest. O let him have
> The peace he lent us, in his grave,

If that no Naboth all his reign,
Was for his fruitful vineyard slain;
If no Uriah lost his life,
Because he had too fair a wife;
Then let no Shimei's curses wound
His honour, or profane this ground.
Let no black mouth'd, no rank breath'd cur,
Peaceful JAMES his ashes stir.
Princes are Gods; O do not then
Rake in their graves to prove them men.
For two and twenty years long care;
For providing such an heir,
Who, to the peace we had before,
May add twice two and twenty more;
For his days travels and nights watches;
For his craz'd sleep, stoln by snatches;
For two fair kingdoms join'd in one;
For all he did or meant to have done;
Do this for him, write on his dust,
" JAMES, THE PEACEFUL AND THE JUST."

His body was, for the greater state, conveyed from Theobald's to Denmark house, by torch-light, where it rested from the 23d of April to the 4th of May, and then was interred at Westminster, with great solemnity. Upon his coffin was engraven this memorial:

DEPOSITUM,

" Invictissimi Principis Jacobi, Magnæ Britanniæ
Franciæ & Hiberniæ Regis; qui rerum, apud Scotos,
annos 59. menses 3. dies duodecim; apud Anglos, annos
22. & dies 3. pacifice ac fæliciter potitus; tandem
in Domino obdormivit; 27 Die Martii, Anno a Christo
nato 1625. Ætatis vero suæ 60.

Children of King James the I. Monarch of Great Britain, by Ann, daughter of Frederick II. King of Denmark, his Queen.

I. Henry, born at Stirling the 19th of February 1594, and on the day of his baptism created Duke of Rothsay and Earl of Carrick; and, after his father's coming to the Crown of England, created Duke of Cornwal and Prince of Wales, and installed Knight of the Garter, an. 1609. In the 18th year of his age, he fell sick of a fever, which deprived him of his life, upon the 6th day of November 1612. He was buried at Westminster the 7th of December, the funeral pomp being completed by the tears and lamentations of the people. He was a Prince of vast hopes and extraordinary virtues; his death being universally lamented, both at home and abroad.

II. Robert, died an infant.

III. Charles, Duke of Albany, Marquis of Ormond, Earl of Ross, Lord Ardmanoch, Duke of York, and Prince of Wales, succeeded his father in the Monarchy of Great Britain.

IV. Elizabeth, born the 19th of August 1596, and was married to Frederick Count Palatine of the Rhine, Duke of Bavaria and Silesia, in February 1613. Thus strengthened by an alliance with the king of Great Britain, he was thought a fit person to be king of Bohemia, and accordingly was elected by the states of that kingdom: but he was no sooner invested in the crown, but the Emperor, with great force, assaulted him in Prague, and not only drove him with his wife and children from thence, but took also from him his own patrimony, the Palatinate. King James, his father-in-law, sent his ambassador to the Emperor to solicite his restauration, but to no purpose. This exiled Prince, the King of Bohemia, died at Mentz, an. 1632.

Children of Elizabeth, Queen of Bohemia.

I. Frederick, Count Palatine, crowned King of Bohemia: He died sans issue, an. 1629.

II. Charles, Count Palatine, married Charlotte, daughter of William Landgrave of Hesse-Cassel; by which lady he had, (1) Charles, Count Palatine, who died an. 1685, without succession; (2) Charlotte, married to Philip Duke of Orleans, only brother to Louis XIV. the present French King, and had issue by him Philip now Duke of Orleans, and a daughter, Elizabeth, married to Leopold Duke of Lorrain.

III. Rupert, Count Palatine: he came into England an. 1642, and was elected a Knight of the Garter; and being looked upon as a fit man for action, was made General of His Majesty's horse, and, an. 1642, created Duke of Cumberland and Earl of Holderness. But the king's forces, at last, being totally dispersed, he transported himself into France; and upon the restauration of King

Charles II. he returned to England, and was installed a Knight of the Garter. Having served Admiral in several naval expeditions against the Dutch, he gave many signal proofs of his great courage and conduct. He died in the year 1682, unmarried.

IV. Maurice, Count Palatine, came over to England, where, in the wars of King Charles I. he behaved himself with much valour and conduct. He died in the year 1654, without any succession.

V. Edward, Count Palatine; he embraced the Romish religion; and died at Paris, an. 1663, leaving issue, by Ann his wife, daughter and heir of Charles Duke of Nevers in France, three daughters; (1) Ann, married to Henry Julius Prince of Conde, and hath issue; (2) Benedicta Henrieta Philippa, married to John Duke of Brunswick and Hanover, and had issue, two daughters; Charlotte, married to Rainauld Duke of Modena; and Willielmina Æmilia, to Joseph the present Emperor; (3) Louisa Mary, married to Charles Prince of Salms, and had issue.

VI. Elizabeth, eldest daughter of Frederick King of Bohemia, by Elizabeth daughter of King James VI. was Abbess of Herwerden in Westphalia, but of the reformed religion; she died an. 1680, without issue.

VII. Louisa; she embraced the Romish persuasion, and became Abbess of Monbaisson in France, but died without issue.

VIII. Sophia, born 1630, married to Ernest Augustus Duke of Brunswick and Hanover. Her Highness, being nearest heir to the crown of Britain in the Protestant line, is nominated successor to Her present Majesty Queen Ann, in case she have no issue.

Issue of Sophia, Dutchess Dowager of Hanover, and Grand-daughter of King James VI.

I. George Louis now Duke of Hanover, born in the year 1660, married Sophia daughter of William Duke of Zell; by whom he hath George, born in an. 1683, and a daughter, Dorothea, married to Frederick William Prince of Prussia.

II. Frederick, was slain in Transilvania, fighting against the Turks, in the year 1690, unmarried.

III. Maximilian, now living, unmarried.

IV. Charles, slain at the battle of Casnock, fighting against the Turks, in an. 1690.

V. Ernest now living at the Court of Hanover.

VI. Sophia, married to Frederick Marquis of Brandenburgh, now King of Prussia, and hath iusse.

CHARLES I. Second Monarch of Great Britain, only surviving son of King James, born at Dunfermling in Scotland, on the 19th of November 1600: so weak an infant, that his baptism was hastened without the usual solemnities, that otherwise would have attended that occasion. In the second year of his age 1601, he was created Duke of Albany, Marquis of Ormond, Earl of Ross, and Lord Ardmanoch. In the year 1603, when King James his father was preparing for his remove from Scotland to the throne of England, there was a certain Scots gentleman made such an augury of his future greatness and succession to the crown, as I thought deserved here to be related. The gentleman came to take his leave of the court, and was for that purpose admitted into the bed-chamber, where the King, Queen, and the royal children were present. Having addressed himself to the king, with a great deal of affectionate wishes, he then, overlooking Prince Henry, the king's eldest son, applied himself directly to Duke Charles, and kissed his hand, with so much ardency and affection, as if thereby he meant to pay him some extraordinary honour. The king to correct his supposed mistake, directed him towards Prince Henry, as the apparent heir of his crown. The gentleman replied, he was not mistaken, he knew to whom he addressed himself. This child (says he) "shall convey your Majesty's name and titles to succeeding generations." An historian [1] observes, that this then was conceived to be dottage; but the event gave it the credit of a prophecy. In the year 1604, the Duke was brought to England, and then made Knight of the Bath; and on the 16th of January 1605, was created Duke of York: on the death of Prince Henry, his brother, he was honoured with the Dukedom of Cornwal; and, November 3d 1616, was created Prince of Wales. His father dying the 27th of March 1625, the same day Prince Charles was proclaimed King at Westminster, and at Edinburgh the 31st of the same month.

In the first year of His Majesty's reign, he instituted a new hereditary title of honour, that of Baronet, inferior to that of a Lord Baron; (which King James intended before his death, for advancing the plantation of Nova Scotia in America, and for settling a colony there,) to be conferred by patent under the great seal. The number, according to the first institution, was not to exceed 150; he promised that neither he or his successors should ever create,

[1] History of the Life and Reign of King Charles I.

in time coming, any other dignity, under that of a Lord of Parliament, that should be equal to them. They were to take place of all ordinary Knights, called " Equites Aurati," though not of Bannerets, (that is such as are, or should be, created under the royal standard in the king's army, the Sovereign being present,) who should have precedency of the Baronets during their lives, the honour not descending to their posterity. In the several patents, His Majesty did dispone to each of these knights a certain portion of land in Nova Scotia, erecting the same into a free Barony. They had precedency according to the priority of their creations, and were allowed to wear about their necks an orange taunie Ribban, and pendant to it, on a Shield Argent, a Saltyre Azure, circumscrib'd with this Motto, " Fax mentis honestæ gloria ;" and, as an augmentation to their Coat of arms, an ensign of Nova Scotia, viz. Argent, a Saltyre Azure, charged with a Scutcheon of the royal arms of Scotland; Or, a Lion Rampant Gules, within a double Tressure, flower'd and counter-flower'd; with an imperial crown above the shield.

In the year 1633, His Majesty was pleased to honour his native country with his presence; he arrived at Edinburgh the 15th day of June, and was crowned at the Abby Church of Holy-rood-house, the 18th thereafter. At which solemnity he promoted several to new honours, viz. William Earl of Angus he created Marquis of Douglas, George Viscount of Duplin, Earl of Kinoul; William Viscount of Air, Earl of Dumfries; William Viscount of Drumlanrick, Earl of Queensberry; William Lord Alexander and Viscount of Canada, Earl of Stirling; John Lord Kinloss, Earl of Elgin; David Lord Carnegie, Earl of Southesk; John Lord Traquair, Earl of Traquair; John Lord Weems, Earl of Weems: William Lord Ramsay, Earl of Dalhousie; Sir John Gordon of Lochinvar, Viscount of Kenmure; Sir Robert Douglas of Spot, Viscount of Belhaven; Sir James Livingston, son to Alexander Earl of Linlithgow, he created Lord Almont; Sir James Johnston of that-ilk, Lord Johnston; Sir Alexander Forbes of Pitsligo, Lord Pitsligo; Sir David Lindsay of Balcarras, Lord Balcarras; Sir George Forrester of Corstorphine, Lord Forrester; Sir John Frazer of Muchel, Lord Frazer; and Sir Robert Maclellan of Bomby, Lord Kirkcudbright.

In this Parliament His Majesty urged that the ratification of his royal prerogative, and his right of appointing the apparel of Churchmen, might pass by the same vote. Many of the members agreed to the clause of the prerogative, but dissented to that of Churchmens apparel, as being apprehensive it would bring

[1] Sir James Balfour's Annals, in MS.

in the English surplice. His Majesty also was solicitous for an uniformity in publick worship, between his three kingdoms; and to pave the way for this, he recommended to some of the Bishops, the compiling of a Liturgy for Scotland, which differed little from that of the English; only it excluded the lessons out of the Apocrypha, and made use of the last version of the Psalms, the word Presbyter being used instead of Priest, to make it the less offensive[1]. According to His Majesty's command, it was finished in the year 1636, and ordered to be read in the Churches; at which great offence was taken, even by many that were Episcopal in their judgement, that this Service Book should be imposed by the civil power, without being presented and approven by the General Assembly, as had been done in the restitution of Episcopal Government, and introduction of the five Articles of Perth. So Easter-Day, in 1637, was appointed for the first reading of the Liturgy; but, upon some considerations, it was deferred to the 23d of July. As soon as it began to be read in the High Church of Edinburgh, a number of the meaner sort of people fell into clamour and confusion. The Bishop of Edinburgh, Dr. Lindsay, who was to preach that day, stept into the pulpit and endeavoured to appease the tumult, but without any success. The like disorders happened in many other Churches where the Service book was attempted to be read: upon which the Lords of Council put out several proclamations, for repressing such disorders for the time to come, but little obedience was yielded to them. The Council, a few months after, was petitioned in name of divers of the nobility, gentry, ministers, and commons, for removing the Service-book, Book of Canons, and the High-commission-Court. These keeped frequent meetings, which were called the " Tables:" They proceeded in framing and subscribing the Covenant, under this title, " The " Confession of Faith of the Kirk of Scotland, subscribed at first by the " King's Majesty, the Council and the Court, in the year 1580, and by persons of all ranks, in 1581." In which all the corruptions of the Church of Rome were particularly abjured, with a protestation, " That that declaration was made without any mental reservation or equivocation whatsoever."

The Council, alarmed at these proceedings, agreed to send Sir John Hamilton to the king, to acquaint him with the state of affairs, and to declare that they thought the cause of the general combustions in the country were the fears apprehended of innovation of religion, from the Service-book, Book of Canons and High-commission-Court; and therefore His Majesty may please that he would take trial of his subjects grievances, and in the mean time not

[1] Sir Philip Warwick's Memoirs. [2] Guthrie's Memoirs.

to urge the practice of the Liturgy: Which the king was pleased to yield to, by his Proclamation, over the Market-Cross of Edinburgh, discharging the Service-book, the Book of Canons, and High-commission-Court; aud indicted a General Assembly, to sit at Glasgow, the 21st of November 1638, and a Parliament at Edinburgh, the 15th of May thereafter. At the time appointed the Assembly sat down, the Marquis of Hamilton being His Majesty's High Commissioner, and Mr. Alexander Henderson chosen Moderator. The 2d day of the Assembly a Declinator was presented to the Commissioner[1], in name of the Bishops of St. Andrews, Glasgow, Edinburgh, Galloway, Aberdeen, Ross, Brichen, and Dunblain, against the Assembly: it being put to the vote, whether or not they were a free and lawful meeting, notwithstanding the Bishops Declinator; it was carried in the affirmative. The Assembly proceeded, and condemned the Service-book, the Book of Canons, and the High-commission-Court, together with the Five Articles of Perth, viz. I. " That the Lord's Supper be receiv-
" ed kneeling. II. That sick persons might receive it at home. III. That
" Baptism might be administered in private houses, in case of necessity. IV.
" That Christmas-day, Good-Friday, Easter-day, Ascension-day, and Whitsun-
" day, should be religiously observed. V. That children, well instructed in
" Christianity, should be confirmed by the Bishop." They likeways abolished the Episcopal Government; and having cited the Bishops before them, they, not thinking fit to compear, were deposed from the Episcopal Function; and the eight that signed the Declinator were excommunicated. The Commissioner, seeing how matters went, took occasion in a speech to shew the illegality of their proceedings, declaring his resolution to dissolve the Assembly; which, on the 8th of December, he did in his Majesty's name, discharging their further proceedings, under pain of Treason. The Moderator told his Grace, " They were sorry he should leave them, but their consciences bore them wit-
" ness, they had done nothing amiss, and could not desert the work of the
" LORD." So they continued sitting, and went on, declaring six former Assemblies to be null and void. The king published a declaration against their proceedings, dated December 8th. To which the Assembly made a protestation[2], and continued sitting until the 20th of the same month.

The king, offended with these proceedings of the Covenanters, resolved by force to reduce them to obedience; to effect which, he levied an army of 6000 horse, and about the same number of foot, and sent a fleet by sea, under the command of the Marquis of Hamilton. On the 27th of March His Ma-

[1] History of the General Assembly 1638.   [2] History of King Charles I.

jesty began his journey northward. The Covenanters also took the field, with an army of about 16000 men, under the command of General Lesly; and marching towards England, encamped at Dunse: The English army, by this time, was advanced within seven miles of that place; but neither army attempting any act of hostility. Upon the 2d of June, the Scots sent their humble supplication to the king, by the Earl of Dunfermling, for a treaty, which His Majesty granted, by the mediation of the Marquis of Hamilton, whose affection to his country made him employ his whole interest with the king for procuring a gracious answer; and so it happily ended in a peace, on the 18th of June. The chief Articles agreed on were, " That there should be a full and free As-
" sembly holden at Edinburgh, the 12th of August, and a Parliament the 26th
" of the same month; that His Majesty's Castles should be delivered up to
" him; and that both armies should be disbanded¹." So, upon June 20th, each of them disbanded, and retired peaceably homeward.

The Assembly met at the time appointed, wherein they condemned Episcopacy as unlawful and contrary to the word of GOD; and ratified the Covenant, ordaining the same to be sworn and subscribed by the whole nation. All which acts were confirmed in the subsequent Parliament. But the king refusing to allow the Assembly of Glasgow 1638 to be a lawful meeting, (though His Majesty ratified the same acts past in the Assembly at Edinburgh 1639) the imprisoning the Lord Loudoun, one of the chief of the Covenanters, whom they had sent to Court, with their Petition for redress of grievances, highly incensed that party: and Laud, Arch-Bishop of Canterbury, with the rest of the hot men in England, pusht His Majesty to a second rupture; whereupon he raises an army; the Covenanters likewise got a good army together, which entered England the 21st of August 1640, under the command of General Lesly. Encountering a part of the king's forces, under the conduct of the Lord Connoway, they obtained a signal victory at Newburn, August 28th, and on the 30th they took the town of Newcastle. The King, in this strait, summoned the Peers to meet him at York, the 24th of September; by whose council a treaty was commenced at Rippon, where Commissioners, appointed by both nations, met the first of October 1640. The English were, the Earls of Bedford, Hartford, Essex, Salisbury, Warwick, Bristol, and Holland; and Lords Wharton, Paget, Kimboltoun, Brook, Paulet, Howard of Escrick, Savel, and Dunsmore. The Scots Commissioners were, Charles Earl of Dunfermling, John Lord Loudoun, Sir William Douglas of Cavers, ... Hepburn of

¹ Bishop of Dunkeld's Memoirs.

Wachtoun, Mr. Archbald Johnston of Waristoun, John Smith, Alexander Wedderburn, and Mr. Alexander Henderson Minister of Edinburgh. They concluded upon a cessation of arms; and that the treaty should be removed from Rippon to London, to be prosecuted there.

In the year 1641, His Majesty having indicted a Parliament in Scotland, which he resolved to honour with his presence; he arrived at Edinburgh the 16th of August, and on the 19th made the following speech to the Parliament.

My Lords and Gentlemen,

" THERE hath been nothing so displeasing to me, as those unlucky differ-
" ences, which have happen'd between me and my people; and nothing that I
" have more desired, than to see this day, wherein I hope, not only to settle
" these unhappy mistakings, but rightly to know, and to be known to, my native
" country.

" I need not tell you, for I think it is well known to most, what difficulties
" I have passed through and overcome, to be here at this present. Yet this I
" will say, if love had not been a chief motive to this journey, other respects
" might easily have found a shift, to do that by a commission, which I am come
" to perform myself.

" And this considered, I cannot doubt of such real testimonies of your
" affections, for the maintenance of that Royal power which I enjoy after an
" hundred and eight descents; and which you have professed to maintain; and
" to which your own national oath doth oblige you; that I shall not think any
" pains ill bestow'd.

" Now the end of my coming is shortly this: To perfect whatsoever I have
" promised; and withal, to quiet the distractions which have and may fall out
" amongst you: And this I mind, not superficially, but fully and chearfully, to
" perform. For I assure you, that I can do nothing with more chearfulness,
" than to give my people a general satisfaction. Wherefore, not offering to
" endear myself unto you in words, which indeed is not my way, I desire, in
" the first place, to settle that which concerns the Religion and just Liberties of
" this my native country, before I proceed to any other act."

The most material things, done in this Parliament, were the ratification of the treaty of Rippon; an act for raising an army to be sent to Germany, for the service of the elector Palatine: and that His Majesty should nominate the officers of state, Privy Counsellors and Lords of the Session, with consent of Parliament: all which the King ratified, and ended the Parliament with conferring several honours. Archbald Earl of Argile, he created Marquis of Argile: General Alexander Lesly, Earl of Leven; John Lord Loudoun, Earl of Loudoun; James Lord Almont, Earl of Callender; Sir John Scrimzeor of Dudop, Viscount of Dundee; Sir Robert Arbuthnot of that-ilk, Viscount of Arbuthnot; and Sir Andrew Murray of Balvaird, Minister at Ebdie, he created Lord Balvaird. On the 18th of November, His Majesty took journey for London, and arrived there the 25th day of that month.

In 1642, a breach falling out betwixt the King and the Parliament of England, they both take arms: the King march'd with his army to Nottingham, where he set up his standard, declaring the reasons of the war, related at large by the English Historians. The Parliament, to strengthen themselves against the King, resolved to send for assistance to Scotland; and chose, out of both Houses, Commissioners to negotiate a treaty of alliance, who came to Edinburgh August 7th 1643, and brought with them a declaration of the Lords and Commons of the Parliament of England to the Estates of Scotland, and another to the General Assembly of the Church there. . They promised to aid their brethren in England, upon condition of uniformity in Church Government, and a solemn League and Covenant; they transmitted a form of it to the two Houses at Wesminster, where it was consented to, August 28th: ordered to be printed and published, September 21st: and the next day it was taken by the House of Commons. His Majesty publish'd a proclamation against taking of it, dated October 19th. Notwithstanding of this, it was imposed on people, as they would escape the brand of malignancy. Upon this confederacy, the Scots army, under the command of General Lesly, then Earl of Leven, entered England, January 15th 1644. The Parliament, by their assistance, obtained that great victory at Marston-moor. In the mean time, His Majesty gave commission to James Marquis of Montrose, to be Governour of Scotland, and to raise an army to give a diversion to the Covenanters. He fought successfully in that character, in the several battles of Tipermure, Alford, Aldern, Aberdeen, Innerlochie, and Kilsyth, but was defeat at Philiphaugh; all which are at large related by Doctor Wishart, late Bishop of Edinburgh, in his Memoirs of the Marquis of Montrose.

Upon the 5th of May 1646, the king, leaving Oxford in disguise, in company of Dr. John Hudson, a Divine, and Mr. John Ashunburn, riding as a servant to the latter, with a cloakbag behind him, came to the Scots army at Newark, and the next day they took their march northward. His Majesty being with Lieutenant General David Lesly in the van, came, the 13th of May, to Newcastle, where they received a message from the Parliament of England, requiring that his Majesty's Person might be delivered up to them. In this, as the Lord Holies says, appeared the wisdom of the Scots Nation, foreseeing the inconveniencies which would have followed, had they been positive at that time in detaining the king; therefore, they made for him the best conditions they could, for the safety and honour of his person: and, to avoid greater mischiefs, they were necessitated to leave him in England, and so march away, which they did in February 1647. The Parliament presently voted him to be brought to Holmby-house; thereafter, he was removed to Hampton Court, and thence, to the Isle of Wight, where he was kept prisoner; during which time the Parliament of Scotland met, in March 1648, wherein James Duke of Hamilton made overture for raising an army, in order to His Majesty's rescue. The Parliament voted to raise an army of 30000 foot and 6000 horse, to be sent to England, under the command of the Duke of Hamilton; and, to obtain the favour of the church, they declared for the Covenant. A rendezvous of the army was appointed at Annan, near the borders of England. An insurrection against this enterprize was intended, but they were defeat at Mauchlin in Kyle, before they got to a head, by Middleton and Hurry, on the 4th of July 1648. On the 8th of July the Scots army marched into England; but by the time they got to Preston in Lancashire, the horse and foot being at a considerable distance, Cromwell and Lambert fell upon them with such advantage that they were overthrown the 17th of August[1], and the Duke taken prisoner. On the 6th of February 1649, he was brought to his trial before the High Court of Justice, for that he, as Earl of Cambridge, had invaded the nation in an hostile manner, and levied men to assist the king against the kingdom and people of England: for which he received sentence of death, the 6th of March; and, upon Friday next ensuing, lost his head.

After the defeat of the Scots army, General Cromwell sent Colonel Evers to bring the king from the Isle of Wight to Hurst Castle, and from thence to Windsor, the 10th of December; and January 19th following, the king was brought from Windsor to St. James's, and on the 28th ensuing, Cromwell, the grand Rebel, brought an ordinance into the House of Commons, nominating diverse persons for trial of the king, which being tendered to the House of Lords, it was refused, and protested against by the Parliament of Scotland. Notwithstanding, the Commons, on the 4th of January, voting the Supreme

---

[1] Life of James Duke of Hamilton.

authority to be in the people, and consequently in them, as their representatives, proceeded without the Lords, and ordered their Commissioners, for trial of the king, to meet on Monday the 10th of January 1649; appointing Sergeant Bradshaw to be President of the Court. One Ask, a common Lawyer, and Dr. Dorislaus, a Dutch Civilian, were pleaders against him.

This infamous Court met at Westminster-hall, the 20th of January; whereupon Bradshaw commanded Sergeant Dandy to fetch in the prisoner, who immediately brought the king, attended by a guard of partizans, and placed him in a chair, and then acquainted him, " That the commons of England, assembled in Parliament, being sensible of the great calamities brought upon the nation, and of the innocent bloodshed, which was referred to him as the author of it, according to that duty which they owe to God, the nation and themselves, and that fundamental power and trust reposed in them by the people, have constituted this high Court of Justice, before which he was now brought; and that he was to hear his charge, upon which the Court will proceed according to Justice." Thus, having brought His sacred Majesty to that pretended judgement-seat, the solicitor, in name of the Commons of England, did accuse Charles Stewart, King of England, of High Treason and Misdemeanors. His Majesty, preparing to give fitting answers to their accusations, could not be heard. Four times was he brought before this pretended Court of Justice. Upon the 27th of January, contrary to all Law, Reason, Religion, Oaths of Allegiance, and Covenants, he was, by the mouth of that infamous Regicide, John Bradshaw, sentenced to be beheaded, upon the 30th ensuing [1]. The fatal day being come, at ten of the clock, attended by a regiment of foot and a guard of partizans, His Majesty was conveyed through a window of the Banqueting-house to the scaffold, covered with black, where he beheld the executioner in a mask, at which he was not at all affrighted, but declaring himself to the world, to die an innocent man and a good Christian, according to the profession of the Church of England, praying that his enemies might repent, and that his death might not be laid to their charge. After which, with a Christian magnanimity, he endured the fatal stroke, which separated his head from his body; both were put into a coffin, and carried into his lodgings at Whitehall, and from thence to St. James's, and put into a leaden coffin, and on the 7th of February, interred by James Duke of Lenox, the Marquises of Hartford and Dorchester, the Earl of Lindsay, and Dr. Juxton, Bishop of London, in a vault in the Abby of Westminster, with this inscription upon the coffin, in capital letters:

[1] Sanford's Genealogical History of the Kings of England.

KING CHARLES, 1648.

Several mournful elegies and epitaphs have been celebrated to the memory of this great Prince. This following, so universally esteem'd, done by the great Marquis of Montrose, I thought fit to subjoin.

" Great, good, and just, could I but rate
" My grief to thy too rigid fate!
" I'd weep the world in such a strain,
" As it would once deluge again.
" But since thy case much rather cries
" For Briareus hands, than Argus eyes,
" I'll tune thy elegies to trumpet sounds,.
" And write thy epitaph in blood and wounds!"

Issue of King Charles I. by Maria Henrieta his Queen, Daughter of Henry IV. of France.

I. Charles, born the 29th of May 1630, succeeded his father, in his kingdoms.

II. James Duke of York, born the 14th of October 1633, afterwards King of England. In 1646, after the taking of Oxford, by the Parliament's forces, he was by them brought to London, and committed to the charge of the Earl of of Northumberland; but, in anno 1648, was carried, in women's habit, by Colonel Bamfield, to his sister the Princess of Orange, in Holland. At the 20th year of his age, he entered into arms, serving under the Mareschal De Turenne, and became a Lieutenant General in the French King's army; notwithstanding, upon a treaty between the said King and Oliver Cromwell, he was advertized to depart that kingdom by a day prefix'd. Taking his leave of that Court, he travelled towards Flanders, upon the invitation of Don John of Austria, who offer'd him, in the name of the King of Spain, all possible service and assistance. His Royal Highness took arms under him against the French, who then were leagued with the grand usurper, Oliver Cromwell, in opposition to Spain. He returned with his brother at the Restauration 1660, and was made Lord High Admiral of England; and soon after installed a Knight of the Garter. But his succession to the Crown, upon the death of his brother, and unfortunate reign, I leave to the relation of our most fam'd historians. And, in regard, I design to conclude the history of the Royal Family with the death of King Charles II. I shall insert the posterity of King James VII. in this place.

Issue of King James VII. by the Lady Ann Hyde, eldest daughter of Edward Earl of Clarendon, Lord High Chancellor of England.

I. Charles Duke of Cambridge, born 22d October 1650, died an infant.

II. James Duke of Cambridge, born 12th July 1663, deceased in his infancy.

III. Charles Duke of Kendal, born 4th July 1666, died a child.

IV. Edgar, Duke of Cambridge, born the 14th September 1667, died the 8th of June 1671.

V. Mary, born the 30th of April 1662; a Princess endowed with many eminent virtues; she was married, in Anno 1677, to William, Prince of Orange, afterwards King of England; she died Queen of England, childless, in 1694.

VI Ann, born at St. James's, 6th February 1664; and, upon the death of His late Majesty King William, March 8th 1702, pursuant to an act of Parliament pass'd in the first year of the reign of the said King William, intituled, " An Act declaring the rights of the subject, and settling the succession of the crown," she was proclaimed Queen of England, Scotland, France, and Ireland. The glories of her reign I leave to the better hands of our more able historians; and I pray GOD long to preserve Her Majesty, to be the support of the Protestant religion at home and abroad, and a lasting blessing to these nations, over whom she now happily reigns. Her Majesty was married, July 28th 1683, to his royal Highness, George Prince of Denmark, only brother to Christian V. late king of that kingdom; and by him her Majesty had a numerous issue, but none of them now living: that most hopeful Prince, William Duke of Glocester, the last of her children that survived, dying in July 1700, much lamented. Her Majesty became a widow, by the death of her royal consort, the Prince, October 28th, 1708.

Issue of King James VII. by Mary D'Este, daughter of Alphonso, Duke of Modena, his second wife.

I. Charles, Duke of Cambridge, born 7th November 1677, died December following.

II. Catharine, born 10th January 1674, died in her infancy.

III. Isobel, born 28th of August 1676, died 2d March 1680.

IV. Charlotte Maria, born 15th August 1682, deceased an infant.
V. James, of whom the Queen was delivered the 10th of June 1688.
VI. Louisa, said to be born at St. Germans, upon the 18th of June 1692.

III. King Charles I. had a third son, Henry, born the 8th of July 1640, and created Duke of Glocester the 13th of May 1645; who being partaker with his royal brothers, during the usurpation, had at length the happiness to see the king peaceably restored to the throne of his ancestors, accompanying him into England 1660. Upon the 13th day of September next ensuing, he departed this life, unmarried, greatly lamented.

IV. Mary, eldest daugter of King Charles I. born 4th of November 1631, espoused William of Nassau, Prince of Orange, who died 1650, and nine days after his death (4th November) she was delivered of a posthumous child, William Prince of Orange, afterwards King of England; who married Mary, eldest daughter of King James VII. They were proclaimed King and Queen of England, France, and Ireland, February 13th, 1689, and of Scotland the 11th of April the same year. He deceased without any issue, the 8th of March 1702.

V. Elizabeth, second daughter of King Charles I. born 1635, died 1650.

VI. Henrieta, third and youngest daughter of King Charles I. born the 16th of June 1644. During the troubles in England she was carried to France, where she embraced the Romish religion: She married Philip Duke of Orleans, only brother to Louis XIV. the present French King.

Issue of the Princess Henrieta, Dutchess of Orleans, daughter to King Charles I.

I. Maria Louisa, born 27th of March 1662, married Charles II. King of Spain; she died without issue.

II. Ann Mary, born 1669, married Victor Amadeus, Duke of Savoy. Her children were, (1) Victor Amadeus, Prince of Piedmont, born in 1698; (2) Charles Emanuel Duke of Aoast, born 1701; (3) Emanuel Philibert, Duke of Chamlais, born in December 1705; (4) Mary, married to Louis Duke of Burgundy, eldest son to Louis the Dauphin, and grandson to Louis the present French King, and hath issue; (5) Maria Louisa, born in 1688, married to Philip Duke of Anjou, second son to Louis, Dauphin of France.

CHARLES II. eldest son of King Charles I. after the barbarous murther of his royal father, by unquestionable right, succeeded him in the crown of

Scotland, England, and Ireland. The usual ceremonies of proclamation and coronation were not to be expected, as affairs were then transacted; for on the day that King Charles I. was murthered, an act was passed to disinherit the son, ordaining, "That no person whatsoever should presume to proclaim Charles "Stewart, son of Charles Stewart, late King of England, commonly called "Prince of Wales, or any other person, to be King or chief Magistrate of Eng- "land, or Ireland, under pain of being adjudged a traitor." This inhibition did not affright His Majesty's loyal subjects of Scotland from doing their duty; for, having a just abhorrence of that unparallel'd and astonishing murder of the king, they proclaimed Prince Charles King of Scotland, the 3d of February 1649, at the Market-Cross of Edinburgh; and about this time, called home their Commissioners from England, who, at their departure, sent an expostulatory declaration to the sitting Members of the English Parliament, wherein they put them in mind of all their oaths, vows and protestations, for maintaining of the king's person and just rights, and upbraided them with their shameful and detestable abjuration, and infringement of them, by what they had lately acted against the sacred person of His Majesty: which was so ill resented by the sitting Members, that they imprisoned the messenger that brought it, voted the paper scandalous and seditious, sent after the Commissioners, and secured them, till a copy of the paper was sent into Scotland, to know if the Parliament there would own it: upon which a Commissioner was sent from Scotland, to justify what their Commissioners had done. In the month of September 1649, the Estates of Scotland dispatched Sir John Windram of Libertoun to the king, who then was at Jersey, in preparation to a treaty; who, being admitted to the king's presence, delivered his message, the substance of which was, "That the king would be pleased to acknowledge the Parliament, "and especially the two last Sessions of it, to be a lawful assembly; and then "they would treat of the means to re-establish peace and obedience to his "authority in that kingdom." So Mr. Windram was sent back with the following letter.

CHARLES R.

" WE have received your letter by Mr. Windram, and graciously accept all
" the expressions of affection and fidelity to us, with your tender resentment
" of our present condition, and the just indignation which you profess to have
" against the execrable murder of our father: and we believe that your inten-

" tions are as full of candour towards us, as we are, and always really have
" been, desirous to settle a clear and right understanding between us and our
" ancient subjects of Scotland, which may be an assured foundation of their
" happiness and peace for the time to come, and an effectual means to root
" out all the seed of animosities and divisions caus'd by these late troubles;
" and also, to re-unite the hearts and affections of our subjects one to another,
" and all of them to us, their King and lawful Sovereign; that thereby we may
" be put into a condition to maintain them in peace and prosperity, and to
" protect them in their religion and liberty: Therefore we have thought fit to
" command and desire you, to send us Commissioners sufficiently authorized,
" to treat and agree with us, both in relation to yourselves, and what we may
" expect from you, to bring and reduce the murderers of our late most dear
" father of happy memory, to condign punishment, and to recover our just
" rights in all our kingdoms. And we will, that they attend us, on the fif-
" teenth day of the month of March, at the town of Breda, where We intend
" to be, in order to a treaty with them."

To the same effect, was a letter written also to the kirk. When Sir John Windram returned with the king's letter into Scotland, the Council of State and the Committee of the Kirk, having duly considered the matter, they choose Commissioners, and dispatched them to Breda. For the Committee of Estates were, John Earl of Cassils, Robert Earl of Lothian, Robert Lord Burleigh, Sir John Windram of Libbertoun, John Smith, and John Jaffries. For the Committee of the Church were, Sir John Brody of that-ilk: Mr. John Livingstoun, and Mr. James Wood, Ministers. They arrived at Breda, and, the first day of their audience, the Earl of Cassils addressed himself to the King, in name of the Commisssioners of Parliament, in a speech to this effect, " That the king-
" dom of Scotland had sent him and his colleagues with propositions to him,
" not that they thought to take advantage of his necessities, or weary him by
" their importunities, but by making their humble submissions, in which they
" hoped their desires would appear so just and reasonable, that he would soon
" condescend to grant them; and that in their humble address they did mani-
" fest to the world their loyalty and constancy to him." Mr. John Livingstoun, in name of the Church made a speech also, wherein " he desired his Ma-
" jesty to hearken to the joint desires of the Estates and Kirk of Scotland,
" that so he might enjoy the blessing of GOD, and be received by his people
" in comfort and peace, to promote the work of the LORD, and to make
" them happy." Then they produced their Commissions and letters, with

the propositions of the Estates and Kirk of Scotland, which were as follows. " I. That he would be pleased to remove, from any access to the Court, all persons excommunicated by the Kirk. II. That he would be pleased to declare, that he would by solemn oath, under his hand and seal, allow the National Covenant of Scotland, England, and Ireland; and that he would prosecute the ends thereof in his royal station. III. That he would ratify and approve all Acts of Parliament, engaging to the Solemn League and Covenant, and establishing Presbyterian Government, the Directory of Worship, Confession of Faith, as they are already ratified by the General Assembly and Parliament; and that he would give his Royal assent to the acts of Parliament, enjoining the same in the rest of his dominions; and that he would observe the same in his own practice and family, and never endeavour any change thereof. IV. That he would consent, that all matters civil might be determined by the present and subsequent Parliaments; and to all matters ecclesiastical, as ordered by the General Assembly." The treaty with the King being concluded, the Estates of Scotland sent a solemn invitation to His Majesty that he would be pleased to hasten his speedy coming into Scotland, declaring that they would hazard their lives and fortunes to restore him to the possession of his other kingdoms. The King complying with their requests, took shipping at Scheveling in Holland, in the beginning of June; and, escaping a double danger, first of a storm, that cast him upon the coast of Denmark, and afterwards of the Parliament of England's fleet, that were set out to intercept him in his passage, he landed safe at Speymouth, the 16th ensuing. His Majesty's safe arrival was congratulated with the greatest demonstrations of joy and affection; and he was proclaimed King a second time, at the cross of Edinburgh.

The Commonwealth of England, having notice of these occurrences, were advised by Cromwell to invade Scotland, to prevent their invasion of England, contrary to their Solemn League and Covenant, under the command of Oliver Cromwell, then General of the English forces; and, towards the end of July, he entered Scotland with an army, consisting of 12000 effective men, and advanced to Haddingtoun, where he published a declaration, in the name of the commonwealth of England, to justify their proceedings against the Scots: but so great was the generality of the affection of the Scots to the King, that his declaration signified little. The Scots, against this invasion, formed an army for the King's service, consisting of 6000 horse and 15000 foot, and marched directly against them. Cromwell, seeing the Scots army so strongly entrenched, that it was impossible to force them; after he had faced them a day and a night, marched away to Musselburgh. The Scots, seeing the English retreat, fell upon their rear, commanded by General Lambert, who was wounded, and had like to be taken prisoner; but Cromwell coming to his relief, drove them back to their camp, not without loss on both sides. The next morning early, several squadrons of Scots horse, commanded by Major General Robert Montgomery and Colonel Strachan, came out of the line, with a design to beat up the English quarters about Musselburgh. They surprised the out-guards, and, with a great deal of gallantry, routed the first Regiment that opposed them: but advancing to another body, met with such a stout resistance, that they were forced to retire to their army.

The Scots and English armies, lying near one another without engaging, (the Scots being very advantageously posted) Cromwell's army began to be in great distress for want of provisions, which made him retreat to Pentland hills, and thence, with some difficulty, to Musselburgh; and so to Dunbar, with intention (as is reported) to ship his foot, much wearied by sickness and long marches, and ride away with his horse into England. But the Scots, having notice of his design, pressed so hard upon him with their army, that he could not effect his purpose. On the 3d of September, both armies engaged; the English obtained a signal victory; the Scots having lost 4000 men in the field of battle, and a far greater number taken prisoners.

This defeat obliged the Scots to quit the City of Edinburgh, which Cromwell took possession of; the King retiring to the town of Perth, where the Committee of Estates were assembled. On the first day of January 1651, he was solemnly crowned at Scoon, the usual place of inauguration of our Kings, with as great magnificence and solemnity as the state of affairs could then admit of. His Majesty was conducted from his bed-chamber, by the Earl Marischal on his right hand, and the Lord High Constable on his left, to the church, his train being carried by the Lords Erskine, Montgomery, Newbottle and Mauchlyn, the eldest sons of the Earls of Mar, Eglintoun, Lothian, and Loudoun, under a canopy of crimson-velvet, supported by the Lords Drummond, Carnagie, Ramsay, Johnston, Brichen, and Yester, the eldest sons of the Earls of Perth, Southesk, Dalhousie, Hartfield, Panmure, and Tweeddale: the Crown was carried by the Marquis of Argile, the Sword by the Earl of Rothes, and the Scepter by the Earl of Crawford. When His Majesty was placed in the Chair of State, the Earl of Loudoun, Lord Chancellor, spoke to the King to this purpose.

" SIR,

" YOUR good Subjects desire you may be crowned, as the righteous and " lawful Heir of the Crown of this Kingdom; and that you would maintain " Religion as it is presently established and professed, conform to the National

"Covenant, League and Covenant, and according to your Declaration at Dun-
"fermling, in August last; also that you would be pleased graciously to receive
"them under your Majesty's protection; to govern them by the Laws of the
"Kingdom; and to defend them in their Rights and Liberties, by your Royal
"Power; offering themselves in a most humble manner to your Majesty, with
"their vows, to bestow land, life, and what else is in their power, for the
"maintenance of religion, for the safety of your Majesty's sacred person, and
"maintenance of your Crown: Which they entreat your Majesty to accept,
"and pray Almighty GOD, you may, for many years, happily enjoy the same."

To which His Majesty was pleased to make this return:

"I Do esteem the affections of my people more than the crowns of many
"kingdoms, and shall be ready, by God's assistance, to bestow my life in
"their defence, wishing to live no longer than I may see religion and this king-
"dom flourish in all happiness."

The Coronation Sermon was preached by Mr. Robert Douglass, Minister at Edinburgh, on 2 Kings, chap. xi. 12, 17. "And they brought forth the King's "Son, and put the Crown upon him, and gave him the testimony, and they made "him King, and anointed him, and they clapped their hands, and said, GOD "save the King. And Jehoiada made a Covenant between the Lord, and the "King and the people, that they should be the Lord's people; between the "King also and the people¹."

In this month of January 1651, His Majesty was pleased to make several promotions; Sir James Carmichael of that-ilk he created into the dignity of Lord Carmichael; Sir Robert Colvil of Cleish, Lord Colvil; Sir Thomas Ruthven of Freeland, Lord Ruthven; Sir James Rollo of Duncrub, Lord Rollo; Sir Alexander Sutherland of Duffus, Lord Duffus; Thomas Rutherfoord, of Hunthill, Lord Rutherfoord.

After the solemnity of the coronation was over, the Scots nation began vigorously to act, in raising an army for the king's service; and, having gathered their forces, they encamped at Stirling, with intention to march into England, while Cromwell endeavoured all he could to prevent it, by drawing them

¹ " The Form and Order of the Coronation of Charles the Second."
Aberdeen, 1651.

to an engagement in Scotland. In pursuance of which design, he landed part of his army in Fife, under the command of Colonel Overton: to drive the English thence, 4000 horse and foot were commanded to march against them, under the conduct of Sir John Brown of Fordel; which Cromwell having notice of, sent over Lambert and Oakey, with two Regiments of horse and two of foot, to join the former; and, engaging near Innerkeithing, overthrew the Scots. Sir John Brown, charging the enemy with undaunted courage and resolution, received a wound; and, falling into their hands, died a few days after. This, with the loss at Dunbar, very much weakened His Majesty's affairs; and the English, having over-run a great part of Scotland, forced him to the northern parts, where finding he could not long subsist, he and the Scots army, consisting of about 15000 horse and foot, were obliged to march directly unto England, and was so closely followed by Cromwell's army, that his English friends were thereby hindered from a conjunction with him; so that, having marched as far as Worcester, His Majesty was there encountered by Cromwell, upon the 3d of September, the same day of the month that, the year before, he had won the battle of Dunbar. The King having charged on the head of one of the bodies, with great gallantry and conduct, Cromwell gave the Scots army an absolute defeat. The English write, there were slain about 2000 in the fight. William Duke of Hamilton, who had charged the enemy with extraordinary courage and resolution, received a shot in his thigh, and falling into their hands, died the next day of his wounds; a few minutes before his death, he expressed a great chearfulness, that he had the honour to lose his life in the King's service.

The King, being now obliged to provide for the safety of his royal person, departed from Worcester that evening, leaving Colonel Carles in the rear, to keep the enemy in dispute, that the approaching night might favour his escape, and so made all possible speed to a place called Whiteladies, twenty-five miles from Worcester, and there committed himself to the fidelity of John and Richard Pendrels, two brothers, who immediately put him into the habit of a wood-cutter, and set him to work all day, September 4th, and in the night following, Richard Pendrel carried him to the house of Mr. Woolf of Madley, and thence guided him to Boscobel wood, whence he hid himself in an oak, in the day-time, and stole into the house at night. Hence John Pendrel brought him, in the habit, and on the horse, of a miller, to Mr. Whitegrave's house at Mosley, and so to Bently, where Colonel Lane contrived, that the king should ride as a servant before Mrs. Jean Lane his sister, to Bristol, and conducted hence, by the Lord Wilmot, to the house of Colonel Wadham, at Trent in Dorsetshire, where he continued three weeks, not without the privity of six or seven persons in the family, on expectation of a passage from Lime; but, being disappointed from this place, it was resolved the King should go to Bridport; but, fearing a discovery, he hasted back to Colonel Windham's, thence, to the house of Mr. Hyde at Heatall; and, after strange escapes, came to Brightmanstead, where there was a ship hired for carrying him over to France. His Majesty landed safely at Diepe, on October 21st: a very signal mercy of God in his miraculous protection! A Providence not to be paralleled in history. Having wandered in disguise about England, for the space of six weeks, a sum of money being promised to those that should discover him, and a penalty of High Treason inflicted on any who should not discover him; yet, notwithstanding he was both seen and known, by no less than fifty-two persons being privy to his escape, he passed unmolested, till at length he found an opportunity of transporting himself into France.

From the year 1651 to 1659, His Majesty travelled in Germany, Spain, and Flanders, until the year 1660; at which time his Majesty, being at Brussels, within the Spanish dominions, observing an universal inclination and disposition of all his subjects to receive him, he removed to Breda, and thence to the Hague, where, after an hearty invitation by the English Commissioners, sent from their Convention at Westminster, he embarked at Scheveling, the 23d of May, and landed at Dover the 25th; and on the 29th following, being his birth-day, and then 30 years of age, he made his entry into London, being received with the greatest and most universal joy and acclamations that possibly could be expressed: and, with what cordial and universal joy His Majesty's Restoration was welcom'd by the Kingdom of Scotland, is yet in remembrance.

He summoned a Parliament to sit at Edinburgh, the 1st day of January 1661; Lieutenant General John Middleton of Cadham, as a reward of his many eminent services during the Usurpation, was created into the dignity of Earl of Middleton, and made Lord High Commissioner. In this first Session of Parliament, the Solemn League and Covenant was condemned as an unlawful oath, imposed on the subject, by a prevailing faction, contrary to authority; and an act past annulling the Parliaments from the year 1640 to 1649. The transactions concerning the King's majesty at Newcastle, in the years 1646 and 1647, condemned; Duke Hamilton's engagement declared to have been an honourable, just, necessary, and seasonable discharge of that duty, whereunto the Kingdoms were, by the Law of God, by the Law of Nature and Nations, obliged to preserve the sacred person of their King; and the forfaultures of the Marquises of Huntly, Montrose, and others, who had suffered for their loyalty to the King, rescinded. His Majesty moreover declared, that he would maintain the true reformed Protestant Religion, in its purity of doctrine and worship, as it was established during the reigns of his father and grandfather: and, as to the government of the Church, he would settle and secure that, in such a form as should be most agreeable to the word of God. And, in the mean time, doth allow the present administrations, by Sessions, Presbyteries and Synods. In this Parliament, Archbald, Marquis of Argile, was indicted of high treason, for compliance with Oliver Cromwell, for which he was condemned, and beheaded the 27th of May 1661.

In the 2nd Session of Parliament, begun at Edinburgh the 8th of May 1662, the Earl of Middleton His Majesty's High Commissioner, an act was made, restoring the episcopal government, as it was exercised in the year 1637. The King called to court, Dr. James Sharp, Professor of Divinity in the University of St. Andrews; Mr. James Hamilton, Minister at Camnethan; Mr. Robert Lighton, Principal of the College of Edinburgh; and Mr. Andrew Fairfoul, Minister at Dunse; where they were first ordained Deacons and Presbyters, and then consecrated Bishops: by which act they expressly renounced the validity of their former ordination. Dr. Sharp was promoted to the Archbishoprick of St. Andrews, Mr. Fairfoul to the Archbishoprick of Glasgow, (who died a few weeks after his promotion;) Mr. Hamilton to the Episcopal See of Galloway, and Dr. Lighton to the Bishoprick of Dunblain. And upon their return home, they consecrated the rest; Dr. George Wishart, who had formerly been Minister at Lieth, before the year 1638, was promoted to the Bishoprick of Edinburgh; Mr. Thomas Sydferf, formerly Bishop of Galloway, and the only Bishop then alive of all them who had been laid aside by the assembly of Glasgow, 1638, was translated to the see of Orkney; Dr. David Mitchel, one of the Ministers of Edinburgh before the year 1638, was advanced to the Bishoprick of Aberdeen; Mr. George Haliburton, Minister of the Gospel at Perth, was promoted to the Bishoprick of Dunkeld; Mr. John Paterson, Minister at Aberdeen, to the Bishoprick of Ross; Mr. Murdoch Mackenzie, Parson of Elgin, to the Episcopal See of Murray; Mr. David Strachan, Parson of Fettercairn, to the Bishoprick of Brichen; Mr. Patrick Forbes was promoted to the Bishoprick of Caithness; Mr. David Fletcher, Parson of Melross, to the bishoprick of Argile; and Mr. Robert Wallace, Minister at Barnweel in the shire of Air, was made Bishop of the Isles.

In this session of Parliament an Act past, commanding all ministers to repair to their Diocesian Assembly, and concur in all acts of church-discipline, as they should be required by the Bishop of their respective diocess, under pain of being suspended from their office and benefice. And whereas, by the Presbyterian discipline, the right of patronage was removed from the Patrons, the Parliament did provide, " That all ministers, who had entered into the cure of any paroch, since the year 1649, could have no right to uplift the rents of the respective benefices, for this instant year, nor following, unless they obtain a presentation from the patron, and have collation from the Bishop of the diocess, before the 20th of September next." Moreover, the Parliament formed a declaration to be subscribed by all in publick office, to this effect ; " That it was unlawful, upon any pretence whatsoever, to enter into leagues and covenants, or to take up arms against the king, or those commissioned by him ; and that these oaths (whereof the one is called the National Covenant, and the other intituled, The Solemn League and Covenant) were, and are, in themselves unlawful oaths, and were imposed on the subjects of this kingdom, against the laws and liberty of the same ; and that there lieth no obligation on the taker of the said oath."

The same year (1662) His Majesty consummated his marriage with Donna Catharina, Infanta of Portugal, daughter of John IV. of that name, King of Portugal. The Marriage was solemnized by proxie, at Lisbon, by the Earl of Sandwich. She embarked for England, attended by a Squadron of the Royal Navy, and, at Portsmouth, was received by the King, and married there by Dr. Gilbert Sheldon, Bishop of London [1].

In the year 1666 fell out that Insurrection of Pentland Hills, which had its rise in the stewartry of Kircudbright, in the shire of Galloway, occasioned by Sir James Turner's too warmly executing his commission upon the Dissenters in these bounds, who, gathering together to the number of about 60 horsemen, marched to Dumfries, took Sir James prisoner, and disarmed the soldiers: they, encreasing to the number of about 7 or 800, came to Lanerk, where they renewed the Covenant ; and, upon their march to Edinburgh to petition the Council for redress of their grievances, they were encountered by General Thomas Dalziel, who dispersed them [2], on the . . day of November 1666, many of them being slain in the field. The Non-Conformists, continuing under pressures, for their not complying with Episcopacy, were rendered desperate. A field meeting, for the worship of God, at Loudon Hill, in the shire of Air, was assaulted by Colonel John Grahame of Claverhouse, with three troops of horse and dragoons, whom, at Drumclog, the 1st day of June 1679, they repulsed, and killed about 30 of the king's soldiers upon the place. The Dissenters consulting what was expedient for them in that juncture, whether to

---

[1] History of the life of King Charles II, in the late English History. [2] Manuscript History of the Church of Scotland.

disperse or keep together, the result was, that they judged it most safe in that extremity, for some time not to separate; representing their purposes were in defence of the reformed religion, as they stood obliged thereto by the covenant. When the King had notice of this insurrection, he gave present direction for his forces in England to march northward, the Duke of Monmouth being made General, who arriving in Scotland the 18th of June 1679, marched with the King's army against the enemy, who were encamped in Hamilton-park, to the number of 1500. Bothwel-bridge was the only passage to it, which they had barricado'd and well lined with musqueteers. Some of them came and presented their declaration to the Duke, and a petition signed by Robert Hamilton, who commanded them. But the Duke refusing to treat with them upon any other terms, than laying down their arms and submitting to the King's mercy; some skirmishing began at Bothwel-bridge, on the 22d of June ensuing. They behaved themselves well enough at first, but wanting arms, ammunition and conduct, being also divided among themselves, they were quickly dispers'd; about 300 were killed and 1100 taken prisoners [1].

Upon the 2d of February 1685, His Majesty was suddenly seized with a violent fit of an apoplexy, and on the 6th ensuing departed this mortal life, without any lawful issue, and was privately interred, on the 14th following, at the Abby of Westminster. On the coffin was affix'd a silver plate gilt, with the following inscription:

DEPOSITUM

AUGUSTISSIMI ET POTENTISSIMI PRINCIPIS

CAROLI SECUNDI

ANGLIÆ SCOTIÆ FRANCIÆ ET HIBERNIÆ REGIS

FIDEI DEFENSORIS

OBIIT SEXTO DIE FEBRUARII ANNO 1684

ÆTATIS SUÆ QUINQUAGESIMO QUINTO

REGNIQUE SUI TRICESIMO SEPTIMO.

Natural issue of King Charles II. by Lucie, daughter of Richard Walters of Haverfoord, Esq;

I. James, born, at Rotterdam in Holland, anno 1649, and bore the sirname of Croffts; in anno 1662 he came over to England, and was created into the dignity of Duke of Orkney in Scotland; and, upon the 14th of February 1663,

---

[1] Life of James Duke of Monmouth, page 278.

created Baron of Tindale, Earl of Doncaster and Duke of Monmouth, and elected a Knight-Companion of the most Noble Order of the Garter. In 1668 he was made Captain of the King's Life-Guard of Horse, and soon after constituted Captain General of His Majesty's forces, and Lord Lieutenant of the East Riding of York. But, in the latter end of the reign of King Charles, falling out with the Court, he retired to Holland, and resided at the Hague until the King's death. And, upon King James's accession to the throne, he invaded England in an hostile manner, and proclaimed himself King. His army, consisting of about 5000 horse and foot, was routed by His Majesty's troops, under the command of the Earl of Faversham; the Duke apprehended, was conveyed, under a strong guard, to London, committed to the tower, and beheaded the 15th of July 1685. His Grace was married unto the Lady Ann Scot, daughter and sole heir of Francis Earl of Buccleugh; whereupon they were created Duke and Dutchess of Buccleugh, and he assumed the sirname of Scot, as the custom of Scotland is; where he, who marries any considerable heiress, takes her sirname to preserve the family. He left issue, by his Dutchess; (1) James Earl of Dalkeith, who was received by her Majesty Queen Ann, on the 7th of February 1704, a Knight of the most Noble Order of St. Andrew of Scotland, called the Thistle; and died on the 14th of March 1705, leaving issue, by the Lady Henrieta, daughter of Laurence Earl of Rochester, Walter, Lord Scot, now Earl of Dalkeith, apparent heir of her Grace Ann Dutchess of Buccleugh, his grandmother: (2) Lord Henry Scot, who was, by her present Majesty, created unto the dignity of Earl of Delorain, Viscount Hermitage, and Lord Goldyland, in Scotland, 29th of March 1706.

II. Mary, natural daughter of the King, married to William Sarsfield of Lucan, Esquire; and, surviving him, she married William Fanshaw, Esquire, Master of Requests to King Charles II.

A natural son of King Charles II. by Catherine, daughter of Thomas Peg of Yeldersly.

Charles, sirnamed Fitz-Charles, created Earl of Plymouth: He died at Tangier, anno 1680, without succession.

Natural children of King Charles II. by Barbara Villiars, Dutchess of Cleveland, daughter of William, Viscount Grandison in Ireland.

I. Charles, sirnamed Fitzroy, first created Earl of Southampton, but afterwards by letters patent, bearing date at Westminster, the 10th of September, 1675, created Duke of Southampton; and by Alice, his wife, daughter of Sir William Poultney, hath issue, William Earl of Chichester.

II. Henry Fitzroy, created, first, Earl of Eustoun, an. 1672, and, by letters patent, dated the 11th of September 1675, he was further advanced to the dignity and title of Duke of Grafton, and elected a Knight of the most noble order of the Garter, an. 1680. He was killed at the siege of Cork in Ireland, an. 1690, leaving issue by Isobel his wife, daughter and heir of Henry Earl of Arlinton, Charles, now Duke of Grafton, his son and heir.

III. George Fitzroy; he was by letters patent, bearing date at Westminster, October 1st, 1675, created Earl of Northumberland; and, in 1682, he was further advanced to the dignity of Duke of Northumberland; and, on the 10th of January 1683, he was elected Knight of the Garter. He married Catharine, daughter of Robert Wheatly of Brecknock, Esquire, by whom he hath, as yet, no issue.

IV. Ann, sirnamed Fitzroy, married to Thomas Lennard, Earl of Sussex, and had issue.

V. Charlotte Fitzroy, married Henry Earl of Litchfield, and hath issue.

A natural son of King Charles II. by Eleonor Gwin.

Charles, sirnamed Beuclerk, created Earl of Burford, the 28th year of the reign of King Charles II. and by letters patent, dated January 10th 1684, created Duke of St. Albans. He was Captain of the Band of Gentlemen Pensioners, and Master Falconer of England; and in the year 1697, soon after the peace of Ryswick, he was sent over, by the late King William, to congratulate the French King, upon the marriage of his grandson the Duke of Burgundy. He married Diana Vere, daughter and coheir of Aubrey de Vere, Earl of Oxford, by whom he hath issue, Charles of Earl of Burford, his son and apparent heir, and several other children.

A natural son of King Charles II. by Louise de Querouaille, Dutchess of Portsmouth, a French Lady.

Charles, sirnamed Lenos or Lenox, created Earl of March and Duke of Richmond; and by other letters patent, he was created Baron of Methven, Earl of Darnly, and Duke of Lenox in Scotland. On the 20th of April 1681, he was instituted Knight of the Garter; and upon the removal of Monmouth, he was made Master of the horse to King Charles II. in which office he continued until the King, his father's death.

A natural daughter of King Charles II. by Elizabeth, Viscountess of Shanon, daughter of Sir William Killegrew, Knight.

Charlotte, sirnamed Fitzroy, was married to William Earl of Yarmouth, and had issue.

A natural daughter of King Charles II. by Mary Davis.

Mary, sirnamed Tudor, was married to Francis Earl of Derwentwater, and had issue; and after his decease, to Henry Grahame, Esquire.

Arms of the Royal Family of Stewart.

Or, a Fess Checquie, Azure and Argent.

STEWART DUKE OF LENOX.

Having thus finished the Genealogical history of the Royal family of Stewart, I come now to that collateral branch, the illustrious and noble family of Lenox, descended of Robert Stewart, a younger son of Walter II. High Stewart of Scotland [1], in the reign of King Alexander III. Which Robert, by the gift of Walter his father, had the Lordship of Torboltoun in the shire of Air [2]. He took to wife . . . . daughter and heir of Robert de Croc, Lord of Crocstoun and Darnly, and obtained with her that fair Lordship, leaving issue, Robert Stewart Lord of Crocstoun, his son and heir, Bailie to the High Stewart of Scotland, in the Barony of Renfrew. I found him so designed in a precept, by Walter, High Stewart of Scotland, for infefting the Monks of Pasly in several lands within that Barony, in the year of our Lord 1313 [3], the 7th year of the reign of King Robert Bruce. Sir Allan Stewart of Darnly and Crocstoun, his successor, was one of those noble patriots, who assisted that renowned Prince, in recovering the liberties of his country, against the oppression of King Edward I. of

---

[1] Lesly de Reb. Gest: Scotorum. [2] Reg. de Pasly. [3] Lesly.

England; and, in reward of his good services, he obtained from that Prince a grant of the Barony of Dreghorn[1]. He was slain at the battle of Hallidonhill against the English, in the year 1333. To him succeeded Sir John Stewart of Darnly, his son; father of another Sir John, who was one of the Hostages sent to England, for the ransom of King David Bruce, taken prisoner at the battle of Durham, in the year of our Lord 1358; and, upon the accession of King Robert II to the Crown, he obtained a Charter of the Lordship of Darnly, Inchennan and Perthick-Scot, upon his own resignation, to himself in liferent, and to Robert, his son and apparent heir, in fee, and to the heirs male of his body; which failing, to Walter Stewart his brother-german; and, he failing, to Alexander his brother; dated at Darnly the 31st of January 1361. But Sir John and Robert his son, dying without issue, the Lordship of Darnly devolved upon Sir Alexander, his brother: Which Sir Alexander, added to his paternal inheritance the Barony of Galstoun, by marriage of Janet, daughter and heir of Sir William Keith of Galstoun; by whom he had John, his successor, and Alexander of Torbyne, of whom issued, (as I am informed) the Stewarts of Halrig; and, of a third son, descended the Stewarts of Barscube in Renfrewshire[2]. Sir Alexander Stewart, dying in the year 1406, to him succeeded,

Sir John, his son and heir. During the Government of Robert Duke of Albany, he accompanied Archbald Earl of Douglas and John Earl of Buchan, with 4000 Scots auxiliaries, to the assistance of the French against the English, where they did eminent service at the siege of Beauge; the Duke of Clarence, the English General, being killed, with 2000 of his men, and the town won. The Earls of Douglas and Buchan being slain at the battle of Vernoil, an. 1424, he was made Commander of the Scots forces, and a Mareschal of France; and, further to reward his good services, Charles VI. of France created him into the dignities of Count d'Evreux, and Seigneur de Concorsant. He was sent ambassador, from France, to King James I. of Scotland, 1436, to renew the ancient league betwixt the two crowns, and negotiate a marriage between the Dauphin and the Lady Margaret, King James's daughter: and, upon his return to France, King Charles was pleased, as a mark of his royal favour, and to perpetuate the memory of his services to that crown, to allow him, as an augmentation to his Coat of arms, the royal bearing of France, viz. Azure, three flowers-de-luce, Or, within a Border engraled. And, in the year 1429, fighting with an undaunted

---

[1] Carta in Publicis Archivis. [2] Hist. of Stewart of Darnly, in Bib. Jurid.

courage and resolution, at the battle of Herrings near Orleans, had the hard fate to be there slain: leaving issue by Isobel his wife, daughter of Sir William Seton of that-ilk, ancestor to the Earl of Winton, (1) Allan his son and heir: (2) John, Lord Aubigny in France, father of Bernard Stewart, Lord Aubigny, the famous General in the Neapolitan wars, under Charles VIII. and Louis XII. of France. By the last he was created unto the titles and dignity of Duke of Terra Nova, Marquis de Gyralle and Squilazzo, Count of Acri, Grand Constable of Sicily and Jerusalem, Vice-Roy of Naples, Governour of Calabria, Captain of the Guard-de Corps, Lieutenant General of the French army in Italy: and being sent ambassador from France to King James IV. of Scotland, on his way from Edinburgh to Stirling, died at Corstorphine, in the year 1508: (3) Sir Alexander of Beilmouth.

To Sir John Stewart of Darnly succeeded Sir Allan his son, who lived in the reign of King James I. and II. He was slain by Sir Thomas Boyd of Kilmarnock, at Falkirk, in the year 1439. In revenge of which, Sir Alexander Stewart his brother, killed Sir Thomas Boyd, at Craignacht-hill in Renfrewshire. The said Sir Allan was married unto Lilias Lenox, second daughter and one of the co-heirs of Duncan last Earl of Lenox; by whom he had two sons; Sir John his successor; and Alexander, ancestor of the Stewarts of Galstoun. I have seen, by the favour of George Ross now of Galstoun, a grant of the lands of Galstoun, by John Lord Darnly, in the year 1452, to Alexander Stewart his brother-german: which family continued, for several ages, in great reputation, and failed, in the reign of King Charles II. in the person of Lodovick Stewart of Galstoun, who died without succession, in the year 1650, and disponed his estate to George Ross of Haining, his uncle, whose son and heir is George Ross now of Galstoun.

Of the Stewarts of Galstoun descended several of good note. Allan Stewart of Threpwood, Provost of Edinburgh, in the reign of King James the V. and Captain of His Majesty's Guards, was a younger son of this family. And in King James VI.'s time, Colonel William Stewart of Houston in West-Lothian, frequently mentioned by our historians, was brother to Thomas Stewart of Galstoun, and father of Frederick Stewart, Lord Pittenweem.

But the first of the noble family of Darnly, who laid the foundation of that honour, which his successors ever since enjoyed, was Sir John Stewart of Darnly; who, standing highly in favour with King James II. was, by that Monarch created a Lord of Parliament, with the title of Lord Darnly, in the year of our LORD 1445; and continuing in the same favour with King James III. he obtained the Earldom of Lenox with the dignity, about the year 1481. This noble Earl married Christian, daughter of Alexander, first Lord Montgomery, ancestor to the Earl of Eglintoun; by whom he had (1) Matthew his successor; (2) Robert Lord Aubigny, who was a Marsechal of France; (3) William, Governour of Milan, and Captain of the Scots Gens d'Armes in France. Beside these sons he had moreover several daughters; (1) Elizabeth, married to Archbald Earl of Argile, of whom His Grace the present Duke is lineally descended; (2) Marion, married to Sir Robert Crichton, son and heir to Sir Robert Crichton of Sanquhar, ancestor to the present Countess of Dumfries; with whom he obtained the sum of 1200 merks of portion, as appears from the contract, dated at Edinburgh, the 28th of May 1472, (3), ... married to Sir John Murray of Tillibardin, ancestor to the Duke of Athol. John Earl of Lenox departing this life, an. 1491, his estate and honours devolved upon Matthew his son and heir.

Which Matthew was of the Privy Council to King James IV.; and accompanying his Sovereign to the battle of Floudoun, had the hard fate to be there slain, with the flower of the Scots nobility and gentry, upon the 9th day of September 1513; leaving issue, by the Lady Elizabeth Hamilton his wife, daughter of James first Earl of Arran, and of the Lady Mary his wife, daughter of King James II. (1) William Master of Lenox, who married Margaret Grahame, daughter of William Earl of Montrose, but died without succession; (2) John his suceessor: He had likewise two daughters; (1) Margaret married to John Lord Fleming, sans issue, and afterwards to Alexander Douglas of Mains, and had issue; (2) Elizabeth, to Sir Hugh Campbel of Loudoun, and had issue Sir Matthew Campbel of Loudoun, father of Sir Hugh Campbel, created Lord Loudoun, by King James VI. in the year 1604.

John, son and heir of Matthew Earl of Lenox, is of the Privy Council to King James V. and one of the Peers appointed to attend that Prince, after he took upon him the administration of the Government. But the Earl of Angus having taken the entire management upon himself, retaining the king in effect a prisoner, the Earl of Lenox, endeavouring to rescue him, was defeat in the attempt, and killed in the field, near Linlithgow, in the month of September 1526; leaving issue, by Ann his Lady, daughter of John Stewart, Earl of Athol, first, Matthew, who succeeded him; second, John, Lord Aubigny in France, Captain of the Scots Gens d'Armes, and Governour of Avignon; third, Robert, Bishop of Caithness; and one daughter, Eleonor; married first to William Earl of Errol, and had issue; secondly to John Earl of Sutherland, and had issue.

Matthew, Earl of Lenox, served in his youth in the French wars in Italy, where he behaved himself with a great deal of gallantry. Upon the death of King James V. he was sent for to France, and cajoll'd with hopes of marrying the Queen Dowager, to support her against the factions of the nobility at home; but was afterwards accused by the Queen and Cardinal Beatoun, as too much favouring Queen Mary's marriage with Edward Prince of Wales, King Henry VIII. of England's son; which obliged him to make an apology for himself to the French King: and, after a disadvantageous rencounter with the Earl of Arran, then Governour of Scotland, at the city of Glasgow, in the year 1545, his estate was forfaulted, and he fled into England, where he was honourably entertained by King Henry VIII. who bestowed upon him in marriage his niece, the Lady Margaret Douglas, only daughter of Archbald Earl of Angus, by Margaret, eldest daughter of King Henry VII. of England, and Dowager of James IV of Scotland; by whom he had two sons, Henry Lord Darnly, and Charles, afterwards Earl of Lenox.

Earl Matthew being restored to his estate and honours, by Queen Mary, in the year 1563; in 1565, Henry Lord Darnly, his son, was married to Queen Mary of Scotland, by whom she had issue James the VI. first Monarch of Great Britain.

Matthew Earl of Lenox, after his return home, did not meddle in public affairs until the murther of his son, that he prosecuted the Earl of Bothwel as guilty thereof. And, upon the death of James Earl of Murray, he was elected Regent to King James VI. his grandson, upon the 12th of July 1570. The first thing he did, during his Regency, was his pursuing the Earl of Huntly, then at the head of a small army for the interest of Queen Mary; from whom he took the Castle of Brichen, which he had garrisoned: he afterwards took the Abby of Pasly, which Lord Claud Hamilton had taken from the Lord Semple. The impregnable Castle of Dunbarton held out, by the Lord Fleming, for Queen Mary, was surprised upon the 2d of April 1571, by the prudent conduct of Captain Thomas Crawford of Jordanhill. The Regent having called a Parliament at Stirling, was surprised, and barbarously murther'd in a scuffle, by one Captain Calder, the 4th of September 1571, and was interred in the Chapel of the Castle of Stirling.

To Matthew Earl of Lenox succeeded Charles, his second son and heir, who deceased in the 21st year of his age, 1579; leaving issue, by Elizabeth his wife, daughter of Sir William Cavendish of Chatsworth, and sister to the Earl of Devonshire, one daughter, Arabella, a lady of many rare virtues: she secretly married William Seymour, Marquis of Hartford. They were both committed prisoners to the Tower of London, where the Lady Arabella ended her life upon the 27th of September 1615. Charles Earl of Lenox, thus dying without male issue, his estate and honours devolved on Robert Bishop of Caithness, his uncle, who resigned the Earldom of Lenox with the dignity, in lieu whereof he received the stile of Earl of March. He married Elizabeth Stewart, daughter of John Earl of Athol, and died upon the 29th of August 1586, without any succession.

The Earldom of Lenox was bestowed by King James VI. upon Esme Stewart, Lord Aubigny, son and heir of John Lord Aubigny, brother of Matthew Earl of Lenox, cousin-german to the King's Father, who coming from France, anno 1579, was, a few days after his arrival, created Earl of Lenox, and in anno 1580 made Lord High-Chamberlain of Scotland, and next year Duke of Lenox. He was in so great favour at Court, that, to prevent the Duke of Guise the King's kinsman, from employing his interest with the King in favour of the Popish faction, (though Lenox had publicly renounced Popery) that diverse of the nobility surprised the King at Ruthven, in the year 1582, and removed Lenox from him, who retired to France, and died at Paris, the 26th of May 1583; leaving issue, by Catharine de Balsac his wife, sister to the Sieur d'Entragues, two sons, Ludovick his successor, and Esme Lord Aubigny; as also two daughters, first, Henrieta, married to John I. Marquis of Huntly, and had issue; the second, Mary, to George Earl of Mar, and had issue.

Ludovick, son and heir of Esme Duke of Lenox, was Lord High-Chamberlain and Admiral of Scotland; and upon King James's coming to the Crown of England, accompanied his Majesty thither. He was, by the favour of that monarch, created a Baron of England, by the title of Lord Steringtoun, and improven to the dignity of Earl of Newcastle and Duke of Richmond: he was also a Knight of the most Noble Order of the Garter. This great Duke was married, 1st, to Sophia Ruthven, daughter of William Earl of Gourie; 2dly, to Margaret, daughter of Sir Matthew Campbell of Loudoun; 3dly, to Frances, daughter of Thomas Viscount of Bindon; but by none of these had any surviving issue. And departing this life the 16th of February 1624, his estate and honours devolved upon Esme, Lord Aubigny, his brother and heir.

Which Esme took to wife Catharine, daughter and sole heir of Gervaise Lord Cliftoun, by whom he had James his successor; George [*], Lord Aubigny, putting himself in arms for the King, was killed at the battle of Renton, 23d October

---

[*] This Lord George left a daughter Lady Catharine, who carried on the line of the family now represented by her descendant the Earl of Darnley. See the continuation article Lenox,

FAMILY OF STEWART.

1642; John, kill'd at the battle of Brandon, anno 1644. As also he had three daughters; 1st, Elizabeth married to Thomas Howard Earl of Arundel; the 2d, Ann, to Archibald Lord Angus, son and heir of William, Marquis of Douglas, and had issue; the 3d, Frances, to Jerome Earl of Portland. He departed this life upon the . . . day of . . . 1625. To whom succeeded James his son and heir, who was Lord High-Admiral of Scotland, one of the Gentlemen of the bed-chamber, and a Knight of the most Noble Order of the Garter. He died upon the 30th of March 1655[1], leaving issue, by the Lady Mary his wife, only daughter of George Duke of Buckingham, Esme, who succeeded him in his honours, but died in his minority, anno 1660; and a daughter, Mary, married to James Earl of Arran in Ireland, son to the Duke of Ormond; his estate and honours descending to Charles Earl of Litchfield, his cousin-german, son of George Lord Aubigny; who, being Ambassador Extraordinary from King Charles II. of England to the Crown of Denmark, died at Elsinore in that kingdom, the 2d of December 1672, without issue: his estate in Scotland did fall to the King by succession, who bestowed the same, with the dignity of Duke of Lenox, anno 1675, upon Charles, one of his natural sons by Louisa de Querouaille, Dutchess of Portsmouth. His Grace hath married Ann, daughter of Francis Lord Brudnel, eldest son of Robert Earl of Cardigan, by whom he hath issue Charles Earl of Darnly.

ARMS.

Two Coats, quarterly: First and Fourth; Azure; Three Flowers-de-luce, within a border engraled, Or: Second and Third; Or; a Fess checquie, Azure and Argent; within a border, Gules, charged with 8 Buckles, Or: over all, in a Surtout, the Coat of the antient Earls of Lenox; viz. Argent; a Saltyre engraled, betwixt four Roses, Gules. Supporters, Two Wolves: Crest, a Bull's Head breathing fire: Motto, " Avant Darnly."

[1] Dugdale's Baronage of England.

STEWART DUKE OF ALBANY.

The first who enjoyed this honour, was Robert Stewart, second son to King Robert II. by Elizabeth Mure: he was created unto the dignity of Earl of Monteith, in the year 1370, and obtained the Earldom of Fife from Isobel Macduff, daughter and heir of Duncan last Earl of Fife. For authority of this, I have seen an indenture betwixt Robert Stewart Earl of Monteith, on the one part, and Dame Isobel, Countess of Fife, and spouse to Walter Stewart, brother to the said Robert, on the other; wherein she obliges herself to resign the Earldom of Fife in the King's hands, in favours of Robert Earl of Monteith, for the annuity of £145 Sterling. Which indenture bears date, at Perth, the penult of March 1371. After this, he is commonly designed Earl of Fife and Monteith; he was appointed Governour of Scotland by his father; and, on the accession of King Robert III. his brother, to the Crown, he continued in the government of the kingdom, and was created Duke of Albany, in the year 1399. During whose administration the English invaded Scotland, and wasted the southern countries, but were repulsed by the Earl of Douglas. So much as to his civil actions: as to his works of piety, I find this memorable note; that he gave the third part of the Barony of Rosyth, for maintenance of a qualified priest, to celebrate divine service, at the altar of St. Michael the archangel, in the church of Inverkeithing; which grant he expresses to be made " pro salute animarum Malcolmi, Wilhelmi & Alexandri regum Scotiæ." This donation bears date, at Faukland, the 28th September 1406. He founded also a chaplainry in the Chapel of the Castle of Stirling, for the safety of the souls of Robert and David Bruce, Robert Stewart his father, and Robert Stewart his brother, all Kings of Scotland; and for the safety of his own soul, &c. This great Duke departed this life the 1st day of September 1419, with the reputation of a person of noble accomplishments, equally fit for the weightiest affairs of peace and war. He married Margaret, daughter and sole heir of Murdoch Earl of Monteith, by whom he had; first, Murdoch his son and heir; 2d, John Earl of Buchan, Constable of France, slain at the battle of Vernoil, 1429, married to Elizabeth, daughter to the Earl of Douglas; by whom he had only one daughter, Jean, married to Sir George Seton of that-ilk, of whom George Earl of Wintoun is the lineal heir; 3d, Sir Robert, slain at Vernoil. Besides these sons he had several daughters; first, Isobel, married to Alexander Earl of Ross; by whom she had one daughter, who was deformed: she resigned the Earldom of Ross in favours of

John, Earl of Buchan, her uncle, and retired to a Cloister. The Countess of Ross was married a second time with Walter Haliburton, Lord of Dirltoun. 2d, Marjory, married to Sir Duncan Campbell of Lochhow, first Lord Campbell. For this I have seen [1], a charter of the lands of Menstrie, by Robert Duke of Albany, " dilecto filio suo Duncano Campbel, domino de Lochhow ;" of whom his Grace John Duke of Argile is the lineal heir. 3d, Elizabeth, to Sir Malcolm Fleming of Cumbernauld. My authority for this is a Charter granted by Robert Duke of Albany, in the year 1418, of the Barony of Bigar ; " Malcolmo Fleming, " Militi, & Elizabethæ, sponsæ suæ, filiæ nostræ charissimæ [2] :" of whom the Right Honourable John Earl of Wigtoun is lineally descended.

To Robert, Duke of Albany, succeeded Murdoch his son and heir ; he was chosen Governour of Scotland upon the death of his father, which he enjoyed till the restauration of King James I. when, being attainted of treason, he and two of his sons, Walter and Alexander, were sentenced to lose their heads, which was accordingly execute at Stirling, an. 1424. He married Isobel, eldest daughter and co-heiress of Duncan Earl of Lenox, For authority of this, I have seen an indenture, dated at Inchmyrin, the 17th of February 1391, betwixt Robert Earl of Fife, on the one part, and Duncan Earl of Lenox upon the other ; wherein it is agreed, that Murdoch Stewart, eldest son to the Earl of Fife, shall have to wife Isobel, the eldest daughter of the said Earl of Lenox. Upon which there is a Charter of that Earldom, by King Robert the III. in Anno 1393 [3], to Duncan Earl of Lenox, and to his heirs male, whom failing, to Murdoch Stewart and Isobel his wife, daughter to the said Earl ; and to the heirs lawfully to be procreate betwixt them. By the said Isobel he left issue three sons, Walter, James, and Alexander ; the first and last being execute with their father, James fled to Ireland, where he died [*].

For illustration of this, I have seen a mortification, by Isobel, Dutchess of Albany and Countess of Lenox, to the Convent of the Gray Friars of Glasgow, of the lands of Balagan ; which grant she expresses to be made " pro salute " animæ nostræ, & salute quondam recolendæ memoriæ Domini Murdaci Ducis " Albaniæ, dilectissimi Sponsi nostri ; necnon pro animabus quondam Domini

---

[1] Carta penes Jo. Ducem de Argile.
[2] Carta penes Ja. Com. de Wigtoun. [3] Carta penes Burgum de Dunbartoun.

[*] But his posterity have been continued down in a direct male line to the present day, being now Earls of Castle Stewart in Ireland, See the Continuation of Ochiltree.
Editor.

" Duncani Comitis de Lenox, Progenitoris nostri, & pro animabus Walteri,
" Jacobi & Alex: quondam filiorum nostrorum." Dated at Inchmyrin, the
18th of May 1451.

STEWART LORD OCHILTREE.

The first of this family was Andrew Stewart, grandchild of Murdoch Duke of Albany, by James one of his younger sons: He was, by King James II. created Lord Evandale, in the year 1455, upon the forfaulture of the Earl of Douglas. He was Chancellor to King James III. and obtained a Charter from that Prince of the Earldom of Lenox, for life, in the year 1470. He died in Anno 1489, his estate and honours descending on Alexander Stewart his nephew, son of Walter Stewart of Morphy, his brother-german. For this I have seen a grant by King James III. of the Lordship of Evandale, an. 1485, and of the lands of Easter Leckie and Shirgarton in Stirlingshire, to Andrew Lord Evandale in liferent; and to Alexander Stewart his nephew, son to Walter Stewart of Morphy, his brother-german, in fee. Which Alexander, Lord Evandale, was father of Andrew Lord Evandale, who was of the Privy Council to King James IV. He married Margaret Kennedy, daughter to . . . by whom he had three sons; first, Andrew his successor; second, Henry, created by King James V. unto the dignity of Lord Methven; third, Sir James of Doun, ancestor to the Earl of Murray.

Andrew, second Lord Evandale, exchanged Evandale with Sir James Hamilton of Finnart, for the Barony of Ochiltree, in the year 1534, which is ratified by an Act of Parliament, in 1543, and he allowed the stile of Ochiltree, with the precedency of Evandale. He married Margaret, natural daughter of James Earl of Arran, by whom he had Andrew his son and heir, commonly called "The good Lord Ochiltree," who was a chief instrument in our happy reformation. He took to wife Agnes Cunninghame, daughter to the Laird of Capringtoun, by whom he had two sons, I. Andrew, Master of Ochiltree; who died before his father. II. James, the great favourite of King James VI. in his minority. He was Constable of the Castle of Edinburgh, Captain of His Majesty's guards, and Lord High Chancellor of Scotland. The family of Hamilton being forfaulted in Morton's Regency, he was created Earl of Arran, in the year 1581. Which dignity and offices he enjoyed until the Road of Stirling 1585, that the family of Hamilton was restored to their estate and honours. Captain Stewart was killed by Sir James Douglas of Torthorald, in revenge of the Earl of Morton's death, whom the Captain had accused as accessory to the death of King Henry, for which he lost his head.

To Andrew, Lord Ochiltree, last mentioned, succeeded immediately Andrew his grandson, viz. son of Andrew, Master of Ochiltree, his eldest son. Which Andrew, was Governour of the Castle of Edinburgh, in the year 1606, and Comptroller of His Majesty's household, in 1608. He married Margaret, daughter of Sir John Kennedy of Blaquhan, by whom he had Andrew his successor, who transferred his estate and honours to Sir James Stewart of Killeth, his cousin-german, and retired to Ireland, where King James VI. bestowed on him several lands in the county of Tyrone, and created him a Lord of Parliament in that kingdom, with the designation of Castle-Stewart, by Letters Patent, bearing date, November 9th 1619 [1]. He died about the year 1634, without succession.

Sir James Stewart of Killeth, son and heir of Captain James Stewart, sometimes stiled Earl of Arran, by Elizabeth his wife, daughter of John Earl of Athol, became Lord Ochiltree upon his cousin's resignation, in the year 1615. The Lordship of Ochiltree was acquired from him, in the year 1642, by Sir Archbald Stewart of Blackhall, who sold the same to William Earl of Dundonald; and so ended the Stewarts of Ochiltree.

STEWART LORD DOUN, NOW EARL OF MURRAY.

From the family of Ochiltree the Stewarts of Doun derive their descent. Sir James Stewart of Baith, their ancestor, was a younger brother of that noble family. He obtained from King James the V. the hereditary command of the Castle of Doun, with the Stewartry of Monteith, in the year 1534. He married Margaret Lindsay, Dowager lady Innermeath, by whom he had two sons; James his successor; and Henry, author of that branch of the Stewarts of Burray in Orkney, whose lineal heir is Sir James Stewart, Baronet.

[1] Cambden's Annals.

Sir James, son and heir of Sir James Stewart of Doun, upon the dissolution of the Monasteries and their dependencies at the reformation, obtained the lands belonging to the Monastery of St Colm, erected into a temporal Lordship, and was created a Lord of Parliament by King James VI. in the year 1581. He married Margaret, daughter of Archbald, fourth Earl of Argile, by whom he had two sons; James his successor; and Henry, Lord St. Colm, who died without succession.

James, second Lord Doun, became Earl of Murray in right of Elizabeth his wife, daughter and sole heir of James Earl of Murray, Regent of Scotland; and by her he had issue; James, his successor; 2d, Sir Francis, who was made Knight of the Bath, at the creation of Henry Prince of Wales, in the year 1608. His daughters were; 1st, Margaret, married to Charles Earl of Nottingham, an English Peer; and surviving him, she married Sir William Mounson, Viscount of Castlemain in Ireland, sans issue: 2d, Mary, married to Alexander Lord Saltoun: 3d, Grissel, to Sir Robert Innes of that-ilk, and had issue. This Earl of Murray was kill'd by George Earl of Huntly, the 7th of February 1592, his estate and honours devolving on James his son and heir.

Which James wedded Ann, daughter of George Marquis of Huntly, by whom he had James his successor, and a daughter, Margaret, married to James Grant of that-ilk, and had issue; and departing this life, . . to him succeeded James, Earl of Murray, his son, who married Margaret, daughter of Alexander Earl of Home, by whom he had two sons and four daughters; 1st, Alexander his successor; 2d, Archbald, ancestor of Stewart of Dunern: his daughters were; 1st, Mary, married to Archbald Earl of Argile, and had issue; 2d, Margaret, married to Alexander Lord Duffus, and had issue; 3d, Henrieta to Sir Hugh Campbell of Calder, and had issue; 4th, Ann to David Ross of Balnagoun.

To James succeeded Alexander, Earl of Murray, his son; he was a Privy Counsellor to King Charles II. and advanced to be Secretary of State for Scotland, by that monarch; and, upon King James's coming to the Crown, he was His Majesty's High Commissioner to the second Session of Parliament, in 1686, and one of the extraordinary Lords of the Session, and a Privy Counsellor of England; and, upon King James's reviving the order of St. Andrew, called the Thistle, he was elected a Knight of that most noble order. He married Emilia, daughter of Sir William Balfour of Pitcullo, in Fife, Lieutenant of the Tower of London; by whom he had, I. James Lord Doun, who died before his father; leaving issue, by Catharine his wife, daughter of Sir Lionel Talmash of Helengham, two daughters; Ann, married to Alexander Grant of that-ilk, but had no succession; and, Amelia, to John Earl of Crawfurd; II. Charles his successor; III. Francis, who married Margaret daughter of John Lord Balmerinoch, and hath issue. Earl Alexander, departing this life in 1701, he was succeeded by Charles his son and heir. Which Charles, Earl of Murray, hath married the lady Ann Campbell, daughter of Archbald Earl of Argile, Dowager of Richard Earl of Lauderdale; but as yet hath not any issue.

His Lordship's armorial bearing is; Three Coats Quarterly; 1st and 4th, Or, a Lion Rampant within a double Tressure, flowered and counter-flowered, Gules; within a Border, componed, Azure and Argent: 2dly; Or, a Fess Checquie Azure and Argent; 3d; Or; Three Cushions within a Double Tressure flowered and counter-flowered Gules; supported by two Grayhounds: for Crest, a Pelican feeding her young: Motto: " Salus per Christum Redemp- " torem."

STEWART LORD METHVEN.

ANOTHER illustrious branch of the family of Ochiltree, was Henry Stewart, younger brother of Andrew Lord Ochiltree. He was Master of the Ordnance to King James V. by whom he was also created unto the dignity of Lord Methven, in the year 1539. He married Margaret, daughter of King Henry VII. of England, and Dowager of King James IV. of Scotland; and divorced from Archbald Earl of Angus; but by her he had no issue. He afterwards took to wife Janet Stewart, daughter to John Earl of Athol, and widow of Alexander Master of Sutherland; by whom he had Henry his successor, and two daughters; I. Jean, married to Colin Earl of Argile, sans issue. II. Dorothea, to William first Earl of Gourie, and had a numerous issue, of whom many noble families are descended.

To Henry Lord Methven succeeded Henry his son, who was killed at Broughtoun, by the shot of a cannon ball from the Castle of Edinburgh, an. 1572; and having no succession, his estate came to the Crown.

STEWART LORD LORN AND INERMEATH,

DESCENDED, according to our best antiquaries, from Sir Alexander Stewart, a younger son of Sir Robert Stewart of Darnly, by the heiress of Crocstoun[1]. Which Sir Alexander, standing loyal to King Robert Bruce, as a reward of his good service, obtained from that Prince a grant of the lands of Garmeltoun and Dunning in Perthshire[2], which continued with his posterity for many ages. The Stewarts of this race became possessed of the Lordship of Lorn, by marriage of an Heiress of the sirname of Mackdougal, and continued to make a considerable figure in this kingdom for several centuries, and came to a period in the person of John Lord Lorn, created a Lord of Parliament by King James II. an. 1445. The Lordship of Lorn came to be shared betwixt his three daughters and coheirs; Isobel the first, married Colin Earl of Argile; for which reason, that noble family carry the Gally quarterly, in their achievement: Margaret, the second, married Sir Colin Campbel of Glenorchie, a younger son of Duncan, the first Lord Campbell, and ancestor to the Earl of Breadalbin, who carries the arms of Stewart Lord Lorn, quartered with his paternal bearing. The third daughter was married to Archbald Campbell, a younger brother of the noble family of Campbell, ancestor of the old Campbells of Otter.

He had a natural son, Dougal, predecessor of the Stewarts of Appin, of whom Robert Stewart of Appin, is now the lineal successor. . . .

Upon the decease of John Lord Lorn, in the reign of King James the III. Walter Stewart of Inermeath, laid claim to his estate and dignity, and accordingly was seased in the Lordship of Lorn, upon the 21st of March 1469[1]. For, the further illustration of this, I have seen (by the favour of the learned and curious antiquary Mr. Alexander Campbell, Advocate, brother to the laird of Craignish, my very worthy friend) an indenture, dated 30th November 1469, wherein, Walter Lord Lorn, obliges him to resign the Lordship of Lorn in the king's hands, in favours of Colin Earl of Argile; in exchange of which Argile resigns the lands of Kildoning, Baldoning, and Innerdoning, in Perthshire; the lands of Coldrain, in Fife, the lands of Culkerny, in Kinrosshire. Moreover he obliges himself to procure for the Lord Lorn the title of Lord Inermeath, with the precedency of Lorn.

[1] Genealogy of the Lord Lorn, by the famous Antiquarian Mr. Will. Hamilton of Wishaw. [2] Carta in Rotulis Rob. L

The family of Inermeath continued until the reign of King James the VI. that James Lord Inermeath, having married Mary Stewart, daughter of John Earl of Athol, was, by the favour of that monarch, created Earl of Athol, upon the 25th day of March an. 1596; but he died without succession, an. 1605.

STEWART EARL OF ATHOL.

HAVING done with that branch of the house of Lorn, I come now to take notice of the descendants of Sir James Stewart, commonly called the Black Knight of Lorn, a younger brother of that noble family. He married Jean, daughter of John Earl of Somerset, and Dowager of King James I. of Scotland, by whom he had three sons, I. John; II. James, Earl of Buchan; III. Andrew, Bishop of Murray.

John, son and heir of Sir James Stewart was, by the favour of King James II. his uterine brother, created Earl of Athol. He obtained from that Prince a Charter of the Lordship of Balveny, in portion with Margaret Douglas (commonly called The Fair Maid of Galloway) daughter to the Earl of Douglas, in the year 1460. The reducing of that formidable rebel, Donald, Lord of the Isles, who, in the minority of King James III. proclaimed himself king of the Isles, was chiefly owing to Athol's courage and valour; for, being made His Majesty's Lieutenant, he brought him to submit to the king's clemency; from which action he got that motto, " Furth fortune and fill the fetters."

From him, John Earl of Athol was the fifth Earl in a direct masculine line; who departed this life the 8th of November 1594, leaving issue, by Mary his wife, daughter of William first Earl of Gourie, three daughters; I Dorothea, married to William first Earl of Tullibardine, and had issue; II. Mary, to James Lord Inermeath, who thereupon procured the title of Earl of Athol; but he died without succession, the dignity devolving upon Dorothea, Countess of Tullibardine, his lady's sister; of whom John Duke of Athol is the lineal heir, who carries the coat of Stewart, quartered with the paternal coat of Murray. III. Jean, married to Henry Lord St. Colm, sans issue.

STEWART EARL OF BUCHAN.

THE next collateral branch of the Stewarts of Lorn is Sir James Stewart, second son of Sir James Stewart, commonly called The Black Knight of Lorn. He was created Earl of Buchan, by King James II. about the year 1457, and became possessed of the Lordship of Auchterhouse, in right of Margaret his wife, daughter and sole heir of Sir Alexander Ogilvy of Auchterhouse, by whom he had Alexander, Earl of Buchan, his son and heir; whose grandson, John master of Buchan, being killed at the battle of Pinkie, his estate and dignity came to Christian, his daughter and sole heir; who took to husband Robert Douglas, son of William Douglas of Lochlevin, and younger brother of William Earl of Morton.

STEWART EARL OF TRAQUAIR.

THE first of this family was James Stewart, son of James first Earl of Buchan, who became possessor of the Barony of Traquair, by marriage of Catharine Rutherford, one of the daughters and coheirs of Rutherford of that-ilk, in the reign of King James IV.

He obtained a Charter of confirmation of the Barony of Traquair, in the year 1492. By the said Catharine Rutherford, his wife, he left issue, William his son and heir, who obtained from King James IV. his lands of Traquair and others erected into a free Barony, by a Charter, dated at Edinburgh, the 11th of August, 1512 [1]. Which William took to wife Christian Hay, daughter of Lord Yester, by whom he had Robert his son and heir; who obtained a Charter of the Barony of Traquair, upon his father's resignation, an. 1538 [2].

But the first of this family who arrived to the dignity of Peerage, was Sir John Stewart of Traquair, who, being a Baron of an opulent fortune, and a Privy Counsellor to King Charles I., was, by the favour of that Prince, first advanced to the dignity of Lord Stewart of Traquair, by his letters patent, bearing date the 19th of April 1628; and, in 1630, he was constitute, first, Thesaurer Depute,

---

[1] Carta in Publicis Archivis.   [2] Ibid.

and then, Lord High Thesaurer of Scotland. At the solemnity of His Majesty's coronation, he was further dignified with the title of Earl of Traquair, Lord Lintoun and Caberstoun, by letters patent, bearing date at Holy-rood-house the 23d of June 1633. He was also His Majesty's High Commissioner to the Parliament 1639, and bore the same character in the General Assembly of the Church that year. This great Earl deceased in the year 1659; leaving issue, by Elizabeth his wife, daughter of David first Earl of Southesk, Charles his successor; and two daughters: 1st, Mary, married to James Earl of Queensberry, and had issue; the 2d, . . to Patrick Lord Eliebank.

John, Earl of Traquair, his son, married Ann, daughter of George Earl of Wintoun, by whom he had Charles now Earl of Traquair, his son and heir; who hath married the lady Mary Maxwel, daughter of Robert Earl of Nithsdale, by whom he hath issue, Charles Lord Lintoun.

ARMS,

Four Coats, Quarterly; first, Or, a Fess Checquie, Azure and Argent; secondly, Azure, Three Garbs, Or; thirdly, Sable, a Mollet, Argent; fourthly, Argent, in chief of an Orle Gules, three Martlets, Sable: supported by Two Bears proper: Crest, a Crow sitting on the top of a Garb; motto, "Judge naught."

STEWART LORD GARLIES AND EARL OF GALLOWAY.

ANOTHER illustrious branch of the family of Stewart, were the Stewarts, promiscuously designed of Dalswintoun and Garlies, whose original ancestor was Sir Walter Stewart; who, as a reward of his good and faithful services, obtained the lands of Dalswintoun from King Robert Bruce, as appears from the original yet extant[1]. And standing loyal to King David Bruce, he obtained from John Randolph, Earl of Murray, his nephew, a grant of the lands of Garlies. John Stewart of Dalswintoun was his son, who lived in the reign of Robert II.

Whose successor, Sir Walter Stewart of Dalswintoun, was cotemporary with King Robert III. and having no heirs male, Marion, his only daughter, became his heir. For authority of this, I have seen an indenture, in the Scots language, dated at Dumfries, in the year 1396, betwixt Sir Walter Stewart, Lord of Dalswintoun, on the one part, and Sir William Stewart, Sheriff of Teviotdale,

[1] In Rotulis, Rob. L.

descended of the house of Darnly) on the other; wherein it is agreed, that John Stewart, son and heir to the said Sir William, shall marry and have to wife Marion Stewart, the only daughter to the said Sir Walter, with whom he obliges himself to give sixscore of merks in tocher; and, if it should happen that he have no other heirs of his body, that the said Marion shall be his heir.

Like as it is plain, from the archives of the kingdom, that Sir William Stewart of Dalswintoun and Garlies made a considerable figure in the reign of King James II. and that he left three sons; 1st, Sir Alexander his successor; the 2d, Walter, ancestor to the Stewarts of Tonderghie in Galloway; the 3d, Sir Thomas, who obtained the lands of Minto and Morbottle in Teviotdale from his father, with consent of Sir Alexander Stewart his eldest son, which is confirmed by King James III. and became possest of the lands of Wester-Partick, and several others, in the neighbourhood of the City of Glasgow, by marriage of Isobel, one of the daughters and coheirs of Sir Walter Stewart of Arthurly. Of whom the Right Honourable Walter Lord Blantyre is the lineal heir.

Of the family of Minto, several other ancient families descended; as the Stewarts of Fintilloch and Barhills in Galloway; as also the Stewarts of Shambellie in Dumfriesshire; the Stewarts of Heisilside and Bowhouse in Clydsdale; and the Lord Montjoy, in the kingdom of Ireland, descended of Sir Robert Stewart, a gentleman who did, in a singular manner, distinguish himself in his loyalty to his sovereign King Charles I.

To Sir William Stewart of Dalswintoun succeeded Alexander Stewart, designed of Garlies, his son, who obtained the honour of Knighthood from King James III; and, departing this life an. 1490 [1], he was succeeded by Alexander his son and heir.

Which Alexander was Knighted by King James IV. and, accompanying that Prince to the fatal battle of Flouden, in the year 1513, had the hard fate there to lose his life: leaving issue by . . . Douglas his wife, a daughter of the family of Cavers, Alexander his son and heir, commonly called The White Knight, from his complexion; who obtained the honour of Knighthood from King James V. by whom he was also commissioned Ambassador to King Henry VIII. of England. He married, first, Margaret, daughter of Sir James Crichton of Cranstoun-Riddle, but had no issue; secondly, Margaret, daughter of Sir John Dunbar of Mochrum, by whom he had Alexander his successor; and of a younger son descended the family of Phisgill. Thirdly, he married Catharine Stewart, daughter of the laird of Barclaie, by whom he had a son, William, author of that branch of the Stewarts of Clairie.

Alexander Stewart younger of Garlies, in the minority of King James the VI. offered to combat with that daring Hero Sir William Kircaldy of Grange,

---

[1] Genealogy of the family of Garlies, by Mr. David Sympson.

FAMILY OF STEWART. 237

Governour of the Castle of Edinburgh, (then in the interest of Queen Mary) who gave a challenge to any of the adverse party that durst fight him. He was killed in that scuffle at Stirling, where Matthew Earl of Lenox, Regent, lost his life, the 4th of September 1571; leaving issue, by Catharine Herris his wife, daughter and one of the co-heirs of Andrew Lord Herris, Alexander, who immediately succeeded his grandfather, and took to wife Christian, daughter of Sir William Douglas of Drumlanrig, ancestor to the Duke of Queensberry; by whom he had, 1st, Alexander his son and heir; 2d, William of Mains, who married Barbara, daughter and sole heir of James Stewart of Burray in Orkney; of whom Sir James Stewart of Burray is lineally descended.

To Sir Alexander, above-mentioned, succeeded Sir Alexander his son, who, being a Baron of an ample fortune, was, by the bounty and favour of King James VI. created a Baron of this Realm, by the designation of Lord Stewart of Garlies, September 2d 1607; and by the same Monarch improven to the dignity of Earl of Galloway, by Letters Patent, bearing date at Whitehall, the 9th of May 1623 [1]. And departing this life, in the year 1649, he left issue, by Grissel his Lady, daughter of Sir John Gordon of Lochinvar, ancestor to the Viscount of Kenmure, James his successor, who, during the civil wars was very active for the royal cause. He married Nicola, daughter of Sir Robert Greir of Lagg, by whom he had; 1st, Alexander his successor: 2d, Robert of Remestoun: 3d, William of Castle-Stewart, who married Elizabeth, daughter and heiress of John Gordon of Cardoness; and a daughter, Grissel, married to Alexander Viscount of Kenmure, and had issue.

Alexander, third Earl of Galloway, wedded the Lady Mary Douglas, daughter of James Earl of Queensberry, by whom he had Alexander and James, successively Earls of Galloway; 3d, Colonel John of Sorbie; 4th, Andrew, who died in the expedition to Darien, an. 1699; 5th, William; 6th, Robert. Besides these sons, he had likewise two daughters; 1st, Margaret, married to John Clark of Pennicook, one of the Barons of His Majesty's Exchequer in Scotland, and had issue; 2d, Henrieta, to William Earl of Glencairn, and hath issue.

To Alexander, Earl of Galloway, succeeded Alexander his son; but he dying without succession, his estate and honours devolved on James his brother and heir: Which James hath married the Lady Catharine Montgomery, daughter of Alexander Earl of Eglintoun, by whom he hath issue Alexander Lord Garlies.

ARMS.

A Fess Checquie, Azure and Argent; surmounted of a Bend Gules; with-

[1] Genealogy of the family of Galloway, by Mr. David Sympson.

in a double Tressure flower'd and counterflower'd of the last: supported on the Dexter by a Savage, and on the Sinister by a Lion Rampant. Crest, a Pelican feeding her young. Motto, " Virescit vulnere virtus."

STEWART EARL OF BUTE AND LORD MOUNT-STEWART.

Though none of this family did arrive to the dignity of Peerage, until the 2d year of the reign of our most Gracious Sovereign Queen Ann; yet were they Barons of great eminency, and honoured with several matches from diverse noble families, for many ages before: they lineally descended of Sir John Stewart, (commonly called The Black Stewart, from his complexion) son to King Robert the II. the first of the family of Stewart, who enjoyed the crown of this Realm. He obtained from King Robert III. a Charter, confirming a former grant of the Sheriffship of Bute and Arran, therein designed, " dilecto " fratri suo." This Sir John left issue, by his wife . . . . . three sons, 1st, Robert his successor; 2d, Andrew, ancestor of the Stewarts of Roslin and Balinshangrie; of whom Sir John Stewart of Roslin, one of the Gentlemen Ushers to King James VI. did lineally descend; 3d, William, of whom issued the Stewarts of Finnock: for this I have seen a Charter granted by King James II. confirming a former, " dilecto consanguineo suo Willielmo Senescallo, filio Johannis Senescalli Vicecomitis de Bute & Arran," dated in the year 1444.

To Sir John Stewart, Sheriff of Bute, succeeded Robert his son, who was of the Privy Council to King James II. I have seen him so design'd in an indenture betwixt the King's Majesty, on the one part, and Sir Robert Erskine of that-ilk, on the other, dated at Stirling the 10th of August 1440.

To Robert Stewart of Bute succeeded Ninian his son, who, standing highly in favour with King James IV. obtained from that Prince a grant of the hereditary command of His Majesty's Castle of Rothsay, with a salary of 40 merks out of the feu-farms of the lands of Bute, Kintyre, and Cowal, as is evident from a Charter in the Publick Records, dated at Edinburgh, the 5th of August 1498. He married Elizabeth Blair, daughter to the Laird of Blair. For this, I have seen a Charter granted by King James V. an. 1529, to Ninian Stewart, Sheriff of Bute, and Elizabeth Blair his spouse, of the lands of Ambrismore, in liferent, and to Robert, their son, in fee.

Whose successor, James Stewart, Sheriff of Bute, obtained a Charter of his lands, on his own resignation, in the year 1541. He was made Chamberlain of Bute, to which office the king's forest within that isle was annex'd, anno 1549. And, at the same time, he obtained a Charter of the lands of Kirktoun in the Isle of Cumbray [1]. He married, 1st, Mary Campbel, daughter of Archbald, Earl of Argile [2]; and 2d, Marion, daughter of John Fairly of that-ilk, and widow of Thomas Boyd of Linn, brother of Robert Lord Boyd, (and ancestor of Thomas Boyd, now of Pitcon); by whom he had John his successor; who took to wife . . . . Campbell, daughter and heiress of John Campbell of Skipnish [3]; (a brother's son of the family of Argile.) And 2dly, he married Fynewald Macdonald, a daughter of Macdonald of Yla; and departing this life an . . . to him succeeded John, his son and heir.

Which John obtained the honour of Knighthood from King James the VI. about the year 1616, and added to his ancient inheritance the Lands of Foord in East Lothian, by marriage of Elizabeth, eldest of the two daughters and coheirs of Mr. Robert Hepburn of Foord; by whom he had Sir James his son and heir.

Which Sir James was married with Elizabeth, daughter of Sir Dougal Campbel of Auchinbreck, and of Isobel his wife, daughter of Thomas Lord Boyd; by whom he had two sons; Sir Dougal his successor; and Sir Robert of Tillicultrie, one of the Senators of the College of Justice, created a Baronet by Her present Majesty Queen Ann, upon the 24th day of April 1707.

To Sir James Stewart of Bute succeeded Sir Dougal his son, who married Elizabeth daughter of Sir Thomas Ruthven of Dunglass, by . . . . Lesly, daughter of Alexander first Earl of Leven; by whom he had Sir James his successor; and Mr. Dougal of Blairhall, one of the Senators of the College of Justice, and one of the Lords of Her Majesty's Justiciary. He married Mary Bruce, Heiress of Blairhall.

Sir James Stewart of Bute succeeded his father: he was, by the bounty and favour of our present Sovereign, created unto the dignities of Earl of Bute, Viscount of Kingarth, Lord Mount-Stewart, Cumbray and Inchmarnock, by letters patent, dated at St. James's, the 14th day of April, in the year 1703. He married, 1st, Agnes, eldest daughter of Sir George Mackenzie of Rosehaugh, by whom he had James Lord Mount-Stewart, and one daughter, Margaret, married to John Viscount of Garnock, and mother of Patrick now Viscount of Garnock: 2d, he married Christian, daughter of Mr. William Dundas of Kinçavel, by whom he hath a son, Mr. John.

[1] Carta in Publicis Archivis. [2] Genealogy of the family of Bute. [3] Id.

ARMS.

Or; a Fess Chequie, Azure and Argent; within a double Tressure Flower'd and Counter-flower'd, Gules: supported on the Dexter by a Horse, and on the Sinister by a Red Deer. For Crest, a Demi-Lion Rampant, eshewing out of an Earl's Coronet. The Motto, "Nobilis ira."

Of the family of Bute several other antient families descended, as the Stewarts of Kilcattan, in the shire of Bute, now extinct; which hath furnished some considerable cadets, as the Stewarts of Ascog in Bute: to document this, I have seen a contract of marriage, in the year 1584 [1], betwixt John Stewart of Ascog, son to William Stewart of Kilcattan, and Marion Fairly, daughter of David Fairly of that-ilk, by Catharine his wife, daughter of Laurence Crawford of Kilburny, ancestor to the Viscount of Garnock; whose lineal heir is John Stewart now of Ascog, making from him the fifth, in a direct male line.

STEWART LORD BLANTYRE.

The paternal ancestor of this noble family was Sir Thomas Stewart of Minto, one of the younger sons of Sir William Stewart of Dalswintoun and Garlies, ancestor to the Earl of Galloway, in King James the III.'s time: which Sir Thomas obtained the lands of Wester-Partick, Househill, &c. by marriage of Isobel, second daughter and coheiress of Sir Walter Stewart of Arthurly, a branch of the illustrious family of Darnly. I have seen a Charter by John Earl of Lenox, of the lands of Corsehill, to Thomas Stewart of Minto, and Isobel Stewart his spouse, daughter and one of the coheirs of Sir Walter Stewart of Arthurly, on the resignation of Janet Cameron, relict of the said Sir Walter [2], in the year 1489.

In the reign of King James VI. Sir Walter Stewart of Blantyre, son of Sir John Stewart of Minto, being one of the Lords of Council and Session, and Lord High-Thesaurer of Scotland, was, by the special favour of James, first monarch of Great Britain, created unto the dignity of Lord Blantyre, the 10th of July 1606. Of whom Walter Lord Blantyre is the lineal heir. (Vide Lord Blantyre, page 53.)

[1] Carta penes Patricium Vicecomitem de Garnock. [2] Charter in the Publick Register of Charters.

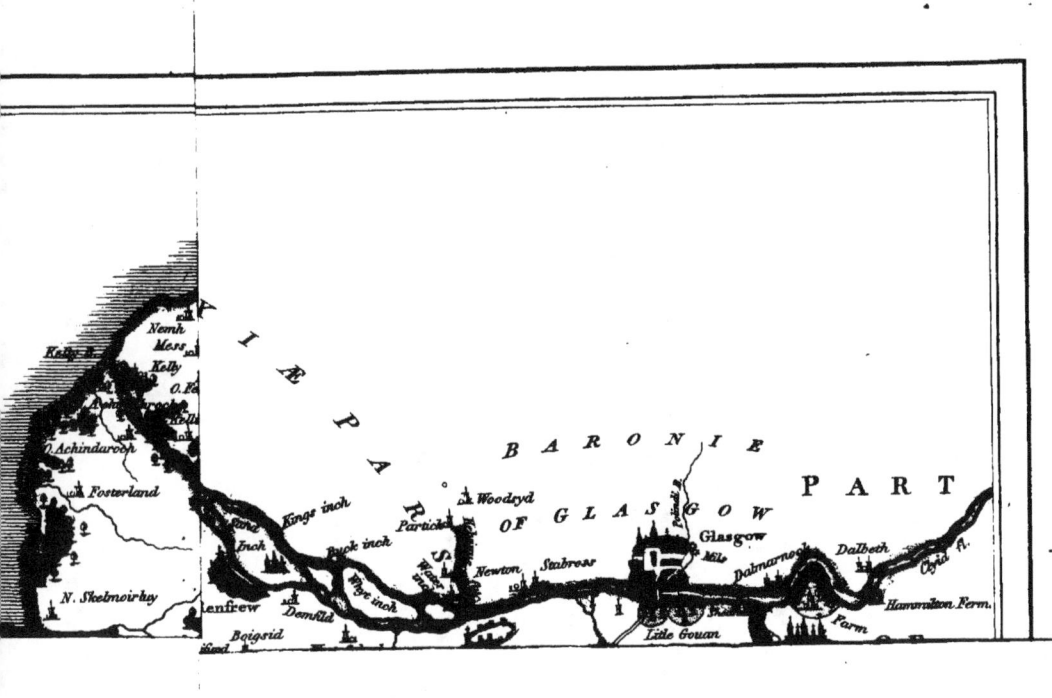

CONTINUATION

OF

THE HISTORY OF RENFREWSHIRE.

PART I.

GEOGRAPHICAL STATE AND CIRCUMSTANCES.

Situation and Extent.—The shire of Renfrew is situated between 55° 41' 40", and 55° 59' 25" of N. Lat. and is stretched out along the south shore of the river and frith of Clyde, from half a mile east of the city of Glasgow, to 28 miles due west from that town. There is a detached part of the shire of Lanark, that comes betwixt it and the Clyde, in a narrow stripe opposite to Glasgow, and extends about five miles farther west, as may be seen in the map. The county extends about 31 miles from S. E. to N. W. the general direction lengthways; and its greatest breadth is about 13 miles in a cross direction from S. W. to N. E. The whole is contained in an area of about 241 square miles; or more precisely, amounts to 154,166 English acres, according to Ainslie's great map of the county. In this are included 1294 acres on the north side of the river; and from 750 to 1000 acres under fresh water lakes, in different places still undrained. An endeavour shall be made to ascertain the quantity of cultivated and uncultivated lands respectively, in the short topographical description of the county, parish by parish, in Part II.

General Aspect.—A range of hills, with little interruption, forms the southern boundary with the county of Ayr. The most easterly of these, in the parish of Eagleshame, are covered with heath. There are some of the same hue, towards the west, in the parishes of Lochwinnoch, Kilmacolm, and Innerkip. The intermediate hills are in general fine green pasture; some of them naked rock. The highest in the county, the Mistylaw, is 1240 feet. Of the others, few exceed 900 feet, but are more generally from 500 to 700 above the level of the sea. There is a range of rising grounds along the shore, in the parishes of Erskine, Kilmacolm, Port-Glasgow, and Greenock, from 300 to 500 feet in height, either green pasture, bare rock, or beautifully fringed with wood. The rest of the county, which is the greater part, is nearly all in cultivation, stretched out into winding vallies and level plains, or diversified, by gently swelling eminences, into heights and hollows, full of towns, villages, and gentlemen's seats, all highly ornamented with woods and plantations.

State of Cultivation.—In Crawfurd's History there is no notice whatever taken of the state of cultivation in this county. The natural state of fertility is, however, very correctly defined; that the lower parts of the county abounded with corn, and the higher with choice pasturage. What is understood now by improvements in agriculture did not then exist. There is no evidence on record, that ever any thing of the kind was attempted. The cultivation up to his day, had, in all probability, remained in the same state as in the days of King David, or of Malcolm Canmore; or, more probably, it had declined. There is at least evidence, that wheat was anciently cultivated in many places in Scotland, where it is hardly yet brought again into cultivation. There is one solitary instance, however, of an attempt at improvement; and a curious fact it is, by a Lord Napier, who took out a patent for improving lands, by sprinkling them with salt. A project that does not seem to have succeeded, as it is no more heard of. This was in 1598, a hundred years before Crawfurd's time. See Wood's Peerage, article Napier.

But Semple, who published a continuation of this History in 1782, takes notice, in the introductory part of the work, of considerable alterations that had taken place in the state of the cultivation since 1710, (the date of Mr. Crawfurd's original publication,) or rather, that were beginning to be introduced in his own times. In particular he mentions, that improved implements of husbandry had been invented: new species of crop introduced, and new modes of management adopted: from all which, great improvements had been made in the general state of the cultivation. The effects of which, at that time, were to raise the rents from six shillings to 20 shillings an acre; the wages of farm servants from

£12 or £16 Scots, to £3 or £4 Sterling in the half year; while the farmers themselves lived better than ever. He takes notice also, that the country gentlemen bore a very active hand in all the improvements, more particularly, that they paid great attention to the roads and bridges; that they exerted themselves greatly in inclosing their lands, which, previous to 1755, were entirely open; that they were beginning to make plantations of wood, and even introduced a more refined system of culture into their gardens. In short, that in every department of rural affairs, there was exhibited a very general spirit of improvement. All this taking place in his own day, and before his own eyes, excited his admiration, and called forth his praise.

Since that time, now 35 years ago, the improvements that have been effected in the cultivation of the soil, and general embellishment of the country, have been still more remarkable, and have been followed with the most beneficial consequences; and which extend not merely to the people immediately connected with the operations, but to every rank and class in society, whether in town or country. The improvements which Semple saw as little more than commencing, may be said to be now completed. For, owing to the increasing energy exhibited, and more judicious means of cultivation employed, there is hardly a single acre susceptible of improvement, that has not been rendered greatly more productive. The whole arable part of the county, has long been inclosed, and the fields minutely subdivided either with hedge rows, or with stone walls. The first, in the lower districts, the latter in the higher lands. Every gentlemen's seat, and even many of the farm hamlets, stand now encircled with plantations. Even many of the hill sides and hill tops, originally bleak and barren, are now waving with forest trees. The very climate has hence become improved, and rendered more propitious to the fruits of the earth.

This favourable change of circumstances has been remarkably apparent in Renfrewshire. But it is not limited to it alone. The same may be observed, more or less, wherever the country is susceptible of such improvements, in every county in Scotland.

The result of the whole has been precisely what was in contemplation from the measures employed; an increase in the food of man. The legislative encouragements that, for the last hundred years, have been held out to cultivate and improve the soil, have occasioned a gradual increase in the produce of land, not only in quantity, but in a much greater variety than was ever before known. This increase of food has alone enabled the country to maintain its greatly augmented population, and has been itself the original cause of the increase. For had not the food of man been augmented, the population neither could have been increased, nor so well maintained, even if it had remained stationary. In Crawfurd's days, about the time of the union of the two kingdoms, Scotland did not contain more than 1,200,000 inhabitants, and had not, in fact, food to maintain more, notwithstanding the penurious style in which they were then compelled to live. In that scanty number too, according to the intelligent Fletcher of Saltoun, there were not fewer than 200,000 mendicants, begging their bread from door to door, none of them having a house of their own, under which to put their head: whereas the population now exceeds 1,800,000, all better lodged, better clothed, and much better fed than ever, whilst there is not one-tenth part of the former number of vagrants to pester the country. All this is imputable to the measures that have been adopted to encourage the cultivation of the soil. Withdraw this encouragement, and more rapidly than ever it arose would be the decline of agriculture; and the country would again dwindle down to its former state of thinly scattered population, and deplorable poverty.

Civil Government.—The hereditary sheriffship of the county, which, at the time Crawfurd wrote, was vested in the family of Eglinton, was, in 1748, on the general abolition of heritable jurisdictions, purchased by the Crown from Alexander tenth Earl of Eglinton, who was allowed £5000 as a remuneration for his surrendered rights in this county. The Crown now appoints the county magistrates. The Right Honourable George, Earl of Glasgow, is Lord Lieutenant and High Sheriff; John C. Dunlop, Esq; Sheriff Depute; Alexander Campbell, Esq; Sheriff Substitute in Paisley; and Claud Marshal, Esq; Sheriff Substitute in Greenock.

CONTINUATION

OF

THE HISTORY OF RENFREWSHIRE.

PART II.

Topographical description of the County, Parish by Parish.

EAGLESHAME PARISH. *See page 23.*

Situation, Extent, and present state of Property.—This Parish is situated in the south-east corner of the County, and contains 15,436 English acres. It continues still to belong, nearly all, to the Earl of Eglinton. The lands of Achinhood (containing the farms of Netherton, Holehall, Holemuir, and Maulouther) which, in Crawfnrd's time, belonged to a cadet of the noble family of Eglinton, have since, in   been reunited to the other property of its chief. There are only four other heritors in the Parish, and their properties are comparatively small, and who hold them as vassals in feu of the Earl. Namely,

I. *Millhall;*—John Mather, whose father acquired this small, but pleasant spot, by marrying Mary, the only surviving child of Robert Dunlop of Millhall, whose ancestor was a younger son of Dunlop of that-ilk. The extent is about 10 acres of fertile land, on which there is a neat small mansion, and also a mill, pleasantly situated on the water of White Cart, about a mile S. E. of the village of Eagleshame.

2. *Boreland.*—William Brown, a more considerable property, about half a mile N. of Eagleshame, all good land, acquired by succession, about 150 years ago, from a family of the name of Anderson.

3. *Muirhouse, East,* James Mather. ⎫ purchased in 1742, by their grand-
4. *Muirhouse, West,* John Mather. ⎭ father, from Baron Mure of Caldwell.
These two properties, lying conterminous to each other, are situated about two miles west from Eagleshame, and partake much of the nature of the muirish country they are surrounded with, being partly cultivated, partly natural meadow, and partly wild enough unreclaimed lands, well stocked with muir-fowl.

The extent of property in the whole Parish may be stated thus:

	Acres English.	Valued Rent Scots.
1. The Earl of Eglinton's, about	14,900,	£.2979 : 13 : 4
2. Millhall,	10,	
3. Boreland, pendicle,	40,	53 : 13 : 4
4. Muirhouse, East,	250,	20 : 0 : 0
5. Muirhouse, West,	250,	20 : 0 : 0
Total,	15,450	3073 : 6 : 8

Soil, and how occupied.—The whole is incumbent on a sub-soil of Basaltic, or, as it is provincially called, whinstone rock, which here, as every where else, is the most kindly of all soil. The arable land is accordingly very productive, and the pastures remarkably nourishing. The chief dependence of the husbandmen is on the dairy, and they have an excellent breed of milch cows. The produce is chiefly applied in churned milk and sweet butter, made up for the Glasgow market. There is little or no natural wood; but, of late, there has been made some Plantations, chiefly of Larch, and other of the Pine race, which are thriving so much, as to give every encouragement to extend them. The muirs are among the best in Scotland for game, both feathered and footed.

The whole may be arranged as under:

	Acres.
1. Arable, in tillage, or, in cultivated grass land, about,	6100
2. Natural pasture and meadow, do.	3960
3. Moss and muir, &c. little susceptible of cultivation, do.	5330
4. Plantations, chiefly on knols inaccessible to the plough, do.	60
Sum as before,	15,450

Aspect and Temperature.—As a considerable proportion of the surface consists of dark muirish soil, hence the general aspect is not very inviting, more especially as it rises into hilly lands in the back ground, perhaps 1000, or 1200 feet above the level of the sea. The general exposure being to the north-east, to which ungenial direction nearly all its streamlets flow, has also a tendency to render the climate cold, especially in the spring and harvest months. In other respects, particularly during summer, the parish of Eagleshame is remarkably rural and pleasant, and at all times very healthy.

Succession of Ministers.—To Mr. Stewart, mentioned by Crawfurd, succeeded Mr. William Parlane, in 1727, who died in August, 1740. He was succeeded by the Rev. Colin Champbell, in June 1741, who was translated to Kilmaronock, in Dumbartonshire, in Dec. 1761, and afterwards to Renfrew. He was succeeded here by the Rev. Henry Greive, who, in June 1767, was succeeded by the Rev. Thomas Clark, who died 23d. Aug. 1783; Mr. Mitchell then got the presentation but was not ordained, on account of unpopularity. The Rev. .... Dobbie, Minister of Glasford, was translated from thence and settled here, on the 5th Jan. 1786; he died on the 26th April 1799, when the Rev. William Finlay (formerly his assistant) succeeded him; he died on the 26th April 1816; and the Rev. Hugh Davidson was settled on the 24th April 1817.

Dissenters.—There is only one meeting-house in the parish, viz. of the Burgher Seceders, whose Pastor (the Rev. James Dickson,) is very highly esteemed. There are different other dissenters from the establishment, as Antiburghers and Cameronians, whose respective places of worship are situated in other parishes in the neighbourhood.

Village of Eagleshame.—A new village was begun here in 1769, as formed by Alexander the tenth Earl, two years before. It is on a singularly pleasant plan. Two rows of houses in straight lines face each other, at the distance of 300 yards at the west-most or upper end of the town, and of 250 yards at the lower or east end; not precisely opposite, of course, as the nature of the ground does not well admit of nearer or more parallel approximation. Midway betwixt them, there is a limpid stream, to which, from each side, the banks shelve downwards, and are, in some parts, formed into washing greens, and in others embellished with plantations. The houses are handsomely built of good masonry, but so far left to the taste of the owners as to be, in some cases, but of one storey height, though more generally of two, whilst some are covered with slate and some with thatch. Every house has an excellent kitchen garden at the back, and generally a considerable plot of potatoe ground. The feu duty, or rather ground rent, on a 999 year lease, is at the moderate rate of 3d. the fall, or 40s. the Scotch acre. These favourable circumstances soon led to a rapid increase in the size of the town; for, instead of 20 or 25 houses, as at the period mentioned, it now contains about 130 houses, and in 1811 there were 943 inhabitants, the town extending nearly half a mile in length, besides a few houses in a cross direction, and some in a back street parallel to the main one. There is a handsome church with an elegant steeple, furnished with a good clock, and a fine toned bell. The inhabitants are of various occupations, but mostly employed in the cotton manufacture. There were here two cotton spinning mills, belonging to two distinct companies; but these erections, which in almost every place where they have been established, become hotbeds of vice and forerunners of a dissolution of manners, have been remarkable here only as unfortunate establishments, both having been burnt down, once and again, before there was full time to induce the contamination of principle, which the collecting of so many uneducated young people, into one place, never fails in the end to accomplish.

The Earl of Eglinton has a commodious small mansion here (Punnoon Lodge) where he usually passes a few days once or twice a-year, among his chearful vassals, who ever hail his return among them with hearty gratulation. Eagleshame is situated 9 miles due south from Glasgow. The direct road from Edinburgh by Hamilton to Kilmarnock and Ayr passes through it. There is no other village in the parish. The rest of the population is scattered over the whole in single farm-steads. The amount in the parish altogether, in 1811, was 1424; but for this see the statistical tables at the end.

Descent of Families.—MONTGOMERY EARL OF EGLINTON. The account of this noble family, as given by Crawfurd, (p. 23.) is generally correct so far as it goes; but more recent researches have disclosed many additional circumstances. To state the principal occurrences relating to it, is the object of this short memoir.

That the family of Montgomery is of Norman origin is indisputed. Roger de Montgomery vicompte de Hiesmes, said to be cousin-german to Robert Duke of Normandy, father of William the Conqueror, commanded the van of the Norman army at the battle of Hastings, 1066. He was after exalted to the dignity of Earl of Arundel and Shrewsbury, and was otherways rewarded by most extensive grants of territory in the south and west of England; more particularly in Shropshire, as nearly the whole of that extensive and fertile county was conferred on him. To these possessions he himself (literally by conquest) added a considerable tract of fine country in Wales, called after his own name, the shire of Montgomery, perhaps the richest county in the whole principality. Much of these vast domains was afterwards lost by his successors taking part with Robert

Courthose, the eldest son of the Conqueror, against the youngest son, Henry I. who, prevailing in the contest, confined his brother in prison, and seized on the property of his adherents.

The first of this family who came to Scotland, was

I. Robert de Mundegumbri, who accompanied Walter the High Stewart from Wales, (hence called by the Highlanders in their Gaelic to this day, Maccumbric, or the Son of the Welchman,) and obtained the manor of Egleshame in this county, the first lands the family had in Scotland, and which has continued, undiminished, their property to this day. He died about the year 1177.

II. John de Montgomery, supposed to be his son. He married Helen, one of the three co-heiresses of Robert de Kent, with whom he obtained a third part of the lands of Inverwick in East Lothian. He was succeeded by his son,

III. Alan de Montgomery in the lands of Inverwick, and in Renfrewshire. He is witness to several charters; in particular, to one with Walter the Bishop of Glasgow, betwixt the years 1208 and 1232. He was succeeded by his eldest son.

IV. Robert de Montgomery, who was witness to a donation of the Earl of March in 1258, to the Monks of Coldingham. He was succeeded by his brother.

IV. John de Montgomery, who died in 1285. He had four sons; 1st, John; 2d, Murthaw, the reputed ancestor of the Montgomeries of Thornton; 3d, Thomas; 4th, Alan, designed of Stahare, or Stair, who was murdered by the English at Ayr in 1297, along with Sir Reginald Crawfurd, father-in-law of Wallace.

V. John, the eldest son, is among the list of those who swore fealty to Edward I. in 1296. He is there designed " of Lanarkshire;" but that county then comprehended the shire of Renfrew.

VI. Alexander de Montgomery is supposed to have been his son and successor. He must have been a man of considerable rank and power, as he obtained a passport from England to go abroad with a retinue of 60 horse and foot. This was in 1358. It is thought he was the father of,

VII. John de Montgomery of Eglisham. He married Elizabeth, daughter and sole heiress of Sir Hugh de Eglinton of Eglinton, by whom he obtained the extensive estates of Eglinton and Ardrossan in Ayrshire, still belonging to the family.

The Eglintons had long been a family of great distinction. Ralph de Eglinton was one of those *Magnates Scotiæ*, who swore fealty to Edward I. in 1296. Sir Hugh de Eglinton was Justiciary of Lothian in 1361. He married Egidia, daughter of Walter, sixth High Steward, and sister of Robert II. and had different charters dated 1361, 1371, and 1373, of various lands, of which the greater part still remain in the family to this day. Sir Hugh de Eglinton is supposed to have died soon after 1376; and the Baronies of Eglinton and Ardrossan became the property, through his daughter, of John Montgomery of Eglisham, and who, from this time quartered, along with his own, the arms of Eglinton.

Ardrossan was long the property of a family who assumed their name from these lands. There is an Arthur de Ardrossan, witness to a charter in 1226; a Godfrey de Ardrossan, who swore fealty to Edward I. in 1296; a Fergus and a Robinus de Ardrossan, who signed an instrument of recognition of the same Edward in 1304; and a Hugh de Ardrossan, who was fined three years rent of his estate by the same King in 1305. A proof that he had not agreed very cordially to the presumptive claims of that ambitious prince. It does not appear at what precise time the lands of Ardrossan were acquired by the family of Eglinton; but it is understood that it was through an heiress of Ardrossan married into the family of Eglinton, during the reign of David II. and previous to the marriage of Sir Hugh de Eglinton with the daughter of the High Steward. It seems not improbable, that this Sir Hugh was the son of that marriage. The date of the reign of David II. is from June 1329, till February 1370-1. An Ardrossan of Ardrossan is witness to a charter in this reign, but without a date; and soon after 1376, on the death of Sir Hugh de Eglinton, his daughter Elizabeth, by the Scottish Princess Egidia, carried both estates to her husband Montgomery of Eglisham.

This Sir John Montgomery of Eglisham, in company with the Douglas, signalized himself at the battle of Otterburn in 1388. He took Henry Percy prisoner, and with his ransom built the castle (now in ruins) of Pulnoon, as related by Lesley and other historians.

By his Lady Elizabeth de Eglinton, he had his successor, and three more sons.

VIII. John de Montgomery of Eglisham, Eglinton, and Ardrossan, succeeded his father after the year 1392; but the precise date is not known. He was employed on several important missions into England, and in 1423 was one of the hostages for the ransom of James I.; at which time the annual revenue of his lands was estimated at 700 merks, whilst that of Lord Hamilton was estimated at 500, and Campbell of Loudon at 300. He married Margaret, daughter of Sir Robert Maxwell of Caerlavrock, by whom he had, 1st, Alexander his successor; 2d, Robert, ancestor of the Montgomeries of Stanhope and Macbethhill; 3d, Anne, married to Robert Lord Kilmawrs.

IX. Sir Alexander de Montgomery, the eldest son, was also much employed at Court, and on several embassies to England, in the reigns of James I. and II.;

and was raised to the Peerage during that period. By Wood, this is said to have been before 31st January 1448-9, when his son was invested in the office of Baillie of Cunninghame; by Crawfurd, that it was in 1445; and by Pinkerton, that in November 1437, the *Lords* Gordon and Montgomery were sent on an embassy to England along with some *Commoners* specified; from which it may be inferred, that he was in the rank of Peers, at least, before that time. He died soon after June 1461. By his Lady, Margaret, daughter of Sir Robert Boyd of Kilmarnock, he had issue; 1st, Alexander; 2d, George, ancestor of the Montgomeries of Skelmurely; 3d, Thomas, Rector of Eagleshame; 4th, Margaret, married the Earl of Lennox: 5th, Elizabeth, married Lord Kennedy; and 6th, Anne, married Cunningham of Glengarnock.

X. Alexander, Master of Montgomery, died 1452, before his father. By his Lady Elizabeth, daughter of Sir Adam Hepburn of Hales, he had issue; 1st, Alexander; 2d, Robert of Braidstane, ancestor of the Viscounts Montgomery, afterwards Earls of Mount Alexander in Ireland; 3d, Hugh of Hislot (Hazlehead); 4th, Margaret, married Lord Home.

XI. Alexander, the eldest son, was second Lord Montgomery. He had a charter dated 25th October 1465, of the lands of Bonington and Piltoun in the county of Edinburgh. He married Catherine, daughter of Lord Kennedy, by whom he had issue; 1st, Hugh; 2d, James Montgomery of Smithston.

XII. Hugh, third Lord Montgomery, born about the year 1460. In October 1488, he got a remission from the Crown for throwing down the house of Kirrielaw, (now Grange, near Stevenston,) and carrying off goods from it. It belonged to his adversaries the Cunninghames of Kilmawrs, who treasured up the injury in their minds till an opportunity occurred of retaliation about 40 years after, which they did not let slip. He attached himself to the party of James IV. and was, by that Prince, raised to the dignity of Earl of Eglinton in 1507. The feuds betwixt him and the family of Glencairn continued to increase in spite of all that their mutual friends could do to prevent them; insomuch that the partizans of the latter set fire to the Castle of Eglinton, and burnt it to the ground, and with it all the family charters and papers. This is stated in a new charter for the whole, granted by James V. in January 1528. His Lordship, after a life of great activity, and having been in many a rencontre, died quietly in his bed in June 1545, in the 85th year of his age. He married Lady Helen Campbell, daughter of Colin Earl of Argyle, and by her had issue; 1st, Alexander, Master of Montgomery, who died before his father was raised to the Peerage; 2d, John, Master of Eglinton; 3d, Sir Neil Montgomery of Lainshaw, who, by marriage with Margaret Mure, heiress of Skeldon, got that estate also. He was, in the spirit of the times, killed in a feud by Lord Boyd, at Irvine, in 1547; 4th, William Montgomery of Greenfield, who, by marriage with Elizabeth, daughter of Robert Francis of Stane, acquired that property near Irvine, which continues still in the family; 5th, Hugh; and 6th, Robert, Bishop of Argyle in 1530.

The daughters were; 1st, Lady Margaret, married to Lord Sempill; 2d, Lady Marjory, married to William Master of Sommerville; 3d, Lady Matilda, married to Colin Campbell of Ardkinglas; 4th, Lady Isobel, married to John Mure of Caldwell; 5th, Lady Elizabeth, married to John Blair of Blair; 6th, Lady Agnes, married to John Ker of Kersland; 7th, Lady Janet, married to the Laird of Cessnock; 8th, Lady Catherine, married to George Montgomery of Skelmurly.

XIII. John Master of Eglinton; he also was engaged in feuds with the Cunninghames, and was himself killed in Edinburgh, on the 28th April 1520, by the adherents of the Earl of Angus, in the fray, known by the name of Cleanse the Causey. He married Elizabeth, daughter of Sir Archibald Edmonston of Duntreath, and by her had issue. 1st, Archibald Master of Eglinton, who died unmarried in 1526; 2d, Hugh, second Earl of Eglinton; 3d, Christian, married to Sir James Douglas of Drumlanrig, to whom she had a son, his successor, and four daughters all well married.

XIV. Hugh, second Earl of Eglinton, succeeded his grandfather in 1545, but died next year, September 3. 1546. He married Mariotta Seyton, only daughter of George Lord Seyton, relic of the Master of Borthwick, by whom he had issue. 1st, Hugh; 2d, Lady Agnes, married to Thomas Kennedy of Bargancy.

XV. Hugh, third Earl of Eglinton. He was engaged in the battle of Langside, on the part of Queen Mary, for which he was declared guilty of treason, by the Regent's Parliament; but the sentence was suspended. He was afterwards in great consideration, at the Court of James VI. To that infamous association and bond, 19, April 1567, entered into by many of the chief nobles of the kingdom, recommending the Earl of Bothwell, as a proper husband to Queen Mary, he was induced at first to be present, unapprized, as many of the rest were, of the object of the meeting; but as Keith remarks in his History, p. 382.—" Eglinton subscribed not, but slipped away." No fewer than 20 other of the nobility were enveigled into this unprincipled transaction, while none but himself had the sagacity to foresee the consequences, or the address to make an escape. He died in 1685. He married Margaret, daughter of Sir John Drummond of Innerpeffry, by whom he had issue; 1st, Hugh; 2d, Robert

Montgomery of Giffen; 3d, Lady Margaret, married to Robert first Earl of Winton, of whom afterwards; and 4th, Lady Anne, married Lord Sempill.

XVI. Hugh, fourth Earl of Eglinton, a young nobleman greatly esteemed, but who did not enjoy the titles a full year, as he was shot dead by the ancient enemies of his house, the Cunninghames, on the 18th April 1586, near to Stewarton. A murder that was deeply revenged by his kinsman, the Laird of Skelmurly, as will be noticed afterwards. He married Egidia, daughter of Lord Boyd, by whom he had one child.

XVII. Hugh, fifth Earl of Eglinton, who, during his minority, was under the tutorage of his maternal uncle, Robert Boyd of Badenheath. His Lordship married his cousin Margaret, daughter of Robert Montgomery of Giffen, but having no issue, he made a settlement of the Earldom of Eglinton, and Lordship of Kilwinning, on Sir Alexander Seton, son of his aunt, Margaret, Countess of Winton; and to secure this destination of titles, and also of property, made a resignation of his honours to the Crown, and took out a new charter, in confirmation of this settlement, with the original precedencies in 1611. He died in 1612.

XVI. Lady Margaret Montgomery, as above, Countess of Winton, had issue. 1st, Robert, second Earl of Winton; 2d, George, third Earl of Winton; 3d, Alexander, sixth Earl of Eglinton; and two other sons and a daughter, who married, first, the Earl of Perth, and secondly, Francis Stewart Earl Bothwell. Her third son,

XVII. Alexander, sixth Earl of Eglinton, (the Grey Steel in popular fame) succeeded to the titles and estates on the death, as above, of Hugh the fifth Earl, in 1612. He took the part of the Parliament in the civil wars, in the reign of Charles I. and was a keen covenanter at that period; but disgusted with the violence that the republicans manifested in the course of the unhappy contest, he very early joined Charles II. in 1650, when he came to Scotland, in the attempt to recover his throne. He brought with him a chosen body of horse, and was appointed by His Majesty captain of the horse guards. He lay, however, under the odious charge, at that time, (among the hot-headed zealots) of being a malignant, and Charles, greatly against his own judgement, was compelled to dismiss him and his troop from the army, four days before the battle of Dunbar, (see Walker's Journal). He thus escaped all participation in that ill conducted action. But next year he was overcome at Dumbarton by the enemy, and sent prisoner, first to Hull and then to Berwick, where he was kept in confinement till the restoration. He died in January 1661, in the 73d year of his age.

His Lordship married Lady Anne Livingston, daughter of the Earl of Linlithgow, by whom he had issue. 1st, Hugh, the seventh Earl; 2d, Honourable Sir Henry Montgomery of Giffen; 3d, Honourable Colonel Alexander, who died without issue; 4th, Honourable Colonel James Montgomery of Coilsfield, of whom afterwards; 5th, Honourable Major General Robert Montgomery. He also took the side of the Parliament against the king, and acquired a high reputation in arms. He joined, however, Charles II. in 1650, and was among the few who distinguished themselves at the battle of Dunbar, on the 3d September that year. He was also at the fatal battle of Worcester, on the 3d September 1651, as Major General of horse, where he received several wounds, and was taken prisoner and sent to Edinburgh Castle. He escaped from thence in 1659, and went abroad. He returned at the restoration with Charles II. and was appointed one of the Gentlemen of His Majesty's bed-chamber. He was a religiously disposed and conscientious gentleman, and did not escape the extortion of the unprincipled Scottish Ministry, in the latter end of the reign of Charles II. for his non-compliance with their tyrannical acts. (See Wodrow's History.) 6th, Lady Margaret, married, first, the Earl of Tweddale, by whom she had a son William, from whom is descended the family of Hay of Drumelzier. Secondly, she married the Earl of Glencairn, High Chancellor of Scotland—without issue.

XVIII. Hugh, seventh Earl of Eglinton, succeeded his father. He took the side of the king in the civil wars, and fought at Marston Moor in 1643, while his father was in the same battle, on the part of the Parliament. Walker, in his Journal of Transactions in 1650, relates that, when the king's army was lying betwixt Leith and Edinburgh, and Cromwell's on the west side of the Esk, near Musselburgh, Colonel Montgomery, son to the Earl of Eglinton, on the 28th of July, fetched a compass, with a strong party of horse, and broke in upon Cromwell's quarters, and routed six or eight parties of horse, wounded Lambert, killed many, and took several prisoners, and that Cromwell himself was fain to fly in his drawers across the river—but being unsupported, the Colonel was compelled in his turn to retire. Whether this Colonel was the eldest son or one of his three brothers, who were all Colonels, is not said. But that he was very obnoxious to Cromwell, appears from this, that he was excepted out of his Act of Grace and Pardon in 1654; and that the Castle of Ardrossan, at that time a family seat, was razed by Cromwell, whilst the family retired to their Castle in the Isle of Cumbra. This Earl died in 1669, in the 56th year of his age. He married, 1st, Lady Anne Hamilton, daughter of the Marquis of Hamilton, by whom he had issue, a daughter.

Lady Anne, married, first, a son of Sir Robert Seton of Hailes; 2d, James, third Earl of Findlater, by whom she became maternal ancestor of the present Earls of Hopetoun and Seafield, connecting them both with the House of Eglinton.

His Lordship married, 2dly, Lady Mary Lesley, daughter of the Earl of Rothes, by whom he had issue; 1st, Alexander the eighth Earl; 2d, Hon. Francis Montgomery of Giffen; 3d, Lady Mary, married to the Earl of Wintoun; 4th, Lady Margaret, married to the Earl of Loudon; 5th, Lady Christian, married to Lord Balmerinoch; 6th, Lady Eleanora, married to Sir David Dunbar of Baldoon. It is recorded by Wodrow, to the honour of this lady, that in the reign of Charles II. she concealed and sustained two presbyterian clergyman, in a house in Kilwinning, several years, from the infuriated rage of persecution in these unhappy times. Indeed, it must be granted, to the credit of the Eglinton family, that they never countenanced persecution on account of religion, nor oppression on any account, and preserved their influence at Court notwithstanding: 7th, Lady Anne, married to Sir Andrew Ramsay of Abbotshall.

XIX. Alexander, eighth Earl of Eglinton, succeeded his father in 1673. He came early into the Revolution, and was one of King William's Privy Councillors. He died in 1701. He married, first, Lady Elizabeth Crichton, daughter of the Earl of Dumfries, by whom he had issue; Alexander, the ninth Earl, and Lady Mary, who married Sir James Agnew of Lochnaw. He married, 2d, in 1698, Catherine, daughter of Sir William St. Quintin of Harpham, in the county of York. She was then 90 years old. The most singular instance of the prolonged powers of female attraction perhaps on record. Lord Eglinton was her fourth husband.

XX. Alexander, ninth Earl of Eglinton, succeeded his father in 1701. He was a Privy Councillor both to King William and to Queen Anne; and was a representative of the Scottish Peerage in the Parliaments that sat down in the years 1710 and 1713. He was very active in supporting Government during the rebellion 1715, having at one period, in conjunction with the Earls of Kilmarnock and Glasgow, and Lord Sempill, assembled 6000 trained men at Irvine, ready to support King George against the Pretender, and all other enemies. He was a nobleman of talents; prudent and careful: cleared the estate of debt, and increased its value by several purchases. He died in March 1729. His Lordship was thrice married; 1st, to Margaret, daughter of Lord Cochrane, son of the Earl of Dundonald, by whom he had issue, two sons who died young, and four daughters; 1st, Lady Catherine, married the Earl of Galloway; 2d, Lady Euphemia, married to George Lockhart of Carnwath, M.P.; 3d, Lady Grace, married to the Earl of Carnwath; 4th, Lady Jean, married to Sir Alexander

Maxwell of Monreath; all of whom had issue: 2dly, to Lady Anne Gordon, daughter to the Chancellor Earl of Aberdeen, by whom he had one daughter, Lady Mary, married to Sir David Cunninghame of Milncraig and Livingstone, and had issue: 3dly, Susanna, daughter of Sir Archibald Kennedy of Culzean, by whom he had issue; 1st, James Lord Montgomery, who died young unmarried; 2d, Alexander, tenth Earl of Eglinton; 3d, Archibald, eleventh Earl of Eglinton; 4th, Lady Elizabeth, married to Sir John Cunningham of Caprington, to whom she had issue two sons. Her Ladyship lived to the very advanced age of 93, dying in February 1800; 5th, Lady Helen, married the Honourable Francis Stuart, son of the Earl of Moray, and had issue a son, who died unmarried; 6th, Lady Susan, married to John Renton of Lammerton, and had issue; 7th, Lady Margaret, married to Sir Alexander Macdonald of the Isles, and had issue three sons; Sir James, Sir Alexander, afterwards Lord Macdonald, and Sir Archibald, Chief Baron of the Court of Exchequer in England. Honourable Diana, daughter of Lord Macdonald, married the Right Honourable Sir John Sinclair, whose issue by her are thus connected with the House of Eglinton; 8th, Lady Frances; 9th, Lady Christian, married to James Moray of Abercairny, and had issue three sons, who in succession became Lairds of Abercairny; 10th, Lady Grace, married Cornet Byne of Bland's Dragoons in March 1751, and died in June following. Susanna, Countess of Eglinton, survived her husband 51 years, dying at Auchans in March 1780, in her 91st year.

XXI. Alexander, tenth Earl of Eglinton, succeeded his father in 1729. He was appointed Governor of Dunbarton Castle in 1759, and one of the Lords of the Bed-chamber to his present Majesty in 1760, which office he resigned in 1767. He was chosen one of the sixteen representatives of the Scottish Peerage in 1761 and again in 1768. Many of the valuable improvements made in the agriculture of the west of Scotland are owing much to his Lordship's refined and correct taste. His own farm of Eglinton, extending with new plantations in the vicinity, to perhaps 1500 scotch acres, was the subject of great embellishment, and although it was destined, at a future period, from the exquisitely fine taste of a succeeding Earl, to be still more decorated, yet was by him rendered one of the noblest and most beautiful parks, around an ancient family seat in Scotland. Nor were his exertions in beautifying the country limited to any particular district, but were extended over all his domains wherever situated. Thus his extensive Baronies of Eagleshame and Eastwood, in this county, (the most ancient patrimony of the family) were highly improved and adorned by the judicious means he employed. His death, which was considered as a severe public loss, was occasioned by a gun-shot wound he received in an unfortunate rencounter near Ardrossan with Mungo Campbell, an excise officer, who had been tresspassing in hunting over his grounds. This was on Tuesday the 24th Oct. 1769, about half an hour past 12 o'clock. He was carried to Eglinton Castle in his coach, where he arrived about 2 o'clock, and, although he had speedily every requisite medical and surgical assistance, he died about 1 o'clock next morning. His Lordship's death was long and deeply deplored, by every good man, and every friend to humanity. He died in about the 46th year of his age, unmarried, and was succeeded by his only surviving brother.

XXI. Archibald the eleventh Earl of Eglinton. He was Major of the 36th Reg. in 1751. In 1757 he raised a regiment of Highlanders (then the 77th) and accompanied them to America, where he served with distinguished reputation, more especially in an expedition at the head of 1200 men against the Cherokees. Here, after displaying much circumspection and great energy (qualities peculiarly requisite in such a warfare) he brought the affair to a successful conclusion with comparatively little loss. In 1761 he was elected Knight of the Shire for the county of Ayr, and same year he was appointed equerry to the Queen, an office he held till his accession to the titles. He was appointed Governor of Dumbarton Castle in 1764, and Deputy Ranger of St. James's and Hyde Parks in 1766; and in 1767, Colonel of the 51st regiment. He was chosen one of the sixteen Scottish Peers in 1776, and again in 1780, 1784, and 1790. He was appointed Governor of Edinburgh Castle in 1782, and Colonel of the Scots Greys in 1795. He had the rank of Major-General in 1772; of Lieutenant-General in 1777; and of General in 1793. He died at Eglinton Castle, 30th October 1796. He married first in 1772, Lady Jean Lindsay, eldest daughter of the Earl of Crawfurd. Her Ladyship died without issue in 1778, aged 21 years. He married, 2dly, Frances, only daughter of Sir William Twisden of Roydon Hall in Kent, and by her had two daughters.

XXII. Lady Mary Montgomery born 5th March 1787; married, first, 28. March 1803, Archibald Lord Montgomery, eldest son of Hugh, twelfth Earl of Eglinton; thus uniting the lineal and male branches of the family. By him her Ladyship had two sons (vide infra). His Lordship dying in Alicant, in January 1814, her Ladyship married, 2dly, Charles Montolieu Burges of Beauport, in the county of Sussex, eldest son of Sir James Bland Burges, by Anne, daughter of Colonel Montolieu, to whom she has a son; Charles James Savile, born 7th October 1816; 2d daughter, Lady Susanna, born 26th May 1788, and died November 16, 1805.

Archibald, the eleventh Earl, dying without male issue, was succeeded by his eldest daughter in a great proportion of his very extensive landed property. The titles and the greater part of the family estates devolved on Hugh Montgomery of Coilsfield, who is descended thus: (See page 254.)

XVIII. The Hon. Colonel James Montgomery, fourth son of Alexander, sixth Earl of Eglinton, acquired (by purchase, with the tocher of his Lady) the estate of Coilsfield in Ayrshire. He died about the month of October 1675. He married the only child of Æneas Lord Macdonald of Aros, by whom he had issue; 1st, Alexander who succeeded him, but died soon after unmarried; 2d, Hugh Montgomery, afterwards of Coilsfield; 3d, Margaret, married to John Chalmers of Gadgirth; 4th, Mary, married to Dunbar of Machrimore; 5th, Elizabeth, married to Kennedy of Kirkmichael.

XIX. Hugh Montgomery, on the death of his brother, succeeded to the estate of Coylsfield. He married, first, Jean, daughter of Sir William Primrose of Carrington, by whom he had three daughters; the eldest married Hamilton of Letham; the second, Thomas Girven, Esq.; the third, Burnet, Esq; He married, 2dly, Catherine Arbuckle, widow of Hamilton of Letham, by whom he had a son, Alexander, who succeeded him, and a daughter, Margaret, married to John Hamilton of Jamaica, (brother of Bourtreehill) of whom Hamilton of Sundrum is descended.

XX. Alexander Montgomery of Coilsfield married Lilias, daughter of Sir Robert Montgomery of Skelmorley. This distinguished branch of the House of Eglinton, (See p. 251.) is descended from George, (X.) second son of Alexander, first Lord Montgomery, who had, from his father, the lands of Lochliboside, Hartfield and Colpley, in Renfrewshire, 1461. He married Anne, daughter of Sir John Houston of Houston, and died in 1505, leaving issue, his successor, John (XI.) of Skelmorley, who married the heiress of Montgomery of Lochranza. He was succeeded by his son Cuthbert, (XII.) who was killed at Flodden, 1513. He left two sons; the youngest, Alexander, designed of Portray; the eldest, George (XIII.) of Skelmorley, married Catherine, daughter of the first Earl of Eglinton, and by her had his successor, Robert (XIV.) of Skelmorley, so designed in 1572. He was deeply engaged in the family feud betwixt the powerful houses of Eglinton and Glencairn, in which he killed Alexander, Commendator of Kilwinning, son of the Earl of Glencairn; and, in revenge, was killed himself, and also his eldest son, in 1584, by Maxwell of Newark, whose mother was a Cunningham. By his wife, a daughter of Lord Sempill, he left two sons, the youngest, George, was ancestor of the Montgomeries of Kirktonholme. The eldest, Sir Robert (XV.) of Skelmorley, pursued the feud against the Cunninghames, (who about this time murdered Hugh the fourth Earl of Eglinton) with great animosity and much bloodshed; for which, in his latter days, he was seized with remorse, and, in expiation, performed many acts of charity, and even of mortification, as he frequently passed the night, immured in the sepulchral vault of the family in the church at Largs. He was created a Baronet in 1628, and died in 1651. He married Margaret, daughter of Sir William Douglas of Drumlanrig, and by her had a son Robert (XVI.) who died before his father; but by his wife Lady Mary, daughter of the Earl of Argyle, left a son, Sir Robert (XVII.) of Skelmorley, who succeeded his grandfather in 1651. He was a gentleman of high reputation, and died in 1684. He married Antonia, daughter and a co-heiress of Sir James Scot of Rossie, and had two sons; 1st, Sir James, (XVIII.) 2d, Sir Hugh. Sir James of Skelmorley, the eldest, after entering warmly into the Revolution, on some disgust, engaged in a conspiracy against King William, and went over to King James, at St. Germains; he was disgusted there also, for, on account of continuing firm in the protestant religion, he did not meet with the reception he expected, and died, it is thought of vexation, in 1694. He married Lady Margaret, daughter of the Earl of Annandale, by whom he had a son, Sir Robert, (XIX.) who was Governor of a garrison in Ireland, and who died in 1731. He married Frances, daughter of Stirling of Keir. She died at Skelmorley in 1759. They had three daughters, the eldest, Lilias, (XX.) inherited the estate; and, as before stated, married Alexander Montgomery of Coylsfield, to whom she brought the estate of Skelmorley, and with it the representation of that ancient branch of the original Eglinton family, sprung from the House of Montgomery, before it was connected with the House of Seton. It ranks still the first in order among the titles of the present Earl. This Lady died at Coylsfield on the 18th November 1783, and her husband Alexander Montgomery of Skelmorley and Coylsfield, died on the 28th of December following. They had issue, 1st, Hugh, twelfth Earl of Eglinton; 2d, Alexander Montgomery of Annick Lodge, who was in the naval service of the East India Company. He died in 1802. (He married Elizabeth, daughter of Dr. Taylour of the East India Companies service, and by her had issue: 1st, William, in the naval service of the East India Company; 2d, Alexander, a Captain in the Royal Navy; 3d, Hugh, in the civil department of the East India Company; 4th, Thomas, in the military department of the East India Company; 5th, Archibald; 6th, Elizabeth, married in 1804 to the Right Honourable David Boyle, Lord Justice Clerk, and has issue: 7th, Hamilla married in. 1815, West Hamilton, Esq.; 8th, Charlotte; 9th, Frances :) 3d, Thomas, died at Dumfries in Virginia, 18th August 1793; 4th, Archibald Montgomery of Stair, was in the civil service of the East India Company on the Bengal establishment, on which he was placed in 1770. (He married Miss Maria Chantry, by whom he has issue; 1st, Alexander, an officer in the Bengal native Cavalry, died in 1813; 2d, Archibald, an officer in the Bengal native Infantry; 3d, William, in the civil service of the East India Company; 4th, Edmond;) 5th, James Montgomery went early into the army; is now a Lieutenant-General, and Colonel of the 74th regiment; was Governor of Dominica, and served with distinction several years in the West Indies; 6th, Frances, married in 1758, James Ritchie of Busbie, had issue; 7th, Lilias, married to John Hamilton of Sundrum, has issue; 8th, Margaret, married in 1772, to John Hamilton of Bargeny, died without issue.

XXI. Hugh, twelfth Earl of Eglinton. Entered into the army in 1756; served during the greater part of the seven years war in America, and was fourteen years a Captain in the 1st regiment of Foot, or Royal Scots. In 1778 he was appointed Major, and afterwards Lieutenant-Colonel of the Argyle Fencibles. In 1780, he was elected Knight of the Shire for the county of Ayr, and again in 1784. In 1789 he vacated his seat in Parliament, by accepting of the office of Inspector of Military roads in the Highlands, the duties of which office he executed with great judgment and decision; rendering the lines shorter, more accessible, and made at less expense than was till then conceived to be possible. In 1793 he raised the West Lowland Regiment, of which he was Colonel, and soon after raised a regiment of the line, called the Glasgow Regiment, which was reduced in 1795. In the same year he was appointed Lieutenant-Governor of Edinburgh Castle; at the general election in 1796, he was the third time chosen Knight of the Shire for the county of Ayr; but his seat became vacant immediately after by his accession to the titles of Eglinton. In 1798, on a vacancy, he was chosen to represent the Scottish Peerage in Parliament; and again at the general election in 1802, and in 1806, was created a British Peer, by the title of Baron Ardrossan in Ayrshire. His Lordship is Lord Lieutenant of the county of Ayr, and a Knight of the Thistle. Before the abolition act in 1748, the Earls of Eglinton were hereditary sheriffs of Renfrewshire, and baillies of the Regalities of Cunningham and Kilwinning, for which Alexander the tenth Earl was allowed, in compensation, £7,800. He succeeded in 1817, to the estate of Bourtreehill, on the death of his sister-in-law, the Dowager Lady Cathcart of Carleton. His Lordship married his cousin Eleanor, fourth daughter of Robert Hamilton of Bourtreehill, a lady singularly happy in disposition, and of inestimable virtues. She died on the 18th January 1817, and her remains were deposited in the family vault in Kilwinning church. The issue of this marriage have been, 1st, Archibald Lord Montgomery; 2d, Hon. Roger Montgomery, who was a Lieutenant in the royal navy. He fell a victim to pestilential disease, when on the public service, at Port-Royal in Jamaica, in January 1799; 3d, Lady Jane; 4th, Lady Lilias, married, first, in 1796, Robert Dundas Macqueen of Braxfield, who died on the 5th August 1816, in consequence of a fall from his horse. Of this marriage no issue. Her Ladyship married, secondly, on the 21st August 1817, Richard Alexander Oswald, younger of Auchincruive.

XXII. Archibald Lord Montgomery was born 30th July 1773; entered early into the army as an Ensign in the 42d regiment or Royal Highlanders. He was Lieutenant-Colonel of the Glasgow regiment, reduced in 1795; and afterwards Colonel of the Ayrshire militia, which he resigned in 1807. He was promoted to the rank of Major-General in the army, in October 1809. He served in Sicily in the years 1812 and 1813, where, in the absence of Lieutenant-General Lord William Bentink, he represented His Britannic Majesty at the Court of Palermo. Removing thence, on account of bad health, he died on the 4th January 1814, at Alicant in Spain, from whence his remains were removed, and finally interred at Gibralter. His Lordship married Lady Mary Montgomery, (vide supra) now only surviving daughter of Archibald the eleventh Earl of Eglinton, by whom he had issue two sons.

XXIII. 1. Hugh, born 24th January 1811, at Coylsfield, and resided afterwards at Eglinton Castle, under the more than paternal solicitude of his venerable grandfather the present Earl. No cares, however, can avert the evils incident to human nature. He was cut off in the seventh year of his age, on the 13th of July 1817, after a short illness, by that fatal disease, the croup, (Cynanche Trachealis) to which children are peculiarly liable.[1] He was a youth of the greatest hopes and most manly dispositions. Strongly indicative of that energy of character, which has continued unabated in the family from the time it arrived

---

[1] In a sequestered spot not far from the castle, the Earl has erected a column to his memory. It is of the Doric order, fluted; composed of white marble; the shaft one entire block; the whole, including base and capital, about 13 feet high. On the pedestal is inscribed this simple though feeling inscription:

TO THE MEMORY OF HIS BELOVED GRANDSON
HUGH:
WHO DIED THE 13TH JULY 1817,
AT THE AGE OF SIX YEARS AND A FEW MONTHS;
A CHILD OF PROMISE:
ON THIS SPOT, ONCE HIS LITTLE GARDEN,
THIS STONE IS ERECTED,
BY HIS AFFLICTED AND DISCONSOLATE GRANDFATHER,
HUGH EARL OF EGLINTON.

in Britain, more than 750 years ago, and through a course of twenty-three generations in succession.

XXIII. 2. Archibald William, born at Palermo, in Sicily 29th September 1812, came to Scotland in 1814, and has since resided in Eglinton Castle. He is the apparent heir of both the Eglinton and the Montgomery estates; and the 23d generation of all the three branches of this great family. The Eglinton direct, the Coylsfield and the Skelmorley, which last is the chief of the whole.

CATHCART.

Situation and Extent.—That part of it which is included within the County of Renfrew, is a narrow stripe of arable land, little more than a mile broad, and about four miles long from the north, where it approaches to the Clyde, about a mile above Glasgow, to the confines of the Parish of Mearns on the south.

Soil and General Aspect—There is little Basaltic subsoil in this Parish, nearly the whole being incumbent on clay or pretty adhesive gravel, some of it is alluvial, having been formed from the occasional overflowings of the White Cart, and this may be said, to be the most fertile soil of the whole. From its near neighbourhood to Glasgow, from whence the street raikings and other manure has long been brought in considerable quantity—the soil in general, has become more fertile than it would otherwise have been naturally, and some very superior crops of wheat and other grain are produced, as well as potatoes, turnips, and artificial grasses, to which the lands are generally applied, the grazing system not prevailing here, so much as further up the country. There are considerable stools of natural wood, as well as plantations on the steep banks of the Cart, from Cathcart upwards, and some very thriving belts of wood in the vicinity of the gentlemen's seats in other parts of the Parish; on the whole, the general aspect of this Parish is chearful, the air mild, and the soil well cultivated and fertile.

State of Property—BARONY OF CATHCART. This fine property having been alienated by its ancient Barons, to a cadet of the family of Sempill, these retained possession to the seventh generation, as territorical Barons of Cathcart. The last of them mentioned by Crawfurd, Sir William Sempill of Cathcart being the fifth in succession, was retoured heir to his father in December 1653. He had the honour of Knighthood conferred on him by Charles II.

and married Margaret, daughter of Sir James Hamilton of Broomhill, and was succeeded by James Sempill his eldest son, who married Margaret, daughter of Sir Samuel Baillie of Lamington, by whom he had a son, Bryce Sempill of Cathcart, who alienated these lands in   to John Maxwell of Williamwood. Bryce Sempill, left only one surviving son, Samuel, to represent his family who went to Ireland, and acquired considerable property in the Counties of Wicklow and Dublin. The Barony of Cathcart continued in the Williamwood family, till about the year 1788, when, being sold in parcels, the old Castle and principal messuage were acquired by the late Mr. James Hill, writer in Glasgow, whose representatives in 1801, disponed them to the present Earl of Cathcart, the direct male heir of its ancient Lords, and who has since bought the conterminous lands of Symshill. There is here a modern house, (Cartside), situated upon the banks of the Cart, adjacent to the old Castle, and which commands, perhaps, the most beautiful and romantic scenery in the country, built by the former proprietor, and to which a large addition had been made by the late Alexander Campbell, Esq; who occupied, as tenant, the whole of his Lordship's property in this Parish. The arms of the Cathcart family, quartered with those of Stair, have lately been prefixed to the front of this addition. These are handsomely sculptured on a stone, that had been inserted in front of the house of Sundrum in Ayrshire, while the Cathcart family possessed that mansion and property, and this stone was presented by Mr. Hamilton of Sundrum, to Lord Cathcart, when he heard that he had purchased as above, the ancient family seat of his ancestors. The rest of this Barony has become the property of different owners, of whom Sir John Maxwell of Pollock, has by much the greater proportion.

Langside—Is divided among several proprietors. The finest portion of the whole is, perhaps, that possessed by George Brown Esq; It is pretty extensive, and rises considerably, and on the highest part of it, there was erected in 1778, one of the most showy mansions in the county, amid some very thriving plantations, and commanding a very extensive prospect. There is another elevated portion of it, possessed by Robert Thomson Esq; on which there is also a handsome dwelling, called Camphill, overlooking a great extent of country. But Sir John Maxwell has the greatest proportion of this beautiful quarter of the Parish, whilst there are several portioners, who occupy a considerable part of it among them in villas. Indeeed, the whole has a most inviting appearance.

Bogtoun—Once the property of a very ancient and honourable family, the Blairs of Blair, (on which they had at one time, a stately Castle on an eminence, rivalling in splendour, the Castles of Crockstoun on the one hand, and Cathcart on the other), has passed from them several generations ago, and has for more than forty years back, been possessed in portions, by three distinct proprietors, namely, Hamilton of Holmehead, the Rev. James Hall, and the representatives of Mr. Pagan. The Rev. Mr. Dow, Minister of Cathcart, has also a small part of it, on which, at what is called Woodend, he has erected an elegant and very commodious mansion. In describing the respective estates in this and other Parishes, where the property is laid off in many divisions, I purposely omit the relative situation of each, referring the reader for this to the map, which will more explicitly point it out.

The lands of Newlands, mentioned by Crawfurd, have long been the property of the family of Nether-Pollock.

Williamwood—On which is a handsome mansion, situated on a gently swelling bank, amid some thriving plantations, is now the property of James Stewart, Esq; merchant in Glasgow. This is a pretty extensive estate, but is more remarkable for embellishment from plantations, than for fertility of soil.

Lee—A small property situated pleasantly on the banks of the Cart, belongs to ———— Watson Esq;

Hagtonhill—Formerly part also of that Barony, belongs now to the representatives of the late Alexander Campbell Esq; who died in May 1817.

Holmehead.—In Crawford's time, (see page 30) the proprietor, James Hamilton, was designed of Aikinhead, and part of Langside. These lands have been alienated, but the family still retain considerable property in the parish, being part of the lands of Bogtoun and those of Holmehead, which last is now the designation, and on which there is a small modern mansion in the vicinity of the old village of Cathcart. James Hamilton of Aikinhead, last-mentioned by Crawfurd, died soon after, 1710, and was succeeded by his son, James Hamilton of Aikinhead, who married Ann, daughter of John Porterfield of that-ilk, by Jean, daughter of Sir James Hamilton of Broomhill. He died in 1740. He was succeeded by his eldest son, James Hamilton of Aikinhead, who died before the year 1782. He married Marion, daughter of Major Roberton of Earnock, by whom he had James Hamilton, now of Holmehead, his successor; and a son, John Hamilton, in the East Indies; and four daughters, Elizabeth, Mary, Marion, and Ann.

The places of residence, and more extensive properties belonging to Mr. Hamilton, are situated in other parts of this county, or in the conterminous counties of Lanark and Ayr. Part of the Holmehead property has been lately disposed of in feu to Mr. Macrone, writer in Glasgow.

Crosshill.—This house and lands, which, in 1782, belonged to William Rowan, Esq; of Billyhouston, (by succession through relationship of a preceding race of proprietors of the name of Thomson) were acquired about six years ago by Mr. Robert Clark, the present proprietor.

Polmadie.—This estate, formerly the property of Colin Rae, Esq; of Little Govan, was acquired about 16 years ago by Moses Steven, Esq. It approaches in one point to the Clyde, and is situated in the parish of Govan.

There are several other places in this parish not particularly taken notice of, but the whole is comprehended in the following table:—

TABLE OF PROPERTY.

Estates, &c.	Proprietors.	Valued Rent Scots. £.	s.	d.	Eng. Acres.
Cathcart Castle and Syme's Hill,	Earl Cathcart,	75			126
Part of Cathcart, }		396	6	8	
Part of Langside, }	Sir John Maxwell, Baronet,	153			706
Newlands, }		374			
Hagton Hill, &c.	Heirs of Mr. Campbell,	112			160
Camphill,	Robert Thomson, Esq;	29	7		50
Westfield,	Sundries,	21			32
Clincart,	Heirs of Ben. Barton,	46	10		90
Hangingshaw, part of,	Shaw, Mann, Auld,	57	7		30
Milnbrae,	Thomas Finlay,	29	12		5
Langside Proper,	George Brown, Esq;	108			105
Hangingshaw, part of,	Sundries,	68	9		78
Burnstile,	Robert Watson,	32	7		20
Bogtoun, part of,	Rev. J. Hall,	73			88
Do. do.	Heirs of Mr. Pagan,	58			64
Lee,	Arthur Watson,	54			64
Williamwood,	James Stewart, Esq;	240	12	4	415
Holmehead,	James Hamilton, Esq;	278			178
Bogtoun, part of,	Do.				88
Crosshill,	Robert Clark,	36			76
Glebe,	The Minister,				5
Total of Cathcart in Renfrewshire,		2242	11		2380
Polmadie, in Govan parish, but in Renfrewshire, Moses Steven, Esq;		144	5		225
Total in this account,		2386	16		2605

The whole surface may be arranged thus —
1. Arable, in tillage, or in cultivated grass lands, ... 2450
2. Natural pastures, limited almost exclusively to water-sides, ... 10
3. Wastes, or occupied by houses, roads, waters, &c. 25
4. Natural woods and plantations, ... 120

Amount as above, ... 2605

Note.—The valued rent is taken from the county books, as made up in 1817. This varies from time to time, as properties become divided, or, as they may be united, by sale or purchase; but the total valued rent of the parish, and of the whole county, never alters. The extent of the different properties, supposed to be stated nearly to the truth, is not warranted to be precisely correct. The proportion of arable and pasture lands, &c. is stated by probable conjecture from the best authorities that could be obtained. These remarks apply to all the parishes, and will not be repeated.

Succession of Ministers.—Mr. Robert Hamilton died minister of Cathcart in 1628. He was succeeded by Mr. Gavin Forsyth; his successor was Mr. John Colquhoun; he was succeeded by Mr. John Stevenson, about the year 1700; his successor was Mr. William Love, who was settled 24th October 1710; he was succeeded by Mr. George Adam, who was settled 23d April 1738; to whom succeeded Mr. John Hamilton, who was settled on the 30th August 1759, who died in 1784, to whom succeeded the present clergyman, Mr. David Dow, who was settled here on the 1st September 1785.

Villages.—The most populous village in the parish is that which is known by the odd kind of name of Cross-my-loof, on the confines of this parish with Eastwood, about half a mile from the town of Pollockshaws, on the road to Glasgow. It was, till lately, remarkable chiefly for being a resort of vagrants who did not conceive themselves to be so little liable to be taken notice of in any place more populous or less obscure. It has become now more respectable from an increase in the number of its inhabitants, who amount to about 500. The next, in point of population, is the ancient village of Langside, which may contain from 20 to 30 families, set down in a commanding situation, amid its fine little gardens on an eminence, overlooking a great expanse of cultivated country at hand, and high towering mountains in the distant view. At the Kirktown of Cathcart, there was formerly a considerable country village, but as the great road from Glasgow to Kilmarnock, which formerly went through it, has been led, by an easier access, a considerable way from it, the town has dwindled down to six or eight families, from this very cheerful situation, and is gradually replacing itself by the new way-side, devoid of every other inducement to a change of settlement.

Manufactures.—In addition to the various branches of the weaving manufactory, which is spread through the whole county, there have long been some extensive establishments for making paper, which continue still to thrive, adding to the population of the place, as well as to the general prosperity. The popuiation has increased greatly, but for this see the tables at the end of this part of the work.

Descent of families.—CATHCART. This highly distinguished and very ancient family having again acquired the old castle, and part of the domains originally belonging to it in this county, the history of it shall here be resumed, and brought down to the present times, by an abridgement correspondent to the size of this work, from that excellent history of the Peerage of Scotland, by John Philip Wood, Esq; to which those are referred who may be desirous to see it more at large, as no publication hitherto on the subject is so perspicuous and enlightened. To John, second Lord Cathcart, and eleventh generation of the family on record, succeeded not the son Alan, (as stated by Crawfurd, for he fell at the battle of Flodden with two of his brothers, 9th September 1513.) but his son

XIII. Alan, third Lord Cathcart, who succeeded his grandfather in 1535. He fell at the battle of Pinkie, 10th September 1547, and by Helen his wife, daughter of William, second Lord Sempill, he had

XIV. Alan, fourth Lord Cathcart, his successor, who was a hearty promoter of the reformation, and signalized himself at the battle of Langside against Queen Mary, in 1568. He died in December 1618, having married Margaret, daughter of Wallace of Craigie, by whom he had a son.

XV. Alan, Master of Cathcart, who died before his father in 1603, leaving by his wife Isabel, daughter of Thomas Kennedy of Bargeny, a son.

XVI. Alan, fifth Lord Cathcart, who succeeded his grandfather in 1618, and died in December 1628; and by his second Lady, daughter of Sir Alexander Colquhoun of Luss, had a son.

XVII. Alan, sixth Lord Cathcart, born in the same year his father died. He died in June 1709, in the 81st year of his age. He married Marion, daughter of Boswell of Auchinleck, and by her had three sons, of whom the eldest

XVIII. Alan, seventh Lord Cathcart, succeeded him in 1709, being then in his 62d year, and died in 1732, in his 85th year. He married the Hon. Elizabeth Dalrymple, daughter of the first Vis. Stair, and by her had three sons. The eldest son, Alan, perished at sea, greatly lamented; the 3d son, James, was killed in a duel by Gordon of Ardoch; and the second son,

XIX. Charles, eighth Lord Cathcart, succeeded his father in 1732, being then about 46 years old. He entered early into the army, and was in due time promoted to be Lieutenant-Colonel of the Scots Greys; was at the battle of Sheriff Muir in 1715, where he contributed greatly to the gaining of the victory over the left wing of the rebel army, by promptly wheeling the dragoons under his command, and attacking the enemy in flank. He afterwards rose through several steps, till in 1740, he was appointed Commander-in-Chief of all the British forces in America, and sailed in October same year, at the head of a great armament on an expedition against the Spanish Main, but died on the 20th December following, and was buried on the beach of Prince Rupert's Bay, Dominica, where a monument is erected to his memory. His death is still considered to have been a great national misfortune.

His Lordship married, first, in 1718, Marion, only child of Sir John Shaw of Greenock, from whence his successors have added the name and arms of Shaw to their own, and latterly have taken Greenock as their second title in the Peerage; and enjoy about £900 a-year of feu duties, part of the Shaw estate in that town. By this Lady, his Lordship had two sons, and two daughters who survived him: viz. the 4th, Charles, of whom after; and the 5th, the Hon. Shaw Cathcart, an Ensign in the Guards, who fell at the battle of Fontenoy, 30th April 1745, unmarried.

His Lordship married, secondly, in 1739 Mrs. Sabine, being her third husband, who, fourthly, married in 1745, an Irish officer in the Hungarian service, Hugh Macquire, for whom she purchased a Lieutenant-Colonel's commission in the British army, but was not encouraged by his treatment to verify the Poesy in her marriage ring. "If I survive, I will have five." The Colonel took her over to Ireland, where he kept her in close durance till his death in 1764. This true story is taken notice of in the fictitious story of Castlerackrent by Miss Edgeworth. Her Ladyship returned immediately to England, where she enjoyed life very happily to a late period, dying at Tewing, 1789, in the 98th year of her age, having enjoyed the life-rent of that manor from one of her former husbands 56 years. Charles, the eighth Lord Cathcart, was succeeded by his 4th son.

XX. Charles, ninth Lord Cathcart, who was bred also to the army, and saw a great deal of severe service, particularly at Fontenoy, where he was dangerously wounded. He went through all the gradations of military rank, to that of Lieutenant-General in the army, to which he was raised in 1760. He was in many various appointments, civil, military, and diplomatic, all which he filled with the most unqualified approbation. He died in August 1776, in his 56th year, no less distinguished (to use the words of Wood) for the virtues which adorn private life, than eminent for all those that adorn a public character. His Lordship married, in 1753, the Hon. Jean Hamilton, daughter of Lord Archibald Hamilton, and by her had seven children, who lived to the years of maturity, and who were all as much distinguished by talent or personal accomplishment, as by the honours of birth, the dignity of rank, or the splendour of fortune. (See Wood, article Cathcart.)

XXI. William Shaw, the eldest son, who succeeded his father, and was the tenth Lord Cathcart, was born in 1755; accompanied his father in 1768 to Petersburgh, where he carried on his classical studies under Mr. Richardson, afterwards professor of humanity in the University of Glasgow; and after his return home, studied the law of Scotland, and was admitted a member of the Faculty of Advocates in 1776, in which year he succeeded his father. His Lordship next year, in the martial spirit of his ancestors, applied himself to a military life, and made his entry as a Cornet in the 7th Reg. of Dragoons, with which, proceeding to America, he distinguished himself much; and, rising rapidly in rank, became Major Commandant of the British Legion, (a Corps peculiarly of his own training,) with the provincial rank of Colonel in 1778. From this time his Lordship rose through all the remaining gradations of rank, till in 1805 he was appointed General of a combined Army on the Continent, of British, Russian, Swedish and Prussian Troops, with continued increase of military renown. In 1807 he was selected to command the very important expedition against Copenhagen, where the Fleet under Admiral Gambier disembarked his army in the vicinity of that strongly fortified city, on the 16th of August, and which capitulated on the 6th September following. The energetic conduct of his Lordship on this occasion, was so justly appreciated, that among other marks of approbation, His Majesty was pleased to raise him to the British Peerage, by the title of Baron Greenock and Viscount Cathcart, both in the County of Renfrew. The talents of Lord Cathcart, however splendid they have appeared in a military point of view, have not been limited to that profession alone, but in a civil, a legislative, and a diplomatic capacity, he has been highly distinguished as the general annals of the country abundantly testify. His Lordship has been farther advanced in the Peerage by the title of Earl of Cathcart and Lord Greenock, in 1814.

His Lordship married in 1779, Elizabeth, daughter of Andrew Elliot of of Greenwells, uncle to the present Earl of Minto, by whom he has had ten children, of whom the eldest son, The Hon. William Cathcart, a most gallant Naval Officer, fell a victim to the yellow fever, in Jamaica, 1804, at that time Captain of the Clorinda frigate. Unmarried.

XXII. Hon. Charles Murray Cathcart, an Officer in the Army, and who has been in much severe service; now Lord Greenock. Hon. Frederick Cathcart, a Captain in the Scotch Greys. Hon. George Cathcart. Hon. Adolphus Frederic Cathcart, the youngest, born in 1803, and three daughters living.

Arms.—Azure, three Cross-Crosslets fitchee issuing out of as many Crescents, Argent: Crest. A dexter hand couped at the wrist, issuing out of a wreath, holding up a Crescent, Argent: supporters, two Parrots proper. Motto, "I hope to Speed." Chief Seat in Scotland, Cartside by Cathcart Castle, in Renfrewshire[1].

I. *Maxwell of Williamwood.*—John Maxwell, (see p. 31.) mentioned by Crawfurd, married Eizabeth, daughter of Henry Wardrop of Dalbeth, by whom he had issue: 1st, James, of whom afterwards. 2d, Henry, Sheriff Depute of Renfrewshire, died without issue. 3d, John, who died without issue; and a daughter, Anna, married to William Thomson of Corsehill, died also without issue.

II. James Maxwell of Williamwood, his eldest son, married Annabella, daughter of Gavin Ralston of that ilk, by whom he had issue: John, of whom afterwards, and 4 daughters. 1st, Ann, married to Charles Maxwell of Merksworth, and had issue, 2 sons, James and Henry, and 5 daughters, of whom, John the eldest, will be taken notice of afterwards. 2d, Elizabeth, died unmarried. 3d, Annabella, married to Archibald Crawfurd, merchant in Greenock, and had issue. 4, Jacobina, married to John Baird, merchant in Glasgow, but had no surviving issue.

III. John Maxwell, the only son, succeeded his father as Laird of Williamwood. He married Martha, daughter of John Baird of Craigton, in Dumbartonshire, and had issue: three sons, the two younger of whom died young, or unmarried. He was succeeded by the eldest son.

IV. James Maxwell of Williamwood, he was Major in the 26th Regiment Dragoons. In 1788, he sold the lands of Cathcart, which had been for a considerable time in the family. He married Mary, daughter of John Campbell of Wellwood in Ayrshire, but died without issue in 1806.

The succession now came to his cousin, Miss John Maxwell, as above, eldest daughter of Charles Maxwell of Merksworth, and representative of that family, her two brothers having died, the one young, and the other unmarried. This lady, in the year 1812, sold the estate of Williamwood, to Major George Morrison, who in 1817, sold it to James Stewart Esq; merchant, of the house of Messrs. James Finlay, & Co. Glasgow, the present proprietor. Miss Maxwell died in 1815, unmarried. The family is now represented by her nephew, James Maxwell Graham, eldest son of her next sister, Janet, who married James Graham, merchant in Glasgow, second son of the late James Graham of Tamrawer, Stirlingshire, decended of Dundaff, (of whom the Montrose family, see p. 46.) and who is also the lineal representative of the family of Merksworth.

---

[1] The Cadets direct of this Noble family, are Cathcart of Carbieston, (of whom Cathcart of Greenfield, Lord Alloway) Cathcart of Carleton, and Cathcart of Genoch.

Arms.—Quarterly; 1st and 4th, Or, a chief Ermines, three Escallops of the first for Graham; second, Argent, on a Saltire Sable, an annulet, Or, Stoned Azure, within a border of the second for Williamwood: third, Argent, on a Saltire Sable, a marlet, Or, within a border, invecked Gules, for Merksworth: Crests, an eagle reguardant, rising from a rock, all proper, with the motto, " Souvenez;" on the left, a stag's head, cabossed, with the motto, " Prospero " sed curo."

Brown of Langside.—Thomas Brown, born in Ayrshire, was bred to the medical profession; lived several years in London, and returning to Scotland, purchased from Robert Crawfurd of Possle, part of the lands of Langside in 1775. He married Martha, eldest daughter of George Bogle Esq; of Daldowie, by whom he had four sons and one daughter now living. He died in 1782, and was succeeded by his eldest son,

George Brown, Esq; the present proprietor of Langside.

Battle of Langside. This rencounter, which decided the contest between the adherents of the unfortunate Mary Queen of Scots, and the party of the Regent Murray, took place in this Parish, and being followed by very important consequences, shall here be taken notice of, from the account given of it by Hollinshead, a cotemporary Historian: Dr. Thomas Robertson, in his History of Queen Mary, and other authorities and memoirs of the times.

On Sunday, the 2d of May 1568, at supper time, says the minute Hollinshead, the Queen escaped out of a Castle on an Island in Lochleven, by means of George Douglas, brother to the laird of Lochleven; and who, the better to elude a discovery, carried with him the keys of the Castle, and threw them into the Lake. (Supposed to be the same bunch of keys that was lately thrown ashore in a storm, and which is now in the custody of the Magistrates of Kinross). The Queen on reaching the shore, found ready waiting, the Lord Seaton, the laird of Riccarton, and James Hamilton of Orbiston, who conveyed her on horseback, the same night, by Queensferry, to Nidry Castle, a seat of Lord Seaton's in west Lothian, a distance of twenty miles. Resting there only three hours, she early next morning came to Hamilton, thirty miles further, where, so well had the enterprize been planned, that she found the Earls of Argyle, Rothes, Eglinton, and Cassillis, with several other nobles, and a thousand armed men ready to receive her.

The Queen, with her wonted celerity, took instant measures for reinstating herself on the throne. Partly from sentiments of loyalty, and of personal attachment to her, and partly from hatred to Murray, a great body of the nobles, with their followers, flocked to her standard. Six days only after her escape, she found herself at the head of six thousand men. Nothing could exceed the zeal which now burst forth; no expectations could be more sanguine, than what her friends entertained in her cause.

In the mean time, Murray, who was then at Glasgow, was in no small alarm. He appeared at first to have resolved to retreat to Stirling, but, suddenly changing his purpose, he determined to remain where he was, being persuaded that if he should seem to shrink back ever so little, it would encourage his adversaries, and dishearten his own party. Many of the latter had indeed, by this time, deserted his cause, some on one pretext, and some on another. Among others, the Lord Boyd, who had already, more than once changed sides, went, on the 8th of May, to the Queen at Hamilton. Murray, however, had still with him a force, amounting to four thousand steady adherents, among whom was a Regiment of six hundred able bodied young men raised in Glasgow, and paid by the City, the inhabitants of which entered into his party with the utmost zeal. Another advantage still he possessed—this army was accustomed to his command, and had confidence in his abilities.

The army of the Queen, formed of less compact materials, was deluded also, with an over-confidence in its own strength. She herself had advised the leaders to avoid coming to battle with Murray, notwithstanding of her superiority in numbers. She meant to wait some considerable time, till she could not only collect more forces, but regain still further, the obedience of her subjects, and in the meanwhile, to retire to the Castle of Dumbarton, where she could remain in safety. She even wanted to come to such an accommodation with her opponents, as might prevent altogether the shedding of blood. But her friends had not the same judgement and moderation. They agreed, indeed, for her security, to convey her to the Castle of Dumbarton, as a strong hold, where she could repose with safety, but they were little disposed to terminate their quarrel with Murray, without coming to blows. For, dazzled with the prospect of overthrowing him, who was their own enemy, as well the Queen's, nothing could restrain their impetuosity. At the same time, they neglected the necessary precautions, and despised the enemy from its greater inferiority in numbers. Thus, under this delusion, they gave themselves up to carelessness and security; errors among the most fatal that can be committed in war. Murray, on the other hand, had judgement sufficient to see, that it was his interest to come to an action with the forces of the Queen, before their numbers should be further increased; and, profiting by their folly, he took the first opportunity that offered of attacking them with advantage. This happened, at Langside, on the 13th of May, being only eleven days after the escape of the Queen from her captivity in Lochleven.

Hollinshead gives a list of the chiefs of both parties, who appeared on the field on this eventful day. On the part of the Queen, there were the Earls of Argyle, Rothes, Eglinton, and Cassillis, Lord Claud Hamilton, son to the Duke of Chatelherauld; the Lords Seaton, Sommerville, Yester, Borthwick, Livingstone, Herries, Maxwell, Sanquhar, Boyd and Ross. Of lairds and knights, Lochinvar, Bass, Wauchton, Dalhousie, and Rosslin; the Sheriff of Ayr, Sir James Hamilton (of Evendale), and many others.

On the part of the Regent, the principal were Morton, Mar, Glencairn, Monteith, the Master of Graham, the Lords Home, Lindsay, Ruthven, Sempill, Ochiltree, and Cathcart; of lairds and knights, Bargeny, Blairquhan, Drumlanrig, Cessford, Luss, Buchanan, Tullibardin, Pitcur, Grange, Lochleven, Lethinton, and Sir James Balfour.

The Earl of Argyle was appointed commander of the Queen's army, with the title of Lieutenant-General, the highest military distinction at that time known; and, in pursuance of the Queen's desire, they determined on marching by Glasgow to Dunbarton, where they proposed to leave her, and afterwards to protract the war, or to give battle to Murray, as they might see cause; as they had no notion that the Regent would dare to interrupt their progress, or force them to fight at his will.

The Regent, who was so far apprized of their motions, as to know that they were about to march, drew up his men, at first on the moor of Glasgow, on the north side of the Clyde, where it was believed they would pass; but finding that they kept on the other side, at a considerable distance, he immediately ordered his army to cross the river, and when that was accomplished, (the horse, by fording it, and the foot by the bridge,) he came up to them by a rapid march, near to the village of Langside, about two miles south of Glasgow.

The ground here rises into two distinct gently swelling eminences, about 100 or 150 feet above the level of the surrounding plain. The one next to Glasgow is the highest, and is known by the name of Camp-hill, from the vestiges, still to be observed, of what is supposed to have been anciently a fortified camp. About a quarter of a mile farther south is the hill of Langside, not altogether so high, nor so well adapted for a military station. Between them, in a hollow, is situated the small village of Langside, from which the battle has its name. The first hill, being the most commanding situation, it was an object with both parties to get possession of it. This the Regent, with the usual vigour and rapidity of his motions, obtained, in spite of his opponents; who, finding themselves baffled in the attempt, retired to the other, where they arranged their order of battle. The Regent in the mean time pushed forward a detachment of Musketeers, who took post in the village, which the forces of the Queen had neglected to secure.

Another loss, which was irretrievable, also befel them. Their General, Argyle, at the very commencement of the action, fell into a fit of apoplexy, so that they became destitute of a Commander, and for which so very little previous arrangement had been made, that they had neither a second nor a third to supply his place. How this misfortune was remedied is no where mentioned. It is only said, that both parties, before coming into close contact, played on each other with their ordnance, (the Queen having 7 pieces and the Regent 6[1],) and that the Regent's being better served, drove the Queen's artillery-men, after half an hour's cannonade, from their guns; but the Queen's cavalry, being the more numerous, put to flight the cavalry of the Regent; and, when encountering with the foot, the archers[2] poured in upon them such a shower of arrows, as compelled them to fall back and fly in their turn. The Queen's infantry then advanced, but were held in check, and afterwards beaten back by the Harquebussiers, (as they were then called) that Murray had planted in the village. Both parties getting then into the open plain, mingled with one another, pell-mell, striving together, man with man, for the space of half, or, according to Hollinshead, three quarters of an hour, with such eagerness, and personal animosity, that they whose spears were broken, continued still the fight, by throwing stones and sticks, or whatever else came to hand, in the faces of their opponents. The result of the whole was a compleat rout of the army of the Queen, which fled from the field, with the loss of about three hundred killed, and as many taken prisoners, among whom were the Lords Seaton and Ross.

On the part of the Regent, it is said that there was only one man killed. This is altogether incredible—that 6000 men should fight unremittingly, hand to hand with their enemies, for the space of half an hour, and not be able to kill more than one man among them all, even although they should have had during part of that time only sticks and stones to fight with. The circumstance acknowledged by M'Ure, in his account of this battle, that Murray returned so fast back to Glasgow, as not to be able to bring all his men with him, (some of them, as he says, having followed the chase too far,) may lead us to believe that the victory was not so cheaply purchased; at any rate, he had abundance of glory in discomfiting an army so much superior, in number, to his own.

[1] Calderwood. [2] The last time archers are known to have been in any battle in Britain.

"In this battle," says Hollingshead, "the valiance of an Highland gentle-
"man, named Macfarlane, stood the regent's part in great stead; for in the
"hottest brunt of the fight, he came in with 200 of his friends and countrymen,
"and so manfully gave in upon the flank of the Queen's people, that he was a
"great cause of the disordering of them '." This circumstance itself, may shew
that the defeat of the Queen's party was not such an easy matter as the historians of the Regent pretend; who at the same time were not aware that the less they made the resistance, the less must be the renown of the victory.

The consequences of this decisive action to the unfortunate Queen, were abundantly deplorable, and are well known. Her party, however, soon made their peace with Murray. Only Lord Seaton, who was probably the contriver of the escape, as he was undoubtedly a great actor in it, seems to have suffered more from his resentment. He was obliged to leave the country, and took refuge in Flanders, where, for two years, his only means of living was by driving a four-horse waggon. (See Wood's Peerage, Title *Winton.*)

On the other hand, the friends of the Regent did not fail of their reward. Among others, the city of Glasgow, which had distinguished itself, not merely by raising a regiment for him, but by supplying at this time his whole army with wheaten bread, in reward, got a charter from him, for erecting flour-mills, (which it enjoys to this day) on the water of Kelvin, at Partick, two miles west from the town. Previous to this, the bakers had their wheat grinded at private mills, on the same water, not only at a greater expence, but by machinery not so well adapted to the purpose.

EASTWOOD.

Situation and Extent.—This parish is situated west from Cathcart; south from Govan; east from Paisley; and north from Mearns and Neilston, these being the different parishes by which it is surrounded. The outline is extremely irregular, but the extent altogether appears to be 6,345 English acres, including a part of the parish of Govan, that is included in the county of Renfrew.

---

[a] Other accounts say, that the Macfarlanes fled shamefully at first, and that Lord Lindsay said "Let them go, I will better fill their place;" but when the rout of the Queen's party became certain, they returned and pursued most manfully. Keith, 480.

Soil and general Aspect.—The soil is chiefly an adhesive, thin till, more indebted for its produce to the arts of cultivation than to natural fertility. Except it be some lands, still under its original growth of dwarf wood, (oak, hazel, aller, &c.) it may be considered as nearly all arable, and under the dominion of the plough. It is very little adapted to pasture. The whole surface is remarkably diversified into gently swelling heights and easy descending hollows, and none of it much elevated above the sea. Perhaps none of it more than 150 feet. The air, of course, is mild, but not remarkably salubrious.

State of Property.—The greater part belongs to Sir John Maxwell, Bart. of Nether-Pollok; and this is also the best land and the most ornamented. The stately mansion of that family is set down here, amid highly embellished pleasure grounds, and much beautiful plantation.

The estate next in extent to this, was Eastwood Proper, when it belonged to the Earl of Eglinton, in whose family it had been more than 300 years. It was sold in 1812 to the late John Anderson, Esq; W. S. who soon after parcelled out a great part of it by sale to sundry gentlemen :—as

To the Rev. David Dow, minister of Cathcart, who got Braidbar, amounting to 150 English acres, including a small pendicle of Giffnock that he had purchased a few years before; Mr. Machaffie, who got the rest of Giffnock, Orchard and part of Wood of Eastwood, amounting in all to about 350 acres; and Mr. Graham and others, who got to the extent of about 190 acres, chiefly in the wood of Eastwood. See the table.

Succession of Ministers.—In 1602, William Wallace. In 1626, John Maxwell. In 1630, Hew Blair, who in 1643 was translated to the Tron Church of Glasgow. In 1645, John Maxwell. In 1652, Hew Smith; in 1676, fined and imprisoned for holding conventicles, In 1679, Matthew Crawfurd, privately called by the parish; wrote a History of the Church of Scotland in two volumes folio, now the property of the church; died in 1701. In 167 , ——— Maclean, afterwards Bishop of Argyle; died in 1687. In 1703, Robert Wodrow ordained; author of the History of the Church of Scotland. In 1735, Robert Wodrow, his son, seems to have succeeded him; resigned in 1757. In 1758, James Simson. In 1786, John M'Caig, ordained assistant, and succeeds him on his death in 1790, and survived him only 11 months. In 1791, Stevenson M'Gill ordained; translated to Glasgow Tron Church, 1797, and is now Professor of Divinity in Glasgow College. In 1798, Robert Anderson, from Symingtoun, in Biggar Presbytery, admitted; afterwards translated to Edinburgh. In 1802, George Logan, the present minister, was admitted. He was previously minister of the Chapel of Ease at Ardoch in Strathearn.

TABLE OF PROPERTY.

Estates, &c.	Proprietors.	Valued Rent Scots. £.	s.	d.	Eng. Acres.
Pollok-Nether,	}	1066	13	4	
Darnley,	} Sir John Maxwell,	400			3690
Do.	}	904	2	8	
Auldhouse,	}	213	6	8	
Mains of Eastwood,	Lady Montgomery,				132
Crawfurd's Mains lands,	Heirs of Mr. Govan,	73	6	8	44
Lavron Shields, Wardhill, &c.	Earl of Glasgow	80	4	0	150
Eastwood, in parcels,	Rev. D. Dow, and others,	255	13	1	692
Eastwood, remaining,	Heirs of John Anderson, Esq; W.S.	366	8	11	742
Total of Eastwood Parish,		3366	13	4	5450
Add Haggs, Titwood, and Shiels, in the parish of Govan, hitherto omitted in all maps of Renfrewshire, but still in the county,	} Sir John Maxwell,	200			895
Total in this account,		3566	13	4	6345

The whole surface may be arranged thus —

1. Arable, or cultivated land, ... 5800
2. Natural pastures, or meadow, ... 25
3. Site of houses, roads, waters, &c. 95
4. Natural woods and plantations, ... 425

                                                          6345

Villages and Manufactures.—Pollokshaws, one of the largest villages in the county is in this parish. It was lately erected into a Burgh of Barony, with a magistracy, consisting of a provost, a bailie, and six councillors, to preside over and keep peace and good order among its numerous inhabitants. These, in 1811, amounted to 3084, and are now supposed to be not fewer than 3,500. It is chearfully situated by the Water of Cart, which also affords great facility to various branches of manufacture, which are carried on here with great activity and ingenuity, such as bleaching, dyeing, and tanning, &c. The greatest source of employment, however, is in the cotton manufacture. Much work is also done by the aid of steam machinery, even to the weaving of cloth. From 200 to 300 looms are put in motion by one engine alone. It is from this ingenuity of machinery, that the British manufacturer is enabled to undersell all the world; and so far is it from diminishing the population (as the patriotic misleaders of the populace pretend) that it has actually been the means of increasing the number.

Thornlybank.—This is a very flourishing village also, and of very recent origin. It is set down upon the Shaws burn, about a mile and a half up from Pollokshaws. Here Messrs. Alexander and James Crum, by their own well directed exertions, with the aid of machinery, have established a muslin or other cotton manufactory in all its branches, including printing, which now gives bread to 1200 or 1500 people, where, 30 years ago, three families did not exist. Deprive this place of its machinery, and it would soon dwindle down to less than three families again.

There is no village at the old church of this parish, nor any particular village in it known now by the name of Eastwood. Even the wood, from which it originally derived its name, is nearly all rooted out; and the ground on which it grew converted into arable land.

It should seem that Eastwood was at one time two parishes, Pollok and Alchous (corrupted to Auldhouse). See Chartulary of Paisley, f. 57. p. 18.

Family Descent.—MAXWELL OF NETHER-POLLOK.—The family of Maccusville, by corruption Macus-well, or, Maxwell, may be regarded as one of the most ancient and distinguished in Scotland.

They are, generally, stated to be descended from Maccus, the son of Undwynd, evidently of Saxon origin, who, in 1116, witnesses the inquisition of David Earl of Cumberland, afterwards David I. into the possessions of the church of Glasgow. The deed concludes as follows:—" Has terras jurarerunt fare " pertinentes, Ecclesie Glasguensi regalu et imperio, supradicti Principis, uctred " filius Waldef, &c. Hugus testes sunt, et audièntes et videntes Matildis " comitissa quæ exparte sua concessit Gullielmus Nepos ipsius Principis, Go- " spatricio patre dolfin. Maccus filius Undwynd." (Original Chartulary of Glasgow, fol. 1. 6.) Mr. Chalmers infers, that he gave his name to the property he acquired in the county of Roxburgh, the original seat of the Maxwells, and hence, derives the names of the places Maxwell and Maxton, formerly written, Maccus-ville, and Maccuston, (Cal. I. p. 510.)

He left a son, patronimically designed like himself, " Lyolphus filius Mac- " cus," who is a witness to the Charter by Malcolm IV. in 1158, to the High Stewart.

The first, perhaps, who assumed the surname of Maccuswell, was Herbert, a prominent character in his day. He was Sheriff of Roxburghshire, and proprietor of the Barony of Maxwell, contiguous to the towns of Roxburgh and Kelso, retained by his descendents till the year 1696. He lived in the middle of the 12th century, in the reigns of Malcolm IV. and William the Lyon, and mortified to the Abby of Kelso, his church of Maccuswell, confirmed by King Malcolm, in the year 1159. (Anderson's Dip. and Char. of Kelso.)

His successor, John de Maccuswell, was also Sheriff of Roxburgh, and held the office of Chamberlain of Scotland in the reign of Alexander II. (Crawf. Off. of State p. 261.) He was one of the Ambassadors to England in 1215 and 1220, and a guarantee of the marriage treaty between Alexander II. and Johanna of England, (Rymer's Fed. 241 at 252.) He died 1241, and was buried in the Abbey of Melross.

After him, we have Humeras, or Aymer de Maccuswell, also Chamberlain of Scotland, and the first of the family connected with Renfrewshire, according to Crawfurd, (Off. of State). He married the heiress of Rolland de Mearns, and thereby acquired that property in this county. Rolland de Mearns does not, however, appear in record; but that there was an old family of this name, appears from a Charter to Paisley in 1250, to which Robert de Mearns is a witness. (Chartulary of Paisley Ad. Lib.) It was either during his time, or in that of his predecessor, that the family fixed themselves in Dumfriesshire, where their principal estates were situated, or in the conterminous county of Galloway, where they still have great possessions.

In the year 1258, this Aymer Camerarius Scotiæ, with other Barons, engaged that Scotland should not make a separate peace, without consent of the Welsh. He figures in many public transactions, and died after the middle of the 13th century. His eldest son, Herbert, was the ancestor of the Maxwells of Caerlaverock, so celebrated in Scottish history and in Chivalry; afterwards raised to the dignities of Lord Herris and Earl of Nithsdale. Their direct male line failed in the person of John Lord Maxwell, son of William the fifth Earl, forfeited in 1715. The estates, however, are still possessed by Marmaduke Constable Maxwell of Nithsdale, the undoubted heir general of the family.

John the second son, was the ancestor of the family of Nether-Pollok, who, until very lately, held that estate of the house of Nithsdale, and are styled their cousins and relations in innumerable deeds, dated at different periods. He first appears in a mortification by his elder brother, to the Abbey of Paisley, entered in the original Chartulary of that foundation, of which the following is an extract:—

" Omnibus, &c.—Herbertus de Maxwell miles, Salutem en domino Sempiter-
" nam, noverit universitas vestra me dedisse et concessisse et hac presenti
" Charta nostra confirmasse Deo et ecclesia sancti Jacobi et sancti mirini de
" Passelet et monachis ibidem deo servientibus unliberam puramet perpetuam
" elemsionam octo acras et demidiam et viginte octo perticatas terræ in nova
" villa de mernis quas minsurari feci, &c. incujus rei testimonium presens scrip-

"tum sigillo mea una cum sigillo venerabilis Patris Domino Roberto Dei gratia Episcopi Glasguensis feci robora Itis testibus Domino Johanne et Alexandro fratibus meus." There is another donation to the same Abbey, by the same individual of—" sex Marcas argenti annui reddibus, &c. &c. Testibus Domino Adda rectore ecclesia de Liberton, Domino Allano perpetuo vicario de Nerris Dom Johanne de Maxwell, Domino de Pollock inferiore Waltero filio Gilberti," &c.

These documents, affording a noble monument of the antiquity of this branch of the Maxwells, are without date; but, from the names of the witnesses, it is evident that they must have been executed considerably previous to the year 1300.

Of the above John, did Sir John Maxwell of Nether-Pollok descend, who lived in the reign of David II. and who, by his alliances and acquisitions in no small degree aggrandised himself and his descendants. He married Isobel Lindsay, daughter of Sir James Lindsay of Crawfurd, ancestor of the Earls of Crawfurd, by Egidia his wife, sister of Robert II. He obtained charters from that Prince, " Dilecto et fideli nostra Johanni de Maxwell militi, et Isabellæ de " Lyndsye sponsa suæ Nept Nostrie," of the lands of Lyandors and Aikenhead, in the Sheriffdom of Lanark in 1372; also, in 1373, a confirmation of the easter half Badvale, (or Bardrule,) and part of the lands of Baddynheth, with part also of the lands of Glenfromidy in Strathearn, with many others still extant on record, and elsewhere. He had also the lands of Schitym in Aberdeenshire, and of Hawkshaws, Glengourin and Finglen, in the shire of Peebles, and of Calderwood, and Drips in Lanarkshire, &c. &c. In 1388, he exchanged with Sir Bernard Haldane of Gleneagles, his lands of Bardrule in Strathearn, for the lands of Jackton in Lanarkshire; and, in the reign of Robert III. he mortified to the Abbey of Kilwinning, his estates of Brummerlands and Lyons Cross.

He died soon after 1401, leaving, by his wife, as above, whom he survived; 1. Sir John, of whom afterwards; 2. Sir Robert, to whom, in 1401, he conveyed his lands of Calderwood. To this deed his seal is appended, exhibiting the Arms of Pollok as now borne, with two Lions as supporters, and, for a Crest, a Savage Head, in profile, bound with a fillet. He also acquired, in right of his wife, Elizabeth, one of the two daughters, co-heiresses, of Sir Robert Denniston of that ilk, extensive property in the shires of Lanark, Renfrew, and Dumbarton, and was progenitor of the most numerous branches of the house of Maxwell; as from him are descended the present knightly family of Calderwood; the Earl of Farnham, in Ireland; the Maxwells of Newlands, in Galloway, of Newark, of Dargavel, of Blackstone, and the respective cadets of them all, also, Sir David Maxwell of Cardoness, Bart.* 3d, William, ancestor of the Maxwells of Aikenhead, long since extinct; 4th, a daughter, Janet, married to Thomas Murray of Culbyres. Sir John, the eldest son, during his father's lifetime, entered into a treaty of partition of the family estates, with him and his son Robert, as appears by a curious indenture in old Scotch, among the most ancient instances of the kind, dated, at Dumbarton, 18th Dec. 1400, in the presence of " Nobillmen and Mychty, that is to say, Maister Valtyre of " Danyelstone, Thomas Boyd Lord of Kilmarnock, Patrick Flemyng of Bord; " Schir Johne of Hammiltoun Knycht, Lord of .... Umfray of Colquhowne " lord of that ilk, with sindrie wther witnes." This curious Deed remains among the family papers in the charter chest of Nether Pollok. He succeeded his father soon after 1401, and died sometime previous to 1441, when we meet with his successor,

Thomas Maxwell of Pollok, in a deed relative to the lands of Aikinhead, who must have died before the year 1452, as we find an indenture between Herbert Lord Maxwell, superior of Nether Pollok, relating to those lands, dated 6th Feb. of that year.

After him there seems to have been a succession of Lairds of Nether Pollok, of the name of John, but whether more than two, is not evident, down to the year 1500. There is a decreet of the Lords of Council, ordering John Maxwell, son and heir apparent of John Maxwell of Pollok, to give up the lands of Govanhaggs, to John Lord Carlile and Janet his spouse, in 1480. There is an instrument in the year 1495, whereby Lord Maxwell remits part of his relief duty, to John Maxwell of Nether Pollok. There is a remission granted in the year 1500, to John Maxwell of Nether Pollok, and his son and apparent heir, John, for the murder of Hector Mure, son to the Laird of Caldwell. This elder John Maxwell, may rationally be concluded to have been the grandson of the John Maxwell, ascertained as above, to have been the Laird of Nether Pollok, in 1452; he had a brother Hugh, of whom hereafter. He married Lady Elizabeth Stewart, daughter of John, Earl of Lenox, by whom he had issue, four sons; 1st, John, of whom afterwards; 2d, George of Cowglen, who died not long before 1521. He left a son, John, of whom, afterwards; 3d,

---

* He was a brave and valiant knight, and was one of those intrepid 7000 Scottish Auxiliaries, whom John Stewart, Earl of Buchan, (afterwards constable of France) carried over to France in 1420, to the assistance of Charles VII. and who, by their valour, turned the tide of victory against the English. He fell at the battle of Vernuil, on the 17th Aug. 1424, and was buried in the church of the predicant friars, Angiers.

Robert, Bishop of Orkney. He was Rector of Tarbolton in 1521, next Provost of the Collegiate Church of Dumbarton, and at last promoted to the See of Orkney. He built the stalls in his Cathedral, which are curiously engraven with the Arms of his predecessors in the See, and he furnished the steeple with a set of excellent bells. In 1526, when James V. made his famous progress through the Scottish isles, he was nobly entertained by this bishop in his palace of Kirkwall. In an inventory of his Geir, the following is a catalogue of his Library.

" The Names of ye Bukis.

" Item, ane prent pontificall; Ane small text of ane pontificall; Item, ane auld written pontificall; Item, Seculinorum Scripturam; Cathena Aurea Sancti Thome; Item, Psalterium cum Commento Edward Episcopi; Biblæ in pergameno Scripta; Ane Inglisse Buke of Goweir; Ane Inglisse Buke of ye Histories of Saintis liffis and Stories of ye Bible; Item ye Cornakillis."

4th, William of Govansheils and Carneweddrick. He married Janet Cathcart, and left issue by her, a son, John.

John, the eldest son, succeeded his father, and (as stated by Crawfurd, page 33.) he married a daughter of Houstoun of that ilk; he died sometime previous to 1521, and was succeeded by his only child, Elizabeth. In 1535 she married her cousin, John Maxwell, son of George of Cowglen, (vide supra.) the male representative of the family. This gentleman was knighted by Queen Mary, and adhered zealously to her interest. After her escape from Lochleven, 1568, he being a person in whom this princess had great confidence, was required to attend her at Hamilton, with his friends, " boden in fier of Wier," as the original letter bears, yet extant among the family writs, as well as other letters from the Sovereigns of Scotland to the Lairds of Nether Pollok, and special invitations to Royal marriages, christenings, and other festivities, not forgetting the usual exactions of contributions, which, as feudal aids, the Barons of the kingdom were bound to render on such occasions. Sir John died in 1577, and by his Lady, the heiress, who was alive, 1598, he left six sons; John, George, William of Cowglen, Robert, Patrick and Walter.

John, the eldest, afterwards Sir John, was retoured to his father in Jan. 1578. He fell in 1593, at the conflict of Lockerby, assisting his chief, Lord Maxwell, against the Johnstons, the ancient enemies of his house. He married Margaret Cunningham, a daughter of the family of Caprinton, by whom he had one son, John, and a daughter, Agnes, who was married in 1611, to John, eldest son of John Boyle of Kelburn, and of this marriage is descended the present Earl of Glasgow, now heir general of the family of Pollok.

Sir John Maxwell of Pollock was retoured heir to Sir John his father in 1604. In the year 1613, he and the Laird of Calderwood discharged the painful duty of attending their chief, the Lord Maxwell, in his last moments on the scaffold *. He was, before 1642, raised to the dignity of a Baronet of Nova Scotia. He died in 1647. He married, first, Isobel, daughter of Sir Hugh Campbell, (according to Wood, but Crawfurd says Sir Matthew) and, 2dly, Grizel, daughter of Blair of Blair. By one of these ladies he had a daughter, who was imbecile, to whom he left a competent provision, and having no other children, he was succeeded by

George, eldest son of John Maxwell of Auldhouse, his cousin, descended, according to Crawfurd, from Hugh Maxwell, brother of that John Maxwell who was laird in 1500, (vide supra) lineal ancestor of John Maxwell of Auldhouse, who, on the 20th June 1546, upon the death of his father, John, was entered in the lands of Auldhouse by the Abbot of Paisley. (See Original Rental Book of that Abbey.) In 1553 he acquired from John Stewart of Kilcruise the lands of Meikle Glanderston, and Freeland Stewart, (this last in Inchinnan parish) also, on the 2d June 1572, a royal confirmation of two previous charters by the Archbishop of St. Andrews, Abbot of Paisley; the one, in November 1562, of the dominical lands of Eastwood, the other, an extended grant of the estate of Auldhouse, on the 12th December same year. (Reg. Mag. Sig. lib. 33. No. 18.)

He was alive in 1578, as he was then on the inquest that served John Maxwell of Nether-Pollok heir to his father. By his wife, a daughter of Robert Dunlop of Hapland, son of John Dunlop of that-ilk, he had issue,

---

* The crime for which this nobleman suffered, was for murdering Sir James Johnston of that-ilk, who was married to his own cousin, the Hon. Sarah Maxwell. His own father, John, sixth Lord Maxwell, was killed about fifteen years before by the Johnstons in a rencontre on the 7th December 1593. A long and bitter feud had existed betwixt the families previous to this; and it was thought to have been made up by the above marriage and forgotten. But it requires little to rekindle old animosities. At a meeting on the 6th April 1608, at which were present only the Lord Maxwell, Sir James Johnston, and Sir Robert Maxwell of Orthardton, who was married to a sister of Sir James Johnston, and each of them with one attendant only. These attendants quarrelling, Sir James turned about to separate them, when Lord Maxwell, probably thinking he was not quite impartial in his interference, drew a pistol and shot him in the back with two bullets. He immediately absconded, but returned to Scotland in 1612, when a pursuit being raised upon him, he fled north to Caithness, thinking he might escape that way to Sweden; but he was betrayed by the Earl of Caithness, brought to Edinburgh, tried and condemned; and afterwards beheaded at the cross of Edinburgh, as above. His brother was restored to the title and lands five years afterwards.

George Maxwell of Auldhouse, who married, first, Janet, daughter of John Miller of Newton, by Giles, daughter of Pollok of that-ilk, by whom he had John his successor. He married, 2dly, Jane, daughter of William Mure of Glanderston, by whom he had

William, ancestor of the Maxwells of Springkell, Baronets. He married, 3dly, Janet Douglas, daughter of the Laird of Waterside, by whom he had

Hugh, who married Marion, heiress of Maxwell of Dalswinton. He was succeeded by his eldest son, John Maxwell of Auldhouse, who was infeft in Auldhouse and Church lands of Eastwood, 4th June 1632. He married Elizabeth, daughter of James Stuart, Tutor of Blackhall, by whom he had, 1st, George, his successor; 2d, Zacharias, of Blawarthill, whose descendants afterwards carried on the line of the family; 3d, Jane, married to Thomas Crawfurd of Cartsburn.

Sir John Maxwell, as above, dying without habile issue, in 1647, was succeeded by George, eldest son of the above John Maxwell of Auldhouse. He had the honour of Knighthood conferred on him in 1649. He died in 1677. He married Annabella, daughter of Sir Archibald Stewart of Blackhall, by whom he had, 1st, John, his successor; 2d, Marion, first, married to William Stewart of Rossythe: no issue; 2dly, to Sir Charles Murray; 3d, Annabella, first, married to John Cathcart of Castleton, without issue; 2dly, to Sir Robert Pollok of that-ilk, and had issue; and 4th, Margaret, married to Alexander Maxwell, younger of Calderwood.

Sir John Maxwell of Pollok the only son, succeeded his father, as above, in 1677, and on the 12th April 1682 was created a Baronet of Nova Scotia, to him and the heirs male of his body. He was chosen Commissioner of the Shire of Renfrew to the Convention of Estates in 1689; was nominated a Privy Councillor in 1696; a Lord Commissioner of the Treasury of Exchequer, &c. 1699; a Senator of the College of Justice and Lord Justice Clerk. In 1707, he obtained a new patent of the Baronetage, extending the dignity to the heirs of entail. He died sometime previous to the 3d November 1732. He married Marian, daughter of Sir James Stuart of Kirkfield, by whom he had no children. He was succeeded in his lands and title by his cousin and heir male, John Maxwell of Blawarthill, son of Zacharias before-mentioned, to whom we now return.

Zacharias Maxwell, second son of John Maxwell of Auldhouse, and brother of the above Sir George Maxwell of Pollok, was designed of Blawarthill, (see p. 67.) from that property in the parish of Renfrew, on the north side of the Clyde. He died before the year 1702. By his wife, Jean, only daughter of John Maxwell of Southbar, and Elizabeth, daughter of William Cunningham of Craigends, he had two sons, James and John.

James, the eldest son, succeeded him in Blawarthill. He died in 1706, having had no issue by his wife, Anne, daughter of Sir James Stuart of Goodtrees, he was succeeded by his brother,

John Maxwell of Blawarthill, who, on the death of the Lord Justice Clerk, Sir John Maxwell, as above, in 1732, succeeded him in his lands, and thus became Sir John Maxwell, the second Baronet of Nether-Pollok. He died about the year 1758. He married, first, Lady Anne Carmichael, daughter of John Earl of Hyndford, by whom he had John, his successor, and a daughter, Beatrix, who died unmarried. He married, 2dly, Barbara, daughter of Walter Stewart of Stewarthall, son of Sir Archibald Stewart of Blackhall, by whom he had, 1st, George of Blawarthill, Advocate, who died unmarried before 1757; 2d, Walter, afterwards Sir Walter; 3d, James, afterwards Sir James; 4th, Annabella, died unmarried; 5th, Jean, married to James Montgomery of Lainshaw; no issue. He married, 3dly, Margaret Caldwell, by whom he had no issue.

Sir John Maxwell, the third Baronet, succeeded his father, about 1753, but died unmarried in 1758. He was succeeded by his next surviving brother,

Sir Walter, the fourth Baronet. He died in 1761, leaving, by his lady, Darcy, daughter of Thomas Brisbane of that-ilk, an infant child,

The young Sir John, called the fifth Baronet, who died in nine weeks after the death of his father. The representation now devolved on his uncle,

Sir James, the sixth Baronet. He died in 1785, leaving, by his lady, Frances Colquhoun, daughter of Robert Colquhoun Esq; of St. Christopher's, four children; 1st, John his successor; 2d, Robert Maxwell, who died a Captain in the army; 3d, Frances, married to John Cunninghame of Craigends, but died without issue; 4th, Barbara, married to the Rev. Greville Ewing.

Sir John Maxwell, the eldest son, succeeded his father in 1785, and is the seventh Baronet. He married Hannah Anne, daughter of Richard Gardiner Esq; of the county of Norfolk, by whom he has had four children; 1st, Harriet; 2d, Mary, who died in infancy; 3d, John Maxwell Esq; younger of Pollok; and 4th, Elizabeth, married to Archibald Stirling Esq; of Kenmuir, and has issue.

Arms, Argent, on a Saltier Sable, Annulet; Or, stoned Azure, with the badge of a Baronet of Nova Scotia. Crest, a Deers head erazed proper. Supporters, two Lions, motto, " I am ready."

MEARNS PARISH. *(See page 35.)*

Situation and Extent.—It is situated to the southward of, and adjacent to Eastwood, having the Parish of Eagleshame to the eastward—Neilston to the westward, and its southern border is bounded by part of Ayrshire. In length, it is about seven miles from S. W. to N. E. and about half as broad in a cross direction—reckoning on the longest sketch in both cases. The contents, in all, are nearly 11,000 English acres.

Surface and Soil.—The surface is remarkably diversified into heights and hollows; but, with the exception of a few moorish hills on its southern extremity, the whole is either already cultivated, or may soon be so; for, with the above exception, it is all accessible to the plough. The general exposure is to the northeast, and as the surface rises considerably from that quarter to the southwest, the climate would be rather ungenial, were it not moderated by the shelter which each small hill in front affords to the heights immediately behind it. The soil, towards the lower end, next to Eastwood, partakes a good deal of the nature of the thin adhesive soil of that parish; but it becomes more and more fertile farther up the country, where it is incumbent on rotten rock, and is remarkably productive naturally, more especially when in pasture, to which, at least three-fourths, even of the cultivated land of the whole parish is applied.

State of Property.—The great estate of Upper-Pollok is still in the possession of the ancient family of Pollok, on which they have a stately old mansion, embossomed among its own full grown timber, situated on an eminence that overlooks the whole country. The ancient castle of Mearns is still an entire but deserted fabric, with a considerable Barony attached to it, which remains, as Crawfurd left it, in the posssession of the family of Stewart, Baronet of Blackhall. The lands of Balgray, with a suitable mansion, remain also, as formerly, with a branch of the house of Upper-Pollok. The lands of Fingalton, have been in various hands since Crawfurd wrote—they are now possessed by a family of the name of Logan—but Fingalton itself, exists now only in the name of its mill. The lands are known by the names of Walton and Langton. The Newton lands have changed masters several times since the days of Crawfurd. They are at present parcelled out to different feuars, as may be seen in the Table of Property.

The principal other estates in this parish are Capelrig, with a commodious mansion on a small streamlet in a hollow, about a mile and a half north from the Kirk of Mearns—Greenbank on a hill side, under shelter of thriving plantations, about the same distance north east, and Southfield, under similar circumstances, about half a mile south. The other numerous properties of this parish, are each set down all over the parish in snug situations, more or less under shelter of plantations. The whole of these occupy their own lands, without the intervention of tenantry, and form a most respectable body of yeomanry, many of whose families have occupied their respective possessions for ages.

TABLE OF PROPERTY.

Estates, &c.	Proprietors.	Valued Rent Scots. £.	s.	d.	Eng. Acres.
Upper Pollok barony,	Lady Crawfurd Pollok,	1431	19	4	4810
Mearns Castle, &c.	Sir Michael Shaw Stuart, Bart.	490	11	1	700
Southfield,	Hugh Hutchison, Esq;	205	19	2	375
Capelrig,	George Brown, Esq;	182	6	8	375
Shaw, &c.	Arthur Robertson, Esq;	157	9	10	226
Langton, and part of Walton,	Mrs. Logan,	156	16		314
Greenbank, and part of Flenders,	John Hamilton, Esq;	151	15		250
Netherhouse, Bissland, and Broom,	John Smith Wilson, Esq;	150	17	4	208
Middleton,	Richard Henderson, Esq;	131	5		440
Craigton, Blackhouse, and Titwood,	James Pollock, Esq;	129	13	2	150
Hazleton and Crofthead,	John Howie, Esq;	112	17	8	214
Walton, Duncarnock, &c.	Archibald Spiers, Esq; Elderslie,	109	14	10	250
Malletsheugh, and part of Walton,	John Gilmour,	103	6	8	175
Burnhouse, Waterford, and part of Newton,	William and James Mather,	99	1	4	108
Townhead of Newton and Pidmire,	James Russell,	73	7	6	94
Newton,	James Warnock,	65	5	10	42
Humbie,	Rev. George M'Latchie, D.D.	57	3	4	75
Rabshill,	John Graham,	57	3	4	75
Broadlees,	Andrew Foulds,	53	13	4	88
Kirkhill and part of Broom,	John Watson,	46	5	6	50
Hazleton,	Patrick Reid,	45	14	8	82
North Walton,	Robert Pollock,	43	15	0	126
Malletsbeugh, part of,	Robert Allason,	43	13	4	57
Craig of Carnock,	William Carsewell,	42	17	4	57
Carsebridge,	Andrew Park,	42	17	4	92
Malletsheugh, part of,	John Gemmill,	33	15		50
Do. do.	James Howie,	33	15		50
Flenders,	John Pollock,	33	6	8	63
Carsebridge,	John Allason,	33	6	8	75
Craigton,	Janet Russel,	29	3	4	50
Do.	James Russel,	29	3	4	50
Knaprock, or Broom,	John Lithgow,	27			30
Broom, part of,	Mrs. Clyde,	26	13	4	32
Hillhead, South,	Andrew Gilmour,	26	13	4	70

TABLE OF PROPERTY CONTINUED.

Properties.	Proprietors.	£.	s.	d.	Acres Eng.
Broom, part of,	Mrs. Clark,	25	13	4	30
Fawside,	Thomas Pollock,	25	3	8	63
Cairn,	Robert Gilmour,	25	6		150
Titwood,	John Watson,	24	6	8	25
Floak,	John Gilmour,	18	15		63
Maidenhill,	John Douglas, Esq;	18	9	8	57
Floak,	Robert Howie,	18			25
Kirkhill,	Robert Pollock,	15			57
Newmill,	Thomas Everet,	13	14	5	30
Flenders, Renwick's,	John Dick,	13	6	8	13
Hillhead, North,	Arthur Gilmour,	12	10		57
Hillhead, South,	Andrew Foulds,	12	10		57
Bonnyhouse,	James Hill, Esq;	12			20
Wilson's Newton,	Andrew Thomson,	12			7½
Rodinhead, or Ritchie's Broom,	John Strang,	12			28
Floak Titwood, Norris's,	Mr. Bryson,	9	5	10	13
Kirkhouses, or Kirkland,	James Strang,	10			25
Little Greenlaw,	Robert Harvie,	8			16
Commonty, appropriated,	Alexander Graham, Esq;				250
Do. do.	Alexander Picken,				23
Do. do.	Mathew Stewart,				6½
Do. do.	James Cuthbertson,				5
Do. do.	Earl of Eglinton,				21
Glebe,	The Minister,				5
		4766	10	8	
					10,950

Which may be arranged thus —

1. Arable, or in cultivation, ... 7250
2. Natural pastures, and meadow, ... 2400
3. Moss, or moor, waters, roads, &c. 1200
4. Plantations, none very extensive, but every where belts and small clumps of wood by the mansions of the numerous proprietors, ... 100

10,950

Succession of Ministers.—In 1602, the Rev. George Maxwell, designed of Auldhouse. In 1653, the Rev. William Osborn Thomson. In 1688, the Rev. John Glen ordained; died in 1691. In 1691, the Rev. James Macdowal ordained; died 1712. In 1713, the Rev. Henry Hunter, designed of Hunterston. In 1733, the Rev. George M'Vey. He was opposed, but this not persisted in; died in 1751. In 1752, the Rev. Alexander Cruikshank ordained. In 1789, the Rev. George Maclatchie was ordained his assistant, and succeeded him on his death in 1791; now the Rev. Dr. Maclatchie.

Village.—The town of Newton of Mearns is perhaps the only village in the parish that has more than 50 inhabitants. The number in it, in 1811, was 280, and it does not seem to be on the increase. It is a handsome town, however, formed of a single street on the top of an eminence, commanding a fine view over the country, and with a neat little kitchen-garden to each house.

Manufactures.—Besides a due proportion of weavers in the Newton, and in almost every hamlet in the parish, there are several very thriving establishments for bleaching cloth; induced to be set down here, from the excellency of the water, which, in different streams, flow through this part of the county. These are, 1. Wellmeadow, in which are employed 22 men and 95 women; 2. Netherplace, 20 men and 45 women; 3. Balgray, eight men and 12 women; and 4. Greenfield, four men and nine women. There are also cotton-works at Busby, in which are 4000 mule and water spindles, and which give employment to 140 persons, men, women, and children. In one part of the buildings are 80 weaving looms set in motion by water.

Family Descent.—POLLOK OF THAT-ILK. This family is, without question, among the most ancient in Scotland. The first of which (anciently called Pulloc) whose existence can be proven by written evidence, was,

I. Fulbert; he had three sons, Peter, Robert, and Hellias. Peter, the eldest, was a man of great eminence in his day, (see page 37.) but he died without male issue. Hellias, the third son, was in holy orders.

II. Robert, the second son, seems to have been a companion of Walter the Stewart of Scotland. He was one of the witnesses to the charter of Paisley, in 1164, (see page 136). He appears to have been succeeded by his son,

III. Robert (see an instance of his munificence to the Paisley Monks, page 37). He appears to have been succeeded by his son,

IV. Peter de Pulloc, who is a witness to a resignation by Dungallus, son of Christinus, Judge of Lennox, of the lands of Cullbuth, supposed to be Kilbowie, in the district of Lennox, and of a piece of ground near the Kirk of Kilpatrick, to the Abbey of Paisley. Among the witnesses, he is set down immediately after Alano de Cathcart, and, from the Chartulary, it would appear that this was about the year 1234.

V. The next in the course of succession, appears to be Thomas de Pulloc, who, in 1270, is witness to a resignation by John de Wardroba Bernaird de Erth, &c. in favour of the Abbey of Paisley, of the Lands of Cachmannock, supposed now Cochnoch, Femballoch, Edenbarnon, Bachannet, Drumgreave, &c. He is set down among the witnesses after John de Knox. He appears to have been succeeded by,

VI. John de Pulloc, who lived in the time of Edward I. of England, and, unfortunately for himself and family, took part with Baliol against Bruce. He appears, from Pryne's Collection, p. 662, to have sworn fealty to Edward; and in the reign of Robert Bruce, about 1310, there appears to have been a grant by Robert of his moveable goods to the Abbey of Arbroath, for his joining the English.

Probably, from this cause, and at any rate about this period, a part of the family estate appears to have been ravished from the Polloks of that-ilk, and to have been seized by the Maxwells, Lords of the Mearns [*].

VII. Robert de Pollok, successor to the above John, espoused Agnes, daughter of John Maxwell, Lord of the Mearns. He appears to have been succeeded by,

VIII. John de Pollok his son, and accordingly there is in the charter-chest of Over Pollok, an original charter, dated 3d May 1372, granted by John Maxwell, Lord of the Mearns, with consent of Robert de Maxwell his son, and heir to his beloved kinsman, John de Pollok, heir of Robert de Pollok, son of Agnes Maxwell, deceased, the daughter of the said John Lord of the Mearns. He appears to have been succeeded by,

IX. John Pollok, designed of that-ilk, in an instrument of resignation in the charter-chest of Lord Dundonald, dated 30th March 1441, bearing to be granted by the said John Pollok and Walter Spreul of Cowden, in favour of Thomas Spreul, of the lands of Cowden and Uply. To him succeeded,

X. Charles Pollok, and of this date (28th July 1486), John Maxwell, Lord of the Mearns, granted a charter of the lands of Over Pollok to the said Charles, designing him his kinsman, and to Margaret Stewart his wife, daughter of the Laird of Minto, (see page 38.) in conjunct fee and liferent, and to the heirs male procreated betwixt them, whom failing, to the superior on Charles's own resignation. He had two sons, 1. John; 2. David, of whom afterwards.

---

[*] From the donations of the churches of Mearns and Pollok by the Polloks of that-ilk, to the Abbacy of Paisley, it seems extremely probable, that the barony of Mearns and lands of Nether Pollok were their property; and this opinion is very considerably strengthened, if not evident, from the circumstance of the lands of Nether Pollok bearing their name.

The eldest son, John, died in his father's life-time. He married Janet Spreul, a lady of the family of Cowden, by whom he had a son, John, who succeeded his grandfather, but, dying in his infancy, the estate, in terms of the investiture to heirs male, devolved upon

XI. David, the second son of Charles, who obtained from the superior a charter, dated the last July 1527, altering the Investiture from heirs male to his heirs whatsoever. He married Marion, or rather Margaret, (see page 38.) daughter of William Stewart of Castlemilk, by whom he left John Pollok, his son and heir, who, in consequence of a particular agreement entered into by his father, married Margaret, daughter of Gabriel Sempill of Cathcart. Crawfurd says that David left a younger son, of whom the Polloks of Balgray were descended; but I have not been able to see any evidence of this descent, though I see he had a younger son, Charles Pollok, and this Charles was afterwards designed of Greenhill, and by Janet Stirling, his spouse, Charles left a son John. David Pollok appears to have died in 1545, and was succeeded by his son,

XII. John, who, dying in 1564, left a son and heir.

XIII. John Pollok, who married Janet Mure, (see page 38), daughter of William Mure of Glanderston, and he appears to have died before March 1577, and was succeeded by his son,

XIV. John Pollok, who married, 1. Maud Montgomery, daughter of Neil Montgomery of Lainshaw; and it would appear, that certain differences having arisen betwixt them, a divorce had taken place, and it appears he was afterwards married to Dorothea Stuart of Cardonald, by whom he had, 1. Robert; 2. Mary, who married James Williamson, brother of Robert Williamson of Murieston. Being at the conflict at Locherby, in the year 1593, assisting his kinsman, Lord Maxwell, against the Laird of Johnston, was there slain, and was succeeded by his son,

XV. Robert, who was married to Jean, daughter of James Mowat of Busby, and by her had his eldest daughter, name unknown, married to John Pollok of Balgray, whose issue seems to have failed; also, 1. Robert; 2. Helen, married to Robert Marshall, writer in Glasgow, by whom she had no surviving issue. This Robert acquired the superiority of the estate from the Earl of Nithsdale, and came thereby again to hold it of the Crown. He died in 1657, and was succeeded by his son,

XVI. Robert, who, in 1660, married Jean Crawfurd, daughter of Cornelius Crawfurd of Jordanhill, by whom he had; 1. Robert, and several other children, of whom there is no issue, except by a daughter, married to Semple of Beltrees. He died in 1676, and was succeeded by his son,

XVII. Robert Pollok, who was married, 1. to Annabella, daughter of Sir George Maxwell of Nether Pollok; 2. to Annabella, daughter of Walter Stewart of Pardovan. He was, by Her Majesty Queen Anne, created a Baronet of Nova Scotia, 30th November 1703, to him and to the heirs male of his body; it proceeds upon a recital of the antiquity and flourishing condition of the ancient family of Pollok of that-ilk, for 600 years then by-past, since the reigns of David and William, Kings of Scotland; also, upon a recital of the many illustrious and faithful services of the said Robert, now Sir Robert of that-ilk, the representative, without interruption of that ancient family. As also, his faithful and zealous services, in defending the reformed religion at the time of the Revolution, and that, when bearing the king's commission, he had been taken, and confined in the most barbarous and uncivilized places of the Highlands, during the space of nine months, because he would not renounce his allegiance to King William. By his second wife, he had four sons and three daughters; 1. Robert, an Officer in the army, who died before his father, without issue; 2. Walter, of whom afterwards; 3. John, a Captain in the army—was killed at the battle of Fontenoy. He was married to Ann, daughter of John Lockhart of Lee, by whom he left one daughter, Robina, of whom afterwards; 4. William, who died without issue. 1. Elizabeth, married to Alexander Hamilton of Grange, and had issue; 2. Jean, married to James Pollok of Arthurlie, and had issue; 3. Annabella, married to James Hamilton of Newton, surgeon in Glasgow, who had an only son, James, who died without issue. Sir Robert Pollok died in 1736, and was succeeded by

XVIII. Walter Pollok, the second son, who married ——— Bogle, daughter of ——— Bogle of Daldowie, merchant in Glasgow; by the said lady, 1. Robert; 2. Walter, who died unmarried; 3. John, an Officer in His Majesty's service, who also died unmarried; 4th, Elizabeth, who died unmarried; 5. Jean, of whom afterwards; Walter, having predeceased his father, his eldest son,

XIX. Sir Robert, succeeded to his grandfather. He was married to Ann Crawfurd, daughter of the Rev. Cornelius Crawfurd, son of Laurence Crawfurd of Jordanhill, Esquire, by whom he had an only daughter, Cornelia, and he dying, 1783, was succeeded by

XX. Cornelia Pollok, his only child, who survived her father but a very short time, having died in her infancy, on the 28th Feb. 1785, and was succeeded by her aunt,

XIX. Jean Pollok, who died unmarried, in 1807, and was succeeded by her cousin,

XIX. Robina Pollok, only child of Captain John Pollok of Balgray, and relict of Sir Hew Crawfurd of Jordanhill, Bart. There exist of this marriage, 1. Sir Robert Crawfurd, Bart. married Miss Mushat: no issue.

XX. 2. Hew, a Captain in the Army, married Jane, daughter of the late William Johnston, Esq; of Headfort, in the county of Leitrim, Ireland, by whom he had issue,

XXI. 1. Hugh, an Officer in the Army; 2. Robert; 3. Jane Pollok; 4. Maria; 5. Anne.

3. Mary, married to Colonel Hamilton of Bardowie, no issue; 4. Robina, unmarried; and 5. Lucken, married to General John Gordon Cumming Skene, of Pitlurg Dice, &c. Aberdeenshire, issue, four sons and five daughters.

HAMILTON OF PRESTON AND FINGALTON.—The Barony of Fingalton was originally of great extent, and, as stated by Crawfurd, one of the oldest possessions of the family of Preston, the most ancient Cadet of the House of Hamilton; having been granted to Sir John Fitz-Gilbert de Hamilton of Rossaven, the original ancestor of that branch, by his nephew, Sir David Hamilton of Cadyow, in 1339;—" Patruo Suo Domino Johanni de Hamiltoun de Rossaven militi." An extract of this charter has been preserved by Baillie of Carnbroe, in his M.S. " History of the House of Hamilton," the original, along with all the private documents of the family, having been destroyed when the Castle of Preston was sacked and burned by the English army under Cromwell, after the battle of Dunbar.

This estate, along with the Barony of Preston, the lands of Rossaven, &c. was sold by Sir William Hamilton, in 1681, before he retired into Holland to join the party of the Prince of Orange. Since that period it has been possessed by many different proprietors, and has been subdivided into several parcels.

The following is the descent of this family *.

I. Sir John Fitz-Gilbert, second son of Sir Gilbert de Hamildown, the original founder of the house of Hamilton in Scotland, (see Abercorn) was born before 1270, and died before 1345. Besides the barony of Fingalton in the county of Renfrew, he acquired the lands of Ross, or Rossaven, in the shire of

---

* The following pedigree of this family, which had long the lands of Fingalton in this county, is an abridgement of a more detailed narrative, communicated by Sir William Hamilton, wherein all the facts are established on the authority of Public Records, private Charters, contemporary Historians, &c. It has, however, been found necessary to abstract the Genealogy alone, as the history and authorities would have occupied too considerable a space.

Lanark, from the monastery of Kelso. He is said, by Crawfurd, to have married a daughter of Sir Robert Cruck of Crucksfie, but the authority is unknown.

II. Sir John II. succeeded his father before 1345. He acquired the barony of Preston, in East Lothian.

III. Sir John III. succeeded his father before 1376. He left a younger son, Walter.

IV. Sir John IV. succeeded his father about 1400. He married Anna, sixth daughter of Sir William Seton of that ilk, by whom he had,

V. Sir James I. who succeeded his father before 1438. By his spouse Margaret, daughter of James first Lord Hamilton, he left three sons: Sir William and Sir Robert, successively barons of Preston, &c. and John, founder of the family of Ellershaw.

VI. Sir William I. succeeded his father before 1450. He left only daughters, of whom, Margaret, the eldest, was, in 1455, married to William, second son of William, second Lord Somerville, and founder of the family of Plain.

IV. Sir Robert I. succeeded his brother before 1460. He left a younger son, Adam of Preistgill.

VII. Robert II. succeeded his father in 1479. In 1484, he was appointed a Conservator of the peace with England. By his spouse, Marion, daughter of Johnston of that-ilk, he had three sons: Sir Robert, his successor, Sir Patrick, and James.

VIII. Sir Robert III. succeeded his father in 1488. He married, first, Marion, daughter of Sir David Crichton of Cranston-Riddell, and, secondly, Dame Ellene Shaw, Lady Dirlton, daughter of Sir James Shaw of Sauchy, and relict of Archibald, master of Haliburton. By his former marriage he left four sons: Robert, his successor; John, founder of the family of Airdrie, of whom again; David of Oliestob, married to Margaret, daughter of George Lord Seaton, but left no issue; and James.

IX. Robert IV. succeeded his father in 1522. By his wife Katharene Tweedy, a daughter of the House of Drumelzier, he had two sons; Sir James of Fingalton, who died in his own lifetime; Sir David, his successor; and three daughters; Janet, married, 1st, to John Hamilton of Broomhill, and, 2dly, to John Carmichael of Edram; Elizabeth, to Robert Dalziel of that ilk; and, Gelis, to John Stewart of Halcraig.

X. Sir David, Knight Banneret, and Marischal Deputy of Scotland, succeeded his father before 1538. By his spouse, Janet, daughter of Sir William Baillie of Lammington, he left two sons: George, his successor; and Patrick;

and four daughters: Margaret, who died unmarried; Katharene, married to Robert Wallace of Carnell; Joane, to John Hamilton of Stenhouse; and, Elizabeth, to Robert Hamilton of Heuchead. Sir David died in 1584. His political actions are commemorated by Buchanan, Knox, Pitscottie, &c.

XI. George. In 1563, he married Barbara, daughter of Sir John Cokburne of Ormiston. By her he had four sons: Sir John, his successor; Robert, of whom again; David and George, who died unmarried; and five daughters; Joane, married to Sir John Lindsey of Dunrod; Helen, to John Muir of Caldwell; Margaret, to Andrew Hamilton of Lethame; Alesone, to James Roberton of Earnock; and, Mary, to Robert Cokburne, a son of the house of Clerkington. George died in 1608.

XII. Sir John V. was born in 1565.—In 1587, he married Joane, daughter of Sir Thomas Otterburne of Ridhall; in 1619, Katharene Howison; and, in 1632, Dame Helen Lumisdaine, of the family of Airdrie in Fife, and relict of Sir Archibald Douglas of Whittingham. By his first wife he had three sons: Sir James, his successor; and Robert and George, who were both Officers of rank in the army of Gustavus Adolphus. Sir John died in 1643. He is distinguished in history as a zealous Presbyterian, and his resolute opposition in Parliament to the five Articles of Perth, is minutely detailed by Calderwood.

XIII. Sir James II. was born in 1590. He married Barbara, daughter of Sir Robert Muir of Caldwell, by whom he had two sons. Robert, who died without issue in his father's lifetime. He married Anne, daughter of Sir Thomas Henrysone of Chesteris; 1. John, his successor, and two daughters; 2. Jean, married to Robert Montgomery of Hazlehead; and, 2. Anne, married to her kinsman, Sir Thomas Hamilton, who succeeded her brother as heir male of the family. Sir James died in 1644.

XIV. Sir John VI. In 1641 he married Margaret, daughter of Sir John Seton of Saint-German, but died in 1647 without issue. On his death the estates and representation devolved on Captain Thomas Hamilton of Brotherstaines, son of

XII. Robert, second son of George Hamilton of Preston, (See XI.) In 1606 Robert married Janet, daughter of Sir John Johnstone of Elphinstone, by whom he had, besides daughters, a son Thomas.

XIII. Sir Thomas was born in 1618. In 1637 he married Margaret Murray; in 1645 Anne, daughter of Sir James Hamilton of Preston, his cousin; and, in 1665, Rachel, daughter of Robert Burnet Lord Crimond, sister of Bishop Burnet, and relict of Sir Thomas Nicolson of Cockburnspath, King's Advocate. By his second spouse he left two sons; Sir William and Sir Robert, successively of

Preston, &c. and four daughters; Janet, married to Sir Alexander Gordon of Earlston; Margaret, to Sir James Oswald; Jane, to Sir Thomas Young of Rosebank; and Anne, who died unmarried. Sir Thomas died in 1672. His exploits, as a royalist, are recorded by Burnet and others.

XIV. Sir William II. was born in 1649. On the 5th September 1673, he was created a Baronet of Nova Scotia, the title being in favour of him and of his heirs male whomsoever. In 1670, he married Rachel, daughter of Sir Thomas Nicolson of Cockburnspath. By her he had three daughters; Rachel, who died unmarried; Anne, married to Thomas, eldest son of Sir James Oswald; and again to Gilbert, son of Sir Thomas Burnet, and nephew of the Bishop; and Jane, to George Stirling of Lethame. In 1681 Sir William confidentially sold all his estates to Sir James Oswald his brother-in-law, and retired into Holland. He engaged in the designs of Monmouth and Argyle, and accompanied the latter, in his expedition to Scotland, in 1685. He again escaped into Holland, where he found great favour with the Prince of Orange, in whose army he held a high command in the invasion of England in 1688. He died, however, of a sudden illness at Exeter during the march to London.

XIV. Sir Robert V. was born in 1650. He was a character of no small note in his day, being General of the Covenanters in the insurrection of 1679, when he commanded their army, in the battles of Drumclog and Bothwell-bridge. He escaped to Holland, where he continued until the revolution, when he returned into Scotland, and succeeded to his brother's title. He died unmarried in 1701. On Sir Robert's death, and the more proximate male descendants, having previously failed, the representation of the house of Preston, devolved on Robert Hamilton of Airdrie. His descent is as follows:—

IX. John, second son of Sir Robert Hamilton of Preston and Fingalton, third of that name, (see VIII.) acquired the lands of Airdrie, in Lanarkshire, from the Monastery of Newbottle, in 1503. He fell at Flouden, in 1513, leaving, by his spouse, Ellene, daughter of John Crawfurd of Ruchsulloch, two sons, Methusalem and William.

X. Methusalem died in 1566. By his wife, Christian Bell, he had two sons, John, who died before himself; and Gavin; also, a daughter, Janet, married to James Dalzell, a son of the family of Dalzell of that-ilk.

XI. Gavin, died in 1591, leaving, by Isabell his wife, daughter of James Roberton of Earnock, four sons; John, his successor; Gavin, James, and Archibald.

XII. John was born in 1569, and died in 1648. By his spouse, Janet, daughter of Robert Hamilton of Torrance, he had John, who married Margaret, daughter of John Hamilton of Udston; but, who predeceased his father without issue; and Gavin, also a daughter, Jean, married to John Fleming of Cardorroch.

XIII. Gavin died in 1687, leaving, by his spouse, Jean, daughter of Robert Montgomery of Hazlehead, Robert, his successor, and William, afterwards principal of the University of Edinburgh. From William, among other distinguished descendants, are sprung, in the male line, Robert Hamilton, L. L. D. the present celebrated Professor of Mathematics, in the King's College, Aberdeen, and James Hamilton, M. D. a physician of the first eminence in Edinburgh, whose sister was married to the late Benjamin Bell, Esq; Edinburgh, a surgeon of distinguished talents, in his profession; the issue of which marriage, have thus flowing in their veins, a due portion of the blood of the Hamiltons of Preston:— and, in the female line, was descended, the late learned Samuel Horsley, Bishop of St. David's.

XIV. Robert VI. he succeeded his father in the estate of Airdrie, and his kinsman, Sir Robert V. in the representation of the house of Preston and Fingalton, and in his right to the title of Baronet. This, however, he did not assert, his estate being greatly burdened by his exertions for the Covenant. He died in 1705, leaving, by his spouse, Elizabeth, daughter of William Cochrane of Rochsoles, William, his successor, and Louisa, married to ——— Balfour of Pilrig.

XV. William III. was born in 1681, and died in 1749. By his spouse, Margaret, daughter and heiress of John Bogle of Kilbowie and Sandyhills, he left four sons: Robert, his successor; John and James, whose male descendants failed in the first generation; and Thomas, of whom again.

XVI. Robert VII. was born in 1714, and died in 1756. By his wife, Mary, daughter of John Baird, Esq; of Craigton, he left three sons, William; James, who died young; and Robert: and two daughters, Grizel, married to John Arnot, Esquire; and Mary, to Thomas Cochran, M. D.

XVII. William IV. was born in 1748, and died unmarried, in 1770. The remnant of the Barony of Airdrie was sold in his minority. He was succeeded by his brother Robert.

XVIII. Robert VIII. was born in 1754, and died unmarried in 1799, at St. Helena, during his return from India. On his demise, the representation fell to the grandson of

XVI. Thomas, who was fourth son of William III. (see XV). He was born in 1728, and died in 1781. He was professor of Anatomy in the University of Glasgow. By his spouse, Isobell, daughter of Dr. William Anderson, he left one son,

XVII. William, who succeeded his father in his chair. He was born in 1760, and died in 1793. By his spouse, Elizabeth, daughter of William Stirling, Esquire, heir male of the family of Calder, he left two sons, William and Thomas. The latter is an officer in the army.

XVIII. Sir William V. is now the twenty-fourth male representative of the house of Preston, Fingalton, and Ross, and the eighteenth generation from Sir Gilbert de Hamyldoun, the original founder of the family of the house of Hamilton in Scotland. On the 24th July 1816, in order legally to establish his right to the title of Baronet, and to the representation of the family, he was served heir male in general, to Sir Robert Hamilton of Preston, Baronet, fifth of that name. He is an Advocate, having been admitted a member of the faculty in 1813.

Arms—three cinque foils Argent, in a field Gules; Crest, an armed man from the middle, brandishing a sword aloft, Proper; motto, " Pro Patriæ."

Supporters—two men in armour, bearing each a banner of the family.

Brown of Capelrig.—The late Mr. Barclay of Capelrig, acquired these lands in 1776, from Baron Mure of Caldwell. He died at Southampton in England in 1783, and was succeeded by his niece, Mary Anderson Barclay, only daughter of Robert Anderson of Over-Gru, and Alison Barclay, Mr. Barclay's sister. This lady married George Brown, Esq; merchant in Glasgow, who, in consequence, is now the proprietor of this very chearful property. They have five daughters living; Ann, Mary, Janet, Barclay, and Alison. Mr. Brown, since his marriage, has added considerably to the property by the purchase of lands in the neighbourhood, all included in the table of property under the name of Capelrig, and has beautified the whole by improvements both profitable and ornamental.

NEILSTON.

Situation and Extent.—This parish is situated to the westward of, and in the immediate vicinity of, the Mearns. It is bounded otherways by part of the shire of Ayr on the south; a small part of Lochwinnoch on the west; and the parishes of Paisley and Eastwood on the north and north-east. The greatest length is about seven miles from S. E. to N. W. and it is nearly half as much in breadth in a cross direction at an average. The extent, in all, amounts to about 12,500 English acres.

Surface and Soil.—The surface, like to the preceding parish, is also remarkably diversified into heights and hollows, and still farther varied by hill and dale. The hills of Ferenize are situated nearly all in this parish, on its western side, and rise pretty steeply to 400 or 500 feet in immediate view above the level of the surrounding country, and 200 or 300 feet higher further back, and from which there is a very widely extended prospect in all directions, embracing great variety of scenery. Adjacent to these, on the east, is stretched out a delightful vale, watered by the Levern and its tributary streamlets, full of population, and manufacturing establishments. The soil is chiefly of that naturally fertile kind, derived from rotten rock, and adapted to almost any crop; but, like to the greater part of the higher lands in this county, is applied more to pasturage than to corn. Although there be a considerable portion of hilly country here, there is little of it unproductive, as even the least fertile is sound grazing land.

State of Property.—The valuable and extensive estate of Arthurlie, in Crawfurd's time had recently passed from a great branch of the family of Darnley Stewart, into that of Pollok, in which it continued two or three generations. In 1780, the greater part of it came through a marriage with the heiress, to Ralston of that-ilk. He soon after feued out a village on part of it, called Newton-Ralston, which has since become considerable. The whole has now been parcelled out to various proprietors, as per table of property. It has become a great seat of manufactures, and it is embellished with several elegant villas, among which, perhaps, that of Arthurlie proper, Mr. Lowndes, may be esteemed the principal. Glanderston, in Crawfurd's time, possessed by a br..nch of the Mures of Caldwell, was afterwards sold to a Mr. Wilson, from whom it was acquired, in 1774, by the father of the present proprietor, Archibald Spiers, Esq; of Elderslie. Kirkton of Neilston, then possessed by Mr. Millar, became afterwards the property of a family of the name of Craig, with which it still remains. Neilstonside, then belonging to the family of Wallace, belongs now to Archibald Spiers, Esq; of Elderslie, whose father purchased it in 1775. Syde, which then belonged to Montgomery of Skelmorley, became afterwards the property of the Laird of Milliken, and now belongs to Fulton of Hartfield, and is no more known by its former name. Caldwell-Easter, belongs still to Mure of Caldwell. Caldwell-Wester, and Cowdon, which then belonged to the Earl of Dundonald, became, in 1725, the property of the Marquis of Clydesdale, in right of his mother, a daughter of the Earl of Dundonald, and were sold by the Hamilton family, about the year 1766, to Baron Mure of Caldwell, and are now the property of that family. Auchinback belongs to the Earl of Glasgow by succession, and as representing the ancient family of Ross Lord Ross.

CONTINUATION OF THE

TABLE OF PROPERTY.

Properties.	Proprietors.	Valued Rent Scots. £.	s.	d.	Eng. Acres.
Easter Caldwell	William Mure, Esq.	230			
Wester Caldwell,		°66	13	4	
Cowdon Commore,		500			
Glanderston and Neilstonside		383	6	8	
Caldwell, part of,		40			
Neilstonside,		322	10		
4 different parts of Commore,	Archibald Speirs, Esq; of Elderslie,	210	16	8	
Glanderston Dike,		53	6	8	
Part of the £17 land of Arthurlie,		186			
Do. do.		34			
Anderson's part of Caldwell,	Heirs of Wood,	30			
Auchinback,		418	6	8	575
Dubs, Park, and Boghall,	Earl of Glasgow,	113	6	8	
Laigh Lyon Cross,		20			
Maxwell's Lyon Cross,	Lady Pollok,	120			
High Lyon Cross,	Heirs of Mrs. Cuthbertson,	20			
Airston's Arthurlie,	Mr. Lowndes,	53	6	8	
Kirkland's part of do.	Mr. Wilson,	13	6	8	
Do. do.	Airston of Greenhill,	6	13	4	
Pollok's Arthurlie,	Mr. Dunlop,	136			244
Part of do.	Mr. Lowndes,	16	6	8	
Do. do.	Mr. Airston,	32	13	4	
Part of £17 land of do.	Mr. Craig of Kirkton,	109			
Do. do.	Mr. Airston,	22			
Do. do.	Mr. Finlay,	25			
Do. do.	Mr. Stevenson,	37			
Do. do.	Allan Stewart,	47	6	8	147
Do. do.	James Cuthbertson,	23	15		
Do. do.	James Finlay, and others,	71	5		
Do. do.	Mr. Airston,	44			
Do. do.	Andrew Spreul,	84			44
Do. do.	Mr. Anderson,	30			65
Hartfield,	Robert Fulton, Esq	633	6	8	
Ferenize,	Mr. Graham,	440			
Extent of lands, not ascertained,					12443
Total in Neilston parish,		4823	6	8	12518
Add, in the parish of Beith,					
* Shutterflatt,	Mr. Stevenson,	59	6		
Do.	Feuars,	10.	7	8	534
		162	16	8	
Also, in Dunlop,					
Knockmade,	William Mure, Esq; Caldwell,	500			904
Total in this account,		5486	3	4	3956

* This place is famed for an insurrectionary meeting of the oppressed covenanters, in the

Which may be arranged thus —

	Acres.
1. Arable, or in cultivation,	10500
2. Natural pastures, and meadow,	200
3. Mosses, moor, waters, roads, sites of houses, &c.	800
4. Wood and Plantations,	1000
	12,950

reign of Charles II. which, as it was productive of the most serious consequences to the gentlemen concerned it is presumed that a concise account of it will not be unacceptable.

Meeting at Chitterfleet.—On Sunday, the 23d November 1666, being three days before the battle of Pentland hills, a number of gentlemen and others on horseback, amounting to 39 in all, met on the lands of Chitterfleet, on the confines of Ayrshire, about a mile and a half west from the present house o' Caldwell. In this number, the following are mentioned as proprietors in the Shire of Renfrew:—William Mure of Caldwell, Easter; the Goodman younger of Caldwell, Wester, or of that-ilk; William Porterfield of Quarrelton, and his brother, Alexander Porterfield of Denniston; and the Laird of Blackstone, whose name is not mentioned, but must have been Maxwell. The object of the meeting was to raise the country and join the covenanters, then in full march to Edinburgh, under Colonel Wallace of Auchens; Major Learmonth of Newholme, Major Macleland of Barscob; Major John MacCulloch, and Captain Andrew Arnot. It does not appear that they succeeded in raising many men, nor that any of the Renfrewshire gentlemen, as above, had got forward in time to be at the battle. But having been so far implicated in the rising, they found it necessary to leave the country. It appears, however, on record, that (with the exception of Blackstone), they were in absence, with many others, tried on the 16th August 1667, at Edinburgh, before a jury of landed proprietors, chiefly of Lothian, and found guilty, and condemned to death, and their whole estates forfeited. They saved their lives by flight, but the forfeitures took place. The estates of Mure of Caldwell were gifted by the Crown to General Thomas Dalziel, by a deed, dated 26th September 1670. These consisted at that time of the following subjects;—the five pound land of Kockward, (now Knockewart), and five merk land of Douniflat, in Ayrshire; the five pound land of Knockmade, and five merk land of Easter Caldwells, in Renfrewshire; the ten merk land of Killochside, in Lanarkshire; also, the tiend sheaves and parsonage, tiends of the same lands of Kittochside, and of Caldwells: also, of the lands and tiends of Kippelrig, in Renfrewshire, all holden of the Crown, or of the Prince of Scotland—and the following lands, holding of a subject superior, viz. The ten pound land of Beith, with pertinents, &c. in the parish of Beith; the ten merk land of Cowdam, in the parish of Symminton; the ten merk land of Thorntoun, in the parish of Kilmaurs; all in Ayrshire, and the four merk land of Newland, in Eastwood parish, and the five merk land of Glanderstoun, in the parish of Neilstoun, in Renfrewshire. Major Learmonth's lands of

Succession of Ministers.—In 1602, the Rev. Andrew Law. In 1632, the Rev. John Law; deposed in 1649, when William Semple from Ireland preaches during the vacancy, which does not appear to have been filled up till 1657, when the Rev. Hugh Walker is ordained, who was outed, probably for non-conformity, in 1662. In 1688, the Rev. David Brown is ordained, who, in 1701, was translated to Glasgow. In 1703, the Rev. John Millar is ordained. In 1733, the Rev. Alexander Clerk is presented by Lord Dundonald, is opposed by some of the people, but the presbytery sustain the call, which is confirmed by the General Assembly; he died in 1736. In 1737, the Rev. Henry Millar is ordained; died in 1771. In 1772, the Rev. John Wilson is ordained; died in 1784. In 1785, the Rev. John Monteith is ordained, but translated to Houston in 1797. In 1798, the Rev. William Hood was ordained; died in 1804, and in the same year the Rev. Alexander Fleming was ordained, the present minister.

Villages.—There is, perhaps, no country parish in Scotland that abounds so much in thriving and populous villages as Neilston; and all has arisen from the rapid increase in the population, owing to the recent introduction of manufacturing establishments on a great scale, and whose main movements are impelled by powerful water-fall, or by steam-engine machinery. It is greatly to be regretted, that these should at the same time have such a strong tendency to foster a contamination of principle among the crowds of thoughtless people employed. Neilston, the Kirk town, has long been a place of note. It is situated in a most cheerful and healthy spot, on the brow of an eminence, overlooking a great expanse of country. The population, in 1811, amounted to 683. Barrhead and New town Ralston, erected at a period not remote, and at a small distance from each other, have now grown into one village, having a population, in the same year, of 1230. Grahamston, in the near neighbourhood of them, had then 448. Gateside and Chapel 394. Crofthead 327, and West Arthurlie 305. Thus, in these larger villages, there is a conjoined population of 3064 souls, where, in 1791,

Newholme, in the parish of Dolphintoun; and of Kirklahill and Slainie lands, in the parish of Skirling, were gifted to His Majesty's Lovit, William Hamilton of Woulshaw, (Wishaw). William Porterfield of Quarreltoun's lands were gifted to John Hamiltoun younger of Halcraig. They were called the ten merk land of Easter Cochran. Alexander Porterfield's lands of Denniston, were gifted also, to the same John Hamilton. The different farms on that property, are particularly enumerated, all holding of the Earl of Glencairn, and amounted to L.5 : 1 : 5 in all. Extracted from an old publication, by the covenanters themselves, (apparently soon after the revolution, when the respective estates were restored) of the trials of their chiefs, entitled, " A Bunch of Bitter Wormwood, bringing forth a bundle of sweet smelling Myrrh," in the possession of John Smith, Esq; Swineridgemuir.

the population of the whole parish amounted to only 2330. It is now more than 6000.

Manufactures.—So much is this a manufacturing district, that three-fourths of the population may be stated as manufacturers; the class of husbandmen will not, in number, exceed 1500. In all times there has been a portion of craftsmen intermixed with the cultivators of the soil; but, dispersed in single families among the more numerous class of country labourers, they never were, nor ever had it in their power, to be, more licentious than their neighbours, the cultivators of the soil. It is only when they congregate into numerous associations, that they become troublesome to the community and pernicious to themselves. I shall here, in few words, state the progress of those manufacturing arts, to which the additional population is owing. The chief, and almost only, sources, from whence the population has increased, and with it the general wealth, has been the Cotton-mills and the Bleachfields. In 1791, there were only two small Cotton mills in the parish. One of these, at Dovcotehall, was the second that was erected in Scotland. It was 76 feet long and 28 broad, and one storey high. The other, at Gateside, was two storeys in height, 100 long, and 31 broad; in both these there were only 301 people employed. These soon gave way to larger erections, and were converted into dwellings for the workers. There are now six Cotton mills, all on a larger scale, of four or five storeys in height, displaying immense piles of building, whilst the least of them employs nearly as many people as both of the former. The capital sunk in them is moderately estimated at £80,000, whilst the value of the yarn spun, has, on the average of the two last years, been £194,929 11s. 8d. Neilston parish being copiously supplied, from its numerous streams, with water of a quality adapted to bleaching of cloth, has long been famed for Bleachfields; but all on a moderate scale. In 1791, there were 12 of these, and which employed 92 persons. At present there are 15, and which give employment to 420 people and 31 horses. The extent of these is great. Kirkton Bleachfield, which belongs to John Cochran, Esq; is at present undergoing extensive repairs, and has the prospect of soon being superior to any field in the trade. When finished, it will be capable of bleaching and finishing 1500 pieces a-day.

The amount of goods bleached yearly, in all these works, is 1,560,000 pieces, valued at £1,280,000. The capital sunk in them is estimated at £33,300. There was a Printfield at Ferenize, that in 1791, paid £3000 of excise duty, whilst its yearly expenses, otherways, were about £2000. It has been at a stand for some time back. Laying it, however, out of sight, the capital sunk in these 21 branches of the clothing manufacture, is estimated at £113,300, and the value of goods put through them yearly, at £1,474,929 11s. 8d.

This, when added to £13,072 2s. 4d. the real rental of the parish in 1815, may give some idea of the benefits arising from the extension of manufactures; for, it may be added, that in consequence of these great works, the banks of the Levern, and all other streams in the parish, have been greatly ornamented with villas and pleasure grounds, whilst the surface, especially in the eastern and lower parts, has become highly improved and enriched in no small degree.

Thus the land-rent of the parish in 1791, which was only £4200, is (now) more than three times that sum. The rent of houses too has risen in nearly the same ratio, for, an ordinary cottage in a village, that then was thought dear at 30s. brings now £3 or £3 10s. of yearly rent. So has also pasture lands increased in rent, and in these, as well as in the farms in tillage, the rent continues to be uncommonly well paid. In truth, (to use the words of the worthy clergyman from whom I take the minutiæ of this account) a more virtuous, or a more sober, industrious, and respectable set of farmers is no where to be found.

MURE OF CALDWELL.—In the papers of this ancient family, the surname is written at different times, More, Mure, Moir or Muir, Moore, and frequently by contraction, Mor and Mr. The etymology of the word is perhaps uncertain. It may naturally be supposed the same with the Galic word signifying Great.

The first person using the name, is Reginald, who is witness to a charter of the lands of Keres in England, in the 12th century[1]. In a charter of Alexander the II. there is mentioned a David de Moore, the head of the house of Rouallane. The estate of Polkelly, belonged to Reginald or Reynaud Mure and his family, and afterwards came, by marriage of the heir female thereof, to Sir Adam Mure of Rouallane, in the reign of King Robert the I. Elizabeth More, the daughter of this Sir Adam, was married to King Robert the II.

In the year 1329, Reginald Mure, a son of Sir Adam's, was the chamberlain of Scotland. This Reginald had a grant from the Crown, on the forfeiture of Sir Andrew Murray, of the lands of Tillibardine, and he acquired the Barony of Abercorn, by marriage of the heir female of Sir John Grahame. The family of Mure of Abercorn, are held among the " Magnates et proceres regni," by Rymour, and certainly appear, from other documents, to have been of great consideration in the kingdom. Sir Reginald left two sons; Sir William More, who succeeded to Abercorn; and Gilchrist More, who married Isobel, daughter of Walter Cumin [2].

[1] M.S. in Advocates Library. [2] M.S. in Advocates Library, by Crawfurd.

Gilchrist More, who is also mentioned in Bagimont's Roll, received from his father the lands of Cowdam in the county of Ayr, which at this day belong to Mr. Mure of Caldwell, to whom they have descended by regular succession. To Gilchrist More succeeded Sir Adam More, his son. As the honour of the Lady Elizabeth More has been by some historians very improperly questioned, and her marriage with King Robert the II. disputed, it may be remarked here, in addition to the other invincible proofs on the subject, that there is a charter in 1392, by King Robert the III. to this Sir Adam Mure, wherein he designs him " dilectus consanguinieus meus," a style which was then by no means usual, although now applied, in royal writs, to the Peers of Parliament in general.

The next in succession is John Mure, the younger brother of the last; and, although it is not exactly ascertained at what time the lands of Caldwell came to this family, yet it is believed that it was by the marriage of this John to the heiress of that property, as he is the first who is designed John More of Caldwell. At least, on the 29th October 1409, there is a letter of remission granted by Robert Duke of Albany, in favour of him and of Archibald Mure of Polkellie, the third son, who must have received that property as a patrimony, and of Thomas Boyd of Kilmarnock, for the slaughter of Mark Neilson of Dalrymple [1].

He was succeeded by John More, Lord of Caldwell, who is witness along with Robert More of Rouallan, and several others, to a charter of the lands of Dreghorn, dated 19th January 1430. From the circumstance of his name being there placed first, it may be supposed, as has sometimes been maintained, that the rank of Caldwell was superior to that of Rouallan. While the family of Rouallan existed, there is said to have been frequent disputes upon this subject between the heads of the Houses. However, from the Caldwell charter-chest, it appears, that the debate did not much disturb the mutual good-will and understanding of the parties; for the heads of Rouallan at the time are witnesses to almost all the marriage contracts of the sons and daughters of the families of Caldwell and of Glanderston. The House of Rouallan is now merged in that of the Earls of Loudon, whose last heir female is married to the Marquis of Hastings.

The next of the House of Caldwell is John, whose charter, under the great seal, is dated in 1476 [3]. The lands of Cowdames appear at this time to have devolved as a patrimony to a younger son of the name of Adam; for there is a sasine by Lord Herries, then the superior thereof, in his favour, dated 10th April 1475 [4]. They returned to the Laird of Caldwell, as appears from the titles,

---

[1] M.S. in Adv. Library. [2] Quond. penes Earl of Kilmarnock. [3] Caldwell Char. Chest. [4] Ibid.

prior to 1534. By Elizabeth his wife, John More had a daughter, Marjory, who was married to Lord Ross of Hawkhead. This lady lies interred with her husband, under an arched niche in the choir of the church of Renfrew. He is in armour, and she in the dress of the times. The Caldwell arms being three mullets on a bend, within a border engrailed, are still to be seen above the tomb.

John was succeeded by his eldest son, Sir Adam Mure of Caldwell, who, as Crawfurd says, " was a gallant stout man, having many feuds with his neigh-" bours, which were managed with a great fierceness and much bloodshed." This was according to the way of the times, however, and he was knighted by King James the IV. and is designed in the crown charters and other deeds, " Nobilis vir Adamas More de Caldwell Miles." He was married to Elizabeth, daughter of Sir Thomas Semple, and sister to John the first Lord of Sempill. The eldest son was Constantine. He had also John, a second son, and Hector, a third, who all died without issue. The last, indeed, was slain in a feud at Renfrew by John Maxwell, the apparent heir of Sir John Maxwell of Nether Pollok, and Hugh, the brother-german of Sir John, as appears from a remission dated in the year 1500, in their favour for this slaughter[1]. He had also a daughter, Elizabeth, married to George Lindsay of Dunrod, then an opulent and ancient family in this county, and a second, Janet, married to John Stewart of Ardgowan and Blackhall. He died before 1516, when he was succeeded by Sir John, his younger brother, who married Lady Janet Stewart, supposed to be a daughter of the Earl of Lennox. He had a daughter Agnes, married to Patrick Montgomery of Giffen. Another, Elizabeth, married to William Ralston of Ralston, and also a son, Alexander Mure. Alexander received a patrimony of the lands of Kittochside, in the county of Lanark, which had been previously in the family. These lands returned again by his failure without issue; the superiority of them is still in the possession of the family. To John Mure succeeded

John his son, in 1539, who married Christian, daughter of Ninian Lord Ross of Hawkhead; a dispensation for which marriage, as being within the degrees of consanguinity, then prohibited by the church, was obtained from the Archbishop of Glasgow in the year 1538. The original of this is also in the Caldwell charter-chest.

To him succeeded his son, also called John. He was knighted by King James V. and was married to Lady Isabel Montgomery, daughter of the Earl of Eglinton. He left three sons, 1. Robert Mure; and, 2. William Mure; and, 3. James. The second son, William, received the lands of Glanderston, which

[1] Quondam penes Lord Pollok. [2] Caldwell Charter-Chest.

were previously in the family. He married Elizabeth, a daughter of Hamilton of Raploch, and aunt to Gavin, Commendator of Kilwinning. He was the founder of the family of Glanderston.

Robert Mure, the eldest son of Sir John, and lady Isabell, succeeded his father, as the oldest son, in the estate of Caldwell. He married, first, Elizabeth Kincaid, daughter to Kincaid of that-ilk, an ancient family in Stirlingshire. By her he had a son, John, married to Helen, daughter of Sir George Preston of Valleyfield, who were then both three years under twenty-one years of age. This John died in his father's lifetime, leaving no issue. Robert had also, by his first wife, another son, James, who is afterwards mentioned. He married, second, Barbara Preston, also of the family of Valleyfield, and relict of Robert Lord Sempill; and he was one of the several gentlemen, who, in 1577, signed a bond to maintain and support the dignity of that family[1]. By her he had one daughter, who was married to Sir William Hamilton of Preston, Baronet.

James Mure, the second son of Sir Robert, was married to Margaret, daughter of Sir William Mure of Rouallan. He died also in the lifetime of his father. He left two daughters, 1. Mary, who was married to Gavin Hamilton of Raploch, and, 2. Margaret, married to Edward Hamilton of Silvertonhill, and of whom lineally descended the Lord Belhaven, &c. His eldest son,

Robert Mure, succeeded his grandfather, Sir Robert, in the estate of Caldwell. In the year 1610, he makes up a title as heir of James Mure, fiar of Caldwell, to part of the lands contained in his father and mother's marriage contract, narrating, that the remainder are still liferented by his grandfather. This Robert married Isabell, daughter of Uchtred Knox of Ramphorlie, by his wife, a daughter of Blair of that-ilk. The family of Knox, was long of an ancient and respectable character in this county, and the celebrated reformer was one of its sons. By this marriage, Robert had a daughter, Euphemia, married to William Mure of Glanderston, also his successor.

Robert Mure, the eldest son, died without issue in 1647. To him succeeded his younger brother James, in the year 1647, who also died without issue in 1654.

To him succeeded, in 1654, the third brother, William. He married Barbara, daughter of Sir William Cunninghame of Cunninghamhead. But this honourable and excellent gentleman, as he is called by Woodrow, had his estate forfeited, for being accessory to the Rising at Pentland. He fled to Holland, where he died, and his estates, upon the forfeiture, were given to General Dal-

---

[1] Caldwell Charter-Chest.

ziel. His lady, although she had a liferent of a part provided to her by marriage settlement; yet, unfortunately, lost her right by neglecting to take infeftment. She afterwards, with her daughters, underwent great hardships[1]. She was long a prisoner in Blackness Castle, during which period her third daughter, Anne, died within a few miles of her at Linlithgow. The eldest daughter, Jane, was married to Colonel John Erskine of Carnock, but died without issue.

The 2d was Barbara. Her father's forfeiture was rescinded a few months after his death, by a special act of parliament, on the 19th of July 1698, setting forth the illegality of criminal prosecutions being carried on, and forfeitures pronounced by the Justiciary, in absence of the party accused, which was his case, otherwise, " he could easily have vindicated himself," as Woodrow informs us. Barbara, on whom the succession thus devolved, married John Fairlie of that-ilk, but died also without issue.

She was succeeded in the estates of Caldwell by her cousin, William Mure of Glanderston, who was then the heir male, and heir of line of the family. This gentleman was married to Margaret, daughter of Sir George Mowat of Ingleston, Baronet. He was the lineal descendant of William the first of Glanderston, and second son of Sir John above-named.

This William had no issue, and his nephew, William Mure, Esq; of Duncarnock, eldest son of his brother, James Mure of Rhoddens, in Ireland, was the nearest heir, and of provision to the estate. The nephew married Anne, daughter of Sir James Stewart of Goodtrees, Bart. Lord Advocate of Scotland. He died in 1722. He had three daughters; Margaret, and Elizabeth, who died unmarried; and Agnes, married to the Honourable Patrick Boyle of Shewalton, brother of the Earl of Glasgow.

His eldest son was William Mure, Esq; who succeeded his grand-uncle in the year 1728. He was chosen representative in Parliament for this county, in 1742; he continued the member to the year 1761, when he was appointed one of the Barons of Exchequer in Scotland. He sold the estate of Glanderston to Alexander Wilson, Esq; and the estate of Caplerig, which also belonged to the family, to Robert Barclay, Esq; and he purchased from the Duke of Hamilton the Baronies of Wester Caldwell and Cowdon. He built the present stately mansion house of Caldwell, which is situated on a rising ground, in the centre of the estates, on a point of the county of Air, and at the distance of about a mile west from the Old Castle of Caldwell, of which only the principal tower is now standing. He enclosed and improved a great part of the

[1] Woodrow's History.

estate, which is well wooded. In 1752, he married Katherine, daughter of Lord Easdale, one of the Senators of the College of Justice. He left four daughters; 1. Catherine, married to James Rennie, Esq; who left one daughter, married to John Swinton, Esq; of Broadmeadows; 2. Anne; 3. Margaret, deceased; and 4. Elizabeth. His second son, James Mure, Esq; of London, married Fredrica, daughter of C—— Metcalf, Esq; of Hasted, in the county of Suffolk, and has issue. He died in 1776, and was succeeded by

His eldest son, William Mure, Esq; presently of Caldwell, and the representative of the ancient family of Abercorn. He married, in 1791, Anne, daughter of Sir James Hunter Blair of Dunskey, Bart. by whom he has issue, three sons; William, James, and David, and six daughters; 1. Jane, married to The Honourable Major General Sir Charles Colville, G. C. B. brother of Lord Colville; 2. Catharine; 3. Elizabeth; 4. Clementina; 5. Jemima; and, 6. Anne.

ABBEY PARISH OF PAISLEY.

Situation and Extent.—It is situated in the heart of the finest part of the county; bounded on the east by the parishes of Eastwood and Neilston; on the south and south-west by Neilston and Lochwinnoch; on the west, by Kilbarchan, and, on the north, by the parish of Renfrew, and part of Lanarkshire. In extent, it is the third in the county; and by far the most valuable. It is stretched out nine miles in length, from N. E. to S. W. and is six miles broad in a direction across. Were it of a regular figure, these dimensions would indicate ean area of more than 34,500 acres; but it is so very deeply indented on all sides, by corners of conterminous parishes, jutting inwards upon it, that it measures little more than 16,000 acres.

Surface and Soil.—Although there is a greater extent of level country included in this parish than in any other in the county, it is nevertheless much diversified in the surface by heights and hollows, and, in part of it, towards the south, rises into pretty high lands, not much adapted to cultivation. The soil, in general, although not originally of the most fertile quality, has become very productive by cultivation, owing to the great inducement held out to the husbandmen, from the prospect of a ready market for every kind of crop, so constantly in demand in this populous county. In the extent, as above-stated, is included the town of Paisley, which, from its increasing population, was, in 1736, disjoined from the ancient parish, and erected into a distinct parish, and is now divided into three different ministerial charges, independent of it. This town contains little territory beyond the extent of its own streets; perhaps not more than a square mile in all, including the ground on which it stands.

State of Property.—HOUSEHILL. (See page 45.) This property was sold by James Dunlop to a Mr. John Blackburn, whose son, Andrew, in 1750, sold it to Robert Dunlop, second son of Robert Dunlop of Garnkirk, in which family it still remains. There is a handsome mansion on it.

Crockston. This ancient patrimony of the Darnley Stewarts, which, in 1710, belonged to the Duke of Montrose, (see p. 46.) was sold by that family about the year 1757, partly to the Earl of Glasgow, and partly to Sir John Maxwell of Nether Pollok, and continues still in these families.

Cardonald belongs to the present Lord Blantyre, in uninterrupted succession from his ancestor, Lord Blantyre, mentioned by Crawfurd. (See page 57.)

Hawkhead, which, in 1710, belonged to Lord Ross, (see p. 55.) is now the property and chief residence of the Earl of Glasgow, by inheritance, through the marriage of his predecessor, John, 3d Earl of Glasgow, with Elizabeth, only surviving sister of William, 14th Lord Ross, who died in 1754.

Raiss, or Logans Raiss, (see page 56.) has long been the property of the Hawkhead family. It is a fine estate, but there is no mansion upon it.

Raiss, or Stewart's Raiss, (see page 56.) was, after the Stewarts sold it, the property of Mr. Robert Fulton, merchant in Paisley; after whose death, in 1766, it was purchased by Robert Arthur & Co. who again alienated it, in 1780, to Mr. Adair, a bleacher,. It belongs now partly to his heirs, and partly to the Earl of Glasgow. The ruins of the mansion are still pretty entire.

Whiteford, which was once the property of an ancient and most respectable family of the same name, and afterwards became the property of the Dundonald family, (see p. 57.) was, in 1670, by the latter, feued out to different people, among whom the principal was William Kibble, farmer in Knock, whose lineal descendant, James Kibble, Esq; of Whiteford, is the present proprietor. There is no mansion now upon it.

Ralston. This very valuable property, long the patrimony of an ancient family of the same name, was alienated by them, about 100 years ago, to the Earl of Dundonald, from whose family it passed, by marriage, to that of the Duke of Hamilton, from which it was acquired, in 1755, by the late William Macdowall of Castlesemple, and who, in 1800, sold nearly the whole of it to William Orr, Esq; now of Ralston. This gentleman built a very elegant mansion on it, upon a rising ground, finely encircled with thriving plantations, and overlooking a great expanse of a highly embellished country. There were two small parcels of it sold to Mr. Gerard, and to Mr. Smith, who have each erected a very pleasant villa on their respective portions of this beautiful estate.

Cochran. This original possession of the Dundonald family, (see page 82,) has long been out of their hands. In 1788, it was purchased by M'Dowall of Castlesemple from the Trustees of Milliken. At present the greater part belongs to Ludovic Houstoun, Esq; of Johnstone. There is hardly a vestige of the old mansion remaining.

Easter Cochran, or Quarrelton, remains still with the same family who enjoyed it in the time of Crawfurd, (see page 86) namely, Houstoun of Johnstone. There was lately an elegant addition made to the ancient mansion, which is set down under the shade of some fine growing timber, the residence of the present proprietor, Ludovic Houstoun, Esq; of Johnstone.

Elderslie, the ancient property of the renowned Wallace, and which, in Crawfurd's time, was still in a branch of his family, passed from them, by marriage, to Archibald Campbell, Esq; of Succoth, who, in 1769, sold it to the father of the present proprietor, Archibald Speirs, Esq; of Elderslie, who takes his designation from it.

Craigmuir. This property (see page 88) has dwindled into a mere farmstead, and is included in the property of Mr. Speirs.

Newton, which, when Crawfurd wrote, was possessed by the family of Alexander, passed from it, about forty years ago, to the late Alexander Speirs, Esq; and is now the property of his son, Archibald Speirs, Esq; of Elderslie.

Fulbar, then belonging to a very ancient family of the name of Hall, was acquired by Alexander of Newton a short time before he sold his own lands to Mr. Speirs, and he sold Fulbar to him at the same time, and it is also the property now of Archibald Speirs, Esq; of Elderslie.

Stanley, remains still the property of the Ross family, in the person of its representative, the Earl of Glasgow.

Bredieland, still remains in the possession of the same ancient family, whose lineal representative, is the present William Maxwell, Esq; of Bredieland and Merksworth.

Woodside, which, in Crawfurd's time, was possessed by a family of the name of Crawfurd, is now the property of John Sheddan, Esq; whose predecessors bought it, in 1755, from the Crawfurds.

Ferguslie, in the immediate vicinity of Paisley, is now in many hands, of whom several are feuars from former proprietors; but by much the greater part of it is the property of J. Campbell, Esq; W. S. Edinburgh. There are some fine situations for villas on this property, part of which overlooks the town of Paisley and whole country.

Merksworth, which belonged, in Crawfurd's time, (see page 92) to a branch of the family of Maxwell of Bredieland, has reverted, on the death of the late Charles Maxwell of Merksworth, who died without male succession, to the family of Bredieland again.

Blackhall, a Barony of considerable extent, in the immediate vicinity of Paisley, towards the south-east, remains still the property of the ancient family of Stewart, Baronet, of Blackhall and Ardgowan, the direct representative of which, Sir Michael Shaw Stewart, has also the property and title of Greenock. The mansion of Blackhall has long been deserted as a family residence, and has, at present, a very dismal appearance, totally devoid of decoration. Of the beautiful planting, taken notice of by Crawfurd, there does not now exist a single shrub.

One great property still remains to be taken notice of; namely, that part of the Lordship of Paisley, belonging to the Marquis of Abercorn. This was originally of very great extent, as appears from the retour of a charter, dated in 1621, to his ancestor, James, fisrt Earl of Abercorn—and which Lordship included much land in other parts of the country, as well as in the parish of Paisley. This was alienated about the year 1650, to Archibald Earl of Angus, eldest son of the first Marquis of Douglas—and he, in 1653, sold it to William, first Earl of Dundonald, and Lord Paisley, for £160,000 Scots. In this family it continued till 1764, when it was repurchased from Thomas, eight Earl of Dundonald, by James, the eight Earl of Abercorn, the immediate predecessor of the late Marquis. It consists now of the lands of Linclave, Barskevan, Laigh Parks, Brownside, and part of Candrens, &c. all mentioned in the original charter, together with the superiority of the New Town of Paisley.

These are all the estates mentioned by Crawfurd, and it seems probable, that, at the time he wrote, they comprehended the whole parish. There are, indeed, several lesser possessions in the present times, that are not taken notice of by him; but we may conclude, that these at that period formed part of those he described, and were included in them without specification. The number of small properties in this parish is, indeed, very great, as may be seen from the table of property; for, owing to the increasiug wealth of the manufacturing and mercantile classes, many individuals in these, have, by the accumulation of spare capital, (acquired by assiduous attention to business) been enabled to enrol themselves among the landholders of the county, to a greater or less extent, according as they have been more or less successful in business. Indeed, for many years back, whenever a great estate in this county has come to the market, instead of being purchased, as formerly, by some Baron as great as he by whom it was sold, it is split down into three or four, or it may be into a dozen of parts, in order to accommodate people of lesser capitals, who purchase it among them. To these new proprietors on a lesser scale, much of the improved state of the country is owing; more especially for those elegant villas, that are now every where to be found in the neighbourhood of commercial and manufacturing towns. Few places in Scotland abound more in these than the Abbey parish of Paisley, or where they are more tastefully constructed, with all their accompaniments of lawns, gardens, and plantations.

TABLE OF PROPERTY.

Estates, &c.	Proprietors.	Valued Rent Scots. £.	s.	d.	Eng. Acres.
Part of Darnley,	Sir John Maxwell,	229	6	8	
Ross Mackay's part do.	Earl of Glasgow,	89	6	8	
Oakshaw and Sneddon,	Town of Paisley,	1077	6	8	
Ferguslie, part of,	J. Campbell, W.S.	276	6	8	
Hawkhead, Templeland, &c.	Earl of Glasgow,	194	6	8	
Do. Tennant's part of,	Do.	344			
Copperas Company at Hurlet,	Mrs. Lightbody,	10			
Fergualie, feuars' part,	Lorrain Wilson, Muir, &c.	97			
Logan's Raiss,	Earl of Glasgow,	417			
Hillhead,	Do.	153	6	8	
Ingliston,	Do.	240			
Stainly,	Do.	707			
Lownsdale,	John Craig,	18			
Harecraigs,	John White, surgeon,	5			
Corsebar,	Mrs. Holmes,	10			
Cardonald,	Lord Blantyre,	960			
Whiteford,	James Kibble, Esq;	66	13	4	
Small feus off do.	Do.	24	4		
Auchintorlie,	Matthew Brown, Esq;	51			
Part of do.	Mr. Peock, and others,	4	16		
Househill,	James Dunlop, Esq;	400			
Quarrelton,	Ludovic Houstuon, Johnstone;	400			
Elderslie,	Archibald Speirs, Esq;	350			
Blackhall,	Sir Michael Shaw Stewart,	333	6	8	
Ralston, part of,	Robert Orr, Esq;	265			
Do. two separate parts,	R. Smith, and heirs of Gerard,	85			
Thornlie, part of,	John Wilson, Esq;	101			
Do. called Glen,	Robert Barclay, Esq;	24			
Do. Wetlands,	Young & Wilson,	20			

CONTINUATION OF THE

TABLE OF PROPERTY CONTINUED.

Properties.	Proprietors.	Valued Rent Scots.			Eng. Acres.
		£.	s.	d	
Do. Collinslee,	Mr. Adam,	13			
Do. Potterhill,	Rev. ——— Reston,	59			
Do. High Parks,	Charles James Fox Orr, Esq; W.S.	40			
Lylesland, Todholes, &c.	Mr. Robert Orr, and others,	66	13	4	
Greenlaws,	James Kibble, Esq;	66	13	4	
Brabloch,	James Buchanan, Esq;	33	6	8	
Hunterhill,	Sir M. Shaw Stewart,	46	13	4	
Craigs, and Gallowhill,	Rev. ——— Reston,	80			
Thrushcraig,	Sir M. Shaw Stewart	33	6	8	
Raffles,	Earl of Glasgow,	26	13	4	
Candrens, part of,	Lord Douglas,	266	13	4	
Habsland and Benston,	Ludovic Houstoun, Esq;	30			
Easter Corseflat,	Mr. Brown, and others,	80			
Linclave and Barakevan,	Marquis of Abercorn,	400			
Candrens, part of,	Do.	345			
Laigh Parks,	Do.	280			
Brownside,	Do.	133	6	8	
Gallowhill,	James Kibble, Esq;	100			
Dundonald's Meiklerigs,	Robert Fulton, Esq;	70			
Maxwell's, part of,	John Peock,	28			
Riccarsbar, part of,	Robert Fulton, Esq;	14			
Do. do.	George Storie,	30			
Do. do	Adam Keir, Esq;	16			
Do. do.	Robert Wright,	10			
Bughthills,	Marquis of Abercorn,	26	13	4	
Carriagehill, part of,	Mr. Braid and others,	26	13	4	
Part of Cochran,	Ludovic Houstoun of Johnstone,	224	13	4	
Hartfield,	Robert Fulton, Esq;	100			
Fulbar,	Archibald Speirs, Esq;	160			
Newton,	Do. do.	106	13	4	
Bardrain,	Do. do.	66	13	4	
Leitchland,	Do. do.	50			
Arkleston,	Do. do.	400			
Newland Craigs,	Do. do.	25			
Hillington,	Archibald Buchanan, Esq;	400			
Stewart's Raiss, part of,	Earl of Glasgow,	16	13		
Do. and Fordsmouth,	Heirs of J. Adair,	36	13	8	
Greenend,	Sir John Maxwell,	33	6	8	
Cummin's Muirhead,	Archibald Speirs, Esq;	108			
Woodside, &c.	Mr. Sheddan,	56	8	4	
Miller's part of do.	Mr. Menzies,	18	6	8	
Merksworth,	William Maxwell, Esq;	80			
Meiklerigs,	Do. do.	98			
Bredieland,	Do. do.	50			
Wardmeadow,	Do. do.	16			

TABLE OF PROPERTY CONTINUED.

Properties.	Proprietors.	Valued Rent Scots.			Eng. Acres.
		£.	s.	d.	
Auchlodmont, part of,	William King, Esq.	73	6	8	
Do. do	Archibald Speirs, Esq.	53	6	8	
White's Calside,	Barr and others,	16	13	4	
Knavesland,	Mr Barns,	16	13	4	
Stobbs, part of,	R. Fulton, Esq.	7	10		
Do.	Adam Keir, Esq.	2	10		
Thornly, part of,	Mr. Stevenson,	43			
Craiginfeoch, Sempill.	Archibald Speirs, Esq.	133	6	8	
Craiginfeoch and £100 0 0	Ludovic Houstoun, Esq.	292	13	4	
Cochran, 222 13 4	Robert Fulton, Esq.	30			
Total,		11,765	13	4	16160

Which may be arranged thus :—

1. Arable land, or in cultivation, ... 12500
2. Natural pastures, and meadow, ... 1500
3. Moss, sites of houses, roads, waters, &c. 1160
4. Woods or plantations. Few of great extent, but very general in belts and pleasure grounds around the seats of the numerous proprietors, ... 1000

16,160

Succession of Ministers—1573, Mr. Patrick Adamson, a man of great note in his day. He was at one time Archbishop of St. Andrew's, and is well known in the history of the church; died in 1592. 1578, Thomas Smeaton, principal of the College of Glasgow; died in 1581. 1585, Andrew Knox, a younger son of Ramfurlie, afterwards Bishop of the Isles, and lastly of Raphoe, in Ireland, supposed ancestor of Viscount Northland. 1607, Patrick Hamilton. 1626, Robert Boyd of Trochrig, principal of the College of Glasgow. 1627, John Hay, jun. 1629, John Crichton, a man of a singular character; deprived in 1638. 1668, Henry Calvert. 1653, Alexander Dunlop. 1669, Matthew Ramsay. 1672, William Eccles. 1684, John Fullarton. 1688, Anthony Murray. 1689, William Leggat. 1694, Thomas Blackwell. 1700, Thomas Brown, from the 2d charge. 1709, Robert Millar, a man of great worth; died 1752. 1751, James Hamilton, from the 2d charge; died 1782. 1783, Robert Boog, from the 2d charge.

CONTINUATION OF THE

2d Charge commenced with

1641, Mr. John Fullarton chosen—but went to Kilwinning. 1644, Alexander Dunlop—translated to the 1st charge. 1654, James Stirling. 1686, John Taylor. 1698, Thomas Brown, translated to the 1st charge in 1700. —— *Note*, The place vacant until ——. 1722, Robert Mitchel, translated to the town, 1739. 1740. William Fleming, died 1747. 1751, James Hamilton, translated to the 1st charge. 1754, John Rae, died —— 1758, Archibald Davidson, translated to Inchinnan. 1762, Alexander Kennedy, died 1773. 1774, Robert Boog, translated to the 1st charge. 1783, James Mylne, professor of Moral Phil. Glas. 1797. 1798, James Smith; died Jan. 28, 1817. 1818, Patrick Brewster, admitted April 10,

Villages.—There are several populous villages in the vicinity of Paisley, on the high roads leading into it, as Williamsburg on the east; Lylesland on the south; Ferguslie on the west, &c.; but these are so very little separated from it, that they shall be included in the account of the town of Paisley, the next parish to be treated of, although they are all within the bounds of this; as is also the New Town itself of Paisley, one of its most important quarters. There are many small villages, too, in the more remote parts of the parish, that, in a less populous district, might attract particular notice, but they become, singly, of very little importance in this. The only village of much importance is Johnstone, which is indeed the greatest village in the county, and one of the most recent origin, as it is only 36 years since it began to be feued out on a regular and extended plan. Previous to this it was a small hamlet, consisting of a few cottages by the side of the Black Cart, over which was a bridge on the road leading to the mansion of Johnstone, (now Milliken) from which this small place, chearful enough of itself, was called The Brig of Johnstone, a name still applied in ordinary to the magnificent village that has so very lately been erected in its vicinity. This town is situated three miles west from Paisley, within less than half a mile of the high road to Ayrshire by Beith. It is laid out in a regular plan of one main street from east to west, 40 feet broad, and has now three streets across from south to north, of 40 feet in breadth also; and there is room to extend the town either in length or breadth, as occasion may require, all on nearly a level field, that is elevated a small degree above the adjacent country. The houses are handsomely composed, of good mason work, two storeys high, with slated roofs. To each house there is attached an adequate extent of ground for a garden, which forms one of the most gratifying luxuries that a villager can ave. Johnstone increased so rapidly, that, in 1792, only ten years from its first erection, it had a population of 1434 souls, and continued still so much to prosper, that, in 1811, there were 3,647 inhabitants, and, as it has never ceased to thrive, it is thought that now (1818,) there cannot be fewer than 5000. The great source of employment for all this population, (which is just so many additional inhabitants to the country) is the cotton works. There are some very large buidings, or mills, erected for the purpose, the machinery of which is, in some cases, put in motion by water, and, in others, by steam. In 1792, a Chapel of Ease, capable of containing 1000 people, was built here by subscription, and since that period a clergyman has officiated in it regularly. The projected canal from Glasgow to Ardrossan has been completed as far as this town. From the former, at about 11 miles of distance. On this there is a regular establishment of track boats twice a-day, with excellent accommodation for passengers; and goods of all kinds are transmitted, at all times, as may be required, on long open boats adapted for the purpose ; and it is gratifying to see, that they are very much employed, the traffic being very considerable to and from that great manufacturing and commercial city, and also Paisley, through which the canal passes.

Manufactures.—The account of these in the Abbey parish, will be included in that of the town of Paisley.

Family Descent.—HAMILTON, MARQUIS OF ABERCORN.—This chief branch of the great House of Hamilton, is descended from the Ducal family of that name, whose origin and descent falls first to be discussed; and which shall be as concisely related as consists with perspicuity.

The descent of the House of Hamilton is allowed to have been from the potent Earls of Leicester, whose immediate ancestor was Robert de Bellomonte, Earl of Mellent, &c. who came to England in 1066, with William, Duke of Normandy, and, at the battle of Hastings, commanded the right wing of the Norman army.

What particular branch of this family assumed the name of Hamilton, or at what particular period, the great antiquaries, Dugdale and Archdale, are not agreed; but the first of them, mentioned in Scottish annals, (on the authority of Wood, from whose very interesting work this is abridged) was subscriber to a charter,

I. Gilbert de Hamildun, clerico, recorded in the Chartulary of Paisley, in the year 1272. It seems probable, from other subscriptions in charters, that he was father to,

II. Sir Walter filius Gilberti de Hamilton, who swore fealty to Edward I.

in 1292. His second son, John, had the lands of Innerwick and was ancestor of the Earls of Haddington; his eldest son,

III. Sir David, succeeded him in the lands of Kinniel and Cadyow. He died in 1374; and was succeeded by his eldest son,

IV. Sir David Hamylton, who at that time was proprietor of the lands of Cloneschynach[1], Bernys, and Auldlandis, in the Barony of Renfrew. He was succeeded by his eldest son,

V. Sir John de Hamilton. He had three sons; 1. Sir James; 2. David, ancestor of the Hamiltons of Dalserf, Blackburn, Allershaw, Ladyland, Green, &c. 3. Thomas, ancestor of the Hamiltons of Raploch, Torrence, Darngaber, Stenhouse, Woodhall, Holmhead, Dechmont and Barns; also, the Earls of Clanbrassil, and other families in Ireland.

VI. Sir James of Cadyow, the eldest son, succeeded his father. His son, Gavin, was ancestor of the Hamiltons of Dalziel, Orbistoun, Haggs, Kilbrackmont, Monkland, Bothwelhaugh, Parkhead, and Bar. His eldest son,

VII. Sir James, succeeded his father before the year 1445, when he was created a Lord of Parliament, by the title of Lord Hamilton. In 1454, he joined The Douglas against James II. but left his party very opportunely, on the night before the expected battle; on which the army of Douglas, (40,000 strong) slunk away, every man to his own home, as fast as he could, which occasioned the downfal of that overgrown house, and the further elevation of the House of Hamilton. He died in 1479. By his second Lady, the Princess Mary, daughter of James II. (with whom he got the island of Arran, which the family still enjoys) he had,

VIII. James, second Lord Hamilton and first Earl of Arran. By his third Lady, daughter of Sir David Betoun, he had,

IX. James, the eldest son, second Earl of Arran. On the death of James V. in 1542, Arran was unanimously chosen Regent of Scotland, and next year, by the estates of Parliament, was declared first Prince of the blood, and next heir to the throne, failing Queen Mary or her issue. In 1548, he had the title of Duke of Chatelherault conferred on him by the King of France. He died 22d Jan. 1574-5. He married Lady Margaret, daughter of James, third Earl of Morton, by whom he had issue, four sons.

---

[1] Probably what is now called Abbot's-inch, as belonging at one time to the Abbot of Paisley, or to the Abbot of the order of Clunie, at Paisley. Hence Clunie's-inch, Barns and Allands, are the modern names of the two other places mentioned. All three, are in the neighbourhood of each other, and belong now to Lord Douglas.

X. Lord Claud Hamilton, fourth son of the second Earl of Arran, was a brave and gallant gentleman; and, during the discords that prevailed under the unhappy reign of Queen Mary, he adhered to her interest in all her misfortunes. After the battle of Langside, in May 1568, he was outlawed by the Regent Murray, and his estates forfeited. During the regency of the Earl of Mar, his lands were given to Lord Sempill, and during the regency of Morton, he continued a sharer of the oppressions that bore down the Hamilton family. At last, when the King took the management of affairs into his own hands, he restored to them all their estates and honours; and, in particular, to Lord Claud and his heirs male, or assigns, he bestowed the Lordship and Barony of Paisley, with the pertinents and monastery there, in 1585; and further, raised him to the dignity of the Peerage, by the title of Lord Paisley, in 1587. He died in 1621, aged 78. By his lady, a daughter of Lord Seton, he had a daughter married to the Marquis of Douglas; and had four sons, of whom, the three younger, the Honourable Sir Claud, the Honourable Sir George, and the Honourable Sir Frederick, had all considerable property in Ireland; the last in particular, and who was ancestor of the present Viscount of Boyne, in that kingdom. The eldest son,

XI. James, Master of Paisley, was, in his father's lifetime, created, first, Baron, and then Earl (1606) of Abercorn. He also had a large grant of lands in Ireland, in the Barony of Strabane, on which he built a strong and fair Castle. He died before his father in 1617. By his lady, a daughter of Lord Boyd, he had issue, five sons and three daughters. Of the sons, the 2. Claud, Lord Strabane, and the 4. the Honourable Sir George Hamilton, will be taken notice of afterwards.

XII. James, the eldest son, was second Earl of Abercorn; and when he was a very young man, in his father's lifetime, he was created Lord Hamilton of Strabane, in Ireland, a title that he afterwards resigned to his next brother, Claud, who thus became Lord Strabane. On the death of the last Duke of Hamilton of that name, in 1657, he became the male representative and chief of that family, although the titles, as well as estates, were settled on that Duke's daughter, Anne, Duchess of Hamilton. He married the Dowager, Duchess of Lenox and Richmond, and by her had issue. 1. James Lord Paisley, who predeceased his father. He married Catherine, daughter of Lentthall, speaker of the House of Commons, in the Long Parliament, and by her had an only daughter, Catherine, of whom afterwards.

XIII. George, third Earl of Abercorn, was the eldest son; he died unmarried, and this male line became extinct. The family was now carried on by,

XII. Claud, second Lord Strabane, 2d son of James, the first Earl, who died in 1638. By a daughter of the Marquis of Huntly he had two sons,

XIII. James, the eldest, was third Lord Strabane; he was drowned bathing in 1655; he had no issue.

XIV. George, fourth Lord Strabane, his brother, succeeded him. He died in 1668. He married Elizabeth, sole heiress of Christopher Fagan of Felham, by whom he had two sons.

XV. Claud, the eldest, succeeded his father, and was fifth Lord Strabane. He became also the fourth Earl of Abercorn. He took the part of James II. in the wars in Ireland, at the revolution. He was killed on a voyage to France in 1690. His estate and title of Strabane were forfeited. The title of Abercorn devolved on his brother,

XV. Charles, fifth Earl of Abercorn. He obtained, in 1692, a reversal of his brother's attainder, and succeeded thus to both the title and the estate of Strabane. He married, but had no surviving issue. He died in 1701, and this branch also became extinct. The titles now devolved on the issue of,

XII. Sir George Hamilton, 4th son of James Lord Paisley, (see No. XI.) He was on the side of Charles I. in the civil wars; retired into France, after that King's death; returned, at the restoration, and, from Charles II. had a singular grant (probably a lucrative, though certainly an invidious one) of all the fines that might accrue to the Crown, by reason of plowing, drawing, and working with horses by the tail, contrary to acts of parliament. He married Mary, sister to the first Duke of Ormond, by whom he had six sons and three daughters. Of his younger sons, perhaps, the most distinguished was the third son, Count Antony Hamilton, who was a Lieutenant General in the service of France, and died in April 1720, aged 74, much esteemed by all who knew him. He was the author of the admirable Memoirs de Gramont. His sister, Elizabeth, after refusing several of the best matches in England, preferred that adept in dissipation, Philibert Count de Gramont to them all. He was reckoned the chief ornament in the Court of Charles II.—none could boast a nobler birth—none more worthy of esteem—and none more charming in person. His eldest son,

XIII. James, was one of the grooms of the bed-chamber to Charles II. who made him Colonel of a regiment of foot. He died in consequence of having a leg taken off by a cannon ball, in a sea fight with the Dutch in 1673. He married Elizabeth, daughter of Lord Colepepper, by whom he had three sons. The eldest son,

XIV. James, was brought up also at the Courts of Charles II. and James II.

and had good appointments, but perceiving the intention of the latter was to introduce Popery, he early entered into the party of King William, and served in his armies with distinguished ability during the Irish wars at that time. On the death of Charles, Earl of Abercorn, as above, he became the sixth Earl, in 1701, and also Lord Strabane, which title was raised in his favour to that of Viscount. At the treaty of Utrecht, in 1713, he preferred his claim of indemnification from the French court for the Dukedom of Chatelherault, as being heir male of the first Duke. It seems probable that there was a comprmoise, on this subject, betwixt him and the Hamilton family, who accepted of 500,000 livres for it, from the court of France. He died in 1734, and was buried in Henry VII's. chapel, Westminster. By his Lady, Elizabeth, heiress of Sir Robert Reading, he had,

XV. James, seventh Earl of Abercorn. He died in Jan. 1744. He married Anne, daughter of Colonel John Plumer, and by her he had six sons and one daughter. His second son, the Honourable John Hamilton, bred to the royal navy, he was a very gallant and brave officer. He was lost by his boat oversetting, in going from his ship, the Lancaster, of 66 guns, to Portsmouth, in Dec. 1755. He married Harriet, daughter of Mr. Secretary Craggs; by her had a daughter, who died unmarried, and a posthumous son, John James, of whom afterwards. His eldest son, who succeeded him, was

XVI. James, eighth Earl of Abercorn. His Lordship had no property in Scotland till, in 1745, he purchased the Barony of Duddingston from Archibald, Duke of Argyle, near Edinburgh, where he built an elegant and dignified mansion, and made it his favourite residence. In 1764, he acquired the paternal estate of his ancestors, the Lordship of Paisley, from the Earl of Dundonald. He laid out a new town there, on a regular plan, with one of the best inns in Scotland. He also built a magnificent house at Baron's Court, near Londonderry. He had a seat also at Witham in Essex, where, on the 7th Sept. 1761, he gave a most loyal and hospitable reception to her Majesty Queen Charlotte, who slept there, on her journey from Harwich to London. He was a nobleman who possessed singular vigour of mind, integrity of conduct, and patriotic views. His Lordship died, going from Duddingston to London, on the 9th of October 1789, in the 77th year of his age, and was buried in the ancient family vault in the Abbey of Paisley. He was never married. He was succeeded by his nephew, son of the Honourable John Hamilton of the royal navy,

XVII. John James, ninth Earl of Abercorn, who, on the 1st Oct. 1790, was advanced to the dignity of a British Peer, by the title of Marquis of Abercorn, &c. His Lordship married, first, in June 1779, Catherine, daughter of Sir Joseph Copley of Sprotborough, and by her, who died at the Priory, 13th September 1791, had two sons and four daughters.

XVIII. 1. James, Viscount Hamilton, born 1786, married Catherine, daughter of the Honourable John Douglas, by whom he had issue. His Lordship died in 1814, and his widow married soon after the Earl of Aberdeen; who had previously been married to his sister as below, the Honourable Lady Catherine Hamilton, who died in 1812; 2. Lord Claud Hamilton, died in 1808; 3. Lady Harriet Margaret Hamilton, who died after a short illness, in 1803, after being contracted to the Marquis of Waterford; 4. Lady Catherine Constantia, died in infancy; 5. Lady Catherine, married, in 1805, to the Earl of Aberdeen. Died in 1812, leaving issue; 6. Lady Maria. The Marquis married, secondly, his cousin, Lady Cecil Hamilton, daughter of his uncle, the Honourable George Hamilton, a churchman. This Lady his Lordship divorced in 1799, and she was the same year married to Colonel Copley, a younger son of the family of Sprotborough, of whom his Lordship's first Lady. By this Lady, the Marquis had a daughter; 7. Lady Cecil Frances, born in 1795. His Lordship, thirdly, married, in 1800, Lady Anne Jane Gore, daughter of the Earl of Arran. John James, Marquis of Abercorn, died on the 27th January 1818, and was succeeded by his grandson,

XIX. son of the late James, Viscount Hamilton, and who is now the second Marquis of Abercorn, and 19th generation from Gilbert de Hamyldun, common ancester of all the families of the name of Hamilton.

COCHRAN EARL OF DUNDONALD.—William Lord Cochran, (see p. 85) succeeded his father in 1720, and became fifth Earl of Dundonald. He died in 1725, at the age of 17. He was succeeded by his cousin,

Thomas, son of William Cochran of Kilmaronock, who was the sixth Earl of Dundonald. He died in 1737. He married Catherine, daughter of Lord Basil Hamilton, by whom he had his successor,

William, seventh Earl of Dundonald. He was killed at the siege of Louisburg in 1758. Dying unmarried, the titles devolved on a distant relation, the grandson of the Honourable Sir John Cochran of Ochiltree, who was the second son of William, first Earl of Dundonald, who died in 1686. This was Thomas Cochran of Culross, a commissioner of excise in Scotland, and who had formerly represented the County of Renfrew in Parliament. He now became eighth Earl of Dundonald, and died at his seat of La Mancha, in the Shire of Peebles, in 1778. By his second lady, Jean, daughter of Archibald Stuart of Torrence, he had a numerous issue, of whom, ten arrived at mature age, and several of them have attained to high rank and distinction in the army or navy, or in the civil service of the country in particular.

HISTORY OF THE SHIRE OF RENFREW. 323

The Honourable Sir Alexander Forrester Cochrane, Knight, G. C. B. was bred to the sea, and has been one of the bravest, the most active, and among the most successful commanders in the royal navy, and this, too, in an age when the British flag never before waved so proudly over the enemies of the country.

Archibald, the eldest son, born in 1748, succeeded him, and is the ninth Earl of Dundonald. He went early into the army, but quitted that service for the navy, and afterwards, applying his talents to scientific pursuits, his Lordship, by the strength of his uncommon genius, has made several chemical discoveries, which, in practice, have turned out to be essentially useful. By his first lady, Anne, daughter of Captain James Gilchrist, a brave naval officer, his Lordship has had six children, of whom three sons are still living, all of whom have distinguished themselves most gallantly in the service of their country—more especially his eldest son,

Thomas Lord Cochrane, who was born in December 1775—entered first into the army, and was a Captain in the 106th regiment. But quitting the army for the sea service, his Lordship has performed some of the most daring exploits perhaps on record. Whatever difference of opinion may be formed as to his politics, there can be but one as to the intrepid bravery of his personal character. This very ancient family has no territory now in Scotland attached to the title but the old Castle of Dundonald, and about fifteen acres around it, in the parish of Dundonald in Ayrshire.

Ross LORD Ross, continued from page 56. William, twelfth Lord Ross, took an opposite side in politics from his father. He entered with great zeal into the revolution, and was a privy counsellor to King William and Queen Anne; and was, in 1704, high commissioner to the Church of Scotland, and one of the Lords of the treasury. He was a steady promoter of the Union; and one of the Scottish peers in Parliament. He died in 1738, in the 82d year of his age. He married, first, the daughter and heiress of Sir John Wilkie of Fouldean, and by her had a son, George, 13th Lord Ross, and three daughters; 1. Kon. Eupheme Ross, married the Earl of Kilmarnock, and had issue; 2. Hon. Mary Ross, married the Duke of Atholl, and had issue; 3. Hon. Grizel Ross, married Sir James Lockhart of Carstairs, and to whom she had six sons.

1. Sir William Lockhart of Carstairs. He was killed accidentally at Boroughmuirhead, by leaping out of his carriage in June 1758, on account of the horses having become unmanageable, and left two daughters, one of whom died unmarried; the other married Bertram of Kersewell, to whom she had a numerous issue.

2. Sir James Ross of Balnagowan, who was a Major General in the army, and died without issue in 1760. The third and fourth sons died unmarried. The sixth son was Thomas Lockhart, Esq; a commissioner of excise, who died in 1779, which branch is now represented by the daughters of his son Charles Lockhart of Newhall, who died without issue male in 1804.

The fifth son was Admiral Sir John Lockhart Ross, an officer of great distinction in the British navy, and no less eminent in the arts of peace than of war, as his judicious improvements on the estate of Balnagowan (to which he succeeded in 1760, on the death of his brother Sir James,) bear witness. He died in June 1790, in the 69th year of his age. He married Elizabeth Baillie, heiress of the ancient family of Lamington, (lineally descended of the renowned Wallace, the Guardian of Scotland,) and also heiress of Sir James Carmichael of Boningtoun, both in the county of Lanark. By this lady, (daughter of Robert Dundas of Arniston, late president of the court of session,) he had three daughters, who died unmarried, and five sons; 1. Sir Charles Ross of Balnagowan, who was a Lieutenant-General in the army. He was Knight of the Shire for the county of Ross, from 1796 to 1806. He died in 1813. He married, first, in 1778, Maria Teresa, daughter of Count Lockart, and by her had a son who died young, and a daughter, Matilda, who, on the death of her uncle, Count Lockhart, succeeded to her ancestor, Sir George Wishart's estate of Old Liston, and assumed the name of Wishart. She married, in 1812, Captain Sir Thomas Cochrane, royal navy, to whom she has two children; 1. Maria Teresa; 2. Alexander Dundas Ross. Sir Charles Ross married, secondly, in 1799, Lady Mary Fitzgerald, daughter of the Duke of Leinster, by whom he had five daughters and one son, now Sir Charles Ross of Balnagowan, born 19th January 1811; 2. James, who was a captain in the royal navy. He married Catherine, the only surviving child and heirers of Farquharson of Invercauld. He died in 1809, leaving a son, James, now of Invercauld, and two daughters; 3. George, an advocate, married Grace, eldest daughter of the Rev. Andrew Hunter, D. D. by whom he has issue; 4. John, was a Lieutenant-Colonel in the army, fell at the battle of Talavera in July 1809; 5. Robert, first Major in the 4th regiment of dragoon guards. Lord Ross married, 2dly, a daughter of Lord Wharton; 3dly, a daughter of the Marquis of Tweedale; 4thly, a daughter of Sir Francis Scott of Thirlestane, but no surviving issue now of any of these marriages.

XX. George, 13th Lord Ross, held different appointments under government, and died in June 1754, in the 73d year of his age. He married Lady Elizabeth Kerr, daughter of the Marquis of Lothian, by whom he had, 1. William, 14th Lord Ross; 2. Hon. Charles Ross of Balnagowan, who was killed at the battle of Fontenoy, 30th April 1745, unmarried. That estate devolved on his father; 3. Hon. George Ross, died without issue; 4. Hon. Jane Ross, married John Mackye of Polgowan, died without issue; 5. Hon. Elizabeth Ross, married in June 1755, to the Earl of Glasgow; 6. Hon. Mary Ross, died unmarried.

XXI. William, 14th Lord Ross, succeeded his father in 1754, but enjoyed the honours and estate only two months. He died on the 19th August 1754, unmarried, and the title became extinct. The estate of Balnagowan went to his cousin, Sir James Ross Lockhart, after an ineffectual opposition from Sir Alexander Gilmour, and his other property devolved on his three sisters, and ultimately, on the decease of the eldest, without issue, and youngest unmarried, the whole came to the second, Elizabeth, Countess of Glasgow, and is now the inheritance of her son, the present Earl of Glasgow.

BOYLE EARL OF GLASGOW.—The descent of this very ancient family, as it is comparatively recent in the county of Renfrew, shall commence no farther back than with that distinguished person, who was the first in the family promoted to the Peerage by King William, who was the eighth generation recorded by Wood in the Peerage, from John Boyle of Kelburn, who was killed, on the side of James III. at the battle of Bannockburn in 1488.

David Boyle of Kelburn, son of John Boyle of Kelburn, by a sister of Sir Walter Stewart of Allanton, was member for Buteshire in the convention Parliament, 1689. Was a privy counsellor in 1697, and was raised to the peerage, in 1699, by the title of Lord Boyle. In January 1703, was appointed Treasurer-depute, and in April following, was further dignified with the title of Earl of Glasgow, &c. to him and his heirs male whatsoever. He was a steady supporter of the Protestant succession. He had a principal share in carrying on the treaty of union, and was one in the first set of the representatives of the Peers of Scotland in the British Parliament, in 1707. He represented Her Majesty in the general assembly of the church, from 1706 to 1710 inclusive; he was also appointed Lord Register of Scotland in 1708, and held it till 1714. In the rebellion, 1715, he offered to raise and maintain 1000 men on his own charges for the support of Government. In short, no nobleman in Scotland took a more active part in his day than himself for the best interests of his country, He died in November 1733. By his first Lady, Margaret, sister of the Viscount of Garnock, he had issue: 1. John, second Earl of Glasgow; 2. Honourable Patrick Boyle of Shewalton, a Lord of Session. Died in March 1761, unmarried; 3. Honourable Charles Boyle, died unmarried; 4. Honourable William Boyle, died 1704. His Lordship married, secondly, Jean, daughter and heiress of Mure of Rowallan, and by her had, 1. Lady Jean, heiress of

Rowallan, married Sir James Campbell, K. B. killed at Fontenoy 1745; was mother of Hugh, fifth Earl of Loudon, and grandmother of the Countess of Loudon, now Marchioness of Hastings; 2. Lady Anne, died unmarried.

John, second Earl of Glasgow, succeeded to the titles and property in 1733, died in 1479, in the 53d year of his age. He married Helen, daughter of Morison of Prestongrange, and by her had issue, besides one who died young; 1. John, third Earl of Glasgow; 2. Honourable Patrick Boyle of Shewalton, a gentleman distinguished through a long course of life for every virtuous and honourable disposition. He died at Irvine, 26th February 1788. By his Lady, Elizabeth, daughter of Alexander Dunlop, professor of Greek in the University of Glasgow, he had issue: 1. William, a Lieutenant in the army, died young; 2. Colonel John Boyle of Shewalton; 3. Alexander, in the royal navy, died young; 4. The Right Honourable David Boyle, Esq; Lord Justice Clerk. He was admitted a member of the faculty of Advocates 1793; appointed Solicitor General of Scotland, in May 1807; next month was, at the general election, chosen member of Parliament for the county of Ayr, and was constituted a Lord of Session and of Justiciary, and Lord Justice Clerk, in February 1811. He married, 24th December 1804, Elizabeth, daughter of Alexander Montgomery of Annick Lodge, next brother of Hugh, 12th Earl of Eglinton, and has issue: 1. Patrick; 2. Elizabeth; 3. Helen; 4. Alexander. His daughters were, 1. Helen, married, in 1791, to Thomas Mure of Warriston, descended of the family of Caldwell, and he had issue; 2. Elizabeth, married, in 1800, to John Smollet Rouet of Bonhill, and has issue; and two who died young. The daughters of the second Earl of Glasgow, were six, all of whom died unmarried, except the youngest, Lady Helen, who married Admiral Sir James Douglas of Springwood Park, but died without issue, in 1794.

John, third Earl of Glasgow, was born in November 1714, and succeeded his father in 1740: was bred to the Army: was wounded at the battle of Fontenoy in 1745, and again severely at the battle of Lauffeld, in 1747. He represented his Majesty, as Lord high Commissioner to the general assembly, from 1764 till 1772, inclusive. He died in March 1775. He married Elizabeth, second daughter of George, 12th Lord Ross, who became at last sole heiress to the estates of that opulent and very ancient family. By this Lady, who died in October 1791, he had issue: 1. John, Lord Boyle, who died young; 2. George, fourth Earl of Glasgow; 3. Lady Elizabeth, married, in 1786, Sir George Douglas of Springwood Park, and had issue. She died in February 1801; 4. Lady Jane.

George, fourth Earl of Glasgow, born 26th March 1766. His Lordship has been in various stations, in the fencible and militia service. He resigned the situation of Colonel of the Renfrewshire Militia in 1806. He was constituted Lord Lieutenant of that county in April 1810. He was chosen one of the sixteen representatives of the Scottish Peerage in parliament, at the general election in 1790, and at every subsequent election till, in 1815, when he was elevated to the rank of a British Peerage, by the stile and title of Lord Ross of Hawkhead, in the county of Renfrew, which has been the designation and residence of his maternal ancestors for more than three hundred years.

He married, 4th August 1788, Lady Augusta Hay, born 25th April 1766, third daughter of James, fourteenth Earl of Errol, and by her, who, in 1806, succeeded to her grandfather, Sir William Carr's estate of Etal, has issue,

1. John Lord Boyle, born in August 1789, bred to the royal navy, in which service he signally distinguished himself for valour and intrepidity. He died 6th March 1818. 2. Lady Isabella.

3. James, an officer in the R. N. now viscount Kelburn; 4. Lady Elizabeth; 5. Lady Augusta; 6. Honourable William Boyle.

Titles.—Earl of Glasgow, Viscount of Kelburn, Lord Boyle of Kelburn, Stewarton, Cumbra, Fenwick, Largs, and Dalry, Scottish titles; and Lord Ross of Hawkhead, a British Peerage.

Arms.—Quarterly; first and fourth, Or; an Eagle displayed, Gules, as a Coat of Augmentation, on the Creation of the Earldom, being formerly the Crest of the family: second and third, parted per bend, Crenelle, Argent; and Gules for the surname of Boyle. Over all an escutcheon, three Harts' Horns, Gules; two and one for Kelburn. Crest, an Eagle with Two Heads displayed, parted per pale, Crenelle, Or, and Gules.

Supporters.—Dexter, a Savage, Proper; Sinister, a Lion Rampant, parted her bend, Crenelle, Argent and Gules.

Motto.—" Dominus Providebit."

Seats.—Kelburn House, in Ayrshire; Hawkhead, in Renfrewshire; and Etal, in Northumberland.

Note.—Although the family of Boyle has not been traced farther back than twelve generations to the present Viscount Kelburn, son of the fourth Earl of Glasgow, yet, in Wood's Peerage, it is traced back 200 years farther; but, as a descendant of the house of Ross, his Lordship is the 23d generation direct, as traced by Wood in the Peerage, (from which the account here given, is an abridgement). It is to be remarked, that the Renfrewshire family of Ross Lord Ross, is quite unconnected with the clan Ross in Rosshire, descendants of the ancient family of Ross, Earls of Ross, the main stem of which became extinct

350 years ago. Crawfurd derives the Hawkhead family of Ross, from Ross of Wark, (in Northumberland). Wood derives it from Ros, of Ros, in Yorkshire. In either case, it is evidently of English origin; although, in modern times, a great branch of the family (Balnagowan) has gone to Rosshire, the native country of the Celtic family of Ross.

DUNLOP OF HOUSEHILL.—James Dunlop of that-ilk, (see page 45), had four sons, of whom the eldest succeeded to the ancient family title and inheritance of Dunlop in Ayrshire; the second acquired the estate of Garnkirk, in Lanarkshire; the third, the lands of Craig, in Ayrshire; and the fourth, Thomas, purchased the lands of Househill in 1646. This estate continued in the family till near the year 1750, when it was conveyed to Robert Dunlop, second son of James Dunlop of Garnkirk, who married Janet, second daughter of Archibald Buchanan of Drumhead, Dumbartonshire, by whom he had issue, 1. James Dunlop, now of Househill, Colonel of the Renfrewshire Militia, who succeeded his father in 1762, and who married Elizabeth, daughter of John Buchanan, Esq; of London, second son of Gilbert Buchanan of Bunkle in Stirlingshire, and has four daughters, coheiresses. 2. Robert, who succeeded to the lands of Drumhead, as heir of entail, and married Frances, daughter of Samuel Beachcroft, Esq; London, by whom he has three sons and a daughter; 3. Lilias, married to Robert Muirhead, Esq; of Croy, merchant in Glasgow; 4. Dorothy, married to Robert Finlay Esq; merchant, Glasgow, now deceased, by whom she has a son and —— daughters.

HOUSTOUN OF JOHNSTONE.—Ludovick Houstoun, (see page 82.) married Agnes, daughter of Walkinshaw of that-ilk, by whom he had two sons; 1. George, 2. Ludovick, and three daughters, Jean, Rachel and Anne; the eldest son, George, who succeeded him, died unmarried in 1757, and was succeeded by his nephew, George, the son of the second brother, Ludovick, by Jean Rankine, who died in 1805.

George Houstoun of Johnstone, married first, Mary, daughter of Colonel William Macdowal of Castlesemple, by whom he had two sons, Ludovic and William Macdowall. This lady died in 1782, and in 1805 he married, 2dly, Anne, daughter of Walkinshaw of that-ilk, who died in 1810 without issue. He himself died in 1815, and was succeeded by the eldest son of the first marriage, Ludovic Houstoun, Esq; now of Johnstone. He married, on the 6th November 1809, Anne, daughter of John Stirling, Esq; of Kippendavie, by whom he has issue, George, born 31st July 1810.

The estate was much improved and greatly embellished by the late proprietor, who also, in 1812, made a large addition to the mansion house, and has likewise increased the estate by some very extensive purchases. These will appear in the different tables of property in the parishes of Paisley and Lochwinnoch. Every article, separate from Quarrelton in the county-books, having been recent purchases.

HALL OF FULBAR, from page 88. Robert Hall last-mentioned, married Margaret, daughter of John Maxwell of Dargeval, by whom he had issue John Hall, who succeeded to the estate of Dargeval, and assumed the name of Maxwell. See Dargeval, Erskine parish.

MAXWELL OF BREDIELAND, & MAXWELL OF MERKSWORTH, from page 89. They are said to be a branch of the Maxwells of Caerlaverock. The last-mentioned John Maxwell of Bredieland's grandfather was Gavin, who married Catherine Hamle, a daughter of the family of Roughwood, by whom he had Hugh, his son and heir, who married Janet, daughter of Rowan of Dumbreck, by whom he had three sons; 1. John, the last mentioned by Crawfurd; 2. James; 3. Gavin. John married Marion, daughter of ——— Alexander of Blackhouse, by whom he had a daughter, Janet, who succeeded her father in Bredieland, and married her cousin, John Maxwell of Castlehead, son of her father's brother, Gavin, by whom she had James Maxwell of Bredieland, who married Catherine, daughter of the Rev. William Orr, minister of Spott, by whom he had a son, William, who succeeded him in 1766. He married a daughter of the Rev. Matthew Moncrief of Culfargie in Perthshire, by whom he had issue, 1. James, his apparent heir; 2. Matthew, late a lieutenant in the 70th regiment, who died in the West Indies about nine years ago, leaving a daughter by his marriage with a daughter of Major Lawson. 3. Anne Scott; 4. Catherine, married Richard Jermont, merchant, London. 5. Hope Margaret; and 6. Jean. On the death of his cousin, Charles Maxwell of Merksworth, he succeeded to that branch of the family, which was descended thus:

James, the 2d son of Hugh Maxwell, (vide supra) of Bredieland, acquired the lands of Merksworth, from the Algoes of Easter Walkinshaw. He died without issue, and was succeeded, through his own deed of entail, by his nephew, the 3d son of Gavin Maxwell of Castlehead. He, by his second wife, Janet, daughter of John Leckie of Croy Leckie, in Dumbartonshire, had a son, Charles, who married, Anne, eldest daughter of James Maxwell of Williamwood, (see page 270) by whom he had two sons, James, who died young, and Henry, who died unmarried, He had also five daughters, John, Janet, Ann, Annabella, and Elizabeth. When he died himself, in 1789, the representation not only of Merksworth, but of Williamwood, devolved on his daughter, Miss John, (see Williamwood Genealogy, 270,) but the property of Merksworth, by the preceding deed of entail, fell to William Maxwell of Bredieland, as above, the present proprietor. There is a neat small mansion on the lands of Merksworth, pleasantly situated on the left bank of the Cart, about a mile north from Paisley.

RALSTON OF THAT-ILK.—From page 58. Gavin Ralston of that-ilk, was son of William Ralston of that-ilk, by Ursula Mure, a daughter of the family of Caldwell. He married Anne, daughter of William Porterfield of Porterfield, by whom he had a son, William, and four daughters; 1. Ursula, married Robert Barr of Treehorn, Esq; 2. Annabella, to James Maxwell of Williamwood; 3. Jean, to John Sheddan of Roughwood; 4. Catherine, to the Rev. John Fullarton of Dalry; they all had issue. William, who succeeded him, married Marion, heiress of the Rev. David Ewing, minister of Calder, by whom he had; 1. Gavin; 2. Margaret, who married the Rev. John Fleming, Kilmacolm; 3. Anne, to William Caldwell, Yardfoot, both had issue. He died about 1745, and was succeeded by Gavin Ralston of that-ilk, his only son, who married Annabella, a coheiress of Pollok of Arthurlie, by Jean, a daughter of Sir Robert Pollok of that-ilk, by whom he had issue.

ORR OF RALSTON.—The late William Orr, Esq; of Ralston, was the second son of Robert Orr, manufacturer in Paisley. He went to Ireland in his youth, where, along with his brother, John Orr, Esq; of Dublin, he introduced and brought to great perfection the art of printing linens. There, by an assiduous attention to business, and an integrity in his transactions, that procured him unbounded confidence, he acquired a handsome fortune, with which he returned to his native place about the end of the last century. In 1797, he acquired, from the Earl of Glasgow, part of the lands of Ingliston, on which he built one of the most elegant villas in the county. About two years after, when the late William Macdowall, Esq; of Castlesemple, was disposing of the adjacent Barony of Ralston, about a mile and a half east from Paisley, he purchased the greater part of it—and called his whole property there by the name of Ralston. He married Margaret, daughter of the late James Kibble, Esq; of Whiteford, by whom he had three sons and four daughters. He died in 1812, and was succeeded by his eldest son, Robert Orr, Esq; now of Ralston, who married Miss Anne Duffie of Dublin.

FULTON OF HARTFIELD.—The late Humphrey Fulton, manufacturer in Paisley, was the first that introduced the silk manufacture into that town, which was afterwards carried on to such an extent as to give employment to 5000 looms, and produce £350,000 worth of goods yearly. In the progress of this concern, so highly beneficial to the country at large, he acquired a handsome fortune to himself. He died in 1779. He married Mary Cochrane, by whom he had, 1. William Fulton, now of Park of Inchinnan, who acquired that property in 1789. He maried Marion, daughter of the late Rev. Henry Millar, Minister of Neilston, by whom he has, 1. Henry, a merchant in London; 2. William, a manufacturer in Paisley, who has issue a son and daughter; also a daughter, Elizabeth.

2. Robert Fulton of Hartfield, a property he acquired in 1789, from which he takes his designation, though, as may be seen from the tables of property, he has other possessions of greater value. He married Elizabeth, daughter of the late Rev. Peter Scott, Minister of the Laigh Kirk, Paisley, by whom he has had Robert Fulton, late Lieutenant Colonel of the 79th Regiment, who married Jane, daughter of John M'Kerrell, Esq; of Hillhouse, and has issue; and Anne, who was married to Herbert Buchanan, Esq; of Arden, and died in 1817, leaving issue.

3. Margaret, married to John M'Kerrel, Esq; of Hillhouse, and has issue;

4. Mary, married to the Rev. Robert Boog, D. D. first minister of the Abbey Church, Paisley, and has issue.

ADAM OF COLLINSLEE.—This small property, half a mile south of Paisley, on which is a bleachfield, was acquired from the Duke of Hamilton, in 1755, by Mr. Richard Glen, who died in 1798, and bequeathed it to his grand-nephew, John Adam, who still carries on the business of bleaching to a considerable extent.

BUCHANAN OF HILLINGTON.—Adjacent to the east side of the lands of Ralston, lie the lands of Hillington, which belonged to Archibald Buchanan, Esq; of Hillington, in this shire, and Silverbanks in the shire of Dumbarton; who married Martha, daughter of Peter Murdoch of   by whom he left three sons, 1. Peter, who succeeded him; 2. George; 3. Andrew. His daughter, Mary, married Alexander Speirs of Elderslie, Esq; and had issue. He was succeeded by his eldest son. Peter died without issue, and was succeeded by his brother, George, who, also died without issue, and was succeeded by Archibald, his nephew, eldest son of his brother, Andrew. He married Mary, daughter of Richard Dennistoun, Esq; and has one son, Andrew.

TOWN OF PAISLEY.

Etymology.—It is seldom that the origin of the names of ancient places is so evident as to admit of no doubt. So long, however, as authentic records relating to this place. extend back, Paisley has had nearly the same appellation. Thus, in the year 1160, the church that stood here, was called " Ecclesia de Paselet," latinised into Pasletum, in the records of the ancient monastery. In the statistical account of the Abbey parish, published in 1794, the following etymology is said to have been suggested, by a good Gælic Scholar.—" A ridge " of rocks runs across the river, and forms a beautiful cascade. Prior to the " building of the town, this would undoubtedly be the most striking object the " place could present. The face or brow of a rock in Gælic is, pais-licht. Hence, " in all probability, the original of the monkish Pasletum, and the modern " Paisley." Many received etymologies are much more fanciful.

Ancient State.—The ancient state of this town, is thus taken notice of by Chalmers, in Caledonia, vol. I. p. 156.

" No one has ever denied to Paisley the honour of a Roman station, at Vanduaria, a town of the Damnii. Sir R. Sibbald and Horsley, speak of the visible remains of a Roman station at this place. The expansion of the town, and the cultivation of the country, have almost obliterated the Roman remains. The bowling-green, however, on the commanding height, is said, by tradition, to denote the Prætorium of the Roman camp. The British name of this town seems obviously to have been derived from the vicinity of the White Cart, to which the station extended. Wen-dur signifying, in the British, White-water; and this Celtic appellation was easily latinized by the Romans into Vanduaria, as Esc, was converted into Esica, and Alan into Aluana. Beyond Paisley, on the west, no Roman station has yet been found, though some roads have been traced, and coins and armour, as we have seen."

In the beginning of the last century there existed, at Paisley, the remains of a large Roman camp, with its Prætorium on the rising ground, called Oakshawhead, which overlooks the surrounding country and the town of Paisley. The Prætorium was not large, but well fortified with three fosses, and ramparts of earth, which were then so high, that men on horseback could not see over them. " The camp itself," says Mr. William Dunlop, who was principal of the College of Glasgow and royal historiographer, " took in all the rising ground, " and, by the vestiges, seems to have reached to the Cart. Upon the north " side, the agger, or rampart, goeth along the foot of the hill; and if it be al- " lowed to go as far on the other side, it hath enclosed all the ground on which " the town of Paisley standeth, which may be reckoned about a mile in circuit."

The form of this camp seems to be much the same with the Roman camp at Ardoch. In the vicinity of this station, there are two small posts, somewhat larger than the Prætorium of the large camp, but of the same form; the one on the west, on the lands of Woodside, and the other on the south, on the lands of Castlehead, each about half a mile from the large station.

Situation.—This town is situated about seven miles west by south from the city of Glasgow, and about three miles south of the Clyde. The greater part of it is erected upon one of those gently swelling heights, so generally to be met with in the lower part of Renfrewshire, which give a pleasing variety to the surface, without much diminishing the value, as they are all arable to the top. On the south and east sides of this hill, which is surrounded by a richly cultivated country, the town is built from the bottom, up to the very summit, from whence there is a very extensive prospect. This part of Paisley has every advantage that can arise from a free circulation of air, whilst, from the general declivity of the streets, a ready descent is given to the waters, which, on every shower that falls, washes them clean, and this contributes still further to salubrity. The town, however, is not all included in this elevated site. About 36 years ago, on the great increase of inhabitants, from the rapid extension of trade, a new town was laid out to the eastward, on the extensive plain, near the old Abbey, which was till then included within a high wall, and formed the ancient and very extensive garden of that celebrated monastery. The plan of this new quarter is more modern; the streets are broader, and laid off in straight lines; and the houses are constructed with more regard to uniformity. Along the western side of this new town, the White Cart winds its course, and separates it from the ancient Paisley. Over this water there are three bridges, to facilitate communication. It is a navigable stream, so far as to admit vessels from 60 to 80 tons burden. Besides bestowing the advantage of commercial intercourse by water with the river Clyde, it adds much to the beauty of the scenery in this place, by the variety of form it exhibits as it flows along. In one place smooth as a mill pond, in others ripling along from interruptions, and in another part forming a cataract, gushing impetuously over that brow of rock, which is supposed to have given name to Paisley itself. Along the south side of the town the lately constructed canal from Glasgow to Johnstone, is conducted, which, independent of commercial advantage, is a most enlivening object to every place that has it in view, and this is beginning to induce an extension of the town in that quarter. To the north of the old town, on a plain, similar to that on which the new is erected, there is a quarter laid out for building, on which considerable progress is made, nothing inferior in regularity and uniformity to the other. This is erected on the lands of the ancient Snawdoun, (by some supposed to be the origin of that title among those of the Prince of Wales) and from which some of the streets are now named. To the westward there is a large quarter, called Maxwelltown, laid off with a considerable degree of elegance and taste, and there also is the cheerful appendage of Ferguslie. Such is the main body of the town. There are suburbs, extending further in different directions.

When Crawfurd wrote, in 1710, Paisley was an inconsiderable place. He describes it as consisting of only one single street, about half a mile long, with some lanes. At present it is more than two miles long, and it is about a mile and a half broad. It is however very irregular in the outline, and does not at all correspond in size to a place of the same length and breadth in a square. but still, with the exception of Edinburgh and Glasgow, it is the largest and most populous town in Scotland, and will of course rank as the third in the kingdom. In respect to manufactures, by which it has arisen to importance, it is perhaps the first. Glasgow may indeed dispute this pre-eminence, but no other town can. In one thing it excels almost every manufacturing town in Britain, namely, in the general orderly conduct of its inhabitants. While other populous manufacturing towns are for ever affronting themselves, by getting into a state of riot and commotion on all public questions, whether civil, religious or commercial, the people of Paisley have always had the moderation to make their sentiments known in a peaceable and respectful manner. They are too knowing to become the dupes or the tools of factious and aspiring demagogues.

Population.—Next to a general and well directed spirit of industry, nothing shews more forcibly the importance to the country of any particular place than the population. The following returns of the number of inhabitants in the town and Abbey parish, will shew this not only as at present, but the progress it has made in the course of the last 120 years, at the six different periods mentioned.

In 1695, there were 4,375 souls; 1755, 6,799; 1782, 17,780; 1792, 24,592; 1805, 35,000; 1811, 36,722.

At this latter period, the inhabitants, in the town and suburbs, amounted to 29,541. There has been no census taken since 1811, but as there has been still an increase of people, notwithstanding of a decline in employment, the number is now, on good grounds, supposed to be 36,000.

Rental.—This also shows comparative importance to the State. The rent of houses in the whole parish and town of Paisley, in 1815, was £52,523, of which the town may be stated at £48,000. The house rental of the whole county in the same year would be about £120,000.

Manufactures.—To give an account of these, adequate to the subject, would itself fill a volume. Happily there is the less reason for going deeply into the investigation, as it has already been pretty amply discussed, though in very concise terms, by Mr. Wilson, in the General View of Renfrewshire, published only six years ago; a work containing as much well authenticated information as perhaps any that has been laid before the public in so small a compass. I propose, therefore, without entering into minute detail, to confine myself to general results. To the inhabitants of this county, in which Mr. Wilson's work is very generally known, this will probably be thought sufficient. To subscribers at a distance it is a matter of less interest.

The progress of the linen manufacture (which existed before the Union) is exhibited in the following table, extracted from the stampmasters books.

	Anno.	Yards	Value.		
			£.	s.	d.
In the years ending on the 1st November,	1744	953,407	18,886	15	10
	1748	413,660	23,671	19	7
	1758	649,998	43,665	8	11
	1768	529,022	54,665	12	11½
	1784	1922,020	164,385	16	6¼

The *thread manufacture* commenced in 1722. The general table will shew the progress it has made.

Silk Gauze.—This was introduced in 1759. It was prosecuted at one time to so great an extent, as to give employment to 5000 weavers, and as many warpers, winders, &c. as to amount to 5000 people more, and finished goods to the value of £350,000 yearly. From a fluctuation in fashion, to which all fancy goods are liable, it fell off so much, as, in 1785, not to exceed £9,600 in value. It is beginning now to revive.

Muslin Manufacture.—This has increased greatly in the course of the last 30 years, and is now the greatest manufacturing employment known. It is calculated to give employment to 6,750 weavers by the Paisley manufacturers, whilst each weaver gives employment to two people more, in tambouring, bleaching, &c. These are not all employed in this town, but many of them in the manufacturing villages around, even as far as Saltcoats, Kilwinning, Irvine, &c. in Ayrshire. The Paisley people excel in this branch. The Glasgow manufacturers, with all their acuteness, are not understood to equal them.

Cotton Spinning.—This is carried on to a vast extent by the Paisley manufacturers, but chiefly in the distant villages.

The whole of the principal subjects of manufacture may be condensed into the following table, shewing the number of people employed, and the value of the goods manufactured, as ascertained in 1805.

Species of Manufacture.	Number of people employed.	Value produced yearly.
Muslin,	20,350	£.675,000
Silk,	240	9,600
Cotton Spinning,	7,000	360,000
Thread Making,	1,440	96,000
Distilleries,	60	75,000
Leather, Soap, Candles,	120	85,000
Inkle, or Tape,	100	6,000
Iron Founderies,	50	5,000
Total,	29,250	1,254,700

One very ingenious manufacture is not included in the above enumerated articles, because it was only introduced in that year, and had not then been prosecuted to any considerable extent—namely, imitations of India shawls and plaids. The materials used are silk and cotton, but more generally Merino wool, instead of cotton, as succeeding better with the public taste. These are of different sizes and different degrees of fineness. Thus, respecting size, they are ¼ and ¼ scarfs; ⅚ plaids and ¼ shawls, at the following prices :—

Scarfs from 10s. to 50s.
Plaids from 50s. to 180s.
Shawls from 24s. to 130s.

The number of different hands employed in making a single article of any of these is 11; namely, the dyer, winder, warper, weaver, draw-boy, cutter, sewer, fringer, picker, washer, and dresser.

The annual value of this manufacture, at an average of the last three or four years, is estimated at £.100,000. There are besides this, many other flourishing manufactures, or handicrafts, not brought into account; such as all manner of work by wrights, smiths, coopers, shoemakers, saddlers, &c. &c. and linen weavers, employed by the inhabitants in the town and country, for their own use, and which forms no part of export trade, that were they all to be estimated according to real worth, would, without all question, make the value of goods manufactured by the Paisley people amount to, or rather exceed, the sum of £.1,500,000 yearly.

In addition to the general increase of national wealth, from the labour and ingenuity of the people employed in these manufactures, the circumstances of the individuals themselves are greatly meliorated. This is remarkably apparent from their dress, in which the young men in particular, and the tambouring girls, display no small degree of finery and taste. They seem indeed to be disposed in general to lay out their whole winnings in this way. Far preferable, at any rate, to spending them in dissipation; yet, there are a few among them who reserve a part of their income for a time of trouble or of bad trade, (to which laudable propensity, the lately established saving-banks, afford facility), whilst there are others, who, from their savings, have built houses for their families, and shops for themselves. During a time of good trade, a superior tradesman has been known to earn three guineas a-week or more, while some of the tambouring girls make fifteen shillings in the same period. There is another very prominent trait, in the character of the Paisley weavers, and that is, a pretty general taste for books. If you enter into conversation with them, you will find many of them well informed on several subjects, particularly, general history, natural history, religion, and, of late, politics. They, in general, maintain a high sense of independency, correctly blended with a regard to the rights of others, as well as their own. Some of them indeed, as in all populous communities, carry their ideas of civil liberty to a degree bordering on licentiousness. But the great mass of common sense is on the side of regularity and order.

In religion, though the greater part adhere to the established church, still there are many dissenters of various sects. This, however, far from being inimical to the spirit of the gospel, rather is in conformity to it, by inciting emulation.

The cotton spinning trade, now established in this part of the country, is also highly valuable, on account of the great number of women and poor children who are employed in its various operations. It appears, however, to have no tendency to improve the morals of the country.

Boys and girls are received into this employ, by the time they are eight years old. They receive from two to five shillings a-week; their attendance is, from six in the morning till eight at night. But no time is allowed for education, and after parents begin to receive wages for their labours, few of them think of sending them to school.

In order to correct this baneful effect, a society was formed, at Paisley, for instituting and supporting Sunday schools, of which there are at prerent 37 under its inspection. This has subsisted since the year 1797, and much good has resulted from it; both in checking the progress of vice, and in conveying much important religious, and moral instruction to neglected children. There are likewise several schools opened on the week-day evenings, for teaching those to read who are employed on other works through the day, and cannot obtain education otherwise. From the last account of the numbers attending these benevolent seminaries, they amounted to about two thousand six hundred. All the Sabbath schools are taught gratis, and each of them is attended by a sub-committee. The fund for providing books, fire, candles, and house rents, is collected at the church, where a sermon is preached for the purpose, about once in six weeks, by the ministers of the established church, and the Presbyterian dissenters in rotation. A dispensary also, for the purpose of furnishing medical aid gratis to the poor, has been long established, to the great relief of many, and of late, a very convenient building has been erected in a healthy situation for the benefit of such as are seized with contagious fevers, &c. This institution promises to be of great utility to the poor, and has been the means, under Providence, to check the progress of infectious disorders in many cases.

Succession of Ministers.—LAIGH KIRK, built in 1736, in which year, Robert Mitchel, from the 2d charge in the Abbey parish came to it. In 1736, Peter Scott; died in 1753. In 1754, Robert Finlay, afterwards translated to Glasgow. In 1756, John Witherspoon; went afterwards to America. In 1769, James Morrison, died in 1801. In 1781, Colin Gillies. In 1802, John Reid. In 18— Robert Burns.

HIGH CHURCH, built in 1756, when James Bain was ordained, but in 1766 he joined the Presbytery of Relief; died in 1790. In 1766, George Muir. In 1772, William Taylor, translated to Glasgow in 1800. In 1781, John Finlay ordained.

MIDDLE CHURCH, built in 1781, when John Snodgrass was admitted; died in 1797. 1798, Jonathan Rankin ordained.

Civil State.—Paisley was erected into a burgh of barony by James III. in 1488. It enjoys all the powers necessary to government and police, without any of the burdens to which royal burghs are subjected. The government of the town is vested in a Provost, three Bailies, and seventeen Councillors, who appoint a Treasurer, a Chamberlain, a Town-Clerk, and a Procurator Fiscal. Eight of the magistrates and council are changed at Michaelmas annually. The freedom of the town is conferred on very moderate terms. The revenues are not great, but they have been managed to the best advantage. The town originally held of the Abbot of Paisley, and afterwards of the temporal Lordship, which came in place of the Abbey. This was at first vested in the family of Abercorn, and by purchase from it, came to that of Dundonald. This superiority, in 1658, was purchased from the latter by the magistrates and council, and Paisley has, since that time, held of the Crown.

Sheriff Court.—In Paisley is the supreme sheriff court of the county. Till of late, there were no other sheriff court in it; but now there is a sheriff substitute in Greenock, as there had been one all along here. The court at Paisley consists of a sheriff depute; a sheriff substitute; a procurator fiscal, and a sheriff clerk. There is a faculty of procurators, which was incorporated by royal charter, 24th June 1803. It consists of a Dean, a Treasurer, a Clerk, Three Councillors, three Examinators, and has at present 21 other members, with a Librarian.

Religious Establishments.—There are three established clergymen in the burgh, in three separate churches, and two in the Abbey parish in one church, perhaps the most elegant ancient fabric at this day in Scotland. There is a Gaelic chapel in connection with the established church. There is a Burgher meeting-house; an Antiburgher meeting-house; an old Relief, do.; a new Relief, do.; a Reformed presbyterian or Cameronian meeting-house, and a Roman Catholic chapel.

Police.—The town is divided into nine wards, with two commissioners in each; a general superintendant, a surveyor, a clerk, two sergeants, four corporals, and 12 watchmen. The suburbs are divided into six wards, with one commissioner to each; with a clerk, who is also surveyor. These are under the particular cognisance of the sheriff substitute ex officio. The burgh is under the cognisance of the magistrates. The expense of the whole is defrayed by an assessment.

Town's Hospital.—This is a handsome but plain building, situated in Hospital street, with a large garden at the back. It was first opened for the reception of the poor in 1752. It is supported by annual assessments on the inhabitants, and is under the direction of three members of the town council, and nine gentlemen from the town at large, nominated by the town council. On the 1st June 1817, there were in it, men, 35; women, 60; in all, 95 aged persons. Boys, 24; girls, 13; in all, 37 children. Total 132. The annual expense for the year preceding, was £1,936: 0s: 3d; including clothes.

Glasgow, Paisley, and Ardrossan Canal.—A canal from the Clyde, near Glasgow, to the sea at Saltcoats, or Ardrossan, has long been a favourite contemplation. The distance is about 30 miles in nearly a straight line, and through a deep valley a great part of the way. The neigbouring country is remarkably populous; the city of Glasgow (in number of people, the second in Britain) is at the one end, whilst through the whole tract, at short intermediate distances, is the town of Paisley, with the several lesser towns or villages of Johnstone, Kilbarchan, Lochwinnoch, Kilbirny, Beith, Dalry, Kilwinning, Stevenston, Saltcoats, and Ardrossan, containing in all, not fewer than 160,000 inhabitants, while the country itself is full of minerals, coal, iron, and limestone, in quantity inexhaustible. All these inducements, led Lord Eglinton, in conjunction with a number of respectable gentlemen in the counties of Ayr, Renfrew, and Lanark, to apply to Parliament, which granted them an act in 1805, to enable them to accomplish this important object. The first general meeting of the company was held, at Paisley, 17th July 1806. The operations commenced in May, 1807, and the navigation betwixt Glasgow and Johnstone was opened on the 4th October 1811.

The length of the canal from Port Eglinton to Johnstone, (which is all that has yet been made) is 11 miles, from thence to Ardrossan 21 and three quarters. The breadth of the water 30 feet, and the depth four feet and a half. From Port Eglinton to Johnstone there are 35 stone bridges over it; there are two tunnels through which the trade passes, one under the Causeyside Street of Paisley, 240 feet long, and one through Ralston square near the west end of that town, 210 feet in length; there are five aqueducts, the one across the Cart, near Paisley, is 240 feet long, 27 broad and 30 high, and the span of the arch is 84 feet. There are 18 culverts, for taking off superfluous water; 8 basins; 12 landing places; and a store-room at Paisley and another at Johnstone, besides the one mentioned at Port Eglinton. There are no locks on the canal so far as it is yet made, but eight will be required near Johnstone, to raise it to the summit level, and 13 to lower it down, near Saltcoats, to Ardrossan. Each of these Locks require to be eight feet of rise or fall. The present cut is supplied in water, by several brooks let into it betwixt Paisley and Johnstone. The actual cost of finishing it so far as it has gone, has not been less than £120,000, of which £30,000 was for masonry. This has been greatly more than was originally calculated upon; as 884 shares at £50 each, was then supposed to be sufficient. The rest has been borrowed, on the credit of some of the share holders, trusting to relief from general meetings of the whole.

Exclusive of vessels for the transport of goods, there are three boats for passengers, viz. the Countess of Eglinton; the Countess of Glasgow, and the Paisley, all well employed. These are 68 feet long each, and eight feet wide, and are fitted up in an elegant manner, with every suitable accommodation. They are calculated to hold 120 passengers each. The first boat freighted for passengers, was on the 6th November 1810.

This canal, when finished, will not only be of incalculable benefit to the agricultural and commercial interests of the country through which it passes, but be the means of opening up a more ready communication with Ireland and other ports, from the magnificent harbour of Ardrossan in Ayrshire, constructed by the Earl of Eglinton, on a scale as to extent, and in a style of building, unexampled as a private undertaking in any country, or in any age.

RENFREW.

Situation and Extent.—This parish, lying north from that of Paisley, is about six miles in length from N. E. to S. W. and about two miles and a half, where broadest in an opposite direction. It contains 3,776 English acres, and for so small an extent is remarkably irregular in the outline, and must have been originally very incommodious to the people to attend their parish church, as part of it is situated beyond the Clyde, and part of it beyond the Cart, both unfordable rivers, though now there is an excellent ferry across the first, and one of the finest bridges in Scotland over the other. Part of the neighbouring parish of Govan comes close to the town of Renfrew, at a distance of three miles from its own parish church. But conveniency to the parishioners does not seem to have been much attended to in the laying off parishes.

Surface and Soil.—That part of the parish on the south side of the Clyde, is nearly a perfect level, with a deep and rich soil, formed, much of it, from depositation from waters. On the north of the Clyde, the surface is pleasantly diversified with some gently rising lands, and the soil is deep and fertile.

State of Property.—INCH (see page 67,) was purchased in 1760, by the late Alexander Speirs, Esq; and is now the property of his son, Archibald Speirs, Esq; of Elderslie. There is here an elegant and stately mansion in wich he resides, and it is now called Elderslie, from which he takes his designation in preference to any of the other properties he has in the county.

Blawerthill, (see page 67,) which belonged to the family of Maxwell Pollok, was purchased from it about the year 1777, by the above Alexander Spiers, Esq; and is also the property of his son Archibald Spiers, Esq; of Elderslie.

Scotstoun. (see page 58.) John Walkinshaw, son of William last-mentioned by Crawfurd, lost this property (so says Semple, who published a continuation of this account in 1782) to a person of the name of Crawfurd, whose son John sold it to Messrs. Richard & Alexander Oswalds, merchants, in Glasgow, (of whom Oswald of Auchincruive, in Ayrshire,) with which family it still remains. There is a very pleasant mansion on it, near the north banks of the Clyde.

Jordanhill. (see page 68.) This beautiful property was sold by the Crawfurd's, its ancient barons, in the year 1750, to Alexander Houstoun, merchant, in Glasgow, (said to be of the House of Calderhall in Mid Lothian,) whose son and successor, Andrew Houstoun, Esq; of Jordanhill, built an excellent mansion on it about the year 1730, upon a fine commanding height, surrounded with plantations, overlooking the whole country. He afterwards, in the year 1800, sold the whole to Archibald Smith, Esq; now of Jordanhill, the present proprietor.

Knock or Knox. (see page 61.) This ancient residence of the family of Knox, and from which the name is assumed, is the property of Archibald Campbell, Esq; of Blythesword, and has been a considerable time in his family. It is situated about a mile north from Paisley, and is one of the best situations for a villa perhaps in Renfrewshire.

Porterfield, (see page 62.) belongs now to the town of Renfrew.

Kirkland, (see page 64.) passed from Ross, a Cadet of Hawkhead, into the possession of Lord Ross the chief, from which family it was alienated to the family of Campbell of Blytheswood. It lies very near the family seat of Mr. Campbell, and is now included in the pleasure grounds*

Renfield, or Ranfield, (see page 64.) a very pleasant property on the east banks of the united streams of the two Carts, immediately before their junction with the Clyde. It belongs still, as in the days of Crawfurd, to Campbell of Blytheswood, who is now about building a new mansion, more adequate than the ancient house to be the family seat.

Abbots-Inch. This valuable property has been overlooked by Crawfurd altogether. It is situated on the left bank of the Cart, about a mile below Paisley, and stretching inland till it joins the united streams of the Black Cart and Gryffe, and is all a remarkably deep rich soil, like to the best in the Carses of Gowrie,

---

* On these lands, near to the bridge of Inchinnan, there is a grey stone, still fondly visited by those who admire the ill-fated Argyle, who perished on the scaffold in the reign of James II. There are some reddish veins to be observed in it, which the superstitious conceive to be impressed with that colour in commemoration of his fate. He was taken at this spot when endeavouring to escape by a ford, where the bridge is now built. Laing and Fox and Wood, call this a ford of the Inchinnan. This is a topographical mistake. There is no water of that name. It was the Cart.

Falkirk, or Stirling. There is a small plain house on it, near its eastern extremity, in the vicinity of the White Cart. This property belongs to Lord Douglas.

Walkinshaws, Easter and Wester. (see pages 90 and 91.) These properties have passed through various hands. They are enrolled in the cess books, at present, in the name of Boyd Alexander, Esq; of Southbar. There is a stately mansion, among some full grown wood, at Wester Walkinshaw.

TABLE OF PROPERTY.

Properties.	Proprietors.	Valued Rent Scots. £.	s.	d.	Eng. Acres.
Abbot's Inch,	Lord Douglas,	533	6	8	
Scotstoun,	George Oswald, Esq;	401	13	4	
Blawerthill, &c.	Archibald Speirs, Esq;	458			1297
Jordanhill,	Archibald Smith, Esq;	266	13	4	
Inch,	Archibald Speirs, Esq;	281	5	0	
King's Inch, part of,	Mr. M'Call,	18	15		
Porterfield,	Town of Renfrew,	160			
Walkinshaw, Wester,	Boyd Alexander, Esq;	160			
Do. Middle,	Do.	150			
Do. Easter,	Do.	136	13	4	
Castlehill,	Soap Company,	20			
King's Meadow,	Town of Renfrew, and Blytheswood,	40			
Kirkland and Renfield,	Archd. Campbell, Esq; of Blytheswood,	60			
Part of Walkinshaw,	Boyd Alexander, Esq;	53	6	8	
Total,		2829	13	4	3776

Which may be arranged thus:—

1. Arable land, or in cultivation, ... 3600
2. Natural pastures, and meadow, ... 36
3. Moss, sites of houses, roads, waters, &c. 60
4. Plantations, ... 80

3,776

Succession of Ministers.—In 1576, Andrew Hay. In 1602, John Hay. In 1650, John Maule. In 1653, Patrick Simpson; outed in 1662, and John Hay, re-admitted, In 166 , Francis Ross. 16 , Robert Douglas. In 1690, Patrick Simpson, re-admitted; died in 1715. In 1716, Neil Campbell from Roseneath, translated to Glasgow College, principal. In 1731, Robert Paton from

Haddington; died in 1768. In 1769, Colin Campbell, son of Neil Campbell; died in 1788. In 1790, Thomas Burns from Inchinnan.

Town of Renfrew.—A clean, neat enough cottage-kind of town, consisting, chiefly of a single street, with houses on each side, one storey high, covered with thatch. It does not seem to have increased much, in size or in importance, since the days of Crawfurd. It has, however, a considerable landed property; which, with rents of salmon fishing, and an excellent ferry-boat, produces about £.800 a-year, The population in 1811, amounted to 1637, and it is still the head burgh, (in fact, the only royal burgh) in the county, in so far, that the election for a representative of Renfrewshire in parliament is still held in this town.

DOUGLAS LORD DOUGLAS.—According to legendary story, the origin of this splendid and very widely spreading family can be traced as far back as to the end of the 8th century, about 1050 year ago. But not confiding much in unsupported tradition, we will be walking on surer grounds, by appealing, with the acute Chalmers, to written evidence, and the best of all records—the charters of the family. From these it should appear, that the Douglases are of Flemish origin; as the oldest charter that can be produced, is from Arnald the Abbot of Kelso, granting some lands on the water of Douglas in Lanarkshire, " Theabaldo Flamatico." To Theobald the Fleming, the undoubted ancestor of Lord Douglas. According to the usual practice, at the time, the year in which this charter was granted, is not mentioned, but it must have been betwixt the year 1147 and 1160, the ascertained time in which this Abbot was in office. After all, this is among the most ancient charters in record, belonging to any Scottish family now existing, and establishes a very great antiquity, independent of the reveries of tradition.

In the following short memoir of this very noble family, I omit purposely, for the sake of brevity, the more ancient progenitors, the potent Earls of Douglas, so renowned in story, and commence with the eleventh in descent from Theobald, as above, namely,

XI. Sir William Douglas, second son of Archibald (Bell-Cat), fifth Earl of Angus. He fell at the battle of Pinkie in 1547. He married the heiress of Auchinleck of Glenbervie, by whom he had,

XII. Sir Archibald Douglas of Glenbervie, (of whom Douglas of Inchmalo, and Douglas Lord Glenbervie are descended), by his lady, a daughter of Earl Marischal, he had,

XIII. Sir William Douglas, who claimed the title of Angus, and was adjudged to be entitled to it, in opposition to James VI. who was himself a competitor for it, in right of his descent from Margaret, the daughter of the great Earl. This William, ninth Earl of Angus, by a daughter of Graham of Morphie, had,

XIV. William, tenth Earl of Angus. He died in 1611. By his lady, a daughter of Lord Oliphant, he had,

XV. William, eleventh Earl of Angus, and first Marquis of Douglas, (created 17th June 1633, to him and his heirs male whatsoever). He lived in a state of great splendour, displaying much hospitality and magnificence at his castle of Douglas. He died in 1660. He was ancestor of the Earls of Selkirk, Dumbarton, Forfar, and Orkney, and of the present family of Hamilton. By his lady, sister of the Earl of Abercorn, he had,

XVI. Archibald Earl of Angus. He died in 1655, in his father's lifetime. He married a daughter of Esme, Duke of Lenox, and by her had,

XVII. James, second Marquis of Douglas. He died in 1700. He married first, a daughter of the Earl of Mar, by whom he had James Earl of Angus, a brave commander. In 1689, he raised in one day 1800 men from among the covenanters, called the Cameronian, (now the 26th) regiment. He fell on the 3d August 1692, at the battle of Steinkirk, with nearly his whole regiment, in the 21st year of his age, unmarried. The Marquis married, 2d, a daughter, (lady Mary) of the first Marquis of Lothian, by whom he had, 1. a son, who died in infancy ; 2. Archibald, of whom afterwards, and 3. Lady Jane, born in 1698, married 1746, Colonel, afterwards, Sir John Stewart of Grandtully, to whom she had two sons; 1. Archibald, of whom afterwards; 2. Sholto, who died young.

XVIII. Archibald, third Marquis, and afterwards Duke of Douglas, Marquis of Angus and Abernethy, &c. His Grace died 21st July 1761, in the 67th year of his age. He married Margaret, daughter of Douglas of Mains, but had no issue.

XIX. Archibald, (son of lady Jane Douglas, sister of the late Duke), as heir of line, succeeded to the real and personal estates of his uncle, Duke Archibald. This was contested by the Hamilton family, but was decided in his favour, by a decree of the House of Peers, 27th February 1771. He was created a British Peer, by the title of Baron Douglas of Douglas Castle, 9th July 1790. He married, first, 13th June, 1771, Lady Lucy Graham, daughter of the Duke of Montrose, who died 13th February 1780. By whom he has issue,

XX. 1. Hon. Archibald Douglas, born in 1773, Col. of the Forfar militia ; 2. Hon. Charles Douglas, born in 1775, Lieut.-Col. of the Forfar militia. 3. Hon.

William Douglas, died young; 4. Lady Jane Margaret, married 22d November 1804, Lord Montague, and has issue.

His Lordship married, 2d, 13th May 1783, Lady Frances, sister of Henry, Duke of Buccleugh, and has issue; 5. Honourable Caroline Lucy; 6. Honourable Sholto Douglas—in the army; 7. Honourable James Douglas; 8. Honourable George Douglas—a most gallant sea-officer; 9. Honourable Frances Elizabeth Douglas; also two sons, who died in infancy; 10. Honourable Mary Sidney, born in July 1796.

SPEIRS OF ELDERSLIE.—Archibald Speirs, Esq; second son of the late Alexander Speirs, Esq; of Elderslie, succeeded to his estates in 1782, and married, 24th January 1794, the Hon. Margaret Dundas, eldest daughter of Thomas Lord Dundas, by whom he has issue,

FIVE SONS,

1. Alexander;
2. Thomas Dundas;
3. Archibald William;
4. Peter Charles;

and, 5. Lawrence Dundas.

AND NINE DAUGHTERS,

1. Margaret Bruce;
2. Mary;
3. Charlotte Fitzwilliam; (since dead)
4. Anne Godolphin;
5. Frances Laura;
6. Helen;
7. Dorothea Dundas;
8. Harriot Octavia Isabella;

and, 9. Matilda Isabella Grace.

Mr. Speirs has represented the county of Renfrew in Parliament since 2d May 1810.

CRAWFURD OF JORDANHILL.—Lawrence Crawfurd of Jordanhill (see page 74.) died the 22d September 1723, and was succeeded by his eldest son,

John Crawfurd of Jordanhill. He died unmarried in 1754, and the whole of the male line of Lawrence Crawfurd, his father, being thus extinct, the representation devolved upon the descendants of his uncle James before-mentioned, to whom we now return.

James, second son of Hew, apparent heir of Jordanhill, by Bethia Hamilton, and only brother to the said Lawrence, being bred to the law, was Sheriff Depute of the shire of Renfrew. He married Isabel, eldest daughter, and, at last, only child of William Crawfurd of Boydland. He died in 1695, and was succeeded by his eldest son,

Hew Crawfurd, afterwards of Jordanhill, served heir to his father 30th December 1718; a man of good parts and great integrity; was one of the clerks of His Majesty's Signet, and being eminent in his profession, and in great business, he acquired a handsome fortune. He married Mary, daughter of Mr. James Greenshields, Rector of Fuinoch, in the county of Tipperary in Ireland, He died the 8th of January 1756, and was succeeded by his only son,

Sir Hew Crawfurd of Jordanhill, Bart. served heir to his father 8th December 1756; thereafter, on the 19th July 1765, served heir male to the said Sir John Crawfurd of Kilbirny, Bart. and is the eighteenth generation in a direct line from Gualterus de Crawfurd, ancestor of the families of Kilbirny and Jordanhill, who flourished in the reign of William the Lyon, anno. 1180. He married Robina, only child of the deceased Captain John Pollok of Balgray, second son of the deceased Sir Robert Pollok of Pollok, Bart. by Anne his wife, eldest daughter of James Lockhart of Lee. (See account of the Pollok family, page 293.)

CAMPBELL OF BLYTHSWOOD.—Colin Campbell of Blythswood (see page 64, last line) entailed the lands of Renfield, and his other heritable possessions, on his heirs male. He had only one son, James, who succeeded him, and a daughter, who married William, son of John Sommervile, Provost of Renfrew. James Campbell married Mary, a daughter of Walkinshaw of Barrowfield. He died in 1767, she in 1771, and, having no children, the estate of Blythswood devolved by entail to James Douglas, Esq; of Mains, who assumed the designation of Campbell of Blythswood. He died in 1772. He married Henrietta, daughter of James Dunlop of Garnkirk, by whom he had three sons ; 1. John, who obtained the rank of Colonel in the army, and was killed in action at Martinique in 1794; 2. Archibald, the present proprietor; 3. James, who died a Lieutenant in the 55th regiment at Antigua in 1781. He had also the following daughters: 1. Henrietta, married to Archibald Swinton, Esq; of Manderston ; 2. Agnes; 3. Grace, who died in 1808; 4. Jane ; 5. Mary, and one who died in infancy.

OSWALD OF SCOTSTOUN.—Scotstoun was purchased in the year 1748, from Mr. Walkinshaw's creditors, by Messrs. Richard and Alexander Oswald, brothers, merchants in Glasgow. They were never married, but conveyed the estate of Scotstoun, with their contiguous lands of Balshagrie, in Lanarkshire, to George Oswald, merchant in Glasgow, eldest son of their cousin-german, the Rev. Dr. James Oswald, late minister of Methven in Perthshire, whose second son, Alexander Oswald, Esq; of Shieldhall, died in 1813, and his brother, Richard Oswald, Esq. of Auchencruive, died in 1784.

George Oswald, Esq; succeeded to the estate of Scotstoun in 1766, he married, in 1764, Margaret Smyth, second daughter of David Smyth, Esq; of Methven ; she died in 1792, leaving four sons and seven daughters. viz.

1. Richard Alexander Oswald, Esq; of Auchencruive, in Ayrshire, who

married, first, in 1793, Miss Louisa Johnstone, third daughter of Wynne Johnstone, Esq; of Hillton, in Berwickshire, she died in 1798, leaving a son, Richard, and a daughter, Margaret Hester; he married, secondly, Lady Lilias Montgomery, second daughter of the present Earl of Eglinton; 2. David, went into the army, and died in the West Indies in 1797, unmarried, major of the 38th regiment; 3. James, a Post Captain in the Royal Navy; 4 Alexander, an advocate.

1. Elizabeth; 2. Katherine Cochrane, married to Robert Haldane, Esq; formerly of Airthery, now of Anchengray, in Lanarkshire; 3. Margaret, married to Major General John Wilson; 4. Christian, married to Alexander Anderson, Esq; merchant in London; 5. Mary Ramsay, married to James Dennistoun, Esq; of Colgrain; 6. Camilla, died in 1808; 7. Isabella.

SMITH OF JORDANHILL.—Archibald Smith, youngest son of James Smith of Craigend, in Stirlingshire, acquired the lands of Jordanhill in 1800, as before stated, from Andrew Houstoun of Jordanhill, and made considerable additions to the mansion, and improved the lands. He married Isabella, daughter of William Ewing, Esq; by whom he has had, 1. James, formerly a captain in the Renfrewshire militia, who married Mary, daughter of Alexander Wilson, Esq; (son of the late Dr. Wilson, Professor of Astronomy, Glasgow) by whom he has, Christina Laura; Archibald; Isabella; Alexander. 2. Isabella, married to John M'Call, Esq; 3. William, married Jane, daughter of Alexander Cunninghame, Esq; (son of Sir William Cunninghame of Robertland). She died in 1813, leaving two sons, Archibald and Cunninghame; 4. Archibald.

Arms.—Gules, a Chevron Ermine, between two Crescents, in chief and a Garb in base, within a Bordure Engrailed, Or; Crest, an Eagle's Head erased proper, gorged with a Ducal Coronet, Or. Motto, " Macte."

LOCHWINNOCH.

Situation and Extent.—This is the largest parish but one in the county. It is situated on the confines of Ayrshire, about half way betwixt the most easterly and the most westerly points of the county of Renfrew. It extends about 12 miles from east to west, and, where broadest, is about 6 miles from north to south. The extent in all, is about 19250 English acres.

Surface and Soil.—It is greatly diversified in its general aspect. Part of it consists of high and bleak hills, in the back ground; part of it is a low winding valley, in general of a very fertile soil, and in the heart of it, is the largest loch or lake in the county. This valley, with the shelving country towards it, on both sides, contains nearly the whole population. It is also highly ornamented with plantations, whilst the houses of its numerous small proprietors, are each set down under the shade of a few old trees, in the midst of well cultivated spots of ground. The whole Strath has a warm and cheerful appearance. It is the very vale of Tempe of Renfrewshire.

State of Property.—The fine estate of Castlesemple, (see page 75) the most ancient domain of the great family of Sempill, so renowned in this county, passed from its chief, Hugh, the 11th Lord Sempill, in 1727, to Colonel William M'Dowall, a younger son of Garthland, in the county of Wigton. In this family it continued till the year 1808, when it began to be broken down and parcelled out, which was accomplished in the course of four or five years after, when it was all disposed of to different purchasers. Previous to this, the M'Dowall family had acquired more property than the ancient barony of Sempill in this parish, all which was disposed of at the same time.

The principal part of this combined property, including the mansion and pleasure grounds of Castlesemple, was acquired by John Harvey, Esq; This had always been the finest part of the parish, as well when it remained with its ancient lords, as when it was possessed by the family of M'Dowall. It had indeed been highly improved, while it was in the possession of this last. In particular, the first who acquired it, Colonel William M'Dowall, instead of the old castle, which had become ruinous, had built in 1735, an elegant mansion in a more modern stile, while his successor had enriched the whole territory by extensive and judicious plantations of wood. It seems destined still to undergo further embellishments from the hands of the present proprietor. The situation indeed is the best in the whole county, and the most inviting to decoration.

Another considerable portion of Mr. M'Dowal's estate was acquired by James Adam, Esq; and on which he has not been sparing of improvement. Were this an agricultural report, few places would be more deserving of notice. Of the other properties mentioned by Crawfurd, very few remarks will suffice. Thus, the lands and house of Barr, (see page 74) after being absorbed in the great possessions of M'Dowall of Castlesemple, are now the property of James Adam, Esq.

Millbank, (page 78) came afterwards to a family of the name Orr, in which it still remains.

Balgreen (page 79) became (after being in various hands) part of Mr. M'Dowall's estate, and is now the property of William Fulton.

Beltrees, (page 79) having long remained in the family of Sempill, (Cadet of Lord Sempill) is mostly now the property of Cochrane of Ladyland. See table of property.

Gavin and Risk (page 79) in various hands. See property table.

Ellieston castle (page 80) was also absorbed in Mr. M'Dowall's estate, and is still an appendage of Castlesemple.

The whole property of this parish, which, (with the exception of one or two great possessions) is the most minutely divided of any in the county, will appear in the following table of property :—

TABLE OF PROPERTY.

Baronies.	Particular Lands	Proprietors.	Valued Rent.			Extent English Acres.
Castlesempill.	Castlesempill Proper, South and North Mitchelstone, Markethill, Cowanstone, Elliestone, Bridgend, Gateside, ...	John Harvey, Esq; ..	941	19	1 1/10	725 352
	Peockstone, ...	Alexander Speir, ...	39	19		55
	Lochgrass, ...	James Adam, Esq; ..	61	15	10	382
	Part of Bridgend, ...	Robert Stevenston, ..	1	10	2	
	Do. do. ...	Charles Selkrig, Esq; .	1	3	11	
	Part of Sheills, ...	William Orr, ...		10	10½	
	Part of Markethill, ..	James Clark, ...		9	11	
	Pendicle at Tower of Ellieston, ...	Ludovic Houstoun, Esq;		7	10 1/10	
	Total, ...		1047	16	8	
Corseford and Corseflat.	How-wood, Corsehead, and West Muirdykes, Corseford, Warbuie, How-wood, Coalhouse Hill, and Midtown, ...	John Harvey, Esq; ..				107
	Holmes, ...	Ludovic Houstoun, Esq;	14			
	Auchinreoch, Hallhill, Whitelawmuir, Blackdyke, Whitehills, Mounttop, ... Swinetrees, ...	Fulton of Hartfield, ..	111	3	4	52

HISTORY OF THE SHIRE OF RENFREW.

TABLE OF PROPERTY CONTINUED.

Baronies.	Particular Lands.	Proprietors.	Valued Rent.			Extent English Acres.
	Burnside, ...	Dr. Cochran, ...	22	3	4	35
	E. Muirdykes, ½ Sheep Park, ...	Robert Caldwell, . . .				114
	N. Muirdykes, Broomhead, ...	William Love, ...				52
	South Muirdykes, . . .	Robert Faulds, ...				60
	Burnside, ...	William Peock, ...				35
	Skiff Park, Corsehead and ½ Sheep Park, . .	William M'Dowall, Esq;				112 47
	Little Corseford, ...	Adam Keir, Esq; . . .	25			
	Valued rent not particularized, ...		352	3	4	
	Total, ...		524	10		
Auchinbothie Blair.	Overtown, ...	Robert Pollok, ...	38	6	8	
	Windyhill, ...		14			
	Overtown, ...	Francis Gemmill, . . .	21	6	8	
	Overtown, ...	Robert Pollock, ...	21	6	8	
	Burntfaulds, ... ; .	John Gemmill, ...	10	13	4	
	Spreulston, ...	William Fulton, . . .	64			
	Boghouse, ...	Andrew Clark, ...	40			
	South Castlewalls, . . .	John Pollock, ...	30			
	Tophouse, . . ;	Alexander Pollock, . .	28			
	Walls, ...	Andrew Clark, ...	27			
	Reevoch, ...	John Gemmill, ...	24	6	8	
	Reevoch, ...	Margaret & Jean Allison,	24	6	8	
	Tower & Broomknows,	William Fulton, . . .	20			
	Tower and Fauldhouse,	Margaret Craig, . . .	20			
	Total, ...		383	6	8	
Auchinbothie, Wallace.	Bowfield, ...	John Harvey, Esq; . .	129	6	8	
	Overtrees, ...	James Lata, ...	52	13	4	
	Rashiefield, ...	John Blair, ...	50			
	Trees, ...	Robert Craig, ...	60	13	4	
	Nether Broadfield, . .	Stewart's heirs, ...	55			
	Over Broadfield, . . .	John Robertson, . . .	27	6	8	
	Do. part of, ...	James Stevenson, . . .	25			
	Total, ...		400			
Auchingown, Ralston.	Boydstone and Corsehouse, a feu of, . . .	James Latta, ...	40			
	Netherhouses, ...	James Adam, Esq; . .	32			82

TABLE OF PROPERTY CONTINUED.

Baronies.	Particular Lands.	Proprietors.	Valued Rent.			Extent English Acres.
	Park,		50			
	Muirhead,	General Graham,	42	16	8	
	Muirburn,		48			
	Barrodger,		41	6	8	
	Boutrees,	Mr. Bartlemore,	58			95
	Netherhouses,	Do.	14			38
	Wawkmill,	Mrs. Donaldson,	7	3	4	
	Total,		333	6	8	
	Auchingown, part of,	Robert Fleming,	35	6	8	
	Do. do.	John Reid,	16	13	4	
Auchingown Stewart.	Do. do.	John Henry,	16	13	4	
	Yardfoot,	James King,	41	16	8	
	Wattieston,	John Swan,	35	6	8	
	Newmilks,	John Fleming,	30			
	Wateryet,	John Robertson,	30			
	Burnthills,	John Campbell,	12			
	Knows,	James Love,	33	6	8	
	Burnthills,	John Pollok,	4			
	Middleton,	Mrs. Barr,	26	13	4	
	Barfod,		41	16	8	
	Barfod Nether,	John Stewart,	43			
	Total,		366	13	4	
	Burnthills & Glenhead,	John Pollok,	19	6	8	
	Belltrees Muir,	John Peock,	22			
	Muirend,	John Barbour,	23			
Belltrees.	Lorabar,	John Caldwell,	19	3	4	
	Glenhead & Newhouse,	James Campbell,	40			
	Park and Hall,	Mrs. Barr,	40	13	4	
	Townfoot of Belltrees,	William Caldwell,	52	13	4	
	Do. do.	Cochran of Ladyland,	83	3	4	
	Total,		300			
	Easter Gavin,	Cochran of Ladyland,	84	13	4	
Gavin and Risk.	Mid and West Gavins,	John Harvey, Esq;	64	13	4	
	Risk,	William Orr,	45	6	8	
	Risk, part of,	Mrs. Barr,	38			43
	Townhead,	Do.	50			
	Townfoot,	Do.	45	6	8	
	Lochside,	Do.	40	6	8	

TABLE OF PROPERTY CONTINUED.

Baronies.	Particular Lands.	Proprietors.	Valued Rent.			Extent English Acres.
	Meikle Gavin,	William Caldwell,	61	6	8	
	Earlshill,	Do. do.	36	12	4	
	Wardhouse,	Do. do.	20			
	Mossend,	Allan Pinkerton,	30	6	8	
	Total,		516	13	4	
	Loups,	John Harvey, Esq.	34	7		47
	Bridgend,	Do. do.	11	11		
	Barr, Mains, E. Holmes, Bankend, and Laighhole,	James Adam, Esq.	111	16	4	95
		Do. do.	30	6	8	
	Garpel,	Do. do.	70	3	0	
	Carsefauld,	Do. do.	20	17	0	73
	Burnfoot,	Do. do.	24	6	8	19
Barr.	Caldermills,	Do. do.	36			
	Feu off Barr,	Allan Gilmour,	3			
	Westhills, part of,	William Orr,	29	6		
	Do do.	John Marshall,	30			
	Brannoxhill,	Mrs. Henderson,	22	16	0	
	Sunnyacres,	Do. do.	22	16	0	
	Bridgend,	Do. do.	19	19		10
	Bridgend faulds,	Do. do.	10			
	Bridgend, part of,	Robert Orr,	11	8		
	Braes,	William Brodie,	12	13	4	
	Easthills,	Mrs. Montgomery,	58	13	4	
	Highhole,	John Speir,	40			
	Total,		600			
Lochhead, or Easter Carse	Lochhead,	William Fleming,	57	15	6	76
	Lochhead,	James Allan,	43	6	8	
	Lochhead,	William Miller,	28	17	10	
	Warrandsale,	John Boyd,	5			
	Total,		135			
	Linthills,	John Harvey, Esq.	39	2	2	
	Do. or Muirfauldhouse,	William Glen,	21	17	0	
	Linthills,	John Gemmill,	17	6	8	
	Do. do.	John Orr,	34	13	4	
	Do. do.	John Brodie,	29	3	0	
	Do. do.	William Love,	15	16	2	
	Langstilly,	Robert Kirkwood,	40			

x x

TABLE OF PROPERTY CONTINUED.

Baronies.	Particular Lands.	Proprietors.	Valued Rent.			Extent English Acres.
	Auchinhean,	Robert Kirkwood,	11	2	2¹	
	Do.	Robert Bartlemore,	52			
	Do.	Thomas Orr,	33	6	8	
	Do.	James Latta, and R. Arthur, equally.	22	4	5⅐	
	Gavilmoss,	John Boyd,	13	6	8	
	Do. do.	Robert Arthur,	13	6	8	
	Do. and Gibsyard,	James Latta,	16	13	4	
	Kaimhill,	Robert Kirkwood,	16	13	4	
	Do.	Robert Orr, writer,	33	6	8	
	Kaim,	John Caldwell,	33	6	8	
	Kaim,	William Orr,	32	0		
	Do. 7/7,	William Glen,	22	4	5⅐	
	Do. Byrebush, ⅐,	John Caldwell,	11	2	2⅔	
	Bars of Cloack,	John Barr,	14			33
	Meikle Cloack,	William Montgomery,	42			
	Little Cloack,	John Logan,	16	13	4	
	Do. do.	William Barbour,	8	6	8	
	Do. do.	James Boag,	8	6	8	
Glen.	Glenmill,	Robert Orr,	26	13	4	
	Millbank,	Do. do.	40			
	Narvelston,	William Brodie,	18	6	8	
	Mavisbank,	Do. do.	18	6	8	
	Fairhills,	Do. do.	33	6	8	
	Kerse,	Henry Dunlop,	40	0	0	
	Kerse,	William Brodie,	40	0	0	
	Kerse,	William Brodie,	33	6	8	
	Kerse,	John Blair,	33	6	8	
	Gilesyards,	Robert Pollock,	30			
	Do.	Thomas Clark,	15			
	Do.	William Glen,	15			
	Little Millbank,	Robert Stevenson,	33	6	8	
	Fairhills,	James Orr,	15			
	Fairhills,	William Stirrat,	15			
	Jaffraystock,	James Dunlop,	46	13	4	54
	Do. or Newfaulds,	Thomas Robertson,	16	13	4	33
	Plantilly,	John Boyd,	26	13	4	40
	Auldyards,	John Caldwell,	36	13	4	
	Muirshields, &c. &c.	Andrew Moody, Esq;	28			2494
	Lorabank,	Robert Orr,	20			
	Langyards,	Do. do.	63	6	8	
	Barnaigh, Easter,	Robert Burns,	26			
	Do. 10 sh. land of,	John Aitkin,	26			
	Do. 20 sh. land of,	James Aitkin,	54			

TABLE OF PROPERTY CONTINUED.

Baronies.	Particular Lands	Proprietors.	Valued Rent.			Extent English Acres.
	Do. Wester or Low,	David Clark,	20			46
	Do. High or Newhouse,	John Harvey, Esq;	16			80
	Do. Hill of Barnaigh,	Do. do.	42			130
	Moniabrock,	William Burns, Esq;	26			120
	Do.	Thos. & Rob. Caldwell,	26			
	Do. or Midhouse,	Archibald Campbell,	52			
	Do. or the Ward,	James Brodie,	34			
	Tandlemuir,	James Holms,	40			
	Do.	John Donald,	30			
	Clovenstone,	Robert Jameson,	27	10		
	Edge,	William Wyllie,	22	10		
	Artnox,	Robert Brodie,	8			
	Sandiestone,	John Blackburn,	27			
	Longcraft,	William Peock,	14			
	Balgreen,	William Fulton,	53	6	8	
	Mistylawmuir,	John Harvey, Esq;	100			1763
	Total,		1686	18	4	
Calderhaugh.	Crooks, part of,	John Harvey, Esq;	6	6	8	6
	Do. do.	Robert Smith,	20	6	8	27½
	Do. do.	Widow Hotson,	13	6	8	8¼
	M'Donally,	John Harvey, Esq;	22			
	Langley,	Mrs. Barr,	27	6	8	
	West Sandielands,	James Adam, Esq;	3			
	Knockbartnock,	Fulton of Balgreen,	33	6	8	
	Knockbartnock,	John Lang,	26	13	4	
	Smithy & Strandheads,	Fulton, Buchanan, Pollock,	13	6	8	
	Wellpark,	Robert Jamieson,	5			
	Johnshill, 3 shares £10.	Mrs. Wilson, Crawford, How,	30			
	Do. one share,	James Alexander,	3	6	8	
	Barclay's feu,	Thomas Ewing,		15		
	Do. do.	James Campbell,		15		
	Calderhaugh Lots,	John Harvey, Esq;	34			34
	Do. do.	James Adam, Esq;	30			11
	Do. seven lots,	Sundries,	67	11	8	53
	Total,		337	1	8	
	Sum total of the whole,		6859	14	5	

The whole may be arranged thus :—

	Eng. Acres
Arable, in cultivation,	8000
Sound Pasture on hill sides, &c.	5750
Moss or Muir of little value,	4000
Roads, waters, sites of houses, &c.	500
Plantations, some very extensive about Castlesemple, and a portion of old wood about every seat of the numerous proprietors,	1000
	19250.

Succession of Ministers.—In 158 , Mr. Andrew Knox, translated to Paisley. In 1602, Patrick Hamilton, translated, in 1607, to Paisley. In 1627, Alexander Hamilton. In 1647, Hew Peebles, persecuted, died 1691. In 1691, John Paisley. In 1728, John Pinkerton, died in 1750. In 1750, John Cowper, died in 1787. In 1788, James Steven. In 1802, Crawfurd, from a chapel of ease at Port Glasgow. In 1815, Robert Smith, ordained on a presentation from 69 persons, who had purchased the right of patronage.

Village and Manufactures.—Lochwinnoch is a very thriving village, built on a regular plan of one main street, (which is more than half a mile long) with some streets crossing it at right angles. The houses are generally of two story in height, and covered with slates. The number of people, in 1811, was 1907, and it seems to be increasing, as there have been many new houses erected since. The situation is indeed very pleasant, as it is exposed only to the south-east, being under shelter in all other directions, either by rising grounds or thick plantations. It is supported almost wholly from the cotton manufacture, dependent on Paisley. There are here two very large cotton mills, that give employment to the greater part of the children of the village so soon as they are able to work. The water of the Calder, a stream sometimes of great size, flows close by the south end of this town, and falls into the loch of Castlesemple, about half a mile to the eastward. It is applied to bleaching of cloth, and other manufacturing purposes. There is no other village of any note in the parish, nor, of course, manufactures.

Family Descent.—SEMPILL LORD SEMPILL.—The account of this ancient noble family shall be resumed, from very nearly where Crawfurd brought it, (see page 78), and commencing with the seventeenth generation from their most remote ancestor on record, Robert, the Steward of Renfrew, in the days of Alexander III. who witnessed a charter in the year 1280. Namely,

XVII. Francis, eighth Lord Sempill. He was the first of the family that renounced the errors of popery. He married a sister of the first Earl of Roseberry, but died without issue, in 1684. He was succeeded by his sister,

XVII. Anne, Baroness of Sempill. She married Francis Abercromby of Fetternear, who was created Lord Glasford for life. Lady Sempill died in 1695, leaving issue, three sons who, in succession, became Lords Sempill.

XVIII. Francis, the eldest son, succeeded his mother, and was ninth Lord Sempill. He died unmarried soon after the Union, which he opposed in all its parts. The second son,

XVIII. John, succeeded, and was 10th Lord Sempill. He was very active on the side of government in the rebellion 1715. He died unmarried next year. His only surviving brother,

XVIII. Hugh, became then the 11th Lord Sempill. He entered early into the army, and rose to be Colonel of the 42d, or Royal Highlanders, in 1741. He commanded the left wing of the royal army, at the battle of Culloden, 16th April 1746; and was in every respect an officer of distinguished abilities. He died in November 1746, in consequence of the tendon of his arm being punctured when he was let blood. He married Sarah, daughter and coheiress of ———— Gascoyne, Esq; by whom he had issue; John, who succeeded him; Hon. George, who died in 1779, being then a Colonel, in the service of the East India company; Hon. Hugh, a Captain of Marines, died 1764; Hon. Sarah, married to Crawfurd of Auchinames; Hon. Anne, married Dr. Adam Austin; two sons more, who died young, and four daughters, who died young or unmarried. This Lord Sempill sold Castlesemple, in 1727, and bought North Bar in 1741.

XIX. John, 12th Lord Sempill, succeeded his father, 1746, and died in 1782. He married Janet, daughter and heiress of Dunlop of Bishopton, in 1755, by whom he had issue; Hugh, his successor; Hon. George, a Lieutenant in the army, died 1782; Hon. Patrick, died young; Hon. Sarah, married to Sir William Forbes, of Craigievar, died 1799, had issue; Hon. Janet Sempill, and Hon. Joanna Sempill.

XX. Hugh, 13th Lord Sempill, born July 1758, was in the foot guards. Married in 1787, Miss Mellish, daughter of Charles Mellish of Ragnall, and by her has,

XXI. Selkirk, master of Sempill; born 12th February 1788, who was a Captain in the Renfrewshire militia; Hon. Francis Sempill; Hon. Maria Janet Sempill; Hon. Sarah Sempill.

MACDOWALL OF CASTLESEMPLE.—This highly respectable family requires to be particularly taken notice of. The first that was connected with this county, was

Colonel William M'Dowall, a younger son of M'Dowall of Garthland, in the county of Wigton. In the course of service, he had occasion to be employed in the island of St. Christophers, in the West Indies. There he married   daughter of Mrs. Milliken of Milliken, by her first husband, with whom he acquired a considerable estate or plantation in that island. By this Lady he had a son, William, of whom afterwards. In 1727, he purchased the ancient barony of Castlesemple, in this parish, from Hugh, the 11th Lord Sempill, in whose family it had previously been for many hundred years. He married, secondly, Isabella Wallace, sister of Mr. Biggar (otherwise Wallace) of Woolmet, near Edinburgh, by whom he had, 1. James, who went to the West Indies; 2. John, who succeeded his uncle in the lands of Woolmet. Colonel M'Dowall, the first of Castlesemple, died in 1748. He was succeeded by the son of his first Lady,

William M'Dowall, second of Castlesemple. In 1760, he purchased the family estate of Garthland from his cousin, William M'Dowall, Esq; of Garthland, and, on his death, in 1775, he assumed the title of Garthland, prefixing it to Castlesemple.   He married Elizabeth, daughter of James Graham, Esq; of Airth, by whom he had, 1. William, of whom afterwards; 2. James, a merchant in Glasgow, and at one time provost of that city He married Isobell, daughter of   Peters of Crossbasket, by whom he had issue: William, at present comptroller of the customs at Greenock, and proprietor of Skiff Park, part of the estate of Castlesemple; 3. Dayhort M'Dowall, Esq; of Walkinshaw, Barns, &c. since sold. He married Wilhelmina, daughter of Mr. Graham of Airth. He died in 1809. Issue, William M'Dowall, Esq; Advocate; 4. Hay M'Dowall, a General in the army, died in   ; 5. David M'Dowall, a captain in the navy, who lost a hand in Rodney's memorable engagement, 12th April 1782. Married Miss Grant, heiress of Arndilly, and is now David M'Dowall Grant of Arndilly, Esq; 6. Lawrence since dead Lieutenant Colonel of the Renfrewshire militia; and two who died abroad.

William M'Dowall, Esq; of Garthland, and third of Castlesemple, succeeded his father in 1786. He was appointed His Majesty's Lieutenant of the county of Renfrew, in 1793, and continued in that station while he lived. He also represented the county in five different parliaments, commencing in the years 1783, 1784, and in 1802, 1806 and 1807, in which last he continued till his death, on the second of May 1810. He died unmarried. He was a man singularly endowed with talents, and every good and praise-worthy disposition, as the following resolutions of a very numerous and most respectable meeting of the noblemen, gentlemen, freeholders, magistrates of Towns, and heritors of the county, called together for the purpose, at Renfrew, on the 30th October, 1810, amply testify, in which it was unanimously resolved,—

1st. That it is a tribute justly due to the memory of those, who, placed in eminent situations, have distinguished themselves by zealous and patriotic exertions for promoting the welfare of their country, to record, by some public act, the high estimation in which such patriotic conduct is deservedly held.

2d. That the late William M'Dowall, Esq; during a long series of years discharged, on every occasion, the duties of those important stations to which he was called, with unwearied assiduity, and with uncommon ability and zeal for the public good, and thereby essentially promoted the prosperity, not only of his native county, but of Scotland in general, as has been invariably felt and acknowledged by the commercial, manufacturing, and agricultural classes of this part of the empire.

3d. That, while they, who compose the present meeting, as well as the inhabitants of Renfrewshire in general, during the period of a long and uninterupted intercourse with Mr. M'Dowall, have had the best access to know, and to appreciate his innate worth, and superior talents and accomplishments, and therefore, require no additional aid to keep alive the remembrance of all his public and private virtues; still they consider it their duty, to mark their feelings, on the present occasion, by some deed which may transmit to posterity the high and grateful sense which the county at large entertain of the energy and ability which he uniformly exerted and displayed, in promoting whatever tended to advance the best interests of his country, and which, joined to an enlightened understanding, to a deportment at once dignified and condescending, and a suavity of manners peculiarly his own, rendered him most justly esteemed, respected, and beloved by all.

They accordingly caused a monument to be erected in the Abbey Church of Paisley [1], with the following inscription :—

---

[1] This monument was designed by Flaxam, London, and was exeeuted by Gowans, Edinburgh. It is of white marble, cost £.800, and is placed above the gallery, below the east window.

CONTINUATION OF THE

TO THE MEMORY
OF
WILLIAM MACDOWALL
OF CASTLESEMPLE AND GARTHLAND,
HIS MAJESTY'S LIEUTENANT;
AND
IN FIVE PARLIAMENTS
THE REPRESENTATIVE
FOR
RENFREWSHIRE,
ERECTED BY THE COUNTY,
A MEMORIAL OF ESTEEM FOR
HIS PRIVATE VIRTUES,
AND GRATITUDE FOR
HIS PUBLIC SERVICES.
MDCCCX.

HARVEY OF CASTLESEMPLE.—John Harvey, Esq; of Castlesemple, is son of the late William Rae and Elizabeth Harvey, daughter of John Harvey of Midmar, in the county of Aberdeen. On the death of his uncle, Robert Harvey, Esq; of the isle of Grenada, in the West Indies, he succeeded to his estates there, in consequence of his last will; which farther directed and required that his nephew, John Rae, should take the surname, and bear the Arms of Harvey only. This has been done accordingly, under his majesty's royal licence and authority, dated, at Whitehall, the 4th January 1792.

Arms.—Gules on a bend Erminois, Three Trefoils Slipped Vert; On a chief Argent, a Buck's head Cabossed Azure, between two Mullets of the field. Crest. On a Wreath of the Colours, a Cubit Arm proper, issuing from a Crescent, Or; charged with a Buck'shead Cabossed Azure, in a Hand, a Trefoil as in the Arms. Motto. "Omnia Bene."

ADAM OF GARPELL.—Mr. Adam's paternal grandfather was proprietor of the lands of Kersehead, in the parish of Dalry in Ayrshire, which he purchased in the name of his son, Hamilton Adam, who, in 1759, bought the lands of Burnfoot, from John King of Garpell, and the west Sandilands from William M'Dowall, Esq; of Garthland, in 1785, both in the vicinity of Lochwinnoch. In 1758, he married Janet, daughter of Michael Nasmyth, school-master in Lochwinnoch, who had previously commenced a manufactory of ounce threads, and was the first that introduced that branch of manufacture into that neighbourhood. Of this marriage, the only issue now living, is James Adam, Esq; now of Garpell, which property, on the death of his father, he purchased, having at the same time sold the lands of Kersehead. He has since acquired the lands of Barr, and other lands in this parish, formerly the property of Mr. M'Dowall of Garthland and Castlesemple. He married Miss Sheddon, daughter of Mr. Sheddon of Moricehill, near Beith, and has several children.

COCHRANE OF LADYLAND—The lands of Belltrees, that were previously possessed by Robert Orr, (who acquired them from William M'Dowall, Esq; of Castlesemple, who had purchased them from Robert Semple, mentioned by Crawfurd, page 79) came to this family in this manner.

Robert Orr, as above, married Margaret Cochrane, sister of William Cochrane of Ladyland, and died in 1770, without issue. He was succeeded by his brother-in-law, the said

William Cochrane, Esq; of Ladyland. In 1756, he married Janet Glasgow, daughter of Robert Glasgow, Esq; of Pudevenholme and other lands, part of the estate of Glengarnock, and sister to Robert Glasgow, Esq; of Mount-Grenan, in Ayrshire, by whom he had six sons and four daughters. The eldest son is,

William Cochrane, Esq; now of Ladyland and Belltrees. On the 5th September 1815, he married Catherine Hamilton, eldest daughter of William Hamilton, Esq; of Craighlaw, in the county of Wigton, and of Garvocks in Renfrewshire, sister to William Hamilton, Esq; the present proprietor of these lands, who is at present a Lieutenant in the 10th royal hussars.

KILBARCHAN PARISH.

Situation and Extent.—This parish is situated to the north of the preceding, and adjacent to it. It is of a triangular form, bounded on two sides by waters, (the Black Cart and the Gryfe) and on the third side, by part of the parishes of Lochwinnoch and Kilmalcolm. The length from E. to W. is seven miles, and in breadth it is from a singlepoint on the east, to four miles at the west end. The extent in all is about 9,200 English acres.

Surface and Soil.—The lower part, towards the east, is a flat country, partly fertile land and partly unreclaimed moss. Towards the west it rises into small hills, of which a great part is cultivated. The whole abounds in beautiful scenery from the great diversity in the surface, and it is further embellished with plantations around the seats of its numerous proprietors.

State of Property.—JOHNSTONE, (p. 82), which belonged to a branch of the family of Houstoun, was purchased in 1733, by the ancestor of the present proprietor, Sir William Milliken Napier, and from that time was called Milliken, while the name of Johnstone was transferred by the former proprietor, Mr. Houstoun, to Easter Cochrane, now Johnstone, where he resides.

Craigends, long the patrimony of an ancient branch of the family of Glencairn, (see p. 97), is still the property and place of residence of Cuninghame of Craigends.

Thirdpart, that belonged to the Semples has, for 60 years past, made part of the estate of Castlesemple, which includes a considerable part of the lands lying next to it, in the parish of Kilbarchan.

Achinames, which, for many ages, was the property of a great branch of the original house of Crawfurd, is still retained in that family as superior, but the property has been parcelled out among a great many small proprietors, who pay each an annual feu duty.

Waterstoun, which was long of *that-ilk*, (see p. 96), to a family of the same name, has gone through many hands, and is now included among the possessions of the Napiers of Milliken family.

Bruntchells, has been in many hands since Crawfurd wrote, (see p. 96), and has of late been divided into many different parcels. (See the table).

Ramphorlie, (see p. 95), did not remain long with the family of Dundonald. It was acquired by the family of Aikenhead, (now Holmehead,) with whom it remains in property or in superiority, as specified in the table.

Blackstoun, (see p. 90), is still in the family of Napier. On this property there is a good mansion, pleasantly situated on the left bank of the Black Cart, well sheltered among some ancient wood. The house of Craigends, is a chearful habitation, situated in a peninsula, betwixt the Gryfe and the Locher, having a due portion of old wood and young plantations. The house of Milliken, (ancient Johnstone), was formerly situated on the brow of a height, overlooking a great extent of a very interesting country. The present mansion might enjoy the same prospect, were it not hid amidst its very extensive plantations, which, however, are greatly ornamental to this part of the country. There are other mansions of proprietors in this parish, that enliven the general scenery, from amid their respective plantations, as Bankhead, in the neighbourhood of Kilbarchan, Glentyan, belonging now to Captain James Stirling, R. N. and Forehouse, Mr. Barbour, both in the vicinity of that town; also, Clippens, Dr. Cochran, and several more of lesser note.

TABLE OF PROPERTY.

Properties.	Proprietors.	Valued Rent.			Extent English Acres.
Johnstone or Milliken, ...	Sir William M. Napier,	566	13	4	
Over do. and Kilbarchan estate, ...	Do. do.	666	18	8	
Weetlands, ...	Do. do.	50			
Barr or Barrhill, ...	Do. do.	100			
Thirdpart, Corseford, Corseflat, Clochadrich, Nebanny, &c.	John Harvey, Esq; of Castlesemple, ...	922	13	8	1006
Craigends, Kaimhill, and Fulton's Hallgreen, ...	John Cuningham, Esq; of Craigends, ...	922	13	4	
Blackstoun, Selvielands, &c.	William Napier, Esq.	657	13	4	
Bankhead, ...	Mr. Orr's representatives,	167	9		
Lawmarnock, ...	Mr. M'Call, ...	123	0	3	
Cartside, ...	William Barr, ...	50			
Killoochant, ...	James Clomie, ...	50			
Huthead, ...	James Jackson, ...	43			
Damton, ...	Mr. How, ...	36	13	4	
Gladston, ...	James Jackson, ...	38	6	8	
Roberton, ...	John Speirs, ...	33	6	8	
Pissinlinn, ...	William Fife, ...	33	6	8	
Wardend, ...	John Ritchie, ...	33			
13 Sundry small Lots, .	Sundry people, ...	127	1	1	
Eight old feuars of Burntchells, ...	Sundry people, ...	115	16	8	
Three late feuars of do. ... :	Lang, Graham, Holmes,	100			
Lands of Law. { Law, ...	Mr. M'Call, ...	63			
Goldenknolls, &c....	John Barr, ...	42	13	4	
Wardhouse, ...	John Speirs, ...	38	13	4	
Four lesser Lots, ...	Gardner, Craig, Lang,	64	2		
Ramphorlie, ...	Hamilton of Holmehead,	300			
Barnbrock, feu of do.	Adam Keir, Esq; ...	50			
Barmufflock, do.	Heirs of Capt. Troop,	50			
Barnbeth, do.	John Stevenson, ...	33	6	8	513
Bridge of Weir, do.	James Lyle, ...	26	13	4	
Clovens, Horsewood, do.	John Barr, &c.	40			
Tors, ...	Heirs of Dr. Colquhoun,	260			
Auchincloich and Auchinsales, ...	Mr. M'Call, ...	190			
Manswary, ...	Mr. M'Culloch, ...	52			
Littletown, ...	John Armour, ...	29	3	4	36
Plainlee, ...	James How, ...	26	13	4	
Clippens, ...	Dr. Patrick Cochran,	26	13	4	
Sandholes, ...	John Aitkin, ...	26	13	4	
Burnfoot, ...	James Clark, ...	23	6	8	22
Moss-side, ...	John Speirs, ...	16			
Muirhead, ...	John Jameson's heirs, .	16	13	4	
Total, ...		6278	8	8	9200

Feuars of Achinames.

And which may be arranged thus :—

	Eng. Acres
1. Arable, in cultivation,	5400
2. Sound dry pasture,	2000
3. Moss unreclaimed,	1200
4. Sites of houses, roads, waters,	140
5. Woods and Plantations,	460
Total,	9200

Succession of Ministers.—In 1602, Robert Stirling. In 1605, Andrew Hamilton. In 1649, John Stirling, outed in 1662, for non-compliance. In 1688, James Stirling, translated to Glasgow in 1699. In 1701, Robert Johnstone, died in 1738. In 1739, John Warner, died in 1786. In 1787, Patrick Maxwell, after some opposition; died in 1806. In 1802, Robert Douglas, the present minister, ordained assistant and successor.

Villages.—Kilbarchan, in the year 1740 contained 40 families, or about 200 souls, and would at that time be reckoned a considerable village. In the year 1791, the number of inhabitants had increased so much as to amount to 391 families, or about 1780 souls, (see Stat. Scot. vol. 15.) and in 1811, the number had still increased, but much slower, to 1898. It is probable that the increase has not been much since. It is a town chearfully situated, on a gently rising plain, surrounded by higher grounds on all sides, except to the south-east, to which direction only it is open. The chief source of employment is in the linen and cotton manufactures, including three bleachfields.

Bridge of Weir. This is a very cheerful small village, situated in a hollow, on the banks of the Gryfe, on the great road from Kilbarchan to Port-Glasgow. It owes nearly its whole existence to the cotton manufacture. Perhaps 20 families in it.

Linwood. This is a regular built town on a handsome plan, situated by the Black Cart, on the estate of Blackstoun. It has arisen entirely from a cotton work erected about 30 years ago, of an immense size, calculated to work 25,000 spindles, and, when completed, to employ 1800 people. The whole machinery is put in motion by water. The number of people in this village is about 600.

Family Descent.—CRAWFURD OF AUCHINAMES, (see p. 80).—This is a family of very great antiquity, and purely of native origin, underived from either Norman or other foreign blood. It is also the chief stem of a very numerous class of ancient Scottish Barons, who flourished in the most early period of authentic Scottish history.

From what the most respectable authors on heraldry have delivered, it appears, that the Crawfurds in particular, in the reign of David I. were of great distinction; that two brothers of that name, both Knights, were in the service of that Prince; and that Sir Gregan, the younger of the two, opportunely came to the relief of the king, who had been dishorsed by a stag or deer near Edinburgh, on Holyrood-day, A. D. 1127. That an account of this happy interposition, his armorial bearings were changed from Gules, a Fess Ermine, to Three Stags Heads, erazed Gules, which were carried by all his posterity, except the families of Crawfurd of Kerse and Drumsoy, who carry, (as the more simple achievement) only one Stag's Head, erazed Gules, in a Field Argent.

It further appears, from a variety of evidence, that there were anciently three great families of the name of Crawfurd, viz. I. Crawfurd of Crawfurd, which failed of male issue in the person of Sir John Crawfurd, who died in 1248. He left two daughters; 1. Margaret, married to Archibaldus de Duglas, Dominus loci ejusdem. He got with her part of the Lordship of Crawfurd, and from whom is descended the potent and widely extended house of Douglas; the 2. married Sir David de Lindsay of Wauchopedale, who got with her the remainder of the Lordship of Crawfurd, and from whom are descended the Earls of Crawfurd and Lindsay.

II. The family of Crawfurd. John, who descended from Sir John Crawfurd, the brother of Sir Gregan, and who must have inherited those lands as a portion distinct from the lands of Crawfurd, proper. From this family descended the Crawfurds of Loudon, the families of Achinames, Kilbirnie, &c. The Kilbirny family was by a daughter, who married Barclay, a south country Knight, who assumed the name of Crawfurd, on receiving with his wife, half of the Barony of Crawfurd-John; from them again descended, the Viscounts of Garnock, the Crawfurds of Jordanhill, &c. III. The family of Dalmacgregan, who, as Mr. Crawfurd tells us, in his register of blazons, were called Lords of Dalmacgregan in Nithsdale, and of Torringzean in Kyle. This family and its numerous cadets, are all descended from Sir Gregan Crawfurd, who saved the life of King David, as above.

The Crawfurds of Dalmacgregan, or of the Vale of the the son of Gregan, are also distinguished from other Crawfurds, by their armorial bearings, the Stag's heads, whereas, all the other Crawfurds, carry the original Coat, Gules, a Fess Ermine. Their chief, the Lord of Dalmacgregan, fell with the Douglases, when they were forfeited as Earls of Galloway; but from this family have sprung all the Crawfurds, who bear the Stag's Head, namely, the Crawfurds of Torringzean—of Kerse—of Balquhanny—of Drongan—of Liffhores, and of Camlarg. All the families who carried the Stag's Head, are now extinct, with the exception of Kerse and Drumsoy, now united with Achinames, as shall speedily be shewn.

Many of the original charters and papers, belonging to the ancient families of Kerse and Drumsoy, happening to be in the hands of Ronald Crawfurd, Esq; W. S. a son of the family of Drumsoy, perished in a fire, which burnt his house in Edinburgh 9th May 1741. This is the reason that the following genealogy of these families begins much later than it otherwise would have done. It is collected also, in some parts, from extraneous, but perfectly well vouched authorities, in addition to the charters and other papers that were preserved. The first recorded in these is,

I. Esplin Crawfurd of Kerse, married Sibella Little, as appears from a charter dated 26th January 1488. He was succeeded by his eldest son,

II. Alexander, who is mentioned in a charter in 1505. He was succeeded by his brother,

II. Bartholemew. He married Anne, daughter of Lord Evandale, directly descended from King Robert II. By whom he had,

III. David of Kerse. He had charters in 1526 and 1539 of various estates. He married Catherine, daughter of Hamilton of Sanquhar, by whom he had two sons. From the second of whom, William, descended the Crawfurds of Drumsoy.

IV. David, the eldest son, succeeded him in Kerse. He had a charter in 1583, confirming to him some lands near Sanquhar. He was one of the wardens of the marches, in the minority of James VI. He married Jean, a daughter of Lord Fleming, by whom he had four daughters, married respectively to Gordon of Craiglaw—Boswell of Auchinleck—Wauchope of Edmeston, and Maxwell of Newark. He had no male issue. We return now to his brother,

IV. William Crawfurd of Drumsoy. He married Christian, daughter of James M'Gill, the first Viscount Oxenfurd, by whom he had,

V. Duncan of Drumsoy, who married, about 1600, Margaret, daughter of Sir Robert Fairly of that-ilk, by whom he had his successor,

VI. David of Drumsoy. He married his cousin, daughter of Gordon of Craiglaw, by the eldest daughter of the IV. David Crawford of Kerse, by whom he had, 1. David; 2. Esplin, who died unmarried; 3. Patrick, of whom afterwards. He died about the year 1660, and was succeeded by his eldest son,

VII. David of Drumsoy. He married a daughter of Crawfurd of Ardmillan, by whom he had a daughter, married to Stewart of Fintulloch, who had issue, two daughters, and a son.

VIII. David, historiographer of Scotland to Queen Anne. He was a man of genius and abilities. He wrote a historical defence of Mary, Queen of Scots, which is much esteemed. He was married but left no productive issue. He died in the lifetime of his father. The representation of the family now devolved on his uncle,

VII. Patrick, the third son of David, No. VI. as above. He married, first, a daughter of Gordon of Turnberry, (and niece of David Crawfurd, heir male of the family of Liffnores,) by whom he had, 1. Thomas, who was first Secretary to the Embassy of the Earl of Stair, then charge des affaires, and lastly, Envoy extraordinary to the court of France. He died, in 1724, at Paris; 2. Robert, who died unmarried; 3. a daughter, Anne, to Mr. William Hogg, merchant, Edinburgh, without issue; 4. Margaret, married to John Cochrane, Esq; of Ravelrig, to whom she had one daughter only, who was married to David Ross, Esq; of Inverchastly, a Lord of Session. He married, secondly, Jane, second daughter of Archibald Crawfurd of Achinames, by whom he had seven sons, of whom immediately, (and two daughters who died unmarried,) and in her right, became possessed of the estates of Achinames and Crosbie, &c. by whom he had, 1. Patrick, of whom afterwards; 2. George, died a Lieutenant Colonel of the 53d regiment, in 1758, leaving issue, by Anne, daughter of Randall of Salisbury, a son, Patrick George, who died in 1804. and a daughter, Mary, married to Thomas Gilbert, a distinguished member of Parliament; 3. Ronald Crawfurd of Restalrig, a writer to to the signet. He married in 1743, Catherine, daughter of John Forbes, Esq; of Newhall. He died in 1763, leaving a son, Patrick, who died unmarried, and one daughter, Margaret, married Patrick, Earl of Dumfries, to whom she had a daughter, 1. Elizabeth, married to the Viscount Mount Stewart, by whom she was mother of the present Marquis of Bute, who, in her right, inherits also the estate and honours of Dumfries. 2. Jane, married to William Berry, nephew and heir of Mr. Fergusson of Raith, and has issue, two sons, Robert and Ronald. 3. Annabella, married to William Fullarton, Esq; of Rosemount; and a daughter who died unmarried. 4. James Crawfurd, who was a considerable merchant in Holland. He married Elizabeth, daughter of   Andrews, a merchant in Rotterdam, by whom he had the following children, who attained to mature years; 1. Patrick, who, in 1769, was appointed conservator of Scots privileges in Holland. 2. James, 3. George who, in conjunction with Patrick, supported their father's house and carried on his trade, which was considerable; 4. Ronald, was a merchant in Glasgow, in the house of Speirs and Co. 5. Margaret, married to Macleod of Geanies, and has issue. He died at Rotterdam in 1766; 5. Hugh Crawfurd, who was a merchant in the East Indies, where he died unmarried; 6. Alexander Crawfurd, in the army, died in Lord

Cathcart's expedition to Carthagena ; 7. John Crawfurd, the youngest son, was bred in the army, and was in much active service, and attained to the rank of Lieutenant General. After the peace of 1763, he was appointed Governor of Minorca, where he died unmarried, universally esteemed as a good officer and a most worthy gentleman. Patrick Crawfurd of Drumsoy, Achinames, and Crosbie, &c. died in 1733, and was succeeded by his eldest son,

VIII. Patrick Crawfurd of Achinames and Drumsoy, heir, male, and representative of the family of Kerse, and of all the Crawfurds of Kyle, viz. Camlarg, Drongan, Balquhanny, Torringzean, &c. His mother, who died in 1740, was sole heiress of Archibald, the 12th Laird of Achinames, the male heir of Sir Reginald de Crawfurd of Loudon, who, in the days of Wallace, was murdered by the English at Ayr, whose eldest son had an only daughter, who married Sir Duncan Campbell, progenitor of the Earls of Loudon, and whose uncle, Reginald Crawfurd, was the first Baron of Achinames, from whom Archibald, as above, was descended in a direct line.

The above Patrick Crawfurd of Achinames, was twice chosen Knight of the shire, for the county of Ayr ; 1st, in the Parliament, which met in December 1741; 2d, in the Parliament, which met in November 1747. He sat also in a third Parliament, namely, in that which met in April 1761, in which he represented the county of Renfrew.

He married, first, Elizabeth, daughter and one of the coheiresses of George Middleton, Esq; Banker in London, descended of the renowned family of Fettercairn, Earls of Middleton. By that lady, he had two sons; 1. John, of whom afterwards; 2. James Crawfurd, Colonel in the guards, and one of the Equerries to her Majesty, He was Governor of Bermuda, and died without issue in 1811.

He married, secondly, Sarah, daughter of Lord Sempill, by whom he had a daughter, Sarah, born in 1751, at Errol, in Perthshire. She died unmarried, at Bermuda 1796. He died in 1778, and was succeeded by his son,

IX. John Crawfurd of Auchinames, &c. He was member for Old Sarum in the Parliament that sat in April 1768, and afterwards for the county of Renfrew in the next Parliament which sat in October 1774. He was an intimate friend, and associate of Charles James Fox. He died unmarried 25th May 1814, and was succeeded by his cousin,

X. John Crawfurd, now of Achinames, Kerse, Errol, &c. the eldest surviving son of Patrick George, who was son of Lieutenant-Colonel George Crawfurd, (vide supra). The said Patrick George died in 1804. He married Jane, daughter of Lieutenant-Colonel Donald Macdonald, of the 84th regiment, Brigadier-General in America, by which lady, who died in July, 1811, he left, 1. George, who died unmarried in 1804; 2. John, as above; 3. William Petrie; 4. Donald; 5. Margaret; 6. Catherine.

Patrick, (No. VIII.) father of the late John Crawfurd, feued out, in 1764, the whole of the Achinames estate in Renfrewshire, retaining only the superiority; but the lands of Crosbie, Arniel, &c. in Ayrshire, are still possessed by the family.

John, the present proprietor, married, in 1814, Sophia Marianna, daughter of Major-General Horace Churchill, and has issue, 1. Edward Henry John; 2. Katherina Horatia.

Having thus brought down the genealogy of the family of Kerse and Drumsoy, we shall now revert to that of Achinames, previous to its junction with the former. Should this part of the narrative be considered as rather concisely stated, it must be imputed to the nature of this work, which does not admit of much amplification. It is already stated (see above) that this branch of the family is derived from the House of the ancient Crawfurds of Loudon, in the days of the renowned Wallace, about the year 1300, when a Reginald de Crawfurd, an immediate descendant of that family, was Baron of Achinames. From the loss of a considerable part of the family papers by fire, in 1741, as already stated, there occurs a chasm in the history of the descent of this line, as well as of the others; but that the Crawfurds were in possession of Achinames about the year 1300, appears also from the original history of Renfrewshire, published by Crawfurd in 1710; in which that remarkably accurate annalist stated, (page 80.) that they had been in possession of Achinames well nigh 400 years, which he must have known from an inspection of the family papers then in existence, and this coincides with the account as now given. The next in record in the family papers still preserved, after Reginald, was,

I. Thomas Crawfurd of Achinames, who, in 1401, (see page 81.) modifies a certain sum to an altar in the church of Kilbarchan. He was succeeded by his son,

II. Archibald, who is recorded as obtaining a charter of part of these lands in 1427. His son,

III. Robert Crawfurd of Achinames, gives a charter to his sons, James, Henry, and Robert, in 1483, and is recorded as an arbiter on the part of the Abbot of Paisley in 1448. He fell at the battle of Flodden in 1513. He married, first, Isabel, daughter of George, Master of Angus, by whom he had a daughter, Margaret, married to Sempill of Noblestoun. 2dly, Marion, daughter of Houston of that-ilk, by whom he had three sons. He was succeeded by the eldest,

IV. James of Achinames, who, in 1498, gets a charter of the lands of Corsbie and Munock, and is a party in other charters in 1526 and 1533. He was succeeded by his son,

V. Thomas Crawfurd of Achinames, who, in 1539, obtains a gift of the non-entries of the lands of Auldmuir. He married Marion Montgomery, daughter of the laird of Hazlehead, (of the family of Eglintoun) by whom he left three sons, all successively lairds of Achinames. He was succeeded by the eldest son,

VI. John Crawfurd of Achinames in 1544. He was killed at the battle of Pinkie, 10th September 1547. He married a daughter of the second laird of Craigends, but left no issue.

VI. William, his next brother, succeeded him as laird of Achinames. He is mentioned in a legal deed in 1588. He married 'Annabella, daughter of the laird of Gadgirth, by whom he had a son, James, who died before him; but who previously married Elizabeth, daughter of the Earl of Glencairn, who is infeft in the lands of Corsbie in 1579. By this lady he left an only daughter, Jane, heiress of Corsbie, of whom afterwards.

William, as above, died about the year 1585, the youngest brother,

VI. Patrick, succeeds to Achinames and other lands. He appears in a process, in 1586, about Munock and Gill; and, in 1588, gives a seisine of lands to the laird of Hazlehead. He married a daughter of Frazer of Knock, by whom he had his successor,

VII. William, who married, about the year 1600, Margaret, daughter of Houston of that-ilk, by whom he had a son,

VIII. Patrick Crawfurd of Achinames, for whom his cousin Jane, the heiress of Corsbie, in the strong regard that prevailed in those times for family aggrandisement, reserved herself, and by their marriage, she, at 28, and he, at 18 years, the ancient patrimony of the family was again united. The issue of this auspicious marriage was six sons and two daughters. The daughters were married, one to Sempill of Fulwood, and the other to Frazer of Knock.

IX. William, the eldest son, succeeded his father, and was infeft as his heir in 1649. He married Anna, daughter of Colonel Sir   Lamont of Ineryne, by whom he had issue a son, of whom afterwards, and four daughters; 1.   married to Houstoun of that-ilk; 2.   married to Hunter of Hunterston; 3.   married to Kennedy of Killichangie; 4.   married to Boyd of Trochrig. He was succeeded by his only son,

X. Archibald Crawfurd, the 10th generation here recorded, and 12th laird or baron of Achinames. He married, first, Margaret, daughter of Porterfield of that-ilk, by whom he had a son, William, of whom afterwards, and three daughters; 1. Anna, married James Bruce of Powfouls, without issue; 2. Jane, married (as before stated) to Patrick Crawfurd of Kerse and Drumsoy; 3. Margaret, married James Young of Killicanty, without issue.

XI. William, his only son, married Helen, daughter of Sir Thomas Burnet, M. D. eldest son of Lord Crimond, and brother of Bishop Burnet, but died without issue. On which, his father, unwilling that his estates should pass from the family through a female, married, 2dly, a lady of the family of Shaw Stewart of Greenock, but was in this disappointed, for by this lady he had no issue.

William had previously married of which marriage there was only one daughter, Helen, married to Patrick Edmeston of Newtoun, and as he died before his father, the direct male line of this family ended; but Jane, the second daughter, having married the male representative of the other families of this house, descended of Sir Gregan Crawfurd, and derived all, as there is every reason to believe, from the same original stock, an arrangement was made by which the estates of Corsbie and Achinames were retained to her and her husband, (and who, in a judicial proceeding, was decerned and ordained as heir male of Archibald and William,) who represented the families of Kerse and Drumsoy, so that the representation of the whole centered in the issue of that marriage, as already related in the genealogy of the house of Kerse.

Arms are now quarterly, Argent, a Stag's head, Gules, for Kerse and Drumsoy, &c. and Gules a fess ermine, surmounted of two spears in Saltire, for Achinames. Supporters, two Bulls sable, armed and enguelled, Or; Crest, a Stag's head, erazed Gules, with a cross Crosslet fitchee betwixt the attires. Motto, " Tutum te Robore Reddam."

CUNINGHAME of CRAIGENDS—from page 98, and also, two other sons, William and James; and three daughters; 1. Lillias, married to Thomas Wallace of Cairnhill; 2. Magdalene, married to Mungo Campbell of Netherplace; 4. Elizabeth, married to Gabriel Porterfield of Hapland, all in Ayrshire; William married Martha, daughter of John Robison, merchant, Glasgow, by whom he had an only daughter, Margaret; James died unmarried . He was succeeded by his eldest son,

Alexander Cunninghame, Esq; of Craigends, who married, 1st, Anne, daughter of Sir John Houstoun of that-ilk, by whom he had a son, William, who succeeded him, and two daughters; 1. Christian, married to Boyd Porterfield of that-ilk, and had issue; 2. Joanna, married to Claud Alexander, Esq; of Newton, and had issue, also two daughters, who died unmarried; 2dly, he married

Catherine, daughter of Sir James Campbell of Houstoun, without issue. He was succeeded by his only son,

William Cuninghame, Esq; of Craigends. He married his cousin, Margaret, (vide supra), by whom he had three sons; 1. Alexander; 2. William; 3. John. The eldest son,

Alexander Cuninghame, Esq; of Craigends, succeeded his father, but died in 1790, without surviving issue, and was succeeded by William Cuninghame, Esq; of Craigends, his brother. He died unmarried, and was succeeded by his brother in 1792, the present proprietor, John Cuninghame, Esq; of Craigends, who has considerably increased the family estate, by different purchases of lands in the neighbourhood, (included in the tables of property, in the parishes of Kilbarchan and Houstoun). He married, 1st, in 1794, Frances, daughter of the late Sir James Maxwell, Bart. of Pollok. She died in 1797, without issue. In 1800, he married, 2dly, Margaret, 2d daughter of Sir William Cuninghame of Robertland, by whom he has

FIVE SONS.

1. William;
2. Alexander;
3. John;
4. Boyd Alexander;
5. Robert Charles,

AND SIX DAUGHTERS,

1. Anne Colquhoun;
2. Margaret;
3. Frances Maxwell;
4. Lillias;
5. Janet Lucretia;
6. Williamina

Arms.—Quarterly; first and fourth Argent, a Shake Fork Sable; for Cuninghame; second and third, Or; a Fess Cheque Azure and Argent for Stewart; Crest, a Unicorn's Head, couped Argent, horned and maned, Or; and gorged with a Collar Checque, Argent and Azure; motto, " So, fork, forward."

Napier Milliken of Milliken.—In this family is vested the direct male representation of the ancient house of Napier, by the following line of descent.

I. John Napier of Merchistoun, the celebrated inventor of Logarithms, whose renown reflects a lustre, not only on the family, but on the nation from which he sprung, was the twelfth generation from the first ancestor of the family, who assumed that name from their lands in Dumbartonshire, as recorded by Wood, in the Peerage of Scotland, which may be consulted for a more particular account.

He was born in 1550, at Merchistoun, near Edinburgh, or, as some accounts say, at Gartness, in Stirlingshire, at a time when his father could not have been above 16 years of age. After finishing his studies at St. Andrew's, he is said to have made the tour of France, Italy, and Germany. On his return home, he led a life of great retirement, devoting his time to the study of mathematics and the Holy Scriptures. The first has in all ages been the study of men of science, and the last is at all times of essential importance, but at this particular æra would be more than usually interesting, from having been more recently the subject of general investigation, and which, in a peculiar manner, had at that time agitated the Christian world. His success in the former is sufficiently evinced by his discovery of the Logarithmical Canon, a sublime invention of universal utility, the result of patient and intense meditation. His researches in prophecy were profound, although the result is now known to have been erroneous, at the same time the principles he set out on may have been radically true.

It is not the plan of this work to enlarge much on the characters of individuals, or even to record all the circumstances of their lives. In the present case, it is sufficient to take notice of the following works of this great man.

In 1614, he published, at Edinburgh, Mirifici Logarithmorum, &c. In 1617, appeared his work, entitled, Rabdologiæ, &c. This was the last of his works published in his lifetime.

After his death, his son, Robert, (ancestor of Milliken) to whom he left the care of his M.SS. published, in 1619,—" Mirifici apsius canonis constructio et
" Logarithmorum ad naturales ipsonem numeros habitudines. 2. Appendix de
" alia atque præstantiore Logarithmorum specie construenda in qua scilicet uni-
" tatis logarithmus esto. 3. Propositiones quædam eminentissimæ ad triangula
" sphærica mira facilitate resolvenda."

Besides his superlative genius for mathematical investigations, he was singularly endowed with the powers of mathematical invention, of which many examples, truly wonderful, are well authenticated. With the populace, the exertions of his mind in this line were concluded to have been altogether supernatural. In the vicinity of his seat, near Edinburgh, where he frequently resided, he is still called by the name of Marvellous Merchistoun, and many a wonderful exploit is still recorded of him. At Gartness too, where he occasionally resided, he was viewed in the same light, as he was then believed to have been a warlock or a wizard, a notion not fully rooted out to this day. Mr. Wood observes, that he might amuse himself, by encouraging this belief in his necromancy, as it would have the effect to prevent his neighbours from intruding upon him, and interrupting his studies.

To Napier, Kepler dedicated his Ephemeridas, esteeming him to be the greatest man of his age, in the particular department to which he applied his mind. Indeed, when we reflect that his discoveries were not connected with any analogies that might have led him to them, but the fruit of unassisted reflection, we must consider him as one of the most sublime geniuses that has appeared among mankind. He died 3d April 1617, in the 67th year of his age, and was buried in the church of St. Giles, Edinburgh, where the family burial place is thus inscribed :—

"Sep. familiæ Naperorū interius hic Situm est."

He married, first, Elizabeth, daughter of Sir James Stirling of Keir, by whom he had Archibald, who succeeded him, and a daughter; secondly, he married Agnes, daughter of Chisholm of Cromlix, by whom he had, 1. John, of Easter Torry, who left no issue; 2. Robert, ancestor of Milliken, of whom immediately, 3. Alexander of Torrie, left no male issue; 4. William of Ardmore, ancestor of Craigannet; 5. Adam, ancestor of Blackstoun, of whom afterwards; and five daughters, all well married. He was succeeded by his eldest son, Sir Archibald, who, in 1627, was raised to the peerage by the title of Lord Napier, to him and the heirs male of his own body. He had previous to this (but in the same year) the dignity conferred upon him of a Baronet of Nova Scotia, to him and his heirs male whatsoever. His grandson, the 3d Lord Napier, foreseeing (as he did not incline to marry,) that he would have no issue of his own, took out a new patent of the peerage, with a reversion to the heirs male or female of his father, but his patent of baronetcy remained as it was. Dying accordingly without issue, the title of Lord Napier was carried, by the issue of his eldest sister, into the family of Nicholson of Carnock, and which failing also, was carried by the issue of the second sister, into the family of Scott of Thirlestane, where it still remains; that family having assumed the arms and name of Napier, as well as having inherited the property of the third Lord Napier. The title of Baronet, not being affected by this destination, returned to the next male heir whatsoever, to which we now confine the narrative.

II. Robert, the third son of the illustrious John of Merchistoun, was designed of Culcreugh and other lands. By his first Lady, whose name is not mentioned, he had two sons, 1. Archibald, of Bowhopple, who had a numerous race of descendants, the last of whom, being the fifth generation, died without issue, in 1817; the second son of this marriage left no issue. By his second Lady, Anna Drummond, he had two sons and a daughter, the eldest, William, married and had only one son, who died young; the second son was,

III. Alexander Napier of Culcreugh, who, by a first wife had no issue, but by the second, Margaret Lennox, he had three sons.

IV. John Napier, the eldest, succeeded his father in 1702, and died in 1735. By his Lady, whose name was also Margaret Lennox, he had an only son,

V. Colonel William Napier, of Culcreugh, who married Jean, the eldest daughter of James Milliken of Milliken, of which family the connection with the county of Renfrew shall be here stated in few terms. In 1733, Major James Milliken bought the lands of Johnstone from Mr. Houstoun, the former proprietor, and as Mr. Houstoun chose to retain the title of Johnstone, Mr. Milliken called the barony Milliken, after his own name. He died in 1741. He married Mary Stephen, a widow lady, with an opulent fortune in the West Indies, by whom he had a son, James Milliken, Esq; of Milliken, who died in 1776. By his Lady, Jean, daughter of Alexander M'Dowall, Esq; of Garthland, he had two sons who died unmarried, and two daughters. The youngest, Mary, was married to Dr. Nathan Spens, physician in Edinburgh, and had issue; the eldest daughter, Jean, was married, as above, to Colonel Napier of Culcreugh, to whom she had,

VI. Robert John Napier of Milliken. He entered into the army in 1779, when very young, and went to India with his regiment, the 98th, in the expedition under General Meadows in 1781, and was wounded in the action at Port Praya. In June 1782, he got a company in the late 2d battalion of the 42d, afterwards the 73d regiment, and was with that regiment during all the campaigns on the Malabar coast. He served under the late Lieutenant Colonel Campbell, at the siege of Mangalore. Colonel Campbell having been killed in that siege, the command then devolved on Captain Napier, who made a most gallant defence for three months against a very large army. He was twice wounded in this siege, and did not surrender till, from the failure of provisions, the garrisson was reduced to the last extremity, and was, in consequence of the brave defence made, allowed to march out with all the honours of war. On this occasion the conduct of Captain Napier was so meritorious that he received the thanks of the commander in chief of the district in three different public orders.

In the year 1785, he exchanged into the 63d regiment, the majority of which he got in 1794. He went with it to the continent, in the first expedition under the Duke of York, and was there again wounded.

On the grenadier companies being formed into battalions, at the Camp of Nutscalling, he was, by Lieutenant Colonel Sir Ralph Abercombie, appointed Major of the 2d battalion. He accompanied that General in the expedition to the West Indies, and was wounded at St. Lucie.

In consequence of the many severe wounds that he had received, he was obliged to retire from actual service in 1802, having been upwards of 22 years actively employed. He was promoted to the rank of Lieutenant Colonel in the 69th regiment, and when he died was second senior Colonel in the army.

In the year 1786, he married Anne, daughter of Robert Campbell, Esq; of Downie, in Argyleshire, of which marriage there were four children, only one of whom now survives. He died in 1808, and was succeeded by his only son, William Napier Milliken of Milliken, who married Elizabeth Christian, fifth daughter of the late John Stirling, Esq; of Kippendavie, by whom he has one child, a daughter, Mary.

He is thus the heir of the two families of Milliken of Milliken and Napier of Culcroich; and being descended, as already shewn, from Robert, the third son of John Napier of Merchistoun, the celebrated inventor of Logarithms, he is the direct heir of the family of Napier also, as the second son of that family left no issue, and the eldest failed of issue male in the third generation. It will be seen also from this short genealogical memoir, that he is the seventeenth generation from the first of the Napiers of Napier, who flourished in the reign of Alexander III. King of Scots.

On the 17th of March 1818, before a most respectable Jury, at Edinburgh, he was served heir male general of Archibald, third Lord Napier of Merchistoun, Baronet of Nova Scotia, great grandson of the illustrious Philosopher, and which service carries with it the latter dignity of Knight Baronet, together with the territorial rights attached to it *, by patent, dated second May 1627, in consequence of which he now assumes the stile and dignity of Sir William Milliken Napier of Napier, Baronet, one of the oldest Baronets in Scotland, and the senior Baronet in this county.

Arms.—Quarterly; 1st and 4th, Argent, a Saltier, engrailed Gules, cantoned with four Roses, Gules, for Napier of Merchistoun; 2d, Azure, a Lion Rampant, Argent, crowned, Or; for M'Dowall of Garthland, as heir of line of that family; 3d, Argent, a Fess Azure, voided of the field, between three Demi-Lions, crowned Gules for Milliken, with the Badge of Nova Scotia surrounding the Shield. Crest of Napier of Merchistoun, an arm grasping an Eagles' leg, Proper. Crest of Milliken, a Demi Lion Rampant, Gules, holding a Dagger, Or, with a Sword in his dexter paw. Supporters, two Eagles, with their wings closed proper. Motto, " Sans Tache."

* " In Nova Scotia, beginning at the uttermost point towards the south, next the eastern " side of the barony of Dunypace, lying on the northern side of Argalis Bay, formerly, Great " French Bay, and thence eastward, three miles along the said Bay, and thence northward, " six miles back, keeping six miles in breadth, called Nepar". Vide patent.

NAPIER OF BLACKSTOUN.—For the origin of this branch of the illustrious family of Napier, see the preceding account of Milliken, from which it will appear that it was descended from the renowned philosopher, John Napier, baron of Merchistoun, whose 5th and youngest son, was,

I. Adam, who married Anna Buchanan, by whom he had,

II. Alexander, who was christened on the 3d December 1644, at Holyroodhouse, in presence of Archibald Lord Napier, and Sir George Stirling of Keir, as the record bears. He married Catherine, daughter and sole heiress of John Maxwell of Blackstoun, (see page 90.) by whom he had two sons; 1. John; 2. Alexander; and one daughter, Anne. He was succeeded by his son,

IV. John Napier, Esq; of Blackstoun, who died unmarried, and was succeeded by his brother,

IV. Alexander Napier, Esq; of Blackstoun, who entered into the army, and was a captain in the Scots Greys about the year 1730. He rebuilt the house of Blackstoun in a more modern style. The old house had been burnt by accident. He died about the year 1751. He married Mary Anna Johnstone, a lady from Dumfriesshire, by whom he had Alexander his successor, and five daughters; 1. Catherine, married to John Paterson of Craigton, Esq; 2. Anna, married to William Millar of Walkinshaw, Esq; 3. Jean; 4. Joanna; 5. Henrietta.

V. Alexander Napier, Esq; his only surviving son, succeeded him in the estate of Blackstoun. He entered at first into the army, but relinquishing that profession about the year 1768, he retired to his family estate, on which he made great improvements, and added to it by considerable purchases. He died in 1801. He married Elizabeth, second daughter of the Rev. Henry Millar, in 1774, by whom he had six sons and five daughters; 1. Alexander, of whom afterwards; 2. William, a banker in Greenock, of whom afterwards; 3. Robert, died young; 4. John, who commands a ship in the country trade in India; 5. Andrew, in the medical department of the East India Company, was lost at sea; 6. Johnstone, in the military service of the East India Company, now a Captain in the 15th regiment Madras Native Infantry. The daughters, 1. Henrietta; 2. Mary Ann, died young; 3. Elizabeth Cochran, died young; 4. Catherine, died young; and 5. Anne, married in 1810, to Captain Roger Ayton, late in the 92d regiment, son of General Ayton of Inchdarney, and has issue.

VI. Alexander Napier, Esq; the eldest son, succeeded his father in Blackstoun, on his death in 1801, as above. He entered early into the army, and after being engaged in a variety of services, in the different quarters of the globe, he succeeded to the Lieutenant Colonelcy of the 92d regiment, on the death of Lieutenant Colonel Erskine, on the 13th March 1801, in Egypt, which distinguished regiment, he commanded afterwards in all the various services in which they were engaged, till he himself was killed at Corunna, at the close of the unfortunate campaign of Sir John Moore in 1809. He was succeeded by his brother,

VI. William Napier, Esq; now of Blackstoun.

Arms.—Argent, a Saltier, engrailed Gules, cantoned with four roses, Gules. Crest, a right arm couped from the elbow, grasping a Sabre Proper; motto, " Sans Tache."

How of Damton.—Semple takes notice of a very ancient family in this parish, namely, How of Damton, and states, that the present John How (in 1782) was the 12th John, in direct descent, and the 8th that had been practitioners in medicine. The family still retains the lands of Damton and Plainlees. John How of Damton, surgeon, the same mentioned by Semple, died in November 1816. He had a son, John, a surgeon also, who died in 1797, and the family is now represented by James How, the only surviving son, manufacturer in Glasgow, and a daughter, Jean, married to Mr. Couper, surgeon, Glasgow.

HOUSTOUN AND KILLALLAN.

Situation and Extent.—These united parishes are situated adjacent to, and due north from the preceding, and divided from it in their whole extent, by the winding water of Gryfe. The greatest length is about five miles and a half from east to west, and the breadth from north to south, is from a single point, to three miles and a half. The extent in all is about 7500 English acres.

Surface and Soil.—The lower part of these parishes, towards the east, is among the flattest and the most fertile land in the county. The western part of them rises higher, and is more irregular in the surface, but is pleasantly diversified by heights and hollows. The whole of this division is incumbent on basaltic or rotten rock, which, wherever it is pulverised, by the influence of the weather, or, by cultivation, to a sufficient depth, to admit of the roots of plants getting hold, is uniformly a fertile soil. Some of this still presents bare and rocky points, but in the intervals is productive of sweet and healthy pasturage, and where planted, the young trees are thriving vigorously. About the old church of Killallan, there is a remarkably pleasant and finely sheltered tract of very fertile lands; and from the Kirktown of Houstoun, there is perhaps one of the finest prospects to be seen in Scotland, and from no point in Renfrewshire is the county itself seen to greater advantage. A small portion of the low country in the eastern division of these parishes is still incumbered with thick moss, but this is every year growing less and less from cultivation, when the subsoil, along with a small portion of moss mixed up with it, becomes very productive land.

State of Property.—HOUSTOUN, (see page 98,) the greatest property in the parish, and which had remained many ages in the family of the chief of that name, was alienated by them to Sir John Shaw of Greenock, about the year 1740. From this family it was soon disposed of to a Sir James Campbell of Jamaica, and by his heir, to Governor Macrae, by whose representatives it was sold about thirty years ago, to the father of the present proprietor, Archibald Speirs, Esq; of Elderslie. There was once a large and very ancient mansion upon it, overlooking the whole country, from one of the finest spots in it. There is one wing out of four of the old fabric still remaining, large enough to accommodate any ordinary family.

Barrochan. (see page 102,) This property, the next best in the parish, is still in the same family of Fleming that has possessed it for many ages back; part of it however is alienated to Archibald Speirs, Esq; of Elderslie. There is a good old mansion here, the seat of the family, pleasantly situated on the south side of a craggie hill, well sheltered among its ancient woods.

Fulwood, (see page 103) an estate containing some remarkably fertile lands, was sold by the Porterfields, its possessors in Crawfurd's time, to a branch of the family of M'Dowall of Castlesemple, in 1774, from whom it was acquired about three years after, by the father of Archibald Speirs, Esq; of Elderslie, the present proprietor. The house has been demolished.

Blackburn, (see page 103), which, in the days of Crawfurd, belonged to a branch of the once potent house of Sempill, has undergone nearly the same revolution of proprietors as the last mentioned, only more annihilated, as the very name is lost. It belongs to Mr. Speirs of Elderslie.

Boghall, (see page 104,) which was a decayed house when Crawfurd wrote, still exists under that name, in some farm-steads and cottages. It has been in different hands since that time. The lands, which are pretty extensive, belong now to Boyd Alexander, Esq; of Southbarr. The following table of property will shew the destination of the whole united parishes.

TABLE OF PROPERTY.

Estates.	Proprietors.	Valued Rent.			Extent English Acres.
Houstoun, Fulwood, and part of Barrochan,	Archibald Speirs, Esq; of Elderslie,	2661	2	5	
Part of Houstoun,	John Cuninghame, Esq; of Craigends,	156	1	0	
Barrochan, greater part,	Malcolm Fleming, Esq;	294	2	1	
Do. part of,	Archibald Speirs, Esq; of Elderslie,	179	9	2	
Boghall, Yeatstone, and Haddockstone,	Boyd Alexander, Esq; of Southbarr,	466	13	4	
Gryfe Castle,	Do. do.	126	13	4	
Yondertown,	William Holme and James Lang,	73	6	8	
Mill and Mill-lands of Gryfe,	Patrick Spear,	66	13	4	
Burn-Gill,	William Spear,	33	6	8	
Total,		4057	8		7500

And which may be arranged thus:—

Arable, in cultivation,	4000
Dry pasture,	2500
Unreclaimed moss,	350
Sites of houses, roads, waters,	150
Plantations,	500
Total,	7500

Succession of Ministers.—In 1602, Thomas Hamilton; found unfit. In 1606, Alexander Hamilton. In 1634, Robert Birnie; translated to Largs. In 1643, James Houstoun, deposed for irregularities. In 1655, William Thomson, outed, and a long vacancy ensues. In 1695, Robert Taylor, translated to Currie in 1701. In 1703, William Fleming, died in 1717. In 1720, Robert Carrick, died 1771. In 1771, John Monteith at Killalan, admitted to the united charges of Houstoun and Killalan. In 1781, John Monteith, jun. admitted assistant and successor to his father; in 1784, he was translated to Neilstoun, and in 1797, on the death of his father, he succeeded him in Houstoun and Killalan. Previous to this junction, the ministers in Killalan, succeeded each other in the following order :—In 1602, George Semple, was deposed in 1603. In 1603, John Cuninghame ; translated. In 1626, John Hay, jun. translated to Paisley. In 1627, Matthew Brisbane, a man of great consideration in his time. In 1643, Robert Brisbane, deprived as a malignant. In 1649, James Hutchison—outed in 1662 ; also a man of note; died about 1706. In 1708, John Tork. In 1729, Patrick Bruce, translated next year to Kililough, in Ireland. In 1731, William Pollock—by the parish, in opposition to Barrochan. In 1744, Alexander Scott, translated in 1746, to Innerkip. In 1748, John Monteith, and who, on the junction of this parish with Houstoun, as above, was in 1771, admitted to the charge of both.

Villages.—Houstoun. Old Houstoun, once more extensive than at present, still consists of some very pleasant dwellings, at a considerable distance from each other. The new town is a handsome village, laid off in a regular street ; the houses of good mason work, generally two story in height, and covered with slate. The number of inhabitants in 1811 was 524, perhaps a few more now. The chief employment is the cotton manufactory. There are some cotton-mills in the parish, on the Gryfe, not far from the village. Part of the Bridge of Weir is in this parish, and is included in the notice taken of this very cheerful small town, in the account of Kilbarchan. It is situated on both sides of the Gryfe, which is the boundary there between the parishes.

Family Descent.—FLEMING OF BARROCHAN. Patrick Fleming of Barrochan, (see page 102.) had a son, William, and three daughters.

William Fleming, Esq; of Barrochan, succeeded his father, and died about the year 1762. He married Catherine Durham, by whom he had issue ; 1. Patrick, who died young ; 2. Malcolm, of whom afterwards; 3. Elizabeth ; 4. Mary, both died unmarried ; 5. Catherine; 6. William.

Malcolm Fleming, Esq; of Barrochan, entered early into the army; but, on the death of his father, as above, in 1762, he sold out, and retired to his paternal estate of Barrochan, where he has made considerable improvements, more especially by inclosing his lands, and by plantations. He married, in 1781, Elizabeth, daughter of William Ferguson of Dunholm, Esq; by whom he has issue,

William Malcolm Fleming, younger of Barrochan, one of the Judges in the Honourable East India Company's Service; and three daughters, Elizabeth, Catherine, and Jane.

INCHINNAN PARISH.

Situation and Extent.—This small, but very fertile parish, is bounded on the west by that of Erskine; every where else by unfordable rivers—the Clyde, the Cart, and the Gryfe. It is about three miles long from east to west, and, where broadest, is about two miles and a half from north to south. The whole extends to about 3060 English acres.

Surface and Soil.—The greater part is flat Carse land, more especially in the vicinity of the rivers now mentioned. Part of it, towards the middle, rises into small hills arable to the top, and highly decorated with the plantations in the pleasure grounds of the different proprietors. The soil is almost all excellent, more especially in the lower parts, so resemblant to the rich lands in the Carses of Falkirk, Stirling, or Gowrie, and probably, like to those, has been formed by deposition from water. There is still a small portion of deep moss land unreclaimed, but so very little, as not to require a separate specification in the arrangement of soil.

State of Property.—SOUTHBARR, which had been in the possession of a family of the house of Maxwell, for several hundred years, was acquired about   years ago, by the present proprietor, Boyd Alexander, Esq; It is a most beautiful property, with an elegant mansion that overlooks the whole country, as it is itself one of its greatest ornaments, situated on the south side of some rising grounds, richly clothed with plantations. Mr. Alexander has more recently purchased part of the adjacent very fertile lands of Barnhill and Allands, that belonged, when Crawfurd wrote, (see page 105,) to Graham of Dougaldstone, afterwards to the family of Douglas, and more latterly, to M'Dowall of Walkinshaw.

Barr; or, Northbarr. These lands which, in Crawfurds time, (see page 106) belonged to Mr. M'Gilchrist, were the greater part of them alienated, in 1741, to Hugh, the 11th Lord Sempill, and with them, the ancient mansion. This was afterwards called Sempill House, and is most beautifully situated on the south banks of the Clyde, in the north-west corner of this parish. It remained with this noble family till, in 1798, when it was acquired by Mr. Buchanan, and, about six years ago, was purchased by Lord Blantyre, the present proprietor.

Mr. M'Gilchrist, when he sold the greater part of this property, as above, retained a very pleasant wing of it, nearer to the water of Cart, where, on a rising ground, he erected a very cheerful mansion on a lesser scale, which is remarkable for commanding a very extensive prospect, and is still in the possession of his family. He called it also Northbarr, but is more generally known, from its elevated site, by the name of House of Hill.

Park of Inchinnan.—This property, which belonged to a family of the name of Stirling, (a branch of the house of Glorat), see page 106, was afterwards acquired by Mr. M'Gilchrist of Northbarr, who disponed it to John Sommerville, Esq; sometime Provost of Renfrew, and who, in consequence, took the designation of Park. He died in 1767. Next year, it was acquired by a gentleman of the name of Campbell, (said to be a branch of the house of Breadalbine), who made considerable improvements upon it, and in particular built the present mansion. It continued in this family till 1789, when it was acquired by William Fulton, Esq; the present proprietor. (See page 331). It is a remarkably pleasant place.

The lands of Freeland, (see page 107), that belonged to Mr. Maxwell, of the family of Dargeval, was sold in 1734, to Mr. Robert Fulton, merchant in Paisley, who enjoyed this place till his death in 1766. He was succeeded in it, by Mr. John Kerr, eldest son of Margaret Fulton, his sister, and who disponed it to Matthew Kelloch the present proprietor.

The Palace of Inchinnan, (see page 106) which, in Crawfurd's time, still exhibited some considerable remains, has long since been so utterly demolished, that it is only from conjecture that the site of it can be pointed out. Semple, who published his account of this county in 1782, says, that he "observed "one of the stones built in the gable-end of a corn mill at that place, with "these letters, D. D. F. S. L. H. C. L. 1631. The farm at that place is called "Garnaland where the castle stood."

The valued rent and extent of the different properties in this parish will be seen in the following table of property.

TABLE OF PROPERTY.

Estates.	Proprietors.	Valued Rent.			Extent English Acres.
Inchinnan, Commonsides, Newmains, &c. &c.	Archibald Campbell of Blytheswood, Esq;	900			1220
Barnhill, Allands, &c.	Boyd Alexander, Esq; of Southbarr, & partners,	463	6	8	474
Southbarr,	Boyd Alexander, Esq;	293	6	8	500
Barr and Milltown,	Lord Blantyre,	200			186
Freeland,	Matthew Kellock,	160			105
Park and Barnsail,	William Fulton, Esq;	157	6	8	274
Rashiehill and Muirhouse,	James Maxwell, Esq; Dargeval,	96			200
House of Hill, part of Craigiehall, &c.	Miss M'Gilchrist,	85	6	8	75
Greenhead,	John White,	20			10
Ferrycroft,	Representatives of Thomas Crawfurd,	16	13	4	6
Ladyacre,	Robert Cameron,	6	13	4	2½
Glebe,	The Minister,				7½
Total,		2398	13	4	3060

Which may be arranged thus:—

1. Arable, in cultivation, ... 2600
2. Natural pasture, ... 100
3. Sites of houses, roads, waters, ... 60
4. Wood lands, ... 300

                                                                               3060

Succession of Ministers.—In 1602, Gabriel Maxwell. In 1626, Thomas Law. In 1649, James Wallace. In 1691, John Stirling, translated, in 1694, to Greenock against his will. In 1697, Robert M'Aulay, translated to Stirling, in 1706, against the will of the presbytery. In 1701, Matthew Crawfurd ordained, against the will of the parish; and, in 1721, was appointed Professor of Church History, Edinburgh. In 1722, Patrick Maxwell; died in 1749 [*]. In 1750, Archibald

[*] This gentleman appears to have been directly descended from the House of Maxwell-Pollok, thus: John Maxwell of Auldhouse, (page 283) who married a daughter of Dunlop of Hapland; besides his eldest son, George, (who carried on the line of Maxwell of Nether-

Smith. In 1761, Archibald Davidson, who, in 1786, was appointed Principal of Glasgow College. In 1787, Thomas Burns, translated, in 1790, to Renfrew. In 1791, William Hardie, and in 1793, the present minister, William Richardson, D. D. was ordained.

A very singular circumstance is connected with the ministers of this parish ex officio. They have claimed, as undoubted chaplains of the Altarages and Altars, commonly called, " Our Lady's Altars," founded, and of old situated in the kirk and parish of Inchinnan, to be undoubted superiors of the land called Lady-acre; have granted charters; have received feu duty, and still receive it. They are perhaps the only presbyterian clergymen that have such an office in the Christian world.

Villages.—None in the parish that contains half a dozen families; and no manufactures, though situated in the greatest manufacturing county, for its size, in Scotland.

Inchinnan Bridge. Where the two waters, the White Cart, and the Black Cart meet, near the church of Inchinnan, there was formerly a public ferry. The stream, indeed, is here very considerable. It includes more than 19 parts in 20, of all the flowing waters that rise in Renfrewshire. It is also augmented by the flow of the tide, twice in 24 hours, and is then sufficient to carry vessels of 80 tons burden. In 1759, a bridge of ten arches was thrown over these united waters, a few yards below the point where they joined. The water was 547 feet broad. The bridge was 775 feet long and 19 feet wide. It cost only £.1450. After standing 50 years, it gave way in consequence of a land-flood, in the spring of the year 1809. It was rebuilt in 1812, at an expence of £.17,000. The site has been altered. It is formed into two divisions, and crosses these great streams before they form a junction; resting each of them, with an end, on the peninsula beween them, about 30 or 40 yards up from the point. They do not run in a straight line into each other, but the road takes a bend in the middle where they join, and forms nearly a right angle, as each of them crosses its own water at a right angle also. It is certainly a very magnificent work.

Pollok,) had another son, Patrick, merchant in Glasgow, whose son, Robert, was settled minister at Monktown in Ayrshire, in 1640. He died in 1686, and left a son, Robert, who was father of the above Patrick, minister at Inchinnan. All this is substantiated from a monumental stone in the high church-yard of Glasgow, which relates the circumstances more fully. Patrick, the minister of Inchinnan, was father to Thomas Maxwell, minister of Stewarton, who died in 1796, and who was father to Patrick Maxwell, at present writer in Irvine.

CONTINUATION OF THE

Family Descent.—ALEXANDER OF SOUTHBARR, from page 88. Robert Alexander of Newton, Esq; married his cousin, Margaret, daughter of Robert Alexander, a younger son of the family of Blackhouse, one of the principal clerks to the court of session, by whom he had issue, a son, Claud, and a daughter, Jean, married to Mr. Robert Neilson, merchant in Paisley, and had issue.

Claud Alexander, Esq; succeeded his father in Newton. He married Joanna, daughter of Alexander Cuninghame of Craigends, by whom he had five sons, 1. Robert; 2. Alexander, who died unmarried in Jamaica; 3. Claud; 4. Boyd; 5. John; and six daughters, 1. Catherine; 2. Margaret; 3. Anne; 4. Wilhelmina; 5. Lockhart; 6. Lillias.

He was succeeded by his eldest son, Robert Alexander, who died without issue.

Claud went to Bengal, in the civil service of the Honourable the East India Company, where he held the respectable situation of auditor-general of army accounts, and military paymaster-general. On his return to his native country, in 1786, he found that his friends had purchased for him the estate of Ballochmyle, in Ayrshire, the property and beautiful residence of Sir John Whitefoord, to which he afterwards added various other lands, such as Mauchlin Mains, Kingincleugh, &c. &c. In 1788, he married Miss Helenora Maxwell, eldest daughter of Sir William Maxwell of Springkell, Baronet, by whom he had three sons and five daughters; 1. Claud, who succeeded him in 1809, and has lately married Miss Elizabeth, daughter of Colonel Keatinge, by Lady Martha Brabazon, a daughter of the Earl of Meath; 2. William; and 3. Boyd, both merchants in London. The daughters are, Margaret Maxwell, Joanna, Catherine Maxwell, Helenora, who died young, and Mary.

Boyd went to India, and, on his return, he married his cousin-german, Miss Camilla Porterfield, daughter of Boyd Porterfield of Porterfield, by whom he has no issue. He has purchased the estates of Boghall and Gryfe castle, in Killalan parish, Southbarr, in Inchinnan, and also, in partnership with Mr. Redfearn of Langton Lodge, in Yorkshire, the lands of Walkingshaw, in Renfrew parish, Boghead and Stablebrig, parts of Candrens, in Paisley parish, and Barn and Allans, in Inchinnan.

He has made great improvements at Southbarr, and has added still more to the attractions of that beautiful place. He represented the county of Renfrew in the parliament which assembled in 1796, and the boroughs of Glasgow, Renfrew, Dumbarton, and Rutherglen, in that parliament which sat down in 1802.

John entered the army as an ensign in the 48th regiment of foot, and rose to the rank of Major in the 56th; and which he quitted soon after his marriage with his cousin-german, Miss Jane Neilson, a daughter of Robert Neilson, Esq; of Paisley, and has no issue,

Margaret and Wilhelmina *, remain unmarried.

Lockhart married her cousin-german, Mr. Claud Neilson, by whom she had one son and three daughters.

Claud, a merchant in London, married Miss Clifton of the Island of in the West Indies.

Jane, Lockhart, and Margaret, still unmarried.

PARISH OF ERSKINE.

Situation and Extent.—This parish, which is situated to the westward of, and adjacent to the last mentioned, is stretched out about seven miles along the south shore of the river and frith of Clyde, while the greatest breadth, (near the east end,) is about three miles and a half. It extends in all, to about 6365 English acres.

Surface and Soil.—A ridge of hilly country extends through its whole length, nearly in the centre, betwixt the northern and southern boundaries. From the middle of this elevated ground, the lands on one side shelve pretty sharply towards the sea; on the other side the declivity is more gentle towards the interior. Thus a great proportion is hilly and broken ground, in which part of it is bare rock; in other parts, the natural produce is whins and broom, whilst not a little of it is enriched by plantations which prosper greatly. The arable land, which is still a large proportion, is much scattered in detached fields through the whole, and, as it is all incumbent on sandstone, it is not very fertile by nature, but it is generally in good order. Some of the richest of the whole has lately been obtained by clearing away moss, or by cultivation, converting it

---

* This is the lady whom our favourite Scottish bard, Burns, has celebrated in his beautiful poem of the " Bonny Lass of Ballochmyle."

into arable land. It seems probable, that from the very spirited exertions now making to reclaim this moss land, that it will soon, as moss, disappear altogether. There is, at any rate, not much of it remaining, and, in the arrangement of the contents, it is included in arable land.

State of Property.—DARGAVEL, see page 104. This property still remains in the family, although it has passed by a female to another, which has assumed the name of Maxwell, as descended from the same. See family descent.

Craigtoun, (see page 107), in a similar manner, has passed by a female to another family—see also family descent. Erskine remains with the same noble family who acquired it in Crawfurd's time.—See page 112. It is an extensive and beautiful property, highly improved, in particular by plantations on all the high and less fertile lands. The situation of the ancient mansion, by the shore of the ever varying Clyde, is perhaps the most engaging of any on that interesting river. Fancy can hardly conceive more picturesque scenery.

Bargarran, long the seat of an ancient family of the house of Shaw, (see page 112), was acquired in 1772 by Mr. Glen, from whose family it passed by purchase to Lord Blantyre, in 1812, and now makes a very appropriate appendage to the estate and plantations of Erskine.

Bishopton, from page 113.—Some time afterwards the family of Walkinshaw sold this very pleasant property to Hugh Dunlop, Esq; whose only child and heiress, Janet, was married to John, the 12th Lord Sempill, and brought that estate with her to that noble family, from which it was acquired by the present Sir John Maxwell of Pollok.

Park of Erskine—(see page 114). The lands of Park came afterwards to be the property of the family of Cuninghame of Craigends, and were, in 1801, acquired from the present John Cuninghame, Esq; of Craigends, by the late John King of Millbank, and make now (under the name in the cess books of Craigends Park of Erksine) part of the valuable estate of James King, Esq; of Millbank and Drums.

TABLE OF PROPERTY.

Properties.	Proprietors.	Valued Rent.			Extent English Acres.
Erskine,	Lord Blantyre,	1681	0	0	
Freeland of Erskine,	Do. do.	80	0	0	
Part of Bargarran,	Do. do.	196	13	4	
Mains of Bargarran,	Do. do.	50			90
Northbarr, part of, do.	Do. do.	53	6	8	75
Damside, or Whitesmoss,	Do. do.	13	6	8	
Total,		2074	6	8	
Wishaw's Newark,	James King, Esq;	400			750
Craigends Park of Erskine,	Do. do.	200			375
Lands of Drums,	Do. do.	55			100
Millbank, or part of Kirklands of Formakine,	Do. do.	30	16	0	50
Total of Mr. Kings,	£685 : 16s.				
Remainder of Kirklands,	Wood, Allison, Esdon,	46	4	0	50
Barscubehill, Rossland, Craigton, Ingleston,	Miss Jaffray, as heir of the family of Paterson of Craigton,	410	0	0	500
Earl of Glencairn's lands,	W. C. C. Graham of Gartmore, Esq;	333	6	8	
Bishopton,	Sir John Maxwell,	333	6	8	
Part of do. called Ditch and Barangree,	John Maxwell, Esq; of Dargavel,	286	13	4	525
Little Fulwood,	Lord Douglas,	183	6	8	315
Wester Rossland, Gledston, &c.	Matthew Rodger,	94	0	0	132
Corsehill,	William Renton,	14	0	0	25
Total,		4451	0	0	6365

Which may be arranged thus:—

Arable, in cultivation, ... 3000
Natural pasture, ... 2500
Site of houses, roads, waters, ... 65
Wood, natural or planted, ... 800
                                                                                     6365

Succession of Ministers.—In 1602, William Brisbane, a son of the Laird of Bishopton. In 1642, Matthew Brisbane, son of the former minister, a man of great worth and abilities. In 1649, Thomas Hall from Ireland. In 1660, William Houstoun, and was ejected in 1662. In 1692, William Turner, and was translated to Greenock in 1704. In 1705, Walter Menzies, died in 1741. In 1742, James Lundie. In 1772, Walter Young, died in 1814. In 1815, Andrew Stewart, D. D. from Bolton.

Villages.—Hardly one of any note, and as few manufacturers, beyond a country wright, or smith, or taylor, or shoemaker.

Family Descent.—BRISBANE OF BISHOPTON.—The estate of Bishopton, in the parish of Erskine, and county of Renfrew, has belonged to this family for a period long prior to the date of any charter or records which are preserved.

In Rymer's Fœdera, and Lord Hails' Annals, William Brisbane is mentioned as Chancellor of Scotland, in the parliament held at Edinburgh in 1332.

Crawfurd, in his history of Renfrewshire, has the following notice regarding this family, p. 63, " Half a mile west from Erskine, upon the bank of the river " Clyde, on an eminence stands the house of Bishopton, well planted, the " ancient inheritance of the Brisbanes, chief of that name ; the first of whom " I found any memorable mention, is, Allanus de Brysbane, filius Willielmi de " Brysbane, who obtained a grant from Donald Earl of Lennox of the lands of " Macherach in Stirlingshire, to which Malcolm Fleming Earl of Wigton is a " witness, who was created into that dignity by King David Bruce, in the year " 1334. (Carta penes, burgum de Dumbarton)."

Upwards of two hundred years ago, the family acquired various lands in the parish of Largs and county of Ayr, which, by different charters from the Crown, have been erected into the barony and estate of Brisbane. In all the ancient charters, the same is spelt " Birsbane." It is first written Brisbane, in the charter from the Crown afterwards noticed, dated 28th February 1668.

Access cannot at present be had to the older title deeds of the estate of Bishopton, but the following list of charters and other deeds on record, regarding the estate of Brisbane, will give a correct pedigree of the family for upwards of two hundred years.

1. Charter to John Brisbane, younger of Bishopton, of Killing Craig, &c. 1595 ; 2. Ret. of service of the said John, as heir to his father, 1610 ; 3. Charter to the said John and his eldest son of the above lands, 1631 ; 4. Ret. of service to the said John, younger, as heir of his father, 1635 ; 5. Charter to the said John, of Noddisdale, and his spouse, Margaret Brisbane, on the resig.

of her father and the last named John, 1668; 7. Charter to the said James of Kelsoeland, 1571; Cont. of Mar. betwixt John, son of the said James and Margaret Stewart, daughter of Blackhall, 1685; 8. Charter erecting the barony of Brisbane, 1695; 10. Ret. of service of James, the eldest son of John and Margaret, 1727; 11. Ret. of spec. service to Thomas, as heir of James, 1770.

Sir Thomas Brisbane is the only son of the last mentioned Thomas Brisbane, Esq; and (heir to him in his estates of Brisbane, Bishopton, and others in the counties of Ayr and Renfrew,) by Mrs. Elenora Bruce, daughter of Sir William Bruce of Stenhouse, Baronet. The only children of this marriage are, the General and his sister, Miss Mary Brisbane, neither of whom are married.

Copy Patent from the Lyon Office, in favour of Sir Thomas Brisbane, K.C.B.

To all and sundry whom these presents do or may concern, We, Thomas, Earl of Kinnoull, &c. Lord Lyon, King of Arms, do hereby certify and declare, that the Ensigns Armorial pertaining and belonging to Major General Sir Thomas Brisbane of Brisbane, Knight, Commander of the most Honourable Military order of the Bath, and undoubted representative of the most ancient family of Brisbane of Brisbane, in the county of Ayr in Scotland, being the chief of the name of Brisbane, whose ancestors are recorded to have held lands in Scotland, &c. prior to the year 1350, and one of whom is stated in Rymer's Fœdera to have been Chancellor of Scotland, assembled in a parliament held at Edinburgh in the year 1333, and which Sir Thomas Brisbane, K. C. B. has, for his meritorious services in the island of St. Lucie, the island of St. Vincent, the island of Trinidad, and the island of Jamaica, in the West Indies, and at the battles of Vittoria, Pyrenees, Nivelle, Orthes, Toulouse, and Pampeluna, in Spain and France, and also in North America, received several medals and crosses in testimony of his meritorious conduct as commander of brigades in these actions; for which he was created, by His Royal Highness the Prince Regent of England, a Knight, Commander of the most Honourable Military order of the Bath, and now commands a division of the British army in France, under the Duke of Wellington, are matriculated in the public registers of the Lyon office, and are blazoned as on the margin thus, viz: Sable a Cheveron Cheque, Or and Gules, between three Cushions of the Second; in the Collar point a representation of one of the gold medals conferred upon him by His Majesty; above the shield is placed a helmet befitting his degree, with a mantling gules, the doubling argent; and on a wreath of his liveries is set for crest, a Stork's head erazed, holding in her beak a serpent waved proper; and in an escrole above the crest, this motto: " Certamine Summo." On a compartment below the shield, are placed for supporters two talbots proper, which Armorial Ensigns above blazoned, we do hereby ratify and confirm to the said Major-General Sir Thomas Brisbane, K. C, B. and the heirs male of his body, as their proper arms and bearing in all time coming. In testimony whereof, these presents are subscribed by James Home of Lenhouse, Esq; our Deputy, and the seal of our office appended hereunto, at Edinburgh, this eighth day of February, in the year of our Lord 1816. Lyon Office, Edinburgh, 8th February 1816. This patent is duly entered in the records of the Lyon office, by me, John Ker, Herald painter, and keeper of Lyon records.

(Signed)   JAMES HOME.

MAXWELL OF DARGAVEL.—The lands immediately to the west of the town of Renfrew, belonged to, and were possessed from a remote period, by a family, who, when surnames became general in Scotland, assumed the name of " De Aula," or Hall, and afterwards the designation of " Fulbar." Stephen, son of Nicholas, one of their ancestors, obtained a charter[1] from James, the stewart of Scotland, who succeeded his father in 1263, and died in 1309[2], of all that land " apud " burgam de Reynfru be nesse de Reu: ubi aqua de Grefe descendit in aqm. de Clude."

Thomas de Aula, (first so called,) obtained from Robert II. 1st September, in the first year of his reign, (1370) a charter to him and his heirs of the lands of Fulbar, which had been formerly granted to him for his life-time only, " pro fideli servitio suo[3]." And, on the last day of March 1377, he obtained, from the same king, a charter of confirmation[4] of the lands formerly granted to Stephen, and also of the lands of King's Inch. All these lands are described, " in baronia de Renfrew infra Vicecom. de Lanark."

John de Aula.

Robert de Aula obtained a charter[5] from Robert III. 26th May 1395, of the lands near Renfrew, on the resignation of John de Aula, his brother.

Thomas de Hall.

Adam de Hall, son of Thomas de Hall, infeft in lands and houses in and near Renfrew 26th September 1465[6].

Robyne of the Hall of the Fulbar, married to Janet Stewart, heiress of John

---

[1] Charter penes, John Maxwell of Dargavel. [2] Crawfurd's History of the Stewarts. [3] Charter in the register office. [4] Charter penes John Maxwell of Dargavel. [5] Charter penes John Maxwell of Dargavel. [6] Sasine in the hands of John Maxwell of Dargavel.

Stewart, provost of Glasgow. They, with consent of Adam, their eldest son, mortified to the predicant Friars of Glasgow[1], 24th June 1485, forty shillings and four pennies, out of houses in Walker's-gate of Glasgow, and lands near Glasgow.

Adam, his son, married Elizabeth Ralston[2]. He was killed at Flowdon.

Robert, his son, died before his father. He married Janet Langmuir.

Arthur, son of Robert, was infeft in the lands of Fulbar on a crown charter in January 1513[3]. He had two daughters and a son.

William, who being unmarried, had settled, redeemable only by his heirs male, his lands on Adam Hall of Falquinhill, his cousin and heir male of the family[4]. And on the 21st March 1566, he granted him, under reservation of liferent, a charter of the lands of Fulbar, which charter was confirmed by Queen Mary, 23d March 1567. Adam married Janet Wallace, daughter of Cairnhill, and was succeeded by his eldest surviving son,

Adam, who married Elizabeth Forrest, daughter of John Forrest of Magdalanes, provost of Linlithgow. His eldest son, Arthur, married Elizabeth Brisbane of Bishopton, and predeceased his father without children. James, the second son of Adam, having only one daughter, conveyed the patrimonial inheritance of the family to his brother, William Hall of Kipperminshock, provost of Dumbarton, who married Elizabeth Semple of Fulwood, and left a son, Robert, who married Grizel Hamilton of Torrance, who was succeeded by his son Robert, and he by another Robert, who married Margaret Maxwell, daughter of Maxwell of Dargavel, by whom he had two sons, Robert and John, and a daughter, Jean. Robert was minister of Kilmarnock, and died without children. John, the second son, succeeded to the estate of Dargavel, in right of his mother, and took the name and designation of Maxwell of Dargavel. See p. 104.

The lands of Fulbar were sold about the year 1746, and now belong to Mr. Speirs. The property near Renfrew was sold about the year 1786.

John Maxwell of Dargavel entailed the estate of Dargavel, and, dying without issue, was succeeded by his brother, William Maxwell of Freeland, who, dying unmarried, the estate came by the destination in the entail to John Hall, second son of Robert Hall of Fulbar, and Margaret Maxwell, his spouse, sister of the entailer, which John Hall, in terms of the entail, took the name and designation

---

[1] Principal Inventory of the College of Glasgow Papers, page 45. [2] Vide Abercombie's Martial Achievements. [3] Sasine in the hands of John Maxwell of Dargavel. [4] Crawfurd's History of Renfrew.

of Maxwell of Dargavel. He married Janet Anderson, daughter of William Anderson, merchant in Glasgow, by whom he had several children, who all, except John and Margaret, died in infancy. Margaret married Lawrence Craigie, merchant in Glasgow, and has three sons, Lawrence, John, and Peter, and a daughter, Janet. John, who succeeded his father, married Frances Buchanan, daughter of John Buchanan of Ardoch, by whom he had three sons, 1. John, the present proprietor of Dargavel; 2. William, married to Mary, eldest daughter of John Campbell, sen. Esq; merchant in Glasgow, by whom he has four sons, John Hall, William Craig, Alexander, and Francis; and two daughters, Marion and Frances, who died unmarried *.

PATERSON OF CRAIGTON. (See page 107.) Walter Paterson of Craigton married Jean, daughter of   Freeland of Freeland, Esq; by whom he had a son, Robert, and several daughters, all well married. Robert succeeded his father, and purchased the lands of Barscube, and the lands of Ingleston. He married Mary, daughter of John Kelso of Kelsoland, by whom he had a son, John, also five daughters; 1. Jean; 2. Elizabeth; 3. Anne; 4. Mary; 5. Margaret, who was married to Walter Brisbane, merchant in Glasgow.

John Paterson, the eldest son, succeeded his father in Craigton, and added Easter Rossland to it by purchase from the family of Brisbane. He married   but died without issue, and was succeeded by his two surviving sisters, Anne and Margaret. Margaret (Mrs. Brisbane,) had a son, Robert Brisbane, who purchased the estate of Milton in the parish of Carluke, Lanarkshire, and a daughter, Mary Brisbane, married to Doctor James Jeffray, Professor of Anatomy in the College and University of Glasgow. Robert Brisbane of Milton died before his mother, in 1807, unmarried. Mary Brisbane (Mrs. Jeffray) died before her brother, leaving one child, Margaret Anne Jeffray, who succeeded to the estate of Milton as heiress of her uncle, Robert Brisbane. Margaret Paterson (Mrs. Brisbane) died in 1808. Anne, her elder sister, died 22d November 1817, aged 97, unmarried. The said Margaret Anne Jeffray of Milton, as heiress of these two ladies, her grandmother and grand-aunt, now inherits the estates of the family of Paterson of Craigton.

KING OF DRUMS.—James King of Drums, in the parish of Erskine, died on the 19th February 1809, aged 84 or thereby.

* We are indebted to the kindness of the present John Maxwell, Esq; of Dargavel, for a copy of the ancient charter to his ancestor by Robert II. a fac-simile of which is here presented, in the engraving which accompanies this account.

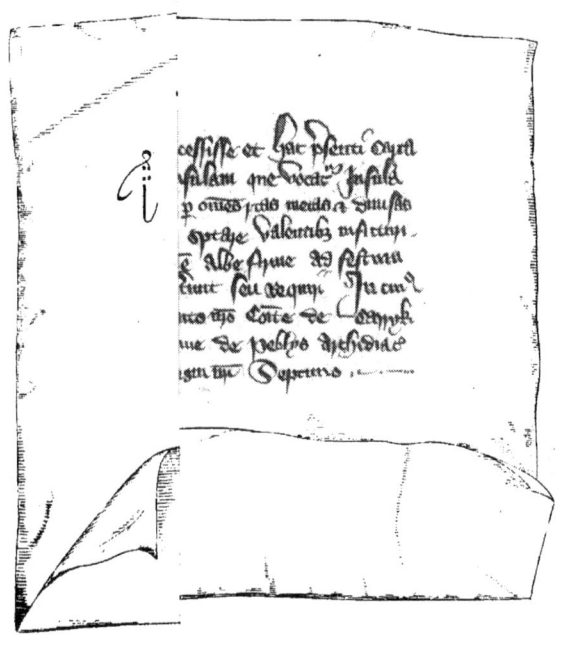

He had four sons, viz. James, John, Matthew, and Thomas, all of whom he survived. James and John predeceased Matthew, unmarried, and Matthew, in his own lifetime, succeeded by a deed of entail of his relation of the same name, to the lands of Millbank in the same parish, and died unmarried in 1793. He had also three daughters. Elizabeth, married to Mr. Cunningham of Bonington; Susan, to Mr. Ewing Cameron, since dead; and Margaret, to William Fulton, jun. Esq;

Thomas succeeded to Millbank, on the death of his brother Matthew, and, having studied the profession of law, was admitted advocate on 1st July 1794.

Having a fortune independent of his father, he, in the year 1795, purchased from the late William Hamilton, Esq; of Wishaw, afterwards Lord Belhaven and Stenton, the estate of Gledoch, commonly called the Ten Pound Land, in the same parish, holding of the Crown, and, with it, a freehold qualification to vote for a member of parliament. This estate has a fine situation on the south banks of the Clyde, nearly opposite to Dumbarton Castle.

In 1801, he purchased from John Cuninghame, Esq; of Craigends, the lands of Park Erskine, in the same parish, lying contiguous to Drums and Millbank.

Having abandoned the profession of the law, he devoted the remainder of his life to rural affairs and the impovement of his estate, and, in 1797, married Christian, third lawful daughter of the deceased John Wallace, Esq; of Kelly, by his last marriage with Mrs. Janet Colquhoun. And on the 22d October 1802, he died at the premature age of 30 years, leaving issue, three children, viz. James, who has chosen the navy for his profession, where he has already seen service in the Pacific and East Indian seas. John Wallace, and Jessie, who have all been educated under the kindest maternal attention of, and are now residing with, their mother in Devonshire in England.

By the death of his father and grandfather, James succeeded to the estates of Drums, Park Erskine, Gledoch, and Millbank, (the name of the last he assumes, conformable to the entail of it) forming altogether an extent of upwards of a thousand acres, 720 of which are arable, exclusive of about 257 acres of shore ground, which might be taken in and improved.

KILMALCOLM PARISH.

Situation and Extent.—This is the largest parish in the County. It is about eight miles in length from east to west, and six and a half, where broadest, from north to south. Part of it, about 2 miles in breadth, stretches down to the

Frith of Clyde, between the parishes of Erskine and Port Glasgow. The whole contains about 19,800 English acres. That quarter next the sea is very steep and rough, but is much beautified by woodlands both natural and planted. A great part of this parish, particularly on the southern and on the western extremities, is moorish land, rising to a considerable height, and very bleak and barren. But the greatest expanse of country, of a uniform feature, is a hollow plain, shelving both from south and north towards the Gryfe, and its tributary streamlets in the centre. This is thickly scattered over with farm hamlets, whilst the soil, which is incumbent on rotten rock, is naturally fine pasture land. Much of it, indeed, is in cultivation, and produces good crops of grain and potatoes, also some clover and turnips. More than 6000 acres of this description of soil, are situated in one unbroken expanse, in the heart of the vale of Strathgryfe in this parish.

State of Property.—The great barony of Duchall, which for many ages was the chief property and place of residence of the ancient and now almost extinct family of Lyle Lord Lyle, and afterwards became the property of the great family of Porterfield of that-ilk, (see page 92,) has of late been divided among a different series of heirs of this last family, and part of which succession is still under the review of the supreme court. It is a property of great extent, situated chiefly in the heart of the parish, but extending on each side of the Gryfe, thence to its southern boundary. The mansion is situated close on the southern bank of that stream; was built in 1768—is a house of considerable magnitude, and is well sheltered amidst some full grown wood.

Cairncurran (see page 94,) remains still in the same family of Cuninghame. The mansion, which was originally situated higher up the country among the moorish lands, has been removed long ago to a milder situation, in the lower end of the parish, and is a great ornament to that part of the country. It is surrounded with much beautiful plantation, and well cultivated lands.

Denniestoun Barony, (long better known by the name of Finlaystone, the chief messuage,) is situated in the northern quarter of the parish, extending down to the Frith of Clyde. The house itself of Finlaystone, (see page 114,) with its extensive woods and plantations, which occupy a great extent along the coast side, has always been esteemed a first rate residence. It has for many ages been the chief mansion of the Earls of Glencairn, and it still remains, with the greater part of the barony of Denniestoun, in the possession of the representative of that noble family, William C. C. Graham, Esq; of Gartmore and Finlaystone.

Newark barony. The greater part of this extensive property is situated in the parish of Kilmalcolm. The ancient castle is in that of Port Glasgow. In Crawfurd's time (see page 119,) it was in the possession of a branch of the family of Dundonald. It came afterwards to be the property of Sir James Hamilton of Rosehaugh, and from that family it came by succession to that of Lord Belhaven, the present possessor.

Craigbett, in this parish, is a very pleasant property, and on which there is a very handsome small mansion, belonging to Alexander Graham Esq. It is situated in the lower end of the parish, on the south bank of the Gryfe.

There are also the following very pleasant Villas on the coast side quarter of this parish, viz. Broadfield, Mr. Crawfurd; Carnegie, Dr. Foster; and Parklee, Mr. M'Iver; also Badreney, rather a deserted like place, but in a pleasant situation on the hill top, about a mile south-east of Port Glasgow.

TABLE OF PROPERTY.

Estates.	Proprietors.	Valued Rent.			Extent English Acres.
Duchal entailed lands,	Mr. Corbett, or Sir M. S. Stewart,	1502	13	4	
Do. unentailed, viz. Blacksohm and Craigends, Dennieston,	Heirs general,	468			11,440
Dennieston's Finlaystone,	William C. C. Graham of Gartmore,	1316	13	4	2225
Do. Feuars,	Foster, Watson, and Mrs. M'Dowall's heirs,	50			63
Part of Newark, in many sundry parcels,	Lord Belhaven,	1191	13	4	3620
Park and Parklee,	John Crawfurd, Esq;	33	6	8	63
Wateryett,	John Whitehill,	25			24
Cairncurran, old and new, and ½ Ladymuir,	Charles Cuningham, Esq;	265			1230
Other half Ladymuir,	Robert Blair,	25			50
Craigbett and Carsemeadow,	Alexander Graham, Esq;	110			252
Halltrick,	Maxwell of Dargavel,	146	13	4	206
Slates,	James Holme,	50			82
Netherwood,	Mr. William Glen,	50			82
Muiredge,	M'Knight Crawfurd, Esq;	26	13	4	150
Over Kilmalcolm, 11 subjects,	11 Feuars from Mr. M'Gregor,	133	6	8	130
Killochries,	Mr. J. Wilson,	36	13	4	50
Newton,	J. and W. Stirrat,	36	13	4	63
Pomillan,	James Blair,	14	13	4	15
Chapel,	Scott —— Adam,	12			30
Coldside,	Robert Erskine,	6			25
Total,		5500			19,800

Which may be arranged thus:—

		Eng. Acres.
1.	Arable, in cultivation,	8500
2.	Moorish pasture, rough but sound,	8000
3.	Moss land of little value,	2500
4.	Sites of houses, roads and waters,	100
5.	Wood, natural or planted,	700
	Total,	19,800

Succession of Ministers.—In 1602, Samuel Cuninghame. In 1626, Daniel Cuninghame. In 1630, Ninian Campbell, was translated, in 1651, to Roseneath. In 1655, James Alexander, eldest son of Robert Alexander of Blackhouse; died in 1669. In 1670, John Irvine—not a very pleasant settlement. In 1672, Patrick Simpson and William Thomson, indulged to preach here. In 1688, James Hay—translated to Kilmarnock. In 1698, James Brisbane. He had a call from Stirling—the Presbytery refuse to translate him, but the commission of the General Assembly appoint him nevertheless. In 1706, Robert Maxwell. Some curious circumstances recorded concerning him. He died in 1735. In 1737, John Fleming, after a great struggle in which the parish prevails, is settled. He died in 1787. In 1788, John Brown, died in November 1817.

Village.—Kilmacolm, the kirk town, is set down in a pleasant enough situation, under shelter of some rising grounds to the north and east. In Mr. Wilson's Survey, it is stated to contain 291 inhabitants, and it seems probable that it has neither much increased nor diminished since that time, in 1812. There does not seem to be any manufactories carried on it beyond the ordinary line of country mechanics.

Family Descent.—EARL OF GLENCAIRN.—William, 12th Earl of Glencairn, (from page 117), supported the treaty of Union, was a privy councillor, and governor of Dumbarton Castle. He made an entail of the estate of Finlaystone to his sons and heirs, whom failing, to his daughters and their heirs, in consequence of which entail that estate is now possessed by Graham of Gartmore, of whom afterwards. He died in 1734. He married Lady Henrietta Stewart, daughter of the Earl of Galloway, by whom he had eight sons, all of whom died young or unmarried, except the 2d son, William, his successor, and two daughters. 1. Lady Margaret, married to Graham of Gartmore, of whom afterwards; 2. Lady Henrietta, married to Campbell of Shawfield, and had issue, of whom is descended the present Shawfield; also two daughters, who died unmarried.

William, 13th Earl of Glencairn, entered early into the army, and went through the various gradations of rank till he attained that of major-general in 1770. He was also governor of Dumbarton Castle, and died in 1775. He married, in 1744, the eldest daughter and heiress of Hugh M'Guire, Esq; of Drumdow, in Ayrshire, by whom he had issue, 1. William Lord Kilmaurs. He had an affair of honour with a French nobleman, in the theatre, at Lyons, which produced severe wounds on both sides, but none of them mortal. He died, at Coventry, in February 1768, in his 20th year. 2. James, 14th Earl. 3. John, 15th Earl, and a son who died young; 1. Lady Henriet, married to Sir Alexander Don of Newton, and had issue, and was also a claimant of the titles—disallowed; 2. Lady Elizabeth, died unmarried in 1804.

James, 14th Earl of Glencairn. He was also in the army. In 1780, he was chosen one of the representatives of the Scottish Peers in Parliament. He died in 1791, unmarried.

John, 15th Earl of Glencairn, was at first an officer in the 14th regiment dragoons, but afterwards took orders in the Church of England. He died, at Coats, near Edinburgh, 24th September 1796, in the 47th year of his age, and is buried at St. Cuthbert's, where a monument is erected to his memory. He married lady Isabella Erskine, daughter of Henry David, tenth Earl of Buchan, but had no issue.

The estate of Finlaystone, (but not the title of Glencairn), now devolved on Robert Graham, Esq; of Gartmore, whose descent from the Glencairn family is thus:

Lady Margaret Cuningham, eldest daughter of William, 12th Earl of Glencairn, (vide supra), was married, on the 2d April 1732, to Nicol Graham, Esq; of Gartmore, to whom she had a son, 1. William Graham, younger of Gartmore, who died before his father in 1774. (He married 25th March 1767, Margaret, daughter of William Porterfield, M. D. by whom he had three daughters;) 2. Robert Graham of Gartmore, who succeeded to the estate of Finlaystone in 1796, in consequence of the deed of entail before-mentioned. He married Anne, sister of Sir John Taylor, Bart. by whom he had the present William Cuningham Graham, Esq; of Gartmore and Finlaystone, and another son and two daughters.

Premier Cadet of the Family of Glencairn.—CUNNINGHAME OF CORSEHILL.—In page 115, it is stated that William, fourth Earl of Glencairn, who died in 1547, left three sons [*]: the first was Alexander, his successor, 5th Earl of Glencairn; the second was,

[*] Wood, whose researches have been more successful than Crawfurd's, has found five sons

I. Andrew Cunninghame, the immediate ancestor of the Cunninghames of Corsehill. This appears from three charters dated successively in 1537, 1538, and 1541, (see Lib. 26, No. 128; Lib. 27, No. 12; Lib. 28, No. 54;) to Andrew Cunninghame, son of Sir William Cunninghame, Knight, Master of Kilmawrs, afterwards, as above, Earl of Glencairn, in which the two Corsehills, in the Lordship of Stewarton and shire of Ayr are particularly specified. The time of his death is not mentioned, but he was succeeded by his son,

II. Cuthbert Cunninghame of Corsehill, who died betwixt the 17th May and 21st December 1616. For his successor, in one public record, of the first of these dates, is designed younger of Corsehill, (Reg. Retours, Lib. 7. Fol. 154.) and in another public record of the last of these dates, (in which he is called Sir Alexander,) he is designed now of Corsehill. So that Cuthbert, the second Baron, must have died in the intervening period. He was succeeded by his son,

III. Sir Alexander Cunninghame of Corsehill. That he was grandson of Andrew, the first Baron, appears further from a charter of confirmation from Charles, Prince and Stewart of Scotland, (Privy Seal Record, Lib. 50. No. 77.) dated 11th December 1622, in which the original charter to his ancestor, Andrew, is recapitulated, and he himself designed, " Nunc de Corsehill legitu-" mum et propinquiorem Hæredum Masculum dicti quondam Cuthberti Cun-" nynghame sui Patris." Which Cuthbert, is there designed legitimate heir male of the late Andrew, his father. From a special retour, dated 19th January 1647, (vol. 19. No. 10, retours) it appears, that this Sir Alexander died in the month of May 1646. He married Anne, daughter of John Crawfurd of Kilbirny, by whom he had a son,

IV. Alexander Cunninghame of Corsehill, whose eldest son,

V. Alexander, died before him, leaving a son,

VI. Alexander Cunninghame of Corsehill. All this appears by a charter 13th April 1663, and confirmation 26th Jan. 1672, (Great Seal Record, Lib. 64. No. 254), in which the last is stiled heir apparent of Corsehill and grandson of Alexander Cuninghame Seniorem de Corsehill. He was created a Baronet of Nova Scotia, by diploma, dated 22d February 1672. He married Mary, daugh-

---

of this nobleman, viz. 1. Alexander, his successor; 2. Andrew, as above, ancestor of the family of Corsehill; 3. Hugh, ancestor of Carlung; 4. Robert, ancestor of Montgrenan; and, 5. William, bishop of Argyle, who is claimed by the the most noble family of Conyngham, Marquis of Conyngham in Ireland, as their immediate connecting ancestor with the family of Glencairn.

ter of Sir Archibald Stewart, Baronet, of Blackhall, by whom he had his successor,

VII. Sir Alexander Cunninghame, the second Baronet of Corsehill, who was retoured son and heir to his father in May 1685, (Retours, No. 38. Fol. 24 and 40.) and took charters to the lands, 26th February 1686, (Record apud Ayr, September 24th 1686.) He married Dame Margaret Boyle, sister to the Earl of Glasgow, and died about the year 1732. He was succeeded by his son,

VIII. Sir David Cunninghame, the third Baronet of Corsehill, who married Penelope, daughter of George Montgomery of Kirktonholm in Lanarkshire, descended at a period not remote from the house of Skelmurly. By her he had a son, designed,

IX. Captain Alexander Montgomery Cunninghame, the first surname he assumed in respect of his mother, through which connection he inherited the lands of Kirktonholm. He married Elizabeth, eldest daughter of David Cunninghame, Esq; of Lainshaw, descended from Hugh, first Earl of Eglinton, about the same time that this family of Corsehill branched off from the family of Glencairn. He was also the direct heir of line by succession through a female of the very ancient and noble family of Lyle Lord Lyle, in the county of Renfrew.

On the death, without issue, of the late James Montgomery, Esq; (son of David Montgomery of Lainshaw, as above) the house of Lainshaw terminated in three ladies, his sisters; of whom the eldest, Elizabeth, married, as already stated, Captain Montgomery Cunninghame, whose male descendants, in consequence, are first in succession to the honours of Lyle, so far as transmissable through a female.

Captain Montgomery Cunninghame died in January 1770, and his father, Sir David, died a few months after at Corsehill. He was succeeded by his grandson, son of Captain Alexander Montgomery Cunninghame,

Sir Walter Montgomery Cunninghame, the fourth Baronet of Corsehill, who died in March 1814, unmarried, was succeeded by his next brother,

Sir David Montgomery Cunninghame, the fifth Baronet of Corsehill, who died in November 1814, and was succeeded by his only remaining brother,

X. Sir James Montgomery Cunninghame, the sixth Baronet of Corsehill, descended thus in a direct line from William the fourth Earl of Glencairn, and of course heir presumptive to his honours, as it does not appear that there is any other descendant by the male line so nearly related. He thus combines in his person the honours of two very noble and very ancient Renfrewshire families, namely, Glencairn, as direct heir male, and Lyle, as direct lineal descendant.

He married, in 1802, Jessie, daughter of the late   Cumming, Banker in Edinburgh, representative of the family of Cumming of Earnside, in the county of Nairn, by whom he has five sons and one daughter.

Arms of the family of Corsehill. Argent a Shake-fork Sable, with a Crescent over it, denoting their descent from a second brother of the Earl of Glencairn, as matriculated in the Lyon Records in the days of Charles II. Motto, " Over, Fork, over."

PORTERFIELD OF PORTERFIELD.—Alexander Porterfield, who succeeded his grandfather in 1690, (see page 64) married, in 1694, Lady Catherine Boyd, daughter of William Earl of Kilmarnock ; 2dly, he married Mrs. Margaret Campbell and with her fortune purchased the estate of Blacksolme about 1735. He died on the 14th May 1743. He had the following issue :—1. William, of whom afterwards; 2. Alexander married an Irish lady, Miss Jollie, by whom he had a son Boyd, of whom afterwards ; 3. Robert, died in his father's lifetime unmarried; 4. Jean, married to James Corbett of Tolcross; 5. Eupham, married to Emanuel Walker, collector of customs at Port Glasgow ; 6. Catherine, married to James Baird, merchant, Glasgow.

William Porterfield, Esq; of Porterfield, succeeded his father in 1743, as above, and died on the 6th November 1752. He married Miss Julian Steele, daughter of Mr. William Steele, minister of the gospel at Lochmaben ; no issue. He was succeeded by his nephew, as above,

Boyd Porterfield, Esq; of Porterfield, who married Christian Cuninghame, eldest daughter of Alexander Cuninghame, Esq; of Craigends, by whom he had issue ; 1. Alexander, of whom afterwards; 2. Boyd; he died in America 1780, or 1781, Captain in the 22d regiment of foot; 3. William, died in infancy ; 4. Margaret, married to Houstoun Nicolson Stewart, Esq; of Carnock, and had issue ; 5. Catherine ; 6. Camilla, married to Boyd Alexander, Esq; of Southbarr; 7. Christian, married to F. Fotheringham, Esq; 8. Anne, married Colonel Thomas Paterson of His Majesty's 22d dragoons, and had issue.

Boyd Porterfield of Porterfield died in 1795, and was succeeded by his eldest son,

Alexander Porterfield, Esq; of Porterfield, who died in 1815, unmarried.

LORD BELHAVEN.—VII. John Hamilton of Udston, the 7th in descent from Sir David Hamilton, the 4th chief of the name, married Helen Whiteford, daughter of Milton, by whom he had, 1. John of Coltness, (and Udston) who carried on the line of the family ; 2. James of Barncleugh, and 3.

VIII. William Hamilton, who became the first of the house of Wishaw; for, in contemplation of his marriage with Beatrix Douglas, daughter of James Douglas of Morton, in 1621, his father disponed to him the lands of Wishaw and others. By this lady he had, 1. James, who, being unfortunate in trade, greatly involved the family estate, and, dying without issue, was succeeded by his only surviving brother, the 2d son,

IX. William Hamilton of Wishaw, who, by his great talents as a lawyer, and prudent management of his affairs, not only retrieved the original estate, but made considerable additions to it. He is also well known for his great knowledge in the antiquities of his country. He married, 1st, in 1660, his cousin, Anne, daughter of John Hamilton of Udston, by whom he had six sons and one daughter; which daughter, Margaret, married Cleland of that-ilk, and had issue. Of the sons, none of them had issue but the 2d, Robert, of whom afterwards, and Archibald the 4th, who married ——— Hamilton, heiress of Dalserf, and had issue. 2d, He married in 1676, Mary, daughter of Sir Charles Erskine of Alva, by whom he had five sons and six daughters. 1. Charles of Wetherby, who married Euphemia, daughter of Sir Archibald Hamilton of Rosehall, by whom he had two daughters. 1. Bethia, who will be mentioned afterwards; 2. Charlotte. 2. John, writer to the signet, who married a daughter of Gartshore of that-ilk and had issue; 3. William, counsellor at law in London, who married Helen Hay, daughter of ——— Hay of Woodcockdale, and had issue. This gentleman was very much in public life; sat in parliament 42 years—was one of the reputed authors of Junius, under the name of Single Speech Hamilton. 5. Alexander, solicitor at law in London, married, 1st, a daughter of Colonel Dalziel; 2d, a daughter of   Lillie, Esq; and had issue by both; 1. Helen, married to Baillie of Parbroath, and had issue; 2. Catherine, married the Rev. Mr. Pitcairn, in Dysart, and had issue; 3. Janet, married ——— Gartshore of that-ilk—had issue; 4. Mary, married Dr. Balfour, son of Denmiln; had issue; 5. Christian died young; 6. Anne, married Mr. James Bogle, receiver-general of the customs, and had issue.

Robert, the 2d son, by the first marriage, married Jean, heiress of William Hamilton of Brownmuir, in Ayrshire, by whom he had four sons; 1. William, of whom hereafter; 2. Robert, minister of Hamilton, who married Cecil, daughter of Mr. Borland, minister of Glasgow, and had issue; 3. John, died unmarried; 4. James of Stevenson, who married a daughter of Baillie of Parbroath, and had issue.

Robert, predeceased his father, William, who lived to an uncommonly advanced age, dying in 1726, and was succeeded by his grandson,

XI. William, eldest son as above, of Robert, who married his cousin, Bethia, daughter of his uncle of Wetherby, by whom he had six sons and one daughter,

Euphemia, married to Alexander Baillie of Parbroath and Luthrie, assistant barrack-master for Scotland. Of the sons, the 4th, James, married Anne, daughter of James Bowie of Holehouse, by whom he had issue. The 5th, John of Bellfield, merchant in Edinburgh, married Isabella, daughter of Sir Henry Stirling of Ardoch, and had issue; two sons died unmarried, viz. William the 2d and Archibald the 6th.

William Hamilton the father was killed by a fall from his horse betwixt Hamilton and Wishaw, on the 16th April 1756, and was succeeded by his son, Charles, who, dying unmarried in 1763, was succeeded by his brother,

XII. Robert Hamilton of Wishaw, who, on the death of James, fifth Lord Belhaven, (descended of James of Barncleugh, 2d son of John of Coltness and Udston) succeeded to this title as heir-general, to which the honours extended. This title had been assumed by another branch of the family, viz. The descendant of the eldest son, John of Coltness, (see No. VII.) but his claim was set aside by the House of Peers, as being found (like to other heritable property) to descend to the representative of the immediate younger brother.

This Robert Hamilton did not, however, take up the honours although justly due. He died in March 1784. He married, in 1764, Susan, daughter of Sir Michael Balfour of Denmiln, by whom he had three sons and five daughters. The younger children afterwards took up the stile of Honourable, as their father was legally entitled to the Peerage, and would have been the sixth Lord Belhaven. By his lady he had, 1. William, his successor; 2. The Hon. Robert Hamilton, colonel in the army; 3. Hon. Peter Douglas Hamilton; 1. Daughter, Hon. Mary Erskine Hamilton, died unmarried; 2. Hon. Jean Hamilton, married, in 1791, to George Ramsay of Barnton, and has issue; 3. Hon. Bethia Hamilton, married to William Ramsay, Esq; Banker in Edinburgh, died in 1809, leaving issue; 4. Hon. Susan Hamilton; 5. Hon. Euphemia Hamilton, died unmarried.

XII. William, seventh Lord Belhaven, born 1765, succeeded his father in 1784, assumed the title in 1799, in consequence of a determination of the House of Peers. His Lordship married, in 1789, Penelope, youngest daughter of Ronald M'Donald of Clan Ronald, by whom he had, 1. Hon. Robert Montgomery, of whom afterwards; 2. Hon. William Hamilton; 3. Hon. Penelope Hamilton; 4. Hon. Susan Mary Hamilton; 5. Hon. Flora Hamilton; 6. Hon. Jean Hamilton; 7. Hon. Bethia Hamilton. His Lordship died in 1814, and was succeeded by his son,

XIV. Robert Montgomery, the eighth Lord Belhaven and Stenton, the fourteenth generation from the Ducal house of Hamilton, and eighteenth from the first establishment of that great family in Clydesdale. His Lordship, in 1815, married Miss Hamilton, daughter of Walter Campbell, Esq; of Shawfield. He has been bred to the army, and has been in very important military service with Wellington in Spain and in France, and was also at the capture of Washington in America. His Lordship is Vice-Lieutenant of the county of Lanark.

CUNINGHAM OF CAIRNCURRAN.—From Crawfurd's History of the Shire of Renfrew (p. 97.) it appears that " Alexander Cuningham Lord Kilmawrs, and " who was created Earl of Glencairn by James III. in 1488, left two sons, Ro- " bert his successor, and William, of whom descended the family of Craigends, " and who obtained from his father the lands of said name. To this William " Cuningham of Craigends succeeded William, his son and heir, who, by Giles " his wife, daughter of Sir John Campbell of Loudon, had three sons, Gabriel, " his successor, William, ancestor of Cairncurran, and Robert, of whom the Cun- " ninghams of Bedland, Auchinharvie, and Suthhook, are descended."

The above ancestor of Cairncurran succeeded to the lands of that name in the year 1534, as appears from a charter from John Lord Lyle, in favour of the before-mentioned Giles Campbell, by whom these lands were conveyed to the said William her son.

William Cuningham, the first of Cairncurran, was succeeded by his son Gabriel, who was succeeded by his eldest son William.

From that time till the decease, in 1807, of William, the father of the present proprietor, there was an uninterrupted succession of Williams in the family of Cairncurran, he being the ninth William Cuningham, from father to son, in a direct line from the said Gabriel Cuningham.

About the year 1722 William Cuningham, Esq; of Cairncurran, the 8th of that name, removed the family residence from ancient Cairncurran to New Cairncurran *, where he built a house and offices, and which were rebuilt afterwards by his successor in 1782.

In 1726 he married Margaret, daughter of the Rev. Charles Coats, minister of Govan, by whom he had four sons, William, Charles, James, and John ; also, two daughters, Margaret and Janet. He died on the 10th May 1734, in the

* These mansions, as well as the peculiar territories connected with each, are quite distinct, and separated by some miles from each other. Ancient Cairncurran is situated far up among the moorish lands, near to the hill that goes by the same name, about three miles south from Port Glasgow. New Cairncurran is situated three miles farther down the country, in a delightful spot, almost close to the boundary burn, betwixt the parishes of Kilmalcolm and Kilbarchan ; and is, without question, one of the most pleasant seats in the parish.

86th year of his age. His widow died 25th February 1770. He was succeeded by his eldest son,

William Cunninghame, Esq; of Cairncurran. In 1768, he married Janet, eldest daughter of Gabriel Lang of Overton, in Dumbartonshire, merchant in Greenock. The following are the names of their children: 1. William, died 25th November 1776; 2. Gabriel, died 24th January 1774'; 3. Charles, of whom afterwards; 4. Margaret, married to John Speirs, physician in Greenock; 5. Janet; 6. William, went to Jamaica and died there, 12 November 1798; 7. Susan; 8. John, went to Jamaica, died there 24 July 1808; 9. Alexander; 10. Grace. The above William Cuningham of Cairncurran, died on the 11th April 1807. He was succeeded by his son,

Charles Cunningham, Esq; now of Cairncurran. In 1802, he married Elizabeth Gray Park, only daughter of Robert Park, Esq; merchant in Glasgow, by whom he has issue:

1. William Charles;
2. Robert Park;
3. Charles;
4. Elizabeth Spens;
5. John.

Arms.—Argent, a Shake Fork Sable: Crest, A Unicorn's Head couped. Motto, "Fork, onward."

DENNISTOUN OF COLGRAIN.—(see page 95.) This family still continues to be represented in the male line.

James Dennistoun of Colgrain, who possessed the estate for many years, died at an advanced age, leaving three sons and two daughters. 1. James, who succeeded him; 2. Robert, who married Anne, daughter of Archibald Campbell, Esq; of Jura, and has issue; 3. Richard married to Christian, daughter of James Alston, Esq; of Westertoun, who has also issue. Eldest daughter, Jane, married to Andrew Buchanan, Esq; of Ardenconnal; second daughter, Mary, married to John Alston, Esq; of Westertoun, who have both issue.

James Dennistoun, Esq; of Colgrain, succeeded his father in 1796. He married, first, Margaret, daughter of James Donald, Esq; of Geilstoun, by whom he had one son, James, his heir; and secondly, Margaret, daughter of Robert Dreghorn of Blochairn, by whom he had four daughters: 1. Isabella Bryson, married to Gabriel Hamilton Dundas, Esq; younger of Duddingstoun; 2. Janet Baird, married to Hugh Maclean, Esq; younger of Coll; 3. Elizabeth Dreghorn, married to Duncan Campbell, Esq; of Barcaldine; 4. Mary Lyon, married to William Baillie, Esq; of Polkemmit, who have all issue.

James Dennistoun, Esq; of Colgrain, succeeded his father in 1816. He married, in 1801, Mary Ramsay, daughter of George Oswald, Esq; of Auchencruive and Scotstoun, by whom he has four sons and five daughters: Eldest son, James; 2. George; 3. Richard; 4. Robert; eldest daughter, Margaret; 2. Isabella; 3. Mary; 4. Elizabeth; and 5. Camilla.

PORT GLASGOW PARISH.

This was formerly a part of the parish of Kilmalcolm, but the magistrates of Glasgow having, in the year 1668, feud about 14 English acres of land here, on which they erected a harbour for the accommodation of their shipping; and foreseeing that it was likely soon to become a populous place, application was made to the proper authorities, and it was, with a few farms in the vicinity, erected into a distinct parish in 1695, by the name of New Port Glasgow, or Port Glasgow, as it is commonly called.

Situation and Extent.—It is about a mile and a half in length, along the Frith of Clyde, and extends about a mile backward up the country. It contains only 844 English acres altogether, and has originally been a barren hilly tract, most of it very steep, and little more than the half of it brought into good cultivation, notwithstanding the great inducement held out from its being in the immediate vicinity of a populous town and excellent market. What is brought into cultivation, consists chiefly of the gardens belonging to the town, and to the pleasure grounds belonging to numerous villas that have recently been erected in the neighbourhood.

The Frith of Clyde, opposite to this parish, is about two miles broad, but it is only a small part of it that is navigable by vessels of burden. This part, called the channel, lies close along the shore of Port Glasgow, and is about 200 yards broad, and is every where so deep, at high water, that the largest vessels that navigate the Clyde can easily be moored in the harbour without discharging their cargo.

The harbour is indeed among the best in Scotland. The ebb tide commonly leaves a depth of about eight feet water, more or less, according as the wind blows, either up or down the Frith. The rise of tide, according to the same circumstance, is from seven to ten feet in ordinary, and in spring-tides sometimes as high as 13 feet, so that vessels from 500 to 600 tons burden have easy access, and can be commodiously birthed, even in ordinary tides.

The first dry or graving-dock in Scotland was built here in 1760, and has since been considerably improved, and now, or lately, yielded a free revenue of more than £500 a year. This circumstance is recorded, not so much to show the pecuniary advantage to the proprietors, (the town council) as the vast advantage it is of to the shipping interest. The extreme length of it, from the gates to the head of the dock on the floor, is 253 feet; width at the gates 31 feet 8 inches, and from the after-block to the head of the dock on the floor, 213 feet. It admits of one vessel at a time of 500 tons, or of two of 300 or 400. The number of vessels belonging to Port Glasgow is just now 133, containing 19,133 tons.

The extent of the shipping of this port, in 1804, including their repeated voyages, was,

		Ships.	Tons.	Men.
Inward,	Foreign Trade,	113	18722	1081
	Coasters,	182	7226	551
	Total,	295	25948	1632
Outward,	Foreign Trade,	177	25137	1692
	Coasters,	119	7202	424
	Total,	296	32339	2116
	Grand Total,	591	58287	3748

Trade continued to increase during the remaining years of the late war so as to amount to half as much more both of tonnage and men. It declined with the peace, but has revived of late so as to be fully equal to the above. Thus, in 1817, it was

		Ships.	Tons.	Men.
Inward,	British,	104	22415	1192
	Foreign,	2	482	21
	Coastwise,	81	5146	362
	Total,	187	28043	1575
Outward,	British,	121	23210	1384
	Foreign,	2	482	22
	Coastwise,	140	9086	537
	Total,	263	32778	1943
	Grand Total	450	60821	3518

Several warehouses for bonded goods are erected near the harbour, but, since the peace, and the West India trade being also diverted into other channels, there is less use for them than formerly.

The extent of commerce may be inferred from the amount of the duties of Customs, thus—

In the year ending 5th January 1807, it was .... £.282,408 5 10
and ditto ditto in 1818, it was .... £.214,724 17 8¼
The amount of excise duties, in 1817, was .... £. 80,780 1 6¼
So much for the harbour of this flourishing place.

The town of Port Glasgow had the advantage, from the first, to be laid off according to a regular plan;—the streets in straight lines, and with a due consideration as to width. The houses too, are constructed with a considerable degree of uniformity, and formed in an efficient stile of good mason work, and all roofed with slate. There has of late been considerable improvements made on the paving and lighting of the streets, and more recently there has been a very handsome town-house erected, containing a hall for the court, an office for the town clerk, a coffee-room; also, a decent jail, for the accommodation of the unfortunate. The whole surmounted by an elegant steeple, with a clock, all from the correct taste of David Hamilton, Esq; architect in Glasgow. The town is a burgh of barony, by a charter in 1775. The government is vested in 13 councillors, of whom, two are bailies, and who are also ex officio, in the commission of the peace. Four of these councillors are changed annually. The revenue of the town, in 1793, (see Stat. Acc. vol. V.) amounted to about £.500, and as it arose chiefly from a tax of 2½ per cent on house rents, and as this was raised in 1803, to 5 per cent, it may be concluded, that the general revenue will now be double—probably, all little enough for indispensible disbursements. The population, which, in 1730, was 1426 persons—in 1811, amounted to 5116, including a very few in the country part of the parish, and is probably considerable more now, as the town is still continuing to prosper.

The country part of the parish has nothing remarkable in it, more than already stated, to attract notice, unless it be that there are several very elegant villas lately erected in the immediate vicinity of the town, and which certainly add greatly to the general beauty of the scenery of all this quarter of the coast side. The old castellated mansion of Newark is in the immediate vicinity. Of it a very correct view is given in this work. It was long the residence of a powerful baron of the house of Maxwell, (see page 118). It now is the property of Lord Belhaven, and with it all the land in the parish, either in direct possesssson, or in superiority. This is part of what was the ancient barony of Newark, the greater part of which, as already stated, is in the parish of Kilmalcolm. That part of it in this parish, is rated thus in the county books:—

TABLE OF PROPERTY.

Properties.	Proprietors.	Valued Rent.			Extent English Acres.
Easter and Wester Devols,	Lord Belhaven and Stenton,	83	6	8	
Easter Douglahill,	Do.	50			
Wester do.	Do.	50			
Dubbs,	Do.	33	6	8	
Braehead,	Do.	33	6	8	
Newark Gardens,	Site of the Town and Feus, &c.	66	13	4	
Total Valuation,		316	13	4	

The surface of the parish may be arranged thus:—

Arable, or forced into cultivation, ... 440
Natural moor and brae pasture, ... 350
Site of the town, roads, brooks, &c. 18
Wood, natural or planted, ... 36
                                                                                    ———
                                                                                    844

Succession of Ministers.—In 1696 this parish was separated from Kilmalcolm. The first minister was Robert Millar, ordained in 1697, and was translated to Paisley in 1709—a long litigation then ensued, about the right of the presentation between the Earl of Glencairn and the town of Glasgow. In 1717, John Anderson—he was translated to Glasgow in 1730. In 1731, David Brown—died in 1754. In 1754, John Anderson—died in 1774. In 1775, John Forrest, the present minister.

PARISH OF GREENOCK.

This parish stretches about four miles and a half along the shore, and nearly as far inland up the country. The cultivated part of it is limited almost exclusively to the coast side, and is not in many places a mile from it, but is more generally less than half a mile in breadth. It has, however, been rendered very fertile, owing to the great encouragement given to cultivation, from the constant demand for country produce by the numerous population. The country inland rises steeply into hills of six or seven hundred feet in height and more, and is very little adapted to any thing but pasturage, and not much even to that, as it is in general very barren moorish land. The whole amounts to about 6365 English acres.

State of Property.—The estates of Easter Greenock, (page 119) of Wester Greenock, (page 124) and Finnart, (page 126) have all descended by inheritance to the family of Stewart of Blackhall and Ardgowan, Bart. as will be seen in the family descent below. The estate of Cartsburn, (page 123), has gone also (by descent) to that of M'Knight Crawfurd of Ratho. See family descent.

TABLE OF PROPERTY.

Estates.	Proprietors.	Valued Rent.			Extent English Acres.
Greenock,	Sir Michael Shaw Stewart, Bart.	1933	6	8	4960
Cartsburn,	Wm. Macknight Crawfurd, Esq;	223	6	8	160
Garvocks,	Wm. Charles Hamilton, Esq; of Craighlaw,	129	2	0	1236
The Glebe,	The Minister's,				9
Total,		2285	15	4	6365

Which may be arranged thus :—

1. Arable, ... 2315
2. Sound dry pasture, ... 930
3. Moorish lands of little value, ... 2780
4. Sites of houses, roads, rivulets, ... 300
5. Woodlands, mostly natural, ... 40

        Total, ... 6365

It is to be observed that a considerable part of the estates both of Greenock and Cartsburn are feued out to different proprietors in the vicinity of the town for villas, as well as in the town itself. Earl Cathcart has about 83 English acres thus in feu, and which is again subfeued at a great additional rate. The minister's glebe too is nearly all feued out at a very high rate, which makes his stipend among the best in the church.

Succession of Ministers.—In 1602, John Lang; is minister in 1628. In 1640, James Taylor. In 1679, Niel Gillies, privately called by the parish. In 1688, ——— Gordon officially, till 1691, when he returns to his old charge of Inverary. In 1694, John Stirling, from Inchinnan, who, in 1701, was admitted principal of the College of Glasgow. In 1704, Andrew Turner, from Erskine; died in 1719. In 1719, his son, David Turner, ordained; died in 1786. In 1786, Allan M'Aulay. In 1792, Robert Steel, the present minister. Town of Greenock, in 1741, disjoined from the parish, when John Schaw was ordained. In 1771, John Adam, from West Kilbride, admitted. In 1793, Thomas Scott, the present minister.

Family Descent.—SHAW STEWART, Baronet of Greenock and Blackhall, continued from page 58, from the family records.

The account given by Crawfurd of this family appears to be quite accurate down to 1650.

IX. Sir Archibald Stewart, (the ninth in direct descent from Robert III. King of Scots) who in that year was Knighted, and made a Privy Councillor by Charles II. (vide supra.) married Margaret, daughter of Bryce Blair of that-ilk, by whom he had,

X. 1. John, who died before his father. He married Mary, daughter of Sir James Stirling of Keir, by whom he had five sons and two daughters: 1. John, who died unmarried before his grandfather; 2. Archibald, of whom afterwards; 3. Walter of Kincarachie; 4. David of Kirkwood; 5. James of Lumloch; first daughter, Mary, who married Sir Alexander Cunninghame of Corsehill, and had issue; 2. Annabella, married to William Porterfield of that-ilk, and had issue.

2. Archibald, who acquired the lands of Scotstoun, by marriage with Margaret, daughter of John Hutcheson of Scotstoun (see page 68) by whom he had a daughter, Annabella, married to Colquhoun of Tillyquhoun; 3. Walter, who acquired the lands of Pardovan by marriage with Elizabeth, daughter of Robert Stewart of Pardovan; and a daughter, Annabella, who married Sir George Maxwell of Pollok, and from whom the present family of Pollok is

descended. Sir Archibald died about the year 1659, and was succeeded by his grandson,

XI. Sir Archibald, the eldest surviving son of his eldest son, John, as above. On the 27th March, 1667, he was created a baronet of Nova Scotia, He died some time after the year 1682. He married, first, Anne, eldest daughter of Sir John Crawfurd of Kilbirnie, (see page 122.) by whom he had, 1. John, of whom afterwards; 2. Patrick, who died without issue; 3. Walter, bred to the bar, and became Solicitor General of Scotland, and ancestor of the family of Stewart-hall in Stirlingshire, and a daughter, Margaret, married, in 1685, to Brisbane of Bishopton, (ancestor of Brisbane of Brisbane) and had issue. Sir Archibald, secondly, married Dame Agnes Dalmahoy, who died without issue; thirdly, Mary, daughter of John Douglas of Kelhead, and had issue, two sons, who died unmarried, and two daughters, 1. Agnes, married to Robert Bogle, Esq; merchant in Glasgow, and had issue; 2. Margaret, married to Peter Murdoch, Esq; merchant in Glasgow, and had issue.

XII. John, the eldest son, was one of the commissioners for Renfrewshire to the Union Parliament. He married Rebecca, daughter of Michael Wallace, Esq; by whom he had, 1. Archibald, of whom hereafter; 2. Michael, of whom afterwards; and four daughters, 1. Anne, married to her cousin, Archibald Stewart of Stewart-hall; 2. Margaret, married to John Peadie, Esq; of Roughill; 3. Rebecca; 4. Johanna, married to the Rev. John Gillies, D. D. minister in Glasgow, (well known for literary abilities,) by whom she had one daughter, Rebecca, married to the Hon. Lieutenant General David Leslie. This John dying before his father, Sir Archibald was succeeded by his grandson,

XIII. Sir Archibald Stewart, the second baronet. He dying unmarried, was succeeded by his brother,

XIII. Sir Michael Stewart, the third Baronet, who was served heir to him in 1724. He was admitted a member of the faculty of advocates in 1735. He was an accomplished scholar, had studied at the Universities at home and abroad, and some fine and curious editions of the classics were added by him to the family library. He was remarkable also for the simplicity of his manners and habits, as well as for the acuteness of his mind and the vivacity of his parts. He died the 20th October 1796, in the 84th year of his age. He married Helen, eldest daughter of Sir John Houstoun of that-ilk, (by Margaret, daughter of Sir John Shaw of Greenock). Through her the descendants of this marriage came to represent the ancient family of Houstoun of Houstoun, as well as of Shaw of Greenock, and Nicolson of Carnock, (her mother being the only daughter of the marriage between Sir John Shaw of Greenock, and Dame Elenor Nicolson, daughter and coheiress of Sir Thomas Nicolson of Carnock.) By this marriage Sir Michael had three sons,

1. John, who, through his mother and grandmother, Dame Helenor Houstoun, and Dame Margaret Shaw, (both then deceased) succeeded to the entailed estate of Greenock, on the death of his grand-uncle, Sir John Shaw, in 1752. 2. Houstoun, who, in the same year, succeeded to the entailed estate of Carnock, on the death of his grand-uncle, Sir John Houstoun, Bart. (it being a condition in the entail of that estate, that it should not be united to the estate of Greenock.) 3. Archibald, who purchased an estate in Tobago, 1770, and was killed in 1779, from the following occurrence :—In the beginning of that year a part of the crew of an American privateer, amounting to 50 men, landed in that island, and burnt two plantations, when this gentleman immediately marched against them with a few men of his own company of militia, who happened to be at hand, and bravely attacked them, and gave them his fire, but was afterwards unfortunately shot himself, and died in a few hours.

Sir Michael had also two daughters, 1st, Margaret, who, in 1764, married Sir William Maxwell of Springkell, Bart. to whom she had four sons, three of whom died unmarried during their father's lifetime, and the 4th, Sir John Heron Maxwell, succeeded to his father, and married Stuart-Mary, daughter and heiress of Patrick Heron of Heron, Esq; by whom he has issue. She has also two daughters, 1. Helenora, married to Claud Alexander of Ballochmyle, Esq; to whom she has three sons and four daughters. 2d, Catherine, married to her cousin, Michael Stewart Nicolson of Carnock, of whom hereafter. This daughter of Sir Michael's, Lady Maxwell, died in March 1816, at the advanced age of 74. His 2d daughter, Helenora, died young. He was succeeded by his eldest son,

XIV. Sir John Shaw Stewart of Greenock and Blackhall, the 4th Baronet. He was elected member of parliament for the county of Renfrew, in 1780, and again in 1786 and 1790. He was remarkable for a powerful and enlarged understanding—for an independent mind—for the most generous spirit, and the most benevolent dispositions—above all, for the most stern and inflexible integrity. His sentiments led him to support the principles of that great statesman, Mr. Fox, with whom, and other illustrious characters of his time he was in habits of intimacy and friendship. He formed his opinions in politics, as on every other subject, with moderation and candour, but he adhered to them on all occasions with the strictest consistency, and acted up to them with undeviating firmness. The improvements he executed at Ardgowan were upon the most extensive scale, and are highly beneficial as well as beautiful in their effect. He built an excellent house, in the modern style, which he surrounded with an extensive park, and the gardens, pleasure grounds, and ample plantations which he planned, afford striking proofs of the excellency of his taste. The old tower of Ardgowan, which formed a part of the ancient mansion, still remains. It is an object beautifully picturesque, and rendered peculiarly interesting, from having been the gift, along with the ground on which it stands, in 1404, of Robert III. to his son the direct ancestor of this ancient family. He married Dame Frances Colquhoun, relict of Sir James Maxwell of Pollok, but had no issue. He died at Ardgowan, August 7, 1812, and was succeeded by the son of his second brother, Houstoun ———— who, as already mentioned, succeeded to the entailed estate of Carnock on the death of his maternal uncle, Sir John Houstoun of that-ilk. He married Margaret, eldest daughter of Boyd Porterfield of that-ilk, through whom (on the death of her brother, Alexander Porterfield, Esq; in 1715, without issue) the descendants of the marriage now represent that ancient family. He had issue by her one son, now

XV. Sir Michael Shaw Stewart, who, on his father's death, in 1785, succeeded to the estate of Carnock, and on his uncle's death, in 1812, as above, became proprietor of his lands also, and the 5th Baronet of Greenock and Blackhall. He married, 24th September 1787, his cousin Catherine, youngest daughter of Sir William Maxwell of Springkell, Baronet, by whom he has issue,

XVI. 1. Michael Stewart Nicolson, who now enjoys the estate of Carnock; 2. William, who died in infancy; 3. Houstoun, a captain in the royal navy; 4. John Shaw, an advocate; 5. Patrick Maxwell, merchant, London; 6. William Maxwell, and three daughters; 1. Margaret; 2. Catherine; and, 3. Helenora.

Shaw of Greenock now represented by Blackhall. John Shaw, who is stated (page 125) to have succeeded to the estate in 1620, acquired, in 1638, from Sir Hugh Montgomery Viscount Airds, (the husband of his aunt) his paternal estate of Broadstone, in Ayrshire, which is still possessed by the family. He obtained a charter, in 1635, erecting the town of Greenock into a burgh of barony. He died in 1679, and was succeeded by his son Sir John Shaw, (see page 125) who died in 1694, and was succeeded by his son Sir John Shaw, who married Helenor Nicolson, eldest daughter of Sir Thomas Nicolson of Carnock, (by Lady Margaret Livingstone,) to which estate she succeeded as co-heiress of Sir Thomas Nicolson, her nephew, (fifth Lord Napier. See Wood) and by her it was so entailed as never to be united to the estate of Greenock. There was issue by this marriage, (besides five sons of whose history nothing is stated) a son John, and a daughter Margaret, (vide infra). He died in 1702, and was succeeded by his son,

Sir John Shaw, who represented Renfrewshire in the first parliament of Great Britain, and was distinguished afterwards by a vigorous defence of the existing government in the rebellion 1715. He married, in 1700, Margaret, the eldest daughter of Sir Hugh Dalrymple of North Berwick, and in the contract of marriage, his father (then living) made a strict entail of his estate on him and the heirs male of his body, whom failing, on his five brothers in succession and their issue; whom failing, on his sister Margaret and her heirs whatsoever; whom failing, on William Shaw of Gannaway in Ireland, the descendant of Robert, mentioned page 125.

By this marriage he had only one daughter, Marion, who, on the 29th March 1718, was married to Charles Lord Cathcart, and whose descendants in consequence (and by a particular family transaction unnecessary here to be explained) inherit sub-feus to a considerable amount in the town of Greenock. His five younger brothers all died before him, without issue; and at his death, in 1752, the succession devolved, in terms of the above entail, on the descendants of his sister Margaret, who was married to Sir John Houstoun of that-ilk, to whom she had issue a son; 1. John, who, in   succeeded his father in the lands of Houstoun, but did not live to enjoy the estate of Greenock, as he predeceased, without issue, his uncle Sir John Shaw in the same year (1752) that he died; 2. a daughter Helenora, (vide infra) and another daughter; 3. Anne, married Colonel William Cunninghame of Enterkine, an officer of great reputation, to whom she had issue, William Cunninghame of Enterkine, Esq; now the only survivor.

The eldest daughter, Helenora, in 1738, married (as above) Sir Michael Stewart, Baronet of Blackhall, to whom she had two sons; 1. John Shaw Stewart, who, on the death of his grand-uncle, Sir John Shaw of Greenock, (his own mother being also dead) succeeded, in 1752, to the estate of Greenock; and on the death of his father, Sir Michael Stewart, as above, in 1796, succeeded to the estates of Blackhall, as already mentioned; 2. Houstoun Stewart, Esq; who, in 1752, on the death of Sir John Shaw of Greenock succeeded to the estate of Carnock, (vide supra).

CRAWFURD OF CARTSBURN.—Thomas Crawfurd, who married Bethia, daughter of Archibald Roberton, Esq; of Bedlay, (see page 124,) had issue by that lady, 1. Thomas, who died without issue in 1642; 2. Archibald; 3. Bethia; 4. Christian, of whom afterwards. He died in 1743, and was succeeded by his son Thomas. He spent much of his time on the continent, and was an able scholar and an accomplished gentleman. He died without issue in 1794, and was succeeded by his aunt, Christian, above-mentioned. She died in 1796. At the time she succeeded to the estate, she was the widow of Mr. Robert Arthur, to whom she had issue, a son Thomas, who died unmarried, and a daughter, Christian, who succeeded her in the estate of Cartsburn, and who was married to the late Thomas Macknight, Esq; of Ratho, (son of the late Rev. James Macknight, minister of Irvine,) to whom she has issue, 1. William Macknight Crawfurd, Esq; who married Jean, second daughter of the late John Crawfurd, Esq; of Broadfield, and has issue; 2. Christian, married to the Rev. Thomas Macknight of Dalbaith, D. D. and one of the ministers of Edinburgh, son of the late Rev.   Macknight, D. D. minister in Edinburgh, and author of The Harmony of the Gospels; 3. Elizabeth.

Arms.—A Fess Ermine, betwixt three Mullets in chief, Argent; and two Swords Saltier ways, in base proper; hilted and pomelled, Or; all within a bordure, waved of the third: above the Shield, a Helmet, with a Mantle, Gules, doubled Argent. Crest, on a Forse, a Sword erected in pale, having a pair of balances on the point; all proper. Motto, "Quod tibe hoc alteri."

Note.—George Crawfurd, the original author of this work, and also of the Peerage of Scotland, was the immediate younger brother of the first Thomas Crawfurd mentioned above. He married Margaret, daughter of James Anderson, Esq; postmaster of Scotland, by whom he had four daughters, Jane, Patricia, Bethia, and Marion. He died 24th December 1748.

TOWN OF GREENOCK.

Although this town as a sea-port ranks among the most important in Britain it is comparatively of very modern origin. In the beginning of the seventeenth century the whole town consisted of only a single row of thatch-covered huts, and with no harbour whatever. Even in the year 1700, it was such an inconsiderable place that, when the inhabitants presented a petition to the Scots Parliament for an aid to assist them in building a harbour, it met with a direct refusal, so very little importance in the public eye was then attached to it.

The inhabitants, however, did not abandon the project. They entered into a contract with Sir John Shaw the superior, to subject themselves to an assessment of one shilling and fourpence Sterling on each sack of malt brewed within the limits of the town, for the purpose of defraying the expense themselves; and, in the year 1707, the work was begun with vigour.

This harbour, divided in the middle by a tongue of land into two, occupied at that time a space of ten Scots acres, and though it cost 100,000 Scots merks, (about £5,555 sterling) to make it complete, yet so efficient was the fund, aided by the harbour dues, that, in the year 1740, the whole expense was reimbursed, and leaving a surplus of £1500 Sterling, which laid the foundation of the present funds of the town. This shews that the spirit of activity, for which the people of Greenock are so remarkably distinguished, was strongly aroused even at this early period; for at this time the population, in all probability, did not exceed 3000; for we know for certain, that in 15 years after (in 1755) the whole population of the parish, including Carts-dyke and the country, was only 3858. At this time the town of Greenock was without a proper form of internal police, but in two years after, viz. in 1757, it was erected into a burgh of barony, governed by a council of nine, of whom two are bailies, and which continues to be its municipal constitution to this day *. These bailies, as also the bailie of the barony (which includes the country) are ex officiis in the commission of the peace. In 1814, a branch of the sheriff court was established here, under a sheriff substitute, a fiscal, and a clerk. In this court there are at present twenty solicitors, who find abundance of employment.

The town of Crawfurd's-dyke, or Carts-dyke, as it is called, (which was originally at a considerable distance from Greenock, though now adjoining,) was erected into a burgh of barony in 1636, about fifty years before a similar form of internal government was conferred on Greenock. There can be no doubt of it being then the most considerable place of the two; yet the number of houses in it long after consisted of only 88, and it was taken notice of as a distinguishing circumstance, that 44 of these houses had outside stairs. Carts-dyke has now other circumstances to be distinguished by than outside stairs, even the houses are among the most elegant of any town in the county.

Greenock, conjoined with this town, in 1811, contained 19,042 inhabitants; in 1801, there were 17,458; in 1792, 15,000; and only 12,000 in 1772. From this may be seen the progressive increase of the town. To these numbers may be added the seamen afloat at the time of the census: in 1811, they were estimated at 3500, making a population in all of about 22,500. It is supposed to

* It had long before this, viz. in 1685, been constituted a burgh of barony, but with such limited powers as to be inadequate to the government of the place.

be still on the increase. In this respect Greenock may be set down as the sixth town in Scotland.

This town (still including Carts-dyke) extends about a mile and a half in a semicircular form along the margin of a beautiful bay. It is hardly in any part a quarter of a mile broad. A great stretch of it is only a single street, open to the sea, and having its fine gardens at the back. Immediately behind the town the ground rises with a pretty steep ascent. And here is erected, in many a varied stile of architecture, those numerous villas for which the vicinity of Greenock is so remarkable. These are set down each amidst its own gardens and pleasure grounds, embracing in the prospect the most picturesque scenery that fancy can well conceive. The Frith is here from two to three miles over. The opposite shore towers upwards, in the most rugged form. The intermediate sea is overspread with sails. Among these, the recently invented steam boats glide swiftly along as if by magic. We would almost suppose ourselves transported into Fairyland.

The harbours of Greenock are under similar circumstances with that of Port Glasgow already stated. The depth of water at ebb-tide and its rise at flood-tide are very little different. The width of the deep channel betwixt the piers and the sand bank is more. It is about 300 yards. This sand bank, which commences as high up as Dumbarton, ends a very little below Greenock. At this end of it, or what is called the Tail of the Bank, there is the best anchoring ground in the Frith of Clyde, and room for hundreds of ships of any burden.

The present harbours occupy an extent of 20 acres. The Carts-dyke harbour is not now used for shipping, much of it is converted into wood-yards.

There are five ship-building yards. In 1791, the largest ship built in Scotland was launched from Mr. Scott's yard here. It was of the burden of 850 tons.

There are two dry-docks at present; each of them can admit a vessel of 650 tons. Two more are projected, one of which is to be on a larger scale.

There is a magnificent custom-house now building. The ground it stands on is part of the old harbour filled up. The estimated expence is £.18000, but it is thought it will cost £.4000 more.

The number of vessels belonging to Greenock is just now 321, containing 42,751 tons, and navigated by 2973 men.

In 1804, the extent of the shipping of this port, including their respective voyages, was,

		Ships.	Tons.	Men.
Inward,	Foreign Trade,	406	53546	3183
	Coasters,	384	21536	1396
	Total,	790	75082	4579
Outward,	Foreign Trade,	352	50366	3673
	Coasters,	739	35155	2438
	Total,	1091	85521	6111
	Grand Total,	1881	160303	10690

In 1817 it was,

		Ships.	Tons.
Inward,	British Ships,	287	49425
	Foreign, do.	15	4168
	Coastwise,	426	22226
	Total,	728	75819
Outward,	British Ships,	372	57054
	Foreign, do.	27	4475
	Coastwise,	489	22748
	Total,	878	84257
	Grand Total	1606	160076

The duties of customs, in 1804, amounted to,.................£208,490
Do.   do.   in 1816,   do.   296,888
The duties of excise, in 1803–4, were ,........................   50,232
These in 1809–10, increased to ....,......   221,854
The harbour revenue, in 1783, was ....,......   111 : 4 : 8
In 1810, it was increased to ....,..............,,.....   4,219 : 15 : 4

The herring fishing also is prosecuted to a great extent. In 1811 there were cleared outwards 144 vessels, containing 6091½ tons, and having a crew of 816, the bounty paid them that year was £2373.

Manufactures. Though Greenock owes much of its importance to its shipping and commercial concerns, it is not without a due share of manufactures. Thus there is a rope-work; a duck-work; three soap and candle-works; two sugar-boiling establishments, and a brewery, all on a large scale. Some tan-works too. That at Lady-Burn, Mr. Hood's is perhaps inferior to none as a complete establishment, in Scotland. There is also a pottery, situated betwixt Greenock and Port Glasgow, that bids fair to acquire celebrity for the manufacturing of table and tea services, and other stoneware of that kind, for which Staffordshire has been so long famed.

Other noticeable Circumstances.—In 1801 a Tontine Inn was built at an expence of £10,000. The subscription for it, at £25 a share, was filled up in two days. There are two public libraries which contain 5000 volumes, and cost £2000. In 1809 an infirmary was opened at an expence of £2394. In 1811 there were admitted into it 150 patients, of whom 108 were cured, 15 relieved, and only 14 died in the course of the year. Revenue of the post-office, in 1811, £5300. Number of cattle slaughtered in 1810 was 1812 Nolt, at an average weight of thirty stones avordupois the four quarters: 2234 veals, at three stones ditto; 7101 lambs at $1\frac{1}{4}$ do. 231 swine, at 8 ditto; three goats at $2\frac{1}{4}$ do. and 10,000 sheep, at $2\frac{1}{4}$ do. making in all, 98,572 stones of butcher meat, at 16 ounces to the pound, and 16 pounds to the stone. The record of this fact will serve two purposes in after comparison—first, the quantity consumed in proportion to the number of people, and second, the weight of the different animals.

Steam Boats.—In 1812 the first steam boat sailed from Glasgow to Greenock. It was invented and built by Mr. Bell at Helensburgh. They have been much improved since, and are probably susceptible of improvement still. The dimensions of them are various, but those most esteemed, are about 75 feet in length, and 15 feet broad, and about 85 tons burden, and cost about £3500. There are 16 or 18 of them that ply betwixt Glasgow, Greenock, and Largs, and intermediate distances—and go frequently to Rothsay, Inverary, and Campbelton, and sometimes to Ardrossan, Irvine, and Ayr. They go at the rate of about 8 miles an hour, even against the wind or tide—when both are in their favour, they have been known to go 12 miles an hour. One can hardly conceive a more pleasant mode of travelling, or more agreeable accommodation than these afford, and it is even cheaper than by any other manner of conveyance.

Of the villas round Greenock, that have a particular name, perhaps the most distinguished for elegance or for situation are the following :—Rosebank, Mr. M'Call; Sea-bank, Mr. Johnston; Glen-park, Mr. M'Naught; Caddel-hill, Mr. Thomson; and Finnart, Mr. Robert Stewart. There are many that have no distinguishing appellation, but are nevertheless as elegant. Such as those belonging to Mr. Robertson, Mr. Thomas Stewart, Mr. Leitch, Mr. Bayne, and Mr. Bannatyne. These are all situated to the westward of the town, and have each a piece of ground attached for gardens, &c. extending from half an acre to three acres, Scots measure. To the eastward of the town there is the elegant mansion (still without a name) belonging to Mr. Gemmill, to which 28 Scots acres are attached. There is also Hillend, Mr. Crawfurd, with nearly five acres; and Lady-Burn House, Mr. Hood, with about two acres, and one, without a name, belonging to Mr. M'Grouther; and, very nearly on the site of the ancient castle of Easter Greenock, Mr. Campbell has erected an elegant small mansion, which he has distinguished by the very unassuming name of Brig-end.

INNERKIP PARISH.

Situation and Extent.—This is the most westerly parish in the county. It is bounded on the north and west by the Frith of Clyde, with a sea-coast in all its windings of about 20 miles; on the south by part of the shire of Ayr; and on the east by the parishes of Kilmalcolm and Greenock. In a straight line, from south to north, it is about five miles long, and it is nearly as broad from east to west. It contains about 12,540 English acres.

Surface and Soil.—There is a beautiful and fertile tract of country about the bay of Innerkip on the west, highly ornamented with the pleasure grounds around the stately mansion of Ardgowan. There is another tract of nearly the same extent, and equally fertile around the bay of Gourock on the north, in the ancient barony of Finnart Stewart, now much embellished with plantations. The other arable lands are limited nearly all to a narrow stripe along the shore, or up the sides of the mountain streamlets, the Kelly, the Daff, and the Kip. The greater part of the parish, however, is wild moorish lands, some of them very high and bleak, and little susceptible of improvement.

State of Property.—The largest portion of the parish, the great estate of Ardgowan, (see page 128) remains still the property of the ancient family of Stewart of Blackhall. It has been greatly improved of late, (vide supra) and is one of the finest estates in the county.

Kelly. This property (see page 129) was purchased in 1792 from the representatives of the former family of Bannatyne, by John Wallace, Esq; of Neilstonside and Cessnock. He built the present house in the year following, and which has since been considerably enlarged by his son, the present proprietor, Robert Wallace, Esq; of Kelly. By him chiefly the place has been formed, not only by his energetic improvements in agriculture, by which he has greatly extended the arable lands, but by extensive plantations of wood both valuable and ornamental. Even the very game on the estate has been improved by the introduction of pheasants among the woodlands, and black-cock in the moors. He has lately acquired a most desirable addition to the pleasure grounds of Kelly, by obtaining a considerable expanse of woodland and other territory on the opposite side of Kellyburn, from the estate of Skelmurly in Ayrshire, by an excambion with Lord Eglinton of other lands that were adjacent to the Earl's mansion on that estate, and equally desirable to his Lordship, so that both places have been improved by the transaction. Kellyhouse, with all its accompaniments, is now one of the finest seats on the Frith of Clyde.

Gourock. This ancient property of the Stewarts of Castlemilk was alienated by them, in 1784, to Duncan Darroch, Esq; the present proprietor, who has made great improvements upon it by enclosing and draining the lands, and building better and more commodious houses for the tenantry, and more especially by plantations of wood, which always ornament an estate as well as add to its value. There is a good old mansion on this property, commanding, from amidst its ancient trees, a beautiful prospect over the town of Gourock and the Frith of Clyde, to the opposite picturesque coast and mountains of Argyle. This gentleman bought, in 1792, the conterminous smaller property also of Fancyfarm, from the heirs of the late Mr. James Donald, formerly merchant in Greenock.

Villas.—There are also some remarkably elegant villas set down on the coast side of this parish, which is uncommonly rich in picturesque scenery. In particular, there are three to the westward of Gourock, near to the Clough-point, and the old castle of Leven, viz. One belonging to Mr. James M'Invoy, merchant in Glasgow, with about two acres and three quarters of pleasure grounds. One belonging to Mr. Adam Crooks, merchant in Glasgow, with two acres and a half; and one belonging to Mr. James Hunter, merchant in Greenock, with one acre, all Scots measure.

Farther south the coast, and near to Kelly House, in Weemes Bay, there are three very commodious and elegant mansions let out from season to season for sea-bathing, for which the situation is admirably adapted.

TABLE OF PROPERTY.

Estates.	Proprietors.	Valued Rent.		Extent English Acres.
Ardgowan,	Sir Michael Shaw Stewart, Bart.	2304	10	
Lunderstown,	Formerly Hyndman, now Sir Michael Shaw Stewart, Bart.	25		
Do.	John Allison,	12	10	
Do.	Robert Jameson	12	10	
Gourock,	Duncan Darroch, Esq;	530		
Fancy-farm,	Do.	70		
Kelly,	Robert Wallace, Esq;	120		
Christwell, or Crosswell, now Langhouse,	Robert Macfie, Esq.	102	10	
Total,		3177		12540

The whole may be arranged thus :—

1. Arable, ... 4500
2. Sound pasture, ... 1500
3. Moss, or moors, of little value, ... 5860
4. Sites of houses, roads, rivulets, ... 140
5. Woodlands, natural or planted, ... 540

    Total, ... 12540

Succession of Ministers.—In 1602, Francis Younger is minister. In 1626, John Hamilton. In 1688, Duncan Campbell. In 1692, William Fleming, died in 1745; John Hyndman presented, but receives a call to the parish of Collington, from whence he was afterwards translated to the West-Kirk, Edinburgh. He was a man of considerable eminence. In 1746, Alexander Scott from Killallan, died in 1787. In 1788, Thomas Brown, the present minister.

Villages.—Gourock. This town is pleasantly situated about two miles west from Greenock, on the west side of the beautiful bay of the same name. The number of inhabitants is about 750, of whom a great proportion are herring and white fishers, there being about 40 small wherries or sloops here manned by three or four men each. There is also a rope-work on a pretty large establishment, which employs 50 or 60 people; and about 25 or 30 men are employed in quarrying whinstone for street-paving, which is in great demand, not only in the neighbouring towns of Greenock and Glasgow, but is exported in considerable quantities (by way of ballast) to Liverpool, and even to America. The rest of the people are in the ordinary line of craftsmen, carpenters, smiths, &c. &c.

The bay of Gourock is esteemed to be among the best anchoring grounds in the Frith, and is much resorted to by shipping of all sizes, as there is neither bank nor shoal to obstruct their way. The place is much frequented in the bathing season, by people from Glasgow, Paisley, and other towns, and more so lately, from the easy conveyance by steam boats, at so cheap a rate as 4s. 6d. for a cabin passenger from Glasgow, which is not above two-pence a mile, and through a country abounding with the most interesting scenery; the very sail itself is worth all the cost for health alone.

Innerkip. The kirk town of the parish is a clean, handsome, and very pleasant village, with a population of about 430 inhabitants. Of these, part are fishers and part cotton manufacturers. This is also a place of resort for sea-bathers, and who have also the inducement of the steam boats, for easy conveyance to and from.

Family Descent.—DARROCH OF GOUROCK.—Duncan Darroch, Esq; of Gourock, was upwards of twenty years in the mercantile line at Kingston in Jamaica. He is chief of the ancient name, the patronymick of which is M'Iliriach. He married, on the 11th April 1791, Janet, daughter of Angus M'Larty, merchant in Greenock, by whom he had the following issue: 1. Malcolm, born the 5th March 1793, and died the 8th May 1795; 2. Donald, born the 21st October 1794; died the 22d October 1809; 3. Helen, born the 26th October 1796; died the 3d February 1797; 4. Malcolm, born the 5th April 1798, and is now an Ensign in the 32d regiment of foot; 5. Angus, born the 24th February 1800, and is now in a mercantile house in London.

Armorial bearings. Argent, a three masted Ship, under full Sail in a Sea, all proper, between three Oak Trees, eradicated and fructuated of the last. Above the Shield is placed a Helmet, befitting his degree, with mantling Gules, the doubling Argent in a Wreath of his Liveries, and set for Crest, a Demy Negro; in his Dexter hand, a Dagger proper, and in an escrol, above the Crest, this motto, " Be Watchful." On a compartment below the Shield are placed, for Supporters, two Alligators proper.

HYNDMAN OF LUNDERSTOWN.—North of the splendid seat of Ardgowan, belonging to the Stewart family, are beautifully situated the Lunderstowns, near to the bay of that name; and, as early as the reign of James the V. we find the Hyndmans in possession of part of them, holding of the Crown. The property of this family was at one time considerable, but has been dilapidated, by sales made from time to time.

Upon the 12th of November 1578, Hector Hyndman of Lunderstown disposed the sixth-part of the lands of that name to his son, John, in conformity to the terms of a marriage contract with his wife, Janet Lanqocht, a name which does not now appear to be in existence in Scotland. This disposition, as appears from the public records, was followed by a crown charter of confirmation in favour of John, dated the 13th December 1459. From Hector the succession flowed in an uninterrupted line downwards to Robert Hyndman of Lunderstown, who was succeeded by his son, John, who married Sophia Campbell, daughter of Campbell of Auchenwillen in Argyleshire, and, upon her death, he married Elizabeth, the eldest daughter of Hunter of Hunterstown in Ayrshire. By these marriages he had a family of 19 children, but few of them attained any great age. He was succeeded by Captain Michael Hyndman of the royal navy, his eldest son, by his first marriage, who died in the year 1792, leaving a son also, named Michael, who sold the lands of Lunderstown to Sir Michael Shaw Stewart of Greenock and Blackhall, Bart. in the month of July 1817, and died shortly after.

Robert, the eldest son of John Hyndman, by his marriage with Elizabeth Hunter, acquired the lands of Springside in Ayrshire, and married Jean Boyd, daughter of Thomas Boyd of Orchard. He died in the year 1796, leaving two daughters, Elizabeth and Marianne, and a son, the present John Blair Hyndman of Springside, who is now the representative of the Hyndmans of Lunderstown.

WALLACE OF KELLY.—(see page 87) Although it does not appear from existing records under what character Wallace of Craigie acquired the lands of Elderslie after the death of Sir William Wallace, the governor of Scotland, yet it is probable that he acquired a right to them both as heir male and as superior; for it is a fact undoubted, that Sir William Wallace was descended in the manner mentioned by Crawfurd, (page 86) from Wallace of Riccarton, afterwards of Craigie, and it is established by authentic writings, that the head of the family of Craigie, was both the superior of the lands of Elderslie, and that the Wallaces, who succeeded Sir William in Elderslie, were of his family of Craigie. With this remark I shall now proceed to trace the descent of the Kelly family from William Wallace, mentioned in page 87, as having obtained a charter of the lands of Elderslie in 1554.

I. In 1586, William Wallace of Elderslie obtained a precept of Clare Constat from his superior, the Knight of Craigie, as heir of his father, William[1]. Also in 1583, he acquired the lands of Helington, and in 1597, those

---

[1] Among the title deeds of Mr. Speirs of Elderslie.

of Ryreswraeths and Windyhill[1]. He married Catherine, daughter of Hugh Crawfurd of Kilbirnie, (see page 122) by whom he had three sons: 1. William, his successor; 2. John, of whom afterwards; 3. James, who acquired, in 1605 and 1612, the lands of Muirhead and Limpetstane, in the parish of Paisley.

II. William, the eldest son, succeeded his father. He had a son,

III. Hugh Wallace of Elderslie, who, in 1637, was served heir to his grandfather, William, in the lands of Windyhill and others. On the 4th April 1640, he had a charter, proceeding upon his own resignation, from his superior, Sir Hugh Wallace of Craigie, in which he is designed "Of Elderslie Dilectus consanguineum nostrum[2]." In 1678 the same Hugh Wallace conveyed the lands of Elderslie to Sir Thomas Wallace of Craigie, who conveyed them to his own second son, Thomas, afterwards (on the death of his eldest brother, Sir William, see page 87) Sir Thomas Wallace of Craigie. In 1700 Sir Thomas Wallace conveyed these lands to Hugh Wallace of Inglistoun, who, with consent of his son Thomas, conveyed them to John Wallace, eldest son of William Wallace, merchant in Glasgow, (brother of John Wallace of Neilstonside) and his spouse, Jean Kennedy, and their heirs male. This John Wallace left no male issue, but only a daughter, Helen, in whose favours a title to the land of her father was made up in 1729. She married Archibald Campbell of Succoth, (vide infra) and in 1769, with consent of her husband, sold Elderslie to Alexander Speirs, Esq; and these lands are now the property and chief title of his eldest son, Archibald Speirs, Esq; of Elderslie. Hugh Wallace of Elderslie, the son of the second William as above, died without issue, on which the representation of the family came to

II. John, the second son of the first William. (vide supra) He married Margaret, daughter of John Hamilton of Ferguslie, of the family of Orbieston[*]. Of this marriage there were three sons.

III. 1. James, who took the title of Lorabank, as the lands of Ferguslie seem to have been purchased about this time by a person of the name of Cochrane; 2. William; 3. Allan.

III. William the second son, married Margaret, daughter of Hugh Stewart of Neilstonside, (see page 41) and by this marriage he acquired the lands of

---

[1] Retours—Renfrewshire. [2] Among the title deeds of Mr. Speirs of Elderslie.

[*] There is on record a charter, dated 9th July 1647, granted by the Crown in favour of John Wallace, who married Margaret Hamilton, bearing to be in implement of their contract of marriage, and containing reference to a former charter granted to him by Lord Abercorn, the date of which is not legible. In the index to the records, mention is made of a charter to John Wallace of Ferguslie, 27th July 1624. The charter itself is however not to be found.

Neilstonside and Drumgrain*. Of this marriage there were two sons; 1. John, who succeeded him †; and 2. William, who became a merchant in Glasgow.

IV. John, the eldest son, had no male issue, having left only three daughters, who sold Neilstonside in 1713, to Alexander Finlayson.

IV. William Wallace, merchant in Glasgow, came thus to be the male representative of the family of Neilstonside, and also of Ferguslie. He acquired the lands of Over-Kirktoun, and others in the parish of Neilston, which he afterwards sold in 1690. He married   daughter of   by whom he had two sons, John and Thomas.

V. John married Jean, daughter of Dr. Thomas Kennedy, physician in Glasgow, by whom he had an only daughter, Helen, who married Archibald Campbell of Succoth, (vide supra) to whom she had Sir Ilay Campbell, Bart. Lord President of the court of session.

V. Thomas, the second son, acquired the estate of Cairnhill in Ayrshire. He married, in 1710, Lillias, daughter of William Cunningham, Esq; of Craigends, by whom he had three sons, 1. William; 2. John; 3. Hugh.

VI. William, the eldest, succeeded to the estate of Cairnhill. He married a daughter of Archibald Campbell of Succoth, by whom he had three sons, who all died without issue, and one daughter,

VII. Lillias Wallace of Cairnhill. She married Captain Ferrier of Summerford, in the county of Stirling, now deceased, and by him had issue, three sons and two daughters.

VIII. The eldest son, John, is heir apparent of Cairnhill.

VI. John, the 2d son of Thomas of Cairnhill, acquired the estate of Cess-

---

* In 1644 John, the eldest son, acquired from Lord Cochran a precept of Clare Constat in the lands of Neilstonside and Drumgrain, as heir of his father William.

† There is upon record (Books of Session, 24th April 1646) a charter by Lord Abercorn, dated 24th April 1646, of these lands in favour of this William Wallace. Allan, the third son of John Wallace of Ferguslie, held a wadset over the lands of Elderslie. James, the eldest brother, after the death of William, the middle brother, expede a service, 9th June 1656, (see Renfrewshire Retours) as heir of conquest to his younger brother Allan in this wadset. John Wallace of Neilstonside, the eldest son of William of Neilstonside, (the second son of John of Ferguslie) was charged by Porterfield, in consequence of a trust bond, to enter as heir of conquest to his uncle Allan in the wadset, and, on the 13th June 1674, obtained decree of adjudication. A title having thus been made up, Porterfield brought a reduction of James' service to Allan as being erroneous, (William the immediate elder brother of Allan being both neir of line and of conquest) and, on the 17th February 1676, obtained a decree of reduction. These facts are established by writings in the charter-chest of Mr. Speirs of Elderslie; and in this way the propinquity of Wallace of Neilstonside and Wallace of Ferguslie is proved.

nock, in Ayrshire, in   He afterwards sold it, when he purchased the lands of Kelly in Renfrewshire. He married Janet, daughter of Robert Colquhoun, Esq; by whom he had several sons, of whom two only survived him, (Robert and James) and several daughters. John was succeeded by his eldest son,

VII. Robert Wallace, now of Kelly, who, in   married a daughter of Sir William Forbes of Craigivar, in the county of Aberdeen.

Hugh, the youngest son of Thomas of Cairnhill, has left several grandsons, and one grand-daughter, by his eldest son, Hugh.

Thus, Mr. Wallace of Kelly is the nearest heir male of the family of Wallace of Cairnhill; in like manner, he is the nearest heir male of the families of Wallace of Neilstonside and of Ferguslie, by direct lineal descent; again, by being heir male of these families, he is the nearest heir male of the Wallaces of Elderslie, his great-grandfather, William, merchant in Glasgow, being the great-grandson of William of Elderslie, who obtained the precept of Clare Constat in 1536; for, as neither Hugh (1st, No. III.) of Elderslie, nor James (2d, No. III.) of Lorabank, nor John (No. IV.) of Neilstonside, nor John (1st, No. V.) of Over-Kirktoun, nor William (1st, No. VI.) of Cairnhill, all the eldest sons respectively of the family at the time, left any of them issue male, the representation falls unquestionably on Mr. Wallace of Kelly, the eldest son of John of Cessnock, the eldest heir male of the family. Lastly, the heirs male of Wallaces of Craigie (the original stock) having failed in the direct line, Mr. Wallace of Kelly becomes of course the nearest heir male of that ancient house, from whence the whole families of Wallace seem to have sprung.

Note.—A gentleman of the name of Wallace, a descendant of the family of Elderslie, mortified, in 1723, the sum of £1200 Sterling to purchase lands, in order to endow a free school in the parish of Closeburn in Dumfriesshire, where he was born; and £200 to purchase five or six acres of land, and build a school and dwelling house for the master; also £200 more to produce a fund to pay an assistant, or doctor, as he called it in the deed of mortification. All this has been done. £1145 was laid out in purchasing land, at some distance, and the remainder in aid of the sum allotted for building the rector's house and inclosing his glebe. The land, in 1792, rented at £90, including £14. 17s. 11d of public burdens, and next year it was let on a new lease, at £.175 yearly. The endowment, in honour of the founder, is named "The School of Wallace Hall," and has long been in high reputation as a seminary of learning. The different branches of education taught at it are, reading English, Writing, Arithmetic, Latin and Greek, all in conformity to the will of the Donor, to which has been added, French, Geography, Mathematics, and Book-keeping. This academy, as it is more generally called, of Closeburn, is indeed among the most celebrated still in Scotland It is free to all the children of the parish, but a number of young gentlemen, from the neighbouring country, are boarded at it, and get their education, for which they pay the usual rates.

CONTINUATION OF THE TABLE OF RENT.

Parishes.	Valuation, Scots.			Rent Sterling, in 1795.	Rent Sterling, in 1810.	Land Rents in 1815.			House Rents in 1815.			Land and Houses in 1815.		
Cathcart,	2586	11	6	2690	8000	5921	19	6	1995	16	6	7917	15	6
Eaglesham,	3073	6	8	2700	7000	9438	13	9	579	1	6	10017	9	3
Eastwood,	3366	13	4	3400	5000	7075	13	10	3101	9		10177	2	10
Erskine,	4451			2980	6000	6931	14	3	561	10		7493	4	3
Greenock,	2285	15	4	3600	10000	5312		2	35360		11	40672	11	2
Houstoun,	4057	8		2750	5500	6124	15		871	15		6996	10	
Inchinnan,	2398	13	4	2100	4500	4806	9	6	267	15		5073	4	6
Innerkip,	3177			2960	4000	3845	17		1478	15		5324	12	
Kilbarchan,	6278	8		4710	8000	10135	4	5	1777	11		11912	15	5
Kilmacolm,	5500			3400	5000	7823	10		326	9	6	8149	19	1
Lochwinnoch,	6831	6	8	7600	9000	12211	3	6	1933	10	9	14144	14	6
Mearns,	4766	19	8	5000	7500	10891	1	5	1131	15	1	12022	16	6
Neilston,	5486	13	4	4860	7000	10115	4	11	3024	7	5	13139	12	4
Paisley Town,	1077	6	8	500	1000	1291	13	6	30229	13		31521	6	6
Do. Abbey Parish,	10741	13	4	9700	23000	22307	6	5	22293	8	3	44600	14	8
Port Glasgow,	316	13	4	200	1000	456	15	6	9958	14		10410	9	6
Renfrew,	2776	6	8	3150	6000	8169	14	10	1753	16	6	9923	11	4
Total, ...	69172		1	62200	117500	132858	16	1	116639	13	9	249498	9	10

Note.—The parish of Cathcart has included in it a small part of Govan, thus,

Cathcart, ...		2242	11
Govan, ...		344	5
		£2586	16

Also, the parish of Neilston has included in it a small part of Beith, also of Dunlop, thus,

Neilston, ...	4823	6	8
Part of Beith, . .	163	6	8
Part of Dunlop, . .	500		
	£5486	13	4

Sum as in the Table,

And this circumstance applies to all the columns as well as to that of the valued rent.

TABLE OF SURFACE IN ENGLISH ACRES.

Parishes.	Arable.	Sound pasture.	Moss or Moors.	Sites of houses, roads, waters.	Wood, natural or planted.	Total.
Cathcart,	2450	10		25	120	2605
Eaglesham,	6100	3960	5200	230	60	15450
Eastwood,	5750	25		145	425	6345
Erskine,	3000	2500		65	800	6365
Greenock,	2315	930	2780	300	40	6365
Houstoun,	4000	2500	350	150	500	7500
Inchinnan,	2600	100		60	300	3060
Innerkip,	4500	1500	5860	140	540	12540
Kilbarchan,	5400	2000	1200	140	460	9200
Kilmalcolm,	8500	8000	2500	100	700	19800
Lochwinnoch,	8000	5750	4000	500	1000	19250
Mearns,	7250	2400	950	250	100	10950
Neilston,	10500	1200	1000	256	1000	13956
Paisley, Abbey, do.	12500	1500	260	900	1000	16160
Port Glasgow,	440	350		18	36	844
Renfrew,	3600	36		60	80	3776
Total,	86905	32761	24000	3339	7161	154166

Explanation of Terms.—1. By arable is meant all lands in cultivation, whether in tillage or in grass. 2. Sound pasture, natural grass distinct from heath, whether on hills or plains. 3 Moss or moors, dark heath and peat mosses in which little or no green pasture is found. 4. Woods, not merely clumps and belts of planting, but hedge-rows, and even single trees whereever growing.

POPULATION TABLE.

Parishes.	1755.	1791-7.	1801.	1811.
Cathcart,	499	697	1059	1449
Eaglesham,	1103	1000	1176	1424
Eastwood,	1142	2642	3375	4845
Erskine,	829	808	847	963
Greenock,	3858	15000	17458	19042
Houstoun,	947	1034	1891	2044
Inchinnan,	397	306	462	641
Innerkip,	1590	1280	1367	1632
Kilbarchan,	1485	2506	3751	3563
Kilmalcolm,	1495	951	1130	1475
Lochwinnoch,	1530	2613	2955	3515
Mearns,	886	1430	1714	1941
Neilston,	1299	2330	3796	4949
Paisley,	4290	13800	17026	19913
Abbey do.	2509	10792	14146	16785
Port Glasgow,	1695	4036	3865	5116
Renfrew,	1091	1628	2031	2305
	26645	62853	78056	91624

The population in 1755 was ascertained at the time by the late Dr. Webster, when making up a scheme of a fund for ministers' widows. In 1791-7 the return from each parish to Sir John Sinclair, when drawing up at that period the statistical account of Scotland. In 1801 and 1811 return to government by the population act.

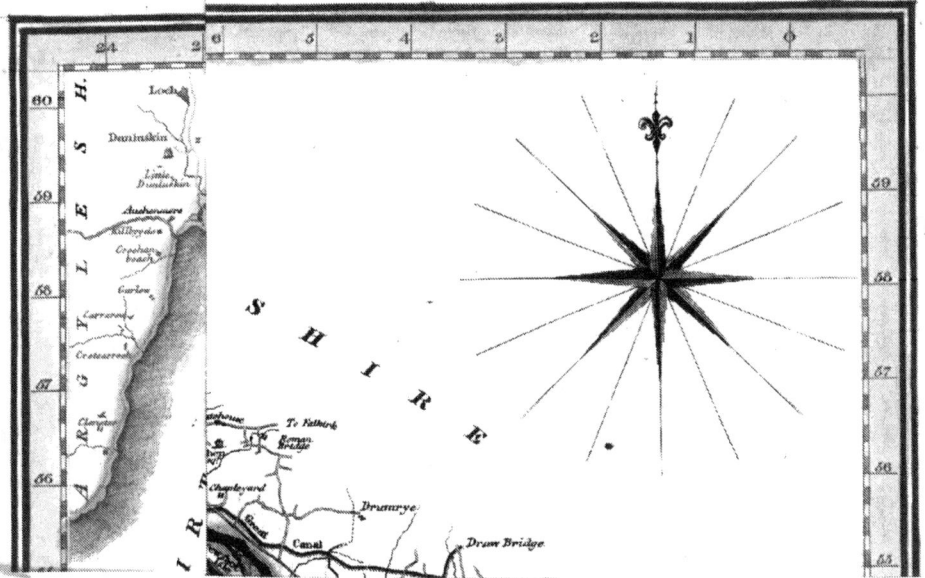

ORIGIN AND DESCENT

OF

THE HOUSE OF STEWART.

THE origin of this illustrious house, like to that of many other great families, is involved in obscurity or disguised in fable. It does not follow, however, because part of its more early history be fictitious, that the whole must be false. That would be too sweeping a conclusion, and would carry incredulity beyond all reasonable bounds. There are two ways in which the history is related.

The first is chiefly traditional, or on the written authority only of Hector Boece; which it should seem has been followed implicitly by succeeding annalists till nearly the present day.

Boece wrote in the beginning of the sixteenth century, about 500 years after the period to which this part of his history refers, and at a time when the legends of tradition were only beginning in this country to give place to the more certain mode of recording events by committing them to writ. The account collected from tradition and from his writings is this :—

1. Ferquhard, Thane (or Maormor, as the more modern antiquaries will have it) of Lochaber, was a younger brother of Kenneth III. King of Scots. His era, without being very scrupulous as to precise dates, is supposed to have been about the year 1000. He had a son,

2. Bancho, Thane of Lochaber, stated to have been cotemporary with the witch-renowned Macbeth, and to have been murdered by his contrivance about the year 1050. He had a son,

3. Fleance, who is said to have fled, on the murder of his father, into Wales, where he married Nesta, daughter of Griffith ap Lewellen, a prince in that country, by whom he had a son,

4. Walter, who lived in the reign of Malcolm Canmore, and was employed in a high station in the service of that prince. His son,

5. Alan, is said to have been a man of note at the court of Henry I. King of England, and to have gone on an expedition to the Holy Land in 1099. He left a son,

6. Walter, who, in the year 1158, was created Lord High Steward of Scotland. The authorities for this origin and descent are stated by Crawfurd, my author, in pages 131, et infra of the original part of this work to which the reader is referred to. From this period forward, the history of this family is supported by written evidence of which the authenticity is not disputed.

But Mr. Chalmers, the erudite author of Caledonia, and whose unwearied researches in that most interesting work has most certainly dispelled much fiction from the early annals of ancient families, has another way of deducing the origin of the Stewarts. He rejects the account of Banquo and Fleance altogether; for as their names are not Gaelic, (as he thinks) such personages could not have existed; and further, setting aside all tradition, and confiding in nothing but direct testimony from writings, he gives the descent of Walter the first High Steward thus:—

I. Flathald, (or Fla-ald, as it is pronounced) whom he will have to be a Norman, had a son,

II. Alan, who, soon after the Norman conquest, obtained from William the castle of Oswestry, with an adjacent territory in Shropshire, that belonged to Meredith ap Blychen, a Briton. He is mentioned as a witness to a charter of Henry I. of England, dated 18th September 1101, which ascertains the time he lived, and this corresponds so nearly to that given by tradition to Alan in the preceding statement, that we may conclude him to have been the same person. This Alan Flaaldi filius, (as Mr. Chalmers finds out to have been his designation) seems to have been the father (as in the first account) of

III. Walter, who, emigrating into Scotland, became Lord High Steward about the same period as mentioned by Boece.

Now, although I am fully convinced from the evidence produced by the learned author of Caledonia, that Alan was the son of Flathald, and that it seems probable that Walter the High Steward was the son of that Alan, yet I doubt very much that Flathald himself was a Norman; on the contrary, I conjecture (for I shall call it by no means more decided) that he was a Briton, and not improbably the very Fleanch of the traditionalists, as there is even a similarity in their names that might lead to that conclusion, independent of other corroborating circumstances *. At any rate the name does not seem to be Normanic. Be this, however, as it may, I shall proceed in few terms to trace the descent of the main stem of the Stewarts from their great patronymical ancestor, the above Walter, the first Lord High Steward, the third link in the chain from the Fla-ald of Mr. Chalmers, and shall leave their more ancient progenitors to rest amid the obscurity of tradition in which they are involved.

This Walter came from England into Scotland in the reign of David I. He is witness to some charters granted by that King, and, although these have no date annexed, yet it must have been betwixt the years 1124, when David

---

* Not trusting to my own conception of the similarity of these two names, I applied to a gentleman of acknowledged abilities in Gaelic literature, requesting to know whether the proper names Bancho and Fleanch had any meaning in the Gaelic language, and whether Fla'ald or Flathald, and Fleanch, had any resemblance in signification to each other? He wrote me as follows:—

1. Bancho, or Banchu, is a compound of two simple Gaelic roots, Ban, adj. and chu, the oblique case of the Sub. N. Cu. Ban, in its primitive sense, signifies white or fair, by metonomy, illustrious. Cu, in modern Gaelic, signifies a dog, but anciently a hero or commander. Now the composite term Banchu, however it came to be pronounced Bancho, forms, as far as etymology is to be founded on, an appropriate appellation for a fair commander, or an illustrious hero.

2. Fleanch; or, as it has been modernised Fleance, may be traced to an origin still existing in the various dialects of the Celtic tongue. In all these Flaitheanas and Flaitheas, means heaven, being also composite terms highly poetical, and combining the ideas of bravery and generosity with happiness, to represent the supreme bliss of departed heroes. From the first of these terms, Flaitheanas, comes its adjective form, Flaitheanach, heavenly, pronounced Fle-hanch, (almost the same with Fleanch) and importing the heavenly, the brave, or the generous, a designation extremely natural to have been given by a partial people to the heir of Bancho, obliged to fly from a bloody usurper for protection to a foreign land.

3. Flathald or Fla'ald. In support of the opinion that it applies to the same person, let it be observed that the Gaelic word for heaven, Flaitheas, with its unquestionable etymon, Flàth, brave, or generous, or happy, admits of the adjective forms Flàthail, Flathaílt, or Flathaild, precisely of the same signification with Flaithenach, heavenly, and the resemblance which the appellation Flathald has to the Gaelic term Fla-thaild, is still more obvious than in the former instance.

These are not fanciful derivations, but perfectly understood by all who are acquainted with the living dialects of the Celtic, and confirmed by the respectable authorities of O'Brian, Luyd, Bullet, and Pelletier.

succeeded to the throne, and 1152, the year in which his son Henry died; for he is a witness also to a charter granted by that prince. The particular year in which he was created Lord High Steward is not mentioned, but he had a charter of confirmation of that office from Malcom IV. dated June 1157. He must have been possessed of immense wealth. This appears from the different properties enumerated in this charter, as follows:—

Names in the Charter.	Modern names, and where situated.	
Renfrew,	the same.	} In Renfrewshire.
Passeleth,	Paisley.	
Polloc,	Pollok.	
Tulloch,	unknown.	
Kerkert,	Cathcart.	} In Renfrewshire.
Le Drep,	The Drip.	
Le Mutrene,	doubtful.	
Eglisham,	Eaglesham.	} In Renfrewshire,
Lauchinache,	Lochwinnoch.	
Innerwick,	the same.	In East Lothian,
Prethe, part of	Partick.	} In Renfrewshire.
Inchenan,	Inchinnan.	
Stemtun,	Stenton.	In East Lothian,
Halestenesdene,	Hassendean.	In Tiviotdale.
Legardsuade,	Legertwood,	} In Lauderdale,
et Birchinsyde,	and Birkhillside.	

Besides all these, which seem to have been the family estates, he had in every burgh and regality in the kingdom a full toft, and with ever toft twenty acres of land for his entertainment, apparently his salary as steward or collector of the royal revenue. (see Crawfurd page 133.) That his wealth must have been very great, appears further from the magnificent Priory (afterwards Abbey) that he founded in Paisley in 1160, and which could not have been built in the present times under £100,000 Sterling of expence, and which he liberally endowed, as may be seen in the charter recorded by Crawfurd, (page 134) besides some valuable donations to the monasteries of Kelso and Dunfermline. He even gave in gift to his friend Robert de Mundigumbri, the lands of Eaglesham in this county, worth just now £10,000 of yearly rent. All this does not betoken a Norman adventurer emigrating still farther from his native land, but is more like to a prince returning, according to tradition, to his own country, and resuming possession of his ancient domains. He died in 1177, and was buried at Paisley. He was succeeded by his son,

IV. Alan II. the 2d. High Steward. He died in 1204, and was succeeded by his eldest son,

V. Walter II. the 3d High Steward. In 1230 he obtained the high office of

Justiciary of Scotland. He died in 1246, and was succeeded by his eldest son,

VI. Alexander, the 4th High Steward. He was one of the regents of the kingdom during the minority of Alexander III. and he was the chief commander at the decisive battle of Largs in 1263. He died in 1283. He was succeeded by his eldest son,

VII. James, the 5th High Steward. He is highly distinguished in Scottish annals, as having borne a very conspicuous part in the momentous struggle for the liberties of his country in the memorable contest about the succession to the crown in the days of The Baliol and The Bruce. He died in 1309, and was succeeded by his eldest surviving son,

VIII. Walter III. the 6th High Steward. He was renowned for abilities and bravery. He married the Princess Marjory, only daughter of Robert Bruce, King of Scots, through which connection his posterity became Kings of Scotland. He died in 1326, in his 33d year, and was succeeded by his eldest son,

IX. Robert, the 7th High Steward. On the death, without issue, of his uncle, David II. King of Scots, on the 22d February 1371, he succeeded to the throne by the name of Robert II. He was then in the 55th year of his age. He was a prince endowed with great vigour both of body and mind; faculties which, on many occasions, he was called upon to exert during the feeble reign of his predecessor. Fordun, the father of Scottish History, who was cotemporary with him, thus describes him. " He was just then in the flower of " his age; exceeding all men in elegance of form; tall and robust in person; " modest and affable; bountiful, cheerful, and sincere; and in whom shone " so much innate goodness and grace, that he was beloved by all, and the delight " of every true Scotsman [1]." This was in 1835, when he was in his 20th year. In his reign happened the celebrated battle of Otterburn, (21st July 1388,) supposed to be the Chevy Chase of legendary song. He died in 1390, and was succeeded by his eldest son,

X. Robert III. whose name was originally John, but which was changed, by advice of the states, to Robert, as a more propitious appellation. He was of a mild and liberal disposition, but of no great energy of character. Fordun, who lived also in his day, says, that " He was tall and straight in his person; " of a comely countenance, with a long and venerable beard as white as snow; " his eyes expressive of cheerfulness and good nature; his face oval and of a " ruddy complexion [2]." He died, at Rothesay, on the 4th April 1406, and was succeeded by his only remaining son,

[1] Lib. XIII. Cap. 22.   [2] Lib. XV. Cap. 19.

XI. James I. at that time iniquitously detained a captive in England. There he remained, till in 1424, when the English court, falling itself into a state of imbecillity, allowed him to return to his own dominions, but not without an enormous ransom. After this he held the reins of government with a steady hand, and displayed great abilities in his administration, till he was murdered in a shocking manner, in the 44th year of his age, on the 21st February 1437-8.

He married an English Princess, the Lady Jean Beaufort, (grandchild of John of Gaunt) whom he thus celebrates in that beautiful poem, the King's Quair (or Book) in the common language of the English and Scottish courts 400 years ago.

> In hir was zouth, beautee, w^t humble aport,
> Bountee, richesse, and womanly faiture,
> God better wote than my pen can report ;
> Wisdom, largess estate, and conynge sure
> In every point so gydit her mesure,
> In word, in dede, in schap, and countenance,
> That nature myt no more her childe avaunce.

James I. was a Prince of great learning and taste, and an excellent poet and musician. To his skill in music we owe that beautiful and correct simplicity in the Scottish airs, which are still the admiration of the musical world. He corrected many abuses in government during the effective part of his reign. He instituted the College of Justice, and introduced many salutary laws, the benefits of which are felt even to this day. He was succeeded by his only surviving son,

XII. James II. who was then in the 8th year of his age; and, after a reign of very little tranquillity, was killed by the bursting of a piece of cannon, at the siege of Roxburgh on the 3d August 1460.

The greater part of the reign of this Prince was a continual scene of domestic warfare, faction, and bloodshed. Most of his own exploits consisted in opposing the overgrown power of the House of Douglas; and the murder, by his own hand, of the chief of that potent family remains a stain on his memory. At same time it may be observed, that the concern which that haughty Lord had in the murder of others, was sufficient to have forfeited his life legally, had the law itself been armed with adequate authority to have brought him to justice. The conduct afterwards of the King in overturning faction and lawless ambition, was full of moderation, justice, and humanity; and the latter part of his life was spent in making salutary laws for the good of his subjects. He was succeeded by his eldest son,

XIII. James III. then in his 7th year, and who, after a most unhappy reign, was killed in battle by rebellious subjects on the 11th June 1488, in the 35th year of his age.

This Prince has been characterised as possessed of neither much personal nor political courage, and too much disposed to allow himself to be influenced by the advice of ignoble minions. But, with all his defects, this unwarlike monarch was a great benefactor to the nation by his distinguished patronage of learning and the fine arts. To him we are indebted, among many other splendid edifices, for the Chapel of Stirling Castle, a noble structure which he embellished with many curious ornaments and devices, and which it has been the destiny of the present age to disgrace itself by destroying. Even Drummond blames this Prince for being "too much given to the building of chapels "and halls, and trimming of gardens." This last circumstance ought to be recorded to his praise; for it is well known that gardens were but partially introduced into England more than 20 years after his death; for previous to the year 1509, the English were in use to import their garden vegetables from the low countries. He was succeeded by his son,

XIV. James IV. then in his 16th year, and who was killed at Flodden on the 9th of September 1513, in the 41st year of his age and 26th of his reign.

The moderation displayed by this Prince in his government, and the interest he took in the welfare of his subjects, conciliated all parties. He appears to have enjoyed a tranquillity almost unknown to his predecessors, and the King of Scots began now to make a considerable figure among the potentates of Europe.

He married Margaret, daughter of Henry VII. of England, an alliance which ultimately led to the union of the two kingdoms; a consummation which the English, more wise than their northern neighbours, had all along desired. He was succeeded by his only surviving son,

XV. James V. a child then 17 months old. He died on the 14th of December 1542, in the 31st year of his age.

He was a great lover of justice, and had the good of the nation much at heart. He new-modelled the court of session, and put it into the form which, till lately, it retained, and with the powers that it enjoys to the present day; and he got many salutary laws enacted in parliament during his reign. His mind was richly stored with learning, and he had an elegant and a correct taste, and his air was noble and majestic. But he was, however, of a thoughtful and melancholy mind, which, with the misfortunes that fell particularly thick upon him in the latter end of his reign, more especially the shameful defeat at Solway, and the preceding mutiny at Fala-moss, quite overcame him, and his spirit died within him in utter despondency of being able to retrieve the affairs of his kingdom. He was succeeded in his throne and in his misfortunes by his only remaining child,

MARY QUEEN OF SCOTS, over the events of whose reign one could almost wish that there were thrown a cloud of impenetrable darkness. She was born on the 7th December 1542, only seven days before the death of her father. She was carried to France in 1548, where she was brought up and educated amidst all the blandishments of that voluptuous and corrupted court. She returned to Scotland in August 1561, among "a barbarous people," (as Buchannan expresses it) "and naturally seditious, who were hardly kept in quiet by the "government of men." In less than six years she was driven from the throne, and resigned her crown on the 24th July 1567. She escaped from her prison on the 2d of May 1568—had a short glimpse of liberty—witnessed the defeat of her army, and with it the extinction of her hopes, at Langside, on the 13th of May following—fled immediately to England, where she was detained in captivity 19 years; and finally, in the 45th year of her age was put ignominiously to death on the 8th of February 1687, by order of her cousin, Queen Elizabeth, whose memory in consequence is doomed to everlasting infamy.

Perhaps no monarch ever entered into the management of affairs under more inauspicious circumstances than this unfortunate queen; and perhaps few were less able from habit and education to rule over a nation like Scotland, at that time torn to pieces by religious controversy and contending factions. Her virtues, however, were eminently calculated to adorn a private station, and it is to be regretted, that she was placed in a situation where her talents and her accomplishments could not be fully appreciated. Had she lived in less turbulent times, and among a people whose minds were less in a state of irritation, and not been thwarted in her measures by the machinations of a neighbouring court, that availed itself of every domestic discord to incite opposition to her government, she might have been esteemed the best of sovereigns, as she surely was the most accomplished woman in the age in which she lived. She was succeeded by her only son,

XVII. James VI. who had been nominally the King of Scots from the 24th July 1567, when his mother was compelled to resign her throne. On the 24th March 1603, on the death of Queen Elizabeth, he succeeded to the Crown of England. He died on the 27th of March 1625, in the 59th year of his age.

With the highest notions of kingly power this King was all his lifetime kept in a state of vassalage. In his youth, by the different factions that contended for, and alternately had the possession of his person;—in his more mature years, by his wife—and at all times by unworthy favourites. But he was a well meaning Prince, and a man of peace. Never before his time did the British nations enjoy so long a period of tranquillity, and never since have they enjoyed so long a peace as during his reign. He valued himself on being an adept in polemic learning and scholastic subtilties, and so was he valued by the learned world in his day. In the present age, he has been accused of pedantry, and the whole race of modern pedants, male and female, censure him for it. But the literary pursuits of James were his glory; for without all question he was the most learned prince of his time. The great object he had in view, all his reign, was (for the sake of peace) to effect a conformity in religious worship among his subjects; as vain an attempt, among a nation of freemen, as it would be to compel them all to be of one complexion, or of one size. It was the bane of his life, and gave him more vexation than all the other cares of government conjoined;—and this being persisted in by his posterity, became ultimately the cause of their ruin. He was succeeded by his only surviving son.

XVIII. Charles I. was born in 1600; succeeded his father as above in 1625. In 1639, a war took place with the Scots, which was soon after terminated. In 1642, the civil war commenced betwixt him and the English Parliament, which raged with fury and alternate success, till, in June 1645, the result of the battle of Naseby put an end to the hopes of the royal party. At last, in the 49th year of his age, on the 31st January 1649, he was brought to the block, not at the instance of the representatives of the nation, whose laws it was alleged he had violated; but by the unhallowed hands of aspiring demagogues, whose usurpation of power is at all times equally unjust, and their deeds equally atrocious, whether it be in London, Paris, or Algiers.

The private character however of Charles I. will bear the strictest scrutiny; neither was he deficient in capacity, nor in fortitude, but eminently distinguished for both.

His political conduct, or exercise of the royal power, however faulty such would appear in the present times, is not to be measured by modern ideas. His was not an age in which the prerogative of the crown and the liberties of the subject were clearly defined. It must be admitted, too, that Charles pretended to no new powers. He was requiring no more than what was willingly yielded to his predecessors on the throne. Even the most popular of them all, the despotic Elizabeth, regulated her conduct with very little regard to a House of Commons.

Had not Charles intermeddled with the religious tenets of his subjects, by which he alienated from him nearly the whole Scottish nation, he would have triumphed over the English commonwealth-men. The great mass of these were little influenced with a regard for civil rights; and, had not their fears been aroused for their religion, their zeal for liberty would have dwindled into nothing; while those demagogues, who wielded that ready-made weapon, the populace, against him, were themselves very faintly actuated by a love of genuine freedom. Even their affectation of religion was downright hypocrisy. To establish their own power on the ruins of the throne was the leading principle of their hearts; and never before, nor since, were the liberties of the subject more trodden under foot than during the time they held the reins of government.

XIX. Charles II. was called to the throne by the restoration on May 29th 1660. On this event, the people of these nations became almost frantic with joy, and were within little of giving up any freedom that was left them. At this time he was in the prime of life, and, with the most affable and engaging manners, was endowed with a great fund of good sense as well as of pleasant humour. He had then the reputation of being a man of abilities and great honesty of disposition. But, on the other hand, he had an indolency about him, and a propensity to indulge in pleasures that were incompatible to that attention to business that the duties of a monarch impose. Hence, he was soon induced to confide the cares of the state too implicitly to his ministers, who were not of a character to revive the almost expiring liberties of their country. From this censure must be excepted the virtuous and upright Chancellor Hyde, (Earl of Clarendon) than whom no minister was more devoted to his country's good, nor more free from corruption. But Charles, with all his indolency, however, never lost sight of the Royal Prerogative, and the nation at one period seemed ready to submit to any privation of liberty that the crown might be pleased to dictate. It was saved unintentionally by the king himself. He fell into the old family error of prescribing a form of religious worship to his subjects. No time could cure the Stewarts of this propensity. This aroused the almost extinct spirit of liberty, and the old Covenanters had the merit, by their undiminished resistance to court influence, to recal, by their example, the nation at large to a regard to liberty of every description.

Charles II. died on the 6th February 1685, in the 55th year of his age and 25th of his reign from the restoration; and, having no legitimate issue, he was succeeded by his only remaining brother,

XX. James II. then in the 55th year of his age.

It would be painful to trace out all the steps that this sadly misled Prince took, from the time he mounted the throne, in February 1685, till his abdication in December 1688. As Bishop Burnet well remarks, " his bad designs were ill " laid and worse conducted, and in conclusion all came under one of the " strangest catastrophes related in history. A great king, with strong armies " and mighty fleets, a vast treasure and powerful allies fell all at once; and his " whole strength, like a spider's web, was so irrecoverably broken with a touch, " that he was never able to recover, what, for want of judgement and heart, he " threw up in a day." He lived after this, nearly thirteen years in exile, in a considerable degree of splendour, by the munificence of Lewis XIV. in the Palace of St. Germains in France, where he died on the 6th of September 1701, in the 68th year of his age.

King James, during his brother's lifetime, was remarkable for the management of his household, and kept his court in great order. At the same time he lived in a stile of great magnificence, as well he might, for he had £100,000 a-year allowed him, which would go farther than £300,000 in the present times. He was also appointed High Admiral of England, an office very suitable to his genius, as he was particularly intelligent in maritime affairs. To him is owing, while in this office, the improvement, if not the invention, of the present system of signals at sea, for regulating the motions of a fleet on a cruize, or directing the various evolutions in a naval engagement.

He was twice married, 1st, to Lady Anne Hyde, daughter of Chancellor Hyde, by whom he had two daughters, Mary and Anne, afterwards Queens of Great Britain.

King James married, secondly, (while Duke of York) in 1673, Maria D'Esté, daughter of Alphonso, Duke of Modena, a marriage that did him no good in the eyes of the nation. By her, who died at St. Germains in 1718, aged 60, he had seven children, of whom none survived her but one son,

· XXI. James Francis Edward, who, on the 10th June 1688, was born to all the titles of High Steward of Scotland, Baron Renfrew, Earl of Carrick and Chester, Duke of Cornwall and Rothesay, and Prince of Wales. The fate of his father involved in it his own, and these dignities became forfeited, while he himself was particularly excluded by act of Parliament from succession to the crown.

His partizans, however, made an attempt to procure the throne for him by force of arms in 1715, not only in defiance of that act of Parliament, but in opposition to the sentiments of by far the greater part of the nation. The very first step that was taken in his name, was not calculated to alter these sentiments in his favour. For in the Declaration addressed to the Scottish nation from Commercy, October 25th of that year, he professed, of his own authority, to dissolve the union of the two kingdoms, that had been effected eight years before. This step being in the same spirit of infatuation that led his father to dispense with the penal laws in England, without consulting parliament, had the same effect on the public mind. It alienated even his friends without conciliating a single opponent, so that this feeble attempt to overturn the legally constituted government came very soon to an unsuccessful end; nor did his own personal conduct (although he was abundantly brave, as he shewed at the battle of Malplaquet) during the short period of less than six weeks that he remained in the country, give much indication of that vigour of mind which such lofty pretensions required. He was glad to regain France in safety, and never afterwards, in person, troubled these nations more. He resided after this, for the most part at Rome, in obscurity, where he died in 1766, in the 78th year of his age. In 1719, he married one of the richest heiresses in Europe, Maria Clementina Sobieski, grand-daughter of the renowned John Sobieski, King of Poland, and by her had two sons: 1. Charles; and 2. Henry.

XXII. Charles Edward Lewis Cassimer, the eldest son, who was born in December 1720, made a very spirited attempt in 1745, to recover the throne of his ancestors, which was not got under without great exertion, and must have required still greater for its suppression, had the conduct of the chiefs of his party been equal to his own. He, too, took upon him to dissolve the Union. The result of the whole, so disastrous to his party, and so beneficial to the country, is well known. After this, he lived chiefly in Italy, in circumstances not very affluent, the patrimony of his family having been greatly reduced in consequence of his efforts to ascend the British Throne. He died, at Rome in 1788, in the 68th year of his age. He had no legitimate issue, but left a natural daughter, the Duchess of Albany, of whom hereafter. He married, in 1772, an accomplished Princess, Louisa Maximiliana of Stolberg, grand-daughter of Lady Charlotte Bruce, (married to a German Prince) daughter of Thomas, Earl of Elgin and Aylesbury. By the bounty of our most gracious sovereign George III. she enjoys a pension of £2000 a year from his Majesty's privy purse. The late Prince Charles, her husband, indignant at not receiving the arrears of the jointure due to his grandmother, Queen Maria D'Esté, Dowager of James II. would never accept of any private donation from that quarter.

XXII. Henry Benedict Maria Clement, the second son, was born in 1725, entered into Italy orders, and was advanced to the Purple, 1747. At the same time he was bishop of Ostia and Frescati, and chancellor of the church of St. Peter. He had also two rich livings in France, the Abbey of Anchin and St.

Amond, together with a considerable pension from the court of Spain, so that for a long period he lived in great dignity and splendour. During the life of his brother, he was known by the name of Cardinal York; but, on the death of Charles, in 1788, he assumed the regal stile, by the name of Henry IX. by the Grace of God King of England, and struck medals with inscriptions to that effect, adding "Sed non voluntate Hominum." In the course of the French revolution, which spared neither the happy nor the unfortunate, this King of England was too good a subject of pillage, and too much within their grasp, to escape the rapacity of the remorseless crew let every where loose upon the rich and the defenceless. He was accordingly stript of his whole living, and reduced to such distress as to be obliged not only to sell the family jewels, that were of great value, but the very lace from his cloak to procure the means of subsistence. In this state, old, infirm, and destitute, he fled, in 1798, from Rome to Venice. Here his circumstances being made known to the British court, by means of Sir John Hippisley Cox, (at that time married on a Stewart of the family of Allanbank) His Majesty George III. with a munificence characteristic of the benevolence of his heart, conferred on him a pension of £4000 a-year, which the good old Cardinal accepted with gratitude, and enjoyed in peace during the remainder of his life. He returned to Rome in 1801, and there died in 1807, at that time Doyen and eldest brother of the sacred college, after having been one of its most respectable and pious members for more than 60 years. He was 82 years old. By his last will he bequeathed to the royal family of England, the different Insignia of the various orders of Knighthood connected with England, that had been in the possession of his family, some of them more than two centuries, which even in his greatest distress he had held sacred, together with some very important M.S.S. connected with British History. A noble return by this venerable and virtuous prince and prelate to his royal relatives, who had so benevolently interferred in his behalf, and gilded down his declining days. The Prince Regent of these realms, it is said, with his accustomed liberality, has also made a handsome subscription towards erecting a monument in Italy to this last branch of the elder stem of the Royal House of Stewart. In his person also became extinct the male line of the House of Stewart Duke of Lennox and Earl of Darnley. This last title however has been revived in the right of a female descendant. See Stewart, Duke of Lennox.

Natural Daughter of Prince Charles Edward.

The Duchess of Albany. This lady was born about the year 1743. Her mother was a Scots Lady of good family (Walkinshaw of Walkinshaw in the county of Renfrew). She was educated in a convent in France. On some difference, which ended in a separation betwixt Prince Charles and his consort, he sent to Paris for his daughter, to do the honours of his house. At his request she had the title of Duchess of Albany conferred on her by the King of France. This assured an acknowledgement of the title, which a creation of his own could not have rendered so universal. Her person was tall and somewhat robust, but her manners were mild and unassuming. At the same time, she lived in a dignified stile. Her equipage was similar to her father's, with the coronet of royalty and the cypher, C. R. on the pannels, and her servants wore the same liveries. In public, her dress was magnificent, and she was adorned with the jewels that had belonged to the Stuart and the Sobieski families, some of which were of immense value. These had been presented to her by her father and the Cardinal York. She was every where treated with great respect, more especially at Rome, where every one seemed to take an interest in her happiness, which she returned with that elegant condescension that is so much calculated to please. The English seemed in particular to be the objects of her attention and regard, and none of them felt any scruples in making due acknowledgements for the honour of her civilities. On the death of her father, in 1788, she went to reside with her uncle, Cardinal York, who, with that benignity of disposition for which he was so much admired, treated her with the greatest affection and kindness. In the year 1789, while on a visit to the Princess Lambertine at Bologna, she was seized with a malignant fever, which cut her off unmarried, about the 45th year of her age.

But to return to the history of the Royal Family of Britain, of the House of Stuart direct or lateral,

XX. WILLIAM AND MARY.

On the abdication of James II. the crown was conferred, by the Convention Parliament, on William Henry Friso, Prince of Orange, and his consort, the Princess Mary Stuart, eldest daughter of the exiled monarch.

William was himself a grandson of England, and half a Stuart, being the son of William II, Stadtholder of the Seven United Provinces, and Mary Stuart, eldest daughter of Charles I. and next heir to the Crown, after the posterity of his father-in-law, James II. He was born on the 4th November 1650, married his cousin, Mary, in 1677, and both in conjunction were declared King and Queen of England, in February 1689, and of Scotland in April the same year. On the death of the Queen, December 28th 1694, in the 33d year of her age, much lamented by the whole nation, he reigned alone under the name of William III, of England and II. of Scotland, till he died, 8th March 1702, without issue, in the 53d year of his age. He was a Prince of great virtues, and the most consummate abilities; and who, by his interposing in the affairs of England, conferred benefits on the British nation never to be forgotten. He was succeeded by his cousin and sister-in-law,

XX. Anne, the youngest daughter of James II. then in her 38th year. She swayed the sceptre with great renown till her death, on the 1st August 1714, in the 50th year of her age, after a reign that had never before been exceeded in glory. She was married, in 1683, to George, Prince of Denmark, who died in 1708, aged 56 years, to whom she had a numerous issue, who all died before herself. She thus became the last, in the direct line of Stuart, who wore the British Crown.

By a special parliamentary destination a collateral branch of the Royal House of Stuart, descended of the Princess Elizabeth Stuart, Queen of Bohemia, daughter of James I. was now called to the throne, namely, her grandson, George Lewis, Elector of Hanover, whose descent from the House of Stewart is thus :—

XVIII. Elizabeth, (the 18th generation) the only daughter of James VI. who attained to mature years, was married to Frederick Elector Palatine, to whom she had,

XIX. Sophia, her youngest child and third daughter, who was married to Ernest August, Duke of Brunswick and Hanover, to whom she had issue, five sons and a daughter, (see page 193) Her eldest son was,

XX. George I. King of Great Britain, son of Ernest August, Elector of Hanover and of the Princess Sophia of Bohemia, grand-daughter of James I. was born 28th May 1660, succeeded his father in 1698, as Elector of Hanover, and to the Crown of England on the death of Queen Anne, 1st August 1714. He died at Osnaburgh, 11th June 1727, in the 68th year of his age, the 13th year of his reign over Britain, and the 30th over Hanover, and his other German territories. He was a Prince of a virtuous and very firm character. During his whole reign, he adhered steadily to those principles which paved his way to the crown, and at no preceding period were the civil and religious rights of the subject better respected or more strictly preserved.

He married, in 1682, his cousin, the Princess Sophia Dorothea of Lunenburg Zell, through whom he obtained a considerable accession of territory. By her, who died in 1726, he had a son,

1. George Augustus, and a daughter; 2. Sophia Dorothea, born in 1685, married in 1706, to William Frederick King of Prussia, whose posterity, by this marriage, are heirs of entail to the British Crown, failing subsequent issue of the reigning family.

XXI. George Augustus II. succeeded his father, as King of Great Britain and Elector of Hanover on the 11th June 1727. He was born 30th October 1683, and died on the 25th October 1760, having nearly completed the 77th year of his age. He was a Prince endowed with many manly virtues, and of a very energetic and decided character. Under him the nation continued to enjoy unmolested the whole of its civil and religious liberties, while it increased in power and in affluence beyond what it had ever done in any former period.

He married, in 1705, Wilhelmina Dorothea Carolina, born 1st March 1683, daughter of John Frederick Margrave of Brandenburgh Anspach, by whom, (known by the name of Caroline) who died 20th November 1737, highly esteemed by the whole nation, he had the following issue :—

1. Frederick Lewis Prince of Wales, of whom hereafter; 2. The Princess Anne, born in 1709, died in 1759.

Her Royal Highness was married in 1734, to William IV. Prince of Orange, from which marriage is descended the present King of the Netherlands, whose family ranks immediately before the royal family of Prussia, in consanguinity to the royal family of Great Britain. 3. Princess Amelia, born in 1711. She lived in great splendour and dignity at the British Court, and died unmarried 21st October 1786; 4. Princess Caroline Elizabeth, born in 1713, and died unmarried in 1757; Prince George William, born in 1717, died at three months old; 6. Prince William Augustus, Duke of Cumberland, born 15th April 1721.

This Prince, the favourite son of George II. is much distinguished in British History, more especially for the memorable battle of Culloden, on the 16th April 1746, in which he cut up in a very decided manner the rebel army which, previous to this, had spread terror and dismay through the nation. He died unmarried on the 31st October 1765, in the 45th year of his age. 7. The Princess Mary, born in February 1723, and died 14th June 1771; married to the prince of Hesse Cassel in 1740, to whom she had three sons. The descendants of this princess, in relationship to the Royal Family of Britain, next after the House of Orange. 8. The Princess Louisa, born in 1724, and died in 1751; was married in 1743 to Frederick V. King of Denmark, to whom she had the late King Christian VII. The descendants of this Princess rank next in order of relationship after the House of Hesse Cassel to the Royal Family of England.

XXII. Frederick Lewis Prince of Wales was born in January 1707, and died 20th March 1751, in the 45th year of his age. He was a Prince, as Smollet observes, possessed of every amiable quality; a munificent patron of the arts; an unwearied friend to merit; well disposed to assert the rights of mankind in general, and warmly attached to the interest of Great Britain. He married, in

1736, Augusta, daughter of Frederick Duke of Saxe Gotha, a Princess of the most exemplary virtues, who died 8th February 1772, and by her had issue,

1. Augusta, Princess Royal of Great Britain, born 11th August 1737; married 17th January 1764 to the renowned Charles William Ferdinand, hereditary Prince, afterwards Duke of Brunswick, to whom she had three sons and three daughters. The descendants of this marriage are next in consanguinity to the reigning family of Britain. This Princess, who was eldest sister to our most gracious sovereign George III. returned to England a few years before her death, which happened on the 23d of March 1813, in the 76th year of her age. She was one of the most virtuous and respectable Princesses in Europe. 2. George, of whom afterwards; 3. Edward Augustus Duke of York, born in 1739, and died unmarried in 1767; 4. Elizabeth Caroline, born in 1740, died unmarried in 1759; 5. William Henry Duke of Gloucester, born in 1743, and died on the 25th August 1805; married, 6th September 1766, Maria Countess Dowager of Waldegrave, by whom he had issue, (1. the Princess Sophia Matilda, born 29th May 1773; 2. William Frederick Duke of Gloucester and Edinburgh, Earl of Connaught. His Royal Highness married, on the 22d July 1816, his cousin, Her Royal Highness the Princess Mary). 6. Henry Frederick Duke of Cumberland, born in 1745, married, in October 1771, the Hon. Anne Luttrell, daughter of Lord Irnham, and died without issue in 1790;. 7. Louisa, born in 1749; died unmarried in 1768; 8. Caroline Matilda, born (after the death of her father) 11th July 1751, married 1st October 1766, Christian VII. late King of Denmark, to whom she had issue; 1. Frederick VI. present King of Denmark; 2. Louisa Augusta, born 7th July 1771, married 27th May 1786, Christian Duke of Holstein Augustenburg.

The amiable Queen Matilda of Denmark, whose marriage was not productive of much domestic comfort, died at Zell, 10th May 1775. Her descendants rank next in order, in connection with the Royal Family of Britain, after those of her elder sister the late Duchess of Brunswick.

XXIII. George William Frederick III. our present most venerable sovereign, was born 4th June 1738. On the death of his father, in 1751, he was created Prince of Wales, &c. &c. On the demise of his royal grandfather, 25th October 1760, the crown of Great Britain devolved on his Royal Highness. His Majesty's reign has already been the longest of any, (without a minority) in the annals of Britain or of Europe, and during it the most eventful occurrences have taken place recorded in History. Never, in any preceding period, has the renown of British arms, the extent of British commerce, nor the general affluence of the nation been carried to a higher pitch; whilst the civil and religious liberties of the subject were never better understood nor more fully enjoyed. His Majesty married, 8th September 1761, the Princess Sophia Charlotte of Mecklenburgh-Strelitz—a marriage singularly productive of domestic happiness. The issue of this marriage has been, 1. George, of whom hereafter; 2. Frederick, born 16th August 1763; elected Bishop of Osnaburgh, 27th February 1764; created, 27th November 1764, Duke of York and Albany, and Earl of Ulster. He married, 29th September 1791, Frederica Charlotte Ulrica Catherina, Princess Royal of Prussia, born 7th May 1767. No issue.

His Royal Highness has seen much active and severe service, and his regulations, as commander-in-chief of the forces, have produced the most salutary consequences, and have been the primary cause of that excellent state of discipline, by which the British army has overcome every power to which it has been opposed.

3. William Henry, born 21st August 1765, Duke of Clarence and St. Andrews, and Earl of Munster. His Royal Highness was regularly bred to the sea service, and went through all the gradations in the royal navy, and served his time as strictly as if he had been the son of a private gentleman. On the death of Sir Peter Parker, in 1813, he was promoted to be admiral of the fleet.

4. Charlotte Augusta Matilda, Princess Royal of Great Britain, born 29th September, 1766. Married, 19th May 1797, Charles William, Hereditary Prince, afterwards King of Wirtemburg, being his second wife, and to whom she has had no issue.

5. Edward, born 2d November 1767, Duke of Kent and Strathern, and Earl of Dublin. His Royal Highness has been regularly bred to the army, and has seen much service.

6. Sophia Augusta, born 8th November 1768.

7. Elizabeth, born 22d May 1770. Married, 7th April 1818, with Philip Augustus Frederick, hereditary Prince of Hesse Homburg.

8. Ernest Augustus, born 5th June 1771, Duke of Cumberland and Tiviotdale, and Earl of Armagh. He married, 28th August 1814, the Dowager Princess of Salms, daughter of Charles, Duke of Mecklenburgh-Strelitz, niece to her Majesty the Queen.

9. Augustus Frederick, born 27th January 1773, Duke of Sussex, Earl of Inverness and Baron Arklow. He married, 3d April 1793, Lady Augusta Murray, daughter of the Earl of Dunmore, by whom he has issue, 1. Augustus Frederick, who takes the surname of D'Esté (the original name of the family) born the 13th January 1794; 2. a daughter. This marriage having been contracted

contrary to the regulations of the royal marriage act, has been declared null and void.

10. Adolphus Frederick, born 24th February 1774, Duke of Cambridge, Earl of Tipperary, and Baron Culloden. His Royal Highness is His Majesty's Vice-Regent of the Kingdom of Hanover.

11. Mary, born 25th April 1776, married 22d July 1816, to her cousin, His Royal Highness the Duke of Gloucester.

12. Sophia, born 3d November 1777. 13. Octavius, born 23d February 1779; died 3d May 1782. 14. Alfred, born 22d September 1780; died 26th August 1782. 15. Amelia, born 7th August 1783; died 2d November 1810.

XXIV. George Prince of Wales, &c. In February 1811 his royal highness was, by parliament, appointed Prince Regent of the British Empire, and persevering in the same wise and vigorous measures, so happily embraced by his royal father, he has, by a series of unequalled exertions, conducted the nation through the most severe contest in which it ever was engaged, to a state again of peace and tranquillity, with a celebrity unknown before in its annals.

His royal highness was born 12th August 1762; married, 8th April 1795, the Princess Caroline Amelia Elizabeth, his cousin, second daughter of Charles William Ferdinand, late Duke of Brunswick Wolfenbuttle born 17th May 1768, by whom he had issue,

XXV. Charlotte Carolina Augusta, born 7th January 1796, married 2d May 1816, to his now royal highness Leopold George Frederick Duke of Saxe, Margrave of Meissen, Landgrave of Thuringuen, and Prince of Cobourg of Saalfield.

Her royal highness, (on whom the eyes of the whole empire were fixed with the fondest hope) after being delivered of a still born male child, at nine o'clock of the evening of Wednesday 5th November 1817, died at two o'clock next morning. No language can express the deep-felt and universal sorrow that this melancholy event occasioned. The whole nation participated in the feelings of the royal family. Amusements of all kind ceased, and a gloom sat on every countenance, as if every family had lost their first-born. On the day of her funeral, (Wednesday, November 19th) all business through the whole land was suspended. The churches, clothed in sable, were every where open, and the people, in the garb of affliction, resorted to them, as on an occasion of the deepest humiliation, to supplicate those consolations which a superintending and benevolent Providence only can confer in such an instance of national calamity. It was indeed A VERY GREAT MOURNING.

This Princess was particularly endeared to the British Nation by many excellent and benevolent dispositions, and above all, by a remarkable strength of mind and independency of spirit, manifested on several occasions. Her refusal of the most popular match with the nation that could have been proposed for her, the Prince of Orange, is an instance perhaps unparalleled of firmness among ladies of her rank, whose destinies are generally made subservient to political purposes. But she had previously fixed her regards upon, and afterwards married the man of her own choice; thus, in this instance, making state policy give way to her own personal happiness. The Prince indeed whom she preferred, is in every respect worthy of the highest estimation; and the domestic manner in which they affectionately lived together, during the existence of the connexion, called forth, and carried with it, the unqualified approbation and praise of the whole empire.

STUART DUKE OF LENNOX. (see page 225.)

This most illustrious branch of the House of Stewart is now represented by Bligh Earl of Darnley, whose descent maternally from it is traced thus:

Lord George Stuart, 4th son of Esme, 3d Duke of Lennox, was killed at the battle of Edgehill, 23d October 1642. He married Lady Catherine Howard, daughter of the Earl of Suffolk, by whom he had issue; 1. a son, Charles, sixth Duke of Lennox, who died without issue in 1672; 2. a daughter.

I. Lady Catherine Stewart, who married Henry Lord Ibrakin, to whom she had an only child.

II. Lady Catherine O'Brien, who married Edward Earl of Clarendon, to whom she had an only child,

III. Lady Theodosia Hyde, who, in 1713, married John Bligh, Esq; who, in 1725, was created Earl of Darnley. By this Lady, the representative of the Stuarts Dukes of Lennox, he had three sons and three daughters; the second son, Edward, who was the second Earl of Darnley, died unmarried, when he was succeeded by the third son,

IV. John, third Earl of Darnley. He married, in 1766, Mary, the daughter of John Stoyte, Esq; of Street, by whom he had issue, 1. John, of whom afterwards; 2. Edward, a Major-General in the army; 3. William, who married, in 1806, Lady Sophia Stewart, daughter of the Earl of Galloway; 4. Mary; 5. Theodosia; 6. Sarah; 7. Catherine, married, in 1804, Lieutenant-General Lord Stewart, and died in 1812. The Earl died in 1781, and was succeeded by his eldest son,

V. John, the fourth Earl of Darnley, who is married, and has a son,

VI. John Lord Clifton, heir presumptive to the honours.

LENNOX DUKE OF LENNOX.—(see page 225.)

This illustrious branch of the family of Stewarts is thus decended.

I. Charles Lennox, son of Charles II. King of Great Britain, by Louise Renée de Penancoet de Keroualle, (of a very ancient and illustrious House in Brittany) Duchess of Portsmouth and Aubigny in her own right, was born in May 1672, and in 1675 created Duke of Richmond and Lennox, Earl of March and Darnley, Baron of Setterington and Tarbolton.

His Grace was elected a Knight of the Garter in 1681, and on the removal of the Duke of Monmouth, was appointed master of the horse to the King, in which station he continued till the accession of James II. when he was deprived of the office, on account that his mother promoted the Bill of Exclusion. He then retired into France and remained there until the revolution, when he returned and declared himself in favour of that measure, and of the civil and religious liberties of the country. He entered immediately into the army, and served in Flanders, under King William, to whom he was Aid de Camp. He died in May 1723, being at that time one of the Lords of the Bed-chamber to George I. His Grace married, in January 1693, Anne, third daughter of Francis Lord Brudenel, and by her, who died December 1722, had three children; 1. Lady Louisa, married to the Earl of Berkeley, and had issue; 2. Charles his successor; 3. Lady Anne, married to the Earl of Albemarle, and had issue.

II. Charles, second Duke of Lennox, succeeded his father in 1723, as Duke of Lennox, &c. and his grandmother, as Duke of Aubigny, in 1734. He enjoyed many high and confidential appointments under the crown. He was also a Lieutenant General in the army, and Colonel of the Blues. He died in 1750. His Grace married, in December 1719, Lady Sarah Cadogan, eldest daughter and co-heiress of William Earl Cadogan, by whom he had twelve children, of whom the following attained to years of maturity; 1. Lady Georgina Carolina, married, in May 1744, to Henry Fox, afterwards Lord Holland, and had issue; 6. Lady Emilia, married, first, to the Duke of Leinster, to whom she had seventeen children; secondly, to William Ogilvie, Esq; to whom she had two daughters; 7. Charles, his successor; 8. Lord George, of whom after; 10. Lady Louisa Augusta, married to Thomas Conolly of Castleton, M. P. without issue. 11. Lady Sarah, married, first, to Sir Charles Bunbury, to whom she had no issue; secondly, in August 1781, to the Hon. George Napier, to whom she has several children.

III. Charles, third Duke of Lennox, &c. was born in Feb. 1735, succeeded his father in 1750, and went soon after into the army, in which he rose gradually through all the subordinate stations to that of the highest, a Field Marshal. He saw much service, but was still more distinguished as a statesman, both in office and out of it. A firm member of administration while in, and a very formidable opponent when out. His Grace married, in April 1757, Lady Mary Bruce, only child of Charles Earl of Elgin and Aylesbury, but had no issue. He died in December 1806, and was succeeded by his nephew, Charles, son of

Lord George Henry Lennox, the only surviving son of the second Duke; was born in November 1737, and in his fourteenth year entered as an Ensign into the army, and rose gradually, during a life of very active and distinguished service, to the rank of General, to which he was promoted in October 1793. He was also distinguished in a civil capacity as a statesman for a steady adherence to those pure principles of civil liberty that give a stability to the throne as well as a security to the rights of the subject. His Lordship died in March 1805, being then a Privy Counsellor, Governor of Plymouth, and Colonel of the 25th regiment. He was member for the county of Sussex in Parliament, from 1767 till 1790, when, on account of bad health, he declined the representation. He married, in December 1759, Lady Louisa Mary Kerr, daughter of William Marquis of Lothian, by whom he had, 1. Mary Louisa; 2. Emily Charlotte, married, in August 1784, to the Hon. Captain Berkeley, and has issue; 4. Georgina, married, in April 1787, to Earl Bathurst, and has issue.

Mary Louisa and Emily Charlotte, received the King's warrant in 1807, to enjoy the rank of Dukes daughters, but not Georgina, who had previously married a Peer.

IV. Charles, who, on the death of his uncle, the third Duke, in 1806, became fourth Duke of Richmond, Lennox, and Aubigny. His Grace has also been bred to the army, and has been in some very severe service. He had the rank of Colonel in the army in 1795; Major-General in 1798; Lieutenant General in 1805, and General in 1814, being the 3d on the list of that year. He is also Colonel of the Sussex, or 35th Regiment, and Governour of Plymouth. He was sworn a privy councillor in 1807, and same year appointed Lord Lieutenant of Ireland.

His Grace married, in 1789, Lady Charlotte Gordon, eldest daughter of the Duke of Gordon, by whom he has had fourteen children, thirteen of whom are living. 1. Lady Mary; 2. Charles, Earl of March and Darnley, a Lieutenant Colonel in the army, and has distinguished himself most gallantly while serving under Wellington in the peninsular war. Married, April 1817, Lady Caroline Paget, eldest daughter of the Marquis of Anglesey; 3. Lady Sarah, married, October 1815, Major General Sir Peregrine Maitland, K, C. B.; 4. Lord John

George, Captain 9th Lancers, A. D. C. to F. M. the Duke of Wellington; 5. Lady Georgiana; 6. Lord Henry Adam, midshipman on board His Majesty's ship, the Blake; was unfortunately killed by an accident on board that ship, off the Island of Minorca in 1812; 7. Lady Jane; 8. Lord William Pitt, Lieutenant in the Blues; 9. Lord Frederick, in the army; 10. Lord Sussex, midshipman on board His Majesty's ship Tonant; 11. Lady Louisa Madelina; 12. Lady Charlotte; 13. Lord Arthur; 14. Lady Sophia Georgiana.

Arms.—Quarterly—the same as the Royal arms, with the descendant distinction. Over all in an Escutcheon for Aubigny, Gules, three oval Buckles, Or. The whole within a Border, Compone Argent and Gules, the first charged with Verdoy of Roses of the Second, barbed and seeded, Proper, for Lennox. Crest, on a Chapean Gules, turned-up Ermine; a Lion Passant, Guardant, Or; crowned with a ducal Coronet, Argent, and gorged with a Collar, counter Compone, Ermine and Azure. Supporters—Dexter, a Unicorn, Or, crowned with a Ducal Coronet, Azure, and gorged with a Collar, counter Compone, Ermine and Azure: Sinister, an Antelope, Argent, Collared as the Dexter. Motto, " En " la Rose Je Fleurie." Supporters, Unicorn, Dexter, Antelope Sinister.

Chief seat, Goodwood in Sussex.

STEWART MARQUIS OF BUTE. (See page 239).

XI. James, the second Earl of Bute, and eleventh in descent from Robert II. King of Scots, inherited the extensive estates of his maternal grandfather, Sir George Mackenzie of Rosehaugh, and succeeded his father, the first Earl, in 1710. He was a nobleman of great talents and virtue, and enjoyed the confidence of his sovereign, and held several offices of great trust under the crown, in the reign of George I. He died in 1723, in the 33d year of his age. He married Lady Anne Campbell, only daughter of Archibald, first Duke of Argyle, by whom he had issue; 1. John, third Earl of Bute; 2. The Right Hon. James Stewart Mackenzie of Rosehaugh, who succeeded (as second son) to the estate of Rosehaugh, and in consequence assumed the name and arms of his great grandfather. He was a gentleman of the most amiable character; full of honour and integrity, and possessed of great literary accomplishments. He sat 42 years in parliament, and was a Privy Counsellor during the last 27 years of his life. In 1758, he was appointed ambassador to the court of Turin, where, for several years, he represented the British Sovereign in great splendour. He was 36 years Lord Privy Seal of Scotland. He died in April 1800, in the 82d year of his age. He married Lady Elizabeth Campbell, fourth daughter of the great Duke of Argyle, by whom he had a son, who died in infancy. He was succeeded, after an appeal to the House of Lords, by his nephew, the Hon. James Archibald Stewart, brother to the first Marquis of Bute; 3. Lady Mary, married to Sir Robert Menzies of that-ilk, without issue; 4. Lady Anne, married Lord Ruthven, and had issue; 5. Lady Jean, married William Courtenay, Esq; and had issue. She died in 1803, in the 83d year of her age. Her son, Captain Courtenay of the royal navy, was killed in the Boston, when engaging, in 1794, the French Frigate, L'Ambuscade, which for this time escaped, but was taken four years after, off the Irish Coast; 6. Lady Grace, married John Campbell, Esq; Lord Stonefield, and had issue. She died in 1783.

XII. John, third Earl of Bute, was born in 1713. He sat as a representative of the Scottish Peerage in four different parliaments. In March 1761, he was appointed one of His Majesty's principal secretaries of state, and the same year was invested with the order of the Garter. On the 29th May 1762, he was constituted first Lord of the treasury, which office he resigned on the 16th April 1763. During his administration he obtained the great object he had in view, namely, the termination of a sanguinary and most expensive war, on terms highly advantageous to the country. This, however, did not save him from the clamour of the factious part of the nation, who at that time could not be satisfied with any measure that originated with a Scottish Minister. From this time, his Lordship lived in great privacy, employing himself chiefly in literary pursuits, more especially in Botany. His superb work on that subject, extending to nine volumes quarto, all in copperplate, was limited to sixteen copies, and can only be found in the libraries of a few select friends.

His Lordship married, August 1736, Mary, the only daughter of Edward Wortley Montague, (a grandson of the House of Sandwich) by the famed Lady Mary Wortley Montague, by whom he had issue, 1. John, first Marquis of Bute; 2. Hon. James Archibald Stuart Wortley. He was bred to the army, and has seen much severe service. He succeeded to his mother's great possessions in England, in 1794, and, on the death of his uncle, the Lord Privy Seal, in 1800, succeeded to his great property in Scotland, and has, in addition to his former names and titles, taken that of M'Kenzie of Rosehaugh. He married, in 1761, Margaret, daughter of the late Sir David Cunninghame of Milncraig.

Of this marriage the issue has been, 1. John, who was an officer in the Guards, and M. P. He died unmarried in 1791. 2. James Archibald Stuart Wortley, an officer in the army. He married, in March 1799, Lady Elizabeth Creichton, daughter of the Earl of Erne, and has a numerous issue. 3. Hon. Frederick; died in 1802, in the 54th year of his age. 4. Hon. Sir Charles, who was a Lieutenant-General in the army, and highly distinguished for active and judicious conduct in much severe service. He died in May 1801, in his 49th year. He married, in 1778, Louisa, daughter and co-heiress of Lord Vere Bertie, and by her had two sons; 1. Sir Charles, born in January 1779, and has been much employed in a diplomatic capacity, and is now British Ambassador at the Court of France; 2. John, who was a Captain in the royal navy, and died in   ; 5. Hon. William, born in 1755, and bred to the church, and is now Archbishop of Armagh and Primate of Ireland. His Grace married, in 1796, Miss Penn, daughter of Thomas Penn, Esq; proprietor of Pensylvannia, by whom he had a numerous issue; 6. Lady Mary, married, in 1761, the Earl of Lonsdale, no issue; 7. Lady Jane, married, in 1768, Earl Macartney, no issue; 8. Lady Anne, married, in 1763, to Earl Percy, (the late Duke of Northumberland) no issue—the marriage was dissolved in 1779; 9. Lady Augusta, married, in 1773, to Captain Andrew Corbet, and died in 1778; 10. Lady Carolina, married, in 1778, to the Earl of Portarlington, and has issue; 11. Lady Louisa.

XIII. John, fourth Earl of Bute, succeeded his father in 1792, and on the death of his mother, in 1794, he became a British Peer, by the title of Lord Mount Stewart. In 1796, he was created Marquis of Bute, Earl of Windsor and Viscount Mountjoy. Previous to all this, he was created a British Peer, 1776, by the title of Lord Cardiff. In 1779, he was appointed Envoy extraordinary to the Court of Madrid. He was again, in 1795, appointed ambassador to the same Court, where he remained till October 1796, when the Spanish Court, under the influence of French Politics, was compelled to declare war against Great Britain. He died in 1814, in the 70th year of his age. His Lordship married, first, in 1766, Charlotte Jean, eldest daughter of Herbert Windsor, Viscount Windsor and Lord Mountjoy, which titles became extinct at his death, in 1758, but have been revived as above, in 1796, as secondary titles of Bute. By that lady he had issue: 1. John, of whom afterwards; 2. Lord Herbert Windsor, born in 1770, unmarried; 3. Lord Evylin James, born in 1773. He entered into the army in 1791, and quited it in 1806, at which time his Lordship had the rank of Colonel in the army. He is M. P. for Cardiff, in Wales; 4. Lord Charles, born in 1775. He was lost in the Leda frigate, in December 1795, being at that time a Lieutenant in the navy; 5. Lord Henry born in   . In 1805 he was appointed Envoy extraordinary to the Court of Wirtemburg: He married Lady Gertrude Villiers, heiress of the Earl of Grandison: He died in 1809, and his lady 11 days after, both in the month of August of that year: They had issue, one son; 6. Lord William, was born in 1778. He was bred to the royal navy, in which service he distinguished himself greatly for energy and professional skill. He had the rank of Captain in 1798, and died in 1814. He married, in 1806, the Hon. Georgina Maude, daughter of Viscount Howarden, and by her, who died in 1801, had one daughter; 7. Lord George was born in 1780. He entered also into the royal navy, and has distinguished himself as a gallant Naval Commander. He was raised to the rank of Captain in 1804. He married, in 1800, Jane, daughter of the late General James Stewart, and has issue; (1. John Windsor; 2. Elizabeth; 3. Louisa, died in infancy; and, 4. Emilia Frances.) 8. Lady Mary Alicia Charlotte; 9. Lady Charlotte, married Sir William Jackson Homan of Dunlum; 10. Lady Elizabeth, died in infancy. The marquis, secondly married, in September 1800, Frances, daughter of Thomas Coutts, Esq; Banker in London, and by her had issue. 11. Lady Frances. 12. Lord Dudley.

XIV. John, Lord Mount Stewart, was born in 1767. He was Lord Lieutenant of the county of Glamorgan, and member of Parliament for the town of Cardiff in 1790. He died in January 1794. His Lordship married, in 1792, Lady Elizabeth Creichton, only daughter and heiress of Patrick, Earl of Dumfries, and by her, who died in 1797, at the age of 25 years, had issue two sons.

XV. John, now Marquis of Bute and Earl of Dumfries, and Lord Lieutenant of the counties of Bute and Glamorgan; 2. Hon. Patrick, a posthumous son, born in August 1794.

STUART EARL OF MORAY.

Referring to the preceding history of this noble family (see page 229) it is necessary to remark, that Sir James Stuart of Baith, there mentioned, was the third son of Andrew, second Lord Avendale, and the sixth generation from Robert II. king of Scots; and that Charles Earl of Moray, the last mentioned by Crawfurd, was the twelfth in descent from that king.

XII. Charles, the fifth Earl of Moray, succeeded his father, Alexander, fourth Earl of Moray, on the 1st Nov. 1700. He died at Dunibirsel on the 7th Oct. 1735, in the 76th year of his age. He married Lady Anne Campbell, daughter of Archibald Earl of Argyle. She died without issue in 1734, in the 76th year of her age. He was succeeded by his brother,

XII. Francis, sixth Earl of Murray, who died at Dunibirsel in Dec. 1739, in the 66th year of his age; a nobleman highly esteemed for great learning and the strictest honour. He married, 1st, Elizabeth, only daughter of the Hon.

Sir John Murray of Drumcairn, a Lord of Session, by whom he had no surviving issue; 2d, Jean, daughter of John, fourth Lord Balmerino, and by her, who died in 1739, had issue five sons and two daughters; 1. James, of whom afterwards; 2. Hon. Gen. John of Pittendriech, who, after a variety of severe service, both at home and abroad, died colonel of a regiment in the service of the Dutch in 1796, in the 88th year of his age. He represented Crail, &c. in Parliament, 1741; 3. Hon. Francis Stuart of Pittendriech: died lieutenant-colonel of the 4th regiment of horse, in Germany, in 1760: was connected by marriage with the Eglinton family, of whom there is now no surviving issue; and again, by a marriage which produced a daughter, married, in 1783, to the Right Rev. T. L. Obierne, bishop of Meath; 4. Hon. Archibald Stuart, a captain in the royal navy, died in 1795; 5. Hon. Henry Stuart, died major of a regiment of dragoons in Germany; 1. Lady Anne, married Stewart of Blairhall, and had issue, died in 1783; 2. Lady Amelia, married to Sir Peter Halket of Pitfirren, a gallant officer, killed at Fort du Quesne in 1755: no surviving issue: she died in 1781.

XIII. James, seventh Earl of Moray, the eldest son, born about 1708, succeeded his father. He was one of the representatives of the Scottish Peerage, from 1741 till his death in July 1767, in the 59th year of his age. He was also a Knight of the Thistle. He married, in 1734, Grace, daughter of Lockhart of Carnwath, by Lady Euphemia, daughter of Alexander, ninth Earl of Eglinton. She died in November 1738. By her he had a daughter, Lady Euphemia, who died unmarried, and a son, Francis, of whom after.

He married, 2d, in 1740, Lady Margaret Wemyss, daughter of David, third Earl of Wemyss, and by her, who died, at Drylaw, much regretted, in August 1779, he had two sons.

1. Hon. James, bred to arms, was Lieutenant Colonel of the Sutherland fencibles in 1793, and depute-governor of Fort George, where he died in 1808, aged 68. He was a gentleman of the most amiable and conciliating manners. 2. Hon. David, a Captain in the royal navy; died in 1784, aged 39. He was married and had several children—none of whom are now surviving.

XIV. Francis, eight Earl of Moray; born in January 1737, and succeeded his father in 1767. He was a great improver of his estates by plantations, having planted upwards of thirteen millions of trees, of which nearly a million and a half were oaks, on his extensive estates in Fyfe, Perthshire, and Moray. He was one of the representatives of the Scottish Peerage in the parliaments that sat down in 1784 and 1790, and was created a British Peer in 1796, by the title of Lord Stuart of Castle Stuart, in the ancient province of Moray, in Inverness-shire. He was Lord Lieutenant of the county of Elgin or Moray, and died, at Drumsheugh, in the vicinity of Edinburgh, in August 1810, aged 74. He married, in June 1763, Jane, daughter of John, twelfth Lord Gray, and by her, who died in February 1786, had issue, 1. James Lord Doun, who died in July 1776; 2. John Lord Doun, who died unmarried in July 1791, aged 24; 3. Francis, of whom afterwards; 4. Hon. Archibald, twin with Francis, who, in 1813, was Lieutenant Colonel of the Dorsetshire local militia. He married, in 1798, Cornelia, youngest daughter of Edmund Morton Pleydell of Milborn, one of the most ancient families in England, and they have a numerous family. 1. Lady Grace, married, in 1789, to Douglas of Cavers, (and have, 1. James; 2. Francis; 3. Jane;) 4. Lady Anne; also one son and two daughters, who died young.

XV. Francis, ninth Earl of Moray, and Lord Stuart of Castle Stuart, succeeded his father in 1810, married, first, whilst Lord Doun, Lucy, second daughter, and one of the rich co-heiresses of General John Scott of Balcomie, sister to the Duchess of Portland, and of the Lady of the Right Hon. George Canning, P. C. and by her, who died in August 1798, had two sons,

XVI. 1. Francis Lord Doun, born November 1795; 2. Hon. John, born in January 1797.

His Lordship married, second, in January 1801, his cousin, Margaret Jane, daughter of Sir Philip Ainslie of Pilton, Knight, by Elizabeth, daughter of Lord Gray, and has issue. 3. Lady Elizabeth, died in 1802; 4. Lady Jane, born in 1802; 5. Hon. James, born in 1804; 6. a son—died in 1805; 7. Lady Margaret Jane, born in 1807; Lady Ann Grace, born in 1809; 9. Hon. Archibald George, born in 1810; 10. Hon. Charles, born April 21st 1812; 11. Lady Louisa Charlotte, born 6th June 1813; 12. Hon. George Philip, born Sept. 4th 1814. Arms. (See page 231.)

STUART OF DUNEARN,

The only surviving Cadet of the House of Moray.—This branch of the family is thus descended: James, third Earl of Moray (the 10th in descent from Robert II. King of Scots) succeeded his father in 1638. He married Lady Margaret, eldest daughter and co-heiress (after the death of her brother) of Alexander, first Earl of Home. Of this marriage the second son was,

I. The Hon. Archibald Stuart of Dunearn, (see page 230) who was Governor of the Castle of Stirling, which he held at the revolution for King William, while his brother, Alexander Earl of Moray, was Secretary of State for Scotland, and Commissioner to the Parliament for James VII. He married Anne, daughter of Sir John Henderson, Bart. of Fordel, by whom he had, 1. Charles, of whom afterwards; 2. Alexander, an officer in the foot Guards; 3. Margaret, married, first, to Sir Archibald Stewart of Burray, and 2dly, after his death, to David Lord Lindores ; 4. Elizabeth, married to Andrew Gillon of Wallhouse, grandfather to the present Colonel Andrew Gillon of Wallhouse ; 5. Amelia, married to Archibald Nisbet of Carfin, grand-father of the late Dr. Josiah Nisbet, whose widow (Frances Herbert Woodward) is the relict of Horatio Lord Nelson.

II. Charles Stuart of Dunearn was an officer in the 3d regiment of Guards, (commanded by William Marquis of Lothian, his first cousin) afterwards Master of Works in the Tower of London, where he died and was buried in 1732. He married, first, Christian, daughter of Sir William Bennet, Bart. of Grubbet, the patron of Allan Ramsay, of Thomson, and other men of genius in Scotland. By her he had one son, Alexander, of whom afterwards. He married, 2dly, Jean, eldest daughter of Alexander Hamilton of Dalziel, his first cousin, by whom he had, 1. Archibald, a young man of great promise and piety, well known to most of the zealous Christians and ministers of that period. He died 17th February 1732, in his 24th year, just before he was to have been licenced to preach in the Church of Scotland, and has left behind him very valuable records of his experience of Christianity, and of his diligent application to understand it himself, and to instruct others in the knowledge of it ; 2. Anne, married to Robert Blackwood of Pitreavie, Lord Provost of Edinburgh ; 3. Mary, married to the Hon. Colonel John Erskine of Carnock, son to Henry Lord Cardross, and uncle to David Earl of Buchan, grandfather to the late John Erskine, D. D. of Carnock ; 4. Jean, married to Mr. William Hogg, merchant in Edinburgh ; 5. Bethia, married to Mr. Archibald Wallace, merchant in Edinburgh ; and 6. James, of whom afterwards.

III. Alexander Stuart of Dunearn, Captain in the 11th regiment of dragoons, and Aid-de-Camp at the battle of Culloden to the gallant General Lord Mark Ker. He was afterwards an alderman, and some time mayor of the town and Governor of the Castle of Ludlow, where he died in February 1786. He married   Boteler, a widow lady of Salop, by whom he had one son, who died in infancy. A very fine collection made by him of paintings, and a library of curious books, were mostly disposed of after his death, and now form part of some celebrated private and public collections in this country. Leaving no issue, he was succeeded by his half-brother,

III. James Stuart, merchant, and frequently a magistrate in Edinburgh. He was Lord Provost of that city in 1764-5, and again in 1768-9. He died 10th June 1777. He married Elizabeth, only surviving child and heiress of Adam Drummond of Binend (son to Adam Drummond of Megginch, descended of the family of Perth) Regius Professor of Anatomy in the University of Edinburgh, and by her, who died 11th November 1752, he had one son, Charles, of whom afterwards; and also a daughter, Margaret, married, in October 1770, to John Gordon, Esq; of Balmuir, W. S. who died in 1789, to whom she had fourteen children. 1. James, married, first, Lilias, daughter of Charles Hunter, Esq; of Burnside, by whom he had a son and a daughter. 2dly, he married Margaret, only child of Robert Haldane, Esq; of Airthrey, now of Auchingray, by whom he has two sons and a daughter; 2. Alexander, a Post Captain in the royal navy; 3. John, who entered Advocate in 1801, but relinquished the bar and entered into the army, and, after hard service, both in Ireland during the rebellion, and in the peninsula, and having been in various battles, died in Barbadoes 22d December 1816, of the yellow fever, being at that time eldest Captain in the 2d regiment of foot; 4. Peter, who also entered the army, and, having received a wound at Buenos Ayres, died from locked-jaw 6th October 1806; 5. Elizabeth, married to Robert Lorimer, L. L. D. first minister of Haddington, to whom she has six children; 6. Helen, married to James Ogilvie, Esq; Accountant, to whom she has three children; 7. Alison; 8. Margaret Jane; 9. Mary Anne, married to John Pringle, agent to the East India Company at the Cape of Good Hope, who died June 24, 1815, leaving two sons. Provost Stuart married, secondly, Alison, daughter of James Spittal, Esq; of Leuchat, who died without issue in October 1813, aged 93.

IV. Charles Stuart of Dunearn, M. D. F. R. S. E. and member of the American Philosophical Society of Philadelphia, who succeeded his uncle Alexander in 1786. He was minister of the parish of Cramond 1773-4-5, but resigned his charge, having separated from the Church of Scotland on account of change of sentiment. He was President of the Royal College of Physicians of Edinburgh in 1807-8-9. He married, October 29, 1773, Mary, eldest daughter of John Erskine, D. D. of Carnock, by the Hon. Christian Mackay, daughter of George Lord Reay. By her, who died 15th April 1817, he had, 1. Christian, born in 1774, died in 1808, a young woman of excellent endowments, natural and acquired, and of singular piety; 2. James, of whom afterwards; 3. Elizabeth Anna; 4. Mary, married to John Burnet, Esq; of Kenmay, to whom she has a son and a daughter; 5. John Alexander; 6. Alison, married to John Wilson Carmichael, Esq; from the isle of St. Vincent, to whom she has a daughter. Dr. Stuart has also had four children, who died in infancy. His eldest son,

V. James Stuart Younger of Dunearn, W. S. married, 29th April 1803, Eleanora Maria Anna, only daughter of the late Robert Moubray, M. D. of Cockairny, whose eldest son, Colonel Robert Moubray of Cockairny, is the representative of the very ancient family of Moubray of Barnbougle, at one time Dukes of Norfolk.

STEWART EARL OF GALLOWAY.

The account of this very ancient branch of the family of Stewart, by Crawfurd, (see page 235) differing in some respects from that given in the Family Tree, the latter account shall here be adhered to, but abridged very considerably.

The second son of Alexander, the fourth Lord High Steward, was,

I. Sir John Stewart of Bonkill, who was killed at the battle of Falkirk in 1298. His second son was,

II. Sir Allan Stewart of Dreghorn and Darnley, &c. Was killed at the battle of Halidown-hill in 1333. Died without issue. His second son was,

III. Sir John Stewart of Jedworth, afterwards of Dreghorn, Darnley, &c. in 1323, 1340, &c. Of three sons, the first and second left no surviving issue, the third was,

IV. Sir Alexander Stewart of Darnley, who succeeded his brother, Sir Walter in 1367. He had two sons; the eldest was ancestor of the Stewarts of Darnley and Lennox; 2. the second son was,

V. Sir William Stewart of Jedworth, mentioned in history from 1385 to 1429, when he was killed before Orleans. He had two sons; 1. John; 2. Sir William Stewart of Castlemilk, ancestor of that family. The eldest son,

VI. Sir John Stewart, married, in 1396, Marion, only daughter and heiress of Sir Walter Stewart of Dalswinton and Garlies, and thus acquired these lands in addition to the original property of the family. He was killed in France in 1419. His eldest son,

VII. Sir William Stewart, succeeded his father in the Dalswinton estates, on his death in 1419, and on the death of his grandfather, (stiled Sheriff of Tiviotdale, by Crawfurd) in 1429, he succeeded to the family estate of Jedworth. He had three sons; 1. Alexander; 2. Sir Thomas of Minto, ancestor of Lord Blantyre, and, as it is supposed, of the Marquis of Londonderry; 3. Walter of Tonderghie.

VIII. Sir Alexander Stewart of Garlies, &c. the eldest son, had three sons; 1. John, who died in his father's lifetime; 2. Alexander; 3. Archibald of Fintaloch, ancestor of the Earls of Blessington, an Irish Peerage that became extinct in 1769.

IX. Alexander, the second son, succeeded to the family estate of Garlies and Dalswinton. His son,

X. Sir Alexander Stewart of Garlies, is mentioned in 1494. He had two sons; 1. Alexander; 2. Walter,

XI. Sir Alexander Stewart, the eldest son, designed of Grenan in 1507. He had the astonishing number of sixteen daughters, all well married, as may be seen in Wood's Peerage, and one son,

XII. Sir Alexander Stewart of Garlies, in 1515 and 1577, &c. His sons were, 1. Alexander; 2. John; 3. Anthony; 4. Robert, who married the heiress of Cardonald.

XIII. Sir Alexander Stewart of Garlies, the eldest son, was slain at Stirling in 1574. His son,

XIV. Sir Alexander Stewart of Garlies, was knighted at the coronation of the Queen of James VI. in 1590. He had issue, 1. Alexander; 2. William of Mains, who married the heiress of Burray.

XV. Sir Alexander Stewart of Garlies, the eldest son, succeeded his father, and, in 1607, was created Lord Garlies, and, in 1623, was created Earl of Galloway. He had issue, 1. Alexander, who died before his father. He had a son, who died young; 2. James; 3. Lady Anne, married to Sir Andrew Agnew of Lochnaw.

The first Earl of Galloway died in 1649, and was succeeded by his second son,

XVI. James, second Earl of Galloway, a nobleman highly distinguished for dignity of manners and courteous disposition. He died in 1681. By his Lady, daughter of Sir Robert Grierson of Lagg, he had issue, 1. Alexander; 2. Robert of Reimston; 3. William of Castle Stewart; 4. Lady Grizell, married to Lord Kenmure.

XVII. Alexander, third Earl of Galloway, celebrated for great integrity and punctuality. He married Lady Mary Douglas, daughter of the Duke of Queensberry, by whom he had, 1. Alexander; 2. James, of whom afterwards; 3. Brigadier-General John Stewart of Sorbie; 7. Lady Margaret, married to Sir John Clerk of Pennycuik; 8. Lady Henrietta Stewart, married to Lord Glencairn.

XVIII. Alexander, the eldest son, succeeded his father, and became fourth Earl of Galloway. He died unmarried in 1698, and was succeeded by his brother,

James, fifth Earl of Galloway. He was a Commissioner of the Treasury, a Privy Counsellor, and a Lord of Police. Notwithstanding these ministerial appointments, he opposed the ministry in their favourite measure, the Union. This is an instance (of which many could be given) that the holding of an office under government does not necessarily imply a servile compliance with court-measures, or that opposition to them is always well founded. He married Lady Catherine Montgomery, daughter of Alexander, ninth Earl of Eglinton, by whom he had, 1. Alexander; 2. James, who was a Major-General in the army; 1. daughter, Lady Margaret, married to the Earl of Southesk; 2. Lady Euphemia, married to Murray of Broughton.

XIX. Alexander, sixth Earl of Galloway, succeeded his father in 1745. He died in 1773. He married, first, Lady Anne Keith, daughter of the Earl of Marischal, by whom he had, 1. Alexander, who died before him unmarried; 2. James, died young; 3. Lady Mary, married to Lord Fortrose, and had issue. His Lordship, secondly, married Lady Catherine Cochrane, daughter of the Earl of Dundonald, by whom he had issue; 4. John, of whom afterwards; 5. Hon. George Stewart, a Lieutenant in the army, was killed at Ticonderago in 1758; 7. Hon. Keith Stewart of Glasserton, bred to the royal navy; was highly distinguished as a sea commander. He died a Vice Admiral in 1795. He married Georgina Isabella D'Aguilar, by whom he had four sons; 8. Lady Catherine, married to her cousin, Murray of Broughton; 9. Lady Susanna, married to the Marquis of Stafford, and had issue; 10. Lady Margaret, married to the Earl of Aboyne, and had issue; 12. Lady Harriet, married to Lord Archibald Hamilton, now Duke of Hamilton, and had a numerous issue; 13. Lady Charlotte, married to the Earl of Dunmore, and had issue.

XX. John, seventh Earl of Galloway, succeeded his father in 1773; was a Lord of Police, a Commissioner of trade and plantations, Knight of the Thistle, and one of the Lords of the Bed-chamber. He was a warm supporter of the Pitt administration, whose measures not only saved Britain, but all Europe. He was representative of the Scottish Peerage in Parliament till 1796, when he obtained a hereditary seat, as a British Peer, by the title of Baron Stewart of Garlies. He died in 1806. To the excellency of his character it is not easy to do justice; to the most friendly and benevolent disposition, he united an activity that was indefatigable; and, whilst he was ever ready to promote the good of his country, and the interest of his friends, he conducted his own matters with a wisdom and a prudence that insured success. He married, first, Lady Charlotte Greville, daughter of the Earl of Warwick, who died of her first child, who died at the same time; secondly, Anne, daughter of Sir James Dashwood, by whom he had issue; 1. Alexander Lord Garlies—died young; 2. George, of whom afterwards; 3. Hon. Leveson Stewart—died young; 4. Hon. William Stewart, a Lieutenant General in the army, and Knight Grand Cross of the Bath, who has been in much severe service, and has signalized himself by great bravery and professional skill. He married, in 1804, the eldest daughter of the Hon. John Douglas, uncle to the Earl of Morton, by whom he has issue; 5. Hon. Charles James Stewart, bred to the church;

6. Hon. Montgomery Granville John Stewart of Grenan, who has sat in different parliaments for the Stewartry of Kirkcudbright. He married the sister of Sir William Honeyman, Lord Armadale, and by her has a numerous issue; 7. Hon. Edward Richard Stewart, bred to the army. Has sat in several Parliaments for the burghs of Wigton, &c. He married the Hon. Catherine Charteris, Grandaughter of the late Earl of Wemyss, and has issue; 8. Hon. James Henry Keith Stewart, bred to the army, and is a Knight companion of the Bath; 9. Lady Catherine, married to Sir James Graham of Netherby; 10. Lady Susan, married to the Duke of Marlborough; 11. Lady Harriet, married to Lord Spencer Chichester; 12. Lady Elizabeth, married to William Phillips Inge, Esq; 13. Lady Georgina, died unmarried; 14. Lady Charlotte, married to Sir Edward Crofton; 15. Lady Caroline, married to the Hon. and Rev. George Rushout; 16. Lady Sophia, married to the Hon. William Bligh, brother to the Earl of Darnley, a descendant of the original house of Darnley.

XXI. George, eighth Earl of Galloway, entered into the royal navy in 1780, under his uncle, the Hon. Keith Stewart, and was with him in the severe action off the Dogger Bank, with the Dutch fleet, in 1781. He was promoted to the rank of Captain in 1793, and to a flag, as Rear-admiral of the Blue, in 1810, and further promoted, in 1813, to be Rear-admiral of the Red, where he now stands second on the list. During a period of unparalleled exertion, his Lordship (in his professional capacity) has distinguished himself among those heroes, who have, in the late wars, raised the glory of the British Flag to a height never before known; and it should seem, as emphatically expressed of him by his commander at the time, in 1794, Sir John Jervis, " In the good old, way," by bringing his ship to action within half musket shot of the enemy. His Lordship was appointed Lord Lieutenant of the county of Wigton in 1807, and a Knight of the Thistle in 1813. He married, in April 1797, Lady Jane Paget, second daughter of the Earl of Uxbridge, and has issue; 1. Lady Jane; 2. Lady Caroline;

XXII. 3. Randolph Lord Garlies, born in September 1800; 4. Lady Louisa; 5. Hon. Keith Stewart, born in January 1814; and two sons and one daughter, who died young. Arms, see page 237.

STEWART EARL OF TRAQUAIR. (See page 235.)

VI. John, second Earl of Traquair, (the sixth in descent from Stewart Earl of Buchan) was born in 1622; succeeded his father in 1659; exerted himself with great gallantry on the side of his unfortunate but ill advised sovereign. He died in 1666. He married for his second wife, (the first had no issue) Lady Anne Seton, daughter of the Earl of Winton, by whom he had two sons, who died without issue, and three daughters, who died unmarried, and two sons, successively Earls of Traquair, first,

VII. William, third Earl of Traquair, died unmarried; second,

VII. Charles, fourth Earl of Traquair, who succeeded his brother. He was a nobleman remarkable for every thing that was good. He died at the age of 82 in 1741. He married Lady Mary Maxwell, only daughter of Robert, fourth Earl of Nithsdale, a most virtuous Lady. They had two sons, successively Earls of Traquair; one daughter, Lady Mary, married the forfeited Duke of Perth; four daughters, who died unmarried, and one daughter, Lady Catherine, married William, the forfeited Earl of Nithsdale, and by whom she had one surviving child, Lady Winifred Maxwell of Nithsdale, the heiress of that very ancient and most respectable family, who married William Haggerston Constable, of Everingham, and by whom she had a numerous issue, still enjoying the great estate of Tereagles in Nithsdale.

VIII. Charles, fifth Earl of Traquair, succeeded his father, in 1741, and died without issue in 1764. He was succeeded by his brother,

VIII. John, sixth Earl of Traquair, who died at Paris in 1779, in the 81st year of his age. He married Christian, daughter of Sir Philip Anstruther of Anstrutherfield, by whom he had, 1. Charles, of whom after; 2. Lady Christiana, married Cyrus Griffin, Esq; and has issue; 3. Lady Mary; 4. Lady Lucy.

IX. Charles, seventh Earl of Traquair, succeeded his father. He married, in 1773, Mary, daughter and co-heiress of George Ravenscroft of Wickham, and by whom he has had, 1. Lady Louisa, and 2. Charles Lord Linton, born in January 1781.

STUART LORD BLANTYRE. (See page 240.)

In addition to the account by Crawfurd of Alexander, the fifth Lord Blantyre, is to be stated, that the third daughter, the Hon. Helen Stuart, was married to John Lord Gray, and had issue; and the fourth daughter, the Hon. Anne Stuart, was married to Alexander Hay, Esq; of Drummelzier, and had issue. He was himself the eighth in descent from Sir William Stuart of Garlies, (see Galloway) and was succeeded by his son,

IX. Walter, sixth Lord Blantyre, in 1704, who was one of the representatives of the Scottish Peerage in 1710. He died unmarried in 1713, and was succeeded by his brother,

IX. Robert, seventh Lord Blantyre, a Major in the army. He died in 1743. He married, first, Lady Helen Lyon, daughter of the Earl of Strathmore, by whom he had no surviving issue. 2dly, Margaret, daughter of the Hon. William Hay of Drummelzier, by whom he had,

1. Walter; 2. William; 3. Alexander; all of whom afterwards.

4. Hon. John Stuart, died unmarried; 5. Hon. James Stuart, Lieutenant-Colonel in the army, killed at the battle of Guildford in 1781; 6. Hon. Charles Stuart, in the civil service of the East India Company, and much distinguished for talents and application; 1. Hon. Margaret Stuart, died unmarried; 8. Hon. Helen Stuart, married Oliver Colt, Esq; of Auldhame, to whom she had a numerous issue; 9. Hon. Marion Stuart, died unmarried; 10. Hon. Elizabeth Stuart, married William Colquhoun of Garscadden; without issue.

X. Walter, eighth Lord Blantyre, succeeded his father. He died in the 25th year of his age at Paris in 1751. He was succeeded by his brother,

X. William, ninth Lord Blantyre, a Colonel in the Dutch service. He died unmarried in 1776, and was succeeded by his brother,

X. Alexander, tenth Lord Blantyre. He died in 1783. He married, in 1773, Catherine, daughter of Patrick Lindsay of Eaglescairny, and had issue, 1. Hon. Margaret Stuart, married, in 1809, the Rev. Andrew Stewart, M. D. now minister of Erskine; 2. Robert Walter, of whom after; 3. Hon. Patrick Stuart of Eaglescairny; 4. Hon. William Stuart; 5. Hon. Charles Stuart.

XI. Robert Walter, eleventh Lord Blantyre, born in 1777; entered as an Ensign into the army in 1795, and has risen gradually through all the subordinate ranks to that of Colonel.

His Lordship served in Holland under His Royal Highness the Duke of York; in the expedition in the Baltic, under Sir John Moore; and in the peninsula under Lord Wellington.

STEUART OF ALLANTON.

The best genealogists derive this family from Sir Robert Stewart, sixth son of Sir John Stewart of Bonkle, or Bonkill, the second son of Alexander, sixth Lord High Steward of Scotland, and great-grandfather to King Robert II[1]. It has been said by some, that it sprung from a younger brother of Darnley and Castlemilk. That is also true; as the Darnley and Castlemilk branches of the

---

[1] See Dun. Stewart's Hist. of the Stewarts, p. 199. Sir Robert Douglas's Genealogical Table of the House of Stewart, &c. and they have been followed by Brown and others.

name (that is, the Darnley and Dalswinton branches) are descended from the eldest two of the seven sons of Sir John Stewart of Bonkle, whereas the Allanton branch is from a younger son [1]. Sir John was killed at the battle of Falkirk, anno 1298 [2].

I. Sir Robert Steuart was born about the year 1280, and obtained the lands of Daldowie, on the Clyde in Lanarkshire, which he held of the Archbishop of Glasgow. It appears that he accompanied his three brothers, Sir Allan Stewart of Darnley, Sir Walter Stewart of Dalswinton, and Sir Hugh, in the expedition to Ireland, under Prince Edward Bruce, and was present at the battle of Dundalk, an. 1318 [3]. He was succeeded by his son,

II. Allan Steuart of Daldowie, sirnamed " Alnwickster." He early attached himself to the House of Douglas, under the celebrated Sir James, commonly called " the Black Douglas," and married into that family. From his bravery in heading a party, which stormed the castle of Alnwick in Northumberland, he obtained the sirname of " Alnwickster [4]."

An. 1385 (according to the traditional accounts of the family) when Scotland was invaded by King Richard II. Allan, although then past sixty, commanded a chosen body of men, consisting of his own tenants of Daldowie, and others levied in the neighbourhood of Ruthglen, and was marching to join the army, then assembling on the borders, under the Earl of Douglas [5], when he encountered, at a place named Morningside, in the moor of M'Morren, a detachment of English horse, which, on account of foraging or plunder, was scouring the country. After a severe conflict, the enemy were routed, but he himself was killed in the action. His remains were deposited in the Chapel of Beuskiag, close by Morningside, a Religious House dependent on the Abbey of Aberbrothic, the Abbot of which was Lord of the District [6]. He was succeeded by his son, who became

III. Sir Allan Steuart of Daldowie and Allanton. He seems to have been born about the year 1365; and, having accompanied his father in this expedition, he succeeded, on his death, to the command of the troops, which he con-

[1] See the foregoing History, p. 127, where Mr. Crawfurd speaks very vaguely, if not erroneously on the subject.   [2] Hemmingford, Tom. I p. 165. Lord Hailes's Annals, p. 260.
[3] Hollinshed's Chron of Ireland, p. 67, 68.   [4] M S. Hist. of the family.
[5] Froissart, L. II. Ch. 149, 150. The English army on this occasion consisted of 60,000 men. The Scotch (says Hume) pretended not to make resistance against such a force; but as soon as they entered Scotland, by Berwick, on the east, the Scotch and French, to the number of 30,000, invaded Cumberland and Westmoreland on the west.—Hist. Vol. III. p. 12, 13.
[6] The ruins of the Religious House existed till within the last 40 years.

ducted successfully to the rendezvous of the army, then about to enter Cumberland. According to the same accounts, at the close of the campaign, he obtained from King Robert II. at Lochmaben Castle, the honour of Knight Banneret, being knighted under the royal standard, together with the addition, to his paternal coat-armorial, of the Lion-passant above his Fesse Chequée. The above tradition is rendered the more probable from the circumstance of the district being from thenceforward named Allcath-Muir, that is, " the Muir of Allan's Battle;" and the stream which waters its southern and western boundary, Alleath-water *; also from the names of various other places immediately adjoining, such as Cathburn, evidently Cathkers, &c. all indicating the site of the engagement, and evidently Celtic compounds. Moreover, from Ponts' M. S. (one of the most authentic Heraldric Records) we find the ancient bearing of Stewart of Allanton to be as above-mentioned †.

The existence, however, of Sir Allan Steuart of Daldowie at this period, is proved beyond a doubt, by his being named as one of the witnesses to a charter, by King Robert III. dated 6th December 1393, and third year of his reign, " to Sir Adam Mure of Rowallan, and Dame Janet Danielston, his spouse, in " conjunct fee, and so to the heirs to be procreate between them, whom failing to " Sir Adam Mure's lawful heirs whatsoever, viz. Sir Reginald Mure of Aber- " corn, and Godfrey Mure of Caldwell, his grand-uncle and cousin, and their " heirs, &c. of the lands of Polnekill, or Polkelly, Green, Dumblay, Ainsoch, " Dardarroch, and Balgray, in Ayrshire, and the lands of Nemphlar, in Lanark- " shire, to be erected into a barony, and to be holden ward ‡."

Some years after, Sir Allan passed over to France in the time of King

---

* *All* is the half of the name of Allan, and *Cath*, in the Celtic, signifies battle. In the same way, " Cathburn," denotes " the Burn of the Battle," or the rivulet where the engagement ceased; " Cathkers," the " field east of the Battle." Spears and Helmets have been found in the adjoining moss, or bog, in which, it is said, many of the English troopers were unhorsed and slain. M.S. hist. of the family.

† Nesbit's Heraldry. vol. II. pp. 53, 299. It unfortunately happens, that the Lion-office, or Herald's College of Scotland, was burnt about 180 years ago; therefore there are no records to be found there of an earlier age than the beginning of the 17th century.

‡ See Robertson's Index to ancient charters, p. 143. This charter is in the possession of either the Earl of Glasgow, or of Lady Loudon. In a memoir found among the papers of the late Mr. George Crawfurd, (by which it appears that he meditated a history of the House of Stewart on a much more extensive scale than that subjoined to his account of Renfrewshire) we find, that he had collected notices of many families of the name, and of that of Allanton among others, in which the latter appeared as witnesses to charters and seasines, from the first one here quoted in 1398, down to the time of Sir Walter Stuart in 1643.

Charles VI. then Dauphin, and served in the Gens d'arms Ecossois of that Prince. He probably bore a part in the disastrous wars in which the French and Scotch were united against the English, in the same period, in the battles of Azincourt, and Baugé; which last was confessedly gained by the valour of the Scotch, under the Earls of Buchan and Douglas, and was the first that turned the tide of success against the English arms.

An. 1421, according to the same accounts, Sir Allan returned to Scotland. He soon visited Daldowie, the religious house at Beuskiag, his father's grave, and the scene of his own early valour. In consequence of which he obtained, from the Abbot of Aberbrothic, under a favourable tenure, lands to a considerable extent in the moor of M'Morren, then Allcath Muir, which, after him, were named Allanton*. There, from an impulse of enthusiasm, and in spite of the superior attractions of Daldowie, he, two years after, fixed the residence of his family, which never afterwards returned to the latter, when Lord Hay of Yester, some years after became the first military vassal of the Abbot for the whole of this extensive district, Sir Allan, of course, held his lands in a similar manner of that nobleman †.

In Paris, he had married a French lady, by whom he had a son, who succeeded him, and was,

IV. James Steuart of Daldowie and Allanton. He was born about 1400, and

---

* The whole of this transaction, and others above stated, are circumstantially described in a M.S. history of the individuals concerned in them, and the account is carefully preserved, and as piously believed by the family. They fairly consider it as good and authentic a record as any other collection of individual memoirs. The grandson of Sir Allan, namely James, sirnamed "the Antiquary," and second of that name, was the first that drew up the narrative. He had seen his grandfather, who lived to a great age, and heard the circumstances from his own mouth; and this history has been continued at different periods to nearly the present time. The original grant of the lands by the Abbot, existed in the beginning of the last century, when it was destroyed by fire, together with several other curious documents.

† When the reformation took place, Lord Yester came in the room of the Abbot of Aberbrothic, and got a gift of the lands from the crown. Lord Sommerville, in his memoirs, says, that Allcath Muir was named "the Out-barony of Camnethan," and that his ancestor, the first Lord, held it of the Abbey of Kelso, or of Melrose, in which he is obviously mistaken; moreover, that he gave this large district to Sir William Hay of Yester, in marriage with his eldest daughter, An. 1427. See vol. I. pp. 168, 169. However that may be, it appears from the chartulary of Aberbrothic, (preserved in the Advocate's Library at Edinburgh) that Lord Yester, and others, were appointed the "Baillies, Commissaries, and Justiciers," of the Abbots, in the extensive regality of Aberbrothic and Ethcarmuir, as early as the year 1494. Fol. 132.

and sirnamed " of Paris," from the place of his birth¹. This James was a pacific character, and diligently cultivated his new possessions. When he married is uncertain; he was followed by his son,

V. James Steuart of Daldowie and Allanton, (and II. of that name) on account of his learning, sirnamed the " Antiquary." He was born about 1433, and educated in France among his grand-mother's relations². He is said to have married a daughter of Sommervile of Camnethan. He had two sons; 1. Adam, who died unmarried, and, 2. Allan, who succeeded him; also two daughters. There is a Charter still extant, by Walter Scott of Westlenflar, to Adam, son and heir to James Steuart of Daldowie, of certain heritages at Lanark, dated 16th August 1493 ³.

VI. Allan Steuart of Allanton. He was born about the year 1485, and married Elizabeth Tait, daughter of Tait of Elington and Little Ernock, or Tait's Ernock, to which estate she succeeded. In an Inquest, held at Lanark, before the sheriff of the county, 19th August 1532, in a proof relative to mails and duties, payable out of the lands of Udston, Tweedie, and Hezzledean, we find Allan to have been one of the Jury*. Also, he attended Lord Yester, and the governor of the kingdom, the Earl of Arran, An. 1547, in the Army which was levied to repel the invasion by the English, under the protector, the Earl of Hertford. There is a will or testament made by him on this occasion. An Inventory is also given of his effects, and is registered in the Commissary-Court of Glasgow, 22d June 1548 †.

Allan had two sons, Adam and Gavin, of whom the former succeeded him, and the latter died unmarried; also one daughter Eupham.

VII. Adam Steuart of Allanton, who married Marion, daughter of James Lockhart of Lee ⁴. He had a son, James, who became his successor; and other children, who died in infancy or unmarried. He died An. 1574.

¹ M.S. Hist. of the family.   ² Ibid.   ³ In the charter-chest of Allanton.

* The original record of this inquest is preserved in the charter-chest of Lochart of Lee. We find, also, an application to the lords of the council, by this lady and her husband, to protect her in her estate against the claims of the Earl of Arran. See Records of Privy Council, an. 1642, 6th July.

† There is an inventory and testament, made about ten years after this period, by Sir Walter Scott of Buccleugh, ancestor to the Duke of Buccleugh, very similar to this curious paper. The debts and effects are inventoried in both in nearly the same simple and homely style, delineating the manners of the times. See Mr. Walter Scott's Border History.

⁴ Testament of Adam Steuart of Allanton, in favours of his lady, Marion Lockhart. In the Testament Register at Edin. 25th Sept. 1574.

During the time of this Adam and his father, the doctrines of the reformation had made considerable progress in Scotland, under George Wishart (who was put to death by order of Cardinal Beaton, an. 1546) and other popular leaders. Wishart was a particular friend of the family, and more than once escaped the pursuit of his enemies by concealing himself at Allanton House. The mode of conducting this dangerous but friendly office was curious. There was an apartment in the old tower of Allanton, formed out of the thickness of the wall; and, when a friend or friends were to occupy it, they arrived during the night. A taylor, who was intrusted with the secret, was immediately set to work, with his back to the concealed door. There he mounted guard as long as it was found needful; and thus the prisoners were subsisted, without the knowledge of the servants of the family. The faithful Taylor's appetite, of course, seemed gigantic; but it is not recorded that any unlucky discovery was ever made [1].

VIII. James Steuart of Allanton, sirnamed " of Langside [2]," (and 3d of that name). He was born an. 1537. By a precept of James E. of Arran, dated at the palace of Linlithgow, 8th August 1579, we find him designed great-grandson of David Tait of Ernock; in which last-mentioned lands he was then infeft. There is also a former charter of the lands of Tait's Ernock, granted by the same David Tait, dated 4th October 1484 [3]. James married, first, Helen, daughter to John Sommervile of Humbie, (a Cadet of the Sommervile family) and secondly, Margaret, daughter to   Spens of Edinburgh.

James was an intimate friend of the celebrated John Knox, whose bold character he admired, and whose doctrines he zealously promoted. By Knox he was introduced to the Earl of Argyle, and the Earl of Murray, misnamed " the good Regent." He enjoyed, as it was said, much of his confidence, and, in fact, became one of the most active partizans of that daring nobleman. At the battle of Langside, an. 1568, (where the unfortunate Queen Mary was defeated) James commanded under him a troop of horse, and by vigorously repulsing the van-guard of the enemy, and gaining, before they could come up, the hill of Langside, he greatly contributed to the success of the action [4].

James had two sons and two daughters. The sons were, 1. James who died before his father an. 1607. The second, James Robert, who was born an. 1595, and obtained the lands of Carbarns on the Clyde; his grandson, William,

[1] M.S. History of the family.   [2] Id. Ibid.   [3] In the Charter-Chest of Allanton.   [4] M.S. of the family. Dun. Stewart, p. 200. See page 271.

purchased the lands of Woodside and Neuk, and thus became the predecessor of several respectable families of the name, viz. the Steuarts of Carfin, Overton, and Brownlee, in Lanarkshire; and of Alderston in East Lothain; also of William Steuart late of Calcutta. James Steuart, now of Carfin, married Mary, daughter to John Sword of Carfin, and has issue; and Robert Steuart, now of Alderston, espoused, first, Margaret, daughter of * * * Johnston of Hilton; and secondly, Louisa Clementina, daughter to Drummond of Logie-Almond, and sister to Sir William Drummond, and has also issue. The two daughters were, 1. Janet, who married Robert Denham of Westshield; 2. Christian, who married Sir James Cleland of Monkland, and both had issue [1].

James died of grief for the loss of his eldest son, an. 1607 [2], and was succeeded by his grandson, the son of

IX. James Steuart of Allanton, (the 4th of that name). He was born an. 1575, and bred to the bar, but he was cut off in early life an. 1607. He espoused Marion, daughter to Walter Carmichael of Hyndford, and sister to the first Lord Carmichael, who was treasurer of Scotland, and predecessor to the Earl of Hyndford [3]. He had three sons and one daughter; 1. James, who died in infancy; 2. Walter, who succeeded his grandfather; and, 3. James, who became Sir James Steuart of Coltness. The daughter, Marion, espoused her first cousin, James Denham of Westshield [4].

James died, as above-mentioned, before his father, an. 1607. His son was,

X. Sir Walter Steuart of Allanton. He was born an. 1606, and married Margaret, daughter to Sir James Hamilton of Broomhill, and sister to the first Lord Belhaven, (who figured as one of the most strenuous opposers of the Union) and to James Hamilton, Lord Bishop of Galloway [5]. During Sir Walter's minority, the lands of Daldowie were, with his consent, sold to clear off encumbrances, although they had been in possession of his ancestors more than 300 years. But he seems to have inherited somewhat of the enthusiasm of his progenitor, Sir Allan, and the partiality of the family to the scene of their early achievements; and accordingly he added to the estate of Allanton by various and extensive purchases. An. 1653, he purchased, on account of his brother,

---

[1] M.S. History of the family. [2] Inventory of goods and gear in the house of Umql. James Steuart, the elder, of Allanton, 12th April 1609, in the Charter-Chest of the Family. [3] Dun. Stewart, p. 200. Crawfurd's Peerage. p. 225. [4] M.S. Hist. of the family.

[5] Mar. Contract, in the Charter-Chest of Allanton, 15th January 1623. Instrument of seasine in favour of Sir Walter Steuart, by Stephen Lockhart of Wicketshaw, 31st May 1628.

Sir James, the estate of Coltness, in the same parish, (namely Camnethan) from the Hamiltons of Udston.

It is recorded, that Oliver Cromwell, in 1650, after the battle of Dunbar, in his progress through Lanarkshire, halted with a few attendants at Allanton House, where he was hospitably entertained by Lady Steuart, and where he passed the night. Sir Walter, being a royalist, took care to be out of the way. On the protector's arrival, as it is said, some choice Canary and other refreshments were presented, but he would suffer nothing to be touched until he himself had first said grace, which he fervently did for more than half an hour, to the great edification of the lady. He then courteously enquired after Sir Walter; and, on drinking the health of the family, observed, that " his mother was a Steuart; and that he always felt a kindness for the name!" This, and several other characterestic anecdotes of the visit are still preserved[1].

Sir Walter had six sons and three daughters. The 4th son, William, succeeded his father. The 5th, James, became James Steuart of Hartwood, in the county of Lanark. The rest died unmarried. The daughters were, 1. Marion, who espoused John Boyle of Kelburn; whose son, by her, was David, the first Earl of Glasgow; 2. Margaret, she married . . . Caldwell of Caldwell. Her eldest daughter married Sir John Maxwell of Pollok; 3. Anne, she espoused Claud Hamilton of Barns, and had issue[2].

Sir Walter lived till after the restoration, and died an. 1672, being succeeded by his eldest surviving son,

XI. William Steuart of Allanton. He was born an. 1640, and married his first cousin, Margaret, only daughter of Sir James Steuart, the first of Coltness[3]. In consequence of his connection with his father-in-law and uncle, Sir James, and his brother-in-law, Sir Thomas Steuart, he was persecuted in the troublesome times which preceded the revolution, and fined by the council, in 1684, £500 Sterling for favouring the covenanters. But afterwards, when his other brother-in-law Sir James became secretary of state, under Lord Melfort, a remission, by King James II. was procured for him, dated an. 1687[4]. In the

---

[1] M.S. Hist. of the family. [2] Crawfurd's Peerage. Mar. Contracts in possession of the family, 1665, 1670, and 1683. [3] Mar. Contr. in the Charter-Chest of Allanton, 28th May 1666. Retour of Service, William Steuart of Allanton, son and heir to the deceased Sir Walter Steuart, 30th November 1672. Charter of Confirmation, by John E. of Tweeddale, 24th July 1673. [4] In the possession of the family. See Act. Records, Privy Council, ad. an. 1684. Also Cruickshank's Hist. of the sufferings of the Church, vol. I. p. 338.

same year, he had the offer of a Baronetage, through the same interest, and, on his declining it, it was given to his cousin Sir Robert of Allanbank[1].

William had three sons and three daughters. The eldest, James, became his father's heir and successor. The rest died unmarried, or in infancy.

William died an. 1700, and was succeeded by his son,

XII. James Steuart of Allanton, (the 6th of that name). He was born an. 1676, and married Cecilia, daughter of David Dunmuir, advocate, and widow of John Lyon of Brigton[2].

James had four sons and seven daughters. The fourth, James, succeeded his father. The others died unmarried. Of the daughters, the 2. Marion, married Andrew M'Dowel of Logan, afterwards Lord Bankton; and, 7. Lillias, married Alexander Murray, brother to John Murray of Lintrose. Her only daughter, Emilia, married, an. 1767, James Guthrie, now of Craigie, and has a numerous issue[3].

James lived to the year 1752, and was succeeded by his son,

XIII. James Steuart of Allanton, (the 7th of that name). He was born an. 1715, and married his relation, Margaret, daughter to Henry Steuart Barclay, of Collerney, in the county of Fife[4].

James was eminent both as an agriculturist and a scholar, and greatly improved his estate, by enclosing and planting, which were beginning to become fashionable in his time in Scotland. He had three sons and a daughter, 1. James, who died in infancy; 2. Henry, who succeeded him; 3. William, born an. 1762. He died in 1775. The daughter was Antonia, born an. 1761. She died also unmarried in 1775.

James died an. 1772, and was succeeded by his son,

XIV. Sir Henry Steuart, Bart. now of Allanton, L. L. D. F. R. S. &c. He was born an. 1759, and married, an. 1787, Lillias, daughter of Hugh Seton of Touch, in the county of Stirling, and has had issue, 1. Elizabeth Seton, born an. 1788, who died in the same year; 2. Elizabeth, born an. 1789. She married R. M'Donald of Staffa, third son to Colin M'Donald of Boisdale, but the eldest by his second marriage.

---

[1] M.S. Hist. of the family. [2] Retour of Service, James Steuart of Allanton, as son and heir to the deceased William Steuart. Mar. Contr. in the Charter-Chest of Allanton. [3] M.S. Hist. of the family. [4] Disposition, James Steuart of Allanton to his son and heir, James Steuart, 13th August 1729. Also, Mar. Contract, 25th April 1754, in the Charter-Chest of Allanton.

She has two sons and one daughter, 1. Henry, born an. 1812; 2. Archibald, born an. 1814; and, 3. Isabella, born an. 1816 *.

STEUART OF COLTNESS,

The second son of James Steuart of Allanton, (the 4th of that name) became

I. Sir James Steuart of Coltness and Kirkfield. He was born in 1608, after his father's death, and was bred a merchant and banker in Edinburgh, by which means he acquired a large fortune. He married, first, in 1630, Anne, daughter of Henry Hope, elder brother to Sir Thomas Hope of Craighall, Lord Advocate of Scotland; and, secondly, in 1646, Marion, only daughter of David M'Culloch of Goodtrees, near Edinburgh, by whom he obtained that estate. She was the widow of Sir John Elliot, son to Gilbert Elliot of Stobbs [1].

In 1653, with the assistance of his brother, Sir Walter, he purchased the lands of West Carbarns, or Kirkfield, from Sir James Sommerville of Camnethan, and, soon after, the estate of Coltness, from John Hamilton of Udston. It had been sold, as early as 1552, by the Sommerviles of Camnethan, to Sir Robert Logan of Restalrig [2].

An. 1649, he was elected Lord Provost of Edinburgh, and, being a zealous covenanter, he was, in the following year, chosen, together with the Marquis of Argyle, and the Earl of Eglinton, on the part of the Scotch, to hold the conference with Oliver Cromwell on Bruntsfield-links. He was also pay-master, and commissary-general to the army, which was defeated by Cromwell, in the same year, at Dunbar, under General Leslie. In 1659, he was again elected Lord Provost, but, on account of his whig principles, dismissed on the restoration in the succeeding year, and sent prisoner, first to Edinburgh Castle, and then to Dundee; and fined first £500, and subsequently £1000 Sterling.

---

* The account of the early ages of this most extensive branch of the House of Steuart is not so fully, or so correctly given, as the Editor would have been able to have done had some very important documents from a respectable quarter arrived in time to have been introduced into this account. Meanwhile, he was unwilling to withhold from his readers a detail much more perfect and curious than is usually to be found amidst the inherent sameness of genealogical disquisition.

[1] Mar. Contr. in the Charter-Chest of Coltness. M.S. Hist. of the family. [2] Charter by John Sommervile of Camnethan to Sir Robert Logan of Restalrig, 30th June 1552. Disposition of the lands of Coltness to Sir Walter Steuart of Allanton, 27th October 1653.

At length, in 1670, through the friendly interference of the Lord Register, Sir Archibald Primrose, (whose life he had saved, after the battle of Philliphaugh) a full pardon and remission, under the great seal, were obtained for him[1]. The well known and excellent Bishop Leighton was brought up, in Edinburgh, under Sir James's care[2]; and the undaunted M'Kell, who was so inhumanly tortured by order of the Privy Council, and afterwards executed, an. 1666, had been Chaplain in his family[3].

By his first Lady, Sir James had seven sons and one daughter. The eldest, Thomas, succeeded his father in the estate of Coltness. The third, Walter, was born an. 1634, and obtained, by marriage, the estate of Westbarns in East Lothian; but this line became extinct after another generation. The fourth son was James, who became Sir James Steuart of Goodtrees, and succeeded his father in that estate. The seventh, Robert, became Sir Robert Steuart of Allanbank. The fifth and sixth sons died unmarried. The daughter was Margaret, born an. 1645. She espoused her cousin, William Steuart of Allanton, and had issue as above.

Sir James had, by his second lady, four daughters. The eldest, Marion, born an. 1650, married Sir John Maxwell of Pollok, Lord justice Clerk. The rest died unmarried, or in infancy[4].

Sir James died in Edinburgh in his 73d year, an. 1681, and was succeeded by his eldest son, who became

II. Sir Thomas Steuart of Coltness. He was born an. 1631, and married, first, in 1654, Margaret, only daughter of Sir John Elliot, and his step-mother, Lady Steuart[5]; and, secondly, in 1677, Susan, daughter of Robert Denham of Westshield, and widow of William Lockhart of Wygateshaw.

---

[1] In the possession of the family. See Records of the city of Edinburgh. History of the times. Records Privy Council.

[2] Bishop Burnet's History of his own times, vol. I. pp. 193, 194. where the character of this most amiable and virtuous prelate is given at length.

[3] Id. Vol. I. pp. 347, 348. M.S. History of the family. The cruel torture, by means of the "Bootikins," is minutely described by Burnet, and the inflexible fortitude and shocking death of M'Kell. This evidently is the original of that inimitable portrait of presbyterian enthusiasm and constancy which, under the name of M'Briar, will live for ever in the imperishable pages of the "Tales of my Landlord," where the whole scene before the Privy Council is highly coloured, and where the Duke of Lauderdale, Lord Dundee, and others are described to have been present, but it is given, at the same time, with perfect fidelity, and with characteristic as well as historic truth.

[4] M. S. Hist. of the family, and Mar. Contracts.

[5] Mar. Contract, in the Charter Chest of Coltness, 10th April 1654.

He was a most zealous presbyterian, and on that account called familiarly "Gospel Coltness[1]." An. 1683, being accused of fighting under the rebel standard at Bothwell Bridge, four years before, though he was actually in Edinburgh at the time, through fear of imprisonment, he concealed himself for some time at Allanton, under the guard of the faithful Taylor, and at length fled to Holland. By the exertions of Sir George Mackenzie, then Lord Advocate, he was outlawed, and his estate confiscated, and given to the Earl of Arran, afterwards Duke of Hamilton [2]. He remained at Rotterdam and Utrecht till 1687, the year of the act of indulgences granted by King James II. when he returned to Scotland, with his brother Sir James, then a favourite at court; and, through his interest, and that of William Penn, the celebrated quaker, (a personal favourite of the King's on account of his father [3]) his pardon was obtained [4].

In the year 1689, after the revolution, Sir Thomas represented the town of North Berwick in the convention of estates; and again, in the first parliament of King William, held in 1690. He was the first who proposed the abolition of episcopacy, and the well known act of that year for regulating the Church of Scotland, was proposed and framed by him. On the meeting of this parliament, he was knighted by the King's Commissioner, and, in 1693, created a Baronet by patent. Soon after, his estate was restored; and he got a grant, in 1696, of £200 Sterling a-year, payable out of the revenues of the Archbishoprick of Glasgow, as a compensation for his losses sustained during the forfeiture [5].

Sir Thomas had, by his first lady, nine sons and three daughters. The eldest was David, who succeeded him. The fourth, Walter, was born an. 1663. He married, first,   King, niece to Sir William Pritchard, Lord Mayor of London; and, secondly, Hannah, daughter to   Quash, also of London. His son Thomas succeeded his uncle Sir David; and a daughter, Martha, of Millhill, in the county of Middlesex, lived down to the year 1784. Sir Thomas's 9th son was Robert, who succeeded his nephew Sir Thomas. The rest died un-

---

[1] M. S. Hist. of the family.   [2] Records Privy Council.

[3] Penn was the son of Sir William Penn, the gallant Admiral, who fought under King James II. when Duke of York, an. 1665, on which occasion he defeated the Dutch, who were commanded by Opdam.

[4] M. S. Hist. of the family. There were in exile with Sir Thomas, at Utrecht, at that time, the Earl of Argyle, the Earl of Loudon, Lord Stair, and his grandson (who afterwards became the well known John Earl of Stair) Lord Melville, the Earl of Leven, the Earl of Marchmont, Sir James's cousin Sir William Denham of Westshield, Pringle of Torwoodlee, and several others.

[5] Rolls of Parliament ad. an. 1689, 1690. Writs in possession of the family.

married, or in infancy. Of the daughters, Anne, the 2d, born in 1661, married Sir Archibald Cockburn of Langton, and had issue. By his second lady, Sir Thomas had five sons, all of whom died in infancy, except the 4th, Archibald, who afterwards succeeded his nephew in the Baronetage, and became Sir Archibald Steuart Denham of Westshield [1].

Sir Thomas died an. 1698, and was succeeded by his eldest son,

III. Sir David Steuart of Coltness. He was born an. 1656—and married, in 1696, his step-mother's daughter, Marion, by William Lockhart of Wygateshaw [2], but had no issue. An. 1685, (the year of the accession of King James II.) Sir David, who had gone with his father to Holland, accompanied Archibald Earl of Argyle in his unsuccessful descent on Scotland, for which the Earl was beheaded at the cross of Edinburgh in the same year. Sir David, on the trial, was condemned to be executed, together with some others; but he then escaped, and was afterwards pardoned [3]. An. 1712, he sold the estate of Coltness to his nephew, Sir James Steuart of Goodtrees, Lord Advocate of Scotland [4].

Sir David died an. 1723, and was succeeded in the title by his nephew,

IV. Sir Thomas Steuart, who was born an. 1708, and was bred a surgeon, in which profession he went out to the West Indies, and died in the island of St. Christopher's, unmarried, in 1737. He was succeeded in the Baronetage by his uncle, who became,

V. Sir Robert Steuart. He was born an. 1675, and espoused Margaret, daughter to Zachary Maxwell of Blawarthill, a cadet of the Pollok family. Sir Robert was a man of science, and became Professor of Natural Philosophy in the University of Edinburgh, which chair he filled with applause till his death [5].

Sir Robert had five sons and three daughters, of whom the whole died either unmarried or in infancy, the 4th excepted, who succeeded his father, and became

VI. Sir John Steuart, L. L. D. He was born an. 1712. Like his father, he was a man of science and learning, and followed him in the professorial chair in the University. But he was better known as Dr. Steuart, as he neglected to

---

[1] M.S. Hist. of the family. [2] Mar. Contr. 3d July 1696, in possession of the family.

[3] Records of the court of Justiciary, 13th July 1685. Cruickshanks's Hist. Vol. II. p. 373.

[4] Disposition and contract of Sale, by Sir David Steuart to Sir James Steuart of Goodtrees, Lord Advocate, and Sir James Stewart, his son, 28th August 1685.

[5] M.S. Hist. of the family, and Mar. Contr. An. 1706.

assume the title of Baronet[1]. He was skilled in metaphysics, and wrote a tract of some merit against the deistical opinions of Mr. Hume, on their first appearance.

Sir John died unmarried, an. 175 , and was succeeded by his uncle,

VII. Sir Archibald Steuart, who was born an. 1683, during his father's exile at Utrecht. He was an advocate, and assumed the name of Denham, on succeeding to the estate of Westshield, in right of his mother. He married Jean, daughter to Sir George Warrender of Lochend, and had one son and a daughter. The daughter died unmarried; and the son, Thomas, after serving as a Captain in the army in Germany, died at Alsfelt an. 1761, without issue[2].

Sir Archibald lived to the age of 90, and died an. 1773; and thus the two Baronetages of Coltness and Goodtrees were united in the person of Sir James Steuart, the 4th of that name,

STEUART OF GOODTREES.

James Steuart of Allanton (the 5th of that name) died, as above, an. 1607, and left two sons. The eldest, Sir Walter, succeeded his father; the younger became

I. Sir James Steuart of Coltness, Kirkfield, and Goodtrees; which last estate he obtained by his marriage to the heiress, Marion, daughter of David M'Culloch of Goodtrees, in the county of Mid-Lothian. He left it to his fourth son, who was

II. Sir James Steuart of Goodtrees. He was born an. 1635, and married, first, Agnes, daughter of the Rev. Robert Trail, minister in Edinburgh; and, secondly, Margaret, daughter to Alexander Air, merchant in Leith[3].

Sir James was bred to the bar, and became one of the most eminent lawyers of his time. His able answer to "Dirleton's Doubts" is well known to the juridical student, and attests his professional ingenuity. In 1660 he first distinguished himself by a bold and masterly defence of his father, at that period under a government prosecution; and this so much exasperated the then rulers that he was forced to abscond. An. 1683, he was condemned and forfeited by the Privy Council, for supplying the rebels, as it was alleged, with provisions, together with his relation Sir William Denham of Westshield, Menzies of Culdares, and several others; and, two years after, they were sentenced to be exe-

---

[1] M.S. Hist. of the family; also Mar. Contr. an. 1706. [2] Mar. Contr. 1724. M.S. Hist. of the family. [3] Mar Contr. in the Charter-Chest of Coltness, 10th November 1681.

cuted as soon as they should be apprehended [1]. It will detract nothing from his reputation to add, that he was actively engaged in the same year (namely 1683) as one of the Scotch coadjutors in the Rye-House Plot, with Baillie of Jerviswood, Fletcher of Salton, and other virtuous patriots of that day [2].

During these perilous times, Sir James was obliged for the most part to keep out of the way; and he concealed himself sometimes at Allanton House, under the safe-guard of the Taylor, and sometimes even in London [3]. At last he was forced to take refuge with his brother Sir Thomas in Holland. There he soon got into favour with the well-known Pensionary Fagel, and the Prince of Orange, afterwards King William; and it fell to the lot of few private individuals to contribute more in bringing about the revolution. His political letters to Fagel, and the grand Pensionary's answer, were celebrated at the time, and he became their principal negociator at the Court of London, to which Penn had prevailed on him to come from very different motives [4]. But such were his extraordinary talents, and his unequalled address in gaining the confidence of all parties, that, although he was known to have been concerned both in the Rye-House plot, and the Duke of Monmouth's, and the Earl of Argyle's enterprizes, yet he was fully pardoned, and sent down to Scotland in 1687 as secretary of state under Lord Melfort. Notwithstanding this, by a singular coincidence, he drew up for Dykevelt, the Prince of Orange's manifesto; was appointed Lord Advocate by King William; afterwards he held the same office under Queen Anne, and in

---

[1] Records of Privy Council, ad. an. 1683, 2d April, and 1685, 13th July. See also Cruickshank's Hist. Vol. II. p. 278. Menzies said pithily of the Test, that "fools made it, and knaves took it;" a remark, of which both the sense and the wit left their sting behind them. [2] Dalrymple's Memoirs, vol. I. part 1. b. 1. p. 39. 8vo edit.

[3] In London he is said to have subsisted after a singular manner. He advertised that intricate law-cases should be solved in writing at half a lawyer's fee, namely 5s. (the fee at that time being half a guinea) and the business was transacted by means of his clerk. The solutions given were so remarkably sound and ingenious, that an investigation was set on foot to discover the author; on which he found it prudent to decamp for Scotland. M.S. Hist. of the family.

[4] M.S. Hist. of the family. Sir James's talents as a political negociator, and an able writer, are noticed by all the historians. Burnet particularly describes the flattering reception which he met with at the court of King James II. although well known to have been a bitter political enemy for more than twenty years. See Hist. vol. III. p. 164—167. D'Avaux's Memoirs. Sir John Dalrymple's Mem. of Great Britain and Ireland, vol. II. pp. 73, 18, 40, &c.

fact, had a principal management in Scotch affairs under all those different princes *.

Sir James had, by his first lady, one son and three daughters. The eldest son was James, and succeeded his father. Of the daughters, Marion, married George Lewis Scott, who became sub-preceptor to George Prince of Wales, and

* Those two eminent men, Sir James Steuart and William Penn, had nearly the same principles, and the same great object at heart, namely, the promoting the civil and religious liberty of their country, although they pursued it by opposite methods; the former, by courting popularity and aiming at power; the latter, by uniformly disdaining both. Dalrymple has preserved a characteristic anecdote of Sir James; but it is given with some additional traits in the family memoirs. Sir James, it seems, from the circumstance of constantly maintaining his ground with every party, was familiarly called "Jamie Wylie," and he took the appellation in perfect good part. At the time of the intended French invasion in 1708, the English fleet appearing suddenly at the mouth of the Forth, was mistaken at Edinburgh for the French, and with Prince Charles, of course, on board. Sir Hugh Dalrymple, the Lord President, (whose daughter had married Sir James's eldest son) was about to fly to England, and he anxiously advised Sir James to do the same: "For recollect (said he) Jamie, you drew up the Prince of Orange's manifesto." "Ay, ay, my dear, that is very true;" (replied Sir James coolly) "and who knows but I may draw up this Prince's too?"—M S. Hist. of the family.

This anecdote is characteristic of the man. The following is characteristic of the times, and paints but too truly how the laws were administered in this kingdom about a century ago. The Lord Chancellor Somers had, after many excuses on the part of this great lawyer, at length obtained his promise to gratify him with a "short account of the Scottish law," which, from such a pen, he justly conceived would be extremely valuable. When Sir James, therefore, next went to London, he put into his Lordship's hands two thick folio volumes, superbly bound and gilt, entitled, " Compend of the Law of Scotland, by Sir James Stewart, her Majesty's Advocate." The chancellor, who began to congratulate himself on possessing what he believed must be such a treasure of law and learning, eagerly opened the book, and, on turning up the first page, found these words: "Show me the man, and I'll show you the law." " Yes, (said his Lordship) a very good motto for a law-book, especially in a feudal country, where personal influence must often prove the most convincing expositor." On proceeding to the next page, and seeing the same inscription repeated, "Very good again, (said he) a true thing is never the worse for being twice told." But, to his great surprise, the entire book contained nothing else, having this significant, but oracular sentence, accurately inscribed upon every page of it! The Lord Chancellor laughed heartily at this new and ingenious method, as he said, of "abridging law-tracts;" candidly acknowledging at the same time, that, had he been called upon to speak of the law of England practically, for the greater part of the past century, he could not have characterized it more truly, or more shortly.—M.S. Hist. of the family.

Anne, married first, James Maxwell of Blawarthill, (see p. 285) and secondly, William Mure of Caldwell, and had issue. By his second lady, he had two sons and four daughters. The elder son was Henry Steuart Barclay of Collerney, in Fife; and the younger was Robert Steuart of Newmains. He married Margaret, daughter of Henry Hamilton of Swanston, brother to Lord Belhaven, and had issue. This family continued for three generations, but is now extinct. Sir James's daughters all died unmarried, or in infancy.

Sir James died an. 1713, in the office of Lord Advocate, having in the foregoing year purchased the estate of Coltness (as above mentioned) from his nephew, Sir David, and established his eldest son there. He was succeeded by that son, who became

III. Sir James Steuart of Goodtrees and Coltness. He was born an. 1681, and married, in 1705, Anne, daughter of Sir Hugh Dalrymple of North Berwick, Lord President of the court of session [1]. Sir James was an advocate. He inherited the whig principles of his family, and, like his father, early distinguished himself at the bar. In 1705, he was created a Baronet. An. 1709, he became solicitor-general for Scotland, and, in 1713, representative in parliament for the county of Mid-Lothian [2].

He had three sons and nine daughters. The 3d, James, succeeded his father; the rest died in childhood. The daughters who married, were, 1. Margaret, born 1715, who espoused Thomas Calderwood of Polton, whose eldest daughter, Anne, married James Durham of Largo, and had a numerous issue; among whom are General James Durham now of Largo, and Admiral Sir Philip Durham, K. C. B. The 2d, Agnes, was born in 1717. She married Henry David, Earl of Buchan, and had several children, namely, David Steuart, the present Earl; Henry, who became Henry Erskine of Ammondell; and Thomas, who became Lord Chancellor of Great Britain in 1806, during the Grenville administration, when he was created Lord Erskine. The 3d, daughter, Marion, was born 1723. She married Alexander Murray of Cringletie, and had two sons, 1. Alexander, and 2. James-Wolf, now Lord Cringletie, one of the senators of the College of Justice, and other children. The six other daughters of Sir James died young or unmarried.

Sir James died an. 1727, and was succeeded by his son,

IV. Sir James Steuart of Goodtrees and Coltness [3]. He was born an. 1713,

---

[1] Mar. Contr. in the possession of the family, 1705. [2] M.S. Hist. of the family. Rolls of Parliament. [3] General Retour of Sir James Steuart of Goodtrees, as son and heir to the deceased Sir James Steuart, her Majesty's Solicitor-General, 3d October 1728.

and married Lady Frances Wemyss, eldest daughter to David, Earl of Wemyss '. Like his two immediate predecessors he was bred to the bar, and early displayed superior abilities, and a commanding eloquence. Endued with a vigour of mind, not inferior to his grandfather's, he possessed more extensive views—more various acquirements—and more profound erudition, and was calculated to have risen to the head of any profession to which he had devoted his uncommon talents, had it not been for the unfortunate rebellion in 1745, in which he was suspected (notwithstanding the whig principles of his predecessors) to have been concerned; and it is believed that he acted as Prince Charles's confidential agent at the Court of France. In consequence of this, soon after the battle of Preston, he privately went abroad; and being included, with some severity, in the list of exceptions to the act of amnesty in 1747, he resided with his family in France, Germany, and Italy, for about eighteen years *.

While thus expatriated, he declined altogether to mix in political concerns. He associated every where with the elegant and the learned †, and became the author of several ingenious and able works, especially a "Defence of Sir Isaac Newton's Chronology," which he published in admirable French ‡; also, a "Dissertation on the Doctrines and Principles of Money, as applied to the German Coin." In 1763, through the interest of two kind and esteemed friends, the late Lord Barrington, and the well known Lady Mary Wortley Montague, he was allowed to return to Scotland; but a formal pardon, under

' Mar. Contr. in the Charter-Chest of Coltness, 1743.

* While he was at Spa, in August 1762, during the war with France, being suspected, though unjustly, as a spy of the British government, 200 French soldiers suddenly surrounded his house; and although in a neutral territory at the time, and owing no allegiance to France, they arrested and carried him off as a state prisoner to the fortress of Charlemont. After a close confinement there of nearly sixteen months, he was at last released, and flattering offers were then made to him to engage in the service of France in a high station. To M. Blain, the intendant of the province, who made the overture, his reply was decisive, and admirably characteristic of the man. "What I have suffered (said he) from my own nation, I had merited by my misconduct; what I have suffered, Sir, from your's, was as unjust as it was unwarrantable, and should never have been inflicted. I would as soon renounce my God, as I would relinquish my country !"—Memoirs of the family.

† Lady Mary Wortley Montague, in her posthumous letters from Italy, (August and November 1758) celebrates the powerful attractions of Sir James's and his Lady's society.—See vol. V.pp. 71, 88, &c.

‡ The Chevalier Ramsay, the late Sir James Steuart, and Mr. Gibbon, the historian, afford, perhaps, the only examples of natives of Great Britain, who published works in the French language, which, by the French themselves, are esteemed pure and correct compositions.

the great seal, was not procured for him till eight years after¹. The interval between his return home and his death was distinguished by various literary and scientific performances; and, among others, an "Enquiry into the State of the Coin and Currency of Bengal," for which the East India Company presented him with a diamond of considerable value² His great work, the "Treatise on Political Economy," delineates a system which is at once original, ingenious, and profound; and although the style is dry and didactic, and less popular than that of the posterior work of Dr. Adam Smith, it will transmit his name to future ages, both as an enlightened statesman and a philosopher, and as the undoubted father of this science in Britain *.

About the year 1756, Sir James disposed of the estate of Goodtrees to John M'Kenzie of Delvin, and it passed, nearly fifteen since, under the name of Moredun, into the hands of Mr. Meason, the present possessor³. An. 1773, on the death of Sir James's kinsman, Sir Archibald Steuart Denham, the Baronetage of Coltness was united, in his person, with that of Goodtrees; and, three years afterwards, William Lockhart Denham (successor to Sir Archibald) disponed to him the estate of Westshield.

Sir James died, an. 1780, and was succeeded by his only son,

V. Sir James Steuart, now of Coltness and Westshield. He married Alicia, daughter of . . . . Blacker, of Carrick, in Ireland ⁴; but has no issue. He is a General in the army, and Colonel of the second regiment of Dragoons, or Scotch Greys; and he represented the county of Lanark in three successive parliaments.

STEUART-BARCLAY OF COLLERNEY.

Sir James Steuart of Goodtrees, Lord Advocate of Scotland, died, as above, an. 1713, and left three sons, of whom the eldest, Sir James, succeeded his father, and the second became

¹ In the possession of the family, dated 1771. ² M.S. Hist. of the family.

* It was among the few blemishes in the literary character of the celebrated author of the "Wealth of Nations," that he disliked this great and amiable man, while he seemed to envy the superior eloquence, variety, and vigour of his conversation. What he borrowed from Sir James's writings, is without acknowledgment; and he does not even notice him as his precursor in the science; a sure proof that he considered him as a formidable rival. Smith used sarcastically to say, that " he understood something of Sir James's system from his conversation, but nothing from his book." His works, literary and philosophical, were collected and published by his son, in 6 vols. 8vo. Lond. 1805.

³ M.S. Hist. of the family. ⁴ Mar. Contract in the Charter-Chest of Coltness,

I. Henry Steuart Barclay of Collerney. He was born an. 1697 [1], and married Antonia, only daughter of John Barclay of Collerney, in the county of Fife, by whom he obtained that estate; and, in consequence, added to his own name that of Barclay [2]. He was bred to the bar, but never followed the profession. About the year 1765, he was appointed secretary to the commissioners of annexed estates in Scotland, which office he held till his death [3].

Henry had seven sons and five daughters. Of the sons two only arrived at maturity; the first, James, who succeeded to his father; and the second, William, who succeeded his brother. The eldest daughter, Margaret, was born an. 1721, and married her kinsman, James Steuart of Allanton, (the 6th of that name) and had issue as above. The rest died unmarried, or in infancy.

Henry died an. 1780, in the 83d year of his age, and was succeeded by his son

II. James Steuart-Barclay of Collerney. He was born an. 1724, and served as an officer in the army, first in Lord Rothes's, and afterwards in Sir John Bruce's regiment [4]. He was distinguished among his contemporaries as an elegant scholar and an accomplished gentleman. He died unmarried in 1780, and was succeeded by his brother,

III. William Steuart-Barclay of Collerney. He was born an. 1736; and married, first, Euphemia, daughter of John Angus, merchant in Edinburgh; and secondly, Elizabeth, daughter to Peter Hay of Leys [5]. William was bred a merchant, and became joint secretary with his father to the commissioners of annexed estates.

By his first lady, he had one son and one daughter. The son died in infancy. The daughter was Elizabeth, born an. 1759, who married, in 1779, Dr. Arthur Robertson, physician in the island of Antigua, and had issue. By his second lady William had two sons and five daughters. The eldest son was Henry, who succeeded his father. The second, Peter, died unmarried. Of the daughters, the eldest, Antonio, married Admiral John Duddingston, and has issue. The second, Lindsay, and the third, Margaret, are still unmarried. The rest died in infancy [6]. William died an. 1783, and was followed by his son,

IV. Henry Steuart-Barclay of Collerney. He was born an. 1765, and was a Captain in the Perthshire militia. He married Elizabeth, daughter to Wilson of Glasgow, but has no issue. He is presumptive heir to the two Ba-

---

[1] Disposition, by Sir James Stewart, Lord Advocate, to his lady and children, 13th April 1711, in the Charter-Chest of Allanton. [2] Mar. Contr. 1717, in do. [3] M.S. Hist. of the family. [4] Id. ibid. [5] Mar. Contracts, in possession of the family, 1756 and 1765. [6] M.S. Hist of the family.

ronetages of Coltness and Goodtrees. About the year 1787, he sold the estate of Collerney to Dr. Balfour, the present possessor,

STEUART OF ALLANBANK.

Sir James Steuart of Coltness and Kirkfield, died, as above, an. 1681. His seventh and youngest son became,

I. Sir Robert Steuart of Allanbank. He was born an. 1643, and married, first, Jean, daughter to Sir John Gilmour of Craigmillar, Lord President of the court of session; and next, Helen, daughter to Sir Archibald Cockburn of Langton[1]. He was an eminent wine merchant in Leith, and partner to his brother, Henry, at Bourdeaux, who dying without issue in 1974, Sir Robert succeeded to his fortune. An. 167 , he purchased from .... Nesbit the estate of Allanbank in Berwickshire; and in 1687 he was created a Baronet by King James II[2].

Sir Robert had, by his first lady, five sons and two daughters. The eldest son, John, succeeded his father; and the others died in infancy or unmarried. The eldest daughter, Margaret, born an. 1686, married Andrew Kerr of Morrison, and had issue. The second, Anne, born 1690, married Alexander Trotter of Kettleshield, in Berwickshire, and had issue, of whom the families of Trotter of Castlelaw, Dreghorn, and John Trotter, Esq; of London, are descended. By his second lady, Sir Robert had one son and five daughters. The son was Archibald, who became Archibald Steuart of Mitcham. The second daughter, Helen, married Sir Gilbert Elliot of Minto, Lord Justice Clerk, great-grandfather to the present Earl of Minto. The rest died in childhood or unmarried[3]. Sir Robert died an. 1707, and was succeeded by his son,

II. Sir John Steuart of Allanbank. He was born[4],   and married Margaret, daughter to . . . Kerr of Morrison[5]. He had six sons and eight daughters. The 3d, son was John, who became his father's heir and successor. All the others died unmarried, or in infancy. Of the daughters, three only were married; the 2d, Jane, to John Coutts of Edinburgh, one of the most eminent bankers of his time, and afterwards Lord Provost of that city. He was father to the present Thomas Coutts, Esq; of London, whose three daughters are the Marchioness of Bute, the Countess of Guildford, and Lady Burdett. The 4th,

---

[1] Mar. Contr. in possession of the family, 1682 and 1693. [2] Patents in the Charter-Chest of Allanbank, by King James II. [3] M.S. Hist. of the family. [4] Special Retour, Sir John Steuart of Allanbank, as son and heir to Sir Robert Steuart, 17th October 1709. [5] Mar. Contr. in the Charter-Chest of Allanbank.

Elizabeth, married her cousin, James Kerr of Morrison, and had issue. The 5th, Lillias, married William Cochrane of Gullan, and also had issue [1].

Sir John died an. 1756, and was succeeded by his son,

III. Sir John Steuart of Allanbank, (the 2d of that name). He was born an. 1714, and married Margaret Agnes, daughter to Charles Smith, wine-merchant at Boulogne [2].

Sir John was an advocate, and was appointed sheriff of the county of Berwick. About the year 1755 he obtained the office of solicitor to the stamp-office in Scotland, a lucrative situation, which, together with the sheriffship, he held till nearly the time of his death [3].

Sir John had eight sons and nine daughters. The eldest, John, succeeded his father. The 6th, Hugh Seton, held, for some years, a considerable office under the secretary of state for the home department. He married Wemyss, daughter of Sir John Dalrymple of Cousland, who died without issue. Of the daughters who arrived at maturity, the eldest, Elizabeth, married, an. 1781, the Chevalier Cicciaporci, a Roman nobleman, and has issue. She was created a Countess, in her own right, of the Holy Roman Empire, by the Emperor, Joseph II. and obtained the order of the Starry Cross. The 2d, Margaret, married Sir John Coxe Hippesley in Somersetshire, and had children. Her eldest daughter, Margaret, espoused Thomas Strangways Horner of Melles-park, in the same county, brother to the present Lady Hippesley, and has a numerous progeny. The sixth daughter was Lillias, who married Alexander Trotter of Dreghorn, in the county of Edinburgh, late pay-master of the navy, during the administration of Mr. Pitt, and has issue. The seventh, Barbara, is still unmarried. The eighth, Frances, married Colonel James Spens of Craigsanquhar, in the county of Fife, and died without issue [4].

Sir John died an. 1796, and was succeeded by his son, who became

IV. Sir John Steuart of Allanbank, (and 3d of that name). He was born an. 1754, and married his first cousin, Frances, only daughter of James Coutts of Whitsomhill, banker in London, and heiress of that estate [5]. He was, for several years, one of the commissioners of excise in Scotland.

Sir John had five sons and six daughters. The sons were, 1. John James, who succeeded his father. The 5th, Robert, is now in the civil service of the

---

[1] M.S. Hist. of the family. [2] Mar. Contr. in the Charter-Chest of Allanbank, 18th March 1752. Charter of resignation, in favour of John Steuart, son and heir to Sir John Steuart, 1755. [3] M.S Hist. of the family. [4] M.S. Hist. of the family. [5] Mar. Contr. in the Charter-Chest of Allanbank, 5th November 1778.

East India Company. The rest died without arriving at maturity. Of the daughters, the 4th, Lillias, and the 6th, Sophia, are unmarried. The others died in infancy.

Sir John died an. 1817, and was succeeded by his eldest son, who was

V. Sir John-James Steuart, now of Allanbank. He was born at Rome, an. 1779, and is unmarried.

STEUART OF MITCHAM.

Sir Robert Steuart of Allanbank died, as above, in 1707. His only son, by his second marriage, was

I. Archibald Steuart of Mitcham, who was born an. 1697, and died in August 1780. He married Grizel, daughter to John Gordon, wine-merchant in Edinburgh[1], and followed the same profession as his father-in-law, by which he acquired a large fortune. In 1745 he was elected Lord Provost of Edinburgh, and being suspected of favouring Prince Charles, and suffering the rebel army to get possession of the metropolis, he was brought to trial in the following year before the court of justiciary, but honourably acquitted[2]. From this time he transferred his business to London, and purchased the estate of Mitcham in the county of Surrey, which became the principal residence of his family.

Archibald had four sons and seven daughters. The eldest son, John, succeeded his father. The 2d, Archibald, succeeded his brother John, just now mentioned. The only daughter that married was Grace, born an. 1743, who espoused Edward Marjoribanks of Lees, and had, 1. the present Sir John Marjoribanks Bart. late Lord Provost of Edinburgh, and now representative in parliament for the county of Bute; 2. Campbell, one of the directors of the East India Company; 3. Steuart, wine-merchant in London; 4. Edward, a partner in the house of Messrs. Coutts & Co.; 5. James, in the civil service in India. He was succeeded by,

II. John Steuart of Mitcham. He was born an. 1728, and followed, like his father, the profession of a wine-merchant in London. About the year 1781, the estate of Mitcham was sold to Lord Loughborough.

John died unmarried an. 1781, and was succeeded by his brother,

III. Archibald Steuart, who was born an. 1741. He served in the regiment of Horse Guards Blue, in which he obtained the rank of Major, and married . . . . Harper, sister to Sir Henry Harper, an English Baronet.

Archibald died an. 1787, leaving issue, one daughter.

[1] Mar. Contr. in the possession of the family. [2] Account of the trial, printed in Edinburgh, 8vo. 1747.

STUART OF CASTLEMILK.

I. Sir William Stuart of Castlemilk, second son of Sir Alexander Stuart of Darnley, lived part of the 14th and 15th centuries; was killed in February 1429, in the siege of Orleans, with his brother Sir John Stuart of Darnley. He left three sons, David, Archibald, and Matthew.

II. David Stuart, eldest son of Sir William, described both as Lord of Fynart and of Castlemilk, succeeded to his father in 1429, and died before 1464.

II. Archibald Stuart, second son of Sir William, succeeded to his brother David before the year 1464: died before 1467, and was succeeded by his son,

III. William Stuart, designed Dominus de Castlemilk, in an instrument, dated 1467. He died 1470, leaving no son, and was succeeded by his uncle,

II. Matthew Stuart, third son of the first Sir William, succeeded to his nephew, and enjoyed the family estates of Castlemilk, Fynart, and Cassilton, and died in the year 1474, leaving two sons, William and John.

III. William Stuart, eldest son of Matthew, designed of Cassilton and Castlemilk, married, before the year 1466, Isabella Norvel, heiress of Cardonald, and died in 1496, leaving two sons, Alexander and John.

IV. Alexander Stuart, eldest son of William, succeeded his father in 1496, and died in 1524, leaving two sons, Archibald and James.

V. Archibald Stuart, eldest son of Alexander, succeeded his father, and enjoyed the three estates of Castlemilk, Fynart, and Cassilton, and died in 1543, and was succeeded by his son,

VI. Archibald Stuart, who married Margaret Maxwell, and died in the year   , leaving three sons, David, Alexander, and John.

VII. David Stuart of Castlemilk, eldest son of the second Archibald, married Janet Cunningham, daughter of William Cunningham of Craigends, and died in 1557, leaving two sons, Alan and Archibald.

VIII. Alan Stuart, eldest son of David, succeeded his father in 1557, and died before the end of that year without issue, and was succeeded by

VIII. Archibald Stuart, second son of David, who succeeded his brother in 1557, and married, in 1570, Janet Stuart, daughter of John Stuart of Minto, and died in 1612, having made up his titles to the estate of Castlemilk, as heir of his grandfather, Archibald, and had a charter and precept from Robert Earl of Lennox, wherein he is described his beloved cousin.

IX. Sir Archibald Stuart, eldest son of the above Archibald, succeeded his father in 1612, and married Anne, eldest daughter of Robert, the fourth Lord

Sempill. He died 12th January 1660, and had issue, two sons, Archibald, the eldest, and James, ancestor of the Stuarts of Torrance.

X. Archibald Stuart, eldest son of Sir Archibald, married, in 1684, Lady Mary Fleming, daughter of John Earl of Wigton, and predeceased his father, leaving one son,

XI. Sir Archibald Stuart of Castlemilk, heir to his father and grandfather, married, in 1666, Mary, daughter of the Master of Carmichael, and granddaughter of Lord Carmichael, created a Baronet by King Charles the II. 1668, and died in 1681, leaving four sons; William, Archibald, Daniel, of whom afterwards, and James.

XII. Sir William Stuart of Castlemilk succeeded his father, Sir Archibald, and married Margaret Crawfurd, sole heiress of John Crawfurd, Esq; of Milton, and died in 1715, leaving two sons; Archibald, the eldest, and John, the second, who succeeded to the estate of Milton.

XIII. Sir Archibald Stuart, eldest son of Sir William Stuart of Castlemilk, succeeded to his father in 1715, married Frances, daughter of James Stirling, Esq; of Keir, by whom he had one son, who died young, and left only one daughter, Anne, who afterwards married her cousin, Sir John Stuart. He died 5th January 1763.

XIII. Sir John Stuart, second son of Sir William Stuart, succeeded to the estates of Castlemilk and Fynart, on the death of his brother, Sir Archibald Stuart in 1763. He married Helen, daughter of John Orr, Esq; of Barrowfield, and died 1st April 1781, and was succeeded by his son,

XIV. Sir John Stuart, eldest son of the above Sir John, who married, in 1766, Anne, only child of his uncle, Sir Archibald Stuart: died without issue 18th January 1797, by which the male representation of the family of Castlemilk in the direct line became extinct, and the estate is now enjoyed by his widow, Lady Stuart, only child of Sir Archibald, as elder heir female.

For the above account of this family, see Genealogical History of the Stewarts, by Andrew Stuart, Esq.

N. B. The estate of Gourock, or Fynart Stewart, was sold to the present proprietor 1784, by the late Sir John Stuart of Castlemilk, the last male heir of that family in direct succession.

Arms were Or, a bend Gules, surmounted of a Fess Cheque, Argent and Azure, with a Badge of Nova Scotia in the Sinister Canton. Crest, A Dexter Hand holding a Sword, Proper. Motto, "Avant."

STUART OF FETTERCAIRN.

This respectable Cadet of the family of Castlemilk is descended thus:—

Sir Archibald Stuart of Castlemilk (No. XI. in the preceding genealogy) married, in 1666, Mary Carmichael, daughter of the Master of Carmichael. By this lady Sir Archibald had four sons, of whom the third,

I. Daniel Stuart, a Captain in the Scots Greys, then commanded by his uncle Lord Carmichael. He was also one of the Commissioners for framing the Treaty of Union in 1707. He married Margaret Wishart, the heiress and only child of Sir George Wishart of Cliftonhall, in the county of Mid-Lothian, by his first wife, Margaret Barclay of Collerney in Fife.

Sir George's Baronetage was to the heirs male of his own body, whom failing, to his heirs whatsoever, and their heirs male, by royal warrant, 19th April 1700, and patent 17th June 1706.

Daniel Stuart died in 1708, leaving three sons, George and James, who died in nonage, and William who, on the death of his grandfather, Sir George Wishart, in became

II. Sir William Stuart. He lived long abroad, married a noble Venetian lady, and died, at Paris, in December 1777, without issue.

Daniel Stuart left also three daughters, Anna, Mary, and Cordelia. Anna and Cordelia died unmarried.

II. Mary Stuart died in 1739. She was married in   to John Belsches of Invermay in Strathern, being his first wife, by whom she left an only child,

III. Emelia Belsches, who married William Belsches of Tofts, in the parish of Eccles, vicecom. Borthwick and of Belsches of that-ilk, in the parish of Liliesleaf, vicecom. Roxburgh, representative of both these ancient families, to whom she had an only son, John, who, on the death of his granduncle, Sir William Stuart, (in 1777, as above) succeeded to his title of Baronet, under the provisions in Sir George Wishart's patent, and afterwards assumed the name and arms of Stuart, in terms of a deed of settlement and entail made by his great-grandfather, Daniel Stuart, (above-mentioned) of date 7th January 1708, recorded in the general register, 18th January 1711, disponing to his children, male and female in succession, nominatum, and to their issue, a very considerable property, which he had acquired partly through his marriage with the daughter of Sir George Wishart, and partly by various lucrative employments he had enjoyed under the crown.

By this deed, it is expressly provided and declared, " that the hail heirs of " talzie, as well male as female, and the descendants of their bodies, shall be " holden and obliged to assume use and bear and constantly retain my surname " and arms of Stuart as their proper surname and arms in all time hereafter."

After the death of Sir William Stuart, (the last surviving son of Daniel) without issue, Mrs. Emelia Belsches, only child of Mary Stuart, his sister, was served and retoured heir to her grandfather, Daniel Stuart, and she and her son obtained his Majesty's Royal Warrant, dated 4th October 1797, for assuming and using the name of Stuart, in conformity to her grandfather's settlement in 1708. She died in 1807, and was succeeded by her only child.

IV. Sir John Stuart of Fettercairn, who thus became the heir of line and of Tailzie and provision of Daniel Stuart his great-grandfather. He represented the county of Kincardine in parliament, from 1797, till 1806 ; and in 1807, was appointed one of the Barons of Exchequer in Scotland. He married, in 1775, Lady Jane Leslie, eldest daughter of David Earl of Leven and Melville, by whom he had an only child,

V. Williamina, married, in 1797, to William Forbes, eldest son and heir of Sir William Forbes of Pitsligo, Bart. She died 5th December 1810, leaving issue by her said husband, two daughters and four sons.

VI. 1. Jane ; 2. Elizabeth ; 3. William ; 4. John ; 5. Charles ; 6. James-David.

CADETS OF BUTE.

I. STEWART OF BLAIRHALL, NOW OF ANNEFIELD.—Dugald Stewart of Blairhall, brother to the first Earl of Bute, was, in 1709, appointed a Lord of Session and Justiciary, by the title of Lord Blairhall, a property he acquired by marriage with Mary, the daughter of John Bruce of Blairhall, near Culross in Perthshire. His second son was,

II. John Stewart, who acquired that estate from his brother, and died in 1760. He married Lady Anne Stuart, daughter of the Earl of Moray, by whom he left three sons and a daughter. The eldest son,

III. Charles Stuart of Annefield, married Mary, daughter of Charles Wedderburn, Esq; of Gosford, by whom he had,

IV. James Stuart, in the West Indies, married, and has three sons and a daughter. The eldest son is

V. James Charles Stuart, a Captain in the army.

STEWART FULLARTON OF FULLARTON.—This family is maternally descended from the Stewarts of Ascog (whose ancestor Robert, the second son of James Stewart of Bute, by a daughter of Blair of that-ilk, branched off from that family about the year 1500.) Thus :—

I. Robert Fullarton, Esq; of Bartonholme, W. S. second son of Fullarton of that-ilk, on the 16th March 1716, married Grizel, daughter of John Stewart, Esq; of Ascog, by whom he had

II. George Fullarton of Bartonholme, Esq; who was an officer in the army, and who had seen much service, particularly in North America, in the seven years war. He married Barbara, sister of James Innes, Esq; of Warrix, by whom he had a son.

III. Stewart Murray Fullarton of Bartonholme, Esq; Colonel of the Galloway militia, who, on the death of the late Colonel William Fullarton of that-ilk, in the year 1808, succeeded as heir male to the estate of Fullarton. He married Rosetta, daughter of the above Colonel Fullarton, by whom he has issue,

IV. 1. George; 2. James; 3. John; 4. Robert; 5. Stewart; and three daughters, 1. Barbara; 2. Mary Anne; 3. Margaret.

He is also heir of line of the family of Cunninghame, Bart. of Cunninghamehead, which branched off from the Glencairn family about the year 1400. The late Colonel William Fullarton, his immediate predecessor, having been served heir to that family on the 17th December 1791.

APPENDIX.

I.

Copy of the Original Charter of the Principality of Scotland.

"Robertus, Dei Gratia, Rex Scotorum, &c. Sciatis quod concessimus charissimo Filio nostro, et Hæredi, Jacobo Senescallo Scotiæ, quod habeat, teneat et possideat, pro toto tempore vitæ suæ, omnes et singulas Terras suas Senescalliæ Scotiæ, viz. Baroniam de Renfreu cum pertinentiis suis; Baroniam de Cuninghame cum pertinentiis suis; Baroniam de Kyle Senescalli cum justis suis pertinentiis, jacen. infra Vicecomitatum de Air; Baroniam de Rathou, cum suis pertinen. Baroniam de Inerwick cum suis pertinen. jacen infra vicecomitatum de Edinburgh: totas et integras terras Insularum de Bute, Arran, Comrey Majore et Minoré: Totas et integras Terras de Couall et Knapdaill cum omnibus suis justis pertinentiis; Totas et integras Terras totius comitatus de Carricke cum omnibus suis justis pertinentiis; Totas et integras Terras de Kyle Regis cum debitis et justis suis pertinentiis jacen infra vicecomitatum de Ayr. in liberam Regalitatam &c. In cujus rei Testimonium, Præsenti Cartæ nostræ nostrum præcepimus apponi sigillum. Testibus, venerabilibus in Christo Patribus, Henrico Episcopo St. Andreæ, Gilberto Episcopo Aberdonensis Cancellario nostro, Roberto Duce Albaniæ Comite de Fyfe et de Monteith Fratre nostro germano, David de Lindesay Comite de Crawfurd, Henrico de St. Claro, Comite Orcadiæ, David Fleming de Biggar, Militibus; et Joanne Senescallo Fratre nostro naturali. Apud Perth, 10 die Decembris, annoque humanæ salutis 1404, et regni nostri anno quarto decimo [*]."

II.

Copy of a Charter from King Robert the III. as Tutor to his son the Prince, of part of the Principality.

"Robertus, Dei Gratia, Rex Scotorum, &c. Sciatis nos verum et legitimum Tutorem charissimi Filii nostri et Hæredis Jacobi Senescalli Scotiæ, cum Avisamento et consensu ipsius, nomine suo et tutorio nomine, Dedisse, concessisse, et hac præsenti carta nostra confirmasse, Willielmo Boyd Filio et Hæredi Willielmi Boyd de Badeynhath, Totas et integras Terras de Gauan et Rich (now Gavin and Reisk) cum pertinen. jacen in Baronia de Renfrew, et infra vicecomitatum de Lanerk, quæ fuerunt dict. Gulielmi Boyd de Badeynhath &c. Tenen et habend

---

[*] This charter is not to be found in record, but Lord Haddington, in his collections of decisions, 10th March 1610, says it was then extant in the register; and Sir James Balfour affirms, that this is the foundation charter of the principality of Scotland.

dictas Terras cum pertinen. dict. Willielmo Boyd filio et hæredibus suis, de Nobis et dict. filio nostro et hæredibus nostris Senescallis Scotiæ, &c. 'De Data 15to die Junii. 1405."

III.

Titles of the Prince of Wales, according to the Charters of the present day, granted by His Royal Highness as Prince and Steward of Scotland.

Georgius Augustus Fredericus, Magnæ Britanniæ Princeps; Brunswiciæ et Lunenburgi Princeps Electoralis; Walliæ Princeps; Cornubiæ et Rothesiæ Dux; Insulæ de Ely Marchio; Comes de Chester, Carrick, et Eltham; Vicecomes de Launceston; Baro de Renfrew et Snawdon; Dominus Insularum, et Scotiæ Senescallus, &c. immediatus legitimus superior terrum aliarumque subscript *, &c.

IV.

Letter from Queen Mary to Sir John Maxwell, before the Battle of Langside, 5th May 1568.

To o^{ur} Traist Friend,
Y^e. Laird of Nether Pollok.

Traist friend, we greit you weill. We dowt not bot ye knaw that God of his Gudenes has put us at libertie; quhome we thank maist heartlie.—Quhairfore desires you w^t all possible diligence faill not to be heir at us in Hamylton w^t all yor. folks friends and serwands bodin in fear of wear as ye will do us acceptable service and pleasure Because we know yor. constance, We neid no^t. at this pnt to mak langar Lre bot will byd yow fair weill.

Off Hamylton y^e. V. of Maij 1568,
(Signed)   MAIRIE R.

Letter from King James VI. to Sir John Maxwell, to attend at Holyrood House, December 1593.

" To o^{ur} right Traist friend,
The Laird of Nether Pollok, &c.

Right Traist friend, we greet you hartlie weill. It hes pleasit God, (to oure greit contentment, and we ar assurit na les to ye comoune lyking of all o^r. weill affected subiecks) to blyss us with appeirance of successioun: oure deirest bed-fellow ye Quene being w^t. chyld and neir hir tyme of delyverie, Qlk and u$''$yr wechtie effairs geving occasioune of a mair necesser deliberatioun and advyse of o^r. nobilitie and estaites, nor at any tyme heir afoir, we have maid

---

* It is now distinctly understood that the principality is strictly limited to the eldest son of the King, and cannot descend to a grandson without a new creation, as it reverts immediately to the crown, on the demise of the Prince before his father, as in the case of the late Prince Frederick of Wales, in the lifetime of his father George II. However extensive the territories are that compose this principality, the emoluments arising from it are little other than merely nominal, as they produce no revenue to the Prince, being barely sufficient to defray the expence of collecting.

speciall chose of you amangis uy"ris quhome we will desyr maist earnistlie, all excuses sett a"pte not to faill to address your selff toward ws here at halyrudhous ye XI. day of Januar nix to cum, at q^r. tyme ye sall be acqueintit with ye p"ticulars motioning your coming, qlk we assuredly luik for as ye will kyth your affectioun in yāt erand, furnishing matir of com"oun reioysing we dout nocht to you and all o^r gude subiectis, and to ye avancement of sic u"yr purposes of greit wecht and importance as ar to be treated and resolved in that conventioun Swa we committ you to Goodis blisset protectioun. From Halyrudhouse XVIII. day of December 1593.

(Signed)   JAMES R.

V.

Letter from James the VI. to the Laird of Caldwell.

To our richt traist freind the Laird of Caldwell,

Richt traist freind, we greit zow hertlie weill Having directit our other lettres unto zou of before desyring zou according to the custome observit of auld be our maist nobill Progenitours in sic caises to haif directed hither to the Queine our bedfallow ane haiknay for transporting of the Ladiis accumpanying hir Quhareuponn we upon zour stay haif tane occasionn to mervell, zit thinking to try forder the conceipt quhilk we haif of zour affectionn in furtherance of sic honourable adois as ony way is concerne ws we are movit as of befoir to visie zou be thir presentis Requeisting zou maist effectuuislie to deliver and direct hither with this berair ane haikney to quhom we haif gevin our comissonn for the samyn effect In doing quhareof ze will do ws richt acceptable pleasour to be rememberit in ony zour adois quhare we may gif zou pruif of our rememberance of zure gud weill accordinglie otherwise uponn the informationn we haif ressavit of sic as ze haif we will caus the reddiest ze haif be taine be our auctority and brocht in till ws Hoping rather ze will do zour deuitie benevolentlie Thus luikeing that our desire tending to the custome observit of auld in sic caises sall be satisfiet and the berair not returne empty we comit zou to the protectionn of God From Haliruid hous the fyrst day of October 1590.

(Signed)   JAMES R.

To our traist freind the Larde of Caldwell.

Traist freind, we greit zow weill, understanding that our weill belovit Robert Archbischope of Glasgu is to repair and travell to the visitationn of all kirkis within the boundes of his dyocis, for ordour taking and reformationn of abuses within the samyn according to his dewitie and charge. We have thairfoir thoucht gude maist affectuouslie to requeiste and desyir zow to accompany assist manteine and concur with him in all thingis requisit, tending to gude ordour and reformationn of all enormiteis, within zour boundes and Parochin And to withstainde all sic as ony way wald seame to impeid or hinder him in that behalf As ze will gif pruif of zour gude affectionn to our service and do ws accepable pleasour Thus we comit zow to God. From Falkland the 22d day of July

(Signed) JAMES R.

VI.

Transcript of the Charter by Robert II. See page 392.

Robertus, Dei Gratia, Rex Scotorum, Omnibus probis hominibus totius terrae sue Clericis et Laicis Salutem: Sciatis nos dedisse concessisse et hac praesenti carta nostra confirmasse dilecto et fideli nostro Thome de Aula surrigico tetam terram nostram quae vocat le Castelbalyr de Ruthirglen et Insulam quae vocat Insula Regis cum pertinentiis infra Vice comitatum de Lanark. Tenend habend. dicto Thoma et heredibus suis de nobis et heredibus nostris in feodo et hereditate per omnes rectas metas et divisas suas cum omnibus et singulis libertatibus commoditatibus aysiamentis et justis pertinentiis quibuscunque, ad dict. terram et Insulam spectantibus seu juste spectare valentibus in futuro libere quiete plenarie integre bene et in pace. Reddendo inde nobis et heredibus nostris dictus Thomas et heredes sui unum denarium argenti nomine albe firme ad festum pentecost. tantum pro wardis releviis maritagiis et aliis servitiis quibuscunque quas de dicta Terra et Insula praedicta cum pertinent. exegi poterunt seu requiri. In cujus rei testimonium presenti cartae magnum praecipimus apponi sigillum. Testibus Venerabili in Christo patre Gulielmo Episcopo Sancti Andreae, Johanne primogenito nostro Comite de Carrick Senescallo Scotiae, Roberto Comite de Fyffe et de Meneteth filio nostro, dilecto Gulielmo Comite de Douglas consanguineo nostro, Majistro Johanne de Peblys Archidecano Sancti Andreae Cancellario nostro, Jacobo de Lyndesay nepote nostro, et Alexandro de Lyndesay Militibus. Apud Sconam penultimo die Martij, anno Regni nostri Septimo.

VII.

Description of the Lordship of Paisley, according to the Charter by King James the VI. dated 3d May 1621, in favour of James, first Earl of Abercorn.

Burgum Baroniæ seu regalitatis et villam de Paislay, Glebariam vulgo appellatam the Mosse of Paislay cum communiis ejusdem, terras de Seidhill cum molendino, et molendino fullorum de Seidhill; terras de Wairdmedow et Walmedow, Snawdown, Hutheide, Hillheide, Garshaw et Brumlandis infra dictum burgum de Paislay; terras de Over et Nether Walkinschawis et Inches cum glebariis lie mosses; terras de Markisworth, Conyngair, Brounes aiker, Munkschaw, Munkschaw-wode, Oxschaw, Dalskeath cum silva, Netherwaird, Overwaird, Guishousland, Bernezaird, Mikilcroftis, Littil croftis, Candrins, Quhytcruick, Blackstoun cum manerio de Blakstoun et decimis; terras de Over Clayfauld, Nether Clayfauld, Over Gallowhillis, Nether Gallowhillis, Knavesland et Erclstoun cum Silva, Hillingtoun, cum maresiis seu Glebariis lie mosses; Inglistoun cum molendino earundem; terras de Grienlaw Easter et

Wester, Coraflattis Easter et Wester, Gaitflattis, Pavatland, Brablok, Lylisland, Toddisholm, Carriagehillis, Ricardsbar cum lacu, Corsbar, Dykbar, Braidlandis, Mikilriggis, Newtoun, Barscavan, Linclive cum maresia seu Glebaria, Woodsyde, Ferguslie, Richbank, Thornlie—Paislay cum nemore, Drumgrane cum molendino; terras de Granes, Auchingown et molendinum earundem, cum molendino de Fulton et multuris, &c. terrarum de Fultones; terras de Middiltoun, Linwoode, Auohenes; Rywraithes, Windiehills, Mureheid; terras de Auldhous, terras Ecclesiasticas de Eistwode, Mernis, Pollok, Neu———n, Lochwynnoche, Kilbarchan, Kilmalcolme, Rutherglen; terras de Glen vocatas Barnechis Eas... Wester, Cambe, Clockis, Linthillis, Auchenheane, Tandlemure, Bar, Brigend, Milnebank, Loc... heid, Easter Kers, Wester Kers, Jaffraystok, Barmuchlock, Mavisbank, Langatallie, Cambehill, Lorabank, Auldzaird, Langzaird, Fairhillis, Gavilmoss, Galliszairds, Clock, Langcraftis Quinsydemure, Monyabroche, cum lie Glen; Morum nuncupatum Mistielaw Mure cum piscariis super lacus de Lochwynnoche ac super aquas Quhyte Cairt Blak Cairt et Gryff: Omnia infra Regalitatem de Paislay et Baroniam de Renfrew; annuum redditum 6s. 8d. de terris de Porterfield; annuum reditum 6s. 8d. de terris de Houstoun in Baroniam de Renfrew; annuum redditum 13s. 4ds. de molendino de Renfrew; annuum redditum 15d. de tenemento in Renfrew; annuum redditum 7sh. tenemento ibidem; annuum redditum 8d. de tenemento ibidem; annuum redditum 8d. de tenemento, ibidem; annuum redditum, 5s. de terris de Monkeyle: 1 libram ceræ de terris de Kilmacolme; 1 libram ceræ de chapel lands de Renfrew; 1 libram ceræ de tenemento de Paislay; 1 libram ceræ de terris de Welmeadow; cum omnibus aliis terris, &c. monastario de Paislay spectantibus et jure regalitatis; Mansionem et Abbaciæ locum Monasterii de Paislay cum avenarum domo lie Cornehous; pistrino et horreis dicti Monasterii, et monte fabrili, vulgo appellato, The Smidie Hill; ac etiam cum horto nuncupato, The Mustert yeard nunc Pomario, alio horto, et fabri ferrarii domo communiter appellato, The Smith's house; et omnibus aliis domibus et hortis ad prædictum Monasterii locum de Paislay pertinentibus extra precinctum ejusdem—decimas Glebas, terras ecclesiasticas, &c. ecclesiarum Parochialum et Parochiarum infra scriptarum, viz. Paislay, Eistwood, Cathcart, Mernis, Neilstoun, Kilbarquhan, Lochwynnoche, Houstoun, Killelane, Kilmalcolm, Innerkip, infra dictam baroniam de Renfrew, cum advocatione predictarum ecclesiarum cum aliis terris in vice comitatibus de Ayr, Dumbarton, Peebles, Roxburgh, Lanark, Argile, Haddingtoun, Berwick and Bute. E. £133 6s. 8d. unitis in dominium baronium, et regalitatem de Paislay.

VIII.

Notes Respecting the Constitution and Records of the Burgh of Paisley.

Paisley was the seat of a Regality Court, but had no corporate rights, or separate municipal jurisdiction, till 1488, when it was erected into a Burgh of Barony, by Charter from James IV. granted to the Abbot of the Monastery of Paisley, who, as superior, was invested with the right of nominating a Provost and Magistrates. In 1490 the Abbot (George Shaw) with consent of the Chapter, disponed the Burgh, with sundry lands and privileges (in feu) to the

"Provost, Baillies, Burgesses, and Community" thereof. Subsequent grants of property and privileges were obtained by the Burgh from the Abbots and their successors, and the Burgh appears to have obtained from the Scottish Parliament, ratifications of certain rights and privileges, in 1491, and 1648.

The Abbacy of Paisley, at the Reformation, being erected into a temporal Lordship, became the property of the Abercorn, and afterwards of the Dundonald, Family. In 1658. " William Lord Cochran of Paisley, and Dundonald" by a transaction and contract entered into, between him and the Magistrates of Paisley, resigned the superiority; and the Burgh, in consequence, obtained an independent tenure from the crown, by Charter of King Charles II. in 1665.

The valuation of the Burgh lands, held of the crown, is upwards of £1000 Scots.

The jurisdiction and privileges, vested in the Magistracy and Community of Paisley, are similar and equal to those usually possessed by Royal Burghs, with the single exception of a vote in the election of a Member of Parliament.

Lands, &c. within Burgh, are held in feu, of the Magistrates, Council, and Community, and, by an ancient and peculiar practice (the validity of which has been recognised by the supreme court) investiture was given in Burgh *lands* by a very simple form. The heir, or other person holding a conveyance to lands, and desiring to be entered or invested in place of the ancestor or granter of the conveyance, appeared personally, or by attorney, and in the usual manner, made symbolical resignation of his right in the hands of the magistrates, for the purpose of obtaining what is termed " new and heritable booking." This booking consists in the registry of the res gesta (including a description of the lands, and a statement of the nature of the parties right, in connection with the person last " booked,") in the Record or Chartulary of the Burgh, and an authenticated copy, or extract of registry, under the hands of the Town Clerk, was held to complete the investiture, without Charter, Sasine, or any other written instrument. This practice, however, became exposed, in progress of time, to great inconveniences, and is now little resorted to, except in the transmission of property in the different churches.

Among a great number of Charters, and other ancient documents in the Charter-Chests of the Burgh, the following may be noticed.

Charter of Confirmation dated, at Linlithgow, on 5th April 1396, by King Robert the III. whereby he " For the welfare of his own soul, and the souls of his ancestors and succes-
" sors, Kings and Stewards of Scotland," gives and confirms " to God and the blessed Virgin
" Mary, and to the blessed James the Apostle, and St. Mirrin the Confessor, also to the Abbot
" and Monks of Paisley, now and to come, all and whole their lands, rents, and possessions in
" our Barony of Renfrew, situated within the county of Lanark : Also all their lands, rents,
" and possessions, in our Barony of Kyle-Stewart, lying within the Shire of Ayr; and their
" five Merk lands of Moll and Huntlaw, and the lands of Hassynden, within the Shire of
" Roxburgh : and their lands of Orde, within the Shire of Peebles, into one entire and free
" Barony, and in pure and perpetual Regality," to be held " by the said monks and their
" successors for ever, of us and our heirs, with power of holding courts, infang-and thief, and
" outfang-and thief," &c. but " reserving the four pleas of the Crown." All other proprietors

of Regalities are prohibited from interfering with the jurisdiction of the Grantees; the Return required for the grant is the prayers of the monks.

Charter by King James the II. dated, at Edinburgh, on 13th January 1451, by which he ratifies the Charter of King Robert III. and the grant of the lands therein described, and farther confirms certain letters of confirmation, "made and granted by the late Malcom, *and* " Malcom, Earls of Lennox, to God, the blessed St. Mirrin, and the Abbot and Convent of " the Monastery of Paisley," of the lands of Kilpatrick, and other lands in the Earldom of Lennox, within the county of Dunbarton, and erects the whole into one Barony and Regality. This grant confers the four pleas of the Crown, which King Robert had reserved; but retains the right to the prayers in behalf of the granter and his successors.

Charter dated, " at Halierude-house" 3d January 1576, by King James the VI. with the consent of James Earl of Morton, Lord Dalkeith, Regent, and Lords of the Privy Council, whereby he, upon the narrative of the good conduct of his subjects, and particularly of the Burgh of Paisley, and because it became him to provide for the erection of a school in the Burgh, "for the initiation of youth in learning and good morals, not only that they might be " useful in the of service God, but in the service of the Burgh," grants and conveys to the Baillies, Councillors, and Community of Paisley, and their successors, " all and whole the altarages " of the Chapels, the lands and manse after-mentioned, farms, annual rents, profits " and duties of the same, pittances, obit silver and common duties under-specified, lying in " the Burgh, parish, and liberty of Paisley, viz. the altarage of St. Mirrin and Columba, " the altarage of St. Ninian, the altarage of the Virgin Mary, the altarage of St. Nicolas, " altarages of St. Peter, St. Catharine, and St. Anne, the Chapel of St. Rock, and the seven " roods of land, or thereby, of the said Chapel, belonging to the same, together with the other " pittances of obit silver or commons, which formerly the Monks of Paisley were in use to " levy and receive; with power to the Baillies, Council, and Community, and their suc" cessors, and their collectors to receive the subjects conveyed in the same way as any pre" bendaries or chaplains could formerly, for the repair and support of a Grammar School, " and support of a Master or Preceptor for the instruction and erudition of youth of the " Burgh and neighbourhood." In terms of the grant, forty merks annually, are to be paid to four poor boys, natives of the Burgh, remaining in the school during the space of five years, and on expiry of that term, and removal of these boys, others are to be put in their place by the Baillies and Council, and the same payment made. The subjects conveyed and confirmed are erected into one body (" corpus") to be called " the King's Foundation of the Grammar School of Paisley," " (Fundationem nostram Scolæ Grammaticalis de Paisley nuncupandam.") Among the witnesses to this Charter appears " our familiar Councillor, Mr. George Bu" quhanane, Pensioner of Corsraguel, Keeper of our privy seal,"

The records or minute books of the Town Council, which are, with little exception, entire from the year 1594, bear distinct references to others of more ancient date now lost, and afford many curious and minute illustrations of the usages of other times, and of the powers exercised by the Council of making acts for the government of the inhabitants.

On the 30th September 1594, an act anent peat stealers was passed, and warrant given to search houses; the peats if found, and not properly accounted for, to be seized, and parties punished, " conform to auld acts made thereanent."

An act of the same date, prohibiting freemen from cutting turfs for rigging, without leave from " baith Baillies;" and unfreemen, without leave of " the Baillies, and maist of the Council," and in the latter case, the Baillies were to be punished at the sight of the Council, if they gave liberty without their concurrence.

In courts held by the Bailies and Council that year, various decrees were passed, whence it appears, that the price of a boll of oat-meal was £4; a threave of oat-straw, 2s. 6d.; a peck of bear, 5s. 6d.; a day's work of two horses, 8s. 6d.; a ewe sheep, 3s. 4d.; a boll of white oats, nine merks 6s. 8d.; a boll of black oats, £4; half a boll of grey corn, 33s.; the fee of a servant maid for half a year, four merks; a boll of malt, twelve merks; plowing an acre of ground, £3; an Angel of gold, £20; a peck of groats, 20s.; a barked hyde, 30s. 8d.; a fourth part of linseed, 6s. 8d.; a side of mutton 11s.; and five quarter fine violet London claith, £10. 16s. 8d. All Scots money.

In 1596, a brief from the " Chancery of Paisley," was directed to the Baillies, to serve William Urie, heir of his brother: and in 1597, the Council passed an act for " warding," i. e. imprisoning, debtors, who had no effects to poind.

8th July 1597. " The which day, the said Baillies and Council understanding perfectly, that the Queen's Majestie is to be shortly in the Place of Paisley, and in respect thereof, for decorations of the kirk and ports of the said burgh, in such sort as may be goodlie done for the present, they have concluded, that there be ane painter sent for to Glasgow, for drawing of some draughts in the kirk, as shall be thought most necessary for the present: secondly, that ane wricht be conducit with, for bigging, mending, and repairing of the ports of the said burgh."

9th March 1602 " Sir James Sempil, Knt. admitted Sheriff Substitute, in presence of the Honourable the Master of Paisley, upon a commission from Robert Lord Sempil, Sheriff Principal of Renfrewshire, and Robert Vass appointed to be Sheriff Clerk.

11th October 1604. Enacted by the Council, " that he that shall happen to give his " nibour the lee, shall pay a fine of forty shillings; and he who gives his nibour a drye cuff, " shall pay five pounds; and the committer of bluid, ten punds."

In 1604, the teacher of the Grammar School was allowed a salary of 100 merks: 40 merks to be paid by the " Master of Paisley," 40 punds by the Baillies and Council, and 13s. 4d. quarterly, by each of the scholars.

By an act in same year, merchants were obliged to shut their doors every Tuesday, during prayers, and to attend church for hearing the word, under the pain of 8s.

Ordered in 1608, that ane silver bell be procured with all diligence for ane horse race yearly, within the burgh; the bounds and the day for running thereof, to be set down by advice of My Lord Earl of Abercorn, Lord Paisley and Kilpatrick.

On 24th June, same year, it was statuted and ordained, that the whole burgesses and inhabitants thereof, specially burgesses, should give their musters sufficiently armed with jak, stailbannett, plet sleives, speir or halbert; and ilk person to give his oath, that the same was their own proper armour, under the pain of ten punds.

16th September 1606.—In presence of James, Earl of Abercorn, with the bailies and council of the burgh, a great number of persons were brought before them for yard breaking;

several of them fined in five punds of money, and put in the stocks, at the Mercate Cross, from ten to twelve; and others to be taken by their parents to the Mercate Cross at same time, with a paper on their head, the space foresaid, and thereafter to be scourged by their said parents, to the effusion of their blood.

29th January 1607, an act passed against any person setting a house to a stranger till they advertise the bailies and council, and have their liberty.

Enacted in 1618, that no merchant within the burgh open his buith door on the Sabbath day to sell any wares, under the pain of an unlaw of 40s.

In 1623, the bailies, with three or four of the council, were appointed to ride to Glasgow, and speak to the provost and bailies thereof, anent the troubling the merchants of this burgh, in using of their calling and trade of merchandize.

On 24th January 1642, an act was made, that no houses be set to persons excommunicated, and that nane entertain them in their house under a pain of ten punds.

Ordered, in 1646, that forty men go to Glasgow with spades, mattocks, and shovels, to-morrow morning, and work four days at the Forts; and that each man get two merks for his trouble, from those who do not go.

On 7th October 1647, the Provost of Glasgow made application to have the College accommodated in Paisley during the plague, which was agreed to.

On the 4th January 1655, the council nominated one of their number to go with all expedition to Edinburgh or Dalkeith, to General Monk, commander in chief of the forces, and to supplicate him for liberty to choose magistrates, and administer justice, and do others of the town's necessary affairs, in respect that one of the Bailies was dead, and the other, to all appearance, dying, and they like to have no obedience of the inhabitants. And, with the General's approbation, but under the superintendence of Sir George Maxwell of Pollok, magistrates were elected in the course of said Month.

In November 1655, the excise of the town and parish was farmed to the bailies and council, at £12 Sterling monthly; and they engaged two collectors at 20s. Sterling per month.

1664, October 19th, " whilk day it is statute be the bailies and council, that whatsomever person hereafter, burgess or inhabitant, liable in payment of any of the town's gudes, and shifting and delaying to do the same, shall have the key of the tolbuith door sent to them by the treasurer, for entering in ward, and remaining therein aye and while they pay that which they shall be liable unto, and that within the space of twenty-four hours after the sending said key; and in case they fail, the officers, as they shall answer upon their peril, shall, upon the first sight of them, put them in ward, therein to remain aye and while they satisfy the debt."

IX.

Supplementary Notices respecting Renfrewshire.

COURTS, PRISONS, &c.

TOWN OF RENFREW.—The burgh of Renfrew, being the only royal burgh of the county, is deemed the head burgh; and there is no reason to doubt that it was the seat of the sheriff court for some time after the barony of Renfrew was erected into a sheriffdom by Robert the III. in 1404. As head burgh, it is the legal place of assembly for the county freeholders, at their annual Michaelmas head courts, and meetings for election of members to parliament; and for the commissioners of supply, at their general annual meeting, for assessing the land-tax, on 30th April. In this county, the Michaelmas head courts of freeholders are held on the second Tuesday after Michaelmas.

The general quarter sessions of the justices of peace are also necessarily held in Renfrew; for though not expressly directed by statute, it has been so decided by the supreme court *. Crawfurd states, that in his time the quarter sessions were held in Paisley; if so, they must have been transferred to Renfrew prior to 1730; for of that date, there is extant a record of their proceedings at Renfrew. But though the particular meetings of justices and commissioners of supply alluded to, must be held at Renfrew, that rule does not apply to adjourned quarter sessions, and these, or other meetings, which are generally held in Paisley.

From the circumstance of the commissioners of supply being nominated by statute, and having a convener elected by themselves, the landholders of Scotland, (who are usually commissioners of supply, if possessed of £100. Scots of valued rent) find it convenient to assemble in this recognized character when any matter of public interest renders it expedient for their convener to call them together. The present convener is Archibald Campbell, Esq; of Blytheswood, who was chosen in 1816, on the decease of the former convener, George Houstoun, Esq; of Johnstone.

The Town House of the burgh of Renfrew, besides the county court room, contains a small prison. The magistrates are in use to hold a weekly court on Saturday, (being the burgh market day) but no practitioners in the law reside in the burgh; and the cases most commonly brought before the magistrates are such as, by the usage of royal burghs, are decided without the intervention of written procedure.

Crawfurd quotes the date of a charter granted by James Lord High Steward of Scotland, (grandfather of King Robert the II.) to prove that this nobleman had his residence at the ancient Castle of Renfrew; but it distinctly appears, from the volume of ancient charters, lately published from the register of the great seal, that King Robert II. did himself reside at Renfrew, both before and after his accession to the crown.

Town of Paisley.—It is not common that the sheriff court of a county should be held elsewhere than in the head burgh; but Crawford has merely mentioned the fact, that this Court was held in Paisley, without giving any information as to the cause; and it remains a subject of enquiry how, and at what period, Renfrew ceased to be the seat of that court, which, though not noticed by Crawford, it undoubtedly once was.

The Town Council records of Paisley, lately explored, show, that, in 1602, Sir James Sempil, knight, was there admitted sheriff substitute, by commission from Robert Lord Sempill, the sheriff principal; and, from the silence of the record, it may be presumed that this was not the first appointment of the kind.

According to Crawford, the office of heritable sheriff was granted by Robert the III. to one

* The quarter sessions are appointed by statute to be held on the first Tuesday of March, May, and August, and last Tuesday of October.

APPENDIX. 507

of the family of Sempill in 1404, (the date at which the barony of Renfrew was erected into a sheriffdom); and the office of heritable bailie of the regality of Paisley * was conferred, by the abbot of Paisley, on another of that family in 1545. The union of these offices in the same family, must have rendered it a matter of evident convenience, that the actual duties of both should be discharged by the same person, in the same place. It would have been incompatible with legal principles, that the courts of the regality should be transferred from Paisley to Renfrew, because the latter was not situated within the bounds of the regality; but there was nothing to prevent the sheriff court from being held in Paisley. It is therefore probable that Paisley became the seat of both courts soon after 1545.

It is stated by Crawford that both of these heritable jurisdictions were acquired by Alexander Earl of Eglinton from Hugh Lord Sempill in 1636, but it appears from the retour of Robert Lord Sempill in 1648, and from that of Hugh Earl of Eglinton in 1661, that the right then acquired by Lord Eglinton was not absolute, but redeemable. In the first of these retours the heritable offices are described as still pertaining to the family of Sempill, and in the latter retour they are stated to be held by Lord Eglinton, along with other subjects, during the "non-payment," *i. e.* in security of "£.5000 Sterling." The Earl of Eglinton received a compensation from Government for this Office, at the abolition of heritable jurisdictions in 1747.

The last person who performed the duties of these offices, by deputation from the Earl of Eglinton, was Mr. Henry Maxwell; and the oldest record extant of the proceedings of these courts, (commencing in 1739) shews that, in conducting the judicial business of the two jurisdictions, little distinction had been observed between them. The record is intitled "Minutes of the Sheriff-Court of Renfrew and Baillie-Court of the Regality of Paisley."

Since the abolition of heritable jurisdictions, the following persons have been Sheriffs Depute of the county, holding commission directly from the crown, and Sheriffs Substitute, holding commission from the Sheriffs Depute.

SHERIFFS DEPUTE.	SUBSTITUTES.
1. Charles M'Dowall, Esq; of Crichen, advocate—commission dated 18 March 1748. Resigned in 1787.	Mr. Thos. Simpson, com. dated 15 Dec. 1748.
	John Campbell, . . . 12 Aug. 1754;
	Robert Paterson, . . . 24 June 1760.
	Hugh Kerr, ... 2 Aug. 1762.
	Robert Paterson, . . . Nov. 1776.
2. Allan M'Connochie, Esq; advocate, afterwards Lord Meadowbank—27 Dec. 1787.	James Blair, ... 4 June 1781.
	James Orr, . , . . . 4 Sept. 1788.
3. John Connel, Esq; advocate, now Judge admiral of Scotland—22 March 1796.	David Hutcheson, . . . 1 Aug. 1796.
	Alex. Campbell, present sheriff sub. } . 4 Aug. 1802.
4. John Colin Dunlop, Esq; advocate, 20 July 1816, present sheriff depute.	Claud Marshall, additional sheriff sub. at Greenock } , May 1815.

† It may be noticed that the regality of Paisley was an extensive jurisdiction, comprehending the domains of the monastery, not only in this county, but in the counties of Ayr, Dumbarton, and others, and had been erected while the barony of Renfrew was yet a district of the sheriffdom of Lanark or Clydesdale.

The number of acting procurators before the sheriff court, at Paisley, is 29.

The prison of Paisley has long been the chief gaol of the county, and is considerably larger than that of Renfrew; but such has been the progress of commerce, manufactures, and population, that these prisons have become quite inadequate for the proper confinement and separation of the numerous prisoners which they are obliged to receive.

The want of a county bridewell or correction-house has been also much felt; for though one was appointed by the act of Parliament, 1672, to be erected in Paisley for the county of Renfrew, the injunction, like many others of the Scottish parliament, was never carried into execution.

The subject of prisons has of late years excited national attention, and, with accustomed liberality, the landed gentlemen of Renfrewshire joining with the magistracy of Paisley, applied for, and obtained an act of parliament in 1815, "for erecting and maintaining a bridewell, "gaol, court house, and public offices for the burgh of Paisley and county of Renfrew." The funds provided by this act were, however, found inadequate for the intended purposes, and a supplementary act has within these few weeks been obtained. The sum of £23,500, is authorised to be levied by assessment, for the purposes of the act, and £2000 more is to be contributed from the corporation funds of the burgh. The management is vested in commissioners. Plans of the intended buildings, upon a respectable scale, with a handsome exterior in the castellated stile, have been obtained from Mr. Elliot, architect of the Edinburgh national gaol, &c.; an area of considerable extent, in a central situation, contiguous to the west bank of the river, between the two lower bridges of Paisley, has been selected as the site; and it is expected that the building will be commenced in the course of the present year. Besides gaol, bridewell, and court house, the buildings are to contain, a county hall, record room, apartments for the sheriff clerk, and Justice of peace clerk, cess office, and depot for the arms, &c. of the county militia; and also a council chamber and apartments for the town clerk and chamberlain of the burgh of Paisley, and for the commissioners of police.

GREENOCK.—The great and increasing importance of Greenock, and the very limited baronial jurisdiction of its magistrates, produced an application to government for having a sheriff substitute settled there; the application was favourably received, and a salary allowed for an additional sheriff substitute. The towns and parishes of Greenock and Port Glasgow, and the parish of Innerkip, were appointed to form a separate judicial district, termed the "Lower Ward of Renfrewshire," and a regular sheriff court was established in Greenock, in May 1815, for that district. Mr. Claud Marshall was appointed sheriff substitute; and soon after received a commission as deputy admiral for the convenience of maritime business.

These changes rendered it expedient that the prison belonging to the magistrates of Greenock should be declared a public gaol, in so far as respected the reception and custody of prisoners, committed by warrant of the sheriff and justices of peace resident in that quarter; which was accordingly done by a clause in the county gaol and bridewell act 1815.

PORT GLASGOW.—The prison of Port Glasgow belongs exclusively to that burgh.

Miscellaneous Notices.

The following notices may serve as additional illustrations of the rapid progress of public improvements in this populous and busy district. Within the short period which has elapsed of the present century, acts of Parliament have been obtained by the towns of Paisley, Greenock, and Port Glasgow, for paving, lighting, and cleansing streets, introducing various regulations of police, and defraying the expence by assessment of the inhabitants.—Foot-paths have been formed along the principal roads, a valuable acquisition hitherto unknown —Two sick hospitals, or infirmaries, one in Paisley, the other in Greenock, as (already noticed) have been founded and maintained by benevolent contributions. That of Paisley is termed the House of Recovery, and its peculiar object is the prevention and cure of contagious diseases among the poorer classes; among whom when once begun, contagion is so apt to spread. It is united with a dispensary of medicines; and, at this time, fever being unusually prevalent, it affords accommodation to more than 40 fever patients.—Provident banks also have been established in Paisley and Greenock, an institution very lately introduced to public notice by the Rev. Mr. Duncan, minister of the parish of Ruthwell, which, for its beneficent influence upon the habits of the labouring classes has already received universal approbation and legislative protection. A safe deposit is thereby afforded for the smallest savings, and interest allowed. The amount of deposits in the Paisley provident bank, established in 1816, at last balance, was L.1247 16s. 10d. chiefly belonging to females.—Public libraries also have been founded in these towns. Those of Greenock have been formerly noticed. The principal one in Paisley contains 3000 volumes, and there are others of respectable extent belonging to operative tradesmen, whose avidity for reading has long been remarked as a distinguishing characteristic.—The spacious coffee-room, lately erected in Paisley, may vie, in appearance, with any other in Scotland.

The revenue from the post-office of Paisley, for the year 1817, amounted to L.3164 3s.— a sum far inferior to that arising from Greenock. The difference between a manufacturing and a commercial population, accounts for a circumstance so oppoite to what the relative size of these towns would have indicated.

The following villas, in the vicinity of Paisley, namely, Greenlaw, Kibble, Esq; Corseflat, Brown, Esq; Whitehaugh, Gerard, Esq; and Barshaw, Smith, Esq; on the road towards Glasgow; Gateside, Burns, Esq; and Sandyford, Caldwell and Gardner, Esqrs; on the road towards Renfrew; Nethercommon, Jamieson, Esq; and Merksworth, Maxwell, Esq; on the road towards Inchinnan; Woodside, Sheddan, Esq; and Ferguslie, Wilson, Esq; on the road towards Beith and Johnstone, render these different approaches towards the town highly interesting.

X.

Commission of the Peace for the County of Renfrew, dated 26th March 1818.

Those marked thus (*n*) were not in the last commission. Freeholders are marked *F.* and Commissioners of Supply, *Com.*

Hugh Earl of Eglinton.
George Earl of Glasgow.
n William Shaw Earl of Cathcart.
n Archibald Hamilton, Esq; commonly called Lord Archibald Hamilton, F.
Robert Walter Lord Blantyre.
n Robert Montgomery Lord Belhaven and Stenton.
n James Boyle, Esq; commonly called Lord Viscount Kelburn, eldest son of the Earl of Glasgow.
Archibald Lord Douglas of Douglas.
n Charles Cathcart, Esq; commonly called Lord Viscount Greenock, eldest son of the Earl of Cathcart.
n The Hon. Archibald Douglas, eldest son of Lord Douglas, F. and Com.
The Hon. Charles Stewart, sometime residing at Erskine House, Com.
n The Hon. Colonel Patrick Stewart.
n The Hon. Colonel William Stewart.
n The Hon. Colonel Charles Douglas.
Sir Robert Crawford of Jordanhill, Bart. F. and Com.
Sir Michael Shaw Stewart of Blackhall, Bart. F.
Sir John Maxwell of Pollok, Bart. F. and Com.
Major-General Sir Thomas Brisbane, Knight Commander of the Bath, F. and Com.
John Airston of Greenhill, Com.
Andrew Anderson, Greenock.
James Anderson, Greenock.
James Adam of Burnfoot and Barr, F.
Boyd Alexander of Southbar, F. and Com.
Archibald Buchanan of Hillington, F. and Com.

n ―― Buchanan, younger of Hillington.
James Buchanan of Northbar, F. and Com.
Herbert Buchanan of Arden.
Robert Barclay, Paisley.
George Brown of Capelrig, F. and Com.
William Blair of Blair, F. and Com.
Thomas Bissland, Greenock.
n James Barclay, Port Glasgow.
n Matthew Brown of Corseflat
n Charles Montolien Burgess of Beauport, F.
n The Hon. Archd. Campbell of Succoth, one of the Senators of the College of Justice, F. and Com.
John Craig of Kirkton, Com.
Archibald Campbell of Blackhouse, F. and Com.
n Alexander Campbell, Paisley.
n Hugh Crawford, at Cartsburn, Greenock.
John Cunningham of Craigends, F. and Com.
n William Cunningham, younger, of Craigends.
n William Carlisle, Paisley.
William Cochran of Ladyland, Com.
Archibald Campbell of Blytheswood, F.
Charles Cunningham of Cairncurran, F. and Com.
William Clark, at Johnstone or Glasgow.
n David Connel, Weemsbay.
n James Crum of Thornlybank, F.
n John Crum of Thornlybank.
n Duncan Campbell, at Millholm, Cathcart.
n Mungo Campbell of Hagtonhill.
n The Rev. David Dow of Braidbar.
James Dunlop of Househill, F. and Com.
Duncan Darroch of Gourock, F. and Com.
n Malcolm Darroch, younger of Gourock.
Alexander Dunlop, at Greenock.

APPENDIX. 511

n John Dunlop, at Greenock.
n John Dunlop, Port Glasgow.
n Henry Dunlop of Arthurlie.
n James Ewing of Keppoch.
n Robert Ewing, Greenock.
Malcolm Fleming of Barrochan, F. and Com.
William Fleming, younger of Barrochan, Com.
Archibald Falconer, Port Glasgow.
Robert Fulton of Hartfield, F. and Com.
Robert Fulton, younger of Hartfield, F. and Com.
William Fulton of Park, F. and Com.
Henry Fulton, younger of Park, Com.
n William Fulton, Paisley.
n James Foster of Laigh Auchinleck.
Alexander Graham of Ferenize, Com.
n Patrick Graham, younger of Limekilns
James Gemmill of Countesswells, Greenock, Com.
William Cunningham Cunningham Graham of Gartmore, F. and Com.
n Robert Buntin Graham, younger of Airdoch.
n Robert Gillespie, Port Glasgow.
n John Gordon of Aitkenhead.
n Alexander Graham of Craigbait, Com.
n Richard Henderson of Middleton, Com.
James Hamilton of Holmhead, F. and Com.
n William Charles Hamilton of Garvocks and Craiglaw, F. and Com.
n John Harvey of Castlesemple, F.
n James Hunter, Greenock.
n James Hill of Busbie.
Ludovic Houstoun of Johnstone, F. and Com.
n George Houstoun, younger of Johnstone.
n William Houstoun, second son of George Houstoun, late of Johnstone.
n John Howie of Shawhill and Hazleden, F. and Com.
n John Hamilton of Greenbank.

n Dr. James Jeffray, Glasgow, F.
n David Johnstone, Port Glasgow.
n Oliver Jamieson of Nethercommon.
n James Kibble of Whiteford, F.
n Adam Keir, Paisley.
n James King of Millbank.
n Alan Ker, Greenock.
William Lowndes of Arthurlie, F. and Com.
Walter Logan of Fingalton, F. and Com.
n Quintin Leitch, Greenock.
n James Leitch, Greenock.
n Major James Lee, residing at Castlesemple, F.
n The Rev. George M'Latchie, D. D. of Humbie, F.
William Mure of Caldwell, F. and Com.
William Mure, younger of Caldwell, Com.
William Maxwell of Bredieland, F. and Com.
n James Maxwell, younger of Bredieland, Com.
William M'Kerrell of Hillhouse, F.
n Fulton M'Kerrell, Paisley.
n John Maxwell, younger of Pollok, F. and Com.
n Andrew Moody of Muirshields.
n James Murdoch at Auldhouse, F.
n William M'Knight Crawford of Cartsburn, F. and Com.
William M'Dowall of Skiff Park, Greenock, Com.
William M'Dowall, late of Walkinshaw, &c. F. and Com.
John Maxwell of Dargeval, F. and Com.
n William Maxwell, second son of the late John Maxwell of Dargeval.
John Mair of Plantation, Glasgow, F. and Com.
Sir William Milliken Napier of Napier, F.
n William M'Fie, younger of Langhouse, Com.
n William Napier of Blackstoun, F.

512   APPENDIX.

n Michael Stewart Nicolson of Carnock, F.
n Robert Orr of Ralston.
John Orr, Paisley.
George Oswald of Scotstoun and Anchincruive, F. and Com.
n Captain James Oswald of the Royal Navy.
n James Oughterson, Greenock.
Thomas Pollock of Fawside, Com.
n Allan Pollock younger of Fawside, Com.
Robert Pollock of Walton.
Gavin Ralston of Ralston, F. and Com.
James Robertson, Greenock.
n George Robertson, Greenock.
Archibald Speirs of Elderslie, F. and Com.
n Alexander Speirs, younger of Elderslie.
n Thomas Dundas Speirs, second son of Archibald Speirs of Elderslie.
n Peter Speirs of Culcroich, F. and Com.
n Archibald Smith of Jordanhill, F. and Com.
n James Smith, younger of Jordanhill, F. and Com.
n Captain Heustoun Stewart of the Royal Navy, F.
n Robert Smith of Barshaw.
n John Shaw Stewart of Over Johnstone, F.
n Robert Stewart of Finnart, Greenock.
n James Stewart of Williamwood.

William Stewart, at Greenlaw, Paisley.
n Robert Thomson of Camphill, F. and Com.
John Wilson of Thornly, F. and Com.
n William Wilson at Cowglen, F.
Robert Wallace of Kelly, F. and Com.
n Captain James Maxwell Wallace, younger son of the late John Wallace of Kelly, F.
Nathan Wilson, Greenock.
n James Watt, Cartsdyke.
n Captain Alexander Young, Paisley.
The Sheriff Depute of the Shire of Renfrew, for the time being.
The Sheriff Substitute, residing at Paisley, for the time being, Com.
n The Sheriff Substitute, residing at Greenock, for the time being.
The Provost and two Bailies of the Burgh of Renfrew, for the time being, Com.
The Provost and three Bailies of the Burgh of Paisley, for the time being, Com.
The two Bailies of Greenock, for the time being, Com.
The two Bailies of Port Glasgow, for the time being, Com.
n The Provost of Pollokshaws, for the time being.

APPENDIX.

The following authentic Memoir, respecting the family of Ross, came too late to be inserted in its proper place, (page 324) and is considered as a document of importance, because it relates to persons of distinction, who, for many centuries had, and still have, property and residence in this county.

ROSS PEDIGREE.

The English Rosses, lords of the baronies of Wark and Belvoir, whose principal estates now centre in the house of Rutland, acquired, at an early period, property in the south of Scotland, and were nearly allied to the royal family of that kingdom.

From the complete similarity of their arms, and this connection, the Rosses of Tarbart and Halkhead have always been regarded as a branch of that family; though, at this distance of time, the precise relationship cannot easily be ascertained.

They certainly had fixed themselves in Ayrshire, as vassals of the Morvilles, soon after the middle of the 12th century; for Sir James Dalrymple expressly says, that he had seen a charter by Richard de Morville, Constable of Scotland, " Henrico de Sancto Claro," of the lands of Hirdmanston, which charter (he adds) must have been granted in the beginning of Richard Morville, who succeeded his father Hugh in the year 1162. Among the witnesses are " Robertus filius Warnebaldi" (the first of the family of Glencairn) and " Godefridus de Ros." Crawfurd, the author of this History, also affirms, in his M.S. Baronetage, that Godfrey de Ros, Reginald de Ros, and James, his brother, test another grant of the same personage to the ancestor of the family of Loudon, in the reign of King William the Lion.

Robert de Ros and Allan de Ros witness a charter, by Allan, the son of Rolland, Constable of Scotland and Lord of Galloway, who lived in the 13th century, to Hugh Crawfurd, of the third part of the village of Stevenston.

Godfrey de Ros is witness to a charter, by John de Lamuelston " Hugoni de Crawfurd" of the lands of Cousland, in the year 1245; also to another by " Hugo de Crawfurd, filius Hugonis de Crawfurd," to Reginald, his brother, of the lands of Kerse, in the reign of Alexander III [1].

These individuals, whose existence may be found by other evidence, were thus closely connected with the county of Ayr, and their estates are known to have been situated in the district of Cunningham, and consisted of Tarbart, Cunninghamhead, Montgrenan, Stewarton, &c. and Stonehouse in Lanarkshire.

Sir Godfrey de Ros, sheriff of Lanarkshire (see chartulary of Kelso) confirms, in the year 1280, under the designation of " Godefridus de Ros miles, filius et hæres domini Godefridi de Ros," a portion of Stewarton, in Cunningham, formerly disponed by a Sir John de Ros to the House of Paisley. He, and his son Godfrey, figure much in the public transactions of the period. They both swore fealty to Edward I. in 1296.

---

[1] M.S. Baronetage of Scotland by Crawfurd. (p. 392) " These writs are in the hands of the Earl of Loudon, which I have seen." Crawfurd.

514   APPENDIX.

Sir Godfrey de Ros, sheriff of Ayr, "*the son*," (see Hailes' Annals, vol. i. p. 314.) so called, in contradistinction to the father, does not appear to have lived long after the year 1300 [1].

His successor, though probably not his son, Sir Godfrey de Roos, also sheriff of Ayr, was extremely vacillating in his public conduct. Fordun informs us, that, in the year 1335, " Godefridus de Ros Vicecomes de Ayre, post tamen aliquam resistantiam, cum universitate de " Carrick Conyngham attractus, seu coactus, placuit senescalli se subdere legi." which circumstance is thus recorded by Wynton,

> Schyre Gotheray ye Ross wes yan
> In Cwnynghame, and Inglis man
> Wes ane Schyrrawe of Are alswa:
> On him richt smertly can yai ga;
> And quhat for lawe, and quhat for awe,
> Til Scottis Pes yai can him drawe,
> So yat in-til a litel qwhyle
> Carryk, Cwnynghame, and Kyle,
> A gret (part) have (beene) wonnyn yen,
> And worthyd all hale Scottismen.

He, finally, adhered to the Baliol or English interest, and thereby forfeited his estates in Scotland [2]. He retired to England, where he spent the remainder of his days. In the year 1341 he obtained from Edward III. at the solicitation of Henry of Lancaster, Earl of Derby, a grant of some land " in recompensationem centum mercatarum terræ in Scotia," besides pensions upon other occasions. He died in exile, previously to the year 1344, leaving issue three sons, Godfrey, John, ancestor of the noble family of Ross, and William. The seniority of these two last is uncertain.

Sir Godfrey, the heir of the family, also stiled " *the Roos,*" received, upon the 6th of July 1344, a pension from the English monarch, to be continued "quousque idem Godefridus, terras " et tenementa in Scotia, que occasione adherentie sue erga nos amisit, recuperavit." He is there called the son of " Godefridus the Roos;" and this pension was in return for services rendered by his father [3].

He was in England as late as the year 1365, soon after which it is probable that he was restored to *a part* of the ancient inheritance in Scotland, as we meet with a Godfrey de Ros of Tarbart, the principal designation, in several deeds about the end of that century. He appears to have been attached to the person of Edward the Third; for that prince, in the year 1369,

---

[1] There were also many younger members. To a charter of the lands of Blair, after 1296, there are as witnesses, " Do-" mino Godefrido de Ros patre, Godefrido de Ross filio, militibus. Reginald de Ross senior et Jacobus filius Godefridi de " Ross junior, et Andreas filius Godefridi de Ross," swear fealty to Edward the I. This last, according to the author of Critical Remarks upon the Ragman Roll, is conjectured to have been the ancestor of the Rosses of Haining, Galston, and Montgrenan.

[2] Charter to William Murray, son of Maurice Murray, of the forfeiture of Godfrey Ross within the barony of Stonehouse, Lanarkshire, (temp. David 2d) Rob. index p. 56.

[3] The above facts are derived from the Rotuli Scotiæ, lately published.

authorized him to transport into England, from Scotland, forty men in arms to assist him in his wars upon the continent [1].

The Rosses of Tarbart existed for a considerable period afterwards, though they alienated their estate of Tarbart in 1450 to their cousins the Rosses of Halkhead.

Upon their failure, the representation seems to have devolved upon the latter family, who, by the express authority of Crawfurd, and indeed of all genealogists, are descended from the John already mentioned, younger son of Godfrey, the adherent of Edward the III [2].

This fact is, besides, in a great measure corroborated by the Rotuli Scotie, in which, upon the 30th of Nov. 1360, a safe conduct is stated to have been granted "Johanni de Roos de Scotia *fratri* dilecti et fidelis nostri Godefridi de Roos." There is also another, 4th November 1362, "Johanni Roos de Scotia venienti de partibus illis usque London cum duobus equitibus, ad loquendum cum Godefrido *fratre suo*, et ad proprias partes redeundum. [3]"

This Sir John acquired, in the year 1367, from King Robert the Second, then Earl of Strathern, the lands of Halkhead in Renfrewshire [4]. He there fixed his residence, and is a frequent witness to many deeds connected with the west of Scotland.

The subsequent generations, down to Sir John Ross of Halkhead, who lived after the middle of the fifteenth century, from the circumstance of the Christian name of the different members being alike, it is not a little difficult to unravel.

There is a royal charter, by Robert the Third, to Sir John Ross, probably the former, of the lands of Auchinback in the county of Renfrew.

A charter by "Adam Fullarton miles dominus ejusdem et de Corsby," in the year 1392, to [5] Paisley, is witnessed "nobilibus viris dominis Johanne de Ross domino de Halkhead, et Johanne Blair de Adamtoun, militibus." To another, by this John Blair of [6] Adamtoun, also to Paisley, Godfrey de Ross dominus de Tarbart is a witness.

John Ross of Halkhead acquired, in 1439, the lands of Arthurlie from William Stuart of Castlemilk, and, in 1445, those of Western-third, and Middlethird, from Robert Lord Lyle [7].

The Sir John Ross of Halkhead, already alluded to, probably entered upon his active career in the year 1449; either he or his father, with James Douglas, brother of the Earl of Douglas, and James Douglas of Lochleven, fought against the Burgundian knights in presence of King James the Second and his court in that year. One or other of them had a charter of the lands of Tarbart in 1450. Upon the 9th of March, a commission passed the great seal, of the office of sheriff of Linlithgow, in favour of Sir John Ross of Halkhead for life. He died before 1501.

---

[1] Rymer's Fœdera, 11 June 1319, Vol. 66. p. 924.

[2] " It is certain this Sir John (of Halkhead) is son of Godfrey Ros of Tarbart." Crawfurd's M.S. Baronetage.

[3] What became of William the other brother does not appear. In the Rot. Scot. there is a safe conduct 13th May 1365, for "Willielmum de Roos de Scotia Scutiferum dilecti et fideli nostri Godefridi de Roos et, duos famulos nos venientes cum quibusdem canibus, et falconibus, ad prefatum Godefridum." There is also a safe conduct to Sir Thomas Somervill from Scotland, *Sir John Ross*, (in all probability of Halkhead) Sir Hugh Eglinton, Sir Duncan Wallays, all from Scotland, to visit Canterbury on the 26th April. Ib. p. 872.

[4] Crit. Remarks upon the Ragman Roll. Nisbet's Heraldry, vol. II. p. 27, new edit. In the charter conveying the property, he seems to have been called " Consanguineus," of the king.

[5] Chartulary of Paisley. f. 228. [6] Ibid. [7] Cart. pen. com. de Glasgow.

He was twice married: The name of his first wife has not been handed down: His second was Marion Baillie, of the family of Lamington, relict of John Lord Somerville, against whom, though apparently without success, he instituted a process of divorce. He had issue, 1. Robert; 2. Patrick, or Calixtus; 3. Nicholas, parson of Renfrew; and, 4. a daughter, Egidia, married to James, son of Sir John Auchinleck of that-ilk.

Robert, the eldest, married Agnes Melvill, daughter and sole heiress of Thomas Melvill of that-ilk, representative of the ancient barons of Melvill in Lothian, thereby adding very considerably to the estates of the family. Predeceasing his father, by her, who also died early, he had only one son.

I. John, first Lord Ross, so created about the year 1503, by James the IV. In the lifetime of his grandfather, whom he succeeded in 1501, he was designed of Melvill. He fell with most of the Scottish nobility, at the battle of Flodden, in the year 1513, leaving, by [1] Christian Edmonstone his wife, daughter of Sir Archibald Edmonstone of Duntreath, upon whom he settled in jointure the lands of Tartrevan, in Linlithgowshire, three sons, Ninian, Thomas, and Andrew.

II. Ninian, second Lord Ross, alternately designed Lord Ross, and Lord Ross and Melvill, was one of the Scotch nobles who, in 1515, were dispatched ambassadors to France to make Scotland a party in the negociations with England. He ratified a treaty with England in 1534. He married, first, Lady Janet Stuart, daughter of the Earl of Lennox, which marriage had taken place, at least as early as the year 1515. Secondly, Elizabeth Ruthven, daughter of Lord Ruthven, relict of William Earl of Errol. He had issue, 1st, Robert, Master of Ross; 2d, James; 3d, John, who had parts of Tartrevan assigned to him; and two daughters; Margaret, married to Andrew Murray of Arngask and Balvaird, without issue; and Christian, married to John Mure of Caldwell, had issue.

Robert the Master, by his wife, Agnes Moncreiff, of the family of Moncreiff of Moncreiff, in the county of Perth, relict of Thomas Scott of Abbotshall, had an only child, Elizabeth, afterwards married to John Lord Fleming. He predeceased his father. By his confirmed testament, still extant [2] at St. Andrew's, it appears that the above lands of Tartrevan had been settled upon him and his spouse, and that he died at the fatal battle of Pinkiecleuch, upon the 10th of September 1547.

By the original investiture, the estate should eventually have descended to Elizabeth his daughter, but Lord Ninian being desirous to preserve the representation in the male line, obtained, in the years 1547 and 1548, upon his own resignation, a new investiture of the barony of Melvill, Tenandry of Halkhead, &c. and with the rest of the estate, to him and his heirs male whatsoever; which conveyance, by the practice of the age, carried the honour also, though not in the slightest manner alluded to. Lord Ninian dying not long after 1555, was succeeded in his estates and dignities by his second son, James.

III. James, third Lord Ross, entered into the association in support of Queen Mary at

---

[1] She was alive in 1549. She maried a George Knellis, from whom, on the score of consanguinity, she was afterwards divorced. Register of Decreets of Consistory of St. Andrew's.

[2] Testament Register, Commissary Court, St. Andrew's.

Hamilton, 8th May 1568, and, dying in 1583, left issue, by Jean, daughter of Robert Lord Sempill, who deceased in 1593, 1st, Robert; 2d, Sir William of Muiriston, who afterwards carried on the line of the family; 3d, Dorothea; 4th, Elizabeth, married to Allan Lockhart of Cleghorn; 5th, Allison; and 6th, Grizzel.

IV. Robert, fourth Lord Ross, married Jean, daughter of Gavin Hamilton of Raploch, by whom he had a daughter Grizzel, married to Sir Archibald Stirling of Keir, and a son James.

V. James, fifth Lord Ross, was served heir to his father in the year 1615. He married Margaret, eldest daughter of Walter, first Lord Scott of Buccleugh, and by her, (who married, secondly, Alexander, sixth Earl of Eglinton, and died in October 1651) had issue. James, sixth Lord Ross; William, seventh Lord Ross; Robert, eighth Lord Ross—and three daughters, 1. Margaret, born 19th December 1615, married to Sir John Stirling of Keir, and died 10th March 1633, æt. 18, leaving one daughter, Margaret, who died 11th May 1633; 2. Jean, married to Sir Robert Innes of Innes, Bart. From them is lineally descended his Grace James Innes Ker, Duke of Roxburgh, now the heir general of James, fifth Lord Ross; and, 3d, Mary, married to John Hepburn of Wauchton, whose issue have failed. She and her sister Jean were, upon the 6th of February 1649, served heirs portioners in the unentailed estates of the Ross family—of James Lord Ross, William Lord Ross, and Robert Lord Ross, their brothers german, and of Jean Hamilton, Lady Ross, their grandmother.

VI. James, the sixth Lord Ross, was served heir to his father in the Lordship and barony of Melvill, &c. 18th September 1634. He died unmarried 17th March 1636.

VII. William, seventh Lord Ross, was served heir to his brother 8th September 1636. He died unmarried in August 1640.

VIII. Robert, eighth Lord Ross, was served heir of his brother William 3d of June 1641. He died unmarried in 1648, when, in terms of the entails of the years 1547 and 1548, the estates and titles devolved on the heir male, Sir William Ross of Muiriston, his granduncle, son of James, third Lord Ross, by Jean, daughter of Lord Sempill.

IX. William, ninth Lord Ross, had a charter, " Domino Willielmo Ross, de Muiriston " Militi," of the lands of Forhead, &c. in 1636; held the office of sheriff principal of the county of Renfrew in the year 1646, and succeeded Robert, eighth Lord Ross in 1648. He was served heir male to him in the Lordship of Melvill, the Tenandry of Halkhead, &c. 20th March 1649. He died in the year 1656. By Helen, his wife, eldest daughter of George, first Lord Forrester of Corstorphin, in whose right his descendants became the heirs general of that family, he had a son,

X. George, tenth Lord Ross.

Upon the 10th of August 1666, he expede, upon his own resignation, a royal charter, which is dated at Whitehall, of the barony of Melvill, the Tenandry of Halkhead, &c. and his entire estate in favour of the heirs male of his body, whom failing, to his eldest heir female of the body, she always assuming the name and arms of Ross; whom failing, to such person whom he might afterwards name—a power which he never exercised.

In this charter it is observable that every thing carried by the investitures of 1547 and 1548 is mentioned; which last, however, determined the descent of the honours. Another royal charter was expede during the lifetime of Lord William his son, upon the 3d of September 1686, of the estate, upon much the same series of heirs, enforcing several stipulations about the honours and dignities.

George, tenth Lord Ross, who died in 1682, married, first, Lady Grizel Cochrane, only daughter of William, first Earl of Dundonald, by whom he had a son, William, eleventh Lord Ross; and a daughter, the Hon. Grizel Ross, married to Sir Alexander Gilmour of Craigmiller. She died at King's Inch, 10th June 1732.

He married, secondly, Lady Jane Ramsay, eldest daughter of George, second Earl of Dalhousie, and by her, (who took to her second husband Robert, Viscount of Oxford) had issue, 1st, " The Hon. Charles Ross of Balnagowan, Colonel of the 5th, or royal Irish regi-
" ment of Dragoons from 1695 to 1715, and again, from 1729 to 1732, who ranked as
" general in the army from 1st April 1712. He entered heartily into the revolution, but
" engaged in Sir James Montgomery's plot for the restoration of the abdicated family in 1690,
" and was committed to the Tower of London. He was one of the lessees of the poll-tax,
" 1693; was member of parliament for the county of Ross in seven successive parliaments,
" from 1707 to 1732, and took an active part in the debates of the house of commons. He
" supported the Tory Administration, and was deprived of his regiment at the accession of
" George I. He was one of the secret committee of the house of commons to inquire into
" the conduct of the South Sea directors, 1720, when Mr. Vernon, member for Whitchurch,
" making corrupt application to him on behalf of Mr. Aislabie, one of the directors, General
" Ross complained of the same to the house, for which he received their thanks, and Mr.
" Vernon was expelled 12th May 1721. Soon after the accession of King George II. General
" Ross was restored to the command of his regiment *, and dying, unmarried, at Bath, on
" the 5th of August 1732, in the 66th year of his age, was buried at Fearn in Ross-shire."

2d, The Hon. Jean Ross, married to William, sixth Earl of Dalhousie, and had issue.

XI. William, eleventh Lord Ross, the eldest son, born about 1656, had a charter of the baronies of Melville, Halkhead, &c. 10th August 1669, to William Master of Ross. " Succeeding his father, 1682, he entered zealously into the revolution, 1689; was a privy
" counsellor to King William and Queen Anne, high commissioner to the Church of Scot-
" land 1704; one of the Lords of the treasury, and a commissioner for the Union, of which
" treaty he was a staunch promoter. He was chosen one of the sixteen representatives of
" the Scottish Peerage, at the general election 1715, appointed Lieutenant of the county of
" Renfrew the same year, and died, at Hawkhead, on the 15th of March 1738, in the 82d
" year of his age †. His Lordship married, first, 7th February 1676, Agnes, daughter and
" heiress of Sir John Wilkie of Foulden, in the county of Berwick, and by her he had two
" sons and three daughters,

1. " George, twelfth Lord Ross, born, at Glasgow, 8th April 1681.

---

* He was advanced to the highest military honours, and was equally famous for the arts of peace and war. Stat. Account Vol. 4. p. 298.

† This venerable Peer resided occasionally at London and Melville Castle, and more frequently at Hawkhead. He took an active part in all public business in the county of Renfrew, and presided at meetings of justices regularly, at the county town, till he was beyond 80 years of age.

2. "The Hon. Eupheme Ross, born 10th November 1684, married to William, third "Earl of Kilmarnock, and had issue,

3. "Hon. John Ross, born 13th July 1687—died young.

4. "The Hon. Mary Ross, born 26th December 1688, married, in 1710, to John, first "Duke of Athol, and had issue.

5. "The Hon. Grizel Ross, born 29tn May 1662, married to Sir James Lockhart of "Carstairs, in the county of Lanark, Bart. and by him had six sons. See an account of this "family in Wood's Peerage, Vol. I. p. 421 and 422.

"Lord Ross married, secondly, a daughter of Philip Lord Wharton, without issue; "thirdly, Lady Anne Hay, eldest daughter of John, second Marquis of Tweedale, by the "daughter of the Duke of Lauderdale, and by her had one daughter, the Hon. Anne Ross, "born 7st April 1714, died in 1774, unmarried.

"Lord Ross married, fourthly, (contract dated 6th June 1731) Henrietta, daughter of "Sir Frances Scott of Thirlestane; but by her, who died, at Edinburgh 16th January 1750, "had no issue.

XII. "George, twelfth Lord Ross, served under the Duke of Marlborough, was ap-"pointed one of the commissioners of excise in Scotland 24th November 1726, and one of "the commissioners of the customs 21st September 1730. He succeeded his father 1738; "made a settlement of his estates, 7th June 1751, on his son and the heirs of his body; "which failing, on his daughters Jane, Elizabeth, and Mary, respectively, and the heirs male "of their bodies; remainder to his nearest heirs and assigns: and dying, on the 17th of June "1754, in the 73d year of his age, was buried at Renfrew. He married Lady Elizabeth "Ker, third daughter of William, second Marquis of Lothian, and by her, who died at "Hawkhead, 22d May 1758, had issue."

1, "William, thirteenth Lord Ross, born 1718-19; 2. Hon. Jane Ross, born 10th "December 1719, of whom afterwards; 3. The Hon. Charles Ross, born 9th February "1721; succeeded, on the death of his granduncle, General Ross, to the estate of Balnagow-"an, in virtue of an entail executed by him in 1727. He was chosen member of parliament "for the county of Ross at the general election 1741; was an officer in the army, and fell "at the battle of Fontenoy, 30th April 1745, unmarried. The estate of Balnagowan de-"volved on his father; and Collins commemorated his untimely fate in a beautiful Ode, "containing these lines,

"O'er him, whose doom thy virtues grieve,
"Aerial forms shall sit at eve,
"And bend the pensive head!
"And, fall'n to save his injur'd land,
"Imperial Honour's awful hand,
"Shall point his lonely bed."

4. The Hon. George Ross, born 7th September 1722, and died young without issue.

5. The Hon. Elizabeth Ross, born 16th April 1725, married, 11th June 1755, to John, third Earl of Glasgow, and afterwards inherited her father's estate of Hawkhead.

6. The Hon. Mary Ross, died unmarried, at London, 22d October 1762, æta. 32.

7. The Hon. Margaret Ross, born 1730–31, died unmarried.

XIII. William, thirteenth Lord Ross, the only surviving son, was an officer in the royal army, commanded by Lord Loudon, at Inverness, in 1745, and, on the march to surprise the Chevalier at Moy, in February 1746, was thrown down by the cavalry, and much hurt. He said he had been in many perils, but never found himself in a condition so grievous as on that day. He succeeded his father in June 1754, but enjoyed the title only two months, dying at Mount-Tiviot, the seat of his uncle, the Marquis of Lothian, of the gout in his head, on the 9th of August 1754, in the 34th year of his age, unmarried. The title became extinct; the estate of Balnagowan went to his cousin, Sir James Ross Lockhart, after an ineffectual opposition from Sir Alexander Gilmour; and his estates of Hawkhead and Melville, devolved on his eldest sister.

XIV. " The Hon. Jane Ross, married, 28th July 1735, to John Mackye, of Palgowan,
" who took the name of Ross, and she died without issue, at Clifton, 19th August 1777.
" Her husband, born in January 1708, was admitted a member of the faculty of advocates
" 1730; was member of Parliament for the burghs of Lanark," &c. from 1741 to 1746, and for the stewartry of Kirkcudbright, in three successive parliaments, from 1747 to 1768: held the office of paymaster of the Board of Ordonance, and afterwards Receiver General of stamp duties, and died, at London, in October 1797, in his 90th year. The estate of Melville, in the county of Edinburgh, was sold in 1760 to Mr. Rennie, the maternal grandfather of the present Lord Viscount Melville.

The estate of Hawkhead, and superiorities in Ayrshire, were retained, some parts of whic are still called Ross-holm and Ross-meadow. After the death of the Hon. Mrs. Jane Ross her only surviving sister,

XV. The Right Hon. Elizabeth Ross, Countess Dowager of Glasgow, succeeded, in 1777, to the ancient estate of Hawkhead. Her husband John, third Earl of Glasgow, " was
" born 4th November 1714; succeeded his father in 1740; was a cornet in the Scots Grays,
" afterwards captain of a company of the 33d regiment of foot; served on the continent; was
" wounded at the battle of Fontenoy, 30th April, 1745; and again severely at the battle of
" Val, or Lauffeldt, 2d July 1747. His Lordship represented His Majesty as Lord High
" Commissioner to the General Assembly of the Church of Scotland, from 1764 to 1772,
" both inclusive; he died, at Kelburn, on the 7th of March 1775, in the 61st year of his
" age; and was succeeded in his titles and estates by his only son George, fourth Earl of
" Glasgow." The Countess Dowager enjoyed the estate of Hawkhead as sole heiress of her father, brother, and sister, and died, at London, the 9th of October 1791. She had issue, two sons and three daughters.

1. " John Lord Boyle, born 26th March 1756, died young.

2. " George, fourth Earl of Glasgow, born 18th September 1765."

3. " Lady Elizabeth, born in 1758, married, at Hawkhead, 16th October 1786, to Sir
" George Douglas of Springwood-park, Bart. M. P. for the county of Roxburgh; and died,
" at London, 15th February 1801, in her 42d year, leaving a son, John James, born 18th

" July 1792. She had also two daughters; 1. Georgiana, born 28th September 1787, died
" 22d August 1795: 2. Helen, born December 1790, died in January 1791.

" Lady Helen, born 1760, died, at London, 1780.

" Lady Jane, born 1764, now residing at Edinburgh.

The Boyles of Kelburn, upon whom the estates and representation of the noble family of Ross have devolved, are well known to belong to the county of Ayr, where, as free barons, they have flourished for more than five centuries. " Robert de Boyvill," or Boyle, was one of the Barons of that county who swore fealty to Edward the First in the year 1296. Robert Boyle was infeft by the Sheriff of Ayr as a crown vassal in the lands of " Caleburn," in the year 1456 which he held blench *. Of him, by indubitable legal evidence, is lineally descended the present Earl of Glasgow, who is in possession of those very lands of Kelburn, which Richard Boyle is proved, by a charter, published in Anderson's Diplomata, to have held in the reign of Alexander the Third. He is also the heir of line of the Maxwells of Pollok, and, through the Rosses, of the noble family of Forrester of Corstorphin.

XVI. George, fourth Earl of Glasgow, born 18th September 1765; succeeded to his father in 1775, and to his mother in 1791; " was a Captain in the West Lowland fencible
" Regiment, 1793; afterwards Major of the Angus Fencibles; Lieut. Colonel of the Rothesay
" and Caithness Fencibles; Colonel of the Renfrewshire Yeomanry, 1796; and Colonel, first,
" of the Ayr and Renfrew, afterwards of the Renfrewshire militia, which he resigned in
" 1806. He was constituted Lord Lieutenant of the county of Renfrew 28th April 1810;
" was chosen one of the sixteen representatives of the Scottish peerage in six successive parlia-
" ments, from 1790 to the present time †;" and in 1815 his Lordship was advanced to the dignity of a Peer of Great Britain, by the title of Baron Ross of Hawkhead.

" He married, 4th March 1788, Lady Augusta Hay, born 25th April 1766, third daugh-
" ter of James, fourteenth Earl of Errol; and by her, who, in 1806, succeeded to her grand-
" father, Sir William Carr's estate of Etal, in Northumberland, has issue:"

1. The Right Hon. John Boyle, Lord Viscount Kelburn, born, at Edinburgh, 12th August 1789; " bred to the sea service, and served on board the Gibraltar in the Mediterranean. He died, at Tunbridge, on the 6th March 1818.

2. Lady Isabella, born 7th July 1790.

3. The Hon. James Boyle, born, at London, 10th April 1792, a Lieutenant in the royal navy, and now the Right Hon. Lord Viscount Kelburn.

4. Lady Elizabeth, born March 1794.

5. Lady Augusta, born 14th August 1801. And,

6. The Hon. William Boyle, born, at Edinburgh, 8th November 1802.

Arms of the family of Ross.

Quarterly: first, and fourth; Or, a Cheveron, Chequé Sable and Argent, between three Water Budgets of the second, for Ross: second, and third; Gules, Three Crescents within

---

* Exchequer roll of that date, Register Office. Compotum Georgii Campbell Vicecomitis de Are, de Lowdon militis (from 3d July 1454 to 26th September 1456). He charges himself with " duplicationem albe firme terrarum de Caleburne " Regi debite, per salsinam datam Roberto Boile de eisdem." † See Wood's Peerage.

a Border Argent, charged with eight roses of the first, for Melville. Supporters, Two Goshawks, proper; armed, jessed, and belled Or.

Crest, a Hawk's Head, erased, proper. Motto, "Think on."

These arms were borne by Ninian Lord Ross, about the middle of the sixteenth century: they are magnificently sculptured upon a fragment of the old castle of Melville, now at Hawkhead, along with a legend bearing his style, " NINIANUS DOMINUS ROSS AC MELVIL." In consequence of certain transactions with the Rosses of Balnagowan, the heirs male of the old Earls of Ross, George Lord Ross, early in the seventeenth century quartered their arms in the second and third coats; and they are thus exhibited in front of the house of Hawkhead.

DUNLOP OF HOUSEHILL.

Robert Dunlop of Househill, second son of James Dunlop of Garnkirk, married, first, Elizabeth Baird, daughter of John Baird, Esq. merchant in Glasgow; by whom he had one daughter, Jean, married to Robert Dinwiddie, Esq. of Jermistoun in Lanarkshire; of which marriage there were two children; Lawrence Dinwiddie, who is succeeded by his son, Robert Dinwiddie, now of Jermistoun; and a daughter, Elizabeth, married to the Rev. Dr. John Lockhart, one of the ministers of Glasgow, by whom there is a son, Captain William Lockhart, in the service of the Honourable East India Company.

Annual Revenues of the Hostages given in Security of the Ransom of James I. in 1424. Rymer X. 327.

	Merks.		Merks.
1. David, son and heir of the Earl of Athol,	1,200	15. James of Dunbar, Lord Frendraft,	500
2. Thomas, Earl of Moray,	1,000	16. Andrew Gray of Foulis,	600
3. Alexander, Earl of Crawfurd,	1,000	17. Lord Robert of Livingston,	400
4. Duncan, Lord of Argyle,	1,500	18. John Lyndesay,	500
5. William, eldest son and heir to the Lord of Dalkeith,	1,500	19. Lord Robert of Lille,	800
		20. James Lord Calder,	400
6. Gilbert, eldest son and heir to William the Constable,	800	21. James, Lord of Cadyo,	500
		22. Lord William of Rothvane,	400
7. Robert, the Marischal of Scotland,	800	23. William Olyfaunt, Lord of Abirdalgie,	—
8. Robert Lord Erskine,	1,000	24. George, son and heir of Hugh Campbell,	300
9. Walter Lord Dirleton,	800		
10. Montgomery of Eglinton,	700	25. Robert, son and heir to Lord Robert de Mautelent,	400
11. Thomas Boyd of Kilmarnock,	500		
12. Lord Patrick of Dunbar, Lord Camnok,	500	26. David Mcignes,	200
		27. David of Ogilby,	200
13. Alexander Lord Gordon,	400	28. Patrick, son and heir to John Lyon,	300
14. Lord William of Abernethy,	500		17,200

Note. It is estimated that each Merk at that time was equal in effect to £10 Sterling at present.

THE END.

J. NEILSON, PRINTER.

ERRATA.

In a work like this, abounding so much in separate subjects, and so many arithmetical figures, errata might be expected; but it is believed that the following are all in which the error makes any material alteration in the sense.

Page.
245 1st paragraph, l. 2. r. 15,450.
281 The foot note applies to Sir Robert of Calderwood.
301 Arrangement of surface, L 2. read 1200 L 3. r. 1286, L 5. r. 13956.
310 Last l. for now, r. late, and, at the end of next sentence add, He was succeeded by his son, Robert Orr, Esq; the present proprietor.
315 Last article in the Table is a repetition (more correctly) of Cochran valuation in the preceding page.
320 Last word of l. 10. from the bottom, r. She
322 Last line, for country in particular, r. country. In particular,
334 l. 8. from the bottom, for, in employment, r. in the wages of labour.
338 l. 11. from the bottom, for James III. r. James IV. L 15. for 1800, r. 1780, l. 19, for 1801, r. 1781, l. 20. for 18— r. 1811.
339 l. 3. for supreme, r. principal
343 Valuation of Scotstoun, £491 : 13 : 4
373 l. 13. from the bottom, for mathematical, r. mechanical.
384 Table, art. 7. for Rashiehill, r. Rashielee; and, for James Maxwell of Dargeval, r. John Maxwell of Dargeval.
388 l. 8. from bottom, after the words, from which, insert, after passing through the hands of more than one purchaser.
390 l. 11. delete the word has.
430 Table of Rental. Valued rent of Paisley parish, should be £11,765 : 13 : 4, and Renfrew, £2829 : 13 : 4.
434. l. 12. delete to, l. 15. for has, r. have, last l. for means, r. terms.
440 l. 21, for 1687, r. 1587.
444 L 3. from the bottom for Italy, r. holy.
448 l. 10. prefix (better) to (known), l. 10. from the bottom, after Britain, add, rank.
493 l. 12. from the bottom, for Borthwick, r. Berwick.

Note.—In page 342, Kirkland is stated to belong to Campbell of Blytheswood. It belongs to Lord Glasgow. The mistake arose from seeing it joined in the Cess Book to Renfield.